W9-AHH-429

Statistical Analysis for the Social Sciences

An Interactive Approach

Philip C. Abrami
Concordia University

Paul Cholmsky
Concordia University

Robert Gordon
Concordia University

ALLYN AND BACON

BOSTON • LONDON • TORONTO • SYDNEY • TOKYO • SINGAPORE

Editorial Director: *Nancy Forsyth*
Executive Editor: *Rebecca Pascal*
Editorial Assistant: *Whitney Brown*
Senior Marketing Manager: *Caroline Croley*
Editorial Production Services: *Chestnut Hill Enterprises, Inc.*
Manufacturing Buyer: *Megan Cochran*
Cover Administrator: *Linda Knowles*
Electronic Composition: *Omegatype Typography, Inc.*

Copyright © 2001 by Allyn & Bacon
A Pearson Education Company
160 Gould Street
Needham Heights, MA 02494

All rights reserved. No part of the material protected by this copyright notice may be
reproduced or utilized in any form or by any means, electronic or mechanical, including
photocopying, recording, or by any information storage and retrieval system, without
written permission from the copyright holder.

Internet: www.ablongman.com

Between the time Website information is gathered and published, some sites may
have closed. Also, the transcription of URLs can result in typographical errors. The
publisher would appreciate notification where these occur so that they may be
corrected in subsequent editions.

Library of Congress Cataloging-in-Publication Data
Abrami, Philip C.
  Statistical analysis for the social sciences : an interactive approach / Philip C. Abrami,
Paul Cholmsky, Robert Gordon.
    p.   cm.
    Includes bibliographical references and index.
    ISBN 0-205-29493-6
    I. Social sciences—Statistical methods.   I. Cholmsky, Paul.   II. Gordon, Robert.
  III. Title.

  HA29 .A287   2000
  519.5—dc21

                                                                    00-057614

Printed in the United States of America

10 9 8 7 6 5 4 3 2 1   RRD-VA   05 04 03 02 01 00

Contents

Preface

Statistical Analysis for the Social Sciences: An Interactive Approach (SASSI) offers instructors additional flexibility in teaching applied statistics and students new and better ways to learn statistics. *SASSI* is both a stand-alone textbook and an interactive multimedia CD-ROM which together emphasize the logic of statistical procedures, fundamental concepts, and the application of quantitative techniques to analytical problems students and researchers are likely to encounter.

The *SASSI* project was initiated to apply advances in instructional design and educational technology to the teaching and learning of applied statistics. In particular, *SASSI* is intended to be accessible, understandable, and engaging, thereby encouraging the learner to actively develop an understanding of statistical analysis for the social sciences.

PREREQUISITES

In preparing *SASSI* we assumed that the student would have limited or no prior experience with statistics, especially inferential statistical techniques. Basic tools and techniques in both descriptive and inferential methods are covered in the first portion of *SASSI*, before specific inferential techniques are covered in the second portion. Furthermore, the mathematical treatment does not place extraordinary demands on students. A reasonable knowledge of basic algebra is sufficient to understand the text and CD-ROM.

THE SASSI TEXTBOOK

The textbook portion of *SASSI* contains a number of key features that make it useful in its own right.

Univariate Statistics

This is a textbook primarily about univariate statistics and, consequently, we treat only a single outcome measure throughout the text. A basic and recurrent theme is variability, including its description and explanation. Wherever we can, we try to link all the inferential techniques we cover to the notion of variability in the dependent or outcome measure and to demonstrate how this variability might be explained by one or more independent or predictor variables.

Explanatory Approach

We have tried a number of things to anchor the learning of statistics in reality. First, we begin virtually every chapter with a commonsensical, often whimsical scenario, which we use throughout the chapter to illustrate the statistical tools covered therein. To the greatest extent possible, we have included small and simple numerical datasets in the scenarios to insure that the reader can easily follow all the computations that follow even without benefit of a calculator or computer.

Second, we provide only derivational formulas, not computational ones. Given that the vast majority of students will end up doing data analysis by computer, we see little need for including the additional complexity inherent in those formulas, which at one time were designed for manual computational ease, rather than ease of comprehension.

Third, we truncate portions of the traditional explanation of hypothesis testing by ignoring tests of single means. In our experience, the actual use of such tests is rare and so we concentrate instead on tests of mean differences.

Integrative Approach

It has been our experience that students learn statistical techniques separately from one another without a sense of how to choose among them in addressing analysis problems. We have tried to address this shortcoming by emphasizing the broad commonalities in techniques, by using similar notational systems (e.g., for analysis of variance and multiple regression), and by pointing out how the techniques differ. Another aspect of this integrative approach is an even-handed emphasis on the statistical tools for the analysis of experiments and for the analysis of correlational investigations. Finally, we show the parallels between the parametric tests that make up the bulk of the text and their nonparametric counterpart, the latter which are also treated herein but in less detail.

Incremental Approach

We know that for the neophyte, the fundamental concepts that underlie many statistical techniques can seem abstract, intimidating, ambiguous, and irrelevant. We have worked hard to counter such claims. We have emphasized explanation wherever we can and taken an incremental approach to the presentation of key concepts by gradually introducing them over succeeding chapters.

Flexible Approach

We realize that for some the material covered in *SASSI* may go beyond what will appear in a single course. Our approach has been to provide explanations, with increasing depth and complexity, of important and frequently used statistics, allowing for abbreviated coverage where desirable. This approach has the added benefits of helping students better understand the statistical techniques they are likely to encounter in published research and which they may need to use in undertaking their own data analysis.

Practical Importance

We have also tried to get away from old-fashioned views of hypothesis testing. For example, we differentiate between point estimation and interval estimation. Emphasis is also placed on the power of statistical tests as well as practical importance in the form of effect size measures and strength of association indices.

Statistics Is a Piece of the Puzzle

We have tried to emphasize how statistics is just one part of the research enterprise. Consequently, we are especially sympathetic to the view that well-articulated and defensible hypotheses and sound research design and methodology have their own crucial roles to play. Although inattention to issues of analysis can destroy a study, proper attention to these issues is not a guarantee that an ill-conceived or poorly executed study can be salvaged. This thinking explains why we cover issues of design early on and emphasize the importance of nonstatistical aspects of good research throughout.

Compatibility with Statistical Packages

We recognize that most readers of the *SASSI* textbook will use computer packages to analyze their data. Although we have not included instructions here for the use of these packages, their existence affected the design and development of *SASSI*. As noted previously, we jettisoned the incorporation of computational formula. We also made sure that our explanations include coverage of idiosyncratic features of computer printouts (e.g., exact probability values, fractional degrees of freedom) that do not normally appear in introductory textbooks. In short, we hope to save everyone the frustration of computer results that don't match the textbook.

Research Integration

We appreciate that many, if not most, of the students using *SASSI* will become consumers of research findings rather than researchers themselves. We believe that it is important, therefore, that statistics be explained in a way that fosters long-term comprehension.

THE *SASSI* CD-ROM

The *SASSI* interactive multimedia CD-ROM is designed to support the *SASSI* textbook and classroom lectures. It is distinct from statistical software such as Statistical Package for the Social Sciences (SPSS) in that it is not designed to serve as a computational tool for data analysis. Rather, it provides a learning environment that enables students to further explore and apply what they learn in the classroom and from the textbook. One of our primary goals in creating it was to provide opportunities for instructors to incorporate discovery learning activities at numerous points throughout the course.

ORGANIZATION

The CD-ROM is divided into two sections: Activities and Problem Generators. Activities generally focus on key concepts in statistical analysis, whereas Problem Generators focus on important procedures. Concepts and procedures were selected based on

1. The importance of the concept or procedure with respect to statistical analysis
2. The frequency and degree of difficulty students have with the concept or procedure
3. The extent to which interactive multimedia can effectively support the concept or procedure

In other words, our concept of the "ideal" activity is one in which interactive multimedia is effectively employed to communicate a key concept in statistics that many students have substantial difficulty in understanding.

Discovery Questions

Students' use of the CD-ROM is structured through embedded "discovery questions." These questions serve to guide students as they perform conceptual experiments within activities, and to focus their attention on key aspects of the onscreen displays. For example, students are first asked to predict the effect degrees of freedom have on the shape of a *t*-distribution, and are then directed to manipulate this parameter and verify whether their prediction was correct by observing the display. Framing the students' interaction with the software in the context of "thought experiments" also helps to promote mindful engagement with the subject matter in place of mindless "clicking" with the mouse.

Interactive Multimedia

Please note that the CD-ROM does not introduce any material that is not covered in the *SASSI* textbook. The textbook/CD-ROM package has been designed to ensure that students who do not have access to the CD-ROM will still receive all of the instruction necessary to succeed in a statistics course. We consider the CD-ROM to be a form of high-tech study guide rather than a replacement for textbooks or lectures. It attempts to harness the power of interactive multimedia to create a learning environment within which students can refine their understanding of, and proficiency with, statistical analysis.

ACKNOWLEDGMENTS

We are grateful to two people, in particular, who have been of assistance in the development of *SASSI*. First, we express our appreciation to Valerie Turner, who helped format the chapters, who proofread, and who offered her judgment on the clarity and pedagogical soundness of the material. She worked tirelessly yet cheerfully to make the textbook better. Second, we are grateful to David Wells, who contributed in the early stages to the design and development of SASSI and who produced the questions and answers at the conclusion of each chapter.

We are also grateful to the following reviewers whose feedback was especially useful during the developmental stages and who helped us identify errors and omissions: Barbara Anderson Lounsbury, Rhode Island College; Michael Biderman, University of Tennessee at Chattanooga; George Domino, University of Arizona; Karen Friedlen, Mount St. Mary College; Glenn Graham, Wright State University; Cleborne Maddux, University of Nevada, Reno; John Muramoto, University of Washington; Michael Nielsen, Georgia Southern University; Thomas Nygren, Ohio State University; David Payne, Monmouth University; Robert Pred, Chestnut Hill College; Margaret Ruddy, The College of New Jersey; Elisabeth Sherun, Georgia Southern University; Philip Smith, University of Wisconsin, Milwaukee; James Starr, Howard University; Eva Szeli, University of Miami; Jennifer Taylor, Humboldt State University; Bruce Thompson, Texas A&M University; Susan Tice-Alicke, Ohio University; Noel Wescombe, Whitworth College; John Young, Rutgers University; Otto Zinser, East Tennessee State University. Finally, we acknowledge the editorial team at Allyn and Bacon who worked with us to make the *SASSI* project into reality.

Philip C. Abrami
Paul Cholmsky
Robert Gordon

chapter 1   Introduction

OVERVIEW

For some people, statistics has a bad reputation. They share the view of Disraeli about the evils of this branch of mathematics. This bad reputation spills over to some students too who have dubbed courses in the area "Sadistics."

To others, statistics has a wonderful reputation as one of the pillars of the social sciences. More than one hundred years ago, Sir Francis Galton, waxing poetic about a key concept in statistical inference, the normal distribution, said it would "have been personified and deified by the Greeks, if they had known of it."

Why are there such wildly different views? Statistics provide us with powerful tools for data summarization and presentation as well as powerful tools for inferential purposes such as hypothesis testing. Like most tools, but especially powerful ones, statistics can be misused and misrepresented. In reply to Disraeli and other critics, it has been said that statistics don't lie, people do.

Whether you are going to be using statistics as tools in your own research or to understand the research of others, you should have a critical understanding of the field. The use of statistics is pervasive both within and outside the social sciences. Most of the time these powerful tools are used wisely, but occasionally they are not. More often, the sense of confusion and fear of being lied to with statistics comes about through lack of critical understanding.

Statistical Analysis for the Social Sciences (SASSI) is about helping you develop that critical understanding. The subtitle, "An Interactive Approach," was chosen purposefully to reflect our belief that to learn with understanding requires that we structure the material in a way that encourages your interaction with it. We have tried very hard to do this, both in the textbook and the CD-ROM that accompanies it. We hope we have succeeded in organizing and presenting the material in ways that facilitate your learning.

Now it is time for you to take over. Our most important advice:

Don't memorize it. Understand it.

In this chapter, we deal with two questions:

1. What is statistics?
2. How do I organize data for statistical analysis?

At several points in each chapter, you will find information on how to use the CD-ROM to help you master concepts in that chapter.

All the chapters in the text begin with a scenario that presents a problem we will try to solve as one of the key activities in the chapter. The Dialing for Dollars scenario and data in Textboxes 1.1a–c set the stage for our discussion of statistics and the organization of data.

Statistics

The word *statistics* comes from the Latin word *status.* Status is also the root for the contemporary political term *state.* What's the connection? Statistics was an important tool of the state. In order to wage war or levy a tax, the ruler or governing body had to know about the population of the state and the extent of citizens' wealth. Gradually the meaning of the word expanded to include any type of data.

Meanings   Today the word *statistics* has a variety of meanings. One meaning of the term remains synonymous with data. That is, the raw data with which one might conduct an analysis are the statistics with which one works. By the way, *datum* is singular and *data* are plural.

A second meaning of the term concerns the functions one performs on data such as computing a measure of central tendency such as the mean or a measure of variability such as the range. For example, in the Dialing for Dollars scenario in Textboxes 1.1a–c, Tom Matthews will be interested in finding the mean of the responses to each of the attitude questions in Part II of the questionnaire.

A third meaning of statistics concerns techniques for the collection, analysis, and interpretation of data for subsequent decision making. For example, this

---

Textbox 1.1a

Scenario: Dialing for Dollars

Tom Matthew is conducting his thesis on wage earner attitudes toward taxation. Part of his thesis includes telephone interviews with heads of households chosen at random from key districts he has identified. The interview is divided into three parts. Part I contains demographic and background information. Part II contains close-ended attitude items in which respondents select from among five equal-interval response alternatives. Part III is a series of open-ended questions to which respondents are free to reply as they wish.

Tom also wishes to learn whether certain political events affect attitudes. He creates two political scenarios: liberal and conservative. His plan is to randomly divide his participants into two groups. One group will be exposed to the liberal political scenario and the other group will be exposed to the conservative political scenario. Then members of both groups will be interviewed.

Tom constructs a draft version of the questionnaire and contacts several participants who agree to help him pilot-test the instrument. He comes to you with the completed pilot interviews and asks you to help him see how he would set things up for data analysis. *Portions* of two of the interviews are reproduced in Textboxes 1.1b & 1.1c.

What advice would you offer Tom about organizing and coding the responses for analysis?

Textbox 1.1b

Scenario: Dialing for Dollars

Attitudes toward Taxation
Pilot Study

Condition: **Liberal**

Part I: Background and Demographic Questions

Respondent: **Jerry Mathers**   Phone: **848-2020**
Age: **37**   Gender: **Male**
Annual family income: **$65,000.00**   Marital status: **Divorced**
Number of dependents: **3**

Part II: Close-ended attitudes

Use the following scale in replying:

  A strongly agree   D. disagree

  B. agree   E. strongly disagree

  C. neutral or uncertain

1. I pay too many taxes for the government services I receive. **(A)**

2. Government services should be privatized. **(C)**

3. The government has the responsibility of providing health and social services to the needy. **(B)**

4. There should be a flat tax rate for everyone. **(B)**

Part III: Open-ended attitudes

1. What reforms, if any, would you like to see to the tax system?

  I would like to see the family tax rate reduced. If government services were cut back and business taxes were increased it could happen.

CD-ROM link 1.1

Activity 1.1: Descriptive Statistics: Seeing the Big Picture
In Activity 1.1, you can explore a fictitious small company's employee database. Do employees with more education tend to make more money? Is seniority more important? Find out by examining the data set from different perspectives using descriptive statistics.

meaning of the term includes the use of statistics to help the researcher in making decisions about hypotheses concerning the data.

Finally, statistics, as a branch of mathematics, is the subject of scholarly study. Statisticians continue to develop new statistical techniques and advance understanding about old ones.

Uses In this book, we will emphasize the use of statistics to serve two broad purposes. One major purpose of statistics is to summarize the important characteristics of a set of numbers (i.e., data). Measures of central tendency, such as the mean, and measures of variability, such as the standard deviation,

---

Textbox 1.1c

Scenario: Dialing for Dollars

Attitudes toward Taxation

Pilot Study

Condition: **Conservative**

Part I: Background and Demographic Questions

Respondent: **Lakie Misot**   Phone: **485-6387**
Age: —   Gender: **Female**
Annual family income: **$18,500.00** Marital status: **Single**
Number of dependents: **0**

Part II: Close-ended attitudes

Use the following scale in replying:

  A strongly agree   D. disagree

  B. agree   E. strongly disagree

  C. neutral or uncertain

  1. I pay too many taxes for the government services I receive. **(A)**

  2. Government services should be privatized. **(E)**

  3. Government has the responsibility of providing health and social services to the needy. **(E)**

  4. There should be a flat tax rate for everyone. **(A)**

Part III: Open-ended attitudes

  1. What reforms, if any, would you like to see to the tax system?

    There has to be greater distribution of wealth. The people paying the lowest taxes are the rich. Government bureaucrats get too much money, too.

CD-ROM link 1.2

Activity 1.2: Populations and Samples
Activity 1.2 uses voter polls in elections to illustrate the relationship between populations and samples. In the activity, you can set the number of people polled (the sample) and see how closely the poll results correspond to the actual election results. If you increase the number of people polled, do you think this will have an effect on the poll's accuracy? Find out in Activity 1.2.

are frequently used descriptive statistics.

A second major purpose of statistics is to make inferences about population parameters from sample values. Statistical tests like the Independent Groups *t*-test and the Analysis of Variance *F*-test are two of many inferential statistical tests we will present in the text. These techniques help one decide whether the data from an investigation represent chance fluctuation that cannot be explained or fluctuation that can be explained.

Variables and Variability

If all the individuals who responded to the questionnaire in the Dialing for Dollars scenario in Textboxes 1.1a–c gave the same responses, there would not be much need to analyze the findings further. But as the findings vary and become more complex, the need to summarize the results accurately becomes important. One may want to explore patterns in the results and speculate why these patterns occur.

The kind of questions one might ask include:

What are the average responses to close-ended questions about taxation?

Are the responses fairly consistent or is there a high degree of inconsistency in the responses?

Does the type of political scenario to which the respondents are exposed explain their reactions to the questionnaire?

Does gender or annual family income relate to respondents' attitudes?

These questions have to do with variables and variability. These are key concepts that appear throughout the text. The following paragraphs define these terms and explain how they will be used in the textbook.

Definitions   A **variable** is a characteristic that can take on different values for different members of a group or set being studied. Height, weight, age, and gender are variables because they would take on different values if, for example, one were to study children in an urban school district. Blood pressure, body temperature, type of ailment, and history of tobacco use would be variables in a study of patients at a large teaching hospital.

Two is the minimum number of different values needed to have a variable. Gender is a good example of a variable that has only two values; family income is a good example of a variable that can take on many values.

In contrast, a **constant** is a characteristic that takes on the same value for all members of a group or set being studied. Type of psychological disorder is a constant if one studies only those patients who suffer from bulimia.

Classification of Variables   Mathematicians classify variables as qualitative or quantitative. A **qualitative variable** consists of attributes or nonquantitative characteristics of objects, people, or events. For example, gender and eye color are qualitative variables.

The categories of qualitative variables are nonoverlapping or mutually exclusive, which means that an element cannot be in more than one category. In addition, the categories must be exhaustive, or comprehensive, so that all the elements can be classified. Finally, qualitative variables may be ordered or unordered. Ordered qualitative variables include military rank and the letter grading system used widely in school. Unordered qualitative variables include eye color, gender, and racial origin.

A **quantitative variable** consists of a count or numerical measurement of the characteristics of objects, people, or events. For example, speed, attendance at the symphony, and intelligence are quantitative variables.

Quantitative variables can be discrete or continuous. A **discrete variable** can assume only a finite number of values; it consists of separate, indivisible categories. No values can exist between two neighboring categories. The number of students attending class, and the rating of a global attitude on a five-point equal-interval scale are examples of discrete quantitative variables.

A **continuous variable** can assume an infinite number of values; it is divisible into an infinite number of fractional parts. The speed of motor vehicles, the distance between stationary objects, and reaction time are examples of continuous quantitative variables.

Variables may be reclassified or recoded for analysis and other purposes. For example, a continuous variable might be recoded into a discrete variable. Or a researcher might wish to reclassify reaction times as fast, medium, or slow or reclassify family incomes as lower class, middle class, and upper class.

Experimental variables   In an experiment, the researcher manipulates an independent variable and then measures the effect of the manipulation on the dependent variable. The **independent variable** is the variable under the experimenter's control. It is the treatment or manipulation whose effects are being studied.

The **dependent variable** is some form of measured behavior ranging from physiological responses, to think-aloud protocols (where respondents think aloud while performing a task), to standardized test results, to unobtrusive recordings of children's fantasy play.

Correlational variables   In a correlational investigation, the researcher measures, but does not manipulate, a predictor variable and also measures the outcome variable. The **predictor variable** is the variable that is hypothesized to explain variability in the outcome variable.

The **outcome variable** in a correlational investigation is also some form of measured behavior. Outcome variables from correlational investigations are not fundamentally different from dependent variables used in experiments.

Experimental and correlational variables are discussed at greater length in Chapter 2.

Variability   Variability is the degree of inconsistency in a set of numbers or distribution of scores. Measures of variability describe the extent to which scores in a distribution are clustered together or are spread out. We emphasize throughout the text that describing and/or explaining the variability in the data lies at the heart of statistical techniques. In particular, we want you to understand the nature of the variability in a single dependent or outcome variable. Thus, *SASSI* covers what is known as *univariate statistics*. Students wishing to go beyond the coverage here might be interested in learning about multivariate statistical techniques that allow for the analysis of two or more dependent or outcome variables.

What is the nature and extent of the variability in the data? How did the fluctuation in scores come about? Did the treatment work? Is there a meaningful relationship between the predictor and outcome variables? These are the types of questions you should be able to answer after developing your understanding of statistics using the *SASSI* textbook and CD-ROM.

Variability is the key concept that helps unify your understanding of statistics. Describing variability is the basic purpose of descriptive statistics. Explaining variability is the basic purpose of inferential statistics. As you read through the text, keeping this in mind will help unify your understanding of statistics from a collection of different summary techniques and test procedures to a collection of tools with similar objectives.

PREPARING DATA FOR ANALYSIS

There's often a big difference between textbook examples of data analysis and the real world of research. Usually textbook examples provide you with data that are already properly set up for analysis with unwanted variables and strange values eliminated. These pure examples are wonderful for helping you learn underlying statistical concepts, because they minimize the extent to which you can get distracted or confused.

The examples we use in the SASSI scenarios go even further. We use very small datasets and, whenever possible, provide data values that make for the simplest computations. We did this to emphasize your understanding of the procedures by cutting down on the manual, computational labor involved in applying them.

Although simple examples help you understand the statistical techniques, they don't necessarily help you deal with the complexities of real data. Often, an investigation will include a host of variables and not just a few. There will be a large number of data values, not just a small set. Some data values will be missing or appear incorrect and need to be checked. Finally, the data collected may not immediately lend itself to analysis. For example, open-ended responses (e.g., written responses and think-alouds) need to be coded into numerical values before statistical analyses may begin.

We realize that for most, if not all of you, the analysis of real data will not be done manually or even with the aid of a calculator. Most of you will turn to statistical packages such as MINITAB, SPSS, and SYSTAT for that purpose. Consequently, it is especially important that you spend some time now learning about how to set up your data for analysis.

Data Coding   The first step in data analysis is to make sure the data you are going to analyze are in numerical form. Although the data might have been collected in another form, as Tom did in the Dialing for Dollars scenario, it will need to be converted into numbers and you will want to use a code sheet or code book for this purpose. We show an abridged example in Textbox 1.2 for the Dialing for Dollars scenario. We discuss some important issues surrounding data coding below.

Code books   A code sheet or book helps ensure that coding is done consistently and that there are rules governing how to treat every type of response. In creating a code book for the Dialing for Dollars scenario, you will want to decide on the values of each of the variables you will analyze. For example, you might want to

---

Textbox 1.2

Scenario: Dialing for Dollars

Attitudes toward Taxation

Pilot Study

Codebook

C1. Condition: 1. **Liberal**

2. **Conservative**

For all variables, missing, illegible, or multiple responses: **Blank**

Part I: Background and Demographic Questions

B1. Identification number: _____

B2. Age: _____

B3. Gender: 1. **Male**

2. **Female**

B4. Annual family income (in thousands): _____

B5. Marital status:

1. **Single**   4. **Widowed**

2. **Married**   5. **Other-sex partner**

3. **Separated/Divorced**   6. **Same-sex partner**

B6. Number of dependents: _____

Part II: Close-Ended Attitudes

Use the following scale in replying:

1. **strongly agree**   4. **disagree**

2. **agree**   5. **strongly disagree**

3. **neutral or uncertain**

A1. I pay too many taxes for the government services I receive.

A2. Government services should be privatized.

A3. Government has the responsibility of providing health and social services to the needy.

A4. There should be a flat tax rate for everyone.

Part III: Open-Ended Attitudes

What reforms, if any, would you like to see to the tax system?

O1. Primary reply

O2. Secondary reply

1. **Reduce family taxes**   4. **Reduce government spending**

2. **Increase business taxes**   5. **Other**

3. **Increase taxes to rich**   6. **None**

have numeric codes for gender such as "1" for male and "2" for female. You could enter alphabetic values for gender such as "M" for male and "F" for female, but you would subsequently have to recode these values for analysis anyway. Note that you would also assign a short but unique name (e.g., C1, A2) to each variable coded.

Protecting participants   You might elect to assign a numerical identification number to participants to protect their identity from being made public. Identification numbers serve other purposes too. They can obscure the identity of participants and minimize any chance of coder bias arising from knowing whose data were being used.

Missing values   Missing responses, multiple responses, and out-of-range or suspect responses often need to be dealt with. Most computer packages have provisions for missing and special responses, and it is important to know what they are.

In the Dialing for Dollars scenario, Lakie Misot did not provide her age (see Textbox 1.1c). It might be wisest to leave the response blank in coding the data for analysis rather than enter the average response for those who did respond. But if the response is blank, you should know how the response is treated and what will happen to the remainder of her data when you conduct the computer analyses.

Will the computer package interpret a blank response as a zero response? If so, that would be a serious error in this instance. Alternately, the package may recognize a blank response as a missing or special value. If so, will the package exclude her data entirely for all the variables, ensuring that the same subset of cases, with complete data, are always analyzed? Or will the package exclude her data partially for a subset of the variables, meaning that the largest number of cases, but not always the same cases, are analyzed?

Open-ended responses   Coding open-ended responses can be both extremely rewarding as well as extremely difficult and time-consuming. Researchers often have to overcome several challenges in developing a coding system. First, the responses have to be interpreted and a small set of numerical values identified to represent them in an unambiguous, comprehensive, and nonoverlapping fashion. Overly verbose responses can be just as challenging to code as responses that are incomplete, where you feel obliged to "fill in the gaps." Second, multiple responses will have to be dealt with. How to code a reply that provides more than a single answer to a question? Will new variables have to be added to the codebook to allow for multiple responses? How will these multiple responses be analyzed subsequently?

Data Matrices   Now that you have created the codebook and coded and verified the data, it is time to input it. To do this, you will create a two-dimensional data matrix. In the columns of the matrix will be the variables. In the rows of the matrix will be the participants. In the cells of the matrix will be the values of the variables for each participant.

Refer to Table 1.1, which is the matrix for the data coded from the Dialing for Dollars scenario. The difficult part of creating a matrix, or *data file,* as it is more

C1	B1	B2	B3	B4	B5	B6	A1	A2	A3	A4	O1	O2
TABLE 1.1 Data Matrix for Dialing for Dollars Scenario											
1	01	37	1	65	3	3	1	3	2	2	1	5
2	02		2	19	1	0	1	5	5	1	3	4

commonly known, is ensuring that you have identified the variables and coded their values properly. In other words, the difficult task is getting the columns right. Once you have entered the data for a few participants and run some test analyses, adding data from other participants, or creating other rows, is straightforward.

Data Verification Once you have created a data file, you should verify the data for freedom from errors. This can be a time-consuming chore and it can seem like a waste of time, given the speed with which computer programs function. Do not compromise on this step. If you do, you will almost certainly regret it later. Remember that getting the computer package to analyze the data is not a guarantee that the results are meaningful unless you have confidence in the data.

What types of problems might you encounter? You might encounter problems attributable to poor data, poor data entry, and the creation of composite variables or unusual responses.

Some problems can be traced to the conditions under which the data were collected and the care with which the respondents participated. Careless responses or other forms of inaccurate responses can be difficult to detect but are worth finding because they can detract from the quality of subsequent analyses. To find them, look for unusual patterns in responses—for example, all positives, all negatives, all neutrals. Try looking for incompatible or impossible replies (e.g., "no computer experience" and "works on computers every day"). Also look for incomplete responses, which can be a special problem when composite measures are being generated.

Some problems may be attributable to data-entry errors. Miscoding or shifting of input (e.g., extra or missing keystrokes) can wreck havoc.

Some of the data problems may be attributable to the creation of composite variables. Such problems are especially likely to occur when a large number of variables are being combined and when missing values are present.

Outliers, or extreme values, may be present, which we will explain more fully later in the text. Suffice it to say for now that even after looking at all the other possibilities, it may still be the case that there is one or more unusual responses which skew the data.

Finally, too many problems with the data may be indicative of a poorly designed or executed study. *Caveat emptor* (let the buyer beware).

Manual Calculations Although statisticians rely less and less on manual calculations to conduct statistical analyses, sometimes it is desirable or necessary to perform manual calculations. Doing so might be necessary when you are learning a statistical technique, verifying that you are using a computer package properly, or when you are unable to obtain results through computer packages.

Being organized, systematic, and neat are the keys to doing manual calculations easily and successfully. Organize the data for the analysis. Plan the calculation steps allowing sufficient space to perform them. Record intermediate and final results and check them for accuracy. Most of all, understand what you are doing and why. Applying procedures by rote usually leads to difficulties.

PUTTING IT ALL TOGETHER

In the chapter we explained why it is important to develop a critical understanding of statistics. We discussed the varied meanings of the term *statistics*, the uses of statistics we emphasize in *SASSI*, and the importance of variables and variability.

We also showed how to prepare data for analysis by first creating a code book and then entering the coded data into a data matrix. We illustrated data preparation using the Dialing for Dollars Scenario as we progressed from questionnaire responses, to codebook, to data file.

KEY TERMS

Variable
Constant
Qualitative variable
Quantitative variable

Discrete variable
Continuous variable
Independent variable
Dependent variable

Predictor variable
Outcome variable
Variability

REFERENCE

Galton, F. (1889). *Natural inheritance.* London: Macmillan & Co., p. 66.

PROBLEMS

Questions

1.1. What are two major uses of statistics?
1.2. Define the term *variable.*
1.3. Define the term *constant.*
1.4. What is the difference between a qualitative variable and a quantitative variable?
1.5. What is the difference between a discrete variable and a continuous variable?
1.6. What is the difference between an independent variable and a dependent variable?
1.7. What is the difference between a predictor variable and an outcome variable?
1.8. Define the term *variability.*
1.9. What is a code (or data) book?

1.10. A researcher is interested in examining the differential effects of three types of instructional delivery: Web-based delivery, video-based delivery, and traditional lecture. Is this an example of a quantitative or qualitative variable?

1.11. In a given study, two groups of day-care children are exposed to different forms of storytelling. The children are then tested verbally on their recollection of major elements of the story. What is the independent variable? What is the dependent variable?

1.12. A researcher has received a grant to investigate the effects of time-on-task on learning, or the amount of time spent actively learning. Four groups of students are exposed to differing levels of time-on-task: one hour; two hours; three hours; and four hours. Is time-on-task a quantitative or qualitative variable? Is it an independent or dependent variable?

1.13. A student taking an introductory research methods course in a graduate program has chosen to determine the extent, if any, of the relationship between undergraduate grade point average and graduate grade point average for a group of students. What kind of investigation does this study represent?

2 Research Methodology: A Primer

chapter

OVERVIEW

The statistical analysis of data is only one phase of the research process. A more complete treatment of research includes the literature review and formulation of research hypotheses or questions, research design and methodology, data collection and analysis, and interpretation and write-up. While we concentrate in this book on data analysis, we need to situate statistical analysis in the larger context. We cannot say too strongly that successful research depends on good quality and integrity at each phase of the research process.

This chapter is a primer on research methodology. It should help develop your methodological skills and help you understand that meaningful data analysis and interpretation depend on the quality of the methods applied to the investigation. If the data used for analysis are of questionable quality, the best statistical tools cannot overcome such a handicap and the meaning of the findings will be blunted.

In covering research methodology some of the key questions we'll answer include:

1. Why is good research design important?
2. How does one deal with research ethics and the proper treatment of participants?
3. What are the two key questions that we ask of every research design?
4. How does one distinguish experiments from correlational investigations?
5. What are the strengths and weaknesses of pre-experiments, true experiments, and quasi-experiments?
6. What are the four scales of measurement?
7. Why are test reliability and validity so important?

We begin with the scenario described in Textbox 2.1.

Textbox 2.1

Scenario: Quigley's Quagmire

Joan Quigley, an early childhood educator, is interested in studying the influence of a self-concept training program on the academic achievement of schoolchildren. Dr. Quigley worked with a team of educators from the local school board and several graduate students to develop the program. After all the development work, they were interested in implementing the

---

continued

---

program. After all the development work, they were interested in implementing the program and determining whether it holds any promise for wide-scale use throughout the school district and elsewhere.

Dr. Quigley received permission from the board, several cooperating teachers, and the parents of 30 schoolchildren to experiment with the training program over the course of an entire school year and then to test the children for academic achievement using a well-established and highly regarded instrument for that purpose. The training program began immediately at the start of classes and continued for almost an entire school year until the children were tested in the spring.

The results on the 200-item test are shown in Table 2.1 for the 20 students who took the test and completed all of the training:*

The arithmetic average or mean of all 20 children's test scores is 90. Is there sufficient evidence of the training program's effectiveness to implement it on a wider scale? If yes, why? If no, why not?

*Data for 10 students are not included because they either did not complete the test and/or did not complete all of the training.

TABLE 2.1   Results of a 200-Item Test

Name	Test Score	Name	Test Score
Fred	75	Bruno	88
Gino	82	Patrice	95
Marta	97	Ishto	69
Alfonso	108	Camille	72
Claudia	78	Yiping	45
Pierre	77	Mohammed	135
Dominique	109	Sam	120
Phil	125	Sally	80
Dorothea	92	Sue	100
Lidya	63	Guillermo	90

THE IMPORTANCE OF GOOD RESEARCH DESIGN

The design of an empirical investigation includes all aspects of a study's methodology. Consideration of research design means that the researcher is attending to the details surrounding the exploration of the research questions or hypotheses of interest. Research design issues focus on answering—after it is clear why the study will occur—how the study will be done, with whom it will be done, when it will occur, where it will occur, and what treatment and measures will be used.

Its important to be specific in describing a study's design, whether as part of a proposal for research or after the research has been conducted and is being written up. The description should be sufficiently complete and clear that another researcher would have little problem replicating the study exactly. A complete description affords others the opportunity to judge the adequacy with which your study was conducted. Remember that even the best research questions depend on the subsequent investigation being well executed for useful knowledge to be generated. Always keep in mind the research equation in Textbox 2.2 to guide the conduct of your own studies as well as your critiques of the research done by others.

Textbox 2.2

The Research Equation

Sound theory + good design + proper analysis = an excellent investigation

---

Statistical Analysis and the Big Picture

Although this text is dedicated to enhancing your understanding of statistics, we want to emphasize that good data analysis is only one patch in the quilt of scientific inquiry. The same care and effort that you place in data analysis should permeate all aspects of an investigation.

The importance of good research design cannot be overstated. Inadequacies in the design of an investigation can seldom, if ever, be overcome by the use of sophisticated statistical techniques. "Garbage in, garbage out" is a tired but true expression that applies to the quality of the statistical conclusions arising from poorly designed studies.

The effort and care that you place on data analysis will be wasted if the data came from a poorly designed study or an investigation that addresses a weak question. Although there are a few techniques for detecting problems with data used for analyses, these techniques are not comprehensive, and although they may detect some errors they do not necessarily lead to foolproof ways to correct those errors. See Textbox 2.3.

It is best if you do not rely on data screening and data modification methods to repair a faulty study. By and large, remember that the methods of data analysis we cover assume that the data come from a well-designed study that used good

---

Textbox 2.3

Bad Data

Error detection ≠ error correction

---

procedures and measurement tools. The extent to which a study's design is flawed and the extent to which a key measure is imprecise is the extent to which unambiguous interpretation of the findings is impossible. See Textbox 2.4.

Textbox 2.4

Good Data

Statistical analysis is only as good as the data.

Ask Good Questions   Even well-designed studies can be pointless if the questions they explore or the hypotheses they investigate are not well formed. Concerns about the theoretical and practical import of the research are important. The investigator should know in advance how the research hopes to make a contribution to knowledge and/or practice, not merely by conducting either a poor replication of phenomena already well studied or a novel investigation of questionable value. A thorough and reasoned literature review is often the basis on which good hypotheses are built. "Good research begins and ends in the library" is meant to emphasize the importance of situating the knowledge gained from well-conceived, -designed, and -executed research within a larger context. See Textbox 2.5.

Textbox 2.5

Link Your Research to What Is Already Known

Good research begins and ends in the library.

An integrative literature review and well-reasoned research questions or hypotheses are not generated in a mechanistic fashion. To synthesize prior knowledge and attempt to expand it through the empirical exploration of hypotheses requires thought, care, and creativity. If research design is the heart of an investigation, then well-reasoned research questions are its soul.

Research Ethics

Much of the data used for analysis in the social sciences are drawn from human participants. Therefore, the ethical treatment of participants, including the care with which the information they provide is treated, are legitimate concerns for social scientists and statisticians.

There are excellent and detailed ethical principles available from professional associations such as the American Educational Research Association (1992) and the American Psychological Association (1992). We urge you to carefully consider the principles and ethical guidelines of your professional field. We briefly summarize several of these principles here, but this summary is no substitution for being completely familiar with all the principles.

In general, the ethical guidelines help insure that researchers respect the rights and dignity of every research participant.[1] These guidelines recognize that participants need to be aware of the nature of their participation and assent to their role, be allowed to discontinue if they feel uncomfortable, and have their rights to privacy and confidentiality protected.

These guidelines apply equally whether the data to be collected are numerical/quantitative or verbal/qualitative. The guidelines apply equally whether the investigator plans to conduct an experimental study or a correlational investigation. The guidelines also apply equally whether the research is conducted in a venue unfamiliar to the participants where they have a heightened awareness of being investigated or a venue familiar to the participants where they have a reduced awareness of being investigated. Finally, the guidelines apply equally regardless of the degree to which the investigator believes the investigation will be of benefit to the participants or others with an interest in the research.

Informed Consent Research participants must be individually informed about what will be occurring during the research study, the nature of the information to be provided to the researcher, and the intended use of the data that are collected. If adults are the participants, they must give their consent. In the case of minors, they might agree to participate but formal consent also must be given by a parent or guardian.

Informed consent often takes the form of a written explanation from the investigator, spelling out the study's purposes and procedures and outlining the participant's role, which is then signed by the participant or parent who indicates a willingness to participate. In cases in which a complete understanding of the research might invalidate the findings, participants must be fully debriefed about the purposes, methods, and expected findings immediately following the study.

Freedom to Discontinue Informed consent does not obligate participants to continue against their wishes, especially if feelings of discomfort or concern arise. Freedom to discontinue must be made explicit to participants and any requests to withdraw should be honored without penalty or prejudice. Participants may withdraw for any reason, whether related to the investigation or not. For example, participants may withdraw because the research raises their anxiety or because they feel the questions are inappropriate to answer. Participants may also withdraw because school, work, or personal issues make their continued involvement difficult or impossible.

Privacy and Confidentiality Participants have a right to know, and should agree with, the researcher's plans for using the information participants provide. How will the data that is collected be stored? Who will have access to individual

---

[1]We discuss the ethics of research involving human participants. Researchers using animals for experimentation also need to ensure that animals are properly treated.

responses? For example, will school personnel see student test results? Will employers have access to employee interviews? What form will the data take when the results are made public? Will individual responses be reported? Will the responses of individuals be recognizable?

It is often desirable to maintain the confidentiality of research participants. Identification numbers can be assigned to participants, making it difficult or impossible for anyone, including members of the research team, to trace the identity of participants. Respecting participants' rights to privacy and confidentiality are especially important now that computer technology makes it easier than ever to mistakenly violate those rights by, for example, allowing data files on diskette to be copied and circulated, even over the Internet.

Similarly, new technologies make it easy to unobtrusively observe and record the behavior of others. Computer conferencing and certain educational software can readily maintain a database of frequency and nature of use. But is it acceptable to allow this electronic form of data collection to take place without asking participants whether they are aware and willing to allow their responses to be used for purposes other than their original intent?

BASICS OF RESEARCH DESIGN

In this section we cover some basics of research design. We discuss the nature of variables and hypotheses used in experimental studies and correlational investigations. We explore the two basic questions that form the basis of the research design treatment developed by Campbell and Stanley (1966). Finally, we present a notational system for describing research designs and distinguishing among them.

Experimental and Correlational Investigations

In its most basic form, an empirical investigation seeks to determine whether there is a nonchance relationship between two variables. There are two basic forms of investigation with which we will concern ourselves: experimental and correlational investigations. Experimental investigations attempt to establish a cause-and-effect relationship between two variables, the independent and dependent variables. Correlational investigations seek only to determine whether the measured relationship between predictor and outcome variables occurred as a function of chance.

CD-ROM link 2.1

Problem Generator: Research Design
To practice identifying the independent and dependent variables in an experiment, select *Research design* from the Problem Generator Menu on the CD-ROM. The Problem Generator will create as many practice problems as you need, and it will provide you with the correct answers so that you can check your work.

Experimental Variables   In an experiment, the researcher manipulates an independent variable and then measures the effect of the manipulation on the dependent variable. The **independent variable** is the variable under the experimenter's control. It is the treatment or manipulation whose effects are being studied. Note that a variable must have no fewer than two values or levels, since one studies *variations* in the independent variable and notes the consequences of these variations on the dependent variable.

The **dependent variable** is some form of measured behavior ranging from physiological responses, to think-aloud protocols, to standardized test results, to unobtrusive recordings of children's fantasy play. The independent variable temporally precedes the dependent variable: the experimenter first manipulates the independent variable and then measures the dependent variable.

Experimental Hypotheses   An **experimental hypothesis** is a statement suggesting that the independent variable causes or produces a change in the dependent variable. An experimental hypothesis is sometimes derived formally from a scientific theory and sometimes derived from less rigorous speculations arising from a practical concern. A true experiment allows the researcher to determine whether a causal relationship exists between the independent and dependent variables. Such an experiment occurs when the researcher is able to study the influence of the manipulated variable in isolation from other extraneous sources of influence. When extraneous sources of influence are not controlled, they serve as potential rival explanations to the effect of the treatment and diminish the certainty with which a cause-and-effect relationship can be established. See Textbox 2.6.

There is great value in knowing whether variables are causally related. Causal explanation is the basic building block of scientific knowledge. In the social sciences, causal explanation helps us understand depression and how to treat it, how children learn to read and how teachers can utilize effective reading instruction techniques, and so on.

A single experiment does not validate a scientific theory or completely support a solution to a practical concern. Often, multiple experiments, with different participants, in varied settings, and using different variables are required to build broad confidence in the applicability of the phenomenon under study.

Textbox 2.6

Experimental Study of Instructor Expressiveness

A researcher hypothesizes that instructor expressiveness affects student ratings of teaching. He conducts a study using a professional actor and a scripted lecture. The actor is videotaped delivering two 20-minute lectures in which he role-plays both a high expressive teacher (e.g., using ample vocal inflection, movement, humor, and hand gestures) and a low expressive teacher (e.g., using limited vocal inflection, lack of movement, no humor, and no hand gestures). One hundred college students volunteer to view the videotapes. Half view the high expressive tape and then complete a multi-item rating form. Half view the low expressive videotape and also complete the rating form. The instructor ratings are significantly higher for the high expressive instructor, and the researcher concludes that instructor expressiveness, the independent variable, affects student ratings of teaching, the dependent variable.

To read more about the study, see: Abrami, Leventhal, & Perry (1982).

Correlational Variables   There are, of course, situations in which it is unethical or impractical to engage in experimentation. For example, experimentally inducing negative teacher expectations may put students at risk of lower school performance and, therefore, it is unethical and unwise to conduct an experiment in which negative teacher expectations are introduced. Nevertheless, it is important to understand whether there is a relationship between teacher expectations and student performance, and so correlational investigations are needed.

Individual difference variables, such as personality traits, are not manipulable. Longitudinal investigations which may last for months or even years seldom control extraneous influences. And there are many instances in which research needs to occur in a natural context rather than in an artificial environment under which most experiments are conducted. These are situations in which correlational investigations are used, where variables are measured, not manipulated.

In a correlational investigation, the researcher measures, but does not manipulate, a predictor variable and also measures the outcome variable. The **predictor variable** is the variable that is hypothesized to explain variability in the outcome variable. Given that predictor variables are measured rather than manipulated, one avoids causal language in speaking of the relationship between the predictor variable and the outcome variable.

Predictor variables and independent variables share the role of explaining variability in another variable. Only independent variables explain the variability in cause-and-effect terms.

The **outcome variable** in a correlational investigation is some form of measured behavior ranging from physiological responses, to think-aloud protocols, to standardized test results, to unobtrusive recordings of children's fantasy play. Outcome variables from correlational investigations are not fundamentally different from dependent variables used in experiments.

Correlational Hypotheses   A **correlational hypothesis** is a statement suggesting that changes in the predictor variable are related to changes in the outcome variable. Because the predictor variable is not manipulated and there is often a lack of experimental isolation and control, correlational investigations are useful for description and prediction but not causal explanation. The nature and uses of correlational investigations are discussed more fully in Chapter 13.

Whether research hypotheses are correlational or experimental, the core of the simplest hypotheses involves the relationship between two variables. Of course, more complex hypotheses can include multiple independent variables or multiple predictor variables as well as multiple dependent variables or multiple outcome variables. Can you find the independent or predictor variable(s) (*A*) and the dependent or outcome variable(s) (*Y*) in the research statements given in Textbox 2.7?

Two Basic Questions

In 1963, Donald Campbell and Julian Stanley published a brief piece on research design that covered pre-experimental, experimental, and quasi-experimental designs as well as ways to critically evaluate the strengths and weaknesses of

---

Textbox 2.7

Find the Independent (Predictor) Variable(s) (*A*) and Dependent (Outcome) Variable(s) (*Y*) in Each Statement

1. Instructor expressiveness affects student ratings of instruction.
2. Negative teacher expectations result in diminished student academic performance.
3. A positive self-concept helps student learn.
4. Successful school achievement is the key to student self-concept.
5. Stock earnings depend on international economic ties.
6. If you use the *SASSI* CD-ROM, you will learn more statistics and enjoy it too.
7. Psychological well-being is a function of genes and the environment.

   Answers: 1. A = expressiveness; Y = ratings. 2. A = expectations; Y = performance. 3. A = self-concept; Y = learning. 4. A = achievement; Y = self-concept. 5. A = ties; Y = earnings. 6. A = CD-ROM; Y = learning, enjoyment. 7. A = genes, environment; Y = well-being.

---

these designs. Their brief treatment became one of the most widely cited in all the social sciences. The concepts and terminology they introduced have become generally accepted among researchers and so we summarize their work here.

When one examines the results of an investigation concerns about the investigation can be organized around two key concerns: the credibility of the conclusions and their applicability or generalizability. The credibility of the conclusions focuses on the following question:

> *Did the researcher really find what he or she claims to have found, or is there another way to explain the findings?*

The applicability of the conclusions focuses on the following question:

> *Will the same results happen all the time with everyone, everywhere?*

Concerns about the credibility of the conclusions focus on the internal validity of an investigation. Concerns about the applicability of the conclusions focus on the external validity of an investigation.

Internal Validity **Internal validity** exists when the experimental treatment has a noticeable impact on the dependent variable in the specific experimental instance under consideration. Internal validity exists when it can be shown that the independent variable, as manipulated, produced a change in the dependent variable, as measured. Threats to internal validity are rival explanations to the effect of the treatment.

In the Quigley Quagmire scenario (see Textbox 2.1), the researcher is hoping to show that the treatment, a self-concept training program, has a causal effect on the dependent measure, student achievement on the 200-item test. In other words, the researcher wants to see whether the treatment or independent variable (i.e., training program) causes some of the variability in the dependent variable (i.e., student achievement). If a study's design allowed you to conclude that there was a causal relationship between the manipulation of the independent variable and the measurement of the dependent variable, you would know that the study was high in internal validity.

External Validity   **External validity** exists to the extent the research findings can be **generalized** across people, settings, treatment variables, and measurement variables. For example, a variety of instruments, techniques, or manipulations may be deemed acceptable with no certainty that a finding with one instrument generalizes to another. Therefore, threats to external validity are limiting conditions to the effect of the treatment, *not* rival explanations to the effect of the treatment.

For example, imagine that you were able to conclude that the self-concept training program produced a learning gain in the 20 students involved in the experiment. The study would be generalizable across populations and settings if you were able to show that the same program produced the same levels of learning when other students at other schools also showed achievement gains due to self-concept training on the 200-item test. But the phenomenon would lack a degree of external validity if you modified either the nature or duration of the program and failed to produce similar results. Likewise, the phenomenon would lack a degree of external validity if you modified the measure of student learning and achievement gains were not evident on this new measure.

Concerns about internal validity and external validity are core concerns. Whether you are critically evaluating your own research or trying to critique the research of others, you must keep these concerns in mind:

- Are the findings believable or is there some other way to explain them?
- Are the findings unique to the conditions of the study or are they widely applicable?

The Great Debate: Internal versus External Validity   Social scientists love to debate whether it is more important to have either internal validity or external validity as the cornerstone of a program of empirical inquiry. Laboratory researchers who rely on carefully controlled experiments as the backbone of their work point out the importance of establishing causal relationships in understanding the nature of phenomena. Whether research is conducted for the purposes of description, explanation, or prediction, laboratory researchers note how essential it is to get a correct understanding of how things "work." Not knowing the underlying, true causes of a phenomenon or being wrong in that understanding means being incapable of proper application—a costly and potentially harmful notion.

Applied researchers who rely on naturalistic and highly generalizable studies as the backbone of their work point out the importance of conducting investigations that are applicable to the persons, setting, and variables one is interested in studying. Stripping away the context of the research denies a chance to inform practice; sterile experimentation offers causal explanations that are meaningless or irrelevant to users.

We believe that the best answer lies between these two extreme positions. Research needs to be controlled if researchers are ever to understand the true nature of phenomena. Research needs to be realistic if researchers are ever to include those factors critical for study. When both internal and external validity cannot be had, the choice as to which type of validity to have may be less dependent on methodological criteria and more dependent on theoretical criteria that guide the variables to be studied and help establish how to study them.

Notational System

In the examples of research designs that follow we will use the simplest versions of research: one independent variable and one dependent variable. Furthermore, the independent variable to which participants are exposed will have only two levels such as experimental (A_1) versus control (A_2), treatment (A_1) versus no treatment (A_2), or, more generally, be differentiable according to some qualitative (e.g., method of instruction) or quantitative (e.g., hours of study time) difference.

The use of the labels "control" or "no treatment" does not necessarily mean that participants are exposed to nothing; more often it means that they are exposed to something more or less traditional, standard, or ordinary than the experimental or treatment condition. Finally, concerns about internal and external validity apply to designs in which the independent variable has more than two levels and to *each* independent variable in a design with multiple treatments (i.e., each independent variable is considered separately when threats to validity are being judged).

Several examples using a notational system for research designs are illustrated in Table 2.2. The notational system helps differentiate among and between pre-experiments, true experiments, and quasi-experiments. We will use the notational system to illustrate and critique these designs from the perspective of Campbell and Stanley (1966). Specifically, we will use this notational system to help you critically examine several types of research designs that have been used to explore whether there is a causal relationship between an independent variable and a dependent variable.

CD-ROM link 2.2

Problem Generator: Research Design
To practice identifying the research design used in an experiment, select *Research design* from the Problem Generator Menu on the CD-ROM. The Problem Generator will create as many practice problems as you need, and it will provide you with the correct answers so that you can check your work.

Types of Designs

The first type of research design is called pre-experimental because pre-experimental studies lack sufficient controls for threats to internal validity. The researcher, then, cannot be confident that his or her interpretation of the data is correct and consequently there may be one or more alternative explanations of the findings. The second type of design is called true experimental because true experimental studies completely control for threats to internal validity such that the researcher can be confident that his or her interpretation of the data is correct, and consequently

TABLE 2.2 Notational System for Research Design	

1. Y_{A11} A_1 Y_{A12} There is a single group of participants observed both before and after the treatment.

2. Y_{A11} A_1 Y_{A12} There are two groups of participants nonrandomly
-------------------------   assigned. All participants are observed simultane-
     Y_{A21} A_2 Y_{A22} ously both before and after the treatment. The first group, receiving A_1, is the experimental group.

3. R A_1 Y_{A11} There are two groups of participants randomly as-
   R A_2 Y_{A21} signed. Posttesting is successive, not simultaneous.

A = introduction of the treatment or manipulation of the independent variable (the subscript 1 refers to the experimental condition and the subscript 2 refers to the control condition).

Y = the observation or measurement of the dependent variable (the subscripts $A1$ refers to the experimental condition and the subscript $A2$ refers to the control condition); the additional subscript 1 refers to the first measurement period, the additional subscript 2 refers to the second measurement period, and so on.)

R = Random assignment of subjects to treatment conditions (see Chapter 6)

– – – – – = lack of random assignment

The *passing of time* is noted by movement from left to right.

there are no alternative explanations of the findings. The third type of research design is called quasi-experimental because quasi-experimental studies typically control most threats to internal validity and are superior to pre-experiments but inferior to true experiments in effectiveness, efficiency, or both.

PRE-EXPERIMENTAL DESIGNS

Pre-experimental designs are attempts at experimentation that are so flawed that numerous possible threats to internal validity often disqualify the research as providing useful scientific evidence. We cover these designs first to help understand how threats to internal validity may affect interpretations of the findings and because pre-experimental designs remain among the most popular research designs in use for applied research purposes. Pre-experimental designs include the One-Shot Case Study, the One-Group Pretest–Posttest Design, and the Static Group Comparison Design. We include correlational studies among pre-experimental designs because simple correlational designs closely approximate the weaknesses (and strengths) of the Static Group Comparison Design.

One-Shot Case Study

The One-Shot Case Study consists of a single group of participants that is exposed to the experimental treatment and then is tested. Using the notational system, the design is represented as:

$$A_1 \qquad Y_{A11}$$

You may already have guessed that the design of the Quigley Quagmire is a One-Shot Case Study and that there are problems interpreting the results that arise from studies of this sort. The general problem with the One-Shot Case Study focuses on the lack of a comparison group. Consequently, all the researcher can do is describe the results of the study; the design does not provide for a comparison of the results and the establishment of a causal relationship. Are the findings good or bad? Better or worse? Did the treatment have any influence? See Table 2.3.

The very minimum for gathering experimental information involves making *at least one* comparison that is, to show that differences in the independent variable, A, produce changes in the dependent variable, Y. Since there is only a single group here measured once, there is no basis for an actual comparison. Instead, a researcher using the one-shot case study makes comparisons based on *hypothetical data* or *common knowledge expectations* or *retrospective recall*:

$$A_1 \quad Y_{A11} \quad \text{(This is the only group actually tested.)}$$

$$(A_2 \quad Y_{A21}) \quad \text{(This is an illusory comparison group.)}$$

In interpreting the Quigley Quagmire scenario, a lot depended on your willingness to make such a hypothetical comparison. If you thought an average score of 90 on the test was high, you probably were tempted to conclude that the self-concept training program worked. In contrast, if you thought an average score of 90 on the test was low, you probably were tempted to reach the opposite conclusion. And if you had no idea what a score of 90 meant, you probably were puzzled and were tempted to conclude that the study lacked critical information for a definitive interpretation.

While the weaknesses of the One-Shot Case Study may seem obvious to you, this design typifies the type of design used in everyday life for making the simplest decisions to the most complex ones. Practitioners will vigorously defend their ability to make such judgments based on their accumulated knowledge and expertise. But is this naive and intuitive science good science? Should important decisions depend on our subjective judgments or is objective evidence always required?

The One-Group Pretest–Posttest Design

Research is most often needed when reasons are not known and answers are uncertain. With this in mind, you might want to urge Dr. Quigley to conduct a further study and come to a more definitive and objective conclusion about the effectiveness of the self-concept training program.

TABLE 2.3   One-Shot Case Study: Quigley's Quagmire

Condition	Posttest
Self-concept training A_1	Mean student achievement $Y_{A11} = 90.00$

If a comparison group is needed, why not compare student learning before training and then again after training? Surely, if differences appear, it must be "proof" that the treatment worked. And doesn't using the same participants for measurement both before and after the treatment help ensure experimental control, because participants serve as their own controls?

In the One-Group Pretest–Posttest Design, a single group of participants is observed prior to the introduction of the treatment and after the treatment has ended:

$$Y_{A11} \quad A_1 \quad Y_{A12}$$

So Dr. Quigley conducts a second study. She finds a new sample of 20 students, tests them at the beginning of classes in the fall (Y_{A11}), introduces the treatment for almost the entire school year (A_1) and then retests the students near the end of the school year in the spring (Y_{A12}). Their average score on the pretest (Y_{A11}) was 60.00. Their average score on the posttest (Y_{A12}) was 90.00. See Table 2.4.

The key question is whether the difference between posttest (Y_{A12}) and pretest (Y_{A11}) is a function of the treatment (A_1) or can the difference be explained otherwise? In other words, is the difference between 90.00 and 60.00 due exclusively to the treatment or can some other factor(s) explain the difference?

Unfortunately, using participants as their own controls only solves one problem with the One-Group Pretest–Posttest Design. It is true that having participants serve as their own controls removes differences between participants as a possible threat to internal validity. However, a host of other threats remain.

Among these threats we will detail three. First, the participants are schoolchildren, and so their academic achievement would be expected to improve merely as a function of maturation or normal growth and development, unrelated to the possible effects of the experimental treatment. Second, the children were also exposed to opportunities for learning other than the experimental treatment, the influence of factors extraneous to the treatment referred to as "history." Third, the gains were apparently small and may have come about in part merely as a function of retesting. It is fairly well known that practice helps improve test performance, even if separated by the passage of time.

There are other possible rival explanations. You may prefer one of these over the explanations offered above. Or you may prefer none of the rival explanations. The point is that one no longer can be certain what accounted for the difference between Y_{A12} and Y_{A11}. It may have been the self-concept training program or it may have been something else. The design of the research is sufficiently flawed that one no longer has confidence that the findings show unequivocally that the treatment worked, causing a change in the dependent variable. See Textbox 2.8.

TABLE 2.4 One-Group Pretest–Posttest Design: Quigley's Quagmire

Pretest	Condition	Posttest
Mean student achievement	Self-concept training	Mean student achievement
$Y_{A11} = 60.00$	A_1	$Y_{A12} = 90.00$

Textbox 2.8

Pre-experiments and Policy Decisions

At first, did you believe that the evidence from the One-Group Pretest–Posttest Design provided empirical validation of the self-concept training program?

Did the magnitude of the difference between the mean pretest scores and the mean posttest scores affect your judgment?

Did the logic behind the self-concept training program influence your beliefs?

What do you now think about the effectiveness of the training program?

If you were an administrator, explain why you would or would not fund the program for adoption throughout the school district.

Static Group Comparison Design

Dr. Quigley may have elected not to use the One-Group Pretest–Posttest Design in favor of the third, but also weak pre-experimental design: the Static Group Comparison Design. In this design, intact groups of participants are exposed to either the experimental (A_1) or control (A_2) conditions. However, participants are not randomly assigned such that the design is represented this way:

$$A_1 \quad Y_{A11} \quad \text{(experimental group)}$$
$$\text{----------}$$
$$A_2 \quad Y_{A21} \quad \text{(control group)}$$

Again the question here is, what accounts for any difference between Y_{A11} and Y_{A21}? Is the experimental treatment accountable for the difference or can the difference be explained otherwise?

The obvious threat to internal validity in the Static Group Comparison Design is the effect of selection. Concerns about selection are that differences preexisting between experimental and control participants, and therefore unrelated to the treatment, are responsible for the difference between Y_{A11} and Y_{A21}. Perhaps the two groups of students differ somewhat in their average ability or in the quality of instruction they received the year *prior* to the experiment. In other words, if the treatment had absolutely no effect whatsoever, a selection effect would still make it seem like the treatment worked because a difference between the groups would be observed when they were posttested.

Imagine that Dr. Quigley had actually conducted a Static Group Comparison Design study. She found a mean (average) score on the achievement test for the control students (Y_{A21}) of 60.00 and a mean score on the achievement test for the experimental students (Y_{A11}) of 90.00. Is the mean difference of 30.00 between the groups attributable to the effects of the self-concept training program, preexisting differences between the two groups of students, or some combination of these two explanations? Not being able to answer with certainty that the treatment caused the difference is what makes this design a weak one for establishing cause and effect. See Table 2.5.

TABLE 2.5 Static Group Comparison Design: Quigley's Quagmire	
Condition	*Posttest*
Control condition	Mean student achievement
A_2	$Y_{A21} = 60.00$
Self-concept training	Mean student achievement
A_1	$Y_{A11} = 90.00$

Simple correlational studies can be considered forms of the Static Group Comparison Design because participants are exposed to varying degrees of one variable but without careful control and random assignment. Therefore, differences in the outcome measure that one may wish to attribute to a single cause may be due to a variety of causes.

All is not lost, however, by using correlational designs. If a strong correlation is obtained, the credibility of the causal hypothesis is strengthened, if not confirmed. In contrast, if a weak or zero correlation is obtained, the credibility of the hypothesis is weakened, if not disconfirmed.

Experimental versus Statistical Control

Our emphasis here is on the experimental control of extraneous influences via well-designed investigations. An alternative to experimental control, when experimental control is impossible or impractical, is statistical control, where the extraneous variable is measured and its influence on the outcome variable removed before the influence of the predictor variable is examined.

Although generally less effective and conclusive than experimental control, statistical control can be used to help reduce or eliminate certain threats to internal validity. The multiple regression techniques described in Chapter 15 lend themselves well to statistical control of extraneous influences. Problems with statistical control include potential measurement problems with the extraneous variable and possible misspecification of the extraneous influence(s). In other words, one may not measure the extraneous factor properly or one may not specify the correct or complete extraneous influence, meaning that alternative explanations are still possible. Furthermore, this type of statistical control only resolves problems with extraneous or third variable interpretations. It does not help the researcher resolve ambiguities associated with reverse variable interpretations.

For example, Dr. Quigley believes that the self-concept training program affects students' learning and provides evidence that self-concept and achievement are correlated. But the correlation itself does not rule out the possibility that the opposite occurs, that achievement promotes self-concept.

Elimination of third variable interpretations in this correlation does not resolve the issue of reverse variable interpretations. To control the likelihood of reserve variable interpretations requires the use of more sophisticated and elaborate techniques, such as cross-lagged panel designs, involving multiple measurements over time.

More on Internal Validity

If you want a more detailed explanation of the possible threats to internal validity than the explanations that appeared above, please consult Textbox 2.9. The likelihood of each of these threats operating in the three pre-experimental designs is given in Table 2.6.

Possible or Probable?

The seven threats to internal validity that may operate in the three pre-experimental designs (see Textbox 2.9) serve as possible rival explanations to the effect of the independent variable on the dependent variable. The particulars of each research situation dictate which of these threats is likely to have operated. Your logical and critical analysis of the situation is essential in deciding which threats may have exerted an influence. Even when a threat is likely, there is no guarantee of its influence nor is there a guarantee that the treatment had no influence. On the other hand, a threat you disregard as unlikely may indeed have exerted an influence. Finally, there is the matter of degree to consider. For example, the loss of a single participant is rarely sufficient to disqualify the findings in a study involving 100 or more participants. On the other hand, if half of the participants drop out of the study, the influence of mortality may be serious.

CD-ROM link 2.3

Problem Generator: Research Design
To practice identifying possible threats to validity, select *Research design* from the Problem Generator Menu on the CD-ROM. The Problem Generator will create as many practice problems as you need, and it will provide you with some sample answers that you can compare to your own.

TABLE 2.6 Possible Threats to Internal Validity in Pre-experimental Designs*

Design	History	Maturation	Testing	Instrumen-tation	Regression	Selection	Mortality
One-Shot Case Study	Yes	Yes	NA	NA	NA	Yes	Yes
One-Group Pretest–Posttest Design	Yes	Yes	Yes	Yes	?	No	No
Static Group Comparison Design	Yes	?	No	No	No	Yes	Yes

*Yes = a threat to internal validity

No = not a threat to internal validity

NA = threat cannot operate due to lack of second measurement

? = may be a threat to internal validity

Seven Major Threats to Internal Validity

We briefly define and give examples of each of the major threats to internal validity, namely: *m*ortality, *r*egression, *s*election, *m*aturation, *i*nstrumentation, *t*esting, and *h*istory. "Mr. Smith" or "Mrs. Mith" are mnemonics for remembering these seven threats.

Mortality is the loss or dropout of participants, especially after the onset of experimentation, which can create group inequivalence. Some also think of mortality as occurring between the pretest and the posttest. But Campbell and Stanley (1966) assume that incomplete data are discarded. If so, mortality is *not* a threat in designs in which participants are repeatedly tested.

Example Fifty corporate trainees are randomly assigned to either of two training programs. The control condition is a standard, in-house program. The experimental program requires at-home computer study via the Internet. A portion of the experimental group fails to do the requisite homework and drops out of the experimental program. A comparison of the remaining participants finds the experimental participants outscoring the control participants. The treatment may have been the cause of the difference, but differential mortality may also explain the findings. For example, experimental participants who did not drop out may have been more highly motivated or otherwise different than the dropouts.

Regression (more fully known as *statistical regression toward the mean*) is a change in scores on retesting when measurement error exists and especially for participants selected on the basis of extreme scores on the pretest. When extreme scores are used at the pretest and a test is not perfectly reliable (has some error of measurement), there will usually be a shift of the Y scores to less extreme scores at the posttest. That is, the scores regress toward the mean or average score, which is the more likely score.

Example Schoolchildren are tested with a locally developed test of mathematics proficiency. It is decided to study the effects of individually paced mathematics instruction on those with either extremely low or extremely high test scores. But because there is some measurement error, not all the test scores will remain the same on retesting. That portion of each high test score and each low test score that is a function of error will tend toward the average or typical score. Hence, regression effects will cause high scores to fall and low scores to rise. As a consequence, the individually paced instruction may appear harmful to those initially identified as high in mathematics proficiency while the instruction may appear beneficial to those initially identified as low in mathematics proficiency.

Selection is the effect of initial group inequivalence often caused by the use of intact groups or volunteers who request the novel treatment. Consequently, the researcher cannot be certain that groups of participants are equivalent at the outset unless they are randomly assigned. Random assignment is not a guarantee of initial group equivalence. By chance, sampling error may create differences between groups. But as you will see, sampling error is taken into account in statistical testing. When it is possible, matching of participants on the pretest followed by random assignment further reduces the risks of initial group inequivalence.

Example A researcher uses two intact classes to study an interactive multimedia computer program for reading comprehension. The experimental class uses the program for half the school year while the control class uses assigned readings. Posttest results reveal higher comprehension scores for the experimental class, but the results may be a function of the two groups initially being unequal in reading.

Maturation includes both short-term and long-term changes to participants, biologically or psychologically, due to normal growth and development. Brief, reversible effects including fatigue, hunger, and irritability are maturational influences as well as sustained, permanent changes such as IQ development or reaction time decay.

Textbox 2.9 (continued)

Example   A researcher studies a new school curriculum by comparing the performance of elementary schoolchildren on an aptitude test taken in September with the students' scores on the test taken the following June. The researcher fails to consider seriously the substantial gain in ability due to normal growth and development and falsely concludes that the new curriculum caused the changes in scores.

Instrumentation is any change in the observational technique or measurement instrument. The mechanical measuring device may deteriorate or malfunction. The human judges may change because of fatigue, experience, or awareness of the study.

Example   A researcher employs two assistants to observe and record the verbal interactions of students working in small groups at the beginning of a biology unit and again at the end of the unit, two months later. The observers are unsure of themselves and miss important interactions at first, but by the end they are more confident and picking up on subtleties. These differences in observer recording over time make it appear as if the verbal interactions among the groups have changed.

Testing effects are changes that occur to the participant, not the instrument, as a function of the initial testing, which affect retesting. The testing influence is due to the reactive or obtrusive nature of the measurement tool or experimental setting in which the investigation occurs.

Example   A group of immigrant children takes a standardized test for the first time and the children have difficulty with the format and timing. On retesting sometime later, the children show fewer problems with the administrative conditions. The change in test scores is attributed to the children's immersion classes, but the performance improvement is mostly a function of their increased familiarity with the testing conditions.

History is the operation of events external to the treatment that occur between pretest and posttest, which may create a change in scores.

Example   A company decides to change its corporate image through a new advertising campaign. It targets 100 clients and gets them to provide pre- and post-campaign attitudinal ratings to determine if the campaign worked. During the campaign, but not part of it, the company announces major price reductions in its products. Is the attitudinal shift a function of price changes or the advertising campaign?

The critical analysis of pre-experimental designs serves to remind everyone that the quality of these designs precludes a definitive conclusion that the treatment worked. The treatment may have operated but the attempt at empirical verification is sufficiently flawed that the finding lacks credibility, even though a statistical test reveals a significant difference between experimental and control groups on the dependent variable (Y).

Is it a certainty that the difference is attributable to the effect of the independent variable, as manipulated, on the dependent variable, as measured? Or is some other factor likely to have contributed to the difference? The degree of doubt that poor research designs raise often disqualifies them from providing useful information to either the scientist or practitioner. If experimentation is worth doing, it is worth doing well. The consequences of an erroneous causal explanation can be damaging to both those who investigate phenomenon and those who apply what is learned to practice.

TRUE EXPERIMENTAL DESIGNS

True experimental designs control for all threats to internal validity. We will cover the two most popular true experimental designs—the Pretest–Posttest Control Group Design and the Posttest-Only Control Group Design—and consider how they control for rival explanations to the influence of the treatment. We will then consider the advantages and disadvantages of the designs and introduce several threats to external validity.

Pretest–Posttest Control Group Design

The Pretest–Posttest Control Group Design is composed of two groups of participants that have been randomly assigned to either the experimental condition (A_1) or the control condition (A_2). Prior to the introduction of the independent variable, both groups of participants are pretested. Following the treatment, both groups are posttested. The Pretest–Posttest Control Group Design is:

R $\quad Y_{A11}$ $\quad A_1$ $\quad Y_{A12}$ $\qquad$ (This group alone is identical to the One-Group Pretest–Posttest Design.)

R $\quad Y_{A21}$ $\quad A_2$ $\quad Y_{A22}$ $\qquad$ (A second, control group is added to the design.)

That portion of this design representing the group receiving the experimental treatment (A_1) is identical to the One-Group Pretest–Posttest Design. Therefore, the critical question is, how does this true experimental design allow researchers to control threats to internal validity while the pre-experimental design did not? Clearly, the answer lies in the addition of the control group receiving A_2.

In the pre-experimental design, we asked whether $Y_{A12} \neq Y_{A11}$ and, if there was a difference between the two groups, it was due to the treatment. Unfortunately, we were not able to conclude whether the difference was a function of the treatment or a function of one or more threats to internal validity.

In the true experimental design, we ask a more complex question:

$$\text{Is } Y_{A12} - Y_{A11} \neq Y_{A22} - Y_{A21}?$$

Any measured difference between the experimental group and the control group is attributable to the only factor that distinguishes the two groups: the independent variable. This will be true even if various threats to internal validity operated. For example, historical influences might have occurred—participants might have matured or been affected by pretesting—and the measuring instrument might have changed over time. There might indeed have been changes from pretest to posttest. But the nature of the true experiment means that *both* the experimental and control group would be affected. If they were affected and the treatment did not work, there would be no differences between the groups. If they were affected and the treatment worked, there would be differences between the groups. And if they were not affected and if the treatment worked, there would be differences between the groups.

The Pretest–Posttest Control Group Design does not control for threats by eliminating their influence on participants. Instead, this true experimental design controls the threats by allowing the researcher to conduct a comparison between the groups where the effect of the treatment can be detected above and beyond the operation of threats to internal validity.

We will use the fictitious data from the One-Group Pretest–Posttest Design that evolved from the Quigley's Quagmire scenario, as previously presented in Table 2.4. To this design we will also add the data from a true control group. As noted in Textbox 2.10, whatever the pattern of findings, one is able to detect

---

Textbox 2.10

Pretest–Posttest Control Group Design: Quigley's Quagmire

Recall that the results on the 200-item test using the One-Group Pretest–Posttest Design were as follows:

Condition	Mean pretest score	Mean posttest score
Self-concept training (A_1)	$Y_{A11} = 60.00$	$Y_{A12} = 90.00$

Now here are three sets of hypothetical outcomes A–C if a true experiment with a control condition (Pretest–Posttest Control Group Design) were conducted. Note that for each of the sets of outcomes the results for the self-concept training group are identical. But the conclusion reached for each of the sets is different.

Outcome A

Condition	Mean pretest score	Mean posttest score
Self-concept training (A_1)	$Y_{A11} = 60.00$	$Y_{A12} = 90.00$
Control students (A_2)	$Y_{A21} = 60.00$	$Y_{A22} = 90.00$

Results: No treatment effect. One or more rival effects operated.

Outcome B

Condition	Mean pretest score	Mean posttest score
Self-concept training (A_1)	$Y_{A11} = 60.00$	$Y_{A12} = 90.00$
Control students (A_2)	$Y_{A21} = 60.00$	$Y_{A22} = 60.00$

Results: A treatment effect. No rival effects operated.

Outcome C

Condition	Mean pretest score	Mean posttest score
Self-concept training (A_1)	$Y_{A11} = 60.00$	$Y_{A12} = 90.00$
Control students (A_2)	$Y_{A21} = 60.00$	$Y_{A22} = 70.00$

Results: A treatment effect. In addition, one or more rival effects operated.

unequivocally whether a treatment effect occurred. Remember that is so because we are now asking:

$$\text{Is } Y_{A12} - Y_{A11} \neq Y_{A22} - Y_{A21}?$$

Posttest–Only Control Group Design

This design is composed of two groups that have been randomly assigned to either the experimental condition (A_1) or the control condition (A_2). Following the treatment, both groups are posttested:

$$R \quad A_1 \quad Y_{A11}$$
$$R \quad A_2 \quad Y_{A21}$$

This design is similar to the static group comparison design. However, in contrast to the pre-experimental design, this true experimental design allows one to conclude that the difference is a function of the treatment. Therefore, the critical question is, how does this true experimental design control threats to internal validity while the pre-experimental design does not?

Selection is a major threat to internal validity in the static group comparison design but random assignment of participants excludes it from consideration in this true experimental design. If mortality affects the design, it would revert to its pre-experimental counterpart. Therefore, since the effects of selection have been removed as a threat to internal validity, it is reasonable to conclude that the difference between $Y_{A11} - Y_{A21}$ is a function of the treatment.

External Validity

If true experimental designs all control for threats to internal validity, how does one distinguish among them? They are distinguished primarily in terms of their ability to control for threats to external validity, or those factors that define the limiting conditions of a treatment's effectiveness.

The existence of pretesting in the Pretest–Posttest Control Group Design means that this design may suffer from the limitations caused by pretest sensitization. Pretest sensitization effects suggest the treatment worked only because the pretest acted as a catalyst that sensitized participants to their condition. Pretesting in a health and conditioning program may operate in such a fashion; not as a substitute for the treatment but as a means for *allowing* the treatment to work. See Textbox 2.11 for the common threats to external validity described by Campbell and Stanley (1966) that distinguish among various research designs. Not on this short list of factors are threats to external validity arising from problems with *treatment generalization* and *outcome generalization*.

Limited treatment generalization means that the treatment works only under selected conditions of implementation. Variations in length, intensity, and quality of the treatment may affect external validity.

Limited outcome generalization means that the treatment works only under selected conditions of measurement. Variations in the methods used for collecting

---

Textbox 2.11

Four Common Threats to External Validity

Multiple-X Interference—In studies with more than a single treatment given to a participant, multiple-X interference is the effect of prior *treatments* on making subsequent treatments work.

Reactive arrangements—The obtrusiveness of the *settings* causes the treatment to work. In a different setting, no treatment effect will occur. May be a problem with all true experimental designs.

Selection and X interaction—The treatment effect is limited to the *sample* studied. May be a problem with all the true experimental designs.

Testing and X interaction—The effect of *pretest* sensitization allows the treatment to work. Without the pretest, the treatment has no or a different effect. Not controlled in the Pretest–Posttest Control Group Design but controlled in the Posttest-Only Control Group Design.

Mnemonic device: MRS T.

---

data, including different forms of tests and alternative measuring devices, may affect external validity.

Dealing with Reality It should be obvious that true experiments have many advantages over pre-experiments when it comes to internal validity and establishing causal relationships. But the advantages of true experimentation often come at the price of more than external validity. What is that price? Practicality. True experiments are extremely difficult to conduct outside of laboratory settings.

Because of their impracticality, some researchers sacrifice external validity by abbreviating treatment intensity and duration, by using nonrepresentative participants, by conducting the study in unnatural environments, and so on. Other researchers sacrifice internal validity in order to conduct research under more natural conditions.

So the debate rages between these methodological choices, a debate that sometimes can be resolved by making choices informed by theory. But what if one did not always have to make such difficult choices? What if there were more practical designs that allowed for control over most threats to internal validity and yet allowed the researcher greater flexibility in design?

Fortunately, these designs exist. They are called quasi-experimental designs and we'll examine two of the most useful.

QUASI-EXPERIMENTAL DESIGNS

Imagine an internal validity continuum with true experiments at one end and pre-experiments at the other end; most people would place quasi-experiments somewhere in the middle of these two extremes. In general, quasi-experiments control for most but not all the threats to internal validity. Compared to pre-experiments, quasi-experiments reduce the probability that a rival explanation is a viable alternative to a treatment effect. Thus, they represent realistic compromises when it is impractical, impossible, or undesirable to conduct a true experiment.

One concern about quasi-experiments is their efficiency. They sometimes require a greater number of groups to study and/or a greater number of observations of those groups than their true experimental counterparts. This concern is readily apparent in the first of the two quasi-experimental designs we'll cover.

Time Series Design

The Time Series Design is a variant on the One Group Pretest–Posttest Design. A single group of participants is studied. However, in place of a single pretest there are two or more pretests taken at various times prior to the introduction of the treatment. In place of a single posttest there are two or more posttests taken at various times following the conclusion of the treatment:

$$Y_{A11} \quad Y_{A12} \quad Y_{A13} \quad Y_{A14} \quad A_1 \quad Y_{A15} \quad Y_{A16} \quad Y_{A17} \quad Y_{A18}$$

The advantages of the Time Series Design are apparent from an examination of Figure 2.1. Here, the design has been implemented with four pretests (i.e., Y_{A1}–Y_{A4}), the introduction of the treatment (i.e., A_1), followed by four posttests (i.e., Y_{A5}–Y_{A8}). Figure 2.1 illustrates eight hypothetical outcomes, A to H. With the exception of the delayed treatment effect shown for outcome D, all the hypothetical outcomes have an important communality: the same mean difference in the

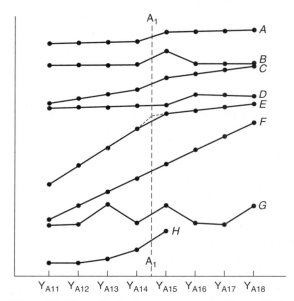

Figure 2.1 Hypothetical outcomes of a Times Series Design (Campbell & Stanley, 1966, p. 38)

outcome measure between the pretest immediately before the treatment (Y_{A14}) and the posttest immediately after the treatment (Y_{A15}).

An examination of the hypothetical outcomes reveals different interpretations of the data. In the topmost outcomes, a treatment effect is a likelihood. In the bottommost outcomes, a treatment effect is *not* a likelihood. And here is why the Times Series Design is superior to pre-experimental designs. Only by using multiple pre- and posttests was one able to determine the likelihood of a treatment effect. Had one only relied on a single pretest and a single posttest, as in the Quigley's Quagmire example shown in Table 2.4, there would be no pattern to the findings over time and one would not be able to distinguish situation *A* from situation *G*.

The Time Series Design, however, is not entirely free from threats to internal validity. In particular, it does not control for threats due to history or the influence of events external to the treatment that are otherwise coincidental with its implementation.

Finally, the Times Series Design requires multiple measurements of participants. Participants should be amenable to this requirement; time and cost factors should also be considered.

Nonequivalent Control Group Design

The Static Group Comparison Design is considered a pre-experimental design primarily because it fails to control for selection effects or the possibility that pre-existing differences between intact groups, and not the treatment, may explain posttest differences. The Nonequivalent Control Group Design minimizes this possibility by measuring participants both before and after the treatment. Thus, the Nonequivalent Control Group Design is similar to the Pretest–Posttest Control Group Design except that intact groups are used and participants are not randomly assigned to conditions:

$$Y_{A11} \quad A_1 \quad Y_{A12}$$
$$\text{-----------------}$$
$$Y_{A21} \quad A_2 \quad Y_{A22}$$

In this quasi-experimental design, one asks the same complex question one asked for the true experiment:

$$\text{Is } Y_{A12} - Y_{A11} \neq Y_{A22} - Y_{A21}?$$

The interpretation of the findings is clearer than if the study had been conducted without a pretest but less clear than a true experiment. Certain threats to validity may operate, but they need to do so *differently* for the experimental group and the control group.

For example, consider the hypothetical data in Table 2.7. The experimental group's average gain is 30.00. The control group's average gain is 20.00. Can one attribute the additional gain to the effect of the treatment?

TABLE 2.7 Nonequivalent Control Group Design: Quigley's Quagmire		
Condition	*Mean Pretest Score*	*Mean Posttest Score*
Self-concept training (A_1)	$Y_{A11} = 60.00$	$Y_{A12} = 90.00$
Control students (A_2)	$Y_{A21} = 40.00$	$Y_{A22} = 60.00$

If, for example, the effects of history were at work here, one might expect that both groups were equally influenced by external events. If so, one would have to conclude that the treatment had some effect on achievement.

If, however, one makes a case for the differential effects of history, one cannot conclude unequivocally that the treatment worked. In this case, differential effects of history may have occurred because control students were less adept at learning the material than experimental students. The two groups reacted differently to the instruction they received in common (i.e., the external event) and that explains why the experimental group gained more than the control group.

The fact that this sort of rival explanation is more complex and less intuitive is the reason why the Nonequivalent Control Group design is superior to pre-experimental designs. Rival explanations are less probable explanations of the findings than a treatment effect.

MEASUREMENT ISSUES

We will cover a potpourri of methodological issues surrounding primarily the reliability and validity of variables from which our measurements arise. As part of that discussion, we want to examine more closely the properties of variables and scales of measurement.

Scales of Measurement

The data collected on variables are the result of measurement. **Measurement** is the process of assigning numbers to characteristics of people, objects, or events according to a set of rules. For example, when you take your temperature, step on the bathroom scale, or place a ruler next to a beam, you are measuring, or assigning numbers in a prescribed way. Both physical objects as well as psychological ones are measured. Intelligence, self-concept, need for affiliation, and locus of control are just a few of the huge number of intangible properties that can be measured.

Not all measurement is the same. Some measurements are more precise than others. In part, this is so because some characteristics are more amenable to precise measurement than others. For example, most psychologists do not think of emotional and affective states with the same precision that physicists conceive of the motion of atoms. And, in part, this is so because some measurement scales are more precise than others. For example, describing people as short or tall is an imprecise measurement of height.

The way in which numbers are assigned to the data determines the scale of measurement being used. S. S. Stevens (1946), a behavioral scientist, identified the four levels, or scales, of measurement widely used today. Arranged hierarchically they are nominal, ordinal, interval, and ratio.

Nominal Scale   The simplest of the four scales of measurement is the **nominal scale.** A nominal scale allows for the classification and labeling of elements or objects into mutually exclusive and exhaustive categories based on defined features. Then the number of objects or elements in each category can be counted.

Categorizing and counting the religious preferences of new immigrants is an example of nominal measurement. From a sample of 100 new immigrants, researchers might find the distribution shown in Table 2.8.

Note that with a nominal scale there is no sense of order or quantity. Elements or objects are merely grouped or classified. There is no sense of one category of the scale being higher or better than another category.

Ordinal Scale   An **ordinal scale** allows for the classification and labeling of elements or objects into mutually exclusive and exhaustive categories based on defined features that are numerically ranked or otherwise ordered with respect to one another. However, equal differences between numbers does *not* reflect equal magnitude differences among the corresponding categories.

Imagine that a departmental committee has to rank five students who have applied for scholarships. After completing its deliberations the committee forwards the following rankings: 1) M. Adelman, 2) S. Donald, 3) N. Levine, 4) P. Alvit, 5) J. Chao. While the committee had a difficult time choosing among the top two applicants, there was a clear difference between those two and the other three students. In other words, the committee was able to order the applicants from strongest to weakest but some of the differences between the ranked candidates were small while other differences were large. With ranking that sense of order would be preserved, but researchers would not have a sense of how much of a difference existed between the categories.

Consider the company executives who have to categorize their employees for pay adjustments and raises. They group 200 employees into three categories as

TABLE 2.8   Religious Preferences of 100 New Immigrants: Nominal Scale

Religious Preference	Number
Christian	30
Jewish	15
Muslim	10
Hindu	10
Buddhist	5
None	30

TABLE 2.9 Ranking Employees for Pay Adjustments and Raises: Ordinal Scale	
Pay Adjustment Category	*Number of Employees*
1. Annual adjustment and raise for outstanding performance	50
2. Annual adjustment for acceptable performance	135
3. No adjustment for poor performance	15

shown in Table 2.9. In order to earn an adjustment and raise, employees needed to exceed all the company's performance indicators. In order to be denied an adjustment, employees needed to fall short of two of the company's performance indicators. The remaining employees received annual salary adjustments.

Interval Scale   An **interval scale** allows for the classification and labeling of elements or objects into mutually exclusive and exhaustive categories based on defined features that are numerically ranked or otherwise ordered with respect to one another. In addition, equal differences between numbers reflect equal magnitude differences between the corresponding categories.

Imagine that you wanted 15 social work supervisors to rate confidentially the quality of care their case workers would be able to provide if financial cutbacks were made to social services and caseloads were to increase somewhat. In order to rate the expected quality of care, the supervisors would be asked to complete a five-point Likert scale, in which the traditional assumption is made that intervals between categories appear equal to the respondents. The results are shown in Table 2.10.[2]

Because the ratings are on an interval scale, it is meaningful to perform most arithmetic operations on the numbers. For example, one can say that the difference between a rating of poor and good is much larger than the difference between good and very good. And one can also find the average of the ratings of the 15 supervisors, which is 2.80. On average, the supervisors believe that their case workers will still be able to do a good job (actually, slightly better than a good job).

TABLE 2.10 Supervisor Ratings of Quality of Care: Equal-Appearing Interval Scale	
Scale Value	*Number of Responses*
1. Excellent	4
2. Very good	3
3. Good	3
4. Fair	2
5. Poor	3

[2]If these intervals do not appear equal to the respondents, different category labels may be required. Some researchers prefer response categories such as: "strongly agree," "agree," "neutral," "disagree," and "strongly disagree" to better ensure that responses are on an interval scale.

But not all arithmetic operations are permissible because the starting point or origin of an interval scale is always arbitrarily defined and does not necessarily correspond to the absence of the measured characteristic. For example, it does not make sense to say that the ratings of the three supervisors who responded "very good" are twice as positive as the two supervisors who responded "fair." In other words, a ratio of interval scale responses is not interpretable.

Ratio Scale   A **ratio scale** allows for the classification and labeling of elements or objects into mutually exclusive and exhaustive categories based on defined features that are numerically ranked or otherwise ordered with respect to one another. Equal differences among numbers reflect equal magnitude differences among the corresponding categories. In addition, the origin or zero point of the scale represents the absence of the measured characteristic. Finally, the ratio of numbers taken from a ratio scale is meaningful.

Imagine that you exposed 10 overweight volunteers at random to either: an experimental exercise and dietary program or a commercial weight loss clinic. After one month, you recorded their weight loss in pounds, as shown in Table 2.11.

The average weight loss can be computed for each group. The average loss for the experimental group was 8.0 pounds. The average loss for the control group was 4.0. Furthermore, it is meaningful to examine the ratio of weight losses. The average loss of the experimental group was twice as large as the average loss of the control group.

Summary of Scales   We conclude this section by offering the summary of the scales of measurement presented in Table 2.12.

TABLE 2.11   Experimental versus Control Weight Loss: Ratio Scale

Experimental Program		Control Program	
Participant	Weight loss (gain)	Participant	Weight loss (gain)
JD	10	SS	5
SR	5	TR	5
NN	0	FU	(−5)
SDA	5	MC	5
DF	20	PA	10

TABLE 2.12   Scales of Measurement

Scale	Properties
Nominal	Categorizes only
Ordinal	Categorizes and orders
Interval	Categorizes, orders, and establishes equal intervals
Ratio	Categorizes, orders, establishes equal intervals, and contains a true zero point

RELIABILITY AND VALIDITY

Tests and Self-Report Measures

Tests and self-report measures are measurement tools used widely to assess the state of individuals or groups. In experimental research, test scores are used to determine whether and to what extent the treatment worked. In correlational research, test scores are used to determine whether and to what extent two or more variables are related. Tests and self-report measures are also used for diagnostic purposes, selection and placement purposes, and prediction purposes.

Definition   A **test** can be broadly defined as any instrument for assessing individual differences along one or more given dimensions of behavior.

Examples of Tests   Common forms of tests and self-report measures include performance tests and personality tests.

  Performance tests assess individual differences in standardized achievement contexts. Examples include the following:

> Intelligence tests (which measure the general capacity for learning and performance).
>
> Aptitude tests (which predict later performance in a specific subject such as language, art, music, and mathematics).
>
> Achievement tests (which measure what has been learned in specific subjects).
>
> Diagnostic tests (which identify specific areas of strength or weakness in a subject).
>
> Performance assessment (which examine performance on tasks that have intrinsic or real-life value).
>
> Measures of creativity (which evaluate divergent thinking).

  Personality tests assess individual differences in such aspects of personality as traits, needs, psychological disorders, values, and attitudes. Examples include the following:

> Specific personality measures (which assess differences in traits and needs).
>
> Projective tests (which provide ambiguous stimuli and freedom of response).
>
> Self-concept measures (which tap thoughts and feelings about oneself).
>
> Learning style inventories (which explore ways individuals approach learning tasks).
>
> Attitude scales (which measure feelings, thoughts, and behavioral dispositions toward people, things, or ideas).
>
> Vocational interest batteries (which explore preferences for various careers and activities).

Other Measurement Tools   There is a wide range of measurement tools that are not tests. Physiological data may be collected from sophisticated devices such as pupilometers, electromyograms (EMGs), electrocardiograms (ECGs), electroencephalograms (EEGs), and so on. Observational methods are often used in lieu of tests, especially when such instruments are inappropriate or provide incomplete evidence. For example, it is often more appropriate to rely on trained observers' recordings of the behavior of children than to rely solely on children's self-reports. Similarly, a better understanding of collaboration may be achieved by observing the extent to which collaboration actually takes place than by measuring someone's personal tendency toward collaboration on a personality measure.

What is especially important about all measurement tools is that they meet good quality standards and are appropriate for the situation to which they will be employed. We discuss the desirable characteristics of standardized tests below, but issues of quality are important regardless of the tool.

Desirable Characteristics of Standardized Tests

The two most important characteristics of a test are its reliability and validity. *Reliability* is the degree a test is free from measurement error. *Validity* is the degree to which a test measures what it purports to measure. These two characteristics are discussed at length below.

Test Reliability

Reliability is the degree a test is free from measurement error or how precise, consistent, or stable a participant's test score is over different testing forms and time spans. Reliabilities are correlation coefficients (see Chapter 13) where the range of scores is from 0 (no reliability) to +1 (perfect reliability). Reliabilities around .9 are considered excellent; reliabilities below .6 are considered marginal.

Factors that may cause measurement error include the following:

The items that comprise the test don't measure the same underlying trait or measure it to varying degrees.

Test administrators fail to administer the test consistently.

Test scorers fail to use uniform scoring procedures.

Testing conditions vary from person to person and time to time.

Individual respondents are affected by personal factors extraneous to the test (e.g., mood, illness, anxiety, or boredom).

There are several major types of reliability estimation, including test equivalence, test stability, internal consistency, and interrater agreement. The following sections will briefly consider each of these types of reliability.

Test Equivalence   **Test equivalence** (alternate-forms reliability) is the correlation *between two different forms* of a test given to the same individuals *at the same* *time.* Knowledge of test equivalence answers questions such as, Do different versions or forms of the test measure the same trait? How closely can I compare student scores on Test Form A with student scores on Test Form B?

Test Stability   Test stability (test–retest reliability) is the correlation between scores *on the same form* of a test given to the same individuals *at two different times.* Knowledge of test stability answers such questions as, How likely would it be for a student who scored 80/100 to get the same score if the test were to be repeated? How confident could researchers be that participants' test scores would be repeatable if testing were to reoccur?

Internal Consistency   Internal consistency is an index of the homogeneity of the items in the test or the degree to which individual test items correlate with one another and the total test score. In other words, to what extent are the test items interrelated, consistent, or homogeneous, and to what extent are they independent, inconsistent, or heterogeneous? There are three major methods for establishing internal consistency: split-half reliability, method of rational equivalence, and coefficient alpha.

Split-half reliability is used to determine reliability when alternate forms of the test are not available. The test is administered and the items are divided in half (odd, even). The scores on the two subtests are computed for each individual, and these two sets of scores are correlated. Since overall test length affects reliability, there is one additional step: the correlation from the two halves of the test must be corrected, through use of the Spearman-Brown prophecy formula, to what it would have been if the subtests were each twice as long.

The *method of rational equivalence* was developed by Richardson and Kuder (1939). They divised several formulas for computing internal consistency, the most famous of which are known as KR-20 and KR-21 (simplified version). The KR [Kuder/Richardson] method applies when test item responses can be marked right or wrong (i.e., on achievement tests but not attitude or interest tests). The KR method represents the average extent to which responses on each test item are related to overall scores on the test.

Without presenting the formula, the closest analogy is to imagine correlating individual responses to each test item (scored right or wrong) with individual total test scores and then averaging all the correlations (one correlation per test item). When test items measure the same trait, these correlations will be high; when they measure different traits, these correlations will be low.

Coefficient alpha was developed by Lee J. Cronbach (1951). It is a method for determining internal consistency based on the work of Kuder and Richardson but applicable to cases in which test items do not have to be scored dichotomously (and thus are useful for attitude questionnaires and interest inventories).

Interrater Agreement   Interrater agreement or intertester reliability is used to determine the extent to which the test administration and/or test scoring is affected by individuals occupying those roles. Test administrator reliability is determined by having several testers administer the test to a sample of individuals and then correlating their obtained scores with one another. Test scorer reliability is determined by having several scorers mark a sample of individual test results and then correlating the obtained scores across different scorers.

What Is the Relationship among the Reliability Estimates? Basically, you may assume that there is no relationship among the reliability estimates. For example, knowing that a test is internally consistent does not provide you with any information on test stability. So, be careful using published information on tests, especially from commercial vendors. Test publishers will usually try to put their tests in the best light. It is up to you to go further and uncover the important information you need.

Test Validity

Validity is the degree to which a test measures what it purports to measure—that is, a test's "truthfulness." Validity is concerned with the appropriateness, meaningfulness, and usefulness of the specific inferences made from test scores. More specifically, there are three broad categories of test validity:

1. Content validity
2. Criterion-related validity (predictive, concurrent)
3. Construct validity

Content Validity **Content validity** is the degree to which the sample of test items represents the content that the test is designed to measure. There are two basic steps in establishing content validity:

1. Define the universe or population of all possible test items (usually, by having content area experts provide their judgments).
2. Show that the test items form a representative sample of all possible test items (i.e., that test items do not overrepresent one area and underrepresent another area).

Occasionally, standardized achievement tests are criticized for lacking content validity *in the context* in which they are used. That is there is an incongruence between what the test measures and instruction (i.e., teaching–testing mismatch).

Criterion-Related Validity **Criterion-related validity** is the extent to which test scores correlate with an external criterion either at present (concurrent validity) or in the future (predictive validity). The test is often used in place of the criterion for practical purposes to save time, reduce costs, increase convenience, and so on. The quality of the criterion measure is a limiting factor in establishing criterion-related validity.

Concurrent validity is the correlation of the test with an external criterion measured concomitantly (i.e., at the same time). For example, a group-administered intelligence quotient (IQ) test is said to have concurrent validity to the extent it is correlated with an established individually administered IQ test given at the same time.

Predictive validity is the correlation of the test with an external criterion separated by a time lapse between measurements. For example, the Scholastic Aptitude Test (SAT) or the Graduate Record Exam (GRE) have predictive validity to the extent they predict future student performance in terms of grade point average at university (undergraduate and graduate, respectively).

Construct Validity   **Construct validity** is the extent to which a particular test can be shown to measure a hypothetical construct, that is, a theoretical construction about the nature of the human condition. Examples of constructs used in testing include self-concept, intelligence, learning style, and introversion–extroversion. They are constructs because they cannot be directly observed but must instead be inferred from behavior.

Because they are constructs, no single investigation is sufficient to establish validity. A series of investigations is usually required to begin to make judgments about construct validity. There is no single external criterion for judging a test's adequacy. For example, "intelligence" will be manifest in a host of ways across a plethora of situations.

Neither does a single test represent the operationalizations of the construct exhaustively—many alternate forms of measuring the construct are possible. For example, there are many different tests of the construct "intelligence."

Other Characteristics of Standardized Tests

In addition to reliability and validity, tests should have several other qualities. We briefly comment on objectivity, conditions of administration, formative data, and other criteria.

Objectivity   The objectivity of a standardized test depends on the degree to which it is uninfluenced or undistorted by the beliefs or biases of the individuals who administer and score it. Interobserver agreement, including procedures for scoring, must be high to call a test objective. (Objectivity may be considered a form of test reliability, because it involves exploring for measurement error introduced by the subjectivity of the test administrator.)

Conditions of Administration   A test may lose a substantial amount of its value if it is administered under widely divergent or suboptimal conditions. A well-developed test specifies many conditions of administration, including the following:

How much time is allowed.

Whether guessing is penalized.

Whether instructions can be repeated.

The nature and extent of tester–testee interaction.

Time of day for administration.

Room conditions (lighting, temperature, desk space, ambient noise).

Normative Data   For norm-referenced tests, the quality, quantity, and appropriateness of comparison group data are important to establishing a test's normative excellence.

Other Criteria

Examinee appropriateness—Is the test suitable for the person being studied?

Teaching feedback—Does the test yield useful information for nonexperts?

Usability—How easily can the test be administered?

Retest potential—Are equivalent forms available for retesting?

Ethical propriety—Does the test involve excess stress to the individual?

PUTTING IT ALL TOGETHER

The emphasis in this chapter was not on statistics but instead on some of the other aspects of research that help to make the subsequent analysis of data useful and meaningful. Our purpose in doing so was to emphasize that the statistical analysis of data is only one piece in the puzzle that is scientific inquiry. We made the case that an excellent empirical investigation depends on the combination of sound theory, good design, and proper analysis.

We covered important issues in research ethics, including informed consent, freedom to discontinue, and privacy and confidentiality. Our introduction to research design centered around two key questions. One question had to do with a study's internal validity: Did the independent variable, as manipulated, produce a change in the dependent variable, as measured? Another question had to do with a study's external validity: To what populations, settings, and variables can the results be generalized? We also distinguished between experimental studies and correlational investigations.

We covered three pre-experimental designs that fail to control for threats to internal validity:

1. The One-Shot Case Study:

$$A_1 \qquad Y_{A11}$$

2. The One-Group Pretest–Posttest Design:

$$Y_{A11} \qquad A_1 \qquad Y_{A12}$$

3. Static Group Comparison Design:

$$A_1 \qquad Y_{A11}$$
$$\text{-----------}$$
$$A_2 \qquad Y_{A21}$$

We also introduced seven threats to internal validity: maturation, regression, selection, mortality, instrumentation, testing, and history.

We next introduced two experimental designs and showed how they controlled for all threats to internal validity:

1. Pretest–Posttest Control Group Design:

$$R \quad Y_{A11} \quad A_1 \quad Y_{A12}$$
$$R \quad Y_{A21} \quad A_2 \quad Y_{A22}$$

2. Posttest–Only Control Group Design:

$$R \quad A_1 \quad Y_{A11}$$
$$R \quad A_2 \quad Y_{A21}$$

We also mentioned four threats to external validity that help distinguish among designs, including multiple-X interference, reactive arrangements, selection and X interaction, and testing and X interaction. Not on this short list of factors are threats to external validity arising from problems with treatment generalization and outcome generalization.

We discussed quasi-experiments as a practical compromise between pre-experiments and true experiments in terms of their control for threats to internal validity. We gave examples of two quasi-experimental designs:

1. Time Series Design:

$$Y_{A11} \quad Y_{A12} \quad Y_{A13} \quad Y_{A14} \quad A_1 \quad Y_{A15} \quad Y_{A16} \quad Y_{A17} \quad Y_{A18}$$

2. Nonequivalent Control Group Design:

$$Y_{A11} \quad A_1 \quad Y_{A12}$$
$$\text{-----------------}$$
$$Y_{A21} \quad A_2 \quad Y_{A22}$$

In the last section we covered some key issues in measurement. We presented four scales of measurement and summarized important similarities and differences between them. A nominal scale is used only for categorization. An ordinal scale is used for placing objects into rank-ordered categories. An interval scale categorizes, orders, and establishes equal intervals. Finally, a ratio scale categorizes, orders, establishes equal intervals, and contains a true zero point.

We summarized several important properties of standardized tests, key among which were reliability and validity. Reliability is the degree a test is free from measurement error or how precise, consistent, or stable a participant's score is. There are several major types of reliability estimation, including test equivalence, test stability, internal consistency, and interrater agreement.

We defined validity as the degree to which a test measures what it purports to measure. We presented three broad categories of test validity: content validity, criterion-related validity (predictive, concurrent), and construct validity.

KEY TERMS

Independent variable	Internal validity	Interval scale
Dependent variable	External validity	Ratio scale
Experimental	Generalizability	Performance tests
hypothesis	Mortality	Personality tests
Predictor variable	Regression	Reliability
Outcome variable	Selection	Test equivalence
Correlational	Maturation	Test stability
hypothesis	Instrumentation	Internal consistency
Pre-experimental	Testing	Content validity
designs	History	Criterion-related
True experimental	Measurement	validity
designs	Test	Concurrent validity
Quasi-experimental	Nominal scale	Predictive validity
designs	Ordinal scale	Construct validity

REFERENCES

Abrami, P. C., Leventhal, L., & Perry, R. P. (1982). Educational seduction. *Review of Educational Research, 52,* 446–464.

American Educational Research Association (1992). Ethical standards of the American Educational Research Association. *Educational Researcher, 21,* 23–26.

American Psychological Association (1992). Ethical principles of psychologists and code of conduct. *American Psychologist, 47,* no. 12, special insert.

Campbell, D. T., & Stanley, J. C. (1966). *Experimental and quasi-experimental designs for research.* Chicago: Rand McNally. (First appeared in: N. L. Gage (ed.) *Handbook of research on teaching,* 1963. Chicago: Rand McNally.)

Cronbach, L. J. (1951). Coefficient alpha and the internal structure of tests. *Psychometrika, 16,* 297–334.

Richardson, M. W., & Kuder, G. F. (1939). The calculation of test reliability coefficients based upon the method of rational equivalence. *Journal of Educational Psychology, 30,* 681–687.

Stevens, S. S. (1946). On the theory of scales of measurement. *Science, 103,* 677–680.

PROBLEMS

Questions

2.1. Why is good research design important?

2.2. How do we deal with research ethics and the proper treatment of participants?

2.3. How do we distinguish experiments from correlational investigations?

2.4. What are the two key questions that we ask of every research design?

2.5. Define *internal validity.*

2.6. Define *external validity.*

2.7. What is a pre-experimental design? List three pre-experimental designs.

2.8. What is the difference between experimental and statistical control? Which control is more effective?

2.9. What is a true experimental design? List two true experimental designs.

2.10. If true experimental designs control for all threats to internal validity, how does one distinguish among them?

2.11. What is a quasi-experimental design? How does it compare to pre-experimental and true experimental designs?

2.12. Define *measurement.* List, and briefly describe, four measurement scales.

2.13. What does reliability refer to, and how is it measured?

2.14. What does validity refer to? List three different categories of validity.

The following scenario is related to questions 2.15 to 2.17.

Officials of the Canadian Omnipotent Bank (COB) are concerned about negative consumer reactions to charges made by politicians in Ottawa of unnecessary bank fees. COB officials decide to investigate ways to change public attitudes toward banks in general and bank fees in particular. They are convinced by an educational technologist that interactive video displays in banks will produce the desired results.

2.15. What is the hypothesis in this example? What are the independent and dependent variables?

2.16. Design a simple true experiment to address the concerns of the COB. Briefly explain how you will manipulate the independent variable. Briefly describe how you will measure the dependent variable.

2.17. Show how the same study could be conducted as a One-Group Pretest–Posttest Design. What are the possible (types of) rival explanations? Which rival explanations are plausible here?

2.18. In what way(s) is the Pretest–Posttest Control Group Design superior to the Posttest-Only Control Group Design, and in what way(s) is it inferior?

2.19. Explain how the testing by X interaction is a threat to external validity and not a threat to internal validity.

2.20. How can test scores be stable but not internally consistent?

chapter **3**

Organizing and Displaying Data

OVERVIEW

Data to the left of me, data to the right of me, data all around me. That's a corny way to introduce some fairly important concepts. Yet there is a ring of truth to the idea that you can be "swamped" by the sheer volume of data which you have collected and want to understand. Organizing data and displaying data are two basic methods for making some sense out of what, at times, appears to be nonsense.

We will try to show you some ways of organizing data to better understand it as well as to screen it for unusual values that may signal a problem. We will also review a few of the popular methods for visually displaying features of data distribution. And we will cover some fairly flexible but less popular methods too.

More specifically, we will try to address questions such as the following:

1. What is the best method for ranking data?
2. What is the difference between percentages, percentile points, and percentile ranks?
3. How do you select a class interval to create a grouped frequency distribution?
4. How do you use a contingency table to present data in tabular form for two variables of interest?
5. What, exactly, are visual displays, and how can they help you understand your data?
6. How can you combine a bar graph and histogram to illustrate the relationship between two variables?
7. How can you make use of pie charts and stem-and-leaf plots or box-and-whisker plots?

We begin with an interesting scenario that describes an experience you should be familiar with. The grading ritual is described in Textbox 3.1, called the Whadya Get? scenario. Most of the chapters in this text begins with a commonsense, often whimsical scenario that contains a small dataset that we use throughout the chapter to illustrate various statistical techniques.

Size, of course, is relative. And our first scenario contains 50 data values. That's a relatively large size when you compare it to the examples in other chapters. But it is small relative to the datasets you might encounter in the "real world." It is large enough for you to realize you probably need some help in the form of organizational tools in understanding it.

Textbox 3.1

Whadya Get? Scenario

You stayed up all night studying for the big exam and the results are finally posted. You rush over to your professor's office to find the 50 examination results for the course, Sex Role Socialization, taped to her door (see Table 3.1). The results are listed by each student's college identification number along with student gender, but every name is obscured. You find your own score of 80 (noted in bold in Table 3.1) but are left wondering how you did in comparison with the others. Did you score in the middle or near the top? How did male students perform compared with female students? With so many student scores, you have a really hard time figuring how well you did. Is there a way to present the exam scores that better organizes and displays the data?

TABLE 3.1   Examination Results for 50 Students and Their Gender Identification (M = Male, F = Female)

60	F	85	M	77	F	69	F	79	M
91	F	30	M	94	M	77	M	80	F
75	F	67	F	79	F	76	M	93	F
82	F	94	F	70	M	84	F	69	F
68	M	81	M	71	M	87	F	79	M
92	M	90	F	73	F	80	F	78	M
74	M	78	F	80	M	65	F	68	M
63	M	64	M	82	F	67	F	68	M
78	M	98	F	88	F	81	M	69	F
61	F	83	M	86	F	92	M	76	F

WHY ORGANIZE AND DISPLAY DATA?

You have conducted an experiment or completed a correlational study and now you are faced with trying to understand the findings. Where and how do you begin to make sense of the evidence you have collected? Begin by organizing the data and sometimes by visually displaying the values.

Having a large amount of data makes it difficult to understand the salient features in the evidence you have collected. In this chapter we will concentrate on ways to **organize and visually display data** in ways that may help you to understand the data better. In Chapter 4, we will consider numerical ways to facilitate your understanding of the data and, in particular, the use of **descriptive statistics** to summarize the important characteristics of a set of numbers. For now, we will concentrate on ways that data organization and display plus the use of percentiles help make large sets of data more manageable and their key characteristics more salient.

As the amount of data in a set grows larger, it becomes increasingly difficult to comprehend each score and its relationship to other scores in the set. For example, in the Whadya Get? scenario we might want to know how unusual a score below 50 is, or how many students in the class scored 90 or higher, or the number of female students with scores of 80 or above. Organizing the data according to one or more important characteristics is a useful means to make sense out of a large number of data values.

Ways of Organizing Data

The organization of data may be done according to only the characteristics of the **measured variable of interest.** For example, student grades might be organized from lowest to highest. In addition, the organization of the data from the variable of interest may also be done according to the **values** of a second variable. For example, examination data might be organized into two subsets, one for female students and a second for male students. In the chapter we will consider both ways of organizing data.

Data Screening

Organizing and displaying the data also allows one to examine the data for unusual or anomalous characteristics. A visual display helps one determine qualities of the shape of a distribution of scores considering their frequency of occurrence. For example, is the **shape of the distribution** flat, indicative that there is widespread variability in the scores, or peaked, indicative that there is little variability? Are there extreme scores or unusual values and, if so, could these scores have occurred because of mistakes in data entry?

A good visual display is useful because it provides both a means to comprehend the data and a means toward insuring that the data have been properly scored and that the data conforms to researchers' assumptions and expectations. In this chapter we will concentrate on the uses of data organization and display for comprehension purposes. We will more fully discuss the uses of data organization and display for screening purposes in subsequent chapters.

ORGANIZING THE DATA

There are several means by which the data may be organized to increase comprehension of it. If the data are at least ordinal in nature, the scores can be arranged by **ranking** in order from lowest to highest, or vice versa. It is often useful to supplement placing the data in order by computing **percentile ranks.** For example, it may be meaningful to learn whether your exam performance placed you in the top 25% of students taking the exam. Another way to organize data is to group the scores and count the number and/or **percentage of cases** in each group. For example, it may help to know how many students in the class got test results in the 60s and 70s. Finally, it may useful to use the values of one variable to organize and group the data from another variable. For example, you could use the gender identity of the students to subdivide the exam results into male and female subgroups. Let's take a closer look at several methods for organizing the data, including ranking, percentiles, and percentile ranks.

Ranking

Ranking the data is a straightforward procedure, especially when every score is unique. Merely arrange the data in ascending or descending order. In practice, however, ranking can be a time-consuming chore when there are many numerical values in the data to be ranked. That is because each score needs to be compared against all other scores for proper placement. See Textbox 3.2.

Ranking Tip   To simplify the chore of ranking the data manually, it is often useful to presort the data into categories. For example, you might first sort the examination results into piles by tens (e.g., 50, 60, 70). Then sort the data again, arranging each exam score in rank order within each pile. Once the data are ranked, you can assign a rank order to each score. The same scores are assigned tied ranks.

Tied Ranks   Life is not always simple. Even ranking the data can be problematic when some data values are not unique. There are two methods for assigning **tied ranks.** In the popular method, the tied scores are all assigned to the highest rank in the category. In the mathematical method, the tied scores are assigned the average rank for the scores that are tied. The differences are illustrated in Table 3.2.

For example, in the Whadya Get? scenario there are three students with exam scores of 80, occupying ranked positions 20, 21, and 22. In the popular method they would all receive the highest rank, 20. This is the method frequently used to award prizes at athletic competitions when scores are tied.

In the mathematical method, the three students would all receive the average rank, 21. Using the mathematical method on a distribution ensures that the sum of the ranks equals the sum of the ordered positions. In contrast, with the popular method one could arrive at a sum of the ranks that was less than the sum of the ordered positions. For this reason, the mathematical method is preferred for data analysis purposes.

An Easy Way to Deal with Ties   An easy way to deal with ties is to begin by assigning ranks to all the ordered scores in the set, regardless of ties. Next, look

---

Textbox 3.2

Using Ranks for the Whadya Get? Scenario

The data for the Whadya Get? scenario have been placed in descending order with popular and mathematical ranks assigned (see Table 3.2). Placing the data in order helps clarify the examination results. Only a handful of students had scores below 65. Your score of 80 places you in the upper half of the class. Note places where there are tied ranks for differences between the popular and mathematical methods. Because the mathematical method takes into account all the locations the tied scores occupy, it may yield rankings that are numerically larger than the popular method.

TABLE 3.2		Examination Results Placed in Descending Rank Order*					
E	*G*	*P*	*M*	*E*	*G*	*P*	*M*
98	F	1	1.0	78	F	25	26.0
94	M	2	2.5	78	M	25	26.0
94	F	2	2.5	77	M	28	28.5
93	F	4	4.0	77	F	28	28.5
92	M	5	5.5	76	M	30	30.5
92	M	5	5.5	76	F	30	30.5
91	F	7	7.0	75	F	32	32.0
90	F	8	8.0	74	M	33	33.0
88	F	9	9.0	73	F	34	34.0
87	M	10	10.0	71	M	35	35.0
86	F	11	11.0	70	M	36	36.0
85	M	12	12.0	69	M	37	38.0
84	F	13	13.0	69	F	37	38.0
83	M	14	14.0	69	F	37	38.0
82	F	15	15.5	68	M	40	41.0
82	F	15	15.5	68	M	40	41.0
81	F	17	17.5	68	M	40	41.0
81	M	17	17.5	67	M	43	43.5
80	M	19	20.0	67	F	43	43.5
80	F	19	20.0	65	F	45	45.0
80	M	19	20.0	64	M	46	46.0
79	M	22	23.0	63	M	47	47.0
79	M	22	23.0	61	F	48	48.0
79	F	22	23.0	60	F	49	49.0
78	F	25	26.0	30	M	50	50.0

*E = examination result; G = gender; P = popular ranking method;
M = mathematical ranking method

over the data for ties and use either the popular method or preferably the mathematical method of assigning ranks to tied scores.

Percentages and Percentiles[1]

Everyone is familiar with percentages—since everyone has taken exams—but you are probably less familiar with percentiles. It is important to keep a clear distinction among a percentile point, a percentile rank, and a percentage.

[1]For the moment we will treat the scores as discrete numerical values (e.g., whole numbers or integers) and calculate percentiles accordingly.

A **percentage** is a proportion times 100. In the Whadya Get? scenario, it is known that 25 of the 50 students are females. Therefore, the proportion of female students is:

$$\frac{25 \text{ female students}}{50 \text{ students}} = .50 \text{ (proportion of female students in the class)}$$

To find the percentage, simply take the proportion and multiply it by 100:

$$.50 \times 100 = 50\%. \text{ (percentage of female students in the class)}$$

Percentages are easy to compute and easy to understand. They are widely used in everyday life to convey useful information about some of the properties of a set of numbers.

But percentages can also be misused if one attempts to misinform rather than inform. A good case in point is the use of change in percentages, either a percent increase or a percent decrease. One can look at the change in percentages over time as one might when pretest scores and posttest scores are compared for a single group or subgroup. One can also look at the change in percentages between groups as one might when one compares the scores of two groups such as the experimental and control groups.

How could using the percent increase present a misleading picture in the Whadya Get? scenario? Three students are known to have scored 94 or higher on the exam. Imagine that in another section of the course, also with 50 students but using a different instructional method and the same examination, there are four students who scored 94 or higher. Therefore, there were one-third, or 33%, more students who scored 94 or higher in the second section of the course. This seems like quite an impressive gain until you consider that it was based on only a single student difference between the two sections.

The **percentile point ($P_\%$),** also called a *percentile* or *centile,* is a point on the original measurement scale at or below which a specified percentage of scores falls. For example, the 10th percentile, or P_{10}, of a set of scores is the point at or below which 10% of the scores fall. In the Whadya Get? scenario, a student who scores at the 10th percentile on the examination knows that only 10% of the students in the class, or five students, received a score as low or lower. For the Whadya Get? scenario, $P_{10} = 64$.

In contrast, the **percentile rank of a score (PR_Y)** is a point on the percentile scale that gives the percentage of scores falling at or below the specified score. For example, the percentile rank of an examination score of 64 is 10.00. That is, $PR_{64} = 10.00$. See Textbox 3.3.

A percentile or percentile rank is *not* a percentage correct. A percentile rank does not indicate absolute performance on a test or measure; it indicates performance relative to other scores in the distribution. For example, a percentile rank of 80 corresponds to a score of 86 on the examination from the Whadya Get? scenario. But $PR_{86} = 80$ does not mean that 80% of the test items were answered correctly. It means that 80% of the students had scores of 86 or lower.

	Textbox 3.3

Using Percentile Ranks to Understand the Data

Table 3.3 contains the rank-order examination results for the Whadya Get? scenario along with the corresponding percentile rank of each score (PR_Y). By placing the examination results in descending order, one is able to determine the percentile point ($P_\%$) associated with each score. One is also able to see that each percentile rank is equal to the **cumulative percentage** for all the scores falling at or below the score in question. Note that no adjustments were made for tied ranks.

TABLE 3.3 Rank Order Examination Results and Corresponding Percentile Ranks (PR_Y)

E	PR_Y	E	PR_Y	E	PR_Y	E	PR_Y	E	PR_Y
98	100	86	80	80	60	76	40	68	20
94	98	85	78	79	58	75	38	68	18
94	96	84	76	79	56	74	36	67	16
93	94	83	74	79	54	73	34	67	14
92	92	82	72	78	52	71	32	65	12
92	90	82	70	78	50	70	30	64	10
91	88	81	68	78	48	69	28	63	8
90	86	81	66	77	46	69	26	61	6
88	84	80	64	77	44	69	24	60	4
87	82	80	62	76	42	68	22	30	2

Quartiles, Quintiles, and Deciles Many researchers use percentiles to assist them when exploring data. In particular, they sometimes calculate the 25th, 50th, and 75th percentiles, because these numbers are useful in summarizing and interpreting the data. The 50th percentile represents the exact middle of the distribution of scores and is the second **quartile**, or Q_2. It is also known as the median and will be more fully described in Chapter 4.

The 25th and the 75th percentiles are also quartiles. You may see them reported as Q_1 and Q_3 to represent the first and third quartiles, respectively. For the Whadya Get? scenario, $Q_1 = 69$, $Q_2 = 78$, and $Q_3 = 84$.

The use of quartiles allows researchers to divide the data into broad categories and to form a general picture. For example, using quartiles allows students to be categorized into several groups according to their examination scores. Using quartiles, you would know that a student scoring 63 was in the lowest performing quartile, earning an exam score that placed him among the lowest 25% of the students in the class.

There are two other methods you may encounter or wish to use for organizing and categorizing the data when it is in the form of centiles. Some researchers and practitioners use **quintiles** as a way to organize and understand the data. Quintiles organize the data into fifths, dividing the data at each 20th percentile.

It is also occasionally useful to report **deciles** or the scores at each 10th percentile. The decile scores for the Whadya Get? scenario are as follows:

$$D_1 = 64 \qquad\qquad D_4 = 76 \qquad\qquad D_7 = 82$$
$$D_2 = 68 \qquad\qquad D_5 = 78 \qquad\qquad D_8 = 86$$
$$D_3 = 70 \qquad\qquad D_6 = 80 \qquad\qquad D_9 = 92$$

Whether you choose to use quartiles, quintiles, or deciles depends on the situation. In some situations where broad categorization is sufficient, you may wish to use quartiles. In other situations, where finer distinctions are appropriate, the use of deciles may be called for. But whether you use quartiles, quintiles, or deciles, you should always be aware that these methods categorize each score or data point relative to the other scores in the set.

Percentiles Are Ordinal Measures   In Chapter 2 we discussed different scales of measurement. It is important to note that percentiles, because they emanate from a ranking of the data, are measured on an ordinal, not interval, scale; thus, the actual difference between scores is lost when percentiles are used, even if the scores were originally measured on an interval scale.

For example, look at the deciles for the Whadya Get? scenario. The difference in actual examination results between the 90th percentile and the 80th percentile is $92 - 86$, or 6. In contrast, the difference in actual examination results between the 70th percentile and the 60th percentile is $82 - 80$, or 2. Consider the lowest scoring student with an examination result of 30. His score is 30 points lower than the next student, yet they are only 2 percentile points from each other. In other words, when the examination results were converted to percentile ranks, information was lost about the actual differences in examination results among the students.

Don't be fooled by percentiles. They only *appear* to provide interval measurement because you normally understand 100-point scales as interval scales. Percentile measurement is ordinal measurement. Fortunately, we will discuss the z-score method of determining the relative position of scores in Chapter 5. This alternative to percentiles maintains the interval scale of measurement of the original scores.

Uses of Percentiles and Percentile Ranks

Percentiles are often used in reporting test results and as a means of conveying information about performance relative to others who have also completed a test or measure. Individual test results, in the absence of any interpretative information, are insufficient to arrive at a judgment of the quality or quantity of performance. For example, merely knowing that you've gotten an 80 on an important examination does not tell you whether you performed well or poorly.

We briefly present below some information on two approaches to interpreting test results: norm-referenced evaluation and criterion-referenced evaluation. Consider these approaches to evaluation as you consider the two situations described in Textbox 3.4. They describe the experiences of a biology teacher using relative standards (percentile ranks) to assign grades and an English teacher using absolute standards (percent correct) to assign grades. Do you think you would raise any objections if the instructor described in the Whadya Get? scenario (see Textbox 3.1) used either set of criteria for the Sex Role Socialization course?

Norm-Referenced Evaluation Percentiles are useful in providing information about one's performance relative to the performance of others. Knowing how

---

Textbox 3.4

A Grading Dilemma

Teacher-made and standardized tests are intended to measure the nature and extent of student learning. Deciding on test content and establishing standards for assigning grades are often difficult and contentious issues. Everyone has probably taken an exam in which he or she thought that the questions were not what was expected and therefore were unfair. Many people have often complained that the teacher's standards for assigning grades were too strict and therefore unfair. Choosing either norm-referenced evaluation or criterion-referenced evaluation is not a guarantee that students will feel that grading is fair. Consider for example, the following two situations.

A biology teacher decides to use norm-referenced evaluation to assign final grades in her honors course for premed students. She decides to use the following *percentile ranks* to assign grades:

75th percentile or higher—*A*

25th percentile to 75th percentile —*B*

25th percentile or lower—*C*

After grades have been assigned on the final examination, three student representatives ask to see her. They complain that all the students worked hard in the course and performed well on the examination. By using norm-referenced evaluation, the teacher was harming the chances of students who wished to enroll in medical school. What would you do?

An English teacher decides to use criterion-referenced evaluation to assign grades in his summer school course for students who failed during the regular school year. He decides to use the following *percentage correct* to assign grades:

80 or higher—*A*

70 to 79—*B*

60 to 69—*C*

50 to 59—*D*

49 or lower—*F*

After grades have been assigned on the final examination, several failing students come to see the teacher. They claim that the teacher's criteria are too strict for a summer school course and failing will mean they will have to repeat a year of school. What would you do?

one has performed relative to a comparison group can help in the interpretation of individual results. Many standardized tests use such comparison groups, called *norm groups,* as one way to index individual results. Well-established standardized tests may have a host of norm groups that can vary according to key characteristics such as age, gender, and ethnicity. This type of evaluation is called **norm-referenced evaluation.**

The appropriateness of the norm group is one key to whether comparative judgments are meaningful. Test results may seem artificially high (or low) if the group to which one is compared is inappropriate. For example, students whose native tongue is not English may seem to perform poorly on aptitude tests when their scores are compared to normative standards generated by students whose native tongue is English.

Achievement tests, which use percentile ranks and norm groups, are also criticized because they tend to engender competition among students for grades. Teachers who assign grades on the basis of percentile ranks guarantee that there will be winners and losers among classmates. For example, norms may be set such that the top 20% of students earn *A* grades, the next 20% earn *B* grades, and so on. If the class is mostly composed of high-achieving and hard-working students, this grading may well seem unfair to some people.

Criterion-Referenced Evaluation   **Criterion-referenced evaluation** is an alternative to norm-referenced evaluation. With criterion-referenced evaluation, individual test results are compared to preset standards of excellence. Grading is determined on the basis of what students know, not how well students compare to their classmates.

In a simplified criterion-referenced system, a predetermined standard may be set for assigning grades. For example, the teacher may decide in advance that a score of 85 is the minimum for an *A,* a score of 70 is the minimum for a *B,* and so on. Preset standards can result in many students who achieve the highest criterion, a problem for college administrators, or few students who achieve the highest standard, a problem for students and a headache for instructors.

As you might suspect, a difficulty in criterion-referenced evaluation is establishing the standards for assigning grades without first looking at the test results. Some critics have argued that it is impossible to establish standards for criterion-referenced evaluation without knowing test results. "Scratch a criterion and you'll find a norm" reflects this view.

Other Uses   Percentiles and percentile ranks are basic tools whose uses extend well beyond educational settings. Although we can all understand the use of percentiles for interpreting examination results, it is important that you don't see their use so narrowly. For example, researchers use percentiles to examine how well participants fared on an outcome measure when they have or have not been exposed to a treatment. Clinicians may use a patient's percentile rankings on a battery of tests to make an initial judgment of psychological well-being. A job counselor may use percentile ranks on placement tests to evaluate an applicant's suitability for a corporate appointment.

GROUPING THE DATA

Merely placing the data in order and computing percentiles may not be sufficient for comprehending large distributions, especially when the spread of scores is also large. A **frequency distribution** is an arrangement of values that shows the number of times a given score or group of scores occurs. A **grouped frequency distribution** is another tool for organizing the data to enhance interpretability. For example, you might want to organize the Whadya Get? examination data by intervals of 20 (e.g., 20–39, 40–59, 60–79, 80–89) or smaller intervals of 10 (e.g., 60–69, 70–79, 80–89), counting the number of examination scores in each **class interval**.

Selecting a Class Interval

Tables 3.4*a–c* show three different frequency distributions for the same Whadya Get? examination

> **CD-ROM link 3.1**
>
> *Activity 3.1: Creating a Histogram*
> How do visual data displays help you to interpret data sets and make decisions?
>   Activity 3.1, based on the Whadya Get? scenario (see Textbox 3.1), shows you how one kind of visual display (the histogram) is constructed. The histogram is an example of a visual representation of a grouped frequency distribution.

TABLE 3.4*a* Grouped Frequency Distribution for Examination Results (Class Interval = 20)

Class Interval	Frequency	Cumulative Frequency	Percent	Cumulative Percent
20–39	1	1	2.00	2.00
40–59	0	1	0.00	2.00
60–79	28	29	56.00	58.00
80–99	21	50	42.00	100.00

TABLE 3.4*b* Grouped Frequency Distribution for Examination Results (Class Interval = 10)

Class Interval	Frequency	Cumulative Frequency	Percent	Cumulative Percent
30–39	1	1	2.00	2.00
40–49	0	1	0.00	2.00
50–59	0	1	0.00	2.00
60–69	13	14	26.00	28.00
70–79	15	29	30.00	58.00
80–89	13	42	26.00	84.00
90–99	8	50	16.00	100.00

TABLE 3.4c Grouped Frequency Distribution for Examination Results (Class Interval = 1)

CI	F	CF	%	C%	CI	F	CF	%	C%
30	1	1	2.00	2.00	65	1	6	2.00	12.00
31	0	1	0.00	2.00	66	0	6	0.00	12.00
32	0	1	0.00	2.00	67	2	8	4.00	16.00
33	0	1	0.00	2.00	68	3	11	6.00	22.00
34	0	1	0.00	2.00	69	3	14	6.00	28.00
35	0	1	0.00	2.00	70	1	15	2.00	30.00
36	0	1	0.00	2.00	71	1	16	2.00	32.00
37	0	1	0.00	2.00	72	0	16	0.00	32.00
38	0	1	0.00	2.00	73	1	17	2.00	34.00
39	0	1	0.00	2.00	74	1	18	2.00	36.00
40	0	1	0.00	2.00	75	1	19	2.00	38.00
41	0	1	0.00	2.00	76	2	21	4.00	42.00
42	0	1	0.00	2.00	77	2	23	4.00	46.00
43	0	1	0.00	2.00	78	3	26	6.00	52.00
44	0	1	0.00	2.00	79	3	29	6.00	58.00
45	0	1	0.00	2.00	80	3	32	6.00	64.00
46	0	1	0.00	2.00	81	2	34	4.00	68.00
47	0	1	0.00	2.00	82	2	36	4.00	72.00
48	0	1	0.00	2.00	83	1	37	2.00	74.00
49	0	1	0.00	2.00	84	1	38	2.00	76.00
50	0	1	0.00	2.00	85	1	39	2.00	78.00
51	0	1	0.00	2.00	86	1	40	2.00	80.00
52	0	1	0.00	2.00	87	1	41	2.00	82.00
53	0	1	0.00	2.00	88	1	42	2.00	84.00
54	0	1	0.00	2.00	89	0	42	0.00	84.00
55	0	1	0.00	2.00	90	1	43	2.00	86.00
56	0	1	0.00	2.00	91	1	44	2.00	88.00
57	0	1	0.00	2.00	92	2	46	4.00	92.00
58	0	1	0.00	2.00	93	1	47	2.00	94.00
59	0	1	0.00	2.00	94	2	49	2.00	98.00
60	1	2	2.00	4.00	95	0	49	0.00	98.00
61	1	3	2.00	6.00	96	0	49	0.00	98.00
62	0	3	0.00	6.00	97	0	49	0.00	98.00
63	1	4	2.00	8.00	98	1	50	2.00	100.00
64	1	5	2.00	10.00	99	0	50	0.00	100.00

CI = Class Interval; F = Frequency; CF = Cumulative Frequency; % = Percent; C% = Cumulative Percent

results. The differences in the tables are due to the class interval—20, 10 and 1, respectively—selected for grouping. As the class intervals grow larger, the examination results are easier to comprehend but a certain degree of detail is lost.

A good mathematical rule of thumb is to create approximately 10 to 20 classes and to adjust the intervals accordingly so that they are equal in size. To estimate the size of each interval, subtract the lowest score from the highest score and divide by the number of class intervals you wish. For example, if income data ranged from $20,000 to $100,000 and 20 intervals were desired, you would create class intervals in increments of $4000. Sixteen class intervals would result in increments of $5000.

Each situation may dictate a deviation from this guideline. There are occasions in which the class intervals are already known or are conceptually meaningful and dividing the data any other way would not be sensible. For example, student grades may be based on the following criteria and it would make sense to use them as the class intervals:

$$90+ = A$$
$$80–89 = B$$
$$70–79 = C$$
$$60–69 = D$$
$$59– = F$$

In contrast, if the instructor had used a finer grading scheme, the following class intervals might be used:

$97–99 = A+$	$77–79 = C+$
$93–96 = A$	$73–76 = C$
$90–92 = A-$	$70–72 = C-$
$87–89 = B+$	$67–69 = D+$
$83–86 = B$	$63–66 = D$
$80–82 = B-$	$60–62 = D-$
	$59– = F$

Tables 3.4*a–c* show frequencies for intervals of size 20, 10, and 1 using the Whadya Get? scenario data. The frequencies and percentages within each interval are reported along with **cumulative frequencies** and percentages. A cumulative frequency is the total number of scores in the class interval and all intervals below it. A **cumulative percentage** is the cumulative frequency divided by the total frequency, all times 100. For example, in Table 3.4*a* the cumulative percentage for class interval 60–79 is:

$$\left(\frac{29}{50}\right) \times 100 = 58.00\%$$

Note especially that as the class interval grows larger, the size of each table grows smaller. There is a point at which the class interval becomes too large and the advantage of using grouped frequencies is lost. There is too little detail and interpretability is hindered. This is probably the case in Table 4.3*a*.

On the other hand, there is clearly a point at which the class interval becomes too small and the advantage of using grouped frequencies is also lost. There is too much detail and interpretability is hindered. This is probably the case in Table 4.3*c*.

Empty Class Intervals   Unusually high or low scores may create situations, as in the Whadya Get? scenario, in which several class intervals are empty. Researchers sometimes eliminate these empty class intervals by combining them. For example, in the Whadya Get? scenario one could combine all the class intervals below 60 into a single class representing a failing grade. Combining class intervals is not problem-free; doing so means the researcher loses precision in representing some of the data. For example, is the single failing grade in the 50s, or is it much lower?

Assumptions   By grouping the data into larger class intervals, the data becomes more manageable and easier to interpret. But inevitably information is lost—in particular, the exact value of the scores. Therefore, whenever anyone represents a grouped frequency distribution or computes certain characteristics of the distribution, this loss of information must be ignored and two assumptions must be made.

The first assumption is that, in a class interval, the scores are uniformly distributed between the limits of the interval and not bunched together around a particular value or values. For example, if there were 20 scores in the interval 60–69, one would expect 2 scores of 60, 2 scores of 61, and so on. One would not expect 5 scores of 60, 0 scores of 61, 10 scores of 62, and so on, *even if the scores were actually distributed in this way.* As you can see, this is one way grouping data loses information.

The second assumption is that whenever a single score must represent a class interval, the interval midpoint is the representative score. In other words, it is assumed that all the scores within the interval can be represented adequately by its midpoint. For example, 64.5 is the midpoint for the class interval 60–69.

To ensure that the midpoint of a class interval is an integer, the class interval should encompass an odd number of scores. For example, the interval 60–64 covers five scores and therefore the midpoint for the class interval is 62.

Estimating Percentiles and Percentile Ranks from Grouped Frequency Distributions

Sometimes the original distribution of scores is not available and one must rely solely on a grouped frequency distribution for information and interpretation. For example, the grouped frequency distribution can be used to *estimate* the percentile and the percentile rank associated with a particular score. To estimate either, the exact limits of the class intervals used in the grouped frequency distribution must be known.

Exact Limits of the Class Interval Although we have recorded the examination scores in the Whadya Get? scenario as discrete values (i.e., whole numbers or integers), imagine that they are actually continuous variables that can take on fractional values. That is, although we recorded the scores as whole numbers, imagine that the recorded value actually represents a value that falls within certain limits, called the **exact limits,** or **real limits.** Thus, the values 79.5 and 80.5 represent the lower real limit and the upper real limit, respectively, for an examination score of 80. Similarly, the values 80.5 and 81.5 represent the lower and upper real limits, respectively, for an examination score of 81.

If individual scores can have exact limits, class intervals can be treated likewise. For example, the exact limits for the class interval 80–89 is 79.5 and 89.5, respectively. The use of exact limits is important when one wishes to estimate percentiles and percentile ranks from grouped data.

Estimating Percentiles The general formula for estimating a percentile from a grouped frequency distribution is given in Equation 3.1

$$\textbf{Equation 3.1: } P_\% = \text{lrl} + \left(\frac{np - \text{cf}}{\text{fi}}\right)w$$

where:

$P_\%$ = percentile to be estimated

lrl = lower real limit of the class interval

n = total number of scores

p = proportion corresponding to the desired percentile (i.e., %/100)

cf = cumulative frequency of scores below the interval containing $P\%$

fi = frequency of scores in the interval containing $P_\%$

w = width of the class interval

CD-ROM link 3.2

Problem Generator: Percentiles and Percentile Ranks

To practice estimating percentiles (Equation 3.1), select Percentiles and Percentile Ranks from the Problem Generator Menu on the CD-ROM. The Problem Generator will create as many practice problems as you need, and will demonstrate each step in their solution so that you can check your work.

Let's see how the general formula is used for estimating a percentile from a grouped frequency distribution. Textbox 3.5 provides an illustration using the Whadya Get? scenario. In this illustration we will work only from the grouped frequency distribution shown in Table 3.4*b,* in which the class interval is 10. In other words, by using the grouped frequency distribution only, information will have been lost about the exact value of each individual score.

Estimating Percentile Ranks One can also use the grouped frequency distribution to estimate the

---

Textbox 3.5

Estimating Percentiles in the Whadya Get? Scenario

Imagine that *only* the grouped frequency distribution was represented in Table 3.4*b* and that you wished to know the score associated with the 75th percentile (P_{75}):

$$P_{\%} = \text{lrl} + \left(\frac{np - \text{cf}}{\text{fi}}\right)w = P_{75} = 79.5 + \left(\frac{[50][.75] - 29}{13}\right)10 = 79.5 + 6.54 = 86.04$$

How does this estimate compare to the percentile point for the ungrouped frequency distribution in Table 3.2? P_{75} from this table is 83.5. Why are the two values of P_Y different? They are different because the *actual* distribution of the data is not equal across the class interval. Remember that it was assumed that the distribution of scores in a grouped frequency distribution is equal. When it is not equal, the estimate made will be (slightly) erroneous.

percentile rank of a score when complete data are unavailable. The general formula is given in Equation 3.2:

$$\textbf{Equation 3.2: } \text{PR}_Y = \left(\frac{\text{cf} + \left[\dfrac{(Y - \text{lrl})}{w}\right]\text{fi}}{n}\right)100$$

where:

PR_Y = percentile rank to be estimated

Y = score for which the percentile rank is to be estimated

lrl = lower real limit of the class interval

n = total number of scores

cf = cumulative frequency of scores below the interval containing PR_Y

fi = frequency of scores in the interval containing PR_Y

w = width of the class interval

Let's see how the general formula is used for estimating percentile ranks from a grouped frequency distribution. Textbox 3.6 provides an illustration using the Whadya Get? scenario. As in the example for estimating percentiles (see Textbox 3.5), in this illustration one will also work only from the grouped frequency distribution shown in Table 3.4*b*, in which the class interval is 10. In other words, by using the grouped frequency distribution only, information will have been lost about the exact value of each individual score.

Qualitative Variables   The construction of frequency distributions for qualitative variables or variables on a nominal scale of measurement is relatively simple. No decisions about class size or number of intervals have to be made. See Textbox

---

Textbox 3.6

Estimating Percentile Ranks in the Whadya Get? Scenario

Imagine that *only* the grouped frequency distribution was represented in Table 3.4*b* and that you wished to know the percentile rank PR_Y associated with a score of 92:

$$PR_Y = \left(\frac{cf + \left[\frac{(Y - lrl)}{w} \right] fi}{n} \right) 100 = \left(\frac{42 + \left[\frac{(92 - 89.5)}{10} \right] 8}{50} \right) 100 = 88.00$$

How does this estimate compare to the percentile rank found using the ungrouped frequency distribution in Table 3.3? The percentile rank in the table is either 90 or 92. (Remember, no adjustment was made for tied ranks.) Why are the estimated and actual values different? Once again, the *actual* distribution of the data is not equal across the class interval. When it is not equal, the estimate made will be (slightly) erroneous.

CD-ROM link·3.3

Problem Generator: Percentiles and Percentile Ranks

To practice estimating percentile ranks (Equation 3.2), select Percentiles and Percentile Ranks from the Problem Generator Menu on the CD-ROM. The Problem Generator will create as many practice problems as you need, and will demonstrate each step in their solution so that you can check your work.

3.7. It shows the frequency distribution for student gender in the Whadya Get? scenario.

Occasionally, researchers will combine the values of qualitative variables into larger categories, especially when responses are infrequent in some of the smaller categories. For example, imagine students were asked to indicate their summer job preferences by selecting one of six choices: no job or vacation; farm worker; office worker; self-employed; laborer or tradesperson; and technical or professional employee. These six categories might subsequently be combined into three categories: unemployed; self-employed, and employed. Collapsing categories in this fashion may aid interpretation with little loss of detail.

Grouping: Advantages and Disadvantages

The major advantage to grouping the data is that it makes the data more comprehensible; that is, there is less information to overwhelm the reader. In addition to making a large distribution more comprehensible, the use of grouped frequency distributions is desirable when either the range of scores is large or the precision of measurement increases. Finally, when computations are done manually, the use of grouped data may ease computational labor.

The major disadvantage of grouping is that it inevitably results in a loss of information. Individual scores lose their identity when they are grouped into classes. Some imprecision in calculating statistics occurs when one relies solely on

---

Textbox 3.7

Distribution of Student Gender in the Whadya Get? Scenario

In the Whadya Get? scenario, one nominal variable was measured: student gender. The frequency distribution for student gender is given in Table 3.5.

TABLE 3.5   Frequency Distribution for Student Gender

Student Gender	Frequency	Cumulative Frequency	Percent	Cumulative Percent
Male	25	25	50.00	50.00
Female	25	50	50.00	100.00

grouped frequencies rather than exact frequencies. Another disadvantage of grouping the data is that there is no single way to determine the class intervals and more than one grouped frequency distribution is possible.

CROSSTABULATION

So far we have emphasized various ways to organize and present, in tabular form, data from a single variable of interest. Using the examination results from the Whadya Get? scenario, we have shown how data on an ordinal, interval, or ratio scale of measurement may be placed in rank order and organized into groups. Similarly, we have briefly illustrated the treatment of data on a nominal scale of measurement using student gender from the Whadya Get? scenario.

Now we will briefly turn our attention to ways to organize and present data in tabular form based on two variables of interest. **Crosstabulation** or the use of a **contingency table** allows the researcher to organize and display the values or levels of one variable according to the values or levels of a second variable. Textbox 3.8 illustrates the crosstabulation of examination results by student gender.

In experimental research, researchers might want to tabulate participants' reactions on the dependent variable separately for each value of the independent variable such as the treatment group and the control group. An examination of the crosstabulated data might help one begin to explore and understand whether the independent variable had an effect on the dependent variable.

In correlational research, crosstabulation is also used to represent the values of the outcome measure separately for different values of the predictor variable. Here too, crosstabulation helps one begin to explore and understand whether there is a relationship between the predictor variable and outcome variable.

Textbox 3.8

Crosstabulation of Two Variables in the Whadya Get? Scenario

Table 3.6 is a contingency table showing the crosstabulation of grouped examination results (class interval = 10) separately for male and female students. The table appears to show a tendency for female students to get somewhat higher grades than male students.

Each cell of the contingency table has four numbers. The first number is the count, or frequency, of scores in the cell. For example, there are 7 male students who scored between 60 and 69. The second number is the row percentage. For example, 32 percent of male students scored between 70 and 79. The third number is the column percentage. Only 3 of 8 male students, or 37.5%, earned exam grades between 90 and 99. The fourth number is the cell percentage of the total. One student, a male, or 2% of all students, scored between 30 and 59.

TABLE 3.6 Contingency Table Showing Examination Results Divided by Student Gender

Count
Row %
Column %
Total %

	30–59	60–69	70–79	80–89	90–99	Row Total
Male	1	7	8	6	3	25
	4.00%	28.00%	32.00%	24.00%	12.00%	50.00%
	100.00%	53.80%	53.30%	46.20%	37.50%	
	2.00%	14.00%	16.00%	12.00%	6.00%	
Female	0	6	7	7	5	25
	0.00%	24.00%	28.00%	28.00%	20.00%	50.00%
	0.00%	46.20%	46.70%	53.80%	62.50%	
	0.00%	12.00%	14.00%	14.00%	10.00%	
Column Total	1	13	15	13	8	50
	2.00%	26.00%	30.00%	26.00%	16.00%	100.00%

DISPLAYING THE DATA

Sometimes it is especially difficult and cumbersome to understand and describe the noteworthy features of a distribution by resorting only to a prose description and numerical summary. A properly prepared visual display can do much to increase comprehension.

Visual displays help one to organize, summarize, and interpret data. A well-constructed graph helps improve one's understanding of the results and aids in explaining them to others. At the same time, visual displays allow the reader to quickly perceive complex trends that would otherwise be difficult to describe in words. For example, it may take a while to read a written description of results but only seconds to form a "picture" of the findings from a graph. Experienced researchers consider graphs an essential feature of any data analysis and report. Truly, one picture may be worth a thousand words—and numbers!

But like text that is poorly worded, a visual display that is ill conceived and poorly constructed can create confusion rather than clarify. Poor visual displays may not aid understanding and may be overly complex to interpret.

Finally, visual displays can mislead if the intention is to exaggerate small differences or to minimize large ones. Common tricks to distort findings include changing the range of scores that are displayed or using an ordinate other than zero. For example, when the apparent range of possible scores on a graph is small, small actual differences may appear large. Alternately, when the apparent range of possible scores on a graph is large, large actual differences may appear small. Compare, for example, Figure 3.1*a* and 3.1*d*. Differences between class intervals are more noticeable in Figure 3.1*a* than 3.1*d* even though the same data are being displayed in each figure.

Such misuses of visual displays are incompatible with sound practice and are contrary to the concepts that form the basis of this book. Although you may see such misuses in the popular press and elsewhere, visual displays that attempt to convey a misleading representation of the data are highly inappropriate and unethical in scientific reports and publications. A good visual display conveys meaning; it does not hide or distort it.

What Exactly Are Visual Displays?

Visual displays include graphs, figures, charts, and plots. Visual displays are non-text, pictorial devices designed to represent the important characteristics of the data. In contrast, textual displays, primarily tables, are used to present written information such as numbers and special text.

Visual displays are used when it is important to illustrate a specific trend in the data or a general relationship among groups. Textual displays are used when it is important that the numerical values of the data be presented exactly.

Graphs   Let's begin the discussion of graphs by outlining some of the key features of graphs in general. The word *graph* comes from the Greek word meaning "to draw or write." Graphs can take many forms but share certain common elements.

Graphs are two-dimensional representations of the important characteristics of the data. The two dimensions of a graph are known as axes, which are drawn at a right, or 90-degree, angle from each other. The horizontal axis is called the **abscissa,** or the *x-axis.* The vertical axis is called the **ordinate,** or the *y-axis.* As a general guideline, the height of the vertical axis, the *y*-axis, should be no more than two-thirds to three-quarters the length of the horizontal axis, the *x*-axis.

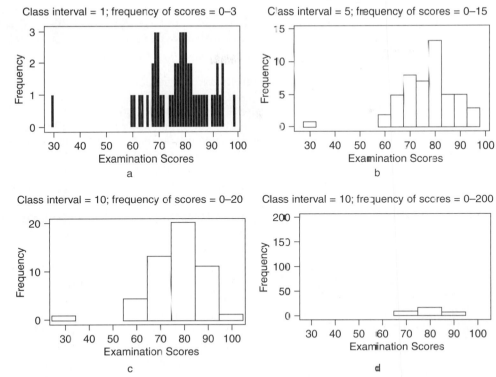

Figure 3.1 Frequency histograms of examination scores from the Whadya Get? scenario

Histograms, bar graphs and frequency polygons are graphs used to display the frequency or percentage of individual scores or scores that have been grouped. These are useful visual displays when one wishes to illustrate how the values of a single variable are distributed. Furthermore, these graphical devices and others may also be used to illustrate the relationship between two variables by showing the frequency or percentages of one variable for different values of a second (and additional) variable.

Histograms   Histograms are used to illustrate the frequency or percentages of values of variables measured on at least an ordinal scale. A histogram is a graph that depicts the frequencies or percentages of individual scores, or grouped scores in class intervals, by the length of its bars. The scale of measurement on the vertical axis, the *y*-axis, is the frequency or percentage of scores. The scale of measurement on the horizontal axis, the *x*-axis, is the range of scores for the variable under consideration. See Textbox 3.9.

Note that for all the class intervals in a histogram, the bars on the prepared graph are touching to highlight the assumption that the scale of measurement for the variable of interest along the horizontal axis,

CD-ROM link 3.4

Activity 3.1: Creating a Histogram
See how a histogram is created from a data set in Activity 3.1 on the CD-ROM.

Textbox 3.9

Constructing Frequency Histograms for the Whadya Get? Scenario

Frequency histograms of individual and grouped examination scores from the Whadya Get? scenario are illustrated in Figures 3.1*a–d*. All four figures illustrate the same distribution of scores, but their appearance differs. Figure 3.1*a* illustrates frequencies for individual scores, while Figure 3.1*b* shows the results grouped by class intervals of width 5. In Figure 3.1*b* the range of frequencies is from 0 to 15, and it does not appear that the frequency of scores in each class interval is similar. Figure 3.1*c* shows the results grouped by class intervals of width 10. Figure 3.1*d* best illustrates how the appearance of the data can change when the range of frequencies changes. Here the range of frequencies is from 0 to 200, and it appears that the frequency of scores in each class interval is similar.

CD-ROM link 3.5

Activity 3.2: Same Dataset, Different Histograms
For a given dataset, is there only one "correct" histogram? Can a histogram misrepresent a dataset?
By varying the width of the class intervals, you can explore how class intervals affect the appearance of a histogram, and how this can affect your interpretation of the underlying dataset.

the *x*-axis, is continuous, not discrete, and that the scores lie in class intervals with exact or real limits (e.g., 79.5–89.5). This is the case whenever the variable of interest is on at least an ordinal scale of measurement or higher (i.e., interval or ratio).

The histograms illustrated in Figures 3.1*a–d* also have the class intervals or bars labeled at their **midpoints** on the *x*-axis. It is also possible to label the class intervals by their lower and upper limits, called **cutpoints.**

Bar Graphs **Bar graphs** are used to illustrate the frequency or percentages of values of a nominal variable. For example, Figure 3.2 is a bar graph for the gender of students enrolled in the course described in the Whadya Get? scenario. Because gender is a nominal variable, the classes or categories that make up each bar are distinct from one another. To reinforce the idea that the scale of measurement in a bar graph is nominal, the bars in the prepared graph are not touching.

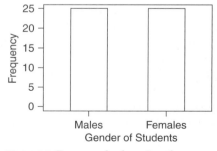

Figure 3.2 Bar graph showing frequency of male and female students from the Whadya Get? scenario

Combination Bar Graphs and Histograms   A combination bar graph and histogram is used to illustrate the relationship between two or more variables. For experiments, we might want to see whether there appears to be differences in the dependent variable when comparing the results for the experimental participants versus the control participants. For correlational studies, we might be interested in whether response frequencies on the outcome variable appear to change for different levels or values of the predictor variable. Note that the use of percentages rather than frequencies may be desirable when the total number of participants varies across levels of the predictor or independent variable. Combination bar graphs and histograms may be used instead of, or in addition to, contingency tables. See Textbox 3.10 and Figure 3.3 for an illustration using the Whadya Get? scenario. Note how clearly the combination bar graph and histogram helps one spot a potential trend in the data.

Frequency Polygons   A **frequency polygon,** also known as a *frequency curve* or *line graph,* is another means to depict a frequency distribution for individual or grouped scores. For the frequency polygon, assume that the scores in the class interval can be represented by the midpoint. For each interval, plot the frequency

---

Textbox 3.10

How Do Male and Female Student Exam Scores Compare?

Imagine you were interested in the examination performance of male versus female students from the Whadya Get? scenario. You can use a combination bar graph and histogram for the group examination scores for male and female students separately. The graph in Figure 3.3 makes it clear that there appears to be a tendency for female students to outperform male students.

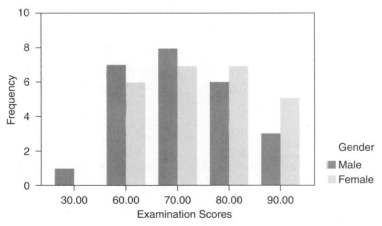

Figure 3.3 Combination bar graph and histogram showing grouped examination scores by student gender (class interval = 10)

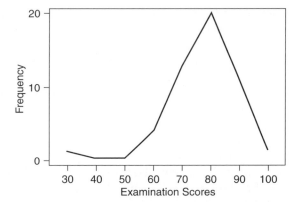

Figure 3.4 Frequency polygon of grouped examination scores from Whadya Get? scenario (class interval = 10)

CD-ROM link 3.6

Activity 3.1 and Activity 3.2
You can see what a frequency polygon (or line graph) looks like in both Activities 3.1 and 3.2 on the CD-ROM.

of scores at the midpoint and then connect the midpoints with straight lines. Note that the shape of the frequency polygon can change depending on the size of the class interval. See Figure 3.4 for an illustration of the grouped examination scores for the Whadya Get? scenario.

A cumulative frequency polygon may also be used to illustrate a cumulative frequency distribution for both individual and grouped scores. A cumulative frequency polygon is also known as an **ogive.** Line graphs may also be used to illustrate percentage and cumulative percentages for both individual and grouped data.

Frequency Polygons for Two or More Groups Frequency polygons may also be used to illustrate the distribution of scores for two or more subgroups of the data. Figure 3.5 illustrates the Whadya Get? scenario examination results, with one line depicting the grouped frequency distribution for male students and a second line depicting the grouped frequency distribution for female students.

Note how the appearance of the line graph for all students combined in Figure 3.4 departs from the appearance of the line graphs for male and female students in Figure 3.5. Although they depict the same data, the figures are organized differently and serve different purposes.

Plots and Charts

There are several other ways to visually represent the data. We will look at pie charts, stem-and-leaf plots, and box-and-whisker plots as useful devices for illustration.

Pie Charts A **pie chart** is a circle divided into sectors that represent the proportionate frequency or percentage frequency of the class intervals. A single pie

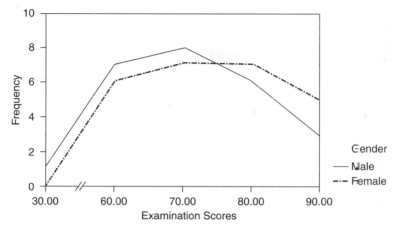

Figure 3.5 Line graph for male and female group examination scores (class interval = 10)

chart can be used to illustrate the distribution of scores on the outcome measure of interest. Two or more pie charts can be used to show the distribution of scores on the outcome measure of interest according to values or levels of a second variable. See Textbox 3.11 and Figures 3.6 and 3.7*a* and *b* for illustrations using the Whadya Get? scenario.

Stem-and-Leaf Plots   A **stem-and-leaf plot** is a means of visual display that allows for exploration of the data and its distribution while retaining the information of the original scores (Tukey, 1977). An important advantage of a stem-and-leaf plot over a histogram is that the plot provides all of the information that is contained in a histogram and, in addition, preserves the values of the individual scores.

A stem-and-leaf plot is easy to construct. The first step in constructing the plot is to specify class intervals. Each class interval is a *stem*, or leading digit, of the plot. The second step is to represent each score by its class interval and, in order, by its trailing digit which is the *leaf*.

Textbox 3.11

Pie Charts Showing Examination Scores

Figure 3.6 is a pie chart for the distribution of examination scores in the Whadya Get? scenario. Figure 3.7*a* and *b* shows the distribution of examination scores separately for males and females. For reasons that are apparent from an examination of Figures 3.7*a* and *b*, it is often more difficult to understand differences among groups using pie charts than using other forms of visual display.

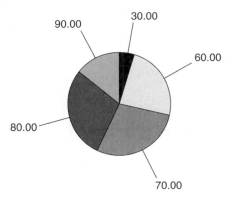

Figure 3.6 Pie chart of grouped examination scores from the Whadya Get? scenario (class interval = 10)

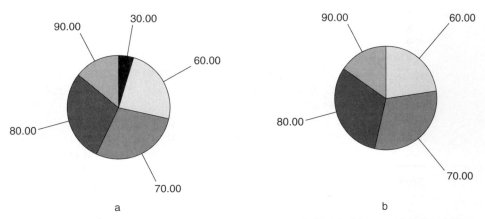

Figure 3.7 Pie chart of grouped examination scores subdivided by gender from the Whadya Get? scenario (class interval = 10). a) male students; b) female students

It is customary to place the smallest class interval at the top of the plot and the largest class interval at the bottom. The frequency is optional. A basic stem-and-leaf plot rotated 90 degrees to the left (i.e., placed on its side) looks much like a frequency histogram. See Textbox 3.12 and Figure 3.8 for an illustration that uses the Whadya Get? scenario.

It is also possible to use the stem-and-leaf plot to represent the distribution of scores for two or more subgroups. Figure 3.9 show the stem-and-leaf plots for male and female students separately. Can you recognize the trend in the data as readily by using the stem-and-leaf plot as by using the combination bar graph and histogram?

Box-and-Whisker Plot A **box-and-whisker plot** is a display that represents information about central tendency, dispersion, and the shape of a distribution all

Textbox 3.12

Stem-and-Leaf Plots

A stem-and-leaf plot for the Whadya Get? examination scores is illustrated in Figure 3.8. Note that there are 15 leaves associated with the "7" stem (i.e., the class interval 70–79). Of these, three leaves are "8." This corresponds to the three examination scores of 78.

Stem	Leaf	Frequency
3	0	1
4		0
5		0
6	0134577888999	13
7	013456677888999	15
8	0001122345678	13
9	01223448	8
		$n = 50$

Figure 3.8 Stem-and-leaf plot of the Whadya Get? examination scores (class interval = 10)

	Male Students			Female Students	
Stem	Leaf	Frequency	Stem	Leaf	Frequency
3	0	1	3		0
4		0	4		0
5		0	5		0
6	3478889	7	6	015799	6
7	01467899	8	7	3567889	7
8	001357	6	8	0122468	7
9	224	3	9	01348	5
		$n = 25$			$n = 25$

Figure 3.9 Stem-and-leaf plots of the Whadya Get? examination scores for male and female students (class interval = 10)

in a single, visual form (Tukey, 1977). The "box" in a box-and-whisker plot refers to the rectangular portion of the display.

The lower horizontal line of the box represents Q_1, the first quartile, or the 25th percentile of the scores. The upper horizontal line of the box represents Q_3, the third quartile, or the 75th percentile of the scores. When there is little overall

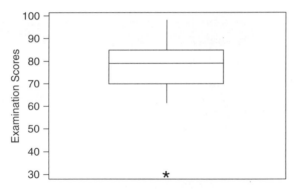

Figure 3.10 Box-and-whisker plot of the Whadya Get? examination scores

variability in the scores, the height of the box will be small. When there is a great deal of overall variability in the scores, the height of the box will be large.

The horizontal line in the middle of the box represents a measure of central tendency, called the *median* (see Chapter 4). When the data are symmetrical about the median, this horizontal line will be in the center of the box. When the data are skewed (i.e., when there are high [or low] scores quite discrepant from other scores), this horizontal line will not be in the center of the box, but generally displaced in the direction away from the longest "whisker."

In most cases, the vertical lines, or whiskers, that extend from the box reflect the spread of the remainder of the data. That is, the lower whisker illustrates the range of scores below Q_1 and the upper whisker illustrates the range of scores above Q_3. In some cases, however, there may be extremely high or low scores called *outliers*. These scores are noted by asterisks. Outliers are usually worth exploring further to determine more about their origins, including whether data entry was erroneous.

An example of a box-and-whisker plot is shown in Figure 3.10 for the Whadya Get? scenario examination scores.

Finally, box-and-whisker plots may be used to display the distribution of scores for two or more groups. See Textbox 3.13 and Figure 3.11 for an illustration using the Whadya Get? scenario.

Textbox 3.13

Box-and-Whisker Plots of Examination Scores Separated by Gender

Figure 3.11 illustrates the Whadya Get? examination scores for male and female students separately. From these plots can be seen three things: (1) females appear to have slightly outperformed males; (2) the male data is slightly skewed; and (3) the female data is slightly more variable.

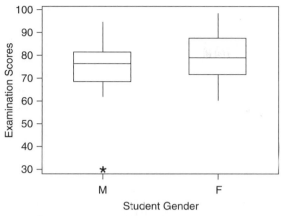

Figure 3.11 Box-and-whisker plots of the Whadya Get? examination scores for male and female students

PUTTING IT ALL TOGETHER

What to do with all these numbers? How to make sense out of the data that has been collected and needs to be interpreted? Organizing and displaying data are two ways to help people understand the salient features of a set of numbers. Organizing and displaying data also allows the data to be examined for unusual or anomalous characteristics. Are there extreme or unusual scores? Could these scores have occurred because of mistakes in data entry?

We presented several means by which a distribution of scores may be organized to increase comprehension of it. If the data are at least ordinal in nature, scores can be arranged in order. Two methods are available for dealing with tied ranks: the popular method and the mathematical method. In the popular method, the tied scores are assigned to the highest rank in category. In the mathematical method, the tied scores are assigned the average rank for the scores that are tied.

One can also supplement the use of ranks by computing percentiles and percentiles ranks. A percentage is a proportion times 100. The percentile point ($P_\%$), also called a percentile or centile, is a point on the original measurement scale at or below which a specified percentage of scores falls. The percentile rank of a score (PR_Y) is a point on the percentile scale that gives the percentage of scores falling at or below the specified score. Percentiles help locate individual scores relative to the rank-order position of other scores in the distribution.

Many researchers use percentiles to assist them when exploring data. In particular, they sometimes calculate the 25th, 50th, and 75th percentiles, or first, second, and third quartiles, because these numbers are useful in summarizing and interpreting the data. For finer divisions of the data, you may use quintiles, which are divisions of the data into fifths, or deciles, which are divisions of the data into tenths.

A frequency distribution is another tool for organizing the data to enhance interpretability. Using a grouped frequency distribution means that the data are arranged into class intervals. A good mathematical rule of thumb is to create approximately 10 to 20 classes and to adjust the intervals accordingly so that they are equal in size. To estimate the size of each interval, subtract the lowest score from the highest score and divide by the number of class intervals you wish.

There are two assumptions made in using grouped frequency distributions. The first assumption is that, in a class interval, the scores are uniformly distributed between the limits of the interval and not bunched together around a particular value or values. The second assumption is that whenever a single score must represent a class interval, the interval midpoint is the representative score.

The general formula for estimating a percentile from a grouped frequency distribution is given in Equation 3.1

$$\textbf{Equation 3.1: } P_{\%} = \text{lrl} + \left(\frac{np - \text{cf}}{\text{fi}} \right) w$$

where:

$P_{\%}$ = percentile to be estimated

lrl = lower real limit of the class interval

n = total number of scores

p = proportion corresponding to the desired percentile (i.e., %/100)

cf = cumulative frequency of scores below the interval containing $P_{\%}$

fi = frequency of scores in the interval containing $P_{\%}$

w = width of the class interval

The general formula for estimating a percentile rank is given in Equation 3.2

$$\textbf{Equation 3.2: } PR_Y = \left(\frac{\text{cf} + \left[\dfrac{(Y - \text{lrl})}{w} \right] \text{fi}}{n} \right) 100$$

where:

PR_Y = percentile rank to be estimated

Y = score for which the percentile rank is to be estimated

lrl = lower real limit of the class interval

n = total number of scores

cf = cumulative frequency of scores below the interval containing PR_Y

fi = frequency of scores in the interval containing PR_Y

w = width of the class interval

Crosstabulation or the use of a contingency table allows researchers to organize and display the values or levels of one variable according to the values or levels of a second variable.

Visual displays include graphs, figures, charts, and plots. Visual displays are nontext, pictorial devices designed to represent the important characteristics of the data. In contrast, textual displays, primarily tables, are used to present written information such as numbers and special text.

Visual displays are used when it is important to illustrate a specific trend in the data or a general relationship among groups. Textual displays are used when it is important that the numerical values of the data be presented exactly.

Graphs are two-dimensional representations of the important characteristics of the data. The two dimensions of a graph are known as axes, which are drawn at right, or 90-degree, angles from each other. The horizontal axis is called the abscissa, or the *x*-axis. The vertical axis is called the *ordinate,* or the *y*-axis. As a general guideline, the height of the *y*-axis should be no more than two-thirds to three-quarters the length of the *x*-axis.

Histograms, bar graphs, and frequency polygons are graphs used to display the frequency or percentage of individual scores or scores that have been grouped. These are useful visual displays when one wishes to illustrate how the values of a single variable are distributed. Furthermore, these graphical devices and others may also be to illustrate the relationship between two variables by showing the frequency or percentages of one variable for different values of a second (and additional) variables.

There are several other ways to visually represent the data, including pie charts, stem-and-leaf plots, and box-and-whisker plots. A pie chart is a circle divided into sectors that represent the proportionate frequency or percentage frequency of the class intervals. A stem-and-leaf plot is a means of visual display that allows for exploration of the data and its distribution while retaining the information of the original scores. A box-and-whisker plot is a display that represents information about central tendency, dispersion, and the shape of a distribution all in a single, visual form.

Textbox 3.14

Data Displays in the Literature

Why do American students not perform as well academically as their counterparts in Asia and in some European countries? Barrett (1990) makes an interesting case that perhaps American students are falling behind because they spend fewer days in school. He presents the data in a simple frequency table. See Table 3.7. As we can see, Japan has the greatest number of school days and the United States is near the bottom.

Meanwhile, researchers have found consistent differences in the academic performance of American, Japanese, and Chinese students. American students consistently score lower on tests of school-related subjects (Chen & Stevenson, 1995). The researchers suggests that Asian students work harder than Americans at their studies primarily because Asian students believe that the effort at studying will lead to academic success while American students believe that other factors, like a good teacher, are more likely to lead to success. See Figure 3.12.

TABLE 3.7 Number of Days in a Standard School Year (Source: Barrett, 1990)			
Japan	243	New Zealand	190
West Germany	226–240	Nigeria	190
South Korea	220	British Columbia	185
Israel	216	France	185
Luxembourg	211	Ontario	185
Soviet Union	200	Ireland	184
Netherlands	200	New Brunswick	180
Scotland	200	Quebec	180
Hong Kong	195	Spain	180
England/Wales	192	United States	180
Hungary	192	French Belgium	175
Switzerland	191	Flemish Belgium	160
Finland	190		

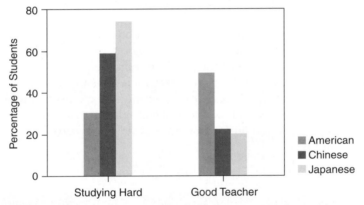

Figure 3.12 Percentage of students who chose "studying hard" or "having a good teacher" as important factors in influencing their math marks
(*Source:* Chen & Stevenson, 1995)

KEY TERMS

Organize and visually display data	Shape of the distribution	Percentage
Descriptive statistics	Ranking	Percentile point
Measured variable of interest	Percentile rank	Percentile rank of a score (PR_Y)
Values	Percentage of cases	Quartiles
	Tied ranks	Quintiles

Deciles	Class interval	Midpoints
Norm-referenced evaluation	Exact limits, or real limits	Cutpoints
Criterion referenced evaluation	Crosstabulation	Bar graphs
	Contingency table	Combination bar graph and histogram
Frequency distribution	Visual displays	Frequency polygons
Grouped frequency distribution	Bar Graphs	Ogive
	Abscissa (*x*-axis)	Pie chart
Cumulative frequency	Ordinate (*y*-axis)	Stem-and-leaf plots
Cumulative percentage	Histograms	Box-and-whisker plot

REFERENCES

Barrett, M. J. (1990) The case for more school days. *Atlantic Monthly,* November, pp. 78–106.

Chen, C., & Stevenson, H. W. (1995) Motivation and mathematics achievement: A comparative study of Asian-American, Caucasian-American, and East Asian high school students. *Child Development, 33,* 518–525.

Tukey, J. W. (1977). *Exploratory data analysis.* Reading, MA: Addison-Wesley.

PROBLEMS

Questions

Section 1   Conceptual/Definition

3.1. What is the purpose of organizing and displaying data?

3.2. What does data screening refer to, and why is it important?

3.3. What are the two methods for dealing with tied ranks?

3.4. What is the difference between a *percentile point* and the *percentile rank* of a score?

3.5. A percentile is an ordinal measure even when the original dataset upon which it was based was interval. Why?

3.6. When you are determining the interval size for a grouped frequency distribution, what two major considerations do you need to take into account?

3.7. What two assumptions are made when data are grouped?

3.8. What are exact or real limits? When are they used?

3.9. What is crosstabulation and why is it important to researchers?

3.10. What is a histogram?

3.11. What is a bar graph?

3.12. What is a pie chart?

3.13. What is a frequency polygon? A cumulative frequency polygon?

3.14. What is a stem-and-leaf plot?

3.15. What is a box-and-whisker plot?

Section 2   Numerical

3.16. Rank the following dataset: 5, 6, 4, 7, 5. For tied ranks, show the results using both the popular method and the mathematical method. In what way do the results of the two methods differ?

Use Data Table 1 to answer questions 3.17 to 3.26. Note: Do not group the data when answering questions 3.17 to 3.19.

Data Table 1:

77	70	68	65	77
59	47	79	62	64
48	66	55	61	64
63	49	56	66	63

3.17. Determine P_{20}, P_{40}, P_{60}, P_{80}.

3.18. Determine PR_{64}, PR_{70}.

3.19. Determine Q_1 and Q_3.

3.20. Using Data Table 1, create a grouped frequency distribution. Use an interval size of 5 and create 7 classes. Start your lowest category at 45.

3.21. Using Data Table 1, create a grouped frequency distribution. Use an interval size of 5 and create 7 classes. Use exact limits to form the intervals. Start your lowest category at 44.5. Determine Q_1 and Q_3 using the exact limits of the grouped frequency distribution. Determine PR_{70} using the exact limits of the grouped frequency distribution.

3.22. Create a histogram using the grouped frequency distribution from question 3.21.

3.23. Create a pie chart using the grouped frequency distribution in question 3.21.

3.24. Create a frequency polygon and a cumulative frequency polygon using the grouped frequency distribution in question 3.21.

3.25. Using Data Table 1, create a stem-and-leaf plot.

3.26. Using Data Table 1, create a box-and-whisker plot.

Data Table 2 (includes the gender of each of the subjects from Data Table 1):

77 (M)	70 (F)	68 (F)	65 (M)	77 (M)
59 (F)	47 (F)	79 (M)	62 (M)	64 (F)
48 (F)	66 (M)	55 (M)	61 (F)	64 (M)
63 (M)	49 (M)	56 (F)	66 (F)	63 (F)

3.27. Using Data Table 2, create a bar chart for the nominal variable gender.

chapter 4 Descriptive Statistics

OVERVIEW

We began Chapter 3 by suggesting that you can be "swamped" by the sheer volume of data which you have collected or otherwise tried to analyze. Organizing data and displaying data are two basic methods for making some sense out of what, at times, appears to be nonsense. Now we want to turn your attention to numerical methods for summarizing the important characteristics of a distribution or the collection of scores called *data*.

Our mission is to summarize without losing important information. In fact, the wise use of descriptive statistics may reveal things about the data that would not otherwise be understandable. The collection of descriptive statistics we will present are powerful tools. And, like all powerful tools, they can be misused, sometimes by error, and on some rare occasions, by choice.

Imagine taking thousands of numbers and being able to distill them into a few meaningful statistics. That's a pretty potent ability, which explains why descriptive statistics are so prevalent. Imagine if you couldn't talk about "averages" or "variability" and weren't able to discuss what was typical or how much people or things varied from one another.

There are good reasons to understand the nature of descriptive statistics. In explaining them, we will answer several key questions such as the following:

1. Why summarize the data?
2. How does one use summation notation?
3. What are the measures of central tendency?
4. What can shapes of distributions reveal?
5. What are measures of dispersion?
6. What information do moments about the mean give?
7. How can one measure bivariate relationships?

We begin with the scenario described in Textbox 4.1.

Textbox 4.1

Scenario: Jerry's Meander,* or How to Lie with Statistics

You and Jerry, a classmate, are conducting field research for a course in political science. The objective of your research is to determine if the political boundaries of a district have been reconstructed in such a way as to ensure that the district will vote in a liberal way in future elections. You know that liberal voters are generally those from blue collar working families, those whose family incomes are modest. In contrast, you know that conservative voters are generally those from white collar business families, those whose family incomes are substantial. Government census data say that the average family income for two adults and two children in the district is $35,000 annually. That is not anywhere near poverty level, but it is also not indicative of families with large disposable incomes. As you and Jerry meander about the district, map in hand, you notice what appears to be striking differences among homes in different areas. While most of the homes are of modest size and appointment, a select few in a small portion of the district are large and sumptuously appointed. Has a large area been divided up and conservative votes neutralized by redistributing them among liberal strongholds? To explore this possibility you receive permission from your professor to collect data on family income in the district by canvassing adults door-to-door who agree to volunteer this information anonymously and only for course purposes. A sample of the data you and Jerry collected is given in Table 4.1. From this evidence, can you say that there is cause for concern about gerrymandering?

*Gerrymandering is the unnatural and arbitrary redistricting of a state, county, or district. The name derives from the combination of then–Massachusetts governor's name *Gerry* and the sala*mander*. It was originally applied to a Massachusetts district whose odd shape was formed during Gerry's term in office.

TABLE 4.1 District Family Incomes, in Dollars (× 1000), in the Jerry's Meander Scenario			
10	15	20	25
10	20	25	25
10	20	25	25
15	20	25	150
15	20	25	200

WHY SUMMARIZE THE DATA?

In Chapter 3, we presented a variety of visual means for making large datasets or distributions of scores more manageable and interpretable. The purpose of Chapter 4 is the same, except that instead of using visual methods to organize the data we will use numerical methods, namely descriptive statistics, to do so.

A good visual display makes the data more manageable and hence interpretable without losing important information or otherwise creating a false impression of the data. Visual displays are often needed when the dataset is large.

A good **descriptive statistic** summarizes the important characteristics of a set of numbers numerically, not visually.

In this chapter, we will discuss at some length two classes of descriptive statistics: measures of central tendency, or how much the scores in a distribution bunch together, and measures of dispersion, or how much the scores in a distribution spread out. We will only briefly cover here a third class of descriptive statistics, namely, measures of bivariate relationship. A more complete presentation of bivariate relationships will be given in later chapters on correlation and regression.

Look at the district family incomes in Table 4.1. How would you summarize the important information contained in the 20 incomes? More than likely you would want to say something about the typical or average income. But only reporting the average income would not tell enough about the 20 incomes. After all, how would the average tell you whether individual incomes were highly similar to one another or highly different from one another? In addition to a measure of central tendency, you would want to compute and report a measure of dispersion, a mathematical means to represent the degree to which the incomes were similar to one another.

Summation Notation

There are many statistical procedures that depend, in part, on summing numbers. To make this notion both clear and brief, we will use the symbol $\sum$ (capital Greek sigma) to symbolize summation. The symbol $\sum$ is read as "the sum of" and tells the reader to take the arithmetic sum of the values represented by the expressions following the symbol. For example, $\sum Y$ means "take the sum of all the values of the variable Y."

Imagine you used Y as the variable name for district family income from the Jerry's Meander scenario. Then $\sum Y$ would be the sum of all the values of district family income found in Table 4.1, expressed in dollars: $\sum Y = \$700,000$.

The more precise form of this **summation notation** would look like this:

$$\sum_{i=1}^{N} Y_i \quad \text{which here means the same as } \sum Y$$

The precise notation says to take the sum of ($\sum$) every one of the i values of Y starting from the first one ($i = 1$) and finishing with the Nth, or last one. We will resort to more precise notation when we feel it is necessary for clarity. When it is not, we will use simpler forms of the notation.

MEASURES OF CENTRAL TENDENCY

In the first section, we consider the basic and well-known measures of **central tendency:** mean, median, and mode. Make sure you have a good understanding of the basics before going on. In the second section, we review some other measures of central tendency, used much less often, including weighted mean, harmonic mean, trimmed mean, and geometric mean. In the third section, we consider the advantages and disadvantages of each of the basic measures of central tendency.

The Basics

Describing any collection, whether it is a collection of objects or numbers, involves trying to identify the most prominent features of the collection. Often, it is desirable to identify one attribute that best describes the collection as a whole. Identifying what is typical or average is one way to do so.

Identifying what is typical about a collection of numbers can be done mathematically in several ways. There are, therefore, three measures of "typicality," called *measures of central tendency:* the mean, the mode, and the median.

Mean   The **arithmetic mean,** or **mean,** for short, is the arithmetic average of all the scores in a distribution. It is computed by adding together all the scores in the set and then dividing by N, the total number of scores. We will use the symbol $\overline{Y}$ (pronounced "Y bar") to stand for the arithmetic mean from a sample of scores.[1] The formula for the mean is as follows:

$$\text{Equation 4.1: } \overline{Y} = \frac{\sum_{i=1}^{N} Y_i}{N} = \frac{\sum Y}{N}$$

For the Jerry's Meander scenario the formula would be as follows:

$$\overline{Y} = \frac{\sum Y}{N} = \frac{\$700,000}{20} = \$35,000$$

The Mean as the Center of Gravity   Imagine you had placed all the scores in a distribution on a balancing beam or seesaw. The scores would be arranged in order and separated by the magnitude of their differences on the scale you had used to measure them. In other words, imagine you had taken a frequency histogram of the scores and put the histogram on a seesaw. Where is the pivot point, or fulcrum location, under the histogram where the seesaw would be perfectly balanced? See Figure 4.1, which illustrates how the mean can be thought of as the center of gravity.

CD-ROM link 4.1

Problem Generator: Descriptive Statistics
To practice calculating the mean, select Descriptive Statistics from the Problem Generator Menu on the CD-ROM. The Problem Generator will create as many practice problems as you need, and will demonstrate each step in their solution so that you can check your work.

CD-ROM link 4.2

Activity 4.1: Measures of Central Tendency and Dispersion
In Activity 4.1, you can change individual values in a dataset. As you move a data point, observe how the mean of the dataset changes as a result.

[1]In Chapter 6 we will make the distinction between summary statistics used for descriptive purposes and summary statistics used for inferential purposes.

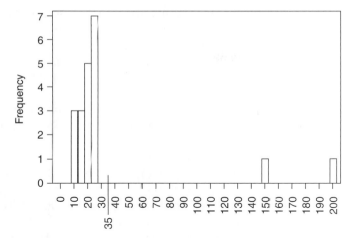

Figure 4.1 Frequency histogram of district family incomes, in dollars (× 1000)

Remember, not only the number of scores to the left and right of the pivot point or fulcrum location are important. Also making a difference is how far the scores are from the pivot point. A score close to the pivot point has much less impact on the balance of the seesaw than a score far from the pivot point, that exerts a greater influence.

The mean is that point at which the scores on the left side of the seesaw are balanced with the scores on the right side of the seesaw. The mean, therefore, can be considered to function as the center of gravity for a collection of scores.

Deviations about the Mean   Now consider Textbox 4.2. Was a mathematical error made in the calculations? How can the mean represent a typical score when, in this example, none of the family incomes were the same as the mean and most of the incomes were below the mean?

We did not make a mistake in our calculations! But was there a mistake in logical inference? Because the mean is the arithmetic average of all the scores in a distribution, it is sensitive to influence by scores that are discrepant, either mostly higher or mostly lower, than the other scores in the distribution. We will consider this more fully when we look at skewness.

Textbox 4.2

Mean of the District Family Incomes in the Jerry's Meander Scenario

The frequency histogram in Figure 4.1 notes the location of the fulcrum, or mean, for the district family incomes of $35,000. Note that *none* of the families reported an annual income of $35,000. Also note that the vast majority (18/20) reported family incomes *below* the mean. Only two families reported incomes above the mean.

In the Jerry's Meander scenario in Table 4.1, there are two scores that are both positively discrepant from the others. These two family incomes are much higher than the others and tend to pull the mean in their direction.

Another way to think about why this discrepancy occurs is to consider each score in a distribution as a deviation score (d_i) from the mean. That is: $d_i = Y_i - \overline{Y}$

The Sum of the Deviations about the Mean   In any distribution of scores for which we have calculated a mean, the sum of the signed deviations about the mean is zero:

$$\textbf{Equation 4.2: } \sum d_i = \sum (Y_i - \overline{Y}) = 0$$

See Table 4.2 for the sum of the deviations about the mean calculations for the Jerry's Meander scenario. Try adding all the positive deviations. The sum of the two positive deviations is 280. Now add the negative deviations. The sum of the 18 negative deviations is -280. Taken together, all the deviations sum to zero.

Because the deviation of a set of scores about the mean must always sum to zero, positive deviations from the mean need to be balanced by negative deviations from the mean. A single large positive deviation can be balanced by an equally large negative deviation or several small negative deviations. In the case of the Jerry's Meander scenario in Table 4.1, the two large positive deviations were balanced by many small negative deviations. The consequence for the mean was a value larger than most of the family incomes.

The mistaken inference, then, may have been in assuming that the word *typical* meant something different than average, such as "most frequent." Fortunately, there is a measure of central tendency that allows us to describe the most frequent score.

Mode   The **mode** is the most frequently occurring score in a set or distribution of scores. It is the numerical value, or interval of values in the case of a grouped frequency distribution, which has the highest frequency of occurrence. We will use the symbol Y_{MO} to stand for the sample mode of a distribution of scores. See Textbox 4.3.

Often encountered are distributions with only a single mode, as illustrated in Figure 4.2*a*. But it is possible for a distribution to have no mode (see Figure 4.2*b*).

TABLE 4.2   District Family Incomes in Dollars ($\times$ 1000) and Deviation Scores in the Jerry's Meander Scenario

Y_i	$Y_i - \overline{Y}$	Y_i	$Y_i - \overline{Y}$	Y_i	$Y_i - \overline{Y}$	Y_i	$Y_i - \overline{Y}$
10	-25	15	-20	20	-15	25	-10
10	-25	20	-15	25	-10	25	-10
10	-25	20	-15	25	-10	25	-10
15	-20	20	-15	25	-10	150	115
15	-20	20	-15	25	-10	200	165

Textbox 4.3

Modal Income in the Jerry's Meander Scenario

In the Jerry's Meander scenario, the mode is $25,000. Of the family incomes reported in Table 4.1, $25,000 is the most frequently reported income. Seven of 20 families report this as their family income. The frequency histogram in Figure 4.1 visually confirms $25,000 as the modal family income.

A distribution of scores can have no mode only when all the values occur with equal frequency (i.e., there is no clear "winner"). For example, a distribution would have no mode when the same number of families reported earning $25,000 as the number of families who reported earning $30,000, as the number of families who reported earning $35,000, and so on.

> **CD-ROM link 4.3**
>
> ***Problem Generator: Descriptive Statistics***
>
> To practice identifying the mode, select Descriptive Statistics from the Problem Generator Menu on the CD-ROM. The Problem Generator will create as many practice problems as you need, and will demonstrate each step in their solution so that you can·check your work.

It is also possible for a distribution to have more than one mode (see Figure 4.2c). In a distribution with two modes, called a bimodal distribution, the larger mode is called the *major mode* (i.e., there is a "winner") and the smaller mode is called the *minor mode* (i.e., there is a "runner-up"). For example, the largest number of families might report incomes of $60,000 and the second largest number of families might report incomes of $150,000 per year.

Median   Exactly 50% of the scores in a distribution are at or below the **median** and exactly 50% of the scores in a distribution are at or above the median. In other words, the median is the 50th percentile of the scores when the scores are arranged in order. We will use the symbol Y_{MD} to stand for the sample median of a distribution of scores. See Textbox 4.4 for the median of family incomes from the Jerry's Meander scenario.

The Median Balances the Number of Scores   Imagine you had placed all the scores in a distribution on a chemist's or miner's scale in which each score, or nugget of ore, had the same weight as any other score. In other words, higher

---

Textbox 4.4

Median Income from the Jerry's Meander Scenario

The median for the family incomes from the Jerry's Meander scenario is $20,000. When the incomes are arranged in order from lowest to highest, $20,000 is the value at which the incomes are divided into two equal halves.

scores have the same weight as lower scores, regardless of their value. In this case, it is the *number* of scores, not the *magnitude* of the scores, that makes a difference in balancing the scale. To balance the scale means that the same number has to be on the left as on the right.

Now consider finding a single value, the median, when the number of scores in a distribution is odd versus when the number of scores in a distribution is even. When N, the number of scores, is odd, the median corresponds to the score for case $(N + 1)/2$ when all the scores are arranged in order. For example, when there are 15 scores, the median is score number 8, that is, $(15 + 1)/2 = 8$.

The Median for an Even Number of Scores　When N is even, the median corresponds to the value *midway* between the score for case $N/2$ and the score for case $(N/2) + 1$. For example, when there are 20 scores, the median is between case 10, that is $20/2$, and case 11, that is $20/2 + 1$. (Remember the balance of a scale. We have 10 scores on one side and 10 scores on the other side. The median needs to be midway between the two sides.)

In the Jerry's Meander scenario, there are 20 scores arranged in order from lowest to highest in Table 4.1. The tenth score is $20,000 and the eleventh score is also $20,000 so the median is clearly $20,000.

If, however the tenth score were, say, $20,000, and the eleventh score were, say, $30,000, the median would be midway between these two values, or $25,000. In other words when there is an even number of scores, any difference between the middle two values has to be split to ensure that scores are equally balanced on the left and right of the scale.

CD-ROM link 4.4

Problem Generator: Descriptive Statistics

To practice calculating the median, select Descriptive Statistics from the Problem Generator Menu on the CD-ROM. The Problem Generator will create as many practice problems as you need, and will demonstrate each step in their solution so that you can check your work.

Selecting a Measure of Central Tendency

The three most frequently used measures of central tendency—mode, median, and mean—do not always yield identical values and are not equally applicable in all situations. How do we choose one over the other? What do we do when the measures do not coincide? Let us consider the advantages and disadvantages of each measure and the situations in which each measure best applies.

Mode　The mode is generally regarded as the easiest measure of central tendency to compute. Because the mode is determined only from counting the frequency of scores in a class or interval, determining the modal value of a distribution is fairly easy. In addition, the mode is the most flexible of the three measures and can be used even when the scale of measurement is nominal. For example, it is meaningful to ask the modal value for hair color in a class of third graders. But it would be meaningless to try and compute the mean hair color, since hair color is a nominal variable. The final advantage of the mode is that it is the least likely measure of central tendency to be affected by extreme scores, as we will see when we discuss skewness in greater detail.

There are several disadvantages to the mode as a measure of central tendency. First, there is the possibility that in any distribution of scores there may be more than one modal value, such as in bimodal or multimodal distributions, or no clear mode whatsoever, such as in a rectangular distribution in which all the scores occur with equal frequency. Although this does not happen too often, in situations where it does, the mode loses some of its value as a way to characterize succinctly the distribution as a whole.

Second, the mode is very sensitive to the size and number of class intervals for grouped frequency distributions. Even though the underlying data do not change, modifications to the size and number of class intervals may readily cause the mode to "jump around" from value to value. For example, for the Jerry's Meander scenario, the modal family income was $25,000, because this amount is the income reported by the most families (e.g., seven). However, imagine that we placed the family incomes in intervals such as $0–$24,999; $25,000–$49,999; $50,000–$74,999; and so on. Now, the modal value is in the first class interval because there are 11 families reporting incomes in this range. Moreover, if you choose to represent the mode as a single numerical value, it would be the midpoint of this class interval, namely, $12,500.

Third, the mode is not very dependable or stable. Values of the mode fluctuate much more than the other measures of central tendency fluctuate. For example, if you were to take a second, third, and fourth sample of family incomes in the Jerry's Meander scenario, most likely the modal family incomes from each of these samples would vary more than either the means or the medians from the same samples would vary.

For these reasons, use of the mode is usually restricted to a situation in which either the data are from a nominal scale of measurement, and neither the median or mean may be used, or when only the simplest and most easily computed measure of central tendency is needed.

Median The median has a few advantages as a measure of central tendency. First, it can be used when the scale of measurement is ordinal, an advantage when compared to the mean, which requires the data to be on at least an interval scale of measurement. Second, the median is much less sensitive than the mode to the distribution's grouping into class intervals. Third, the median is generally more useful and informative than the mode when one is making inferences about a population from a sample of scores. Finally, the median is less affected by extreme scores than the mean. In the Jerry's Meander scenario the mean family income is affected by two large scores; the mean family income is $35,000. The median family income is relatively unaffected by the two large scores; the median income is $20,000.

The disadvantages of the median can be understood relative to the mean. The median has mathematical properties making it difficult to work with, while the mean is more readily computable. Sample medians from a population are likely to fluctuate more than sample means taken from the same population. In other words, the median is less dependable and less stable than the mean. Finally, the median is less often used for inferential statistics than the mean. Consequently, the median is most often used when researchers are concerned about the influence of extreme scores or when the data are on an ordinal scale of measurement.

Mean   By far the most used and familiar measure of central tendency is the mean. It is the only one of the three measures that reflects the value of each score. And it is the most dependable or stable measure of central tendency. However, it is affected by extreme scores and can be used only when the data are measured on no less than an interval scale. Nevertheless, because the mean is the arithmetic average it has desirable mathematical properties. It is amenable to arithmetic and algebraic manipulations in ways that the other measures are not.

Other Measures of Central Tendency

There are several other measures of central tendency, but they are used less frequently than the mean, median, and mode. These measures include weighted and unweighted means, harmonic means, geometric means, and trimmed means.

Weighted and Unweighted Means   There are situations in which two or more means need to be combined. To do so, one may use either a **weighted mean** ($\overline{Y}_W$, or simply $\overline{Y}$) or an **unweighted mean** ($\overline{Y}_U$).

Equation 4.3: $\overline{Y}_W = \dfrac{n_1\overline{Y}_1 + n_2\overline{Y}_2 + \cdots + n_g\overline{Y}_g}{N}$ where $N = n_1 + n_2 + \cdots + n_g$

Equation 4.4: $\overline{Y}_U = \dfrac{\overline{Y}_1 + \overline{Y}_2 + \cdots + \overline{Y}_g}{g}$ where g is the number of groups

To understand the difference, imagine you had computed the mean family incomes for two groups of unequal size. Group 1 has a mean of $100,000, based on the incomes of five families. Group 2 has a mean of $50,000, based on the incomes of 10 families.

Now a single value is wanted to represent the incomes of these two groups together. If you computed an unweighted mean, you would merely take the two group means, add them, and divide by 2. This has the effect of weighting the group means equally, regardless of differences in group size (n). In this case, $\overline{Y}_U = \$75,000$.

However, you can also compute a mean that weights each individual income equally when the data are combined. This has the effect of weighting the group means unequally so long as group size (n) varies. In this case, $\overline{Y}_W = \$66,666.67$.

The choice of weighted versus unweighted mean depends on the purpose to which the data are to be used. If one wishes the mean to represent all the *individual scores* equally, a weighted mean would be the most appropriate choice. If, however, one wishes the mean to represent all the *group scores* equally, then an unweighted mean would be the most appropriate choice.

For example, circumstances sometimes make it difficult to collect data with equal ease for all groups, resulting in differential group sizes. The computation of an unweighted mean ensures that each group has equal representation overall.

Finally, you may recognize one of these means as one that we have covered already. The weighted mean $\overline{Y}_W$ yields an average that is always identical to the basic mean $\overline{Y}$ we introduced at the outset of the chapter.

Harmonic Means   When the influence of extreme values is to be minimized, sometimes one uses the **harmonic mean** $(\overline{Y}_H)$.

$$\text{Equation 4.5: } \overline{Y}_H = \frac{N}{\sum \frac{1}{Y}}$$

For the family incomes from the Jerry's Meander scenario,

$$\overline{Y}_H = \frac{N}{\sum \frac{1}{Y}} = \frac{20}{1.04} = 19.20$$

Trimmed Means   Another way to minimize the influence of extreme scores is to compute a **trimmed mean** $(\overline{Y}_T)$. A trimmed mean is one in which some percent of the lowest and highest scores are eliminated and the arithmetic mean is then calculated from the values that remain. For example, a 5% trimmed mean removes both the smallest 5% (rounded to the nearest integer) and the largest 5% and then averages the rest.

For Jerry's Meander scenario, $\overline{Y}_T = 27.20$.

Geometric Means   When one wishes to find the average of ratios, sometimes one uses the **geometric mean** $(\overline{Y}_G)$.

$$\text{Equation 4.6: } \overline{Y}_G = (Y_1 Y_2 Y_3 Y_4 \ldots Y_N)^{1/N}$$

The geometric mean is the product of all the values with the Nth root taken. For the Jerry's Meander scenario, $\overline{Y}_G = 23.16$.

Shapes of Distributions

We saw in Chapter 3, how a good visual display helps to make large distributions more manageable and their key characteristics more salient. Therefore, we will use a frequency polygon or line graph of hypothetical family incomes to help us illustrate various shapes of frequency distributions. This should further aid the understanding of measures of central tendency and set the stage for a discussion of measures of variability. We will focus on three characteristics that help describe the shape of frequency distributions: mode, skewness, and kurtosis.

Frequency Distributions and the Mode   Figure 4.2*a* is a frequency polygon, which illustrates a hypothetical distribution of family incomes with one mode, called a **unimodal distribution**. There is only one value of family income that occurs with greatest frequency.

Figure 4.2*b* illustrates a hypothetical distribution of family incomes with no mode, called a **rectangular** (or *uniform*) distribution. All the values occur with equal frequency. No one value is more frequent than the others.

Figure 4.2*c* illustrates a hypothetical distribution with two modes, called a **bimodal distribution.** The taller peak is called the *major mode.* The smaller peak is called the *minor mode.* In other words, there are two values that occur more frequently than the others.

Skewness and Measures of Central Tendency   Another characteristic of a distribution is its symmetry. A **symmetric distribution** occurs only when it is possible to divide its graph at the center into two identical halves, wherein each half is a mirror image of the other. Figures 4.3*a* and 4.3*b* illustrate symmetric distributions. In symmetric distributions, the mean is always equal to the median. However, Figure 4.3*b* illustrates that the mode(s) do not always equal the mean or the median in a symmetric distribution. Symmetry is not sufficient to guarantee that all the measures of central tendency will be equal. When, however, a distribution has one mode and is symmetric (see Figure 4.3*a*), all the measures of central tendency will be the same value.

A nonsymmetric distribution is sometimes described as skewed. A **skewed distribution** means that the distribution is lopsided, containing relatively few

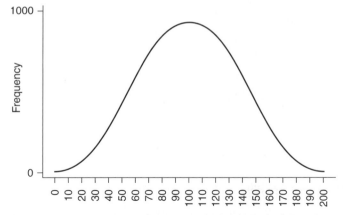

Figure 4.2*a* Hypothetical unimodal distribution of family incomes times $1000

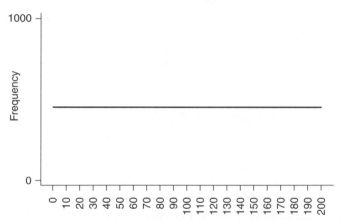

Figure 4.2*b* Hypothetical rectangular distribution of family incomes times $1000

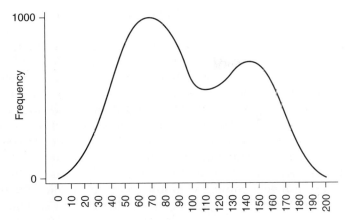

Figure 4.2c Hypothetical bimodal distribution of family incomes times $1000

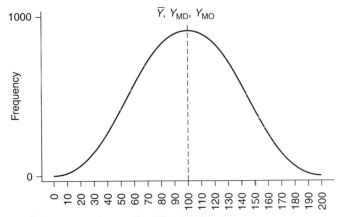

Figure 4.3a Hypothetical symmetrical distribution of family incomes times $1000 ($\overline{Y} = Y_{MD} = Y_{MO}$)

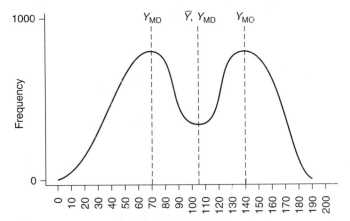

Figure 4.3b Hypothetical symmetrical distribution of family incomes times $1000 ($\overline{Y} = Y_{MD} \neq Y_{MO}$)

extreme scores toward only one end, with the bulk of the scores in the central section.

As Figure 4.3c illustrates, a *negatively* skewed distribution contains relatively few extremely low scores, with the bulk of the scores higher. The tail of a negatively skewed distribution "points" towards lower values. In a negatively skewed distribution, the median is larger than the mean.

As Figure 4.3d illustrates, a *positively* skewed distribution contains relatively few extremely high scores, with the bulk of the scores lower. The tail of a positively skewed distribution "points" toward higher values. In a positively skewed distribution, the mean is larger than the median.

The pattern of values for the measures of central tendency means that positive or negative skewness can be identified without actually examining the frequency distribution of scores. When $\overline{Y} = Y_{MD} = Y_{MO}$, the distribution is symmetric *and*

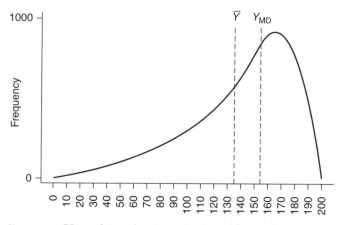

Figure 4.3c Hypothetical *negatively* skewed distribution of family incomes times $1000 $(\overline{Y} < Y_{MD})$

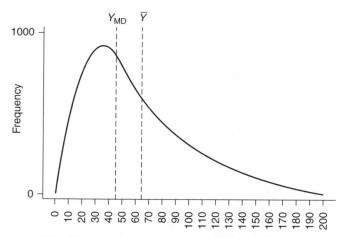

Figure 4.3d Hypothetical *positively* skewed distribution of family incomes times $1000 $(\overline{Y} > Y_{MD})$

unimodal. As a general rule, when $\overline{Y} < Y_{MD}$, the distribution is negatively skewed. And, as a general rule, when $\overline{Y} > Y_{MD}$, the distribution is positively skewed.

Figures 4.3c and d help to illustrate why the mean is affected more than the median by extreme scores. Otherwise, imagine that one of the high incomes from the Jerry's Meander scenario data in Table 4.1 was replaced with a much larger one (e.g., $1,000,000) such that the tail of the distribution of scores was even longer. Replacing this one score would have no effect on the median; there would be no change to the midmost score when the scores were arranged in order. But replacing this one score would have an effect on the mean; there would be an increase in the size of the arithmetic average. Change this one score yourself and recompute the measures of central tendency to see what happens.

CD-ROM link 4.5

Activity 4.2: Moments About the Mean
In Activity 4.2, you can change a distribution's shape and see how the change affects the skewness of the distribution.

Skewness and the Mode In many statistics textbooks, you will see all three measures of central tendency used to describe skewness. However, because the mode is not a very stable or dependable measure of central tendency, the value of the mode relative to the mean and median is not always indicative of skewness in every data distribution. That is, positive skew is sometimes indicated when $\overline{Y} > Y_{MD} > Y_{MO}$, but not every time. (See Textbox 4.5.)

Kurtosis and the Spread of Scores A third characteristic of a frequency distribution is its **kurtosis.** Kurtosis describes the extent to which a frequency distribution of scores is bunched around the center or spread toward the endpoints. The more the scores are bunched around the center, the less variability exists in the distribution and the more the distribution appears peaked. The more the scores are spread toward the endpoints, the more variability exists in the distribution and the more the distribution appears flat.

A frequency distribution with bunched scores that give the appearance of peakedness is called *leptokurtic*. A frequency distribution with widely spread scores that give the appearance of flatness is called *platykurtic*. A frequency distribution with scores that are neither bunched nor widely spread, and that does not appear either peaked or flat, is called *mesokurtic*. These three types of frequency distributions are illustrated in Figure 4.4a to c.

Textbox 4.5

Skewness in the Jerry's Meander Scenario

If you have been using the Jerry's Meander scenario to follow the discussion about skewness, you will now notice a discrepancy between the $\overline{Y} > Y_{MD} > Y_{MO}$ rule and the data, illustrating our point. What you find is $\overline{Y} = \$35,000$, $Y_{MD} = \$20,000$, and $Y_{MO} = \$25,000$. The data are positively skewed, yet the measures of central tendency are not in the "right" order—the mode is larger than the median. This illustrates our preference for using only the values of the mean and median to indicate skewness.

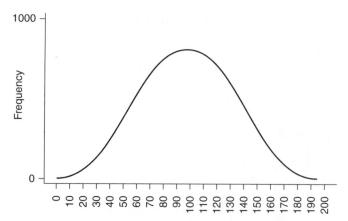

Figure 4.4a Hypothetical mesokurtic distribution of family incomes times $1000

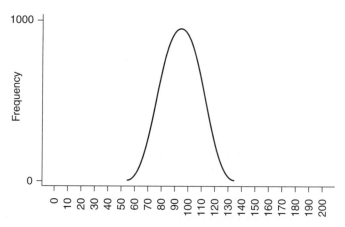

Figure 4.4b Hypothetical leptokurtic distribution of family incomes times $1000

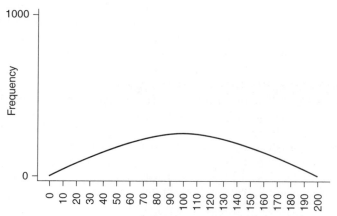

Figure 4.4c Hypothetical platykurtic distribution of family incomes times $1000

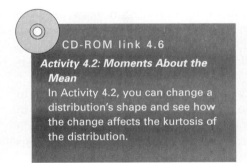

CD-ROM link 4.6

Activity 4.2: Moments About the Mean

In Activity 4.2, you can change a distribution's shape and see how the change affects the kurtosis of the distribution.

How Do I Determine Skewness and Kurtosis for My Data?   Whether a distribution of scores is skewed, as well as the direction and degree of skew, can be determined in two ways: visually and mathematically. The nature and extent to which a distribution of scores departs from mesokurtic can also be determined visually and mathematically. Examining the frequency polygon for your data is the visual way to determine skewness and kurtosis. And you also know that when $\overline{Y} < Y_{MD}$ a distribution of scores is negatively skewed, while when $\overline{Y} > Y_{MD}$ a distribution of scores is positively skewed. Unfortunately, there is no simple mathematical equivalent for determining kurtosis. And these simple methods do not tell one the precise degree of skewness or kurtosis. Therefore, we will discuss more complex mathematical means to determine skewness and kurtosis when we cover the moments about the mean.

MEASURES OF DISPERSION

There are three basic, widely used **measures of dispersion:** range, variance, and standard deviation. We will cover these basic descriptive statistics first and in some detail. There are other measures of dispersion used less frequently: semi-interquartile range, coefficient of variation, and index of dispersion. We will treat these briefly after covering the basics.

The Basics

While measures of central tendency such as the mean, median, and mode offer a useful descriptive statistics concerning a distribution of scores, knowing about central tendency alone is insufficient to form an accurate impression of the data. As well as understanding what in the distribution of scores is typical, one also wants to know the nature and extent to which the scores vary. In other words, one wants to know about the dispersion, spread, or variability in the distribution of scores.

In the Jerry's Meander scenario, for example, you do not get a complete picture of the data by only knowing that $\overline{Y} = \$35,000$, $Y_{MD} = \$20,000$, and $Y_{MO} = \$25,000$. You also want to know something about how the scores vary one from another. Are the family incomes more or less the same, or are they quite different from one another? Do some of the families need social support? On the other hand, might some of the families be interested in and able to afford additional municipal services? Measures of central tendency do not tell you that. And you often want to know about the variability in scores; it is a useful way to describe a dataset.

Consider another example. The mean daytime temperature in Montreal, Canada, is probably around 60 degrees Fahrenheit. If this were all that were known about the daytime weather in Montreal, Montrealers would all walk around with light jackets on throughout the year. But in winter, the daytime temperature can go

CD-ROM link 4.7

Activity 4.1: Measures of Central Tendency and Dispersion
Why are measures needed for both central tendency and dispersion? What are the advantages of having more than one measure for each? Activity 4.1 shows you how the mean, range, variance, and standard deviation each represent a particular aspect of a dataset.

below zero. And in the summer, on many days the temperature can climb into the 90s. It is useful to know what the average temperature is, but it is also important to find out the extent to which the temperatures vary.

Another type of descriptive statistic is needed to summarize the extent to which there is variability in the distribution of scores. Measures of dispersion (variability or spread) allow one to describe this quality of a set of numbers.

Range   The **range** (R) is the simplest measure of dispersion to compute. It is merely the difference between the highest score and the lowest score.[2] For example, in the Jerry's Meander scenario, the range is $190,000 (i.e., $200,000 − $10,000). Note that the range is a single value, not the two extreme values as is sometimes mistakenly given.

The range can be particularly useful when it is important to know something about the maximum extent to which scores can vary. For example, traffic engineers need to know how traffic volumes in rush hour differ from traffic volumes in late night. The range of vehicle sizes and weights in that traffic might also be useful.

Although it is wonderful to have a basic descriptive statistic that is so easy to compute, the range is not an especially good measure of dispersion. It is a measure wholly dependent on the two most extreme scores in the data; it does not take into account any of the other scores, no matter how many there are.

One consequence of the inability of the range to consider more than the two extreme scores is that the range is not an especially stable descriptive statistic; it can fluctuate, depending on the values of the highest and lowest scores, which may be unrepresentative, unlike other scores in the distribution. For example, if one of the households in the Jerry's Meander scenario contained a lottery winner, the largest income might have been much higher, increasing the range substantially.

CD-ROM link 4.8

Problem Generator: Descriptive Statistics
To practice calculating the range, select Descriptive Statistics from the Problem Generator Menu on the CD-ROM. The Problem Generator will create as many practice problems as you need, and will demonstrate each step in their solution so that you can check your work.

Variance (and Mean Deviation)   Clearly, a measure of dispersion is needed that does a better job representing the spread of all the scores in the distribution and not just the two scores at the extremes. How might this be accomplished and a single descriptive statistic arrived at that is intuitively appealing?

If you think about it for a moment, you might realize that the measures of dispersion are designed to complement the measures of central tendency. The mea-

[2]The inclusive range is the difference between the real upper limit of the highest score and the real lower limit of the lowest score. The inclusive range is the range plus 1.

sures of dispersion capture something that the measures of central tendency miss. For example, if all the scores were the same as the mean, there would be no need to compute a measure of dispersion. If, on the other hand, the scores varied considerably, the mean would be less useful at representing the important characteristics of the set of scores. In this situation, the mean by itself is a poor fit to all the data.

Remember that a descriptive statistic is a single number that represents an important characteristic of a set of numbers or distribution of scores. What type of calculation needs to be performed to arrive at this single number, taking into account all the data in the set? Perhaps some number that represents the total variability in the dataset or the average variability in the dataset? But how would this variability be computed? Variability from what?

Since we have already introduced the notion of central tendency, why not compute the variability relative to a measure of central tendency? For example, why not compute the variability of each of the scores from the mean? That is, find the deviation of each score in the set from the mean score: $d_i = Y_i - \overline{Y}$. (See column 2 in Table 4.3.)

Note how the deviation scores reflect the extent to which any value is close to or far from the mean value of 35 (or, more correctly $\times$ \$1000 = \$35,000). Incomes close to the mean have small deviation scores; incomes far from the mean have large deviation scores.

But what should one do with the deviation scores? How does one reduce the deviation scores into a single, descriptive statistic? Unfortunately, whenever the deviation scores about the mean are added, the total is always zero. The positive deviations about the mean always cancel the negative deviations about the mean.

$$\text{Equation 4.7: } \sum d_i = \sum (Y_i - \overline{Y}) = 0$$

At this point, two choices are available, and both choices affect the sign $(+/-)$ of each deviation score. All the deviation scores can be converted to their absolute value and then added together, or the deviation scores can be squared and then added together. In either case, no longer will the converted scores always sum to zero. (See columns 3 and 4 in Table 4.3.)

The sum of the **absolute deviations** is as follows:

$$\text{Equation 4.8: } \sum |d_i| = \sum |Y_i - \overline{Y}| = 560$$

The sum of the **squared deviations** or sum of squares is as follows:

$$\text{Equation 4.9: } \sum (d_i)^2 = \sum (Y_i - \overline{Y})^2 = 45,350$$

Either the absolute deviation method or the squared deviation method overcomes the obstacle presented by the deviation scores about the mean summing to zero. There will now only be one situation in which the absolute deviation method and the squared deviation method will each sum to zero—when all the scores in the distribution are identical. Otherwise, both the absolute deviation method and the squared deviation method will be greater than zero.

| | | | | | | | | TABLE 4.3 Deviation, Absolute Deviation, and Squared Deviation Scores for Jerry's Meander Scenario ($\times$ $1000) |

Y_i	$d_i = Y_i - \bar{Y}$	$\lvert d_i \rvert = \lvert Y_i - \bar{Y} \rvert$	$(d_i)^2 = (Y_i - \bar{Y})^2$
10	-25	25	625
10	-25	25	625
10	-25	25	625
15	-20	20	400
15	-20	20	400
15	-20	20	400
20	-15	15	225
20	-15	15	225
20	-15	15	225
20	-15	15	225
20	-15	15	225
25	-10	10	100
25	-10	10	100
25	-10	10	100
25	-10	10	100
25	-10	10	100
25	-10	10	100
25	-10	10	100
150	115	115	13,225
200	165	165	27,225
$\sum Y_i = 700$	$\sum d_i = 0$	$\sum \lvert d_i \rvert = 560$	$\sum (d_i)^2 = 45{,}350$

You have now arrived at a point where you have two descriptive statistics, each of which summarizes in a single value all the variability in a distribution of scores. But you are not done yet. Summing either the absolute deviation scores or the squared deviation scores means that comparing the variability in datasets of different sizes will be difficult. All other things equal, the sum of either of these deviation scores will become larger and larger as the size of the dataset grows. Therefore, if you tried to compare the sums of two datasets that differed in size only, you might mistakenly conclude that the degree of variability in the larger dataset was greater than the degree of variability in the smaller dataset. However, the truth is that the "extra" variability came about only because there were more scores to consider. Therefore, a measure of variability is needed that takes the size of the dataset into account.

The solution is easy enough. Rather than find just the sum of the deviation scores, also find the average of the deviation scores. Doing so allows the average variability in one distribution to be examined and compared with the average variability in another distribution, regardless of the number of scores each distribution contains.

The mean of the absolute deviations is as follows:

$$\text{Equation 4.10: MAD} = \frac{\sum |d_i|}{N} = \frac{\sum |Y_i - \overline{Y}|}{N}$$

The mean of the absolute deviations is known as the *mean deviation* (MAD) for short.

For the Jerry's Meander scenario: MAD $= 560/20 = 28$

The mean of the squared deviations is as follows:

$$\text{Equation 4.11: } S^2 = \frac{\sum (d_i)^2}{N} = \frac{\sum (Y_i - \overline{Y})^2}{N}$$

The mean of the squared deviations is known as the **variance** (S^2).

For the Jerry's Meander scenario: $S^2 = 45{,}350/20 = 2267.50$

At a basic level, these two methods of describing variability are equally attractive. They include all the data in their calculations, are averages and therefore are not affected by the number of scores in the distribution, and both result in a single value to represent the variability in the dataset. And for both, the greater their value, the greater the variability or dispersion among the scores in the distribution.

Unfortunately, the mean deviation method is limited because absolute values are used in the computation. More advanced statistical procedures require algebraic manipulations that are difficult, if not impossible, to carry out with absolute values. The variance does not suffer from this shortcoming and is, therefore, a much more widely used measure of dispersion than the mean deviation.

CD-ROM link 4.9

Problem Generator: Descriptive Statistics

To practice calculating the variance, select Descriptive Statistics from the Problem Generator Menu on the CD-ROM. The Problem Generator will create as many practice problems as you need, and will demonstrate each step in their solution so that you can check your work.

Steps in Computing the Variance

1. Compute the mean: $\overline{Y} = \dfrac{\sum\limits_{i=1}^{N} Y_i}{N} = \dfrac{\sum Y}{N}$

2. Compute the individual deviation scores: $Y_i - \overline{Y}$

3. Square the individual deviation scores: $(Y_i - \overline{Y})^2$

4. Sum the squared deviation scores: $\sum (Y_i - \overline{Y})^2$

5. Find the average squared deviation score by dividing the sum of squared deviation scores by N, the number of scores $S^2 = \dfrac{\sum (d_i)^2}{N} = \dfrac{\sum (Y_i - \overline{Y})^2}{N}$

Standard Deviation   A problem with the variance is that it is the average of the *squared* deviation scores. It would be preferable if one also had an index of variability that was in the original unit of measurement. Fortunately, that's easy enough. To return to the original unit of measurement, merely take the square root of the variance, called the **standard deviation** (or *S*). (See Textbox 4.6.)

$$\textbf{Equation 4.12:}\ S = \sqrt{\frac{\sum (d_i)^2}{N}} = \sqrt{\frac{\sum (Y_i - \overline{Y})^2}{N}}$$

For the Jerry's Meander scenario: $S = \sqrt{2267.50} = 47.62$

Note that the standard deviation can never be negative, regardless of whether the mean is negative and regardless of whether all the original scores (Y_i) are negative. If you get a negative value for *S*, you have made a computational error. Finally, note that both the variance and standard deviation require data that is on at least an interval scale of measurement. The variance and standard deviation cannot be used when the data are ordinal or nominal.

Quick Computational Check for S   A handy rule of thumb for providing a quick estimate of *S* is the ratio of the range to the standard deviation. This ratio is rarely smaller than 2 or larger than 6.

In general, $2 < R/S < 6$

If your calculations yield a standard deviation that is well outside this range, there is a good possibility that you have made a computational error and you will need to recheck your calculations.

Division by N or N – 1?   We will say right away that this question is the source of a lot of confusion among students, both new and old, to statistics. We just presented the variance and the standard deviation as averages in which the sum is divided by the total number of scores (*N*).

More precisely, division of the sum of the squared deviation scores, or sum of squares, by the total number of scores (*N*) is the correct computational procedure

---

Textbox 4.6

Variance and Standard Deviation for the Jerry's Meander Scenario

In the Jerry's Meander scenario, $S^2 = \$2{,}267{,}500$ and $S = \$47{,}620$. Using *S* rather than S^2 allows you to understand the dispersion of the family incomes in the original units of measurement. You can immediately relate the value of *S* to the 20 family incomes that were reported. The average variability in family incomes is almost $50,000. But it is harder to see the relationship between S^2 and the family income values. Although it is true that the average squared deviation is about $2,250,000, it is hard to relate that number to the family incomes one started with.

when your intention is only to describe the dispersion in the set of scores with which you are working. In other words, divide by N when you are not interested in making an inference from the existing set of scores, or sample, to a larger group, or population. When the variance and standard deviation are used strictly as a descriptive tool, division of the squared deviation scores by N is proper.

Many times, however, one is interested in using the sample dataset to make an *inference* or best guess about a much larger dataset or population. For example, you might want to use the results of the Jerry's Meander scenario data to infer the variance and standard deviation for the family incomes of *all* the families in the district and not just the 20 whose data were obtained. When a small sample of data is used to estimate the variance and standard deviation of the larger population, the sum of the squared deviation scores is divided by $N-1$. Doing so makes the variance and standard deviation more accurate estimators of the population parameters. When the variance and standard deviation have N in the denominator, they are considered *biased* estimators. When the variance and standard deviation have $N-1$ in the denominator, they are considered *unbiased* estimators. We will cover this again, but in greater detail, in Chapter 6.

To describe the variability in a sample:

$$S^2 = \frac{\sum (d_i)^2}{N} = \frac{\sum (Y_i - \overline{Y})^2}{N}$$

$$S = \sqrt{\frac{\sum (d_i)^2}{N}} = \sqrt{\frac{\sum (Y_i - \overline{Y})^2}{N}}$$

Note that uppercase S^2 and S represent the formula for biased estimators of population parameters.

To estimate population parameters from sample values:

Equation 4.13: $s^2 = \dfrac{\sum (d_i)^2}{N-1} = \dfrac{\sum (Y_i - \overline{Y})^2}{N-1}$

Equation 4.14: $s = \sqrt{\dfrac{\sum (d_i)^2}{N-1}} = \sqrt{\dfrac{\sum (Y_i - \overline{Y})^2}{N-1}}$

Note that the lowercase s^2 and s represent the formula for unbiased estimators of population parameters.

- For the Jerry's Meander scenario:
  $S^2 = 45{,}350/20 = 2267.50$ but $s^2 = 45{,}350/19 = 2386.84$
- For the Jerry's Meander scenario:
  $S = \sqrt{2267.50} = 47.62$ but $s = \sqrt{2386.84} = 48.86.$

From now on, you will need to be on the alert if you are using a calculator or computer software package to compute the variance and standard deviation.

CD-ROM link 4.10

Problem Generator: Descriptive Statistics

To practice calculating the standard deviation, select Descriptive Statistics from the Problem Generator Menu on the CD-ROM. The Problem Generator will create as many practice problems as you need, and will demonstrate each step in their solution so that you can check your work.

Check to see whether the results you get are for the biased variance and standard deviation (division by N) or the unbiased variance and standard deviation (division by $N - 1$).

Fortunately, the mean of a sample is a good estimator of the population mean. Therefore, no adjustment is necessary when it is used as an estimator. In other words, always use N in the denominator when computing the mean, never $N - 1$, regardless of whether it is used descriptively or to estimate a population parameter.

Other Measures of Dispersion   While we have covered the "big three" measures of dispersion and, in passing, the mean deviation, there are still a host of other measures of dispersion. Since they are used less often, we will briefly cover only a few of these, including the interquartile range, the semi-interquartile range, the interdecile range, and the coefficient of variation. Both the interquartile range and the semi-interquartile range, in particular, are used when the data are on an ordinal scale of measurement or heavily skewed. These range statistics are the measures of dispersion which often accompany the median when it is the preferred measure of central tendency.

Interquartile Range   In Chapter 3, we covered the procedures for computing percentiles and then used percentiles to determine quartiles and deciles. Recall that the first quartile (Q_1) is the 25th percentile; the second quartile, or the median, is the 50th percentile (Q_2); and the third quartile (Q_3) is the 75th percentile. Scores at each 10th percentile are called deciles.

The **interquartile range** (IQ) is simply the difference between the first and the third quartiles:

$$\textbf{Equation 4.15: } IQ = Q_3 - Q_1$$

Note that the interquartile range includes those scores making up the middlemost 50% of the distribution: 25% falling to the left of the median and 25% falling to the right of the median. Since the interquartile range is based on the calculation of percentiles, which emanate from the ranking of data, it can be used with ratio, interval, and ordinal data.

Textbox 4.7

Interquartile Range for the Jerry's Meander Scenario

For the Jerry's Meander scenario, $Q_1 = 15.00$, $Q_2 = 20.00$, and $Q_3 = 25.00$.
$IQ = Q_3 - Q_1 = 25.00 - 15.00 = 10.00$ (for family income in dollars $\times$ \$1000)

Textbox 4.8

Semi-interquartile Range for the Jerry's Meander Scenario

$SIQ = (Q_3 - Q_1)/2 = (25.00 - 15.00)/2 = 5.00$ (for family income in dollars $\times$ $1000)

Semi-interquartile Range   When the interquartile range is divided in half, it results in what is known as the **semi-interquartile range** (SIQ), or as it is sometimes called, the *quartile deviation*. Therefore, the semi-interquartile range expresses the range of scores for the 25% of scores closest to the median.

$$\text{Equation 4.16: } SIQ = \frac{Q_3 - Q_1}{2}$$

Strengths and Weaknesses of the Interquartile and Semi-interquartile Range Statistics   Both the interquartile range and the semi-interquartile range are useful measures when a distribution is noticeably skewed by a few extreme scores. These few extreme scores are likely to have a much greater influence on the variance and standard deviation then on either of the range statistics. Why? The range statistics do not include values below the 25th percentile or above the 75th percentile. In contrast, the variance and standard deviation include all the scores in computing a dispersion statistic. When a distribution is noticeably skewed, the median is preferred as the measure of central tendency and the interquartile and semi-interquartile range are preferred as the complementary measures of dispersion.

The interquartile range and semi-interquartile range are reasonably stable measures of dispersion, although they are somewhat less stable than the variance and standard deviation. However, they have limited utility for more advanced inferential statistical procedures; their use is essentially limited to the realm of descriptive statistics. Furthermore, both IQ and SIQ do not permit the precise interpretation of a score within a distribution of scores. As you will learn when we discuss the normal distribution, individual deviation scores, used in computing S^2 and S, allow for this precise interpretation.

Interdecile Range   Occasionally you may wish to read about or to calculate a measure of dispersion called the **interdecile range** (IR). IR is simply the difference between the ninth and the first deciles.

$$\text{Equation 4.17: } IR = D_9 - D_1$$

The interdecile range includes the middlemost 80% of the distribution, 40% falling above the median and 40% falling below the median. IR is usually unaffected by extreme scores (although when the number of scores is small, IR is more susceptible to extreme scores than IQ or SIQ, as our example in Textbox 4.9

Textbox 4.9

Interdecile Range for Jerry's Meander Scenario

For the Jerry's Meander scenario, $D_9 = 137.50$ and $D_1 = 10.00$.

IR $= D_9 - D_1 = 137.50 - 10.00 = 127.50$ (for family income in dollars $\times$ $1000)

shows), so it can be used when the distribution is skewed. It can also be used when the data are ordinal or on a higher scale of measurement.

Coefficient of Variation   Both the variance and standard deviation are averages. But how can one tell if a variance or standard deviation is relatively large or small?

Researchers often make judgments about the relative size of the variance and standard deviation from their knowledge of the research context. Their prior research and other studies in the area provide a useful, if subjective, means for judging whether there is a great deal of variability in a set of scores or very little variability.

The **coefficient of variation** (CV) is an objective means for assessing the relative degree of dispersion in a set of scores. It is a ratio of the standard deviation divided by the mean and then multiplied by 100. (See Textbox 4.10.)

$$\textbf{Equation 4.18: } CV = 100\left(\frac{S}{\overline{Y}}\right)$$

The coefficient of variation can be interpreted like a percentage, where the size of the standard deviation is given relative to the mean. When the standard deviation and the mean are identical, CV = 100.

Why is the coefficient of variation a ratio of the standard deviation divided by the mean? Consider two distributions:

$$\overline{Y}_1 = 10.00 \qquad S_1 = 20.00$$
$$\overline{Y}_2 = 100.00 \qquad S_2 = 20.00$$

Textbox 4.10

Coefficient of Variation for the Jerry's Meander Scenario

$$CV = 100\left(\frac{S}{\overline{Y}}\right) = 100\left(\frac{47.62}{35.00}\right) = 136.06$$

In both distributions the standard deviations are the same. In the first distribution, the relative degree of dispersion seems somewhat large, because the mean is not very large. In the second distribution, however, the relative degree of dispersion seems fairly small, because the mean is large.

The differences are apparent when CV is computed. For the first distribution, CV = 200.00. For the second distribution, CV = 20.00.

Another advantage of the coefficient of variation is that it allows standard deviations of measures that involve different units of measurement to be compared. For example, one might be interested in comparing the dispersion of family income from our hypothetical scenario with the dispersion of educational level for each family's principal wage earner. In this case, it would be meaningless to compare the variability of family income expressed in dollars with the variability of education level expressed in years of schooling. However, the comparison would be more meaningful if the two standard deviations were converted to coefficients of variation.

MOMENTS ABOUT THE MEAN

A complete treatment of distributions would cover numerous summary statistics. The collection of these summary statistics are called the **moments of a distribution.** (By the way, the term *moment* originates in mechanics.) An important type of summary statistic looks at individual scores subtracted from the mean (i.e., deviation scores) raised to different powers. These are the **moments about the mean.**

Average deviation (*AD*) is the first moment about the mean:

$$\textbf{Equation 4.19: } AD = \frac{\sum (Y - \overline{Y})}{N} = 0$$

Variance (S^2) is the second moment about the mean:

$$\textbf{Equation 4.20: } S^2 = \frac{\sum (Y_i - \overline{Y})^2}{N}$$

Skewness (S^3) is the third moment about the mean:

$$\textbf{Equation 4.21: } S^3 = \frac{\sum (Y_i - \overline{Y})^3}{N}$$

Skewness is the extent to which a distribution contains extreme scores in one tail of the distribution only. Recall that raising a value to the third power means that the product can be either positive or negative. In the case of skewness, a zero value for S^3 indicates symmetry: the sum of the deviations about the mean, when raised to the third power, will balance the sum of the deviations below the mean, when raised to the third power. However, if the distribution is asymmetric, the sum of the deviations raised to the third power will not balance. If the distribution is negatively skewed, S^3 will be negative. If the distribution is positively skewed, S^3 will be positive.

Kurtosis (S^4) is the fourth moment about the mean:

CD-ROM link 4.11

Activity 4.2: Moments about the Mean

In Activity 4.2, you can explore how the four moments about the mean (average deviation, variance, skewness, and kurtosis) are related to the shape of a distribution.

Equation 4.22: $S^4 = \dfrac{\sum (Y_i - \overline{Y})^4}{N}$

Kurtosis is the extent to which a distribution is peaked or flat. If a distribution is fairly flat, or platykurtic, it has relatively more large deviations from the mean. Large deviations from the mean, when raised to the fourth power, will contribute substantially to the fourth moment, indicative of a flat distribution.

Mathematical Measures of Skewness and Kurtosis[3]   You can use the third and fourth moments about the mean as a way to gauge the skewness and kurtosis, respectively, of a distribution, but there is an important limitation to doing so. You would not be able to compare the values obtained from one distribution of scores with the values obtained from other distributions when they differed either in variability or the scale of measurement used. In other words, you would not be able to use the moments about the mean for skewness and kurtosis to compare one distribution of scores with another. What is needed is a way to index the values of skewness and kurtosis so that you can say whether there is too much skew or too much kurtosis in one distribution compared to another.

A standardized measure of skewness (Sk) allows you to compare distributions that differ in variability such that a set of diverse measurements (e.g., ounces, intelligence test scores, EKG results, years) can be directly compared:

$$\text{Equation 4.23: } Sk = \frac{S^3}{S^2\sqrt{S^2}}$$

Similarly, a standardized measure of kurtosis (Ku) also allows you to compare different distributions:

$$\text{Equation 4.24: } Ku = \frac{S^4}{(S^2)^2} - 3$$

One subtracts by 3 in the formula for kurtosis to set the value to zero for a mesokurtic distribution such as the normal distribution. For a flat or platykurtic distribution, the value of Ku will be positive. For a peaked or leptokurtic distribution, the value of Ku will be negative. (See Textbox 4.11.)

---

[3]There are measures of skewness and kurtosis other than those described here. For example, computer packages for statistical analysis will not necessarily use the same measures or give the same numerical results.

Textbox 4.11

Analysis of Skewness and Kurtosis for the Jerry's Meander Scenario

Begin by computing the first four moments about the mean for the Jerry's Meander scenario. For computational ease and neatness, all values will be times $1000:

$$AD = \frac{\sum (Y - \overline{Y})}{N} = \frac{0}{20} = 0$$

$$S^2 = \frac{\sum (Y_i - \overline{Y})^2}{N} = \frac{45{,}350}{20} = 2267.50$$

$$S^3 = \frac{\sum (Y_i - \overline{Y})^3}{N} = \frac{5{,}918{,}250}{20} = 295{,}912.50$$

$$S^4 = \frac{\sum (Y_i - \overline{Y})^4}{N} = \frac{918{,}076{,}288}{20} = 45{,}903{,}316.00$$

Notice how the third and fourth moments of the mean are not so readily interpretable. But now that you have the moments about the mean, you can use them to compute the standardized measures of skewness and kurtosis:

$$Sk = \frac{S^3}{S^2 \sqrt{S^2}} = \frac{295{,}912.50}{2267.50 \sqrt{2267.50}} = 2.74$$

Therefore, the distribution is positively skewed.

$$Ku = \frac{S^4}{(S^2)^2} - 3 = \left[\frac{45{,}903{,}816.00}{(2267.50)^2} \right] - 3 = 5.93$$

Therefore, the distribution is somewhat flat, or platykurtic.

Go back and examine Figure 4.1. Note the two very large family incomes, which confirms that the distribution is indeed positively skewed. Notice also how these large family incomes "move" the mean upwards. The large group of modest family incomes is below the mean, and the two large family incomes are well above the mean. In other words, there is a tendency for the scores to be "pushed" toward the tails or extremes of the distribution and away from the mean rather than toward the mean. The tendency for a distribution to have scores in the tails of the distribution also suggests that the distribution tends toward being flat, or platykurtic.

Measures of skewness and kurtosis will come into play when we consider the assumptions underlying some of the inferential statistical procedures discussed later in the text (e.g., Chapter 7). As you will see, many of these inferential statistics assume that the data are distributed normally, in the form of a bell-shaped curve. Large departures from normality, signaled by the measures of skewness and kurtosis, are warning that the assumptions may be violated.

MEASURES OF BIVARIATE RELATIONSHIP

Another class of descriptive statistics summarizes the extent to which two variables or two sets of scores are related. For example, imagine that in the Jerry's Meander scenario, you had measured the average age of the wage earners per household in addition to the family income per household. You would, of course, be able to describe the important characteristics (e.g., mean, variance, standard deviation) of this second distribution of scores for the collection of 20 households in our fictitious scenario. But what if you also wanted to describe the extent to which the two measures, or variables—Average Age of the Wage Earners and Family Income per Household—were related?

There are statistical tools available to describe the nature and extent to which two variables are related. In Chapter 13 we will describe and explain these statistical tools. For now, suffice it to say that the most famous of these statistical tools, the Pearson product moment correlation, describes the extent to which two variables are related. The range of values for the Pearson correlation are −1.00 through 0.00 to +1.00, with all possible fractions in between.

A correlation of −1.00 indicates a perfect negative correlation between two variables, a correlation of 0.00 indicates no relationship between two variables, and a correlation of +1.00 indicates a perfect positive relationship between two variables. Perfect relationships between variables mean that it is possible to predict, without error, the scores of one variable from knowledge of a second variable.

A correlation of +.85 between Average Age and Family Income suggests that there is a strong but not perfect relationship between these two variables. Older wage earners almost always earn more than younger wage earners in the hypothetical district. In contrast, a correlation of −.39 between Average Age and Family Income suggests that there is a modest inverse relationship between these two variables. There is a tendency for younger wage earners to have higher family incomes.

PUTTING IT ALL TOGETHER

As we said at the outset, the purpose of descriptive statistics is to numerically describe or summarize the important characteristics of a set of numbers. What are the important characteristics of a set of numbers or distribution of scores? We place special emphasis on measures of central tendency, including the mean, median, and mode, and measures of variability or dispersion, including the range, variance, and standard deviation. Broadly speaking, measures of central tendency describe what value the scores in a distribution are bunched or clustered, and measures of variability tell about the extent to which scores are spread and disparate. Taken together, the descriptive statistics for central tendency and variability offer both a concise and precise way to accurately summarize a large number of values in a way that we hope is now clear, easily understandable, and useable by you, whether in the conduct of research or for practical purposes.

Measures of Central Tendency

The arithmetic mean—or mean, for short—is the arithmetic average of all the scores in a distribution. The formula for the mean is as follows:

$$\text{Equation 4.1: } \overline{Y} = \frac{\sum\limits_{i=1}^{N} Y_i}{N} = \frac{\sum Y}{N}$$

The mode (Y_{MO}) is the most frequently occurring score in a set or distribution of scores.

The median (Y_{MD}) is a score that divides a distribution exactly in half when the numerical values are arranged in order from lowest to highest.

The sample mean is the most dependable and stable measure of central tendency. The mean is also easier to compute than the median. However, only data on an interval or ratio scale of measurement may be used in computing the mean. Furthermore, the mean is the most sensitive measure of central tendency to the influence of extreme scores.

There are several other measures of central tendency, but they are used less frequently. Such measures include weighted and unweighted means, harmonic means, geometric means, and trimmed means.

Shapes of Distributions

We focused on three characteristics that help describe the shape of frequency distributions: mode, skewness, and kurtosis. We illustrated unimodal, rectangular, and bimodal distributions. We looked at symmetric and nonsymmetric distributions, especially positively skewed and negatively skewed ones, and discussed their effects on measures of central tendency. We also differentiated distributions which were peaked or flat.

Measures of Dispersion

There are three basic, widely used measures of dispersion: range, variance, and standard deviation. There are other measures of dispersion used less frequently: semi-interquartile range, coefficient of variation, and index of dispersion.

The range (R) is merely the difference between the highest score and the lowest score.

The average of the squared deviations about the mean of the scores is known as the **variance** (S^2).

$$\text{Equation 4.11: } S^2 = \frac{\sum (d_i)^2}{N} = \frac{\sum (Y_i - \overline{Y})^2}{N}$$

To return to the original unit of measurement, one merely takes the square root of the variance, called the standard deviation (*S*).

$$\text{Equation 4.12: } S = \sqrt{\frac{\sum (d_i)^2}{N}} = \sqrt{\frac{\sum (Y_i - \overline{Y})^2}{N}}$$

When you use a sample of data to estimate the variance and standard deviation of the larger population, divide the sum of the squared deviation scores by $N - 1$; do not divide by N. Dividing by $N - 1$ makes the variance and standard deviation more accurate estimators of the population parameters:

$$\text{Equation 4.13: } s^2 = \frac{\sum (d_i)^2}{N - 1} = \frac{\sum (Y_i - \overline{Y})^2}{N - 1}$$

$$\text{Equation 4.14: } s = \sqrt{\frac{\sum (d_i)^2}{N - 1}} = \sqrt{\frac{\sum (Y_i - \overline{Y})^2}{N - 1}}$$

Note that lowercase s^2 and s represent the formula for unbiased estimators of population parameters.

Moments About the Mean

An important type of summary statistic looks at individual scores subtracted from the mean (i.e., deviation scores) raised to different powers. These are the moments about the mean, which include the variance (the second moment), skewness (the third moment), and kurtosis (the fourth moment). We arrived at ways to compute mathematically both skewness and kurtosis.

A standardized measure of skewness (Sk) allows you to compare distributions that differ in variability such that a set of diverse measurements (e.g., ounces, intelligence test scores, EKG results, years) can be directly compared.

$$\text{Equation 4.23: } \text{Sk} = \frac{S^3}{S^2 \sqrt{S^2}}$$

Similarly, a standardized measure of kurtosis (Ku) also allows you to compare different distributions.

$$\text{Equation 4.24: } \text{Ku} = \frac{S^4}{(S^2)^2} - 3$$

Measures of Bivariate Relationship

Another class of descriptive statistics summarizes the extent to which two variables or two sets of scores are related. In a subsequent chapter, we will describe and explain these statistical tools. For now, suffice it to say that the most famous of these statistical tools, the Pearson product moment correlation, describes the extent to which two variables are related. The range of values for the Pearson correlation are −1.00 through 0.00 to +1.00, with all possible fractions in between.

Textbox 4.12

Understanding Perspectives: Descriptive Statistics

At what age are children readily able to tell the difference between their own perspective and the perspective of another individual? Understanding difference in perspective is essential if a child is to be a good legal witness. Durkin and Howarth (1997) investigated this ability using a series of television vignettes. In one set of vignettes the child viewer sees a crime being committed (something being stolen) and in the video the victim of the theft also sees and catches the criminal in the act (congruent situation). In a second series of vignettes the child viewer sees the theft but the victim in the video witnesses nothing (discrepant situation). Five-, seven-, and nine-year-old children were asked to identify what the victim knew in each series of vignettes. Children's correct responses were analyzed.

The means and standard deviations for the two conditions and the different ages are presented in Table 4.4. The descriptive statistics enable the results of the investigation to be easily understood. By examining the means, in particular, you can see that as children get older, they appear to make fewer errors at judging what the victim knew, but even at 9 years of age children are not able to correctly identify what the victim knew all the time. You can also see that 5-year-old children appear to have had the most difficulty judging what the victim knew in the discrepant condition.

This preliminary interpretation would have been more difficult to achieve had descriptive statistics not been used to summarize the data. However, to confirm our interpretation of the differences, we will need to use inferential statistics.

TABLE 4.4   Mean Correct Responses and Standard Deviations of Young Children Aged 5 through 9

	Congruent		Discrepant	
	Mean	SD	Mean	SD
AGE				
5	3.00	1.08	0.45	1.05
7	3.35	0.99	2.70	1.49
9	3.65	0.67	2.95	1.15
Total	3.33	0.96	2.03	1.67
Maximum score = 4				

(*Source:* Durkin & Howarth, 1997, Table 1, p. 251)

Key Terms

Descriptive statistic	Geometric mean	Absolute deviation
Summation notation	Unimodal distribution	Squared deviation
Central tendency	Rectangular distribution	Variance
Mean	Bimodal distribution	Standard deviation
Mode	Symmetric distribution	Interquartile range
Median	Skewed distribution	Semi-interquartile range
Weighted mean	Skewness	Interdecile range
Unweighted mean	Kurtosis	Coefficient of variation
Harmonic mean	Measures of dispersion	Moments about the mean
Trimmed mean	Range	

References

Durkin, K., & Howarth, N. (1997). Mugged by the facts? Children's ability to distinguish their own and witnesses' perspectives on televised crime events. *Journal of Applied Developmental Psychology, 18*, 245–256.

Problems

Questions

Section 1   Conceptual/Definition

4.1. Define the three basic measures of central tendency.

4.2. What is a deviation about the mean? What special property exists for the sum of the deviations about the mean for a distribution of scores?

4.3. A distribution of scores can have only one mean. Is this true for the mode? Why?

4.4. Identify several advantages and disadvantages associated with each measure of central tendency.

4.5. In a distribution of scores for which the mean and median do not result in the same value, what can you conclude about the shape of the distribution? Does the shape of the distribution change, depending on whether the mean is larger than the median, or the median is larger than the mean?

4.6. Define *kurtosis*.

4.7. What are the major differences between measures of central tendency and measures of dispersion?

4.8. Define the three basic measures of dispersion.

4.9. In the formula for the variance, there is often confusion as to whether N or $N - 1$ should be used in the denominator. When should N be used? When should $N - 1$ be used?

4.10. What are the four *moments about the mean*?

Section 2 Numerical

Use the following data set for questions 4.11 to 4.13:

12	14	16	10	14
18	16	14	12	

4.11. Determine the mean, median, and mode.

4.12. Is the distribution of scores symmetric? Please explain your answer.

4.13. Prove that the sum of the deviations from the mean for this set of scores equals zero.

Use the following data set for questions 4.14 and 4.15:

75	79	87	78	77
80	84	81	80	72
76	69	76	82	74

4.14. Determine the range, variance, and standard deviation. (Please use $N - 1$ in the calculation of the variance and standard deviation.)

4.15. Determine the four *moments about the mean.*

Use the following data set for questions 4.16 and 4.17:

8	8	10	13	7
7	9	6	9	8
9	12	8	10	10
10	11	9	12	9

4.16. Determine the mean and the standard deviation. (Please use $N - 1$ in the calculation of the standard deviation.)

4.17. Prove that the sum of the deviations from the mean for this set of scores equals zero.

Use the following data set for questions 4.18 to 4.20:

Group 1			Group 2		
10	11	10	7	8	6
11	13	14	8	7	7
12	12	9	9	6	

4.18. Determine the mean and standard deviation for each group of scores. (Please use $N - 1$ in the calculation of the standard deviation.)

4.19. Determine the mean and standard deviation for the entire data set where the scores of the two groups are combined. (Please use $N - 1$ in the calculation of the standard deviation.)

4.20. What potential problem exists with the mean that was calculated in question 4.19? What alternative exists to correct for this potential problem?

5 Building Blocks of Inferential Statistics

chapter

Probability, Chance, Variability, and Distributions

OVERVIEW

In this chapter you will learn a few of the basics of probability theory as one way to build a foundation for your understanding of inferential statistics. We will discuss nontechnically the importance of probability, variability, and sampling for inferential purposes.

We will take another step toward developing your understanding of the basic concepts underlying the use of inferential statistics for hypothesis testing. To do this, you will look first at chance variability and examine the binomial distribution to help build a knowledge base before moving on to a discussion of the normal distribution. You will then identify several important features of the normal distribution and learn how to interpret and calculate z-scores.

You will explore:

1. How does the notion of subjective probability guide everyday decision making?
2. How does social science use empirical and objective approaches to probability?
3. What is the role of probability theory in inferential statistics?
4. What are the relationships between samples and populations?
5. How does one explain variability?
6. What is meant by random events and the nature of error?
7. What is the typical distribution of chance variability?
8. What is the binomial distribution, and what does it tell us?
9. What are the properties of the normal distribution?
10. What is the relationship between the standard normal distribution and z-scores?
11. What other issues are important in understanding and using the normal distribution?

We begin with the scenario described in Textbox 5.1.

Textbox 5.1

Scenario: The Money Tree

In your position as vice president of Gotitall Bank, you periodically inspect the profitability of branches throughout the world. Among other figures, each branch reports quarterly profits (losses) averaged by the number of branch employees. For 400 of the 2000 branches of Gotitall Bank that reported on time, you have the following descriptive statistics:

Mean quarterly profit per employee: $\overline{Y} = \dfrac{\Sigma Y}{N} = \$15,000$

Unbiased variance: $= s^2 = \dfrac{\Sigma (d_i)^2}{N-1} = \dfrac{\Sigma (Y_i - \overline{Y})^2}{N-1} = \$9,000,000$

Unbiased standard deviation: $= s = \sqrt{\dfrac{\Sigma (d_i)^2}{N-1}} = \sqrt{\dfrac{\Sigma (Y_1 - \overline{Y})^2}{N-1}} = \$3000$

You want to use this information to help underperforming branches by establishing a mentorship program. Managers from outstanding branches will be paired with managers from underperforming branches in the hope that collaboration will enhance profitability. To do so, you will first need numerical criteria to identify both high- and low-performing branches. How do you arrive at these criteria?

PROBABILITY: THE FOUNDATION OF INFERENTIAL STATISTICS

There are two basic types of statistics: descriptive and inferential. Descriptive statistics, like the mean and standard deviation, numerically summarize the important characteristics of a distribution of scores. On the other hand, **inferential statistics,** like the *t*-test and *F*-test, allow researchers to make inferences or best guesses about population parameters from sample values. In plain English, people use inferential statistics to help them decide whether the treatment in an experiment impacted on the dependent variable with reasonable certainty. They also use inferential statistics to help them decide whether the observed relationship between predictor and outcome variables in a correlational investigation is so large that it is highly unlikely a function of chance.

Probability

Mathematically, **probability** is the likelihood that a given event will occur relative to all the other events that can occur. Statisticians often determine probabilities (*p*) based on the number or frequency (*f*) with which these events can happen. For example, imagine a single die with six sides marked with dots from 1 to 6. The probability of rolling a four is 1/6:

$$p(\text{four}) = f(\text{four})/f(\text{all sides}) = 1/6 = .17$$

We will draw on this basic notion of probability as we develop your understanding of inferential statistics.

Interpreting the Findings

Why isn't any observed difference in the data between experimental and control groups decisively due to the treatment, especially when an experiment is known to contain no flaws in design? Why is it that one can't conclude there is a relationship between variables whenever one observes a detectable pattern between predictor and outcome measures?

Remember that the purpose is to **infer** and not merely to describe. That means one wants to take the results from a small sample and **generalize** to the larger population. It is in this generalization to the population that one asks about the probability that the sample values represent population parameters. Are the findings a fluke, or can one expect the findings to occur repeatedly? In other words, are the sample findings an accurate representation of what one would find if there were some way to study the entire population?

Experimental Findings   Imagine that you studied an experimental medical treatment for ulcers with a group of laboratory rats and found that 30 of the 50 rats in the experimental group showed signs of recovering while only 10 of the 50 rats in the control group showed signs of recovering. Note the difference between the recovery rates of the two groups of rats. Twenty more rats in the experimental group showed signs of recovering. But is the difference just *described* sufficient for you to *infer* that the medication works as a treatment for ulcers? And what if only 20 of the 50 experimental rats improved compared to 15 of the 50 control rats? Is the second difference, of five more rats improving, sufficient for you to infer that the medication worked?

Correlational Findings   Suppose you studied the relationship between student academic self-concept and school achievement and found there was a moderate, positive relationship between these two variables among a random sample of 20 third graders. What size relationship between self-concept and achievement must you find before you feel confident these two measures are truly related in the population of all third graders?

The Pattern of Results   At the heart of inferential statistics is the notion that any pattern of results obtained might have occurred as a function of chance. But not all patterns are equally likely when chance operates. Some patterns occur with a high probability of occurrence as a function of chance (e.g., 40 times in 100) and other patterns occur with a very low probability of occurrence as a function of chance (e.g., 1 time in 10,000). When the pattern of findings could have occurred by chance only rarely, then one looks to offer an alternative explanation of the findings, such as the treatment had an effect or that two variables are truly related.

Choosing Between Alternatives   As we will explain in detail later, the essence of statistical hypothesis testing lies in choosing between two alternatives. One alternative is that the treatment did not work (or that two variables are truly not related) and the pattern of findings is likely due to the operation of chance.

Another alternative is that the treatment did work (or that two variables are truly related) and the pattern of findings is not likely due to the operation of chance. For example, examining the pattern of findings, is it more reasonable to conclude that the ulcer treatment did not work or that it did work? Or does the pattern of findings suggest that the self-concept and achievement measures are unrelated in the population of interest or that the two measures are related?

In short, the probability of getting particular patterns in the data lies at the heart of inferential statistics. "How likely is this pattern if chance operated?" is a key question that underlies most inferential statistics. Consequently, you need to have a basic understanding of probability theory and a few of its key concepts and principles.

Approaches to Probability

It is a relatively straightforward idea that the outcome of events or predictions about the future cannot always be made with great precision. Guessing about the weather, playing the stock market, or planning a controlled experiment are just three of an infinite number of situations in which events may not always unfold as people think they should. Notions about probability have their place in everyday life, in scientific life, in mathematical life, and in statistical life.

Subjective Approach to Probability and Everyday Life   The truth of the matter is that most people could not function if they did not take advantage of their intuitive sense of probability theory. People use their subjective estimates of the likelihood of events to guide many of their thoughts and actions. In most situations, these best guesses about the likelihood of events are accurate and adaptive. For example, you use your subjective sense of the probability of events to do many simple and complex things from dressing for a day at the beach to operating an automobile on the highway. Sometimes you make mistakes, however, and your subjective probabilities are wrong. It could be windy and cold at the beach but you didn't bring a jacket. Or you could drive too quickly down a familiar stretch of highway and get a speeding ticket because you did not notice the radar trap.

People can also be fooled into forming certain beliefs and holding inappropriate expectations about others. For example, Rosenthal and Jacobsen's (1963) classic study of teacher expectations, *Pygmalion in the Classroom,* led to scores of investigations exploring the influence of teacher expectations on students and their learning. Of course, students' greatest fear is that teachers will form false (low) expectations about them and act toward them in ways that become self-fulfilling prophecies. Whether accurate or not, personal expectations arise out of our subjective estimates concerning the likelihood that certain events will occur.

Objective Approach to Probability and Mathematical Life   The **objective approach to probability** takes advantage of mathematical rules in order to determine the likelihood with which specific events will occur under known conditions. Probability theory has always been associated with games of chance involving dice, playing cards, and so on. Unlike complex phenomenon in which parameters are not known, games of chance have very definite probabilities that can be known, albeit sometimes with a great deal of work.

In very simple games of chance, the objective rules of probability are rather straightforward and obvious. For example, the probability of getting heads (H) on a single toss of a coin is 1/2, or .50. Similarly, the odds of rolling a 3 on a single toss of one die is 1/6, or .17.

But as the games of chance become more complicated and sophisticated, the objective rules of probability are neither straightforward nor obvious. For example, is it immediately obvious what the probability is of getting the exact sequence HTTH when a coin is tossed four times? Similarly, what are the odds of getting "snake eyes" (two single dots) twice in succession when throwing a pair of dice? To more readily answer these and other questions, you need a better understanding of probability theory.

Empirical Approach to Probability and Scientific Life

How would a social scientist approach the problem of estimating the probability or likelihood of events, especially complex events such as the effects of social influence on problem solving or the effects of self-concept on student achievement? A social scientist would estimate the probability of such events empirically by observing the frequency with which they occurred. Some social scientists would attempt to estimate these probabilities via experimental methods using carefully controlled, laboratory settings. Other social scientists would attempt to estimate these probabilities via correlational methods using naturalistic, unobtrusive settings. Either way, the social scientist interested in estimating the probability of events would use far more careful and rigorous means than most people would apply in everyday life when generating subjective probabilities of events.

Empirical approaches to probability estimates are especially advantageous when you are trying to determine the likelihood of complex events when it is difficult, if not impossible, to know all that there is to know about the population of interest. Under such conditions, you would try to take a best guess about the population based on observations of a carefully selected sample. Nevertheless, no matter how careful you were in selecting a sample, or how large in size the sample was, it is possible that your estimates will be wrong.

The possibility of making an error has everything to do with your ability to know, and to specify, the nature of the population and its parameters. Because those factors are not known, in the empirical approach to probability one takes a best guess but is never completely certain that she or he is correct. In contrast, with the objective approach to probability the nature of the population and its parameters are known.

For example, you know that the probability of getting a head on any single toss of a coin is 1/2, or .50. This probability is rather obvious, but it derives from a mathematical equation. You know that there are only two possible events—heads or tails—and you want to know the chances of one of them—heads—occurring. When the possible events are well known, it is possible to use the objective approach to estimate the probability of any one event occurring.

Now imagine that you chose instead to determine the probability of getting a head on any single toss of a coin via the empirical approach. How would you go about this? You might conduct an experiment in which you tossed the same coin 100 times and recorded the number of heads. If you counted 60 heads in the 100 trials (not highly likely, but a possibility nevertheless), you would be tempted to conclude that the probability of getting a head on any one single toss of a coin is 60/100, or .60. In other words, by using the empirical approach you would have incorrectly estimated the probability of getting a head on any single toss of a coin.

By using the objective approach, you know via extrapolation that the greatest likelihood is that you would get 50 heads and 50 tails on 100 tosses of a coin. But this outcome is not guaranteed. There is a chance you will get a different outcome. Slightly less likely will be 51 heads and 49 tails. Even less likely will be 55 heads and 45 tails (or 45 heads and 55 tails). Sixty heads on 100 tosses will occur occasionally, while 70 heads on 100 tosses will occur rarely. And once in a very, very long while, merely as a function of chance, you might get 90 heads on 100 tosses. With objective approaches to probability, the probability of each of these collective outcomes can be determined.

Combined Approach to Probability and Statistical Life   Toward the beginning of this chapter we wrote: "the probability of getting particular patterns in the data lies at the heart of inferential statistics." "How likely is this pattern if chance operated?" is a key question that underlies most inferential statistics. We will use objective approaches, that is, probability theory, as one way of estimating what the pattern of results would be if *only* chance were to have operated in the situation of interest. In other words, probability theory predicts the likelihood of particular events or patterns of events as they occur purely as a function of chance.

In contrast, the empirical approach relies on careful observations of a sample to estimate the likelihood of events in the population. When the objective and empirical approaches offer the same or very similar estimates, one would decide that there is insufficient evidence to conclude that the treatment worked or that two variables are truly related. But when the empirical and objective approaches deviate, then one would conclude with a degree of confidence (but not absolute certainty) that the treatment does work or that two variables are truly related.

The combination of the empirical and objective approaches lies at the core of inferential statistics. By comparing the evidence obtained from scientific observation with the mathematical probabilities associated with certain patterns of findings, one is able to make an educated guess as to the likelihood or probability that the empirical findings occurred only as a function of chance.

THE ROLE OF PROBABILITY THEORY IN INFERENTIAL STATISTICS

Before you can get to the point of using inferential statistics properly, you have to come to a good understanding of some fundamental concepts. Chief among these concepts are samples, populations, and variability.

Samples and Populations

Inferential statistical tests are never needed when the research you have conducted measures the entire **population** of interest. It is only when you are not able to measure the entire population, but only a **sample** of the population, that inferential statistics are necessary. Often when you think about a population you think in terms of people or nations, such as the population of the United States or Canada. But your definition of the population of interest does not have to be confined to humans, nor does it have to be determined only by political or geographic boundaries.

The population of interest for research can be people, objects, events, animals, and so on. The population of interest can be defined quite narrowly (e.g., students in a single school district; employees of a small company; a fleet of taxis; a farm's egg-laying chickens) or more broadly (e.g., infants who have not reached the chronological age of 24 months; all white collar workers in North America; professional athletes; long-stem white roses; annual precipitation; albino rats).

The population of interest is defined and described to ensure that researchers are clear as to whom or what they expect the research findings to generalize. In addition, defining and describing the population is useful for determining whether or not the sample selected for study is representative of the population.

A researcher needs to define and describe the population of interest and then sample from it in a way that ensures representativeness. For example, an educational researcher might randomly sample 100 students for study from those officially registered as of the first day of the school year. This definition of the population of interest excludes those who registered late or transferred into the school district, but it includes those who might have dropped out or transferred out of the district. And it assumes that the children, teachers, and parents will allow student participation.

More on Sample Values and Population Parameters   In Chapter 4, we noted that when one uses a sample of data to estimate the variance and standard deviation of the population, the estimates, noted by the lowercase symbols s^2 and s, are divided by $N - 1$, not N. Division by $N - 1$ makes the estimates unbiased.

Furthermore, when one wishes to describe the *actual*, not *estimated*, population parameters, it is common convention to use Greek symbols to do so. For example, the population mean is μ (pronounced "mu"), the population variance is σ^2 (pronounced "sigma squared"), and the population standard deviation is σ. We will explain these distinctions and their importance more completely in Chapter 6.

Variability

The researcher who uses inferential statistics is almost always interested in understanding and explaining the **variability** in some outcome measure or dependent variable. A large portion of this book is given over to explaining the inferential statistical tools that may be used for this purpose. As you will see from the few examples we give, the appearance of variability is pervasive and important. (See Textbox 5.2.)

We have already covered the important descriptive statistics—including the variance, standard deviation, and range—for summarizing variability. In Chapter 3, we also discussed visual means for displaying variability. We hope it is now clear that describing the variability in a distribution of scores is quite important for descriptive purposes. It is equally, if not more, important for inferential purposes.

Of course, there are many times when researchers will want to know whether the sample results from an experimental or correlational study are likely to hold true

---

Variety Is the Spice of Life

Attitudes

When teenagers' attitudes toward premarital sex are measured, the cumulative responses received to the 50-item questionnaire will not be identical. Respondents' total scores will vary from one to the other, just as the individual item responses will vary.

Achievement

A teacher who walks into her classroom for the first time in late summer knows that the abilities, prior achievements, and motivation of her pupils are all not the same. That same teacher also knows that the rate of achievement for each of those pupils during the school year will vary, despite every effort made to do otherwise. Some will achieve a great deal, others will do reasonably well, and a small number may make little genuine progress.

Profits

The corporate manager of a large department store chain knows that items will not sell uniformly from store to store and that profit margins will vary nationwide. She also knows that certain sales staff have high earnings while others regularly flounder.

Athletics

Athletic performance varies from individual to individual and, for some athletes, from day to day. And so a coach is interested in understanding these differences in performance, their causes, and how he can enhance team members' athletic prowess and accomplishment.

Agriculture

The biologist studies the rate of growth of seeds exposed to different nutrients, water, and light. Rate of growth varies among these different conditions but also within them. How might the total variability be explained?

---

for the population of interest. Did the treatment really work? Is there really a mean difference among groups that is attributable to the treatment rather than chance fluctuation? Does the predictor really explain variability in the outcome measure?

All of these questions are based on the analysis of variability in the dependent, or outcome, measure. They seek to determine whether the independent, or predictor, variable explains enough of the variability that it is reasonable to conclude there is likely an effect or relationship in the population rather than the operation of chance.

One important matter that sets inferential statistics apart from descriptive statistics is the researcher's interest in explaining the variability in the dependent variable or outcome measure. In particular, the researcher wants to know whether some of the variability can be attributed to the treatment or a predictor or whether the variability is more likely a function of chance.

Random Events and the Nature of Error   Games of chance provide a perfect opportunity to emphasize that outcomes often fluctuate or vary, sometimes randomly, meaning one cannot predict or guess with complete certainty when they will occur. These are **random events.** One important recognition of probability theory is that outcomes fluctuate even though some outcomes are more likely than others.

Sometimes outcomes fluctuate because of measurement error or imprecision in the tool used to gather data. Most bathroom scales never seem to give the same weights week in and week out. Even precise scientific instruments do not measure perfectly, although their mismeasurement may be quite small.

Other times outcomes fluctuate because of performance error or instability in the devices, objects, or individuals providing the data. People's weight varies daily not because of their bathroom scales but because they are never precisely the same weight each and every day. For betting games, it is the uncertainty that makes the games fun because the outcomes can never be perfectly known.

There are, of course, a virtually limitless number of events that interest researchers and that demonstrate some degree of variability. In other words, the outcomes of events are not always constant but are more often variable. The job of researchers is therefore twofold: to note the degree of variability and to attempt to explain it.

In order to do so, researchers may well begin with the assumption that the variability in the outcome measure cannot be explained or predicted. And if the variability cannot be explained, then it must have occurred as a function of chance. This is not to say that human outcomes or other events are random; they are often quite purposeful. What we are saying is that the researcher begins not able to explain why the scores in the distribution fluctuate.

Error: Variability the Researcher Cannot Explain   As you develop more of an understanding of inferential statistics, you will come to better appreciate why and how you are attempting to determine whether the variability in the dependent variable or outcome measure can be explained by the treatment or predictor variable. To do so, you will have to find strong evidence that some of the variability you observed is not very likely a function of chance and that there is another way to explain the data—that is, the treatment worked.

We will begin with the statistical notion that all variability in the dependent variable or outcome measure cannot be explained and came about purely as a function of chance. And then we will see if we can show with a degree of certainty that some of this variability can be explained. (See Textbox 5.3)

In brief, we begin by saying that all variability in the dependent variable or outcome measure is random variability, chance fluctuation, or **error variability.** Researchers can use statistical procedures to determine whether and to what extent some of this variability can be explained using treatment or predictor variables. But if they are used, it is up to researchers to include these measures in their investigation. (See Textbox 5.4.)

Now you may begin to appreciate why sampling is so important. If you have not sampled properly, then attributing even some of the fluctuation in scores to the treatment would be difficult. If, on the other hand, you have randomly assigned participants to conditions, you know that a certain degree of score

---

Textbox 5.3

Explaining Variability Statistically

The statistical notion that all the variability cannot be explained is a troublesome concept. When you look, for example, at student examination results in your classroom, you almost always offer subjective explanations for the fluctuations in test scores. "John really studied hard," "Mary is really bright," and "Sam had a heavy date last night" are examples of the types of explanations you might offer for the distribution of test scores. How, then, can you as the statistician begin with the assumption that score fluctuation is random error or chance?

You would maintain this assumption in your model until you were able to statistically account for the extent to which effort (à la John), ability (à la Mary), and extraneous circumstances (à la Sam) are predictors of test results. That is, unless you include the appropriate independent predictors variables in your investigation and measure them, you will assume that their influence either does not occur or operates in an unsystematic fashion. If, on the other hand, you want your statistical model to match your theoretical model, you will need to incorporate these factors into your investigation.

Textbox 5.4

Explained and Unexplained Variability

Imagine that you wanted to determine whether studying alone or studying with other students resulted in better examination performance. You decide to conduct a simple experiment to study the effects of collaboration on learning that uses 100 volunteers randomly assigned to either individual ($N = 50$) or group ($N = 50$) study conditions. After a week of part-time study a common exam is given. Scores for the 100 students range from 55 to 93. In the individual study condition, the mean score is 75. In the group study condition the mean score is 80. But in both groups there has been fluctuation in the scores.

You have manipulated one variable, the independent variable "collaboration" (individual work, group work) and measured a second variable, the dependent variable, "examination results." But even if the treatment "worked," you would already know that collaboration alone does not account for all the variability in examination results.

What might explain the variability? A score of factors might explain it, including each participant's aptitude, motivation, interest, personality, external pressures, and so on. But you have not measured or otherwise controlled for these variables except via the random assignment of participants to the two treatment conditions. Therefore, because you cannot account for the variability attributable to these factors in your study—even though you know they may have operated—you allow that a certain degree of variability is unexplained or a function of chance fluctuation, or simply due to error. In this example, then, you can only attribute the variability in the dependent variable, "examination results," to two possible sources: the independent variable, "collaboration," and chance fluctuation.

fluctuation can be attributed to chance. Large amounts of fluctuation between the treatment groups (e.g., individual learners versus collaborative learners) can occur by chance, but as the degree of the difference between groups grows, the less likely would you be to accept chance as an explanation.

How does one deal with variability within the groups? How does one determine whether the fluctuation between groups is large? At what point does one say this difference is unlikely as a function of chance? These are the some of the key questions we will answer as we explore further the concept and techniques of inferential statistics.

THE SHAPE OF CHANCE VARIABILITY: MORE PIECES OF THE PUZZLE

Having considered the likelihood that certain individual outcomes or single events will occur, we now want to turn our attention to the likelihood of occurrence of certain multiple, combined, or cumulative events. A single toss of a coin or roll of a die is a single event; several tosses of a coin or a die is a multiple or combined event. For a single event, you might ask what the probability is of tossing a coin and it landing on heads next time, or what the probability is of rolling a 3 when the die is thrown just once. For multiple or combined events, you might ask what the probability is of tossing two heads in succession or what the probability is of rolling *both* a 3 and then a 6 together in succession.

Be careful to distinguish between **single outcomes** and **multiple outcomes**. When someone asks about the outcome of the *next* toss of a coin, he or she is concerned about the outcome of a single independent event. In contrast, when someone asks about a particular pattern of outcomes based on *several* tosses of a coin, that person is concerned about the multiple outcomes of several independent events.

As you will see, once the probabilities associated with multiple outcomes or cumulative events are further examined, you will come another step closer to understanding the nature of **chance variability** and about the distribution of scores in a dataset. In particular, you will note that not all multiple outcomes or cumulative events are equally likely. Some events occur rarely (e.g., tossing several heads of a coin in succession), and others occur more frequently (e.g., a mixture of heads and tails on several tosses of a coin). You would, therefore, want to know about the probability associated with these different outcome combinations and how they are expected to distribute themselves over many repetitions or trials. In other words, you would use probability theory to build a distribution of multiple outcomes in which you will estimate how likely each multiple outcome is.

The Binomial Distribution

The single most important distribution in inferential statistics is the **normal distribution,** frequently referred to as the **bell-shaped curve.** This chapter is devoted to developing your understanding of this distribution. To do so we will first consider the **binomial distribution** before turning our attention to the normal distribution.

CD-ROM link 5.1

Activity 5.1: The Binomial Distribution
To save you the effort of flipping 16 coins hundreds of times, Activity 5.1 provides you with an automatic coin-flipper! You can use this activity to create binomial distributions and explore their relationship to normal distributions.

Why begin a discussion of one type of distribution by discussing another type? The binomial distribution allows one to consider the simpler case of a variable with only two discrete values before turning her or his attention to the more complex case of a variable with continuous (infinite) values. *Binomial* loosely means two names. We use it here to refer to a variable that at any one time (trial) can take only two discrete values. The most famous example of the binomial distribution involves coin tosses and their associated probabilities. These are often referred to as Bernoulli trials or Bernoulli experiments after James Bernoulli who wrote about such trials in the early 1700s.

Imagine you were to toss a coin two times. What is the probability that neither of the tosses would be heads? One of the two tosses? Both of the two tosses?

On any one toss of the coin, the probability of a head coming up is .50 and the probability of a tail coming up is .50. The probability of both outcomes combined is 1.00.

What are the possible outcomes from tossing a coin two times? Table 5.1 lists the possible outcomes of tossing a coin two times.

There are four possible outcomes. There is a .25 probability of getting both tosses to be heads (1/4) and a .25 probability of getting both tosses to be tails (1/4). There is a .50 probability that the tosses will result in a head and a tail (2/4). The probability of these outcomes combined is 1.00. The frequency distribution of these outcomes is shown in Figure 5.1.

Next consider the probability associated with getting a different number of heads in four coin tosses. Table 5.2 lists the possible outcomes of tossing a coin four times.

There are 16 possible outcomes. There is a .06 probability of getting all four tosses to be heads (1/16) and a .06 probability of getting all four tosses to be tails (1/16). There is a .25 probability that the tosses will result in three heads and one tail (4/16) and a .25 probability of three tails and one head (4/16). The probability of two heads and two tails is .38 (6/16). The probability of these outcomes combined is 1.00. The frequency distribution of the outcomes is shown in Figure 5.2.

TABLE 5.1 Possible Outcomes from Tossing a Coin Two Times

Toss (Trial A) 1	Toss (Trail B) 2	$P(A + B) = p(A) \times p(B)$
Head	Head	$.5 \times .5 = .25$
Head	Tail	$.5 \times .5 = .25$
Tail	Head	$.5 \times .5 = .25$
Tail	Tail	$.5 \times .5 = .25$

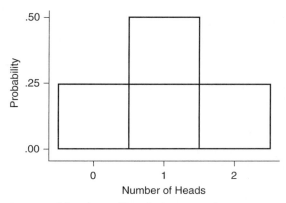

Figure 5.1 Number of heads in two-coin tosses

TABLE 5.2 The Probability Associated with Four Coin Tosses				
Toss 1 (Trial A)	*Toss 2 (Trial B)*	*Toss 3 (Trial C)*	*Toss 4 (Trial D)*	P(A) × p(B) × p(C) × p(D)
Head	Head	Head	Head	.5 × .5 × .5 × .5 = .06
Head	Head	Head	Tail	.5 × .5 × .5 × .5 = .06
Head	Head	Tail	Head	.5 × .5 × .5 × .5 = .06
Head	Tail	Head	Head	.5 × .5 × .5 × .5 = .06
Tail	Head	Head	Head	.5 × .5 × .5 × .5 = .06
Head	Head	Tail	Tail	.5 × .5 × .5 × .5 = .06
Head	Tail	Head	Tail	.5 × .5 × .5 × .5 = .06
Head	Tail	Tail	Head	.5 × .5 × .5 × .5 = .06
Tail	Head	Tail	Head	.5 × .5 × .5 × .5 = .06
Tail	Head	Head	Tail	.5 × .5 × .5 × .5 = .06
Tail	Tail	Head	Head	.5 × .5 × .5 × .5 = .06
Tail	Tail	Tail	Head	.5 × .5 × .5 × .5 = .06
Tail	Tail	Head	Tail	.5 × .5 × .5 × .5 = .06
Tail	Head	Tail	Tail	.5 × .5 × .5 × .5 = .06
Head	Tail	Tail	Tail	.5 × .5 × .5 × .5 = .06
Tail	Tail	Tail	Tail	.5 × .5 × .5 × .5 = .06

Finally, look at the frequency distribution for the probabilities associated with getting different numbers of heads when tossing a coin eight times. See Figure 5.3.

For each frequency distribution, a common pattern emerges. First, each distribution is symmetrical about the midpoint. The left half of each distribution is a mirror image of the right half. Second, the most likely outcome is represented by values in the center of each distribution, and the least likely outcomes are away from the center in the tails of the distribution. For example, for eight coin tosses it

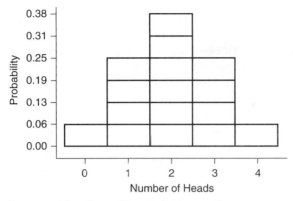

Figure 5.2 Number of heads in four coin tosses

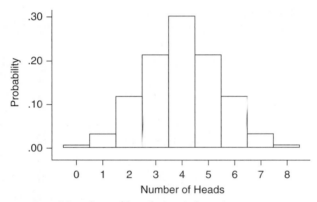

Figure 5.3 Number of heads in eight coin tosses

is much more likely to get four heads (and four tails) than either all heads (8/8) or no heads (0/8). Third, remember that each of the illustrations in Figures 5.1 to 5.3 represents a different binomial distribution and that each binomial distribution is actually a frequency histogram of discrete values. In the cases described here, those discrete values are the number of heads for a set of coin tosses (trials). These are clearly discrete values, because it is nonsensical to speak of a fractional number of heads (e.g., 1.5 heads is not possible) in a set of coin tosses.

Otherwise, the variability represented in each binomial distribution for tossing a coin is a function of chance. Purely as a function of chance one may toss a coin and have it turn up heads eight out of eight times. But such a series of outcomes would happen much less frequently than tossing a coin eight times and getting a mixture of heads and tails.

How It Works: Factorials and Binomial Probability   Figuring out the probable outcomes associated with multiple coin tosses is not too difficult as long as the number of tosses (trails) in the set is small. It was fairly easy to figure out the probability of getting all heads on two coin tosses but more labor-intensive

when the number of tosses (trials) increased to four. Above a few coin tosses fig-uring the "odds" is rather time-consuming using the simple method we illus-trated. Fortunately, there is a fairly straightforward mathematical procedure that takes advantage of factorial mathematics. Factorial means successively multiply-ing a given number by one less than the preceding number until you get to 1. For example, 4! (where ! stands for factorial) = $4 \times 3 \times 2 \times 1 = 24$. Also $0! = 1$.

Taking advantage of factorial mathematics, the formula for finding the prob-ability (P) of any cumulative outcome is:

$$\text{Equation 5.1: } P = \frac{n!}{(r!)(n-r)!}p^r q^{n-r}$$

where:

p = probability of the event occurring on any trial

q = probability of the event not occurring on any trial

n = number of trials

r = cumulative outcome of interest

For coin tosses, p is the probability of a hit, or correct guess (e.g., heads), on any trial, and q is the probability of a miss, or incorrect guess (e.g., tails). Therefore, $p = .50$ and $q = .50$. The number of trials, n, is the total number of coin tosses to be attempted, and r is the number of those tosses that you anticipate will be heads.

Let us begin with a simple example. Using the formula, the probability (P) of getting three heads when a coin is tossed four times is as follows:

$$P = \frac{4!}{(3!)(4-3)!}(.50)^3(.50)^{4-3} = \frac{4 \times 3 \times 2 \times 1}{(3 \times 2 \times 1)(1)}(.125)(.50) = .25$$

There is only a 1/4 chance that in four tosses of a coin, three of the coins will land as heads.

Now let's deal with a more difficult case to determine manually. Using the for-mula, what is the probability (P) of getting six heads when a coin is tossed eight times?

$$P = \frac{8!}{(6!)(8-6)!}(.50)^6(.50)^{8-6} = \frac{8 \times 7 \times 6 \times 5 \times 4 \times 3 \times 2 \times 1}{(6 \times 5 \times 4 \times 3 \times 2 \times 1)(2 \times 1)}(.016)(.25) = .109$$

There is slightly more than a 1/10 chance that in eight tosses of a coin, six of the coins will land as heads.

The Binomial Distribution and Chance   Whether a coin toss results in a head or a tail is a function of chance. (And if you are betting, it had better be!) Sim-ilarly, the likelihood of getting several heads in a collection of coin tosses is also a function of chance. However, not all cumulative outcomes are equally likely. It is more likely to get four heads in total than all heads in eight coin tosses.

Now what do you expect would happen if you tossed a coin eight times over and over again? First of all, you would not expect the results of each set of eight coin tosses to be the same. You might expect to get several heads in each set of eight tosses, but occasionally you will get no heads in a set of eight and occasionally you'll get all heads in a set of eight. Furthermore, you now know the mathematical probability of those cumulative outcomes occurring.

But how can the meaning of those probabilities be interpreted? For example, you know the likelihood of getting six heads in eight tosses is slightly more than a 1/10 chance. Knowing this, if you were to conduct 100 sets of eight coin tosses, would you be certain of getting 6/8 heads in 10 of those sets?

No! You cannot be *certain* that in 100 sets you would get 10 sets with 6/8 heads. You might get 9 sets or 11 sets or maybe as few as no sets with 6/8 heads. Why? The answer lies in the nature of chance and probability. For any collection of trials, you are only making a best guess as to the likely outcome, but you cannot guarantee that pattern of outcomes will occur over the short run, like 100 sets of eight tosses.

For coin tosses and other discrete events, the more sets that are completed, the greater the likelihood that the expected outcomes (e.g., probability of getting 6/8 heads) will match the actual outcomes. In fact, as the number of sets that are completed becomes infinitely large, the expected outcomes become indistinguishable from the actual outcomes. And the opposite of that is also true. If you complete only a few sets, it is more likely that your expected outcome will not match the actual outcome.

Does this mean that you cannot estimate the likelihood of a given pattern of outcomes? Of course not! We just showed how to do so. What this means is that no one can be certain the pattern of outcomes will actually occur according to expectation each and every time. These expected outcomes are only a best guess, not a certainty.

PROPERTIES OF THE NORMAL DISTRIBUTION

When I was a child, author Abrami recalls, our family dictionary was a 1940s version of Funk and Wagnalls' *College Standard Dictionary*. I still have it and use it, although much of the cover is held together with masking tape. It defines *normal* as: "In accordance with an established law or principle. That which is *natural* is according to nature; that which is *normal* is according to the standard or rule which is observed or claimed to prevail in nature" (p. 777).

The **normal distribution**—actually a family of distributions—is a statistical device for helping people visualize and quantify the natural variability among objects or events. The normal distribution, also known as the **bell-shaped curve**, after its shape, is widely used to describe the shape of large distributions. Although the normal distribution is not applicable in all situations, there are many situations in which the normal distribution provides an accurate portrayal of variability.

Binomial Distribution: The Normal Approximation

Now that you have a basic understanding of the binomial distribution, we can finally turn your attention to showing its relationship to the normal distribution. To do so, take the discrete frequency distribution in Figure 5.3 and draw a curve by fitting the midpoints together. See Figure 5.4.

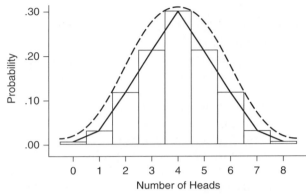

Figure 5.4 Fitting a curve to the midpoints of a binomial distribution

The shape of the curve drawn in Figure 5.4 comes close to the shape of the normal distribution—the famous bell-shaped curve. Indeed, as the number of coin tosses increases, the binomial distribution becomes an increasingly accurate approximation to the normal distribution. The important difference between the two families of distributions is that the binomial distribution is based on variables that have only discrete values while the normal distribution is based on variables that have continuous values.

Many variables are measured on a continuous scale, for example, air temperature in degrees Celsius, automobile speed in miles per hour, and bank branch profitability per quarter. Because they are continuous variables, it does make sense to speak of an air temperature of 28.75 degrees, a car traveling at 51.23 miles per hour, and branch quarterly profits per employee of $8739.67.

Otherwise, the important features of the normal distribution match those of the binomial distribution. (See Textbox 5.5.)

Textbox 5.5

Some Important Features of the Normal Distribution

1. The normal distribution is symmetric about the mean. The left half of the distribution is a mirror image of the right half. Fifty percent of the values or scores fall at or below the mean while 50% of the cases fall at or above the mean.

2. The most likely outcome is represented by values in the center of the distribution (i.e., the mean), while the least likely outcomes are away from the center in the tails of the distribution.

3. The normal distribution is actually a family of distributions. Each distribution can have a different mean and standard deviation, but the areas under the curve are *always* the same.

4. The normal distribution is unimodal and not skewed. Therefore, the mean, median, and mode of the normal distribution are the same value.

Normal Distribution: Some Other Important Properties

For an interesting presentation on the development of the normal distribution and the history of statistics, see Stigler (1986). It now appears that, in 1733, the French mathematician Abraham de Moivre was the first to discover the formula for the normal distribution:

$$Y = \frac{1}{\sqrt{2\pi\sigma^2}} e^{-(X-\mu)^2/2\sigma^2}$$

where:

> Y = height of the curve for any given value of X in the distribution of scores
>
> π = pi (3.1416)
>
> e = base of natural logarithms (2.7813)
>
> μ = population mean of the distribution of scores
>
> σ = population standard deviation of the distribution of scores

de Moivre was a mathematics tutor and he was searching for a shortcut method for computing probabilities for binomial variables. In the process, he derived the function rule for the normal distribution.

But de Moivre's work went largely unrecognized, and it was not until the beginning of the nineteenth century, when a German mathematician interested in problems in astronomy rediscovered the normal distribution. Carl Friedrich Gauss noted that human observations of planetary orbits were subject to error. Gauss found the errors to be distributed in a bell-shaped fashion.

Later that century, discovery after discovery revealed the wide applicability of the normal curve. For example, Adolphe Quetelet believed the normal distribution could be extended to apply to problems in anthropology, meteorology, and human affairs. But arguably the most famous use of the normal distribution was made by the British scientist, Sir Francis Galton. In the latter part of the nineteenth century, Galton began the first serious investigations of individual differences. In his research on how people differ from one another on various mental and physical traits, he found the normal curve to be a reasonably good description in many instances. He became greatly impressed with its application to natural phenomena. Referring to the normal curve as the "Law of Frequency of Error," he wrote:

> *I know of scarcely anything so apt to impress the imagination as the wonderful form of cosmic order expressed by the "Law of Frequency of Error." The law would have been personified by the Greeks and deified, if they had known of it. It reigns with serenity and in complete self-effacement amidst the wild confusion. The huger the mob and the greater the apparent anarchy, the more perfect is its sway. It is the supreme law of Unreason. Whenever a large sample of chaotic elements are taken in hand and marshalled in the order of their magnitude, an unsuspected and most beautiful form of regularity proves to have been latent all along. (Galton, 1889, p. 66)*

Today, applications of the normal distribution are readily found in all disciplines: chemistry, physics, geology, anthropology, meteorology, biology, economics, and, of course, psychology and education. The weight of harvested sugar beets, the crush strength of samples of concrete, the height of cornstalks in a farmer's field, the intelligence of schoolchildren, and the personality traits of military inductees all seem to be normally distributed.

Indeed, the pervasiveness of the normal distribution and its importance in helping to understand the nature of variability was enthusiastically expressed by Galton more than 100 years ago. While Galton went too far in ascribing the character of a law to the normal distribution, his enthusiasm is understandable, since so many variables are normally distributed.

However, it is important to understand that not all variables are normally distributed. Some that are not (they appear somewhat skewed) include human body weight, size of family income, reaction time, and frequency of accidents.

Finally, the preeminence of the normal distribution in statistical theory goes beyond the ubiquity with which the distribution serves to describe the shape of many datasets. In particular, the normal distribution is especially useful in describing the distribution of a collection of sample statistics. For example, imagine that you repeatedly took samples of the same size from a population and computed the means of the samples. The distribution of sample means would tend to approximate a normal distribution, especially as the size of the individual samples grew larger. As you will come to appreciate more fully in Chapter 6, the normal shape of the distribution of sample statistics plays a key role in inferential statistics.

Mathematical Properties of the Normal Distribution   When someone assumes that a set of numbers or the observed values of a variable are normally distributed, she or he knows certain things about their dispersion. That is because the normal distribution is a theoretical distribution based on an infinitely large population that has mathematically derived properties that are widely known. Based on the work of de Moivre and then Gauss, the following facts are known:

- The area from one end or tail of the normal distribution to the mean or midpoint includes 50% of the cases or values (see Figure 5.5a).

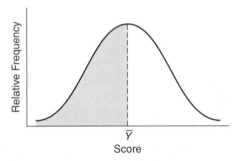

Figure 5.5a The mean of the normal distribution divides the data in half

- The area (see Figure 5.5*b*) from one standard deviation (*s*) unit below the mean ($\overline{Y}$) to one standard deviation unit above the mean includes 68.26% of the cases or values. That is,

$$\overline{Y} \pm 1s = 68.26\% \text{ of the cases.}$$

- A score one standard deviation *above* the mean is at cumulative percentile 84.13. That is,

$$\overline{Y} + 1s = 84.13\%\text{ile}$$

There are only 15.87% of the scores above this value.

- A score one standard deviation *below* the mean is at cumulative percentile 15.87. That is,

$$\overline{Y} - 1s = 15.87\%\text{ile}$$

There are 84.13% of the scores above this value.

- The area (see Figure 5.5*c*) from almost two standard deviation units (actually 1.96) below the mean to almost two standard deviation units above the mean includes 95% of the cases or values. That is,

$$\overline{Y} \pm 1.96s = 95.00\% \text{ of the cases.}$$

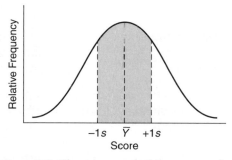

Figure 5.5*b* The area around the mean of a normal distribution from $-1s$ to $+1s$ includes 68.26% of the cases

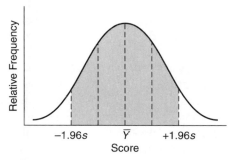

Figure 5.5*c* The area around the mean of a normal distribution from $-1.96s$ to $+1.96s$ includes 95% of the cases

- A score 1.96 standard deviations *above* the mean is at cumulative percentile 97.50. That is,

$$\overline{Y} + 1.96s = 97.50\%\text{ile}$$

There are only 2.50% of the scores above this value.

- A score 1.96 standard deviations *below* the mean is at cumulative percentile 2.50. That is,

$$\overline{Y} - 1.96s = 2.50\%\text{ile}$$

There are 97.50% of the scores above this value.

- The area from approximately 2½ standard deviation units (actually 2.57) below the mean to approximately 2½ standard deviation units above the mean includes 99% of the cases or values. That is,

$$\overline{Y} \pm 2.57s = 99.00\% \text{ of the cases.}$$

- A score 2.57 standard deviations *above* the mean is at cumulative percentile 99.50. That is,

$$\overline{Y} + 2.57s = 99.50\%\text{ile}$$

There are only .50% of the scores above this value.

- A score 2.57 standard deviations *below* the mean is at cumulative percentile .50. That is,

$$\overline{Y} - 2.57s = 0.50\%\text{ile}$$

There are 99.50% of the scores above this value.

Other areas under the normal curve can be found by reference to Appendix A. These are the areas for the unit normal or standard normal distribution, because the mean is zero and the standard deviation is 1. We will show you how to use the tabled values when we cover the standard normal distribution later in this chapter.

The tails of the normal curve extend indefinitely in both directions (i.e., $\pm\infty$), never quite touching the horizontal axis. This means that scores in any distribution can be infinitely smaller than the mean and infinitely larger than the mean. However, the probability of scores being that discrepant from the mean are exceptionally small.

CD-ROM link 5.2

Activity 5.2: Proportions of Area Under Normal Distributions
In Activity 5.2, you will see how the area under a normal distribution can be used to identify the probability associated with sample values. Try changing the normal distribution's mean and standard deviation and see if this affects its other properties.

The Family of Normal Distributions   The normal distribution is not a single distribution but actually a family of distributions. Each of the distributions in this family all share the common characteristics noted above. But normal distributions can have different means and different standard deviations. See Figures 5.6a to c.

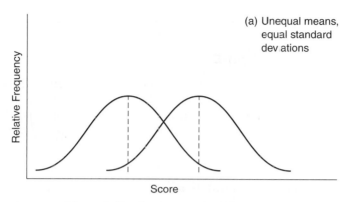

Figure 5.6a Normal distributions with different means but the same standard deviations

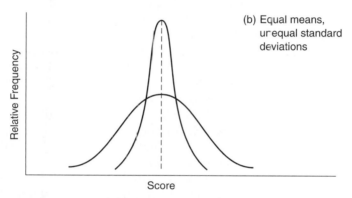

Figure 5.6b Normal distributions with the same mean but different standard deviations

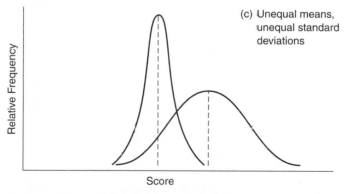

Figure 5.6c Normal distributions with different means and different standard deviations

For example, in the Money Tree scenario in Textbox 5.1, the data are in monetary units with an estimated population mean of $15,000 and an estimated population standard deviation of $3000. Another set of data might also be in monetary units but for the quarterly profits of a competitor's bank in which the mean profit was $14,000 and the standard deviation was $2500. Alternately, another set of data might be in speed units such as miles per hour. For example, we might have the mean speed (105 miles per hour) for the year for all cars racing at Mosport Park and the standard deviation (20 miles per hour).

Each of these examples has a different mean and a different standard deviation, yet you either know or assume that the data are distributed normally or at least approximately so. Knowing or assuming the data are normally distributed means that you can take advantage of the mathematical properties of the normal distribution in simple but important ways.

Areas Under the Normal Distribution

Examine further the key features of the normal curve with reference to the Money Tree scenario in Textbox 5.1. Begin by making the assumption that the data from the scenario is in the shape of a normal distribution (or approximately so). Alternately, one could actually graph the data for the 400 branches that provided quarterly profit statements and either by visual inspection or by using a test of normality determine whether the data actually fit this theoretical distribution.[1] Furthermore, you will want to use our sample data from the 400 branches to estimate the profitability for all 2000 branches of Gotitall Bank.

Figure 5.5*a* illustrates the normal distribution of the Gotitall Bank data and shows the estimated mean value, which is the midpoint of the distribution. The shaded area on the left of the mean represents 50% of the data values. The unshaded area on the right represents the other 50% of the data values.

Figure 5.5*b* also illustrates the normal distribution of the Gotitall Bank data and shows the estimated mean value and ±1 estimated standard deviation from the mean. Because the values of the estimated mean and standard deviation of the Gotitall Bank data are known, and because the data are (assumed to be) normally distributed, you also know that

$$\overline{Y} \pm 1s = 68.26\% \text{ of the scores}$$

$$\$15,000 \pm \$3000 = 68.26\% \text{ of the quarterly profits}$$

In other words, slightly more than two-thirds of the quarterly profits fall in the range of $12,000 to $18,000.

We have used the data from the sample of 400 branches to estimate the population mean and population standard deviation for all 2000 branches of the Gotitall Bank. Because we know or assume that the data are distributed normally (or approximately so) we also know about the areas under the normal curve.

Using this information, you can estimate that 31.74% (100% − 68.26%) of the 2000 bank branches fall outside the area within ±1 standard deviation from the mean. In other words, only 15.87% of the 2000 branches (about 317) had quarterly

---

[1]Statistical analysis programs often contain tests to determine departures from normality in a dataset. These tests include Anderson-Darling, Kolmogorov-Smirnov, and Shapiro-Wilks for small samples.

profits below $12,000 per employee, and only 15.87% of the 2000 branches (also about 317) had quarterly profits above $18,000 per employee.

The area representing ±1s is illustrated as the shaded area in Figure 5.5b. The heavy vertical lines represent −1s, or $12,000, and +1s, or $18,000. The unshaded area in either tail of the distribution is 31.74% of the data values outside ±1s of the mean of $15,000. That is, the lower unshaded area represents all the values *below* $12,000, and the upper unshaded area represents all the values *above* $18,000.

Figure 5.5c also illustrates the normal distribution of the Gotitall Bank data and shows the mean value and ±1.96 standard deviations from the mean. Since the values of the estimated mean and standard deviation of the Gotitall Bank data are known and since the data are (assumed to be) normally distributed, you also know that

$$\overline{Y} \pm 1.96s = 95.00\%$$

$$\$15,000 \pm \$5880 = 95.00\% \text{ of the quarterly profits}$$

In other words, 95% of the quarterly profits fall in the range of $9,120 to $20,880.

In addition, 5% (100% − 95.00%) of the cases fall outside the area within plus and minus 1.96 standard deviations from the mean. In other words, only 2.5% of the 2000 branches (about 50) had quarterly profits below $9120 per employee, and only 2.5% of the 2000 branches (also about 50) had quarterly profits above $20,880 per employee.

The area representing ±1.96s is illustrated as the shaded area in Figure 5.5c. The vertical lines represent −1.96s, or $9120 and +1.96s, or $20,880, respectively. The unshaded area in either tail of the distribution are those 5% of the data values outside ±1.96s of the mean of $15,000. That is, the lower unshaded area represents all the values *below* $9120 while the upper unshaded area represents all the values *above* $20,880.

Not illustrated is the normal distribution of the Gotitall Bank data that shows the mean value and ±2.57 standard deviations from the mean. However, because the values of the estimated mean and estimated standard deviation of the Gotitall Bank data are known, and because the data are (assumed to be) normally distributed, you also know that

$$\overline{Y} \pm 2.57s = 99\%$$

$$\$15,000 \pm \$7,790 = 99\% \text{ of the quarterly profits}$$

In other words, 99% of the quarterly profits fall in the range of $7,290 to $22,710. In addition, 1% (100% − 99%) of the cases fall outside the area within ±2.57 standard deviations from the mean. In other words, only .5% of the 2000 branches (about 10) had quarterly profits below $7,290 per employee, and only .5% of the 2000 branches (also about 10) had quarterly profits above $22,710 per employee.

Now you should be able to apply what you have learned to other data. We will make reference to the normal distribution again as a key concept in statistical inference.

The Standard Normal Distribution and *z*-scores

We noted that the normal distribution is actually a family of distributions, all with the same mathematical properties. Nevertheless, each normal distribution can have a different mean and a different standard deviation yet still belong to the family.

The diversity among these normal distributions can be problematic at times. To avoid having to develop an infinite number of tables, statisticians have made one particular normal distribution the standard. It has a mean equal to zero and a standard deviation equal to 1. It is called the **standard normal distribution.**

The standard (or unit) normal distribution is the distribution whose areas are tabulated in the appendix. Variable values for this distribution are called **standard scores** and are denoted by z_i.

If a variable does not happen to have a mean of zero and a standard deviation of 1, the values of the variable from a distribution of scores may be converted to standard scores in order to use the standard normal distribution table. The conversion is accomplished by the following formula:

CD-ROM link 5.3

Activity 5.3: Standardized Scores
In Activity 5.3, you can see how *z*-scores are calculated and explore the special properties of a standardized dataset.

Equation 5.2: $z_i = \dfrac{Y_i - \overline{Y}}{s}$

One may convert individual values of a variable to determine their relative location on the standard normal distribution. However, there are occasions when it is desirable to convert the entire distribution of scores. It is on these occasions that the converted distribution of scores will have a mean of zero and a standard deviation of 1. Note that **z-scores** take on negative values when the original or raw score is smaller than the mean score. See Textbox 5.6 for an example.

Using Tabled Values of the Standard Normal Distribution   Appendix A provides the areas under the standard normal distribution associated with a wide range of values. There are three columns that provide the following: (1) positive values of z_i; (2) proportions of the area under the normal curve between the mean and the positive value of z_i; and (3) proportions of the area under the normal curve that fall beyond the positive value of z_i. In other words, the table lists only the positive half of the standard normal distribution for z-scores at or above 0.0000. But because the standard normal distribution is symmetrical, one can obtain the negative half of the normal distribution for z-scores below zero with ease. Furthermore, for any z_i, the proportion of the area under the normal curve plus the proportion of the area beyond z_i is .5000. That is, the value in column *b* added to its respective value in column *c* always equals .5000.

Let us begin by using the table to find values that we have already identified, namely:

$$z_i = 0.00$$
$$z_i = +1.00$$
$$z_i = +1.96$$
$$z_i = 2.57$$

Textbox 5.6

Converting Individual Scores to z-scores

Imagine you did a small study and were able to estimate the mean number of times people said "excuse me" during the day and found that the mean was 25.00. You also estimated the standard deviation of "excuse mes" from the sample you studied and found it was 10.00. Your sister claims she says "excuse me" at least 50 times per day on average. What is her z-score and how does she compare to the average in terms of the daily frequency of saying "excuse me"?

On the other hand, you think you make fewer errors or clumsy mistakes than others and therefore you remain silent more often. You excuse yourself only about 15 times per day. What is your z-score and percentile rank?

For your sister:

$$z_i = \frac{Y_i - \overline{Y}}{s} = \frac{50 - 25}{10} = 2.5$$

A z-score this high places your sister near the top .5% of apologizers because she is 2.5 standard deviations above the mean.

For yourself:

$$z_i = \frac{Y_i - \overline{Y}}{s} = \frac{15 - 25}{10} = -1.00$$

A z-score this low places you near the lowest 16% of apologizers because you are 1 standard deviation below the mean.

When $z_i = 0.00$, the area between the mean $\overline{z}$ and z_i is .0000; the $\overline{z}$ values and z_i are the same. The area beyond z_i is .5000 because half of the values are to the right of the mean. Furthermore, .0000 + .5000 = .5000. In addition, the total proportion of cases at or below z_i is .5000; the total proportion of cases above z_i is .5000.

When $z_i = +1.00$, the area between the mean $\overline{z}$ and z_i is .3413 (or half of .6826). The area beyond z_i (i.e., further to the *right* is .1587. Furthermore, .3413 + .1587 = .5000. In addition, the total proportion of cases at or below z_i is .8413 (.5000 + .3413); the total proportion of cases at or above z_i is .1587.

When $z_i = +1.96$, the area between the mean $\overline{z}$ and z_i is .4750 (or half of .9500). The area beyond z_i is .0250. Furthermore, .4750 + .0250 = .5000. In addition, the total proportion of cases at or below z_i is .9750 (.5000 + .4750); the total proportion of cases at or above z_i is .0250.

When $z_i = +2.57$, the area between the mean $\overline{z}$ and z_i is .4950 (or half of .9900). The area beyond z_i is .0050. Furthermore, .4950 + .0050 = .5000. In addition, the total proportion of cases at or below z_i is .9950 (.5000 + .4950); the total proportion of cases at or above z_i is .0050.

CD-ROM link 5.4

Activity 5.4: The z-table
This activity lets you practice interpreting an onscreen table of z-values and relating these values to the z-distribution. Learn to avoid the common errors students make when they look up values in a statistical table

Now let us try to use the table to find the proportions for values of z that have not been previously encountered.

When $z_i = +0.75$, the area between the mean $\bar{z}$ and z_i is .2734. The area beyond z_i is .2266. Furthermore, .2734 + .2266 = .5000. In addition, the total proportion of cases at or below z_i is .7734 (.5000 + .2734); the total proportion of cases at or above z_i is .2266.

CD-ROM link 5.5

Problem generator: z-scores
To practice calculating z-scores and using a z-table, select z-scores from the Problem Generator Menu on the CD-ROM. The Problem Generator will create as many practice problems as you need, and will demonstrate each step in their solution so that you can check your work.

Now imagine you wanted to find that z-score at which .7500 of the values were that value or less and .2500 were above. First, remember that the proportion .7500 can be divided into two parts: .5000 for the area up to the mean and .2500 for the area above the mean. Second, recall that a z-score of 0.00 corresponds to a proportion of .5000. The proportion .7500 is somewhat higher but less than the proportion .8413 (.5000 + .3413) for a z-score of +1.00. Looking at column b of the table, you find the proportion .2500 (actually .2486) and its corresponding z-score: +0.67.

You can also find the proportions for negative values of z in a similar fashion, because the standard normal distribution is symmetrical about the mean. For example, when $z_i = -1.00$, the area between the mean $\bar{z}$ and z_i is .3413 (or half of .6826). The area beyond z_i (i.e., farther to the left) is .1587. Furthermore, .3413 + .1587 = .5000. In addition, the total proportion of cases at or below z_i is .1587; the total proportion of cases above z_i is .8413 (.5000 + .3413).

Comparing Scores on Different Measures   Another practical advantage of converting raw scores to z-scores is that a direct comparison of scores from *different* distributions are more apparent. See Textbox 5.7.

Converting z-Scores to Raw Scores   Just as knowledge of the mean, standard deviation, and an individual score can be used to find a z-score, knowledge of a z-score can be used to find a raw score:

$$\text{Equation 5.3: } Y_i = \bar{Y} + z_i s$$

Textbox 5.7

Comparing Individual Scores on Different Tests

Imagine you wanted to know the performance of a student, John, relative to his classmates in language arts and mathematics. You know the grade level average and standard deviation on term tests in language arts (mean = 70, standard deviation = 10) and mathematics (mean = 120, standard deviation = 20) and John's scores (an 80 out of 150 in language arts and 125 out of 200 correct in mathematics).

John's z-score on the language arts test is +1.00; John's z-score on the mathematics test is +.25. Using the tabled values from Appendix A, you would know that John scored at about the 84th percentile in language arts but only at about the 60th percentile in mathematics.

The Money Tree Scenario: Converting z-scores to Raw Scores

As vice president of Gotitall Bank, you want to define the numerical criteria that identify both high- and low-performing branches in order to identify participants in the mentorship program. Your finance committee recommends that you use fairly extreme scores as the criteria. You elect to use only those branches in the top 1% and those in the bottom 1%. What is the mean quarterly profit criterion for low-performing branches, and what is the mean quarterly profit criterion for high-performing branches? How many branches will serve as mentors?

To find the top 1% and the bottom 1% requires the use of the tabled values of the unit normal distribution given in Appendix A. A z-score of ± 2.33 equals the cutpoints for the highest 1% and the lowest 1% of the branches.

When $z_i = +2.33$, $Y_i = \overline{Y} + 2.33s$.

$$Y_i = \$15,000 + (2.33)\$3000 = \$21,990$$

When $z_i = -2.33$, $Y_i = \overline{Y} - 2.33s$.

$$Y_i = \$15,000 - (2.33)\$3000 = \$8010$$

Only the top 1% of the 2000 branches, or 20 branches, will serve as mentors.

See Textbox 5.8 for an illustration of the conversion of z-scores to raw scores.

Other Issues in Understanding and Using the Normal Distribution

There are two other issues concerning the normal distribution. The first concerns scales of measurement and the problem of using percentiles instead of standard scores. The second concerns ways to use *T*-scores rather than z-scores and convert a set of scores to have any mean and standard deviation.

Problems with Percentiles　So far in this chapter, we have tried to make the case for both the theoretical importance of the normal distribution as well as the practical uses of it. But in order for you to see its practical uses, we have had to introduce what appears to be a rather complex and confusing table and set of calculations. Why bother with these calculations? Isn't there a simpler way? For example, can't we just as easily get by with percentile ranks, which everyone readily understands, and avoid reference to standard deviation units and z-scores?

As you might guess, the answer is often "no." There is an important limitation to the use of percentiles that is avoided when one uses standard deviation units and z-scores. In a normal distribution, percentiles are not on an interval scale of measurement. In contrast, standard scores are on an interval scale of measurement. In other words, percentiles are concentrated around the center of the normal

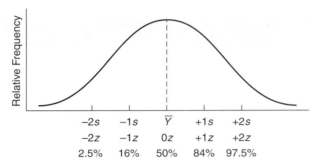

Figure 5.7 Areas under the normal curve: The problem with percentiles

distribution and spread around the tales of the distribution. Standard scores are neither concentrated nor spread. See Figure 5.7.

The ordinal nature of percentiles can be a limitation, especially when raw scores are on an interval or ratio scale of measurement. Comparing different regions of the normal distribution can be problematic with percentiles. See Textbox 5.9.

Textbox 5.9

The Money Tree Scenario: Percentiles Compared to Standard Scores

Imagine the vice president of Gotitall Bank asked all average-performing or below-average-performing bank branches to increase their profitability within two quarters and improve their profitability by increasing their relative standing by 10% over their initial results. In other words, a poor performing branch, with an initial ranking of 1% would need to improve so the branch would have a ranking of 11%. An average performing branch with an initial ranking of 50% would need to improve so the branch would have a ranking of 60%. As you will see, although the percentile rank increase expected of these two branches is the same, the profitability increases are not.

According to Appendix A:

$$.01 = -2.33z$$
$$.11 = -1.23z$$

When $z_i = -2.33$, $Y_i = \overline{Y} - 2.33s$.
$Y_i = \$15,000 - (2.33)\$3000 = \$8,010$

When $z_i = -1.23z$, $Y_i = \overline{Y} - 1.23s$.
$Y_i = \$15,000 - (1.23)\$3000 = \$11,310$

Therefore, the low-performing branches need to increase profits by \$3300. Now look at average-performing branches.

continued

Textbox 5.9 (continued)

According to Appendix A:

$$.50 = .00z$$
$$.60 = .25z$$

$$\text{When } z_i = 0.00, \, Y_i = \overline{Y}$$
$$Y_i = \$15,000$$

$$\text{When } z_i = +0.25z, \, Y_i = \overline{Y} + 0.25s.$$
$$Y_i = \$15,000 + (0.25)\$3000 = \$15,750$$

Therefore, the average-performing branches need to increase profits by $750, a difference of $2550 ($3300 − $750) compared to the low-performing branches. In other words, if percentile improvement is important, the low-performing branches have to increase their profitability more than four times that of average branches. This goal may inadvertently be what the vice president wishes, but it will surely generate a concern over equity among the branch managers!

Finally, remember that the vice-president is looking for percentile improvement. This change in relative standing compared to other branches. It is not the same as a percentage gain or absolute growth in performance.

T-SCORES

Almost all of you have taken a standardized test at one point in your life. Intelligence and achievement tests are the leading candidates. But did you ever stop and wonder how the test constructors arranged the test results so that the average score was always a nice whole number such as 100, and the standard deviation was an equally simple whole number such as 15.

Did these test constructors spend long hours in their offices adjusting the length of the test and the difficulty of the test items so things would work out as perfectly as they had hoped? Or did they do something more simple?

Now that we have covered z-score conversions, which take a set of raw data and convert it to have a mean of 0.00 and a standard deviation of 1.00, you might have guessed that a more general procedure exists that allows one to convert a set of raw data to have any mean and any standard deviation. All **T-scores** are raw scores converted to have any mean and any standard deviation, although they are most frequently used to have a mean of 50.00 and standard deviation of 10.00.

$$\textbf{Equation 5.4: } T_i = \overline{Y}_T + \frac{s_T(Y_i - \overline{Y})}{s}$$

where:

$\overline{Y}_T$ = transformed or desired mean

s_T = transformed or desired standard deviation

For example, imagine a set of scores with a mean of 87.35 and a standard deviation of 13.26. The desired mean is 500.00 and the desired standard deviation is 100.00. If Y_i is 80.00, what is T_i? You would compute T_i as follows:

$$T_i = \overline{Y}_T + \frac{s_T(Y_i - \overline{Y})}{s} = 500.00 + \frac{100.00(80.00 - 87.35)}{13.26} = 444.57$$

PUTTING IT ALL TOGETHER

We began by defining the concept of probability from a mathematical perspective. Probability is the likelihood that a given event will occur relative to all the other events that can occur. We then discussed three types of probability: subjective, empirical, and objective. We concluded that subjective probabilities were used pervasively as a means to determine many events in our lives; that empirical probabilities are more scientific means of observing phenomenon and predicting future outcomes; and that for specific events under known conditions, there could be mathematical rules to determine the likelihood of events. Finally, we offered the idea that the combination of the empirical and objective approaches lies at the heart of inferential statistics.

We also used probability theory along with some other concepts—sampling and variability—to have a nontechnical discussion concerning the basics of inferential statistics. We discussed the need for appropriate sampling procedures when one wishes to make an inference from a subset to the entire population. And we talked about the important, but occasionally confusing, concept that variability in data is assumed to fluctuate randomly or by chance until one has a way to include quantitatively some of this variability in his or her statistical model.

Having considered the likelihood that certain individual outcomes or single events will occur, we turned our attention to the likelihood of occurrence for certain multiple, combined, or cumulative events. We began by considering the simple case of multiple coin tosses and the likelihood that various combined outcomes such as all heads will occur on several tosses.

The Binomial Distribution

Taking advantage of factorial mathematics, the formula for finding the probability (P) of any cumulative outcome is as follows:

$$\textbf{Equation 5.1: } P = \frac{n!}{(r!)(n-r)!} p^r q^{n-r}$$

where:

p = probability of the event occurring on any trial

q = probability of the event not occurring on any trial

n = number of trials

r = cumulative outcome of interest

Whether a coin toss results in a head or a tail is a function of chance. Similarly, the likelihood of getting several heads in a collection of coin tosses is also a function of chance. However, not all cumulative outcomes are equally likely. It is more likely to get four heads in total than all heads in eight coin tosses. However, one cannot be certain that the pattern of outcomes will actually occur according to expectation each and every time. These expected outcomes are only a best guess, not a certainty.

Properties of the Normal Distribution

The normal distribution—actually a family of distributions—is a statistical device for helping people visualize and quantify the natural variability among objects or events. The normal distribution, also known as the *bell-shaped curve*, after its shape, is widely used to describe the shape of large distributions. Although the normal distribution is not applicable in all situations, there are many situations in which the normal distribution provides an accurate portrayal of variability.

The binomial distribution and the normal distribution are quite similar for large sample sizes. The important difference between the two families of distributions is that the binomial distribution is based on variables that have only discrete values while the normal distribution is based on variables that have continuous values.

Some important features of the normal distribution

1. The normal distribution is symmetric about the mean. The left half of the distribution is a mirror image of the right half. Fifty percent of the values or scores fall at or below the mean, and 50% of the cases fall at or above the mean.
2. The most likely outcome is represented by values in the center of the distribution (i.e., the mean), while the least likely outcomes are away from the center, in the tails of the distribution.
3. The normal distribution is actually a family of distributions. Each distribution can have a different mean and standard deviation, but the areas under the curve are *always* the same.
4. The normal distribution is unimodal and not skewed. Therefore, the mean, median, and mode of the normal distribution are the same value.
5. The area from one end, or tail, of the normal distribution to the mean, or midpoint, includes 50% of the cases, or values.
6. The area from one standard deviation unit below the population mean to one standard deviation unit above the mean includes 68.26% of the cases.
7. The area from approximately 2½ standard deviation units (actually 2.57) below the mean to approximately 2½ standard deviation units above the mean includes 99% of the cases or values.
8. Values for other areas under the normal curve can be found in Appendix A.
9. The tails of the normal curve extend indefinitely in both directions (i.e., $\pm\infty$), never quite touching the horizontal axis.

If a variable does not happen to have a mean of zero and a standard deviation of 1, the values of the variable from a distribution of scores may be converted to standard scores in order to use the standard normal distribution table. The conversion is accomplished by the following formula:

$$\text{Equation 5.2: } z_i = \frac{Y_i - \overline{Y}}{s}$$

Just as knowledge of the mean, standard deviation, and an individual score can be used to find a z-score, knowledge of a z-score can be used to find a raw score:

$$\text{Equation 5.3: } Y_i = \overline{Y} + z_i s$$

In a normal distribution, percentiles are not on an interval scale of measurement. In contrast, standard scores are on an interval scale of measurement. In other words, percentiles are concentrated around the center of the normal distribution and spread around the tails of the distribution. Standard scores are neither concentrated nor spread.

T-Scores

There exists a more general procedure that allows one to convert a set of raw data to have any mean and any standard deviation. All *T*-scores are raw scores converted to have any mean and any standard deviation, although they are most frequently used to have a mean of 50.00 and a standard deviation of 10.00:

$$\text{Equation 5.4: } T_i = \overline{Y}_T + \frac{s_T (Y_i - \overline{Y})}{s}$$

where:

$\overline{Y}_T$ = transformed or desired mean

s_T = transformed or desired standard deviation

KEY TERMS

Probability	Sample	Bell-shaped curve
Infer	Representative sample	Binomial distribution
Generalize	Random assignment	Normal distribution
Empirical approach to probability	Error variability	Standard normal distribution
Objective approach to probability	Random event	Standard score
	Single outcome	z-score
Inferential statistics	Multiple outcome	T-score
Population	Chance variability	

REFERENCES

Funk & Wagnall (1947). *The college standard dictionary.*

Galton, F. (1889). *Natural inheritance.* London: Macmillan & Co.

Nunnally, J. C. (1978). *Psychometric theory.* New York: McGraw-Hill.

Rosenthal, R., & Jacobson, L. (1968). *Pygmalion in the classroom.* New York: Holt, Rinehart, & Winston.

Stigler, S. M. (1986). *The history of statistics: The measurement of uncertainty before 1900.* Cambridge, MA: The Belknap Press of Harvard University Press.

PROBLEMS

Questions

Section 1   Conceptual/Definition

5.1. Explain the difference between *descriptive statistics* and *inferential statistics.*

5.2. How is a subjective approach to probability different from an empirical approach or an objective approach?

5.3. The combination of the empirical and objective approach to probability is very important. Why is this true?

5.4. Under what conditions is it unnecessary to conduct inferential statistics?

5.5. Define *error variability.*

5.6. What is the difference between single and multiple outcomes?

5.7. What is the most important distribution in inferential statistics?

5.8. Define *binomial distribution.*

5.9. Is the normal distribution a single distribution? Explain.

5.10. What is the major difference between the binomial and normal distributions?

5.11. List four important features of the normal distribution.

5.12. List some important mathematical properties of the normal distribution.

5.13. What does *standardizing a variable* mean?

5.14. What is a major advantage of using standardized scores rather than raw scores?

5.15. What is a major difference between standard scores and percentiles?

5.16. What is a *T*-score?

Section 2   Numerical

5.17. What is the probability of getting 4 heads when a coin is tossed 7 times?

5.18. What is the probability of getting 5 heads when a coin is tossed 7 times?

5.19. The mean for a set of scores (on a final exam) is 75 and the standard deviation is 8. What percentage of the scores are above 83 (assuming a perfectly normal distribution)?

5.20. For the same exam in question 5.19 above, approximately what percentage of the scores were below 59?

5.21. A set of 50 observations has a mean of 120 and a standard deviation of 12. A single observation from the set has a value of 102. Convert this raw score of 102 to a *z*-score. Assuming that the observations are normally distributed, how many observations in the set were above 102? (You will need to use the table of values for the standard normal distribution, Appendix A, to answer this question).

5.22. For the same set of observations in question 5.21 above, below what observation will .5% of the observations in the set fall?

5.23. For the same set of observations in question 5.21, what *T*-score will be associated with an observation of 130, given that a mean of 50 and a standard deviation of 10 are desired?

5.24. Thirty schools are randomly selected in a study examining high school dropout rates. Among the schools selected, the average dropout rate is 38%, with a standard deviation of 8. Assuming the dropout rates are normally distributed, how many schools have a dropout rate greater than 40%?

5.25. You are a senior administrator in the school board from which the 30 schools in question 5.24 were randomly selected. You believe that schools with a dropout rate in excess of 50% will have to be investigated. Approximately how many schools do you think will have to be investigated?

5.26. You are a senior administrator in the school board from which the 30 schools in question 5.24 were randomly selected. You believe that all schools in your school district with a dropout rate of less than 25% should be given special recognition. Approximately how many schools will be given special recognition?

6 Sampling Distributions

OVERVIEW

We will build slowly here to an exciting climax: our first use of statistics for hypothesis testing purposes. First, we will review and add to what you have learned already about probability, chance, and variability and elaborate on some basic concepts in statistical inference. Second, we will take a more in-depth look at the use of sample statistics to estimate or make inferences about population parameters. Third, we will spend a considerable amount of space covering a critical concept: sampling distributions. Sampling distributions are distributions of sample statistics that one uses to test hypotheses. Finally, we will come to develop some procedures for hypothesis testing and use the normal distribution to help decide whether research findings are "significant."

Some of the questions we will explore include the following:

1. What are the basic concepts and key terms in statistical inference?
2. How do we use sample statistics to estimate population parameters?
3. What are the properties of a good estimator?
4. What are sampling distributions and how are they different from other distributions?
5. What is sampling error and why is it so important?
6. How can you make an interval estimation of a population parameter?
7. What are the statistical procedures for hypothesis testing?
8. How can you use what you have learned to do a simple, statistical test of a hypothesis?

We begin with the scenario described in Textbox 6.1.

Textbox 6.1

Scenario: Flu Bugs

Winter is the time for the colds, flus, and holiday bills, which can make people feel miserable. Recently, a pharmacist believed he had stumbled across an inexpensive, natural treatment for influenza that he suspected caused a different reaction than the over-the-counter medication he usually dispenses. He decided to experiment by recruiting 10 volunteer customers suffering from the flu to participate in his study. The 10 flu sufferers were randomly divided into experimental and control groups. The control group received traditional medication while the experimental group received the pharmacist's newly developed medication. Furthermore, the volunteers were unaware of which medication they had been given.

---

continued

Twenty-four hours after the participants took the medication, the pharmacist's assistant phoned each of them to inquire as to their well-being. He asked them to rate how they were feeling on a 150-point scale, where 0 was miserable and 150 was terrific. The subjective ratings of each participant organized according to which medication they received are as follows:

Experimental: 60, 50, 70, 90, 80

Control: 20, 30, 00, 50, 40

Has the pharmacist discovered a medication that causes a different reaction?

BASIC CONCEPTS IN STATISTICAL INFERENCE

Types of Questions Statistical Inference Asks   We noted that there are two basic uses for statistics. The first use of statistics is descriptive. Statistical procedures can serve to summarize the important characteristics of a set of numbers. Measures of central tendency and variability are examples of statistical procedures that serve descriptive purposes.

The second use of statistics is inferential. Statistical procedures can serve to make a best guess or probabilistic statement about the value of a population parameter based on a value of a sample statistic. For example, in Textbox 6.1 you might want to infer the population mean reaction of all flu sufferers to the pharmacist's new medication from your knowledge of the sample mean which is based on only the five volunteer flu sufferers who took the experimental treatment.

Alternately, you might ask a more sophisticated inferential question about whether the pharmacist's treatment "worked." Such questions ask you to make probabilistic statements about the likelihood with which sample findings could have come about merely as a function of chance. For example, is the difference between the pharmacist's experimental and control group findings so large that it is highly unlikely due to chance? In other words you might ask: How likely is it that chance played a role in making the experimental group reaction to the pharmacist's medication different from the control group's reaction to the traditional medication? Based on the data reported in the scenario, and assuming that the research was otherwise properly conducted, what credibility do you give to the findings?

More precisely:

- What import do you place on the fluctuation in scores among participants within each of the two groups?
- Is the size of the sample of concern?
- What magnitude of difference between the groups would help convince you that the pharmacist's treatment worked differently than the traditional medication?

Estimation and Decision Making   The process of statistical inference is the application of a set of mathematical rules and procedures to the estimation and decision-making processes. Very often, the decision process will focus on whether the differences you observe among groups or the relationship you measure among variables could likely occur due to chance.

In essence, the statistical tests you will use allow you to estimate how likely it is that the results you obtained with a particular sample are due to chance, taking account of such things as group variability, sample size, and the magnitude of mean differences. If there is a low probability that the sample results were a function of chance, then you might infer that something other than chance, such as the effect of a treatment, contributed to the findings. However, in making any inference about the population from a sample, one merely takes a best guess; there is always some likelihood that a best guess or inference is wrong. Inferential statistics allow one to make best guesses only based on the chance probability associated with the sample data. No matter the inference, there is always some likelihood that a guess will be wrong and that an incorrect generalization will have been made about population parameters from sample values.

Finally, it is worth noting that the process of statistical inference, because it is based on a set of mathematical rules and procedures, does not allow one to make judgments about the quality of the research from which those numbers emerge (see also Chapter 2). In most instances, it is often assumed or understood that good research practices have been adhered to. For example, the conduct of a true experiment depends on the random assignment of participants to treatment conditions (e.g., experimental and control groups). Failing to satisfy this condition may lead to differences among groups that are not a function of any treatment but are due to initial group inequivalence. The application of inferential statistical procedures may reveal group differences that are unlikely to have come about due to chance. But the inadequacy of the research design prevents the analyst from reaching a definitive conclusion about causal influence or whether the treatment worked.

Key Terms in Statistical Inference

Purposes of Statistical Inference   Inferential statistics is concerned with the procedures for taking sample findings and making generalizations to populations. Within this general purpose, there are two specific ones: estimation and hypothesis testing. A key problem of inferential statistics is to use some sample value to estimate the value of the population parameter. Another key problem of inferential statistics is deciding whether a hypothesis about a population parameter is or is not tenable. In estimation, the result is a number or an interval bounded by two numbers. In hypothesis testing, the result is a decision about the adequacy or correctness of a hypothesis.

Populations   Remember that a **population,** or universe, is the entire group of persons, events, or objects having at least one trait in common. Extra-inning baseball games played in the major leagues is an example of a population. Diamond engagement rings is another. And people who have influenza is a third. Defining the population at the outset makes it clear whom or what one is interested in or able to offer generalizations or inferences about. For example, the study of third graders would not readily allow one to generalize about college students.

Although populations can be either finite or infinite in size, usually for the purposes of statistical inference, the populations of interest are considered to be theoretically infinite in size. Practically speaking, this assumption reminds researchers that they are seldom in the position to collect data from every person, event, or object in the population of interest and that they are virtually always in the position of making an inference about the larger population from the subset that has been studied.

Finally, the desire to make inferences from samples to populations in hypothesis testing lies close to the heart of scientific inquiry. Replicability, generalizability, and repeatability are terms that come to mind when one is concerned about making inferences. Will the results repeat themselves? Do the findings apply more widely? Are the results merely a strange anomaly or quirk?

Population Parameters   A **population parameter** is any measure obtained by having observed or recorded the entire population. Measures of central tendency, such as the mean, and measures of variability, such as the standard deviation, are population parameters so long as the entire population is observed or recorded on the variable of interest. Furthermore, to ensure that they are distinguished from sample statistics, population parameters are represented by Greek symbols. For example, see Textbox 6.2.

Samples   A **sample** is a subset of the population of interest. It is a smaller number of objects, events, or people taken from the total number making up the population. For example, from the population of extra-inning baseball games a sample would be all those played in the National League during July 1998. The flu sufferers who volunteered to participate in the pharmacist's study would be another example of a sample from the population of all flu sufferers.

The adequacy of a sample is important for inferential purposes. To comfortably generalize from the results of a sample to the population requires that the sample be selected in such a way that it is representative of the population of interest. Representative sampling is one important means to help ensure that the sample being studied is neither biased nor unrepresentative of the population as a whole. A **representative, random sample** is one in which each individual or case

---

Textbox 6.2

Key Greek Symbols for Population Parameters

population mean = μ (pronounced "mu")

population variance = σ^2 (pronounced "sigma" squared)

population standard deviation = σ

in the defined population of interest has an equally likely chance of being included. As you might guess, sampling adequacy is especially important for the purposes of estimation.

Experimental researchers, in particular, often use **convenience samples** for their research. For example, psychologists often conduct experiments with first-year undergraduate students enrolled in introductory psychology courses who have the opportunity to earn extra course credit for research participation. The consequences of convenience sampling can be twofold: (1) either the population to which one hopes to generalize may need to be redefined, or (2) the researcher may have to exercise special caution when generalizing sample findings.

Experimental researchers often consider **random assignment** of participants to be more essential than random sampling. Using random assignment of participants to treatment conditions (e.g., experimental and control groups) helps ensure that prior to the introduction of the treatment, the participants in the groups varied only as a function of chance. That is, random assignment helps ensure the initial equivalence of the groups at the start of research. Random assignment helps prevent selection bias and contributes to the internal validity of the investigation (see Chapter 2).

Nonrandom assignment, then, represents a source of potential bias in making inferences about populations from samples for the purposes of hypothesis testing. As noted, the application of inferential statistical procedures may reveal group differences that are unlikely to have come about due to chance. But the inadequacy of the research design prevents the analyst from reaching a definitive conclusion about causal influence or whether the treatment worked. Because of selection bias due to nonrandom assignment of participants, no one can say why the difference occurred with any certainty. Although there is a chance the treatment may have operated to produce group differences, nonrandom assignment means that the groups may have been different to begin with.

Stratified random sampling helps ensure that certain subgroups in the population will be represented in the sample in proportion to their numbers in the population itself. For example, imagine that you wished to study the influence of mainstreamed versus segregated classrooms on students both with and without special needs. If, in the population of interest, 10% of the children have been identified as having special needs, then use of stratified random sampling ensures that 10% of the sample will be made up by students with special needs.

In **cluster sampling** the unit of sampling is not the individual or case but rather a naturally occurring group of individuals or cases. Cluster sampling is used when it is more convenient to select groups than it is to select individuals or cases from a defined population. For example, imagine that one's defined population consists of all elementary students in Montreal, Canada. Simple random sampling could be used if a complete list of all the elementary school children were available, but such a list does not exist.

One use of cluster sampling would be to divide the city into distinct geographic regions or grids, take a random sample of the regions, and study all the elementary schoolchildren in those areas. A second use of cluster sampling would be to get a list of Montreal's elementary schools, take a random sample of schools, and study all the elementary schoolchildren in those schools. The former method of cluster sampling emphasizes sampling by residential location. The latter method of cluster sampling emphasizes random sampling by school location.

Multistage cluster sampling is a variant of cluster sampling in which one not only takes a random sample based on naturally occurring groups but also takes a random sample within each of the groups selected. For example, you might take a random sample of schools in Montreal and then study a random sample of children enrolled in each of the selected schools rather than all the children enrolled.

Selecting a Random Sample   The process of selecting a random sample must be done unsystematically to ensure that each member of the population has an equally likely chance of being selected. Choosing all the students in a single classroom to represent the entire school is not random sampling. Even selecting participants whose last names begin with the letters *A* to *M* or who were born during the fall or winter months is not random sampling. All these non-random methods of selecting a sample decrease the likelihood that the sample will be representative of the population of interest and an unbiased microcosm of it.

A simple yet effective way to select a random sample is to place the names of the members of the population (e.g., willing participants) on small sheets of paper and stick the pieces of paper in a hat. After the pieces of paper are mixed, participants would be selected until the desired sample size is achieved.

A more elegant way to select a random sample, and one more suited to large populations (i.e., when even a large hat won't do!), is to use either a random number generator found in most statistical packages and some calculators or a table of random numbers. (See Appendix B.)

The first step in selecting a random sample using a table of random numbers is to number all the members of the population and decide what size sample you wish to draw from it.

The second step is deciding where to begin. That, too, can be decided at random. Furthermore, you don't have to use the table from top to bottom or from left to right or a single number at a time. Any order will do.

The third and final step is to use the table to take the sample. For example, imagine you wanted to take a sample of 50 children from a school with a population of 500. All the children are assigned a number from 1 to 500. You pick a starting point somewhere in the table and read downward across three adjacent columns. You ignore all values greater than 5-0-0, selecting those 50 participants whose numbers match the tabled numbers.

Making Assignment Random   Experimental researchers' primary concern is that the assignment of experimental participants to groups (e.g., experimental, control) is done randomly. Use of the table of random numbers to do this is straightforward.

First, place the names of all research participants in random order. Then, starting at a random point within the table of random numbers either read down a column or across a row. If the digit is odd, assign the next participant to the experimental group and the following participant to the control group. Do the opposite if the digit is even. Then find the next random number, continuing until all the participants are assigned in equal numbers to the two groups.

Textbox 6.3

Sample Statistics are Represented by Roman Characters

Sample mean = $\overline{Y}$ (uppercase Y bar)

Sample variance = S^2 (uppercase S squared)

Sample standard deviation = S (uppercase S)

Sample Statistics A **sample statistic** is any measure computed from a sample of observations from the population of interest. Measures of central tendency, such as the mean, and measures of variability, such as the standard deviation, are sample statistics. Furthermore, to ensure that they are distinguished from population parameters, sample statistics are represented by roman characters. See Textbox 6.3 for a few such representations.

Sampling Distributions A **sampling distribution** is a distribution of sample statistics, such as a collection of means, variances, or standard deviations, taken from the population of interest. Not all sample statistics yield the same value; therefore, **sampling error** is the extent to which a sample statistic is discrepant from the corresponding population parameter.

USING SAMPLE STATISTICS TO ESTIMATE POPULATION PARAMETERS

There are two types of estimation in inferential statistics: point estimation and interval estimation. In **point estimation,** the value of a sample statistic, or point, such as the sample mean, is used to estimate or infer the value of a population parameter, such as the population mean. In **interval estimation,** the sample statistic, in combination with an estimate of how much error or imprecision might be associated with this estimate, is used to form a range of values or confidence interval. When there is a great deal of error, the confidence interval is large; when there is little error, the confidence interval is small.

Desirable Properties of Estimators

Although the sample mean is a good estimator of the population mean, it is not necessarily the case that every sample statistic is a good estimator of a population parameter. There are several desirable properties of good estimators: maximum likelihood, consistency, relative efficiency, sufficiency, and unbiased. We will describe each of the properties very briefly. As you have already learned, some sample statistics need to be corrected to deal with one of the properties. Both the sample variance and standard deviation are biased estimators of population parameters.

Maximum Likelihood The principle of **maximum likelihood** says that when you are faced with a choice of several population parameter values, the best choice is that value which makes the sample value have the highest probability among the possible population parameter values.

Consistency   A **consistent estimator** is one that more closely approximates the value of the population parameter as sample size increases. The sample mean, sample variance, and sample standard deviation are consistent estimators, as they tend to be closer to the population value as sample size increases.

Relative Efficiency   A relatively **efficient estimator** is one that has a small sampling error or confidence interval. In other words, when efficiency is high, there is only a small range of estimated values within which the population value is expected to lie. When the population values are distributed normally, the mean is a more efficient estimator than the median. Consequently, the mean is usually the preferred estimator of central tendency.

Sufficiency   A **sufficient estimator** is one that contains all the information about the population; estimation cannot be improved by considering any other aspect of the data. In some populations, such as those whose data are normally distributed, two or more statistics (e.g., mean and variance) may be required for sufficiency.

Unbiased   An **unbiased estimator** exists when it neither consistently overestimates nor consistently underestimates population parameter values. The sample mean is an unbiased estimator of the population mean. However, the sample variance and standard deviation are biased estimators and must be corrected.

Good Estimators

The sample mean $\overline{Y}$ is a good estimator of the population parameter μ. The sample mean is unbiased, is consistent, and, in an important set of circumstances, is relatively efficient. Finally, when used in conjunction with an estimator of the population parameter σ^2, the sample mean is a sufficient estimator.

The sample variance S^2 is a problematic estimator of the population parameter σ^2. The sample variance is consistent and efficient but it is *biased*. For small sample sizes, the sample variance underestimates the population variance. As sample size increases, the sample variance becomes a more accurate estimator of the population variance. (See Hays, 1994, pp. 216–218.)

Correcting the Sample Variance for Bias   The procedure for correcting the sample variance for bias as an estimator is relatively straightforward. Rather than divide the sum of the squared deviations by N, divide by $N - 1$, as we have covered in Chapter 4.

Note that the unbiased variance and standard deviation will be noticeably different from the biased variance and standard deviation when sample sizes are small (e.g., just a few cases). In contrast, when sample sizes are large (e.g., hundreds of cases), there is almost no noticeable difference between the biased variance and standard deviation and the unbiased variance and standard deviation. Division by N versus division by $N - 1$ has a noticeable effect when N is small but not when N is large.

Formulas for Samples, Populations, and Population Estimators

In Textbox 6.4 the formulas for the sample, population, and population estimators are given. Sample statistics describe a subset of the population; population para-

---

Textbox 6.4

Formulas

Sample statistics (i.e., for describing a subset of the population; therefore, N is the number of observations in the sample)

Equation 6.1: Sample mean $\overline{Y} = \dfrac{\sum Y_i}{N}$

Equation 6.2: Sample variance $S^2 = \dfrac{\sum (Y_i - \overline{Y})^2}{N}$

Equation 6.3: Sample standard deviation $S = \sqrt{\dfrac{\sum Y_i - \overline{Y})^2}{N}}$

Population parameters (i.e., when all the population values are known; therefore, N is the number of observations in the population)

Equation 6.4: Population mean $\mu = \dfrac{\sum Y_i}{N}$

Equation 6.5: Population variance $\sigma^2 = \dfrac{\sum (Y_i - \overline{Y})^2}{N}$

Equation 6.6: Population standard deviation $\sigma = \sqrt{\dfrac{\sum (Y_i - \overline{Y})^2}{N}}$

Estimators of population parameters (i.e., when one wishes to use sample statistics to estimate population parameters)

Equation 6.7: Estimated population mean $\overline{Y} = \dfrac{\sum Y_i}{N}$

Equation 6.8: Estimated population variance $s^2 = \dfrac{\sum (Y_i - \overline{Y})^2}{N - 1}$

Equation 6.9: Estimated* population standard deviation $s = \sqrt{\dfrac{\sum (Y_i - \overline{Y})^2}{N - 1}}$

*Although s^2 is an unbiased estimate of σ^2, s is technically not an unbiased estimator of σ, although the problem is slight. For the normal distribution and when N is relatively large, a better but seldom used estimate of σ is

$$\left[1 + \frac{1}{4(N-1)}\right] s$$

meters are used when all the of the population values are known; and estimators of population parameters are necessary when sample statistics are used as estimators of population parameters.

An Example of Estimating Population Parameters: Flu Bugs   From the Flu Bugs scenario in Textbox 6.1 we wish to estimate the population reaction to the pharmacist's flu treatment using the sample data he has collected. More specifically, what are the estimated population mean, variance, and standard deviation? How do these values compare to the sample mean, variance, and standard deviation? Why? See Textbox 6.5.

The sample mean and the estimated population mean are the same value because the sample mean is an unbiased estimate of the population mean. The sample variance and the estimated population variance are not the same value because the sample variance is a biased estimate of the population variance. Similarly, the sample standard deviation and the estimated population standard deviation are not the same value. Because sample sizes are small, the difference between the biased and unbiased estimates is appreciable.

Textbox 6.5

Population Parameter Estimates versus Sample Statistics for the Flu Bugs Scenario (Experimental Treatment Only)

Population Parameter Estimates

$$\overline{Y} = \frac{\sum Y_i}{N} = \frac{350}{5} = 70.0$$

$$s^2 = \frac{\sum (Y_i - \overline{Y})^2}{N-1} = \frac{1000}{4} = 250.00$$

$$s = \sqrt{\frac{\sum (Y_i - \overline{Y})^2}{N-1}} = \sqrt{\frac{1000}{4}} = 15.81$$

Sample Statistics

$$\overline{Y} = \frac{\sum Y_i}{N} = \frac{350}{5} = 70.0$$

$$S^2 = \frac{\sum (Y_i - \overline{Y})^2}{N} = \frac{1000}{5} = 200.00$$

$$S = \sqrt{\frac{\sum (Y_i - \overline{Y})^2}{N}} = \sqrt{\frac{1000}{5}} = 14.14$$

SAMPLING DISTRIBUTIONS

As you will see, sampling distributions are an important part of hypothesis testing. For example, we will use the estimate of a sampling distribution to estimate the likelihood that the obtained findings could have come about as a function of chance or represent either the effect of a treatment on the dependent variable or some relationship between predictor and outcome measures.

Multiple Samples and Sample Statistics   There are situations in which a multitude of samples, all of the same size, can be drawn from the population of interest. For example, the pharmacist from the Flu Bug scenario in Textbox 6.1 might repeat his experiment numerous times, say 100, over the course of the cold weather months each time asking 10 participants to volunteer (i.e., 5 experimental group participants, 5 control group participants). When multiple samples exist, multiple sample statistics (e.g., means, variances) can also be computed.

One important question is whether these sample statistics will necessarily yield the same values. For example, will each of the sample means be equal? Will each of the sample variances be equal? The answer is that there is no guarantee that each of the sample statistics will yield identical values repeatedly. Purely as a function of chance, there will be fluctuation in the value of the statistics from sample to sample. Not all means will be the same; not all variances will be the same.

If there were a sufficiently large number of samples, one could plot the values of each sample statistic in a frequency distribution. Figure 6.1 is the frequency distribution for the 100 experimental group means that the pharmacist calculated.

What can be observed from this frequency distribution? First, the shape of the distribution should be a familiar one. The 100 experimental group means are distributed somewhat normally. Second, the most frequently occurring score is the midmost score in the distribution and is the mean of means. Third, not all the experimental group means are identical; some are large (e.g., 83.07) and some are small (e.g., 56.46). Finally, one could take the collection of 100 experimental group means and compute a second descriptive statistic, the variance of the 100 experimental group means.

A frequency distribution of sample statistics is called a **sampling distribution.** There are a variety of sample statistics for which a sampling distribution can be

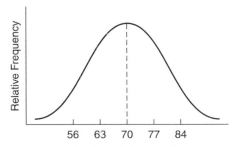

Figure 6.1 Frequency distribution of 100 sample means

created. One might have a sampling distribution of means, a sampling distribution of variances, a sampling distribution of standard deviations, and so on. We will concentrate first on the sampling distribution of means.

Since samples are usually considered to be drawn from populations that are infinitely large in size, it is therefore possible to take an infinite number of samples from the population. Consequently, the number of sample statistics (e.g., sample means) that can be computed is also infinite.

We will denote the population parameters for the theoretical sampling distribution of means as shown in Textbox 6.6.

Sampling Distributions Are Normal in Shape   The fact that the 100 experimental group means are distributed somewhat normally is not accidental. Indeed, as sample size increases, the shape of the sampling distribution for any statistic becomes increasingly like the normal distribution. Furthermore, so long as sample size is large, the sampling distribution is shaped like a normal distribution regardless of the shape of the population from which the samples were taken. It does not matter whether the population from which samples were drawn was rectangular in shape, or heavily skewed, or multimodal; the sampling distribution tends toward the shape of a normal distribution. Knowing that the sampling distribution is a normal distribution is especially useful for hypothesis testing.

Think about that for a moment. It should make sense to you that a collection of statistics, such as sample means, drawn from the same population and with the same sample size, will be distributed normally. Most of the sample means will be quite similar to the overall or grand mean (i.e., the mean of means). Fewer will be somewhat discrepant, either somewhat larger or somewhat smaller than the grand mean. And fewer yet will be greatly discrepant from the grand mean.

Sampling Variances Are Affected by N   Consider next what affects the degree of variability in the sample statistics that make up the sampling distribution. One important factor is sample size. When

> **CD-ROM link 6.1**
>
> ***Activity 6.1: The Law of Large Numbers***
> Activity 6.1 provides you with a laboratory where you can run experiments in probability. After setting the probability of various outcomes of a random event, this high-speed simulation will let you see how closely the actual results match the probabilities you set. Does the number of trials affect the variability in the results?

Textbox 6.6

Population Parameters for the Theoretical Sampling Distribution

Population mean of the sampling distribution of means = μ_M

Population variance of the sampling distribution of means = σ_M^2

Population standard deviation of the sampling distribution of means = σ_M
(also known as the standard error).

each sample is based on a small number of scores, sample statistics vary greatly. In contrast, when each sample is based on a large number of scores, sample statistics vary less

If you took a number of small samples and computed a mean for each of them, you should not be surprised if the means were somewhat different from one another. After all, it makes sense that if each sample is based on only a few cases the chances are fairly high that the means will vary. But if you took a number of large samples and computed a mean for each of them, you would be more surprised if the means were markedly different from one another. You will, therefore, want to take this idea about the influence of sample size into account in dealing with the sampling distribution. This is where the central limit theorem plays a key role.

Central Limit Theorem The central limit theorem is one of the most important concepts in inferential statistics. It combines what we just noted about the shape of sampling distributions and the effects of sample size. See Textbox 6.7.

In summary, there are several important properties of sampling distributions of means:

1. The mean of the sampling distribution of means is equal to the population mean.
2. The variance of the sampling distribution of means for samples of the same size is always the population variance divided by the sample size N (which is the same for each sample).

$$\text{Equation 6.10: } \sigma_M^2 = \frac{\sigma^2}{N}$$

3. As sample size N increases, the shape of the sampling distribution of means more closely approximates a normal distribution *regardless of the shape of the population from which the samples were drawn.*

CD-ROM link 6.2

Activity 6.2: The Sampling Distribution of Means (Part I)
What is a sampling distribution? What is its shape? The first activity in this chapter helps you to discover answers to these and other questions. By rolling sets of dice, you will generate a distribution using the mean of each set. As you roll more and more sets of dice, a familiar shape will emerge from this sampling distribution of means!

CD-ROM link 6.3

Activity 6.3: The Sampling Distribution of Means (Part II)
In Activity 6.3, you will explore one of the more remarkable aspects of the sampling distribution of means. After drawing samples from three different population distributions with non-normal shapes (exponential, bimodal, uniform), you can compare the shape of their sampling distributions of means with one generated from a normally distributed population. When the sample size gets large enough, watch for an interesting phenomenon to occur!

Textbox 6.7

Central Limit Theorem

If a population has a variance σ^2 and a mean μ, the distribution of sample means from samples of N independent observations approaches the form of a normal distribution, with variance σ^2/N and mean μ, as sample size N increases.

Estimators for the Sampling Distribution of Means   Needless to say, one is never in a position to collect an infinitely large number of samples from the population of interest. Therefore, the important parameters of the sampling distribution of means must be estimated. This is a fairly straightforward extension of what we learned from estimating population parameters. See Textbox 6.8.

Estimating the Parameters of the Sampling Distribution of Means: Flu Bugs Scenario   We will use the data from the five experimental Flu Bugs participants in Textbox 6.1 to estimate the mean, variance, and standard deviation of the sampling distribution of means. See Textbox 6.9.[1]

Important Clarification: $s \neq s_M$ It is important to highlight the distinction between the unbiased standard deviation (s) and the standard error (s_M). The standard deviation (s) estimates the average distance *between individual scores* and

---

Textbox 6.8

Estimated Parameters of the Sampling Distribution of Means

Estimated mean of the sampling distribution of means:

$$\text{Equation 6.11: } \overline{Y} = \frac{\sum Y_i}{N}$$

The mean of a single sample is an unbiased estimate of the population mean. The mean of a single sample is also an unbiased estimate of the mean of the sampling distribution of means.
Estimated variance of the sampling distribution of means:

$$\text{Equation 6.12: } s_M^2 = \frac{s^2}{N} = \frac{\frac{\sum (Y_i - \overline{Y})^2}{N-1}}{N}$$

Estimated standard deviation of the sampling distribution of means (also known as the estimated standard error of the mean)

$$\text{Equation 6.13: } s_M = \frac{s}{\sqrt{N}} = \frac{\sqrt{\frac{\sum (Y_i - \overline{Y})^2}{N-1}}}{\sqrt{N}}$$

The variance (and standard deviation) of the sampling distribution are affected by sample size. The larger the sample size, the smaller the estimated variance (and estimated standard deviation) of the sampling distribution.
The variance (and standard deviation) of the theoretical sampling distribution, which is based on an infinitely large number of samples, may be estimated from the variance (and standard deviation) of *only a single sample!*

---

[1]The small sample size ($N = 5$) we used here to simplify computations suggests that this sampling distribution of means will not have the exact mathematical properties of the normal distribution. You will see how good an approximation it is when we discuss the family of *t*-distributions in Chapter 8.

Textbox 6.9

Estimated Population Parameters of the Sampling Distribution of Means for the Flu Bugs Scenario (Experimental Treatment Only)

$$\overline{Y} = \frac{\sum Y_i}{N} = \frac{350}{5} = 70.00$$

$$s_M^2 = \frac{s^2}{N} = \frac{\dfrac{\sum (Y_i - \overline{Y})^2}{N-1}}{N} = \frac{\dfrac{1000}{4}}{5} = 50.00$$

$$s_M = \frac{s}{\sqrt{N}} = \frac{\sqrt{\dfrac{\sum (Y_i - \overline{Y})^2}{N-1}}}{\sqrt{N}} = \frac{\sqrt{\dfrac{1000}{4}}}{\sqrt{5}} = \frac{15.81}{2.24} = 7.07$$

---

the population mean. The standard error (s_M) estimates the average distance between *sample statistics* and the population mean of those statistics. The standard deviation (s) provides an estimate of variability for the individual scores in the population while the standard error (s_M) provides an estimate of variability for the sample statistics drawn from the population.

What Happens with Small Sample Sizes?   Rome wasn't built in a day and neither can you understand statistics in a day. In this chapter we noted that sampling distributions come close to being normally distributed when sample sizes are large (e.g., 30). With smaller sizes, sampling distributions depart from normality. For the time being, we will ignore this complication and allow ourselves the luxury of assuming that our sampling distributions are normally distributed— even those based on small sample sizes. However, we will return to consider the shape of sampling distributions for different sample sizes more completely in Chapter 8. When we do, we will show you some refinements and extensions to the logic and procedures we have laid as a foundation here.

Interval Estimation of the Mean

Why Interval Estimation?   Estimates of central tendency and variability of the sampling distribution of means can be put to good use for interval estimation or estimating the range of values in which the population mean is likely to fall. Although we know that the mean of a single sample is an unbiased estimate of the population mean, we also know that sampling error can operate such that another sample mean might be different from the first. Under such circumstances, it is useful to supplement a point estimation, such as the mean, with an interval estimation, such as a confidence interval. A **confidence interval** is an estimated range of values with a known high probability of covering the true population value.

For example, our best guess at the population mean reaction to the pharmacist's mediation is the mean reaction of the sample of five participants, or 70.00. But this is a single, small sample. Therefore, it seems reasonable to think of using the sample data to estimate a range in which the population mean might lie with a degree of certainty such as 95% certainty.

As you will see, a confidence interval estimate goes beyond what one can learn from an estimated population mean or point estimate in expressing the accuracy with which one's estimates are made. It tells you not only what your best guess is of the population parameter but also gives you a range of scores in which the parameter is likely to fall. A small confidence interval means you have a fairly precise estimate of the population parameter. A large confidence interval says you have a fairly imprecise estimate of the population parameter.

It makes sense, of course, to think that the confidence with which one can make an estimate of the true population parameter from a sample statistic increases as the size of the sample increases. Therefore, interval estimation reflects the importance of sample size, among other things.

But even taking sample size into account, why do samples occasionally yield findings that later appear to be wrong? The statistical answer is that inferential statistics only allow one to make a best guess about population parameters. These guesses can, and occasionally will, be wrong—an example of *sampling error*.

But there is also the research design answer. Sometimes sample estimates prove to be incorrect because there was a methodological problem with the initial investigation that made it different from subsequent investigations. Perhaps your selection of participants was biased. Perhaps there was an unknown or uncontrolled extraneous factor that influenced the results in substantial but undetectable ways. Keep in mind that our statistical models assume that we have avoided these methodological pitfalls. When the pitfalls and weaknesses have not been avoided, that may also explain why findings vary from personal expectations, theory, and/or the results of prior investigations.

In order to estimate a range or interval in which the population mean might lie, take advantage of what you have learned so far about the sampling distribution of means. First, you know that as sample size increases, the sampling distribution of means becomes a close approximation to the normal distribution. Second, you know that the mean of the sample is a good estimate of the mean of the sampling distribution, both of which are also good estimates of the population mean. Finally, you know that you can estimate the variance and standard deviation of the sampling distribution of means using the data from only a single sample.

Interval Estimation and the Sampling Distribution of Means   Remember that the sampling distribution is a distribution of sample statistics, such as sample means, and that the central limit theorem tells you that this distribution increasingly approximates a normal distribution as sample size increases, regardless of the shape of the population from which the sample(s) were taken. Among other things, that means that as long as sample size is reasonably large, you know the sample *means* are normally distributed so that a test of normality is not necessary.

You have already found the point estimate of the population mean. The mean of the single sample of data you have collected or have on hand is your best guess as to the population mean. The mean of this sample is also your best guess as to the mean of the sampling distribution of means.

But your best guess of the population mean need not be your only guess. You know full well that sampling error may operate, allowing the sample mean not to be exactly equal to the true population value. Therefore, you want to qualify your point estimate in some way to indicate the presence and general magnitude of this error. When there is a great deal of sampling error, the confidence interval calculated from any sample tends to be large and the range of values likely to cover the population mean is wide. In contrast, if sampling error is small, the confidence interval calculated from any sample tends to be small and the range of values likely to cover the population means is narrow.

According to the central limit theorem, as sample size increases the distribution of sample means approaches the form of a normal distribution, with variance σ^2/N and mean μ. The standard deviation of the sampling distribution of means (σ_M) or standard error is $\sigma/\sqrt{N}$. Therefore, the probability is about .95 that the true population mean, μ, will fall in the range between the following limits:

Equation 6.14: $\overline{Y} - 1.96\sigma_M$ and $\overline{Y} + 1.96\sigma_M$

The range of values between $\overline{Y} \pm 1.96\sigma_M$ is called the **95% confidence interval.** The two boundaries of the interval, or $\overline{Y} - 1.96\sigma_M$ and $\overline{Y} + 1.96\sigma_M$, are called **the 95% confidence limits.**

You may wish to find other confidence intervals than this. For example, the probability is about .99 that the true population mean, μ, will fall in the range between the following limits:

Equation 6.15: $\overline{Y} - 2.57\sigma_M$ and $\overline{Y} + 2.57\sigma_M$

Notice that the 99% confidence interval is larger than the 95% confidence interval. A wider range of possible values is included, and therefore you can feel increased confidence that the true population mean is covered.

Of course, you do not actually know σ_M. But you can use the data from a single sample to estimate it and therefore estimate the 95% and 99% confidence intervals.

The estimated 95% confidence interval about the population mean is as follows:

Equation 6.16: $\overline{Y} - 1.96s_M$ and $\overline{Y} + 1.96s_M$

The estimated 99% confidence interval about the population means is as follows:

Equation 6.17: $\overline{Y} - 2.57s_M$ and $\overline{Y} + 2.57s_M$

Textbox 6.10 illustrates these estimates using the Flu Bugs scenario from Textbox 6.1.

The confidence interval, by providing a range of possible values, emphasizes the potential operation of sampling error—that there can be fluctuation in mean scores from sample to sample. This is the value of using interval estimation, which is not possible when only point estimation is employed.

Textbox 6.10

Estimated Confidence Intervals About the Population Mean

What is our estimate of the 95% confidence interval (CI) about the population mean of those exposed to the pharmacist's flu medication?

For estimating the 95% confidence interval about the population mean use Equation 6.18:

$$\textbf{(Equation 6.16)} \quad \overline{Y} - 1.96s_M \text{ and } \overline{Y} + 1.96s_M$$

Therefore, 95% CI = 70.00 − 1.96 (7.07) and 70.00 + 1.96 (7.07) or $56.14 \leq \mu_D \leq 83.36$.

The lower limit of the confidence interval is 56.14. The upper limit of the confidence interval is 83.36.

We can say with 95% certainty that the population mean reaction to the pharmacist's medication lies in the range of 56.14 to 83.86. Our best guess as to the population's mean reaction is 70.00. See Figure 6.2.

But what if one wished to estimate the 99% confidence interval instead?

For estimating the 99% confidence interval about the population mean use Equation 6.19:

$$\textbf{(Equation 6.17)} \quad \overline{Y} - 2.57s_M \text{ and } \overline{Y} + 2.57s_M$$

Therefore, 99% CI = 70.00 − 2.57 (7.07) and 70.00 + 2.57 (7.07) or $51.83 \leq \mu_D \leq 88.17$.

The lower limit of the confidence interval is 51.83. The upper limit of the confidence interval is 88.17.

Remember that if the sample size were larger, these confidence intervals would be smaller. Also remember that with the small sample sizes used in this illustration the assumption of normality does not hold, as we will take up in greater detail in Chapter 8.

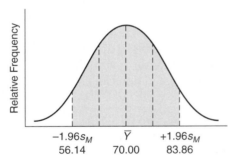

Figure 6.2 Estimated 95% confidence interval about the population mean

Furthermore, note that all other things equal, the size of the confidence interval estimated here would be smaller if the sample size were larger. It should be intuitively obvious that the range of possible means to be estimated grows smaller as sample size grows larger. In the pharmacist's example in the Flu Bugs scenario in Textbox 6.1, few people were studied and, therefore, the confidence interval for the sample means appears to be relatively large in size. For example, if the sample size were doubled but all other statistics remained the same, the size of the confidence interval for sample means would be noticeably smaller.

Other Types of Interval Estimation We have illustrated how to use the sampling distribution of means to estimate a confidence interval. But remember that there are numerous sampling distributions that are possible, depending upon which statistic is distributed. One might have a sampling distribution of variances, a sampling distribution of standard deviations, a sampling distribution of mean differences, and so on.

For each of these sampling distributions, one can estimate a mean and a standard error of the *statistic* based only on the data from a single sample. Furthermore, for each of these sampling distributions the size of the standard error grows smaller as sample size grows larger. Having an estimated mean and an estimated standard error for the *statistic* combined with the use of the areas under the normal distribution, as per the central limit theorem, means that confidence intervals can be computed for these other statistics too. In general, the form for a confidence interval (CI) about a population parameter is

$$\%CI = \text{statistic} \pm (\text{critical value})(\text{standard error of the statistic})$$

As you will see, we will take advantage of the sampling distribution of mean differences when we come to undertake our first statistical test of an hypothesis.

HYPOTHESIS TESTING

When the pharmacist in the Flu Bugs scenario wondered whether his flu medication produced a different reaction than traditional medications, he had formed a hypothesis about the effectiveness of his treatment. Inferential statistics are often used for hypothesis-testing purposes. In essence, inferential statistical tests allow a choice between two hypothetical statements.

Null and Alternative Hypotheses One statement claims there is no effect of the treatment, or independent variable, on the dependent variable. In other words, the treatment did not "work" and the difference between the experimental and control groups likely came about as a function of chance. This is a statement of the **null hypothesis.**

Another statement claims that there is an effect of the treatment, or independent variable, on the dependent variable. In other words, the treatment did "work" and the difference between the experimental and control groups likely did not come about as a function of chance. This is a statement of the **alternative hypothesis.**

In the pharmacist's case, the null hypothesis is a statement that there is no real difference in the population of flu sufferers in terms of their mean reaction to the experimental (A_1) and traditional (A_2) medications. Symbolically, we can represent the null hypothesis (H_0) as

$$H_0: \mu_{A1} = \mu_{A2} \text{ or } \mu_D = 0.0$$

Similarly, we can represent the alternative hypothesis (H_a) as

$$H_a: \mu_{A1} \neq \mu_{A2} \text{ or } \mu_D \neq 0.0$$

Probability Values for Significance Testing In order to help you decide which of these two hypotheses is correct, you will need to use the data from the pharmacist's experimental and control group samples. In doing so, you will need to take a best guess as to whether the population means are the same, indicating no treatment effect, or whether the population means are different, indicating a treatment effect. But because only a tiny fraction of flu sufferers have been studied, you cannot know with certainty whether there is really a difference between the population means attributable to the treatment. You will instead, take an informed guess.

An informed guess will occur something like this. If you believed the difference between the sample means could have occurred by chance fairly often, then you would not reject the null hypothesis. Instead, you would conclude that there is insufficient evidence to believe that the treatment worked. On the other hand, if you believed that the difference between the sample means could have occurred by chance only rarely, then you would reject the null hypothesis and accept the alternative hypothesis. You would conclude that there is sufficient evidence to believe that the treatment worked.

Because no one can ever study the entire population of interest; no one can ever know with certainty whether a decision—either to fail to reject the null hypothesis or to reject the null hypothesis and accept the alternative hypothesis—is correct. But what guidelines should one use to decide which of these decisions to make? Here is where probability values can help.

If you were to choose, say, a probability of 25%, that means that the differences you observed in order to reject the null hypothesis could have occurred by chance less than 1 time in 4. In contrast if you were to choose something smaller, say a probability of 5%, that means that the difference you observed could have occurred by chance less than 1 time in 20.

Traditional researchers use low probabilities (e.g., 5% or smaller) when hypothesis testing. By doing so, they ensure that the sample differences observed are so large that they occur by chance rarely (e.g., less than 1 time in 20). We will note this criterion as the probability value, or **alpha** (α), used for significance testing.

Furthermore, you will need to *exceed* this criterion in order to reject the null hypothesis. When the statistical tests of the observed differences exceed the alpha you have pre-established, you reject the null hypothesis and conclude that the treatment worked with reasonable certainty. One notes that the obtained probability value exceeded the criterion or alpha as follows:

When alpha is pre-established as .10, reject the null hypothesis when the observed probability or *p*-**value** is less than 1 in 10, or $p < .10$.

When alpha is pre-established as .05, reject the null hypothesis when $p < .05$.

When alpha is pre-established as .01, reject the null hypothesis when $p < .01$.

When alpha is pre-established as .001, reject the null hypothesis when $p < .001$, etc.

Sampling Distribution of Mean Differences For the Flu Bugs scenario, the core question we want to explore is whether the difference observed between the experimental sample group mean ($\overline{Y}_{A1}$) and the control sample group mean

$(\overline{Y}_{A2})$ could have occurred by chance less frequently than our criterion alpha which was set as .05. If that mean difference could have occurred by chance only rarely, you would reject the null hypothesis, $\mu_{A1} = \mu_{A2}$ or $\mu_L = 0.0$, and accept the alternative hypothesis. The best guess will be that the treatment worked, causing a different reaction in flu sufferers and that the two estimated means are not from the same population but two different populations. Therefore, the alternative hypothesis is correct: $\mu_{A1} \neq \mu_{A2}$ or $\mu_D \neq 0.0$

Specifically, the observed mean difference $(\overline{Y}_D)$ between the reaction of the experimental group (70.00) and the control group (40.00) is 30.00. Is this difference likely as a function of chance, or is it unlikely?

To answer this question you will need to take advantage of another sampling distribution. (Recall that one can have a sampling distribution for a variety of statistics). Instead of using the sampling distribution of means you will use the sampling distribution of mean differences.

Furthermore, begin with the assumption that the treatment did not work and that the null hypothesis is correct. If the null hypothesis is correct, there will be no difference between the two population means (i.e., $\mu_{A1} - \mu_{A2} = 0.00$). Therefore, the mean of the sampling distribution of mean differences will also be zero.

Stop and think about this for a moment. If the treatment truly does not work and the null hypothesis is correct, there is not going to be any difference in reaction to the pharmacist's medication compared to the traditional medication were one able to test all flu sufferers. However, also realize that studying samples of participants allows for chance variability to come into play.

As you have seen in this chapter, the operation of chance variability results in sample means that are not all necessarily equal to the population mean. Some may be larger and some may be smaller. Occasionally some may be extremely large and some may be extremely small. This fluctuation represents the operation of sampling error.

Similarly, the operation of chance variability results in sample mean differences that are not all necessarily equal to the population mean difference which, if the null hypothesis is correct, equals zero. Some of the mean differences may be positive and some of the mean differences may be negative. Occasionally some of the mean differences may be large positive values and some may be large negative values. This also represents the operation of sampling error.

A critical concern is to determine how likely a function of chance is the mean difference (30.00) observed by the pharmacist. More precisely, you want to know whether the mean difference could have occurred by chance less than 5 times in 100. Remember that it is theoretically possible for any sample mean difference, regardless of its size, to come about as a function of chance when the null hypothesis is correct. However, you have decided in

CD-ROM link 6.4

Activity 6.4: Is the Difference Caused by Chance?
In Activity 6.4, you have an advantage that no researcher has in real life: the ability to vary the mean difference between two populations, and explore how this affects the sampling distributions of mean differences! You will find out that even when there is a large difference between two populations' means, you cannot expect the mean difference between two samples to always be greater than zero.

advance that if the observed difference is large enough that it could occur by chance only rarely, you will reject the null hypothesis. You might be wrong, but you are prepared to say that the observed difference could occur so rarely as a function of chance that a more reasonable explanation is to conclude that the treatment worked.

The question is about the observed mean difference ($\overline{Y}_D$) compared to the population mean difference (μ_D) when one starts with the belief the null hypothesis is correct and the population mean difference is zero. In other words, how does $\overline{Y}_D$ compare to μ_D?

Estimating the Variance and Standard Deviation of the Sampling Distribution of Mean Differences   You have already accepted that the sampling distribution is shaped like the normal distribution especially as sample size increases.[2] And you have already accepted that if the null hypothesis is correct, the estimated mean of the sampling distribution of mean differences is zero. What remains to estimate is the variance of the sampling distribution of mean differences (s_D^2) and the standard deviation of the sampling distribution of mean differences (s_D), also known as the standard error of mean differences. Fortunately, these measures of variability can be estimated from the data for the two sample groups from which data have been collected.

First off, however, we need to state the formula for the variance of the sampling distribution of mean differences:

$$\text{Equation 6.18: } \sigma_D^2 = \frac{\sigma_{A1}^2}{n_{A1}} + \frac{\sigma_{A2}^2}{n_{A2}}$$

You may recognize the sampling variance of the mean differences as the combination of the sampling variance of experimental group means (A_1) and the sampling variance of control group means (A_2).

Now we will show how to estimate the variance of the sampling distribution of mean differences:

$$\text{Equation 6.19: } s_D^2 = \frac{s_{A1}^2}{n_{A1}} + \frac{s_{A2}^2}{n_{A2}}$$

where:

$s_{A_1}^2$ = unbiased variance of the experimental group

n_{A_1} = sample size for the experimental group

Notice an important similarity between the formula for the variance of the sampling distribution of means and the formula for the sampling distribution of mean differences. As sample size increases, the size of the sampling variance decreases.

---

[2]For the moment, sample sizes as small as 5 will be considered to fit this description. In Chapter 8, we will look more closely at the effects of sample size on the sampling distribution of mean differences.

CD-ROM link 6.5

Problem Generator: The Calculated z-value

To practice calculating and interpreting a z-value for a mean difference, select Calculated z-Value from the Problem Generator Menu on the CD-ROM. The Problem Generator will create as many practice problems as you need, and will demonstrate each step in their calculation.

The estimated standard deviation of the sampling distribution of mean differences (or standard error of the mean differences) is as follows:

$$\text{Equation 6.20: } s_D = \sqrt{\frac{s_{A1}^2}{n_{A1}} + \frac{s_{A2}^2}{n_{A2}}}$$

See Textbox 6.11 for computational examples using the Flu Bugs scenario.

Hypothesis Testing Using the z-Test

In Chapter 5, we discussed the use of z-scores to locate points on the normal distribution and the areas which lay beyond these points. We noted that a z-score of ±1.96 included 95% of the area around the mean of the normal distribution. Only 5% of the scores were either less than −1.96 or greater than +1.96. Given that for this example .05 has been selected as the probability value for significance testing, a z-score of ±1.96 will be used as the value needed to be exceeded if you are to reject the null hypothesis. Call this value the **critical value.**

In Chapter 5 we also gave the formula for computing a z-score as follows:

$$\textbf{(Equation 5.2) } z_i = \frac{Y_i - \overline{Y}}{s}$$

Textbox 6.11

A Computational Example of the Estimated Sampling Variance and Standard Error of Mean Differences Using the Flu Bugs Scenario

We can now find the estimated sampling variance and standard deviation of the sampling distribution of mean differences.

$$s_D^2 = \frac{s_{A1}^2}{n_{A1}} + \frac{s_{A2}^2}{n_{A2}} = \frac{250}{5} + \frac{250}{5} = 100.00$$

$$s_D = \sqrt{\frac{s_{A1}^2}{n_{A1}} + \frac{s_{A2}^2}{n_{A2}}} = \sqrt{\frac{250}{5} + \frac{250}{5}} = 10.00$$

Notice that the sampling variance and standard error of the mean differences for the Flu Bugs scenario is not the same as the sampling variance and standard error of the mean for either the experimental group or the control group separately. For example, recall from Textbox 6.9 that the sampling variance for the experimental group was 50.00 and the standard error was 7.07. Adding the sampling variances of means together yields the sampling variance of mean differences.

Suppose you wish to find the location of the observed mean difference on the standard normal distribution when your initial belief is that the null hypothesis is correct and the population mean difference is zero. To locate the observed mean difference on the standard normal distribution you need to know the standard deviation of the sampling distribution of mean differences (σ_M). You could then adapt Equation 5.2 to locate the observed mean difference:

$$z_D = \frac{(\overline{Y}_{A1} - \overline{Y}_{A2}) - (\mu_{A1} - \mu_{A2})}{\sigma_M}$$

Given your initial belief that the null hypothesis is correct and $\mu_{A1} - \mu_{A2} = 0.00$, this reduces to

$$z_D = \frac{(\overline{Y}_{A1} - \overline{Y}_{A2})}{\sigma_M}$$

But you do not know the value of σ_M and must use s_M to estimate it. Therefore, call the estimated value of z_D **the computed or calculated value:**

Equation 6.21: Estimated $z_D = \dfrac{\overline{Y}_{A1} - \overline{Y}_{A2}}{s_D}$

Alternately, the same result is reached via substitution:

Equation 6.22: Estimated $z_D = \dfrac{\overline{Y}_{A1} - \overline{Y}_{A2}}{\sqrt{\dfrac{s_{A1}^2}{n_{A1}} + \dfrac{s_{A2}^2}{n_{A2}}}}$

Equation 6.23: Estimated $z_D = \dfrac{\overline{Y}_{A1} - \overline{Y}_{A2}}{\sqrt{\dfrac{\sum (Y_{iA1} - \overline{Y}_{A1})^2}{(n_{A1} - 1)}}{n_{A1}} + \dfrac{\dfrac{\sum (Y_{iA2} - \overline{Y}_{A2})^2}{(n_{A2} - 1)}}{n_{A2}}}$

See Textbox 6.12 for an illustration of the calculation of z_D using data from the Flu Bugs scenario in Textbox 6.1.

Comparing the Calculated Value and the Critical Value   Having set the probability value for significance testing at .05, you were able to find the critical value for significance testing as ±1.96. In other words, if your calculated value is either greater than +1.96 or smaller than −1.96, you will reject the null hypothesis. Next z_D was computed and found to be +3.00. Because the calculated value (+3.00) is greater than the critical value (±1.96), you reject the null hypothesis and accept the alternative hypothesis. The sample difference the pharmacist obtained is so large that it could occur by chance less than 5 times in 100. This outcome is

---

Textbox 6.12

Calculation of z_D Using Data from the Flu Bugs Scenario

Use Equation 6.22 to calculate z_D for the Flu Bugs scenario.

$$z_D = \frac{\overline{Y}_{A1} - \overline{Y}_{A2}}{s_D} = \frac{70.00 - 40.00}{10.00} = +3.00$$

Alternately, if you have not already computed s_D, you might prefer to use either Equation 6.21 or Equation 6.22. You may wish to calculate z_D using each of these equations to satisfy yourself that they are mathematically identical.

---

unlikely a function of chance, so you conclude that it is more likely that the treatment worked.

Figure 6.3 illustrates a sampling distribution of mean differences. Note that the filled-in portion of the tails of the distribution beyond $\pm 1.96z$ represent the regions of rejection. The calculated value, $+3.00$, lies well within the region of rejection, far enough from a mean difference of zero for you to reject the null hypothesis in this case. The distribution can also be represented in terms of raw scores, with the values along the horizontal axis labeled -19.60, -10.00, 0.00, $+10.00$, and $+19.60$, respectively. The observed mean difference ($+30.00$) falls well outside the critical value of ± 19.60, or $1.96s_M$.

This is the first and basic use of statistical tests for hypothesis testing and inference. This basic statistical test is called the **z-test.**

Factors that Influence the z-Test   The z-test is a ratio. In the numerator of the z-ratio is the mean difference, an indication of variability between the (two) groups. In the denominator of the z-ratio is the standard error, an indication of average variability within-groups further adjusted by sample size. Clearly, the z-test is designed to assess the mean difference relative to both variability within-groups and sample size. What appears to be a "large" mean difference may not be unusual if variability within-groups (i.e., the degree to which the participants

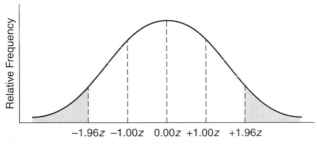

Figure 6.3 Sampling distribution of mean differences (standard scores)

score within each group vary) is also large. Conversely, what appears to be a "small" mean difference may be unusual if variability within-groups is small.

In addition, the size of the standard error decreases as sample size increases. Therefore, all other things equal, the calculated value will be smaller as sample size grows larger. This is sensible; with more and more participants, you should feel more confident that the difference you observe is "real." With small sample experiments, the size of the difference among groups needs to be quite large before one feels comfortable that the difference reflects a treatment effect.

Interval Estimation of the Mean Difference

In a previous section we discussed the idea of interval estimation of the mean. There is a parallel logic to the idea of, and method for, estimating a confidence interval of the mean difference. Although it is known that a single mean difference when properly sampled is an unbiased estimate of the population mean difference, it is also known that sampling error can operate such that another mean difference sampled from the population might be different from the first. It is therefore useful to supplement the point estimate of the population mean difference with an interval estimate of the population mean difference in the form of a confidence interval. In other words, try to estimate a range in which the population mean difference might lie with a degree of certainty.

Equations 6.14 and 6.15 were arrived at to determine the range in which we were 95% certain and 99% certain, respectively, that the true population mean lies. By extension, the probability is about .95 that the true population mean difference, μ_D, will fall in the range between the following:

$$\textbf{Equation 6.24: } \overline{Y}_D - 1.96\sigma_D \text{ and } \overline{Y}_D + 1.96\sigma_D$$

Furthermore, the probability is about .99 that the true population mean difference, μ_D, will fall in the range between the following:

$$\textbf{Equation 6.25: } \overline{Y}_D - 2.57\sigma_D \text{ and } \overline{Y}_D + 2.57\sigma_D$$

Because σ_D, is not known, it has to be estimated using s_D. Therefore, the estimate of the 95% confidence interval is as follows:

$$\textbf{Equation 6.26: } \overline{Y}_D - 1.96s_D \text{ and } \overline{Y}_D + 1.96s_D$$

The estimate of the 99% confidence interval is as follows:

$$\textbf{Equation 6.27: } \overline{Y}_D - 2.57s_D \text{ and } \overline{Y}_D + 2.57s_D$$

Furthermore, this can be made into a general formula for any probability value ($1 - \alpha/2$ for both tails of the distribution) or range of the standard normal distribution (expressed as $z_{1-\alpha/2}$):

$$\textbf{Equation 6.28: } \overline{Y}_D - z_{1-\alpha/2}s_D \text{ and } \overline{Y}_D + z_{1-\alpha/2}s_D = \text{two-sided confidence}$$
$$\text{interval for the estimated mean difference}$$

Textbox 6.13

95% CI for *z*-test of Data from Flu Bugs Scenario

We will use Equation 6.21 to calculate the 95% confidence interval of the mean difference for the Flu Bugs scenario.

$$\overline{Y}_D - 1.96s_D \text{ and } \overline{Y}_D + 1.96s_D$$

Therefore, 95% CI = $30.00 - 1.96(10.00)$ and $30.00 - 1.96(10.00)$ or $10.40 \leq \mu_D \leq 49.60$.

The lower limit of the confidence interval is 10.40. The upper limit of the confidence interval is 49.60.

You are 95% certain that the population mean difference in reactions lies in the range of 10.40 to 49.60. In addition, because the 95% CI does not contain zero, you can reject the null hypothesis and conclude that experimental medication is probably effective.

Finally, notice how interval estimation augments your understanding of the mean difference beyond the point estimation, a mean difference of 30.00. The interval estimation suggests the population mean difference might be much smaller or much larger. Again, the small size of your sample contributes to the wide interval estimate.

Finally, when this confidence interval includes zero (0.0), you also know that the statistical test is not significant, which means the calculated value does not exceed the critical value and that the criterion value of alpha has not been exceeded. In other words, when the interval estimate contains zero, you cannot reject the null hypothesis. Textbox 6.13 shows the computation of the 95% confidence interval for the *z*-test of mean differences.

PUTTING IT ALL TOGETHER

In this chapter, we differentiated sample statistics and population parameters. We also discussed ways to estimate population parameters from sample statistics. We noted that there were several properties of good estimators and that while the sample mean was a good estimator, the sample variance and standard deviation were biased estimators and need to be corrected. We also examined the value of both point estimation and interval estimation of population parameters.

We noted that sample statistics could be drawn repeatedly from the population. According to the central limit theorem, the resulting sampling distribution approaches the form of the normal distribution as sample size *N* increases with a mean equal to the population mean and a variance equal to the population variance divided by sample size. We also showed how to estimate the mean and variance (plus standard deviation) of the sampling distribution from sample statistics. We used these estimates to form a confidence interval to find the range of scores in which the population mean probably lies.

Finally, we used the sampling distribution of mean differences for hypothesis testing. We discussed the null and alternative hypotheses, the probability values for significance testing, and the importance of comparing the calculated value with the critical value. We showed how to use the sampling distribution as the basis for computing the z-test and a confidence interval.

Formulas for Samples, Populations, Population Estimators, Sampling Distributions, and Sampling Distribution Estimators

Sample statistics (i.e., for describing a subset of the population; therefore, N is the number of observations in the sample)

$$\textbf{Equation 6.1: } \text{Sample mean } \overline{Y} = \frac{\sum Y_i}{N}$$

$$\textbf{Equation 6.2: } \text{Sample variance } S^2 = \frac{\sum (Y_i - \overline{Y})^2}{N}$$

$$\textbf{Equation 6.3: } \text{Sample standard deviation } S = \sqrt{\frac{\sum (Y_i - \overline{Y})^2}{N}}$$

Population parameters (i.e., when all the population values are known; therefore, N is the number of observations in the population)

$$\textbf{Equation 6.4: } \text{Population mean } \mu = \frac{\sum Y_i}{N}$$

$$\textbf{Equation 6.5: } \text{Population variance } \sigma^2 = \frac{\sum (Y_i - \overline{Y})^2}{N}$$

$$\textbf{Equation 6.6: } \text{Population standard deviation } \sigma = \sqrt{\frac{\sum (Y_i - \overline{Y})^2}{N}}$$

Estimators of population parameters (i.e., when one wishes to use sample statistics to estimate population parameters)

$$\textbf{Equation 6.7: } \text{Estimated population mean } \overline{Y} = \frac{\sum Y_i}{N}$$

$$\textbf{Equation 6.8: } \text{Estimated population variance } s^2 = \frac{\sum (Y_i - \overline{Y})^2}{N - 1}$$

$$\textbf{Equation 6.9: } \text{Estimated population standard deviation } s = \sqrt{\frac{\sum (Y_i - \overline{Y})^2}{N - 1}}$$

Sampling distribution parameters (i.e., when one has collected all possible samples from the population of interest)

Population mean of the sampling distribution of means $= \mu_M$

Population variance of the sampling distribution of means $= \sigma^2_M$

Population standard deviation of the sampling distribution of means = σ_M (also known as the standard error)

Estimators for the sampling distribution of means

Estimated variance of the sampling distribution of means:

$$\text{Equation 6.12: } s_M^2 = \frac{s^2}{N'} = \frac{\frac{\sum (Y_i - \overline{Y})^2}{N-1}}{N}$$

Estimated standard deviation of the sampling distribution of means (also known as the estimated standard error of the mean)

$$\text{Equation 6.13: } s_M^2 = \frac{s}{\sqrt{N}} = \frac{\sqrt{\frac{\sum (Y_i - \overline{Y})^2}{N-1}}}{\sqrt{N}}$$

Using the sampling distribution for interval estimation

The estimated 95% confidence interval about the population mean μ is:

$$\text{Equation 6.16: } \overline{Y} - 1.96 s_M \text{ and } \overline{Y} + 1.96 s_M$$

The estimated 99% confidence interval about the population mean μ is:

$$\text{Equation 6.17: } \overline{Y} - 2.57 s_M \text{ and } \overline{Y} + 2.57 s_M$$

The estimated 95% confidence interval about the population mean difference μ_D is:

$$\text{Equation 6.26: } \overline{Y}_D - 1.96 s_D \text{ and } \overline{Y}_D + 1.96 s_D$$

The estimated 99% confidence interval about the population mean difference μ_D is:

$$\text{Equation 6.27: } \overline{Y}_D - 2.57 s_D \text{ and } \overline{Y}_D + 2.57 s_D$$

Using the Sampling Distribution for Hypothesis Testing

Follow these steps in hypothesis testing. Remember that the z-test is most accurate when sample sizes are large. Therefore, we will deal with corrections for small sample sizes in Chapter 8.

1. State the null and alternative hypotheses:

$$H_0: \mu_{A1} = \mu_{A2} \text{ or } \mu_D = 0.0$$
$$H_a: \mu_{A1} \neq \mu_{A2} \text{ or } \mu_D \neq 0.0$$

2. Select the probability value for hypothesis testing (e.g., $\alpha = .05$)

3. Compute the calculated value of the z-test:

$$\text{Equation 6.21: Estimated } z_D = \frac{\overline{Y}_{A1} - \overline{Y}_{A2}}{s_D}$$

Alternately, we arrive at the same result via substitution:

$$\text{Equation 6.22: Estimated } z_D = \frac{\overline{Y}_{A1} - \overline{Y}_{A2}}{\sqrt{\dfrac{s^2_{A1}}{n_{A1}} + \dfrac{s^2_{A2}}{n_{A2}}}}$$

$$\text{Equation 6.23: Estimated } z_D = \frac{\overline{Y}_{A1} - \overline{Y}_{A2}}{\sqrt{\dfrac{\dfrac{\sum(Y_{iA1} - \overline{Y}_{A1})^2}{(n_{A1} - 1)}}{n_{A1}} + \dfrac{\dfrac{\sum(Y_{iA2} - \overline{Y}_{A2})^2}{(n_{A2} - 1)}}{n_{A2}}}}$$

4. Find the critical value for the z-test by using Appendix A, which gives the areas under the normal curve.
5. If the calculated value exceeds the critical value, reject the null hypothesis and accept the alternative hypothesis. If the calculated value fails to exceed the critical value, do not reject the null hypothesis.
6. When alpha is pre-established as .10, reject the null hypothesis when the observed probability, or **p-value,** is less than 1 in 10, or $p < .10$.
   When alpha is pre-established as .05, reject the null hypothesis when $p < .05$.
   When alpha is pre-established as .01, reject the null hypothesis when $p < .01$.
   When alpha is pre-established as .001, reject the null hypothesis when $p < .001$.

KEY TERMS

Inferential statistics

Population

Population parameter

Sample

Representative, random sample

Convenience sample

Random assignment

Stratified random sampling

Cluster sampling

Multistage cluster sampling

Sample statistic

Sampling distribution

Sampling error

Point estimation

Interval estimation

Maximum likelihood

Consistent estimator

Efficient estimator

Sufficient estimator

Unbiased estimator

Sampling distribution

95% Confidence interval

95% Confidence limits

Null hypothesis

Alternate hypothesis

Alpha

p-value

Critical value

Computed or calculated value

z-test

REFERENCES

Hays, W. L. (1994). *Statistics.* (5th Ed.). Orlando, FL: Harcourt-Brace.

PROBLEMS

Questions

Section 1   Conceptual/Definition

6.1. In making an inference from a sample to a population, can one draw an incorrect conclusion?

6.2. Do statistical results guarantee meaningful results?

6.3. Define *inferential statistics*.

6.4. Define the terms *population* and *population parameter*.

6.5. Define the terms *sample* and *sample statistic*.

6.6. What is the difference between a *random sample* and a *convenience sample?*

6.7. Why is random assignment important?

6.8. What is the difference between point estimation and interval estimation?

6.9. What is a sampling distribution and how does it relate to sampling error?

6.10. List and describe five desirable properties of good estimators.

6.11. Does the shape of the population from which samples are drawn dictate the shape of the sampling distribution?

6.12. What is the relationship between the variance and standard deviation of a sampling distribution and N size?

6.13. State the central limit theorem as well as three important properties that stem from it.

6.14. What is the difference between the standard deviation and the standard error?

6.15. What is a confidence interval?

6.16. What is the difference between an alpha (α) level and a *p*-value?

6.17. What is the difference between a calculated value and a critical value?

Section 2   Numerical

Use the following data set to answer questions 6.18 to 6.20:

20, 23, 26, 21, 28, 29, 34, 28, 22, 30

6.18. Determine the estimated population mean, variance, and standard deviation.

6.19. Determine the standard error of the mean.

6.20. Determine the 95% confidence interval of sample means about the estimated population mean.

Use the following data set to answer questions 6.21 to 6.23:

38, 40, 36, 40, 37, 37, 32, 44, 45, 39

6.21. Determine the estimated population mean, variance, and standard deviation.

6.22. Determine the standard error of the mean.

6.23. Determine the 95% confidence interval of sample means about the estimated population mean.

The following data exists for both the experimental and control groups in a given experiment. Use it to answer questions 6.24 to 6.27:

Control: 23, 31, 29, 24, 26
Experimental: 31, 34, 35, 29, 37

6.24. Determine the estimated population mean, variance, and standard deviation for both the control and experimental groups.
6.25. Determine the standard error of the mean for both the control and experimental groups.
6.26. Determine the 95% confidence interval of sample means about the estimated population mean for both the control and experimental groups.
6.27. Determine the standard error of the mean differences (s_D) and then use the z-test to determine whether a significant difference exists between the control and experimental groups (using a significance level of .05).

7 Statistical Issues in Hypothesis Testing

OVERVIEW

This chapter is a key chapter. It unlocks the door to understanding the remaining, basic issues in the use of inferential statistics for hypothesis testing. By the conclusion of this chapter you will have gained a solid appreciation of the mathematical logic that is the underpinning, in whole or in part, for all the statistical tests we cover in the remainder of the text. In addition, we will further your understanding of a basic inferential procedure that relies on the standard normal distribution.

The emphasis in this chapter is on the nature and general procedures for hypothesis testing. We also show how to find both two-sided and one-sided confidence intervals and how to use them for hypothesis testing. In addition, we discuss the alternative sampling distribution, in particular, the sampling distribution of mean differences when the null hypothesis is not true. We cover issues associated with the power of statistical tests to detect treatment effects. Finally, we distinguish between statistical significance and practical importance and introduce the effect size measure as a means of detecting the size of effects.

Some of the questions we will answer here include the following:

1. What are the six steps in hypothesis testing and why are they important?
2. What are one- and two-sided confidence intervals and how does one use them?
3. What is the alternative sampling distribution?
4. How does one estimate the power of a statistical test and what are the ways to increase power?
5. How does one know the correct sample size for an investigation?
6. What is the difference between statistical and practical significance and how does one compute an effect size?
7. What are guidelines for the application of statistical methods?

We begin with the scenario described in Textbox 7.1.

Textbox 7.1

Scenario: Devil's Advocate

Two friends decided to settle an argument over whether there is a difference between two recipes for spicy barbecue sauce. John insisted that his family's secret recipe is a winner. Steve was skeptical; he wanted some proof that John's family sauce is better than the gourmet hot 'n' spicy sauce sold in the local supermarket. They decided to have a cook-off to settle the matter. They each agreed to invite their friends over for a blind taste test of pork spareribs cooked with the sauces. A dozen friends agreed to participate and were randomly assigned to John's Devil's Own sauce and Steve's Texas Wildfire sauce. Each participant rated the cooked ribs on a scale from 1 to 10, where 1 was "hog hell" and 10 was "hog heaven." The results for each sauce were as follows:

Devil's Own: 10, 8, 7, 6, 9, 8

Texas Wildfire: 6, 5, 7, 9, 8, 7

Is John right?

STEPS IN HYPOTHESIS TESTING

In this text, we explore the nature of statistical tests to determine whether two or more variables are related. In one simple form of hypothesis testing, we can explore whether an independent variable is significantly related to a dependent variable. If a true experiment has been conducted, finding a statistically significant relationship may lead the analyst to conclude that a causal relationship appears to exist between the manipulated variable and the measured variable; that is, the treatment appears to causally explain a significant amount of variability in the dependent variable. If a correlational investigation has been conducted, finding a statistically significant relationship may lead the analyst to conclude only that a nonchance relationship appears to exist between the predictor variable(s) and the outcome variable.

In Chapter 6, we introduced you to the rudiments of hypothesis testing. In this chapter, we want to explore the procedures and logic of hypothesis testing further. As we noted, basically all uses of statistical inference for hypothesis testing involve the six key steps noted in Textbox 7.2.

State the Null and Alternative Hypotheses

A **statistical hypothesis** is a statement about the parameters of one or more population distributions. For example, a statement about the inequivalence of the means from two populations is a statistical hypothesis. Statistical hypotheses are always about populations, not samples. The statements are hypotheses because they refer to situations that might be true.

There is usually a difference between statistical hypotheses and the scientific hypotheses from which they are derived. Scientific hypotheses are usually statements about phenomena and their underlying bases. Statistical hypotheses, on the other hand, are usually descriptions of population characteristics without explanation of why populations have these characteristics.

Statistical Hypotheses Statistical tests involve the comparison of two hypotheses: the null hypothesis and the alternative hypothesis. The **null hypothesis** is often used to signify a zero, or null, treatment effect or the equivalence of population parameters (e.g., H_0: $\mu_{A1} = \mu_{A2}$) but it can sometimes be used otherwise (e.g., H_0: $\mu = 50.00$). More generally, the null hypothesis is the one that is assumed to be true in generating the sampling distribution used in the statistical test.

The **alternative hypothesis** is often used to signify a nonzero treatment effect or the inequivalence of population parameters (e.g., H_a: $\mu_{A1} \neq \mu_{A2}$) but it too can sometimes be used otherwise (e.g., H_a: $\mu \neq 50.00$). The alternative hypothesis is considered to be true once it is decided that the null hypothesis is false.

The Procedure of Falsification In social science research that relies on statistical testing, a logical procedure called the *procedure of falsification* is used. Falsification depends on the use of a single observation leading to the conclusion that a premise or prior statement is incorrect. For example, establishing the falsehood of "all dogs can swim" is simply the matter of finding a single dog that cannot survive in water. In contrast, establishing the truth of "all dogs can swim" is a daunting task because it requires testing all dogs.

In statistical hypothesis testing, the null hypothesis is presented as the prior statement to be disproved or falsified. That is, one uses the results of research to demonstrate that the null hypothesis is false and, therefore, one tentatively accepts the alternative hypothesis as being a more accurate statement. Furthermore, there are times when one fails to reject the null hypothesis. Failing to reject the null hypothesis, however, is not proof that the null hypothesis is correct. Although there may be insufficient or inconclusive evidence in support of the alternative hypothesis, the lack of evidence cannot be used as support for the null hypothesis.

Textbox 7.2

Steps in Hypothesis Testing

1. State the null and alternative hypotheses.
2. Select alpha: the probability value for significance testing.
3. Select the appropriate test statistic.*
4. Compute the calculated value of the test statistic.
5. Find the critical value of the test statistic.
6. Compare the calculated and critical values in order to make a decision about the null and alternative hypotheses.

*So far, we have covered only one such test: the z-test.

Many factors can contribute to the nonrejection of the null hypothesis, including inadequacy of the sample being studied or measurement problems with the instruments used. Therefore, when a statistical test is nonsignificant, convention suggests that rather than a researcher accepting the null hypothesis it is more accurate to say that the researcher fails to reject the null hypothesis. There is insufficient proof regarding the treatment's efficacy rather than proof that the treatment is ineffective.

Directional and Nondirectional Alternative Hypotheses

A directional alternative hypothesis specifies the form of disagreement with the null hypothesis. For example, a directional alternative hypothesis may specify the direction of inequivalence of population parameters (e.g., H_a: $\mu_{A1} > \mu_{A2}$). Directional alternative hypotheses are also referred to as *one-tailed hypotheses*; nondirectional alternative hypotheses are also referred to as *two-tailed hypotheses*.

CD-ROM link 7.1

Activity 7.1: Directional and Nondirectional Hypotheses
What is a nondirectional hypothesis? What are the two types of directional hypotheses? The first activity in this chapter helps you to master the distinctions between these types of hypotheses and learn how to apply them in making conclusions from a statistical analysis.

Consider, for example, the three sets of hypotheses about two means (or the difference between means) given in Textbox 7.3.

The alternative hypotheses in each set are different and have important implications for the critical values used for significance testing. For Set A, the null hypothesis is rejected and the alternative hypothesis is accepted when the two population means are judged to be inequivalent, either when the mean for group A_1 is greater than the mean for A_2 or when the A_1 mean is less than the A_2 mean. For Set B, the null hypothesis is rejected and the alternative hypothesis is accepted only when the mean for A_1 is greater than the mean of A_2. For Set B, the null hypothesis is rejected and the alternative hypothesis is accepted only when the mean for A_2 is greater than the mean of A_1.

For each set of hypotheses, imagine further that alpha, the probability value used for significance testing, is .05 and that the researcher will employ the z-test even though it is not accurate for the small sample sizes used in the Devil's Advocate scenario. Whether the researcher has stipulated a directional or nondirectional alternative hypothesis affects the critical value used for significance testing. For a nondirectional alternative hypothesis for $\alpha = .05$, the critical value is ± 1.96.

Textbox 7.3

Three Sets of Hypothesis About Two Means

Set A	Set B	Set C
H_0: $\mu_{A1} = \mu_{A2}$ or $\mu_D = 0$	H_0: $\mu_{A1} \leq \mu_{A2}$ or $\mu_D \leq 0$	H_0: $\mu_{A1} \geq \mu_{A2}$ or $\mu_D \geq 0$
H_a: $\mu_{A1} \neq \mu_{A2}$ or $\mu_D \neq 0$	H_a: $\mu_{A1} > \mu_{A2}$ or $\mu_D > 0$	H_a: $\mu_{A1} < \mu_{A2}$ or $\mu_D < 0$

The researcher's calculated value must either be *larger* than +1.96 or *smaller* than −1.96 to reject the null hypothesis. For a positive directional alternative hypothesis, the critical value is +1.65. Only if the researcher's calculated value is *larger* than 1.65 should the null hypothesis be rejected. For a negative directional alternative hypothesis, the critical value is −1.65. Only if the calculated value is *smaller* than −1.65 should the null hypothesis be rejected.

Figure 7.1*a–c* illustrates the critical values and regions of rejection for each of the three alternative hypotheses. Note that for the directional alternative hypotheses, the region of rejection is concentrated in a single tail of the distribution. In contrast, the region of rejection for the nondirectional alternative hypothesis is equally divided between two tails. Therefore, so long as the mean difference is in

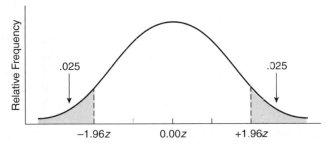

Figure 7.1*a* Regions of rejection and critical values for a two-tailed test of significance ($\alpha = .05$).

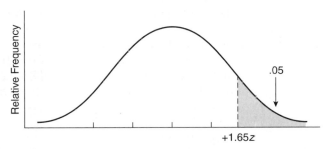

Figure 7.1*b* Region of rejection and critical value for a one-tailed positive test of significance ($\alpha = .05$).

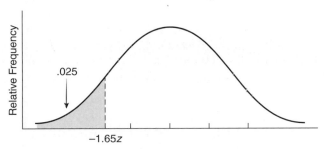

Figure 7.1*c* Region of rejection and critical value for a one-tailed negative test of significance ($\alpha = .05$).

the predicted direction, it is easier to reject the null hypothesis when the alternative hypothesis is directional than when the alternative hypothesis is nondirectional. Of course, if the mean difference is not in the predicted direction, the null hypothesis cannot be rejected in favor of a directional alternative hypothesis regardless of how large the difference is.

Note that a researcher cannot choose to evaluate each of these sets of hypotheses but must select only one in advance of data analysis. The choice of hypotheses is dictated by theoretical or practical considerations. For example, a researcher may only be interested in learning whether a new method of reading instruction improves children's reading ability and not merely whether it has a differential effect on reading performance. If the researcher cannot specify the specific nature of the alternative hypothesis, a two-tailed hypothesis should be used.

Directional alternative hypotheses cannot be stated for all research situations. For example, general or omnibus null hypotheses about *several* levels of a treatment (e.g., H_0: all μ's are equal) have associated with them nondirectional alternative hypotheses (e.g., H_a: all μ's are not equal).

Finally, the calculated value must always exceed the critical value to reject the null hypothesis. In the rare situation in which the calculated value equals the critical value, one fails to reject the null hypothesis.

Example: Devil's Advocate   Often you are not in a position to decide on the null and alternative hypothesis but to interpret what they should be. For example, you may read a research report or journal publication in order to ascertain the statistical hypotheses that should be evaluated. Similarly, you may be asked to analyze the research of others, and to do so, you will need to clarify the statistical hypotheses to be tested.

The Devil's Advocate scenario in Textbox 7.1 is an opportunity to interpret what the statistical hypotheses should be. It should be clear to you that John and Steve are comparing the mean reaction to two barbecue sauces. John believes his sauce is superior to the store-bought variety; Steve does not share this belief. Therefore, the null and alternative hypotheses are as follows:

$$H_0: \ \mu_{A1} \leq \mu_{A2} \text{ or } \mu_D \leq 0$$

$$H_a: \ \mu_{A1} > \mu_{A2} \text{ or } \mu_D > 0$$

Note that the subscript A stands for the independent variable; the type of barbecue sauce. The subscript 1 refers to the Devil's Own level, or value, of the independent variable and 2 refers to the Texas Wildfire level, or value, of the independent variable. The null hypothesis states that mean scores on the dependent measure, the subjective reaction of participants, will be the same regardless of whether the participants ate ribs prepared with the Devil's Own sauce (A_1) or Texas Wildfire sauce (A_2).

Select Alpha: The Probability Value for Significance Testing

Deciding whether to reject the null hypothesis depends on the probability that the obtained sample values could have occurred by chance. If the sample values were likely a function of chance, one will fail to reject the null hypothesis. For example, if the results of the barbecue sauce experiment in Textbox 7.1 could be readily explained by chance, one will fail to reject the null hypothesis and conclude there is insufficient evidence that John's sauce is superior to the gourmet sauce.

Researchers use the estimated sampling distribution to decide the likelihood the obtained sample values occurred by chance. Begin with the assumption that the null hypothesis is correct and use the estimated sampling distribution to determine the probability associated with the sample values actually obtained. Is the mean difference in each group of friends' reaction to the sauces indicative of a treatment effect, or is the difference more likely chance fluctuation?

Given that any sample values can occur by chance, the choice is never a certain one. What, then, is a reasonable probability level to use for significance testing? If you choose a probability value that is fairly high, you must be prepared to risk concluding that the alternative hypothesis is correct even though chance fluctuation is reasonable too. For example, if you choose $\alpha = .25$ as the significance level, you must be prepared to reject the null hypothesis when the likelihood of chance operating to create the results is anything less than 1 in 4.

Selecting large alpha values increases one's tendency to acknowledge trivial or ephemeral tendencies in the data. Unfortunately, if trivial tendencies are to lead one to reject the null hypothesis, one's ideas about what is true may fluctuate continually. Therefore, the conventional rules of hypothesis testing are conservative. Researchers use alpha values of .05 or lower (e.g., .01, .001) especially for research destined for publication. Even small sample, exploratory research or pilot studies seldom rely on alpha values higher than .10.

Decision-Making Errors   Regardless of a researcher's decision concerning the null hypothesis, that person may be wrong. There are two types of decision errors: Type I errors and Type II errors.

1. A **Type I error** occurs when the null hypothesis is rejected but it is true.
2. A **Type II error** occurs when the null hypothesis is not rejected but it is false.

Table 7.1 provides a theoretical categorization of the possible decision outcomes according to knowledge of the true state of the null hypothesis versus the researcher's statistical decision about the null hypothesis. The leftmost column shows the researcher's two possible decisions when the null hypothesis is actually true. The probability value for significance testing is alpha. **Alpha** (α) is also the

TABLE 7.1   The Decision Process and Associated Probabilities

	True State of the Null Hypothesis	
Researcher's Decision	H_0 is true	H_a is true
Fail to Reject H_0	Correctly fail to reject H_0 $(1 - \alpha)$	Type II error (β)
Reject H_0 and Accept H_a	Type I error (α)	Correctly reject H_0 $(1 - \beta)$

probability of making a Type I error or rejecting the null hypothesis when it is true. Consequently, the probability of failing to reject the null hypothesis when it is true is $1 - \alpha$.

The rightmost column shows the researcher's two possible decisions when the null hypothesis is actually false. **Beta** (β) is the probability of making a Type II error or failing to reject the null hypothesis when it is wrong. Consequently, the probability of rejecting the null hypothesis when it is false is $1 - \beta$, which is also known as the **power** of a statistical test.

The probability of making a Type I error is determined by the researcher when the level of significance or alpha (α) is specified. If alpha is specified as .05, the probability of making a Type I error is .05.

The probability of making a Type II error or beta (β), as well as power ($1 - \beta$), are determined by a number of factors:

1. The level of significance, or alpha (α)
2. The size of the sample
3. The size of within-group variability
4. The size of the (expected or actual) treatment effect
5. Whether directional or nondirectional hypotheses are specified

We will explore the consequences of both types of decision errors later in this chapter. In doing so, we hope you come to appreciate that the conventional rules of hypothesis testing may not apply with equal force in all situations nor do they engage completely the tools and logic of current statistical decision making. As a starting point for inquiry, however, these rules have served the social sciences well and will continue to do so.

Select the Appropriate Test Statistic

There are essential similarities among all statistical procedures used for hypothesis testing but there are also important differences. Therefore, a meaningful part of statistical inference is choosing the test statistic that is appropriate for the data and hypotheses to be investigated. The chapters following this one introduce you to the most often used inferential tests, including:

- The *t*-test for two independent samples
- The Oneway ANOVA for a single independent variable with two or more levels
- The factorial analysis of variance for two or more independent variables
- The *t*-test and analysis of variance tests for dependent samples
- Correlation and simple regression for determining the relationship between a single predictor variable and a single outcome variable
- Multiple regression for determining the relationship between two or more predictor variables and a single outcome variable
- Nonparametric procedures for distribution free statistical tests

Compute the Calculated Value of the Test Statistic

The **calculated, or computed, value** is a single number that is derived from the computational procedures applied to the data. In this text, we give you the derivational procedures for these calculations so that you may better appreciate the mathematical logic of each statistical test. We expect that few of you will regularly do these computations manually, especially on large datasets. The speed and ease with which computer programs compute these statistics lessens the value of your learning shortcut computational methods. Nevertheless, it is essential that you understand the logic of these tests in order to use statistical packages wisely.

Find the Critical Value of the Test Statistic

The **critical, or tabled, value** of the test statistic is that number which marks the region of rejection in the sampling distribution. It is the value that must be exceeded to reject the null hypothesis.

For example, ±1.96 is the two-tailed critical value for the z-test when alpha, the probability value for significance testing, is set at .05. The calculated value needs to exceed ±1.96 to reject the null hypothesis.

Using a one-tailed alternative hypothesis changes the critical value, although it has no effect on the calculated value. For example, $+1.65$ is the one-tailed critical value for the z-test when alpha, the probability value for significance testing, is set at .05.

Using an alpha value other than .05 changes the critical value for significance testing. For example, ±2.57 is the two-tailed critical value for the z-test when alpha is set at .01.

Finally, critical values depend on the statistical test used for analysis. Tabled values for a variety of statistical tests are appended to this text.

Compare the Calculated and Critical Values

The calculated value is compared with the critical value in order to make a decision about the null and alternative hypotheses. If the calculated value exceeds the critical value, reject the null hypothesis and accept the alternative hypothesis.

A two-tailed alternative hypothesis means that either a large negative calculated value or a large positive calculated value is needed to exceed the critical value and reject the null hypothesis. For example, if the critical value is ±1.96, a calculated value of -2.45 is sufficient to reject the null hypothesis, but a calculated value of $+1.71$ is insufficient to reject the null hypothesis.

A one-tailed alternative hypothesis means that the size and direction of the calculated values must be considered to exceed the critical value and reject the null hypothesis. For example, if the critical value is $+1.65$, a calculated value of -2.45 is insufficient to reject the null hypothesis, but a calculated value of $+1.71$ is sufficient to reject the null hypothesis. In other words, both the magnitude of the calculated value and the sign of the difference are important when a directional alternative hypothesis is being evaluated. If you have specified a directional alternative hypothesis and the findings are in the opposite direction, you may not reject the null hypothesis regardless of how substantial the findings appear.

Most computer programs for statistical analyses provide the exact probabilities associated with a calculated value. For example, the calculated value +3.00 has a two-tailed probability of .0026 when the z-test is used. The exact probabilities associated with a computed value allow you to make a judgment about null and alternative hypotheses. If the probability value for nondirectional significance testing was set at $p < .05$, the null hypothesis would be rejected because the actual probability of the calculated value (i.e., .0026) is smaller than the critical value (i.e., .05).

An Important Caveat on the Six Steps in Hypothesis Testing

The six steps in hypothesis testing are meant to be followed in sequence. Doing otherwise risks the integrity of the research and may capitalize on chance, yielding spurious findings and unscientific conclusions. In particular, avoid the temptation to modify hypotheses, to choose post hoc among test statistics according to whether they are significant or not, and to alter alpha values to fit the findings. For example, if you argue in advance for the use of a two-tailed hypothesis evaluated at the .05 level of significance, it is not acceptable to modify the nature of the hypothesis or the significance level after the data are analyzed to uncover a "significant" result. Exploratory analyses may be acceptable for preliminary investigations but they have little if any place in carefully designed final investigations. Don't play with the data and your analyses and "fudge" the findings.

Devil's Advocate Example

Let us see whether you can apply the six steps in hypothesis testing to the Devil's Advocate scenario of Textbox 6.1. To do so you need to review and include some of the basic concepts in sampling distributions and the z-test so that you can apply them here.

CD-ROM link 7.2

Activity 7.2: Null and Alternative Distributions
In Activity 7.2, you can put your new knowledge about hypothesis testing to the test! After drawing two samples and comparing their means, you have to decide whether you can reject the null hypothesis. Then, find out if your decision was correct by checking the actual population mean difference.

A Very Brief Review of Sampling Distributions and the z-Test   In Chapter 6 we introduced you to the sampling distribution and the idea that hypothesis testing is begun by making the assumption that the null hypothesis is true. For example, if you begin with the assumption that the null hypothesis is correct, then you begin by assuming that there is no real difference in mean reactions to the barbecue sauces (or the difference is opposite to your prediction). That is, if the null hypothesis is correct,

$\mu_{A1} \leq \mu_{A2}$, the mean population difference in reactions is zero (or negative). We also showed you how to use the results of a single experiment to estimate the variance and standard deviation of the sampling distribution of mean differences. In particular, the estimated standard error of mean differences is as follows:

$$(\text{Equation 6.22}) \; s_D = \sqrt{\frac{s_{A1}^2}{n_{A1}} + \frac{s_{A2}^2}{n_{A2}}}$$

Once you have estimated the mean and standard error of the sampling distribution you can conduct a significance test, the z-test, to determine the likelihood that the observed sample mean difference is attributable to chance fluctuation. In particular, one of several formulas for the z-test is as follows:

$$(\text{Equation 6.23}) \; \text{Estimated } z_D = \frac{\overline{Y}_{A1} - \overline{Y}_{A2}}{s_D}$$

As you can see, z_D is a ratio with the mean difference in the numerator and the standard error in the denominator. This ratio, therefore, allows one to estimate how many standard deviation units the observed mean difference is from an estimated population mean difference of zero under the null hypothesis.

CD-ROM link 7.3

Problem Generator 7: The z-Test
To practice hypothesis testing using a z-test, select z-test from the Problem Generator Menu on the CD-ROM. The Problem Generator will create as many practice problems as you need, and will demonstrate each step in their solution so that you can check your work.

Conducting the z-Test   Let us now apply what is known about sampling distributions and the z-test by using the Devil's Advocate scenario from Textbox 7.1, following the steps in hypothesis testing as shown in Textbox 7.4.

You can use the table of the normal distribution to find the exact probability associated with the calculated value in Textbox 7.4. Given that the alternative hypothesis is directional, the exact probability of a z-score of 1.22 or larger is .1112.

Illustrating the Findings   Figure 7.2 illustrates the estimated null sampling distribution showing the critical value, which divides the distribution into two regions: fail to reject H_0 and reject H_0. In this estimated sampling distribution, given that it is the null distribution, start with the assumption that the estimated population mean difference is zero (or negative). You know that due to sampling error not all sample mean differences will be zero; some sample mean differences will be negative, others will be positive.

The calculated value of z, or the ratio of the obtained mean difference divided by the standard error, can be located on the null sampling distribution. Judging from its location as either far or near from zero, one would be hard pressed or not to reject the null hypothesis.

It is apparent from an examination of Figure 7.2 that the calculated value is not in the region of rejection. Therefore, you should fail to reject the null hypothesis.

Steps in Hypothesis Testing for the Devil's Advocate Scenario

1. State the null and alternative hypotheses:

$$H_0: \mu_{A1} \le \mu_{A2} \text{ or } \mu_D \le 0$$

$$H_a: \mu_{A1} > \mu_{A2} \text{ or } \mu_D > 0$$

2. Select alpha, the probability value for significance testing:

.05

3. Select the appropriate test statistic:

z-test

4. Compute the calculated value of the test statistic:

$$z_D = \cfrac{\overline{Y}_{A1} - \overline{Y}_{A2}}{\sqrt{\cfrac{\dfrac{\sum (Y_{iA1} - \overline{Y}_{A1})^2}{(n_{A1} - 1)}}{n_{A1}} + \cfrac{\dfrac{\sum (Y_{iA2} - \overline{Y}_{A2})^2}{(n_{A2} - 1)}}{n_{A2}}}} = \cfrac{8.00 - 7.00}{\sqrt{\dfrac{\dfrac{10.00}{5}}{6} + \dfrac{\dfrac{10.00}{5}}{6}}} = \cfrac{+1.00}{.82} = +1.22$$

We used Equation 6.25 so that we could show the intermediate values used in the calculations.

5. Find the critical value of the test statistic:

+1.65 (One-tailed region of rejection.)

6. Compare the calculated and critical values in order to make a decision about the null and alternative hypotheses.

The calculated value (+1.22) is not larger than the critical value (+1.65). Therefore, one fails to reject the null hypothesis. In failing to reject the null hypothesis, a Type II error may have been committed.

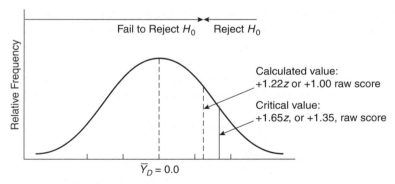

Figure 7.2 Estimated null sampling distribution showing calculated and critical values for Devil's Advocate scenario (one-tailed test)

The critical and calculated values can also be shown in raw-score form by multiplying each z-score by the standard error of the mean differences (s_D). The raw score of the critical value is $+1.65s_D$, or $+1.65(0.82)$, $= 1.35$; the raw score of the calculated value is $+1.22s_D$, or $+1.22(.82) = +1.00$, which is the obtained mean difference.

z-TEST INTERVAL ESTIMATION

In Chapter 6, we gave the general formula for estimating the confidence interval for the z-test. For a two-sided confidence interval the true population mean difference, μ_D, will fall in the range between:

$$\textbf{(Equation 6.28)} \quad \overline{Y}_D - z_{1-\alpha/2}s_D \text{ and } \overline{Y}_D + z_{1-\alpha/2}s_D$$

This formula is appropriate for a nondirectional, or two-tailed, alternative hypothesis. With a nondirectional alternative hypothesis, researchers are concerned with identifying the confidence limit both above and below the estimated population parameter.

One-Sided Confidence Intervals

In contrast, for a directional, or one-tailed, alternative hypothesis, researchers are interested in finding the one-sided confidence interval (Kirk, 1990). For example, with a *positive* directional alternative hypothesis (e.g., $\mu_{A1} > \mu_{A2}$), researchers are interested in finding the interval between the estimated population parameter to some point *below* it. If the interval contains zero (0.0), they fail to reject the null hypothesis. In contrast, with a *negative* directional alternative hypothesis (e.g., $\mu_{A1} < \mu_{A2}$), researchers are interested in finding the interval between the estimated population parameter to some point *above* it. Similarly, if the interval contains zero (0.0), they also fail to reject the null hypothesis.

For a one-sided confidence interval when the alternative hypothesis is *positive*, the true population mean difference, μ_D, will fall in the range between:

$$\textbf{Equation 7.1:} \quad \overline{Y}_D - z_{1-\alpha}s_D$$

For a one-sided confidence interval when the alternative hypothesis *is negative*, the true population mean difference, μ_D, will fall in the range between:

$$\textbf{Equation 7.2:} \quad \overline{Y}_D + z_{1-\alpha}s_D$$

An important difference between the formulas for the one-sided confidence intervals and the two-sided confidence interval is the critical value of z. See Textbox 7.5 for an illustration of a one-sided confidence interval using the Devil's Advocate scenario of Textbox 7.1.

Textbox 7.5

One-Sided Confidence Interval for Devil's Advocate Scenario

Note the null and alternative hypotheses, the latter of which is a positive direction hypothesis:

$$H_0: \mu_{A1} \leq \mu_{A2} \text{ or } \mu_D \leq 0$$
$$H_a: \mu_{A1} > \mu_{A2} \text{ or } \mu_D > 0$$

Consequently, computation of a one-sided confidence interval will be wanted:

$$\overline{Y}_D - z_{1-a}s_D = +1.00 - (1.65)(.82) = +1.00 \text{ to } -.35 \text{ or } -.35 \leq \mu_D \leq 1.00.$$

In addition to the z-test, one can also use the one-sided confidence interval for hypothesis testing. Because the confidence interval contains zero (0.0), one fails to reject the null hypothesis.

STATISTICAL POWER

Beta (β) is the probability of making a Type II error or failing to reject the null hypothesis when it is false. In contrast, **statistical power, or $1 - \beta$,** is the probability of rejecting a false null hypothesis. You will want, therefore, the power of your statistical tests to be high so that the probability of making a Type II error is small. Keeping these definitions in mind, we are ready to explore the idea of power further and discuss ways to estimate it.

What follows is a general discussion of statistical power with illustrations for the standard normal distribution and the z-test. The logic we illustrate here applies to the various statistical tests covered in this book and elsewhere and is of basic importance. However, the particular calculations may vary, depending on the statistical test chosen for data analysis.

The Alternative Distribution

So far, we have concentrated on the null sampling distribution or the distribution of sample mean differences we expect to find under the assumption that the null hypothesis is true and that the population mean difference is zero (i.e., the treatment does not work). But if the null hypothesis is not true, then there must be a sampling distribution associated with the alternative hypothesis for which the population mean difference is not zero (i.e., the treatment does work).

That is, there is a sampling distribution under the alternative hypothesis that has an overall mean difference not equal to zero and a standard error. Furthermore, like the sampling distribution under the null hypothesis, the sampling distribution under the alternative hypothesis includes sample mean differences that vary in size and direction. Finally, the **alternative sampling distribution,** like the null sampling distribution, approaches the form of a normal distribution as sample size N increases.

In choosing between two hypotheses, the null hypothesis and the alternative hypothesis, you are deciding which of the two distributions, the null and alternative distributions, are correct representations of the true influence of the treatment.

Figure 7.3 illustrates hypothetical null and alternative sampling distributions superimposed on one another. The leftmost distribution is the null sampling distribution. The horizontal line is located 1.65 standard errors from the mean (zero) of the distribution corresponding to a directional alternative hypothesis and $\alpha = .05$. The small area to the right of the critical value is the region of rejection (α). The large area to the left of the line is the region of nonrejection $(1 - \alpha)$.

The rightmost distribution is the alternative sampling distribution. Note that it is displaced to the side of the null sampling distribution under the assumption that if the alternative hypothesis is true, then the population mean difference is greater than zero (i.e., the treatment does work). The critical value from the null sampling distribution also divides the alternative sampling distribution into two regions. The shaded area on the left is beta (β) and reflects the probability of making a Type II error. The unshaded area of the alternative sampling distribution is $1 - \beta$ and reflects the probability of rejecting the null hypothesis when it is false. In this illustration, it is clear that the probability of making a Type I error is much smaller than making a Type II error.

The challenge we now face is to estimate both the null and alternative sampling distributions. We have covered how to do so for the null sampling distribution. We will now show how to do this for the alternative sampling distribution so that we can estimate the Type II error rate and power.

If you assume that the alternative hypothesis is correct and then estimate the population mean difference, you can estimate the likelihood of correctly rejecting the null hypothesis. This estimated probability is based partly on your ability to locate the score associated with the critical value from the null sampling distribution on the alternative sampling distribution.

Furthermore, you can estimate power either for research already conducted or for research that is planned. That is, you can estimate power for the study just completed using the sample data for your estimates and answer the question: "What *was* the power of the statistical test to reject the null hypothesis?" Knowing the power of the statistical test you have just conducted affects your confidence in

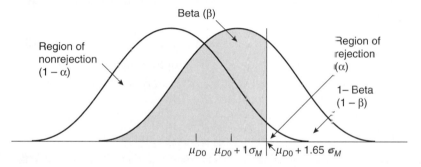

Figure 7.3 Null (leftmost) and alternative (rightmost) sampling distributions

the research findings; one loses confidence when statistical power is low and gains confidence when power is high.

Alternately, you can estimate the power for a study you are planning using prior research or a pilot study and answer the question: "What *will be* the power of the statistical test to reject the null hypothesis?" Knowing the power of a planned investigation helps you determine whether you can be confident in the methodology or whether you need to modify it. For example, you may be convinced to increase the sample size of a planned study to achieve a desired power.

Steps in Estimating Power

There are five steps in estimating power. They are summarized in Textbox 7.6 and explained below.

Estimate the Population Mean Difference for the Alternative Sampling Distribution ($\bar{Y}_{DA}$)

Sometimes you may use the results of research already conducted to determine an estimate of the population mean difference for the alternative sampling distribution. Other times you may need to take an informed guess. In either case, remember that your estimate of the population mean difference under the null sampling distribution is zero.

The informed guess of the population mean difference for the alternative distribution should be done carefully. Guessing too small a mean difference artificially decreases the estimated power of the test, while guessing too large a mean difference artificially increases the estimated power of the test. In certain circumstances, the mean difference might be known from theory or prior research, including either published research or a pilot investigation. In other circumstances, specifying a practically meaningful mean difference might be desirable.

Estimate the Standard Error of the Alternative Sampling Distribution (S_{da})

You can estimate the standard error of the alternative sampling distribution from the investigation you have already conducted, whether that's a pilot

---

Textbox 7.6

Steps in Estimating Power

1. Estimate the population mean difference for the alternative sampling distribution ($\bar{Y}_{DA}$).
2. Estimate the standard error of the alternative sampling distribution (s_{DA}).
3. Find the critical value for the null sampling distribution and convert it to a raw score (CV_R).
4. Compute z_A from CV_R.
5. Find beta (β) and power ($1 - \beta$) by finding the exact probability of z_A.

study to help you plan your primary investigation or the principal study itself. This estimate will be the same as the standard error estimated for the null sampling distribution. You have now estimated the mean of the alternative sampling distribution and estimated its standard deviation. Given reasonably large sample sizes, you also know that the alternative sampling distribution, like the null sampling distribution, is normally distributed according to the central limit theorem. Thus, using what you know about the normal distribution you can find various areas under both the null and alternative sampling distributions.

Why Are the Estimated Standard Errors of the Null and Alternative Hypotheses the Same? Remember that one assumes that the variability of the scores *within* a group is a function of chance. Furthermore, if the null hypothesis is correct, one assumes that the variability of the scores *among* the groups is also a function of chance, because participants were randomly assigned to the groups. In contrast, if the treatment worked, one would expect a treatment effect in addition to some chance fluctuation among the groups.

The standard deviation of the sampling distribution of mean differences is a measure of sampling error. It is assumed not to change, whether the treatment truly has an effect or truly has no effect. Therefore, you can estimate the standard error of the sampling distribution of the alternative distribution from your estimate of the standard error of the sampling distribution of the null distribution.

Find the Critical Value for the Null Sampling Distribution and Convert It to a Raw Score (CV_R)
There are two steps in computing CV_R:

1. Find the critical value.

Using the tabled values of the normal distribution, find the critical value(s) associated with the alpha selected for significance testing There is a directional, or one-tailed, alternative hypothesis in the Devil's Advocate scenario (see Textbox 7.1). Given $\alpha = .05$ for this one-tailed test, the critical value is $+1.65$.

If, however, the alternative hypothesis is two-tailed, use the critical value for one tail only. For example, given $\alpha = .05$ for a two-tailed test, use the critical value $+1.96$.

Note the difference between the critical values for the one-tailed and two-tailed tests. It is easier to reject the null hypothesis with a one-tailed test than a two-tailed test when the mean differences are in the right direction. Therefore, the one-tailed test will be more powerful.

2. Convert the critical value to a raw score.

Remember that the critical value is a point on the standard normal distribution (which has a mean of 0.0 and a standard deviation of 1.0), and so you can treat the critical value as a z-score. We have already presented a formula for converting z-scores to raw scores, which we can press into service here:

$$\textbf{(Equation 5.3) } Y_i = \overline{Y} + z_i s$$

In this situation $\overline{Y} = 0.0$ because it is the expected mean for the null sampling distribution; s in this situation is an estimated standard deviation but of the null sampling distribution of mean differences (and therefore one should substitute the symbol s_D):

$$CV_R = +z_{1-\alpha}(s_D)$$

For example, with the Devil's Advocate scenario, $z_{1-\alpha}(s_D) = +1.65(.82) = +1.35$. We will call this the *critical value expressed as a raw score* (CV_R).

Compute z_A from CV_R   Now that you have calculated CV_R, you need to locate this score on the alternative sampling distribution. This is also a two-step procedure:

1. Find the difference between CV_R and the expected population mean difference of the alternative sampling distribution:

$$CV_R - \overline{Y}_D$$

2. Divide the difference by the standard error. In effect, you compute another z-score (z_A) but for the alternative sampling distribution. Furthermore, because you have converted CV_R to a z-score you are once again dealing with a standard normal distribution with mean 0.0 and standard deviation 1.0.

$$z_A = \frac{CV_R - \overline{Y}_D}{s_D}$$

For the Devil's Advocate scenario:

$$\frac{+1.35 - 1.00}{.82} = +.43$$

What does z_A represent? It is the critical value from the null distribution located as a point on the standardized alternative distribution. If the critical value CV_R were changed, the point where z_A is located on the standardized alternative distribution would also be changed. For example, if you decreased the value of alpha (e.g., from .05 to .01) used for significance testing, the point z_A located on the standardized alternative distribution would be farther away from the center of the distribution and more toward the tail. Why? Because CV_R is a larger value.

Similarly, if you changed the expected mean difference for the alternative sampling distribution, you would also change the value of z_A and hence its location on the standardized alternative distribution. For example, if you increased the expected mean difference (e.g., from $+1.00$ to $+3.00$), z_A would be -2.01.

Find Beta and Power $(1 - \beta)$ You can now find the exact probability associated with z_A by using the tabled values of the standard normal distribution in

Appendix A. The probability associated with the area of the normal curve *below* z_A is your estimate of β. In addition, the area of the normal curve *above* z_A, or $1 - \beta$, is the power of the statistical test you have performed.

Example Power Calculations: Devil's Advocate Scenario

We will use the data from the Devils' Advocate scenario to calculate the Type II error rate and power. See Textbox 7.7 for the calculations. Remember that these calculations are given for illustration purposes only. Because we are using unusually small sample sizes to make calculations easier, we tend to overestimate the power of the statistical test.

In this example, the probability of making a Type I error is equal to α, which is .05. In contrast, the probability of making a Type II error is equal to β, which is .67, many times the size of α. The two sampling distributions that have been estimated are illustrated in Figure 7.4 with the regions associated with Type I and Type II errors.

Finally, Table 7.2 gives the decision process and associated probabilities for the Devil's Advocate scenario with the researcher's decision in bold. The estimate of statistical power (β) is only .33.

Textbox 7.7

Example Power Calculations: Devil's Advocate Scenario

1. Estimate the expected population mean difference for the alternative sampling distribution ($\overline{Y}_{DA}$):

$$\overline{Y}_{DA} = +1.00$$

2. Estimate the standard error of the alternative sampling distribution (s_{DA}):

$s_{DA} = .82$ (equal to the standard error of the null sampling distribution)

3. Find the critical value for the null sampling distribution and convert it to a raw score (CV_R):

$$CV_R = +z_{1-\alpha}(s_D) = +1.65(.82) = +1.35$$

4. Compute z_A:

$$z_A = [CV_R - \overline{Y}_{DA}]/s_D = (+1.35 - 1.00)/.82 = +.43$$

5. Find beta and power ($1 - \beta$):

$$\beta = p(z_A) = .50 + .1664 = .6664 \qquad 1 - \beta = .3336$$

How did we locate z_A? If z_A was 0.00, it would be in the center and be equal to the mean of this standard normal distribution. But it is larger than the mean, and so $p(z_A) = .50 + .1664$.

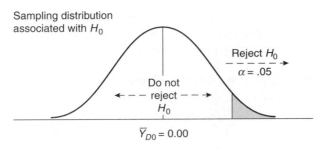

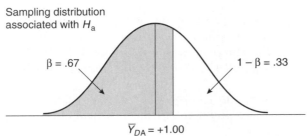

Figure 7.4 Estimated null and alternative sampling distributions for Devil's Advocate scenario

TABLE 7.2 The Decision Process and Associated Probabilities: Devil's Advocate Example

Researcher's Decision	True State of the Null Hypothesis	
	H_0 is true	H_a is true
Fail to Reject H_0	**Correctly Fail to Reject H_0 (1 − α, or .95)**	**Type II error (β, or .67)**
Reject H_0 and Accept H_a	Type I error (α, or .05)	Correctly reject H_0 (1 − β, or 0.33)

INTERPRETATION AND GUIDELINES FOR ACCEPTABLE STATISTICAL POWER

In conducting a statistical test of significance, like the z-test, researchers control the probability of making a Type I error by selecting a p-value for significance testing. Controlling the probability of making a Type II error is not as straightforward as controlling the probability of a Type I error because there are several factors that affect it, including alpha level, sample size, the magnitude of the treatment effect, the size of within-group variability, and the use of directional hypotheses.

Traditionally, the choice of probability values for significance testing considers the consequences of making a Type I error. In medical research, for example, serious consequences can result from incorrectly concluding that a new medication fails to produce undesirable side effects. In this circumstance, there is a tangible consequence of a Type I error and, therefore, researchers often select values of alpha that are quite small (e.g., .001 or smaller).

CD-ROM link 7.4

Activity 7.3: Power
An important part of planning a statistical analysis involves verifying that your experiment has sufficient power to detect the effect you are interested in. This activity will let you vary four different aspects of an experiment (alpha level, sample size, treatment effect size, and within-group variability) so that you can see the effect of each aspect on the experiment's power.

In social science research there are circumstances in which a Type I error is clearly to be avoided and alpha is set commensurately low. For example, serious consequences can result when it is erroneously concluded that novel educational interventions or innovative psychological treatments do not have undesirable consequences.

In other situations the negative consequences of making a Type I error may be less obvious. In addition, there are circumstances under which the consequences of making a Type II error also may be serious. For example, testing either competing theoretical propositions or practical interventions of equal import may not be well served by research of low power. The high likelihood of failing to reject the null hypothesis when it is false may be frustrating to the researcher and may cause problems for both the theoretician and the policymaker.

The ideal solution is to arrange research to minimize the probability of making either types of decision errors—the best of both worlds. Practically, however, research situations may not allow a person complete control over statistical power. For example, access to additional participants may be impossible or impractical.

There is not yet widespread agreement concerning levels of statistical power for social science research. Jacob Cohen (1988), one of the leading advocates of power analysis, recommends that the desirable level of power be .80.

Estimating the Power of Your Research

In advance of conducting a full investigation, it is desirable to estimate statistical power and note whether conditions have been optimized for avoiding decision errors. This is one of the strengths of conducting a pilot study. Pilot studies allow you to estimate treatment effects and within-group variability in the context in which the investigation will occur. Failing that, you may use published research and reports of similar investigations and make an attempt at estimating the power of your investigation from treatment effects and the amount of variability you may expect in the dependent measure.

Ways to Increase Statistical Power

We previously listed five ways to affect the power of statistical tests:

1. The level of significance or alpha (α)
2. Whether directional or nondirectional hypotheses are specified
3. The size of the sample
4. The size of within-group variability
5. The size of the expected treatment effect

Level of Significance   The probability value used for significance testing, or alpha level, has an effect on power. By decreasing the size of alpha (e.g., from .05 to .01), the value of the critical value used for significance testing also increases. This makes the size of CV_R larger, and reduces the size of z_A. Consequently, reducing alpha increases beta, adversely affecting power, and vice versa.

It is generally not a good idea to increase the power of a statistical test by increasing the size of alpha (e.g., from .05 to .10). It is preferable to seek other ways to increase the power of a statistical test than by degrading the test's ability to prevent Type I errors.

Directional Alternative Hypotheses   The size of the critical value is smaller when directional alternative hypotheses are specified than when nondirectional alternative hypotheses are specified. For example, when $\alpha = .05$, the critical value for the z-test is ±1.96 for a nondirectional hypothesis but only $+1.65$ (or -1.65) for a directional hypothesis. The smaller the critical value of the test, the higher the power of the test.

Researchers should avoid changing the nature of the alternative hypothesis solely to increase statistical power. The nature of the alternative hypothesis should be dictated by theory or situational concerns and not adjusted to meet statistical criteria.

Sample Size   Often the easiest way to increase the power of a statistical test is to increase sample size. Recall that the standard error is a function of sample size; the larger the size of the sample, the smaller the standard error. The size of the standard error affects the size of the calculated value of the statistical test as well as CV_R and z_A.

Noticeable increases in power can be obtained when additions are made to small sample sizes. For example, consider the effects on the Devil's Advocate scenario if the size of each barbecue sauce group were increased from 6 to 12 tasters but all other factors were kept constant. If all other things remained the same, including the magnitude of the expected mean difference ($+1.00$), the doubling of sample size would reduce s_D from .82 to .58. The critical value CV_R would be $+.96$, and z_A would be $-.04$. Beta (β), or $p (z_A)$, would be $.5000 - .0160 = .4840$; power, or $1 - \beta$, would be .5160.

Otherwise, the calculated value of the significance test would rise from $+1.22$ to $+1.72$. Where you previously failed to reject the null hypothesis, you would now reject it because the calculated value ($+1.72$) grew larger than the critical value ($+1.65$).

Estimating Sample Sizes from Pilot Studies   It is often the case that researchers will use the results of pilot investigations to estimate the sample size they will need for their main investigation. Under these circumstances, researchers no longer have to use a guess as to the mean difference they expect to find but can use the mean difference obtained in the pilot study.

The formula for determining the appropriate sample size *for each group (n)* is given by the following:

Equation 7.3: $n = \dfrac{(s^2_{A1} - s^2_{A2})(z_\beta - z_\alpha)^2}{(\overline{Y}_{A1} - \overline{Y}_{A2})^2}$

where:

s^2 = estimate of the population variance for each group

z_β = standard score in the alternative distribution corresponding to z_α for the desired power (use one tail only)

z_α = critical value in the null sampling distribution (use one tail only if the test is two-tailed.)

See Textbox 7.8 for an illustration of sample size estimates for the Devil's Advocate scenario.

Otherwise, tables to estimate sample size for desired power are in Cohen (1988).

Within-Groups Variability   The variability among participants in a group, or within-groups variability, affects the size of the standard error and thus the power of a statistical test. The greater the within-groups variability in scores on the dependent variable, the greater the size of the standard error and the lower the power of the test.

Extraneous or unaccounted influences may be responsible for this unwanted variability and can be controlled experimentally or statistically in some cases. For

---

Textbox 7.8

Example of Sample Size Estimates for a Desired Power Using the Devil's Advocate Scenario

Treat the results of the Devil's Advocate scenario as if it were the pilot study for a larger investigation. Follow Cohen's (1988) recommendation and set desired power $(1 - \beta)$ at .80.

The two z-scores may seem difficult to locate.

Remember that, z_α is the critical value in the null sampling distribution that will need to be exceeded in order for the null hypothesis to be rejected. For the one-tailed directional hypothesis, $z_\alpha = +1.65$.

On the other hand, z_β is the critical value of the alternative sampling distribution for a desired power of .80. That portion at or above this critical value represents 80% of the scores in the alternative sampling distribution $(1 - \beta)$, and the portion below this critical value represents 20% of the scores in the alternative sampling distribution (β).

Therefore, $z_\beta = -.84$.

$$n = \frac{(s^2_{A1} + s^2_{A2})(z_\beta - z_\alpha)^2}{(\overline{Y}_{A1} - \overline{Y}_{A2})^2} = \frac{(2 + 2)(-.84 - 1.65)^2}{(8.00 - 7.00)^2} = 24.80$$

Based on the results of the pilot study, approximately 25 participants will be needed in each group for a total of 50 participants to achieve a desired power of .80 in the main investigation.

example, imagine that some of the differences among barbecue sauce ratings were attributable to age differences in the participants, with younger participants giving lower ratings to sauces they did not perceive as sweet. Within-groups variability could be reduced by studying only older adults, which changes the population to which one can generalize, or by incorporating age as a predictor variable in the design.

Within-groups variability can also be reduced by changing the dependent measure used in the investigation or otherwise improving the psychometric quality of the measuring instrument. Excessive within-groups variability can be a signal of poor instrumentation, which can compromise the sensitivity of the statistical test.

Investigations in which only a small amount of variability is attributable to unwanted factors are considered precise. The consequence of such precision is that the researcher is able to detect treatment effects with relatively few observations, while those involving large within-groups variability may require many observations to attain the same degree of power.

Expected Treatment Effect   The size of the treatment effect that the researcher guesses or expects affects the power of the statistical test. All other things equal, the greater the difference among the groups one expects to find, the higher the power of the test to detect those differences. Hays (1994) likens the situation to explorations with a microscope. The microscope's ability to detect gaps in an apparently solid material is made easier when those gaps are as large as possible than when they are small. If you expect to find small gaps, the microscope needs to use high resolution. If you expect to find large gaps, the microscope needs to use low resolution. In other words, it's easier to detect large differences than small ones, so power increases as the size of the expected treatment effect increases.

Another way to consider the influence of the expected treatment effect is to remember the definition of Type II error. A Type II error occurs when the null hypothesis is not rejected but it is false. If you expect a large treatment effect, it follows that you should miss it less frequently than when you expect a small treatment effect.

In the Devil's Advocate scenario in Textbox 7.1, John's guess of a mean difference of 1.0 between his sauce and the store sauce was used. If John had expected a larger difference, power would have been greater. Table 7.3 shows the effect of three different expected mean differences on power in the Devil's Advocate scenario.

TABLE 7.3 Type II Error Rates and Power for Different Expected Mean Differences in the Devil's Advocate Scenario

$\overline{Y}_{DA}$	$+1.00$	$+2.00$	$+3.00$
s_D	.82	.82	.82
CV_R	$+1.35$	$+1.35$	$+1.35$
z_A	$+.43$	$-.79$	-2.01
β	.67	.21	.02
$1-\beta$	.33	.79	.98

Other Considerations

There are two other, related issues we wish to address briefly. The first is a consideration of the choice of the statistical test as it affects power. The second is a consideration of the effect of assumption violations and their influence on power.

Choice of Statistical Tests   It is important to note that the selection of the statistical test used for hypothesis testing can affect power. The majority of the statistical tests we will cover in this text are referred to as *parametric tests* and are among the most powerful statistical tests one can employ. Other statistical tests, called *nonparametric,* or *distribution-free, statistical tests,* are generally less powerful alternatives and we cover them only briefly later in the book. Distribution-free tests are useful when the data to be analyzed are on less than an interval scale of measurement or when the researcher is not confident that the assumptions of the parametric test (e.g., error variability is normally distributed) have been satisfied.

Assumptions and Assumption Violations   Most parametric statistics assume three things: (1) population cases or observations are randomly sampled or experimental conditions are randomly assigned to the cases such that they are independent; (2) the population cases or observations are normally distributed; and (3) the null hypothesis is true. Of course, the null hypothesis is advanced tentatively in the hope that it will be rejected. A fourth assumption is required by some test statistics if the null hypothesis concerns two or more populations—that the population variances are equal or homogeneous.

The parametric tests we cover in this book are not only powerful but generally robust to assumption violations. That means that even though these tests make certain assumptions, they are not greatly affected when the assumptions are not entirely met. We will cover the assumptions in greater detail as we deal with particular statistical tests and show ways to test for assumption violations as well as procedures for reducing their influence.

The effects of assumption violations can be to modify the rate of both Type I and Type II errors from what the researcher expected. When the assumptions of the statistical test are completely met, the actual or empirical probability of Type I and Type II errors is the same as the nominal probability of Type I and Type II errors. However, when the assumptions of the statistical tests are not met, and especially when they are strongly violated, the actual or empirical probability of Type I and Type II errors will be different from the nominal probability of Type I and Type II errors.

For example, a researcher may elect to test the difference between two group means using the z-test with $\alpha = .05$ for a nondirectional alternative hypothesis. However, the variances of the two groups are strikingly different. Because of this marked difference in variances, the real probability of the researcher falsely rejecting the null hypothesis is not .05 but much higher (e.g., .10 or more). At the same time as the empirical rate of making a Type I error increases, the empirical rate of making a Type II error decreases. Because of the assumption violation, the power of the test to detect differences has grown and it may be overly sensitive to group differences. In other words, by violating an important assumption of the test, the researcher may unwittingly have increased the chances of reaching the wrong conclusion either by making the test too liberal or by making the test too conservative.

Statisticians have studied the effects of assumption violations on the empirical probability of making Type I and Type II errors (see, for example, Keselman, Lix, & Kowalchuk, 1998). From these investigations, procedures and guidelines have been developed either for adjusting the statistical tests when it is appropriate to do so or for recommending nonparametric procedures.

EFFECT SIZE AND PRACTICAL IMPORTANCE

Tests of significance tell us whether a nonchance relationship among variables is likely but do not tell us the magnitude of the relationship. Consequently, it is inappropriate to imply a large effect or use the phrase "very significant" when the exact probability of a calculated value is very small.

One of the consequences of significance testing is that power is often low when sample size is small. Under such circumstances, seemingly large effects (e.g., differences among means) can be dismissed as insignificant. Conversely, very small effects can be found significant when sample size is large.

Many researchers, especially those with applied or practical concerns, want to know more than whether there is a nonchance relationship between the independent and dependent variable and more than whether the treatment "worked." Researchers wish to know the magnitude of the relationship between the independent and dependent variable, the size of the treatment effect, or how much the treatment "worked."

The Effect Size

The magnitude of the difference between means is a useful index of the strength of a treatment effect but it does not allow ready comparison across contexts or multiple research findings where different measurement methods may be employed and differences in the degree of chance or unexplained variability may be operative. One needs a standard or common measure.

Cohen (1988) derived such a common statistic and called it the **effect size,** represented by the symbol d, which is a variant of the z-score.

$$\text{Equation 7.4: } d = \frac{\overline{Y}_{A1} - \overline{Y}_{A2}}{s}$$

where s is either the unbiased standard deviation of the control group or the pooled standard deviation.

Cohen (1988) also categorized effect sizes according to their magnitude:

- An effect size around .20 is a small effect.
- An effect size around .50 is a medium effect.
- An effect size around .80 is a large effect.

It is also possible to interpret d as one would a z-score by converting d to a percentile rank. For example, a d of $+1.00$ places the average experimental group participant one standard deviation above the mean or at the 84th percentile of the control group. Interestingly, in analyzing published research, Cohen (1988) found few studies in which d was large.

Effect Size Calculation for the Devil's Advocate Scenario

See Textbox 7.9 for an illustration of the effect size calculation for the Devil's Advocate scenario.

Effect Sizes and Power

There is a relationship between effect size and power. The larger the effect size, other things being equal, the greater the power of the test. Cohen (1988) provides tables for estimating power for various effect sizes, sample sizes, and alpha levels.

These tables are a convenient alternative to the computational procedures we covered earlier. In addition, power curves are also available that graphically represent the relationship among effect sizes, power, and sample sizes for different alpha levels.

Figure 7.5 is a power curve for a two-tailed alternative hypothesis for $\alpha = .05$. It shows groups sample sizes (n) ranging from 8 to 1000. It shows effect sizes from $+.1$ to $+1.4$. Imagine you had computed the effect size ($d = +.7$) and knew the sample size ($n = 15$). What is the estimated power of the statistical test? Reading from the graph, notice that power is approximately $+.45$.

You can also use the power curves to estimate the group sample size you need. To use the curves you will need to estimate the effect size and suggest a desired power, which you should want to be .80 or higher.

Is John Correct?

In concluding the scenario that began this chapter we asked whether John was right that his Devil's Own barbecue sauce was superior to the gourmet brand. In attempting to answer the question, we have elaborated on statistical hypothesis

---

Textbox 7.9

Effect Size for the Devil's Advocate Scenario

$$d = \frac{\overline{Y}_{A1} - \overline{Y}_{A2}}{s} = \frac{8.00 - 7.00}{1.41} = +.71$$

The size of d is between a medium and large effect.

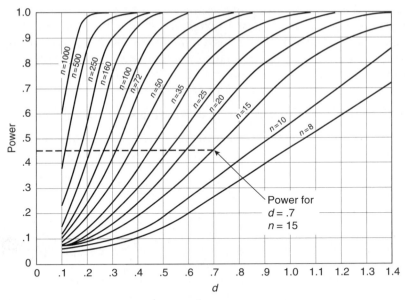

Figure 7.5 Power curves for nondirectional alternative hypothesis and ($\alpha = .05$). (*Source:* Cohen (1988). Figure appears in: Minium, King, & Bear (1993). *Statistical reasoning in Psychology and Education.* (3rd. Ed.) New York: John Wiley & Sons, p. 368.)

testing, confidence intervals, the alternative distribution and power, and effect sizes. Hopefully, you have learned enough to form a cogent answer to the question.

First, the results of the experiment were such that we failed to reject the null hypothesis; the z-test was not significant and our large, one-sided confidence interval included zero (0.0). Second, our estimate of power was not acceptable at .36, based, in part, on John's guess regarding the extent his sauce would be superior to store bought. Third, d was +.71, somewhere between a medium and large effect.

Therefore, one cannot conclude with any confidence that John is right. But one cannot say that he is wrong either. In particular, we have noted the size of the one-sided confidence interval and the magnitude of the effect size. The former suggest that if one were able to reduce the size of the standard error, especially by increasing sample size, one might get both a significant and moderately large effect in a more ambitious investigation.

Store executives might want to be in touch with John. In the interim, it seems like John and Steve should have a larger party and try the taste test again.

GUIDELINES FOR USING STATISTICS

We have now covered a good deal of the basic building blocks of descriptive and inferential statistics. In the next chapters of *Statistical Analysis for the Social Science: An Interactive Approach* we will consider a variety of statistical techniques for different research situations beginning with the *t*-test which is designed to overcome the shortcoming of the *z*-test when sample sizes are small.

But before we cover these techniques we thought it especially useful to provide you with a set of guidelines that should help you better use and understand the place of statistics in the research enterprise. These guidelines were recently developed by the Task Force on Statistical Inference that was convened by the Board of Scientific Affairs of the American Psychological Association.

You will notice that the guidelines are organized around the traditional sections of a research manuscript minus the Introduction but including the Method, Results, and Discussion sections and their subsections. Clearly the board wished to emphasize that the proper use of statistics requires a critical understanding of research more broadly conceived.

The guidelines are listed in Textbox 7.10. For the complete report with the guidelines and explanations, see Wilkinson et al. (1999).

Textbox 7.10

American Psychological Association Guidelines for the Application of Statistical Methods

Statistical Methods in Psychology Journals:
Guidelines and Explanations
Leland Wilkinson and the Task Force on Statistical Inference
APA Board of Scientific Affairs (1999)

METHOD

Design

Make clear at the outset what type of study you are doing. Do not cloak a study in one guise to try to give it the assumed reputation of another. For studies that have multiple goals, be sure to define and prioritize those goals.

Population

The interpretation of the results of any study depends on the characteristics of the population intended for analysis. Define the population (participants, stimuli, or studies) clearly. If control or comparison groups are part of the design, present how they are defined.

Sample

Describe the sampling procedures and emphasize any inclusion or exclusion criteria. If the sample is stratified (e.g., by site or gender), describe fully the method and rationale. Note the proposed sample size for each subgroup.

Assignment

Random assignment

For research involving causal inferences, the assignment of units to levels of the causal variable is critical. Random assignment (not to be confused with random selection) allows for the strongest possible causal inferences free of extraneous assumptions. If random assignment is planned, provide enough information to show that the process for making the actual assignments is random.

---

continued

Nonrandom assignment

For some research questions, random assignment is not feasible. In such cases, we need to minimize effects of variables that affect the observed relationship between a causal variable and an outcome. Such variables are commonly called confounds or covariates. The researcher needs to attempt to determine the relevant covariates, measure them adequately, and adjust for their effects either by design or by analysis. If the effects of covariates are adjusted by analysis, the strong assumptions that are made must be explicitly stated and, to the extent possible, tested and justified. Describe methods used to attenuate sources of bias, including plans for minimizing dropouts, noncompliance, and missing data.

Measurement

Variables

Explicitly define the variables in the study, show how they are related to the goals of the study, and explain how they are measured. The units of measurement of all variables, causal and outcome, should fit the language you use in the introduction and discussion sections of your report.

Instruments

If a questionnaire is used to collect data, summarize the psychometric properties of its scores with specific regard to the way the instrument is used in a population. Psychometric properties include measures of validity, reliability, and any other qualities affecting conclusions. If a physical apparatus is used, provide enough information (brand, model, design specifications) to allow another experimenter to replicate your measurement process.

Procedure

Describe any anticipated sources of attrition due to noncompliance, dropout, death, or other factors. Indicate how such attrition may affect the generalizability of the results. Clearly describe the conditions under which measurements are taken (e.g., format, time, place, personnel who collected data). Describe the specific methods used to deal with experimenter bias, especially if you collected the data yourself.

Power and sample size

Provide information on sample size and the process that led to sample size decisions. Document the effect sizes, sampling and measurement assumptions, as well as analytic procedures used in power calculations. Because power computations are most meaningful when done before data are collected and examined, it is important to show how effect-size estimates have been derived from previous research and theory in order to dispel suspicions that they might have been taken from data used in the study or, even worse, constructed to justify a particular sample size. Once the study is analyzed, confidence intervals replace calculated power in describing results.

RESULTS

Complications

Before presenting results, report complications, protocol violations, and other unanticipated events in data collection. These include missing data, attrition, and nonresponse. Discuss analytic

continued

Textbox 7.10 (Continued)

techniques devised to ameliorate these problems. Describe nonrepresentativeness statistically by reporting patterns and distributions of missing data and contaminations. Document how the actual analysis differs from the analysis planned before complications arose. The use of techniques to ensure that the reported results are not produced by anomalies in the data (e.g., outliers, points of high influence, nonrandom missing data, selection bias, attrition problems) should be a standard component of all analyses.

Analysis

Choosing a minimally sufficient analysis

The enormous variety of modern quantitative methods leaves researchers with the nontrivial task of matching analysis and design to the research question. Although complex designs and state-of-the-art methods are sometimes necessary to address research questions effectively, simpler classical approaches often can provide elegant and sufficient answers to important questions. Do not choose an analytic method to impress your readers or to deflect criticism. If the assumptions and strength of a simpler method are reasonable for your data and research problem, use it. Occam's razor applies to methods as well as to theories.

Computer programs

There are many good computer programs for analyzing data. More important than choosing a specific statistical package is verifying your results, understanding what they mean, and knowing how they are computed. If you cannot verify your results by intelligent "guesstimates," you should check them against the output of another program. You will not be happy if a vendor reports a bug after your data are in print (not an infrequent event). Do not report statistics found on a printout without understanding how they are computed or what they mean. Do not report statistics to a greater precision than is supported by your data simply because they are printed that way by the program. Using the computer is an opportunity for you to control your analysis and design. If a computer program does not provide the analysis you need, use another program rather than let the computer shape your thinking.

Assumptions

You should take efforts to assure that the underlying assumptions required for the analysis are reasonable given the data. Examine residuals carefully. Do not use distributional tests and statistical indexes of shape (e.g., skewness, kurtosis) as a substitute for examining your residuals graphically.

Hypothesis tests

It is hard to imagine a situation in which a dichotomous accept–reject decision is better than reporting an actual p value or, better still, a confidence interval. Never use the unfortunate expression "accept the null hypothesis." Always provide some effect-size estimate when reporting a p value.

Effect sizes

Always present effect sizes for primary outcomes. If the units of measurement are meaningful on a practical level (e.g., number of cigarettes smoked per day), then we usually prefer an unstandardized measure (regression coefficient or mean difference) to a standardized measure (r or d). It helps to add brief comments that place these effect sizes in a practical and theoretical context.

continued

Interval estimates

Interval estimates should be given for any effect sizes involving principal outcomes. Provide intervals for correlations and other coefficients of association or variation whenever possible.

Multiplicities

Multiple outcomes require special handling. There are many ways to conduct reasonable inference when faced with multiplicity (e.g., Bonferroni correction of p values, multivariate test statistics, empirical Bayes methods). It is your responsibility to define and justify the methods used.

Causality

Inferring causality from nonrandomized designs is a risky enterprise. Researchers using nonrandomized designs have an extra obligation to explain the logic behind covariates included in their designs and to alert the reader to plausible rival hypotheses that might explain their results. Even in randomized experiments, attributing causal effects to any one aspect of the treatment condition requires support from additional experimentation.

Tables and figures

Although tables are commonly used to show exact values, well-drawn figures need not sacrifice precision. Figures attract the reader's eye and help convey global results. Because individuals have different preferences for processing complex information, it often helps to provide both tables and figures. This works best when figures are kept small enough to allow space for both formats. Avoid complex figures when simpler ones will do. In all figures, include graphical representations of interval estimates whenever possible.

DISCUSSION

Interpretation

When you interpret effects, think of credibility, generalizability, and robustness. Are the effects credible, given the results of previous studies and theory? Do the features of the design and analysis (e.g., sample quality, similarity of the design to designs of previous studies, similarity of the effects to those in previous studies) suggest the results are generalizable? Are the design and analytic methods robust enough to support strong conclusions?

Conclusions

Speculation may be appropriate, but use it sparingly and explicitly. Note the shortcomings of your study. Remember, however, that acknowledging limitations is for the purpose of qualifying results and avoiding pitfalls in future research. Confession should not have the goal of disarming criticism. Recommendations for future research should be thoughtful and grounded in present and previous findings. Gratuitous suggestions ("further research needs to be done") waste space. Do not interpret a single study's results as having importance independent of the effects reported elsewhere in the relevant literature. The thinking presented in a single study may turn the movement of the literature, but the results in a single study are important primarily as one contribution to a mosaic of study effects.

PUTTING IT ALL TOGETHER

The emphasis here was on the nature and general procedures for hypothesis testing. We also showed how to find both two-sided and one-sided confidence intervals and use them for hypothesis testing. In addition, we discussed the alternative sampling distribution, in particular, the sampling distribution of mean differences when the null hypothesis is not true. We covered issues associated with the power of statistical tests to detect treatment effects. We also distinguished between statistical significance and practical importance and introduced the effect size measure as a means of detecting the size of effects. Finally, we provided the latest guidelines from the American Psychological Association for the application of statistics.

Steps in Hypothesis Testing   We began this chapter by providing the six basic steps in the hypothesis testing process:

1. State the null and alternative hypotheses.
2. Select alpha, the probability value for significance testing.
3. Select the appropriate test statistic.
4. Compute the calculated value of the test statistic.
5. Find the critical value of the test statistic.
6. Compare the calculated and critical values in order to make a decision about the null and alternative hypotheses.

Decision Errors   We also discussed decision-making errors in hypothesis testing and gave the following two definitions:

1. A **Type I error** occurs when the null hypothesis is rejected but it is true.
2. A **Type II error** occurs when the null hypothesis is not rejected but it is false.

One-Sided Confidence Intervals   We illustrated the application of interval estimates and extended it to include the use of one-sided confidence intervals.

For a one-sided confidence interval when the alternative hypothesis is *positive* the true population mean difference, μ_D, will fall in the range between:

$$\text{Equation 7.1: } \overline{Y}_D - z_{1-a}s_D$$

For a one-sided confidence interval when the alternative hypothesis is *negative* the true population mean difference, μ_D, will fall in the range between:

$$\text{Equation 7.2: } \overline{Y}_D + z_{1-a}s_D$$

Estimating Power   We discussed the concept of the alternative sampling distribution and the notion of Type II error rate (β) and statistical power ($1 - \beta$). The steps in estimating power are as follows:

1. Estimate the population mean difference for the alternative sampling distribution ($\overline{Y}_{DA}$).
2. Estimate the standard error of the alternative sampling distribution (s_{DA}).

3. Find the critical value for the null sampling distribution and convert it to a raw score (CV_R).
4. Compute z_A from CV_R.
5. Find β and power ($1 - \beta$) by finding the exact probability of z_A.

Ways to Affect Power   We discussed five ways to affect the power of statistical tests:

1. The level of significance or alpha (α)
2. Whether directional or nondirectional hypotheses are specified
3. The size of the sample
4. The size of within-groups variability
5. The size of the expected treatment effect

Sample Size Estimation   We provided a formula to determining the appropriate sample size for each group in a two-group study:

$$\text{Equation 7.3: } n = \frac{(s_{A1}^2 + s_{A2}^2)(z_\beta - z_\alpha)^2}{(\overline{Y}_{A1} - \overline{Y}_{A2})^2}$$

Effect Sizes   We distinguished between statistical significance and practical significance. We provided a formula for computing the effect size:

$$\text{Equation 7.4: } d = \frac{\overline{Y}_{A1} - \overline{Y}_{A2}}{s}$$

We also showed how to use the effect size to estimate power and sample size using power curves.

KEY TERMS

Statistical hypothesis	Alpha	Critical or tabled value
Null hypothesis	Beta	Statistical power or $1 - \beta$
Alternative hypothesis	Power	Alternative sampling distribution
Type I error	Calculated or computed value	
Type II error		Effect size

REFERENCES

Cohen, J. (1988). *Statistical power analysis for the behavioral sciences.* (2nd ed.). Hillsdale, NJ: Lawrence Erlbaum Associates.

Hays, W. L. (1994). *Statistics* (5th ed.). Orlando, FL: Harcourt Brace & Co.

Keselman, H. J., Lix, L. M., & Kowalchuk, R. K. (1998). Multiple comparison procedures for trimmed means. *Psychological Methods, 3,* 123–141.

Kirk, R. E. (1990). *Statistics: An introduction.* (3rd ed.). Orlando, FL: Holt, Rinehart, & Winston.
Wilkinson, L., and the Task Force on Statistical Inference (1999). Statistical methods for psychological journals: Guidelines and explanations. *American Psychologist, 54,* 594–604.

PROBLEMS

Questions

Section 1   Conceptual/Definition

7.1. List the steps in hypothesis testing.

7.2. What is a statistical hypothesis? How is it different from a scientific hypothesis?

7.3. Social science research uses the procedure of falsification in statistical testing. What is a major shortcoming of this procedure?

7.4. What is a directional alternative hypothesis? What advantage does a directional hypothesis have over a nondirectional alternative hypothesis?

7.5. When does a Type I error occur? When does a Type II error occur?

7.6. What is beta (β)? What is Power? How are the two related?

7.7. What factors determine the probability of making a Type II error?

7.8. Do the null and alternative hypotheses have the same sampling distribution?

7.9. What is the most critical step in estimating power?

7.10. How is the decision to accept or reject the null hypothesis made?

7.11. What is an effect size?

Section 2   Numerical

7.12. What is the critical value of z for a nondirectional hypothesis at $\alpha = .05$? Is the answer the same for a directional hypothesis?

7.13. Which critical value of z—1.96 or 1.65—will produce the larger region of rejection?

7.14. As alpha is increased from .05 to .10, how is Type I error affected?

7.15. As alpha is increased from .05 to .10, how is beta (β) affected?

7.16. In examining the formula for the z-test of the difference between two means, how does the size of within-group variability affect Type II error?

The following data exists for both the experimental and control groups in a given experiment. Use it to answer questions 7.17 to 7.21.

Control: 12, 18, 14, 13, 15

Experimental   16, 17, 16, 19, 22

7.17. Use the z-test to determine whether a significant difference exists between the experimental and control groups.

7.18. Determine the two-sided confidence interval for the estimated mean difference.

7.19. Determine the one-sided confidence interval for the estimated mean difference (for a negative direction alternative hypothesis).

7.20. Determine the effect size, d, for this experiment.

7.21. Determine the Type II error rate and power for this experiment.

8

Testing the Difference Between Two Independent Groups

The *t*-Test

OVERVIEW

You now have all the basic ideas and concepts you will need as the foundation for understanding the inferential statistical techniques we present in this text. What you need is to develop an understanding of the concepts particular to each technique and their applications. At this point, you should have a good understanding of one statistical test: the *z*-test. After completing this chapter, you should have an understanding of a second statistical test, including two models of it: the separate variance model *t*-test and the pooled variance model *t*-test.

As you will see, the *z*-test and the *t*-test both may be used when the researcher is interested in determining whether the mean difference between two groups is significant. The astute reader will immediately recognize that we are indeed presenting a second statistical technique, the *t*-test, that is designed to do virtually the same thing as the first statistical technique, the *z*-test. But why?

In this chapter we will try to answer the following questions:

1. Why are the critical values of the *t*-test and the *z*-test different?
2. Why are the computational values of the *t*-test and the *z*-test identical?
3. When does one use either test?
4. What are degrees of freedom?
5. What is the difference between a critical value and an exact probability?
6. What is the advantage of using a pooled variance approach to estimating the standard error?
7. What are the differences between the separate variance model *t*-test and the pooled variance model *t*-test?
8. What are the underlying assumptions for the *t*-test, and how do you deal with assumption violations?
9. When and how do you use the separate versus pooled variance model *t*-test?

We begin with the scenario described in Textbox 8.1.

Scenario: Drill Press

A professor is experimenting with methods of integrating computer-based instruction into the teaching of cartography: the study of map and chart making. She has two highly recommended software programs. One is a drill and practice tutorial; the other offers a guided discovery approach. Ten students volunteer to help her evaluate the effectiveness of the software in promoting achievement on a test of map-reading skills. Each student is assigned to use one of the programs during geography class period for five days, after which all the students complete a common examination. The results are as follows:

Drill: 60, 70, 80, 65, 75

Discovery: 85, 75, 90, 80, 70

How can you help decide if one of the programs is truly preferable? What are the steps and procedures you will follow to determine whether there is a significant difference between these two software programs? What are the null and alternative hypotheses? What is the significance level you will use? What computational procedure will you employ? What is the calculated value? What is the critical value? How will you decide between the calculated value and the critical value? What types of decision errors might you have made?

WHAT'S WRONG WITH THE *z*-TEST?

In Chapters 6 and 7, we warned you that there was a problem with the z-test when sample sizes were small. We also said we would address the problem more completely in a later chapter. Well, your wait is over. You are finally to a point in your understanding of inferential statistics that you can turn your attention to this issue and understand the problem as well as the solution to it.

As you will see, the resolution of the problem is to recommend a slightly different test, the *t*-test. And because the *t*-test corrects for a problem with the *z*-test for small sample sizes and is identical to the *z*-test for large sample sizes, we will use the *t*-test from now on when we want to examine mean differences among groups.

Review and Application of the *z*-Test

Before we get to the *t*-test, let us review how you would address the questions posed in the Drill Press scenario of Textbox 8.1 using the one statistical test you have learned about so far: the z-test. Then you will be better able to see how the *t*-test relates.

Remember that you wish to find the location of the observed mean difference on the standard normal distribution given your initial belief that the null hypothesis is correct and the population mean difference is zero. To locate the observed mean difference on the standard normal distribution you need to know the standard deviation of the sampling distribution of mean differences (σ_M). Then we can find z_D:

$$z_D = \frac{(\overline{Y}_{A1} - \overline{Y}_{A2}) - (\mu_{A1} - \mu_{A2})}{\sigma_M}$$

Given your initial belief that the null hypothesis is correct and $\mu_{A1} - \mu_{A2} = 0.00$, this reduces to:

$$z_D = \frac{(\overline{Y}_{A1} - \overline{Y}_{A2})}{\sigma_M}$$

But you do not know the value of σ_M and must use s_M to estimate it. Therefore,

(Equation 6.21) Estimated $z_D = \dfrac{\overline{Y}_{A1} - \overline{Y}_{A2}}{s_D}$

See Textbox 8.2 for the hypothesis-testing steps and calculations using the z-test for the Drill Press scenario. Note that by analyzing the data using the z-test,

---

Textbox 8.2

z-Test Analysis of the Drill Press Scenario

In the Drill Press scenario of Textbox 8.1, the null hypothesis is that there is no difference between the groups in examination performance. The alternative hypothesis is that there is a difference between the groups in examination performance. The alternative hypothesis is nondirectional, or two-tailed, because the scenario is not specific in predicting whether drill and practice or guided discovery will be superior:

$$H_0: \mu_{A1} = \mu_{A2} \text{ or } \mu_D = 0.0$$

$$H_a: \mu_{A1} \neq \mu_{A2} \text{ or } \mu_D \neq 0.0$$

There is no indication in the scenario concerning the significance level for hypothesis testing. Use $\alpha = .05$.

Your choice of statistical tests is still limited to the one test you know: the z-test. The calculated value of the z-test is determined from

(Equation 6.21) Estimated $z_D = \dfrac{\overline{Y}_{A1} - \overline{Y}_{A2}}{s_D}$

or, if you prefer more intermediate calculations for s_D:

(Equation 6.22) Estimated $z_D = \dfrac{\overline{Y}_{A1} - \overline{Y}_{A2}}{\sqrt{\dfrac{s_{A1}^2}{n_{A1}} + \dfrac{s_{A2}^2}{n_{A2}}}}$

$$z = \frac{70.00 - 80.00}{5.00} = \frac{70.00 - 80.00}{\sqrt{\dfrac{7.91^2}{5} + \dfrac{7.91^2}{5}}} = -2.00$$

For $\alpha = .05$, the critical value is ± 1.96. Since the calculated value (-2.00) is larger, you reject the null hypothesis and accept the alternative hypothesis. The observed probability is less than .05, or $p < .05$. In making this decision, you may possibly have committed a Type I error.

your decision is to reject the null hypothesis and accept the alternative hypothesis. Your best guess is that there is a difference between the two teaching methods.

As you will see, we come to a different conclusion when the *t*-test is used to analyze the data. For small sample sizes, the *t*-test is more conservative than the *z*-test.

The Contribution of William Gosset

The calculated value of the *z*-test is a ratio that includes two components: (1) the estimated standard error of the mean difference, s_D, in the denominator and (2) the observed mean difference $(\overline{Y}_{A1} - \overline{Y}_{A2})$ in the numerator. This ratio is used to estimate the location of a point on the standard normal distribution. The point estimation from the *z*-test is then used to make a decision about the significance of the observed mean difference between two groups. If the point estimation lies at the extremes of the normal distribution, one will be inclined to reject the null hypothesis and accept the alternative hypothesis.

When σ^2 Is Known versus When σ^2 Is Not Known
When the population variance (σ^2) is known, the sampling variance is also known, because it is the population variance divided by *N*. Obviously, in such a circumstance the standard error is also known. Therefore, when the population variance is known, you do not need to estimate the denominator of the *z*-test and can locate the observed mean difference on the sampling distribution of mean differences.

This is a wonderful idea in theory, but in practice the population variance is never known but must be estimated. When you need to estimate the population variance and the standard error, there is a problem with the *z*-test when sample sizes are small.

Small Sample Sizes and the Sampling Distribution
The *z*-test is fine to use as a test of significance so long as one can be confident that the standard normal distribution represents the actual shape of the population sampling distribution. Remember that according to the central limit theorem, the shape of the sampling distribution becomes increasingly like a normal distribution as sample size increases. But what happens to the shape of the population sampling distribution when sample sizes are small? William Sealey Gosset (aka "Student") was able to demonstrate that as sample size decreased, the shape of the population sampling distribution deviated from the shape of the standard normal distribution.

The Family of t-Distributions

Gosset was a chemist and mathematician in the employ of the Guinness Brewery in England around the turn of the twentieth century. Gosset was conducting research on different strains of yeast used to brew beer. Because of the type of research he was conducting, Gosset did not have large sample sizes to work with. In dealing with small samples, he discovered problems with his statistical tests being too liberal (i.e., too many Type I errors). To correct for the problem, he developed alternatives to the normal distribution for determining critical values for a host of different sample sizes. Gosset called these the family of *t*-distributions when he published his findings in 1908 under the pen name "Student," a name he used to avoid difficulties with the brewery that frowned on the publication of research by its employees.

CD-ROM link 8.1

Activity 8.1: The Calculated t-Value (Part I)

How does the calculated *t*-value express the difference between two datasets? By moving individual data points, you can see how each one is represented in the separate variance model of the *t*-test.

CD-ROM link 8.2

Activity 8.2: The Calculated t-Value (Part II)

The second activity for this chapter is similar to Activity 8.1, but instead of moving individual data points, you can manipulate the entire data distribution directly. This will help you see how the central tendency and variability of a data set is represented in the separate variance model of the *t*-test.

The Calculated Value of t Is Identical to z   The effect of providing these different distributions was to *adjust the critical value upward* as sample sizes decreased. Thus, the mathematical procedures for arriving at the calculated value were not changed. Fortunately, the formula for the calculated value of z is identical to the formula for the calculated value of t, which can be expressed in several forms but yields identical results:

$$\text{Equation 8.1: Estimated } t = \frac{\overline{Y}_{A1} - \overline{Y}_{A2}}{s_D}$$

$$\text{Equation 8.2: Estimated } t = \frac{\overline{Y}_{A1} - \overline{Y}_{A2}}{\sqrt{\dfrac{s_{A1}^2}{n_{A1}} + \dfrac{s_{A2}^2}{n_{A2}}}}$$

$$\text{Equation 8.3: Estimated } t = \frac{\overline{Y}_{A1} - \overline{Y}_{A2}}{\sqrt{\dfrac{\dfrac{\sum (Y_{iA1} - \overline{Y}_{A1})^2}{(n_{A1} - 1)}}{n_{A1}} + \dfrac{\dfrac{\sum (Y_{iA2} - \overline{Y}_{A2})^2}{(n_{A2} - 1)}}{n_{A2}}}}$$

The Critical Value of t Is Not Always Identical to z   The critical value of z is ± 1.96 for a two-tailed alternative hypothesis using $\alpha = .05$. For the *t*-test, the critical value may be as small as ± 1.96 or as large as ± 12.71.

THE SEPARATE VARIANCE MODEL *t*-TEST

Each of Equations 8.1 to 8.3 computes the calculated value in what is known as **the separate variance model *t*-test.** In the denominator of the calculated value for the separate variance model *t*-test you can see that the variance for each group is computed separately and then combined.

Effect of Sample Size on the Critical Value

Examination of the critical values of the *t*-distributions reveal that when sample sizes[1] are small, the correction is substantial. For small sample sizes, the size of the

[1]As you will learn momentarily, it is the degrees of freedom, a concept highly related to sample size, that affects the critical value of *t*.

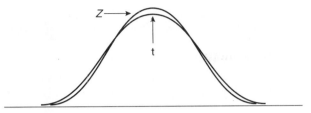

Figure 8.1 Distributions of *t* and *z*

critical values of the *t*-distributions is large compared to the critical value of the normal distribution. Conversely, the magnitude of the difference between the critical values of the *t*- and *z*-distributions gets smaller when sample sizes are large.

Figure 8.1 illustrates two distributions. One is a *t*-distribution for a small sample size. The other is the standard normal *z*-distribution. Note that the *t*-distribution is somewhat flatter, or more platykurtic, than the standard normal *z*-distribution, meaning there is a larger area in the tails of the *t*-distribution. Because there is a larger area in the tails of the *t*-distribution, one must go further from the mean (0.0) of the distribution to find that point—the **critical value**—where group differences occur rarely as a function of chance.

Finally, remember that there is not a single *t*-distribution but many—a family of distributions. The shape of members of the family, and hence the critical value, will vary depending on sample size.

Textbox 8.3 illustrates the effect of sample size on the critical values for *t* compared to the critical value for *z* for $\alpha = .05$ and a nondirectional, or two-tailed, alternative hypothesis. As sample size decreases, the critical value of the *t*-test increases but the critical value of the *z*-test remains unchanged. We will shortly explain how to find the critical values for the *t*-test.

What Happens in Practice?   In many research situations, sample sizes are reasonably large and the results of significance testing with the *t*-test and the *z*-test will tend to agree with one another. However, the discrepancies between the two tests occur more frequently when sample sizes are small because the critical value of *t* grows larger when sample size decreases. For small sample sizes, the critical value of the *z*-test is too liberal and leads to an excessive number of false positive judgments, or Type I errors. The critical value of the *t*-test corrects for these decision errors in the *z*-test. For large sample sizes there is virtually no difference between the critical values of the two tests. Therefore, the *t*-test is more widely used for situations that involve the comparison of two means.

D-ROM link 8.3

Activity 8.3: The Family of t-Distributions
Activity 8.3 allows you to vary degrees of freedom and see the effect on the shape of a *t*-distribution. You can also compare the critical *t*-value associated with a given alpha level with the critical *z*-value for the same alpha.

Degrees of Freedom

As with the *z*-test, the critical value of the *t*-test depends on knowing alpha, the probability value you

---

Textbox 8.3

Critical Values of *t* and *z* for Different Sample Sizes

We will illustrate the effect of sample size on the critical value of *t* using three examples. Note that the critical value of *t* changes with changes in sample size but the critical value of *z* is not affected by sample size.

Small sample size

Imagine a sample of four participants divided into two groups. Using the normal distribution for $\alpha = .05$, one would reject H_0 when the calculated value is greater than $+1.96$ or less than -1.96. However, using the *t*-distribution for $\alpha = .05$, one would reject H_0 when the calculated value is greater than $+4.30$ or less than -4.30. In other words, for sample sizes of two participants per group, the critical value of the *t*-test (± 4.30) is more than twice the size of the critical value of the normal distribution (± 1.96). As Gosset determined, the correction to the critical value needs to be severe when sample sizes are very small.

Large sample size

Now imagine a sample of 80 participants divided into two groups. Using the normal distribution for $\alpha = .05$, one would reject H_0 when the calculated value is greater than $+1.96$ or less than -1.96. Notice that these values are the same as in the previous example, because critical values for the normal distribution do not vary as a function of sample size. However, using the *t*-distribution for alpha $= .05$, one would reject H_0 when the calculated value is greater than $+2.02$ or less than -2.02. In other words, for sample sizes of 40 participants per group, the critical value of the *t*-test (± 2.02) is only slightly larger than the size of the critical value of the normal distribution (± 1.96). As Gosset determined, the correction to the critical value needs to be small when sample sizes are moderately large.

Drill press scenario

Finally, imagine a sample of 10 participants divided into two groups as in the Drill Press scenario in this Textbox 8.1. Using the *t*-distribution for $\alpha = .05$ (two-tailed), the critical value is ± 2.31. Notice that the critical value for *t* is still larger than the critical value for *z*. What effect does this have on our decision about the null and alternative hypotheses? In the Drill Press scenario, the calculated value is -2.00. This value is not larger than the critical value for *t* of ± 2.31. Using the *t*-test, one would *fail* to reject the null hypothesis and, consequently, might have committed a Type II error. The decision arrived at with the *t*-test in this case happens to be opposite to the decision one would have arrived at using the *z*-test.

Remember that with hypothesis testing one is forced to choose between two options: failing to reject the null hypothesis and rejecting the null hypothesis. One can't use phrases such as "almost significant."

---

wish to use for significance testing, and whether the alternative hypothesis is directional (one-tailed) or nondirectional (two-tailed). In addition, for the *t*-test, the critical value depends on sample size. But rather than use sample size directly, you use a concept closely linked to sample size: **degrees of freedom.**

Independent Pieces of Information

In statistics, degrees of freedom, usually abbreviated as df or ν (Greek nu), refers to the number of scores whose values are free to vary. The term comes from the physical sciences, where it refers to the number of planes or directions in which an object is free to move.

As you recall, the variance and standard deviation are both based on a sum of squared deviations about the mean. For unbiased estimates the sum is divided by $N - 1$. In addition, we showed in Chapter 4 that the sum of all deviations about the mean is zero (0.0):

$$\textbf{(Equation 4.2)} \sum d_i = \sum (Y_i - \overline{Y}) = 0$$

Let's take these facts and see if we can apply them to the Drill Press scenario to illustrate and explain the concept of degrees of freedom. In Table 8.1, we have placed the raw scores and the **deviation scores** for four of the five students exposed to the guided discovery software.

In the small dataset in Table 8.1, the first four observations have corresponding deviation scores of 5, -5, 10, and 0, respectively. Given these first four observations and their deviations from the mean, you would know that the fifth observation must have a deviation score of -10 (because the sum of the five deviation scores must be equal to zero). Since you know that the last observation has a deviation score of -10 and you know that the mean of the five observations is 80, you also know that the last observation must have a score of 70.

On the other hand, consider the data in Table 8.2 in which the mean for the entire set of five scores is known but the information for the scores of the last two students has been eliminated. One of the missing scores, let's say Jose's, can be set arbitrarily at any value. This will decide on the score for Moishe but allows you to preserve the known values of the mean and the sum of the deviation scores. If, for example, you arbitrarily set Jose's score at 100 with a deviation score of $+20.00$, you know that Moishe's score *must* be set at 50.00 with a deviation score set at -30.00. Although one of the two missing scores is free to vary, after it is set the final missing score can take on only a specific value if the known values of the mean and the zero sum of the deviation scores are to be preserved.

In sum, given the values of $N - 1$ deviations from the mean, which could be *any* set of $N - 1$ numbers, the value of the last deviation score is completely determined. This reflects the fact that only $N - 1$ of the deviation scores are free to be

TABLE 8.1 Four of Five Raw and Deviation Scores (Guided Discovery Software)

Student	Map Reading Skill Test Score	Deviation Scores (d_i)
John	85	$+5.00$
Mary	75	-5.00
Joseph	90	$+10.00$
Moishe	80	$+0.00$
Jose	**	**
Known values	$\overline{Y}_{A2} = 80.00$	$\sum d_i = 0.0$

TABLE 8.2   Three of Five Raw and Deviation Scores (Guided Discovery Software)

Student	Map Reading Skill Test Score	Deviation Scores (d_i)
John	85	+5.00
Mary	75	−5.00
Joseph	90	+10.00
Moishe	**	**
Jose	**	**
Known values	$\overline{Y}_{A2} = 80.00$	$\sum d_i = 0.0$

any value, and that given these free values, the last deviation is determined. Consequently, it is not sample size per se that determines the distribution of *t* but rather the degrees of freedom that are associated with the estimated variance (and standard deviation) in the denominator of the *t*-ratio.

Degrees of Freedom in the Two-Group *t*-Test   When you compare two groups or samples using the *t*-test, you take into consideration two means and two variances in which each group or sample has its own sample size. While we designate the total sample size for all participants from both groups combined as *N*, we will use *n* to refer to the sample for each group separately. Specifically, we will use n_1 or n_{A1} to refer to the participants or sample making up the group exposed to one level of the treatment (in the Drill Press scenario, it is the drill and practice tutorial) and we will use n_2 or n_{A2} to refer to the participants or sample comprising the group exposed to a second level of the treatment (in the Drill Press scenario, it is the guided discovery approach).

The variance (and standard deviation) for each group has its own degrees of freedom—$n_1 - 1$ and $n_2 - 1$, respectively. Therefore, the total degrees of freedom for a two-group *t*-test is

Equation 8.4: $\mathrm{df} = (n_1 - 1) + (n_2 - 1) = (n_1 + n_2) - 2 = N - 2$

Finding the Correct Critical Value

CD-ROM link 8.4

Activity 8.4: The Critical t-Value
How do you use a *t*-table to find a critical *t*-value? Activity 8.4 provides you with the opportunity to practice looking up critical values based on the alpha level and the degrees of freedom.

One of the steps in determining whether you can reject the null hypothesis is to compare the calculated value with the critical value. If the calculated value exceeds the critical value, you reject the null hypothesis. If the calculated value does not exceed the critical value, you will fail to reject the null hypothesis.

Required Information   Finding the critical value requires that you decide in advance of any calculations whether your alternative hypothesis is directional (one-tailed) or nondirectional (two-tailed). You also need to decide upon alpha, the probability value you wish to use for significance testing. This is all you need to know to find the critical value when you conduct a z-test using the standard normal distribution.

But to find the critical value for the t-test requires that you know more than just the nature of the alternative hypothesis and alpha. Because Student's t is a family of distributions, you must also know the correct degrees of freedom so that you refer to the correct t-distribution to find your critical value. Therefore, to find the critical value in the t-table, you need to know the following:

- What are the degrees of freedom?
- Is the alternative hypothesis one-tailed or two-tailed?
- What is alpha, the probability value for significance testing?

Appendix C contains a table of critical values for the family of t-distributions. Note how the critical values of t in any column get lower as the degrees of freedom get higher. Textbox 8.4 along with Table 8.3 illustrate the use of the table for the Drill Press scenario.

Textbox 8.4

Finding the Critical Value

For the Drill Press scenario, you need to find the critical value of t to which you will compare the calculated value.

Step 1: Determine the degrees of freedom (df):

$$df = (n_1 - 1) + (n_2 - 1) \quad \text{or } (n_1 + n_2) - 2$$
$$= (5 - 1) + (5 - 1)$$
$$= 8$$

Step 2: Locate the row in the table corresponding to the number of degrees of freedom as determined in step 1.

Step 3: Determine whether a one-tail or a two-tail t-test is required. The Drill Press scenario specifies a nondirectional alternative hypothesis, so you will want to find the critical values for a two-tailed test.

Step 4: You need to specify alpha, the probability value for significance testing. For the Drill Press scenario, you will use $\alpha = .05$.

Step 5: Find the critical value of t at the intersection of the column associated with the alpha value and directional test, and the row associated with the appropriate degree of freedom. See Table 8.3.

In the Drill Press scenario, the critical value of the t-statistic is ± 2.31. Because the calculated value (-2.00) is not larger than the critical value, you fail to reject the null hypothesis. In other words, you fail to find evidence that there is a significant difference in the examination performance of students using guided discovery cartography software compared to students using drill and practice software.

TABLE 8.3 *t*-Table Excerpt						

	Critical Values for One-Tail Test					
	0.25	0.10	0.05	0.025	0.01	0.005
	Critical Values for Two-Tail Test					
df	0.50	0.20	0.10	0.05	0.02	0.01
1	1.000	3.078	6.314	12.706	31.821	63.657
2	0.816	1.886	2.920	4.303	6.965	9.925
3	0.765	1.638	2.353	3.182	4.541	5.841
4	0.741	1.533	2.132	2.776	3.747	4.604
5	0.727	1.476	2.015	2.571	3.365	4.032
6	0.718	1.44	1.943	2.447	3.143	3.707
7	0.711	1.415	1.895	2.365	2.998	3.499
8	0.706	1.397	1.860	2.306	2.896	3.355
9	0.703	1.383	1.833	2.262	2.821	3.250
10	0.700	1.372	1.812	2.228	2.764	3.169

Exact Probabilities

In conducting a *z*-test, the computed value you obtain can be located as an exact point on the standard normal distribution. Some of these points are referred to so often that the areas beyond them are well known and may not require use of Appendix A to find them. For example, a *z*-score of ±1.96 has an exact probability of .05 (.0250 × 2) representing the likelihood of a *z*-score of this size or larger. Other scores are less well known and require use of Appendix A. For example, using Appendix A you find that a *z*-score of ±1.85 has an exact probability of .0644 (.0322 × 2).

As you might surmise, there are tables for each *t* distribution that contain the areas under the distribution for each calculated value. And because the *t*-distribution is a family of distributions, you would be correct if you guessed that there was one table for each degree of freedom from 1 to infinity, at least theoretically. That is a very large number of tables and one reason we have not reproduced even a fraction of them here.

Instead of reprinting so many tables, we follow the custom of reporting only a select subset of critical values for many of these distributions. In particular, we report the critical values for one- and two-tailed tests corresponding to frequently used areas, or probability values, in each *t*-distribution.

In many computer statistical packages, however, the areas under the appropriate *t*-distribution for each calculated value are readily obtained and reported. Thus, you will often see the **exact probability** associated with a calculated value of *t*. For example, in the Drill Press scenario the calculated value of *t* is −2.00. For the *t*-distribution with df = 8, the exact two-tailed probability for *t* = ±2.00 is .080 (i.e., *p* = .080).

Use the exact probability reported for the calculated value to determine whether alpha, the probability value you selected for significance testing at the outset, has been exceeded. For example, in the Drill Press scenario you decided in advance to set alpha to .05 for a two-tailed test. The exact two-tailed probability of $p = .080$ associated with the calculated value -2.00 is larger than alpha and, therefore, you would fail to reject the null hypothesis.

Confidence Intervals

Remember that a confidence interval is an estimated range of values with a known high probability of covering the true population value. Using the z-test approach, you were able to *estimate* various confidence intervals for the true population mean difference, μ_D.

z-Test Approach   The general formula for a two-sided confidence interval for a nondirectional, or two-tailed, alternative hypothesis is as follows:

$$\text{(Equation 6.28) } \overline{Y}_D - z_{1-\alpha/2}s_D \text{ and } \overline{Y}_D + z_{1-\alpha/2}s_D$$

For a one-sided confidence interval when the alternative hypothesis is *positive*, the true population mean difference, μ_D, will fall in the range between:

$$\text{(Equation 7.1) } \overline{Y}_D - z_{1-\alpha}s_D$$

For a one-sided confidence interval when the alternative hypothesis is *negative* the true population mean difference, μ_D, will fall in the range between:

$$\text{(Equation 7.2) } \overline{Y}_D + z_{1-\alpha}s_D$$

t-Test Approach (Separate Variance Model)   You know that the z-test tends to be inaccurate for small samples. Therefore, you will substitute t for z in each of these formulas.

The two-sided confidence interval for a nondirectional, two-tailed alternative hypothesis is as follows:

$$\text{Equation 8.5: } \overline{Y}_D - t_{1-\alpha/2}s_D \text{ and } \overline{Y}_D + t_{1-\alpha/2}s_D$$

The one-sided confidence interval for a one-tailed *positive* direction alternative hypothesis is as follows:

$$\text{Equation 8.6: } \overline{Y}_D - t_{1-\alpha}s_D$$

The one-sided confidence interval for a one-tailed *negative* direction alternative hypothesis is as follows:

$$\text{Equation 8.7: } \overline{Y}_D + t_{1-\alpha}s_D$$

Drill Press Example   Textbox 8.5 illustrates the calculation of a confidence interval using a critical value of t instead of a critical value of z. The illustration utilizes the Drill Press scenario.

Textbox 8.5

Computing a Confidence Interval

Because the alternative hypothesis in the Drill Press scenario is two-sided, or nondirectional, use Equation 8.5 to find the 95% confidence interval:

$$\overline{Y}_D = -10.00$$

$t_{1-\alpha/2}$ = the critical value of t, with 8 df and p set at .05 = ±2.31

$$s_D = \sqrt{\frac{s_{A1}^2}{n_{A1}} + \frac{s_{A2}^2}{n_{A2}}} = \sqrt{\frac{7.91^2}{5} + \frac{7.91^2}{5}} = 5.00$$

The 95% confidence interval is as follows:

$$\overline{Y}_D - t_{1-\alpha/2}s_D \text{ and } \overline{Y}_D + t_{1-\alpha/2}s_D = 10.00 - (2.31)5.00 \text{ and }$$
$$10.00 + (2.31)5.00 = -1.55 \text{ and } 21.55 \text{ or } -1.55 \le \mu_D \le 21.55.$$

Conclusion: You can be 95% confident that the population mean difference lies within the range from −1.55 to 21.55.

Remember that a confidence interval is another way of expressing the results of the statistical test. When applied to tests of mean differences, as in the current case, a conclusion can be drawn as to whether significant differences exist by examining the range of values in the confidence interval. When the range includes zero, as in Textbox 8.5, you can conclude that insufficient evidence exists to reject the null hypothesis. When the range does not include zero, you can reject the null hypothesis and conclude that the means of the two groups are significantly different from each other. Compared to a point estimation, interval estimation has the additional advantage of providing a range of values within which the population parameter probably resides.

Effect Sizes Calculations and Power

The procedure for calculating an effect size for the difference between two means depends neither on whether sample sizes are large or small nor on whether one uses the critical values of t or z. Thus, use the formula employed previously:

$$\textbf{(Equation 7.4) } d = \frac{\overline{Y}_{A1} - \overline{Y}_{A2}}{s}$$

Drill Press Example

$$d = \frac{70 - 80}{7.91} = -1.26$$

Remember that the denominator of the equation is the estimated standard deviation and *not* the estimated standard error.

Selecting s   Remember also that you must select an **estimated standard deviation** for the denominator when $s_{A1} \neq s_{A2}$. In the Drill Press scenario, the estimated standard deviation for the two groups are the same. When the estimates are not exactly the same, you may choose one of the following

- The control group standard deviation (if clearly identifiable as such)
- The largest standard deviation (to ensure a conservative estimate of effect size)
- The pooled standard deviation (to be covered later in this chapter)

Interpreting d   Our estimate of effect size suggests a large difference between the groups. Yet according to the results of the *t*-test the differences between the groups may have come about as a function of chance. How can this be so? Doesn't the result of the *t*-test contradict the effect size finding?

The results of these two procedures are not contradictory, although you may think so! The two procedures ask different questions about the data. In the case of the *t*-test, one wants to know whether the observed difference between groups is large enough to make it likely that it did not occur by chance. In other words, one wants to know whether the observed difference had a low probability of occurring by chance.

As we noted when we derived the calculated values of the *z*-test (and also the *t*-test), the test statistic is affected not only by the variability among scores but also by the number of scores or sample size. Why? Because the standard error is the standard deviation divided by the square root of sample size. The larger the sample size, the smaller the standard error.

All other things being equal, it is easier to reject the null hypothesis for large samples than small ones. This makes good intuitive sense; it is easier to imagine mean differences being significant when they are based on a large number of observations than when the mean differences are based on just a few observations.

In the Drill Press scenario, with all other things equal (i.e., means and standard deviations), testing a larger sample would have led to the rejection of the null hypothesis. But you did not test that larger sample and so your decision, based on the data at hand, is not to reject the null hypothesis.

Thus, the statistical test answers the question: "Is the observed difference between groups likely as a function of chance?" or "Is the difference significant?"

An effect size calculation does not allow one to make inferences about whether the observed difference is attributable to chance. It only estimates the size of the difference in standard score form. As such, an effect size is much like a *z*-score because it allows the researcher to compare estimates of effects from disparate studies with different measures, samples, procedures, and so on. Thus, an effect size estimate answers the question "How large is the difference between groups?" or "How large is the effect?"

Power   For all but the smallest sample sizes, the steps for estimating power given in Chapter 7 may be used. However, when sample sizes are small, use of the steps given in Chapter 7 will lead to an overestimate of power. Because the *t*-test is a more conservative statistic when sample sizes are small, use of it has a deleterious effect on power compared to the *z*-test.

The formula for determining the appropriate group sample size given in Chapter 7 may be used whenever the expected sample sizes are moderate in size. Here, too, when the difference in the critical value of t departs substantially from the critical value of z, you can expect the formula to underestimate the desired sample size.

More exact procedures for estimating power and determining the appropriate sample size may be found in Cohen (1988).

CD-ROM link 8.5

Problem Generator: The t-Test
To practice hypothesis testing using a separate variance model t-test, select t-test from the Problem Generator Menu on the CD-ROM. The Problem Generator will create as many practice problems as you need, and will demonstrate each step in their solution so that you can check your work.

The Drill Press Example

We want to conclude this section on the separate variance model t-test by incorporating what we have covered so far in a single example. Textbox 8.6 uses the Drill Press scenario to illustrate the use of the separate variance model t-test and review our coverage to this point.

THE POOLED VARIANCE MODEL *t*-TEST

As you will see, there are two approaches to finding the calculated value of t. We have just covered the separate variance model t-test and we will now introduce you to the **pooled variance model *t*-test.** We will explain the differences between these two approaches and offer some suggestions for choosing between them.

Pooled Standard Error

In the separate variance model t-test, the denominator is the estimated standard error of the mean difference. We estimated the standard error of the mean difference by combining the estimates of the standard error of the mean for each group. Specifically:

$$(\text{Equation 7.19}) \quad s_D = \sqrt{\frac{s_{A1}^2}{n_{A1}} + \frac{s_{A2}^2}{n_{A2}}}$$

However, Hays (1994) showed that rather than using the separate, unbiased sample variances and then combining them to form an estimate of the standard error, there is a real advantage in first *pooling* the sample values and then estimating the standard error. The advantage of using the pooled estimate is that the standard error *tends* to be smaller in size than the separate variance approach.[2]

The formula for estimating the standard error with the pooled variance approach is given below. The pooling procedure is relatively straightforward. It is the weighted average of the estimates from the two samples.

---

[2]The presence of sampling variability means this will not always be the case.

Textbox 8.6

Separate Variance Model *t*-Test Example

Hypotheses

$H_0: \mu_{A1} = \mu_{A2}$ (null hypothesis)

$H_a: \mu_{A1} \neq \mu_{A2}$ (nondirectional or two-tailed alternative hypothesis)

Significance Level

$\alpha = .05$ (probability value for significance testing)

Test Statistic

t-test (appropriate statistical test for comparing the difference between means of two groups)

Calculated Value

$$t = \frac{\overline{Y}_{A1} - \overline{Y}_{A2}}{s_D} = \frac{\overline{Y}_{A1} - \overline{Y}_{A2}}{\sqrt{\frac{s_{A1}^2}{n_{A1}} + \frac{s_{A2}^2}{n_{A2}}}} = \frac{70.00 - 80.00}{\sqrt{\frac{7.91^2}{5} + \frac{7.91^2}{5}}} = \frac{70.00 - 80.00}{5.00} = -2.00$$

Critical Value

For $\alpha = .05$ (two-tailed) and df $= (n_1 - 1) + (n_2 - 1) = (5 - 1) + (5 - 1) = 8$, tabled value of t is ± 2.31.

Exact Probability

Using a computer program, you find that $p = .080$ is the exact probability associated with a calculated value of ± 2.00 and df $= 8$.

Confidence Interval

$\overline{Y}_D - t_{1-\alpha/2}s_D$ and $\overline{Y}_D + t_{1-\alpha/2}s_D = -1.55$ and 21.55 or $-1.55 \leq \mu_D \leq 21.55$.

Effect Size

$$d = \frac{\overline{Y}_{A1} - \overline{Y}_{A2}}{s} = \frac{70.00 - 80.00}{7.91} = -1.26$$

Decision

The calculated value (-2.00) fails to exceed the critical value (± 2.31). You cannot reject the null hypothesis that the drill and practice tutorial has a different impact on student examination performance than the guided discovery approach.

Possible Decision Error

By failing to reject the null hypothesis, you may have committed a Type II error if the null hypothesis was in fact false.

Other

The confidence interval and the effect size are both fairly large, yet you failed to reject the null hypothesis. A study with a larger sample size might offer a more definitive conclusion.

First find the estimated pooled variance (s_P^2):

Equation 8.8: $s_P^2 = \dfrac{(n_{A1} - 1)s_{A1}^2 + (n_{A2} - 1)s_{A2}^2}{n_{A1} + n_{A2} - 2}$

Next, use the estimated pooled variance (s_P^2) to find the estimated standard error of the mean difference (s_{PD}):

Equation 8.9: $s_{PD} = \sqrt{\dfrac{s_P^2}{n_{A1}} + \dfrac{s_P^2}{n_{A2}}}$

When the sample sizes are the same, the pooled variance approach results in the same estimated standard error as the separate variance approach, because the two variances are weighted equally. However, when the sample sizes are different, the pooled variance approach will only equal the separate variance approach if the separate variances are equal. When the sample sizes are unequal and the variances are unequal, the pooled variance approach *tends* to estimate a smaller standard error than the separate variance approach.

To illustrate the difference between the separate and pooled approaches, we will use the Drill Press scenario both with equal sample sizes and with unequal sample sizes. See Textbox 8.7.

Textbox 8.7

Separate and Pooled Variance Approaches to Finding the Standard Error

Equal Sample Sizes

For the Drill Press scenario data given in Textbox 8.1, we have already computed the standard error using the separate variance approach.

Separate Variance Approach

$$s_D = \sqrt{\frac{s_{A1}^2}{n_{A1}} + \frac{s_{A2}^2}{n_{A2}}} = \sqrt{\frac{7.91^2}{5} + \frac{7.91^2}{5}} = 5.00$$

Pooled Variance Approach

Now use the pooled variance approach to compute s_{PD}:

$$s_P^2 = \frac{(n_{A1} - 1)s_{A1}^2 + (n_{A2} - 1)s_{A2}^2}{n_{A1} + n_{A2} - 2} = \frac{(5 - 1)(7.91)^2 + (5 - 1)(7.91)^2}{5 + 5 - 2} = 62.57 = 7.91^2$$

$$s_{PD} = \sqrt{\frac{s_P^2}{n_{A1}} + \frac{s_P^2}{n_{A2}}} = \sqrt{\frac{7.91^2}{5} + \frac{7.91^2}{5}} = 5.00$$

---

continued

Textbox 8.7 (Continued)

The separate variance approach (s_D) and the pooled variance approach (s_{PD}) yield identical results when sample sizes (and variances) are equal.

Unequal Sample Sizes

The two approaches are not always identical mathematically. To illustrate, let us modify the Drill Press scenario slightly (by adding a case to the discovery group), so that both the sample sizes and variances of the two groups are different.

$$Drill: \quad 60, 70, 80, 65, 75$$

$$Discovery: \quad 85, 75, 90, 80, 70, 80$$

	n	Mean	SD
Drill (A_1)	5	70.00	7.91
Discovery (A_2)	6	80.00	7.07

Separate Variance Approach

The separate variances are:

$$s_{A1}^2 = 7.91^2 \qquad s_{A2}^2 = 7.07^2$$

The standard error of the mean difference (separate variance approach) is as follows:

$$s_D = \sqrt{\frac{s_{A1}^2}{n_{A1}} + \frac{s_{A2}^2}{n_{A2}}} = \sqrt{\frac{7.91^2}{5} + \frac{7.07^2}{6}} = 4.57$$

Pooled Variance Approach

The pooled variance is as follows:

$$s_P^2 = \frac{(n_{A1} - 1)s_{A1}^2 + (n_{A2} - 1)s_{A2}^2}{n_{A1} + n_{A2} - 2} = \frac{(5-1)(7.91)^2 + (6-1)(7.07)^2}{5 + 6 - 2} = 55.38 = 7.46^2$$

The standard error of the mean difference (pooled variance approach) is as follows:

$$s_{PD} = \sqrt{\frac{s_P^2}{n_{A1}} + \frac{s_P^2}{n_{A2}}} = \sqrt{\frac{7.46^2}{5} + \frac{7.46^2}{6}} = 4.52$$

When sample sizes are unequal and variances are unequal, the pooled and separate variance approaches are not mathematically identical. Because the smaller variance is associated with the larger group, the pooled variance approach yields a slightly lower estimate of the standard error than the separate variance approach.

Pooled Variance Model *t*-Test

Now that you have another approach to the computation of the standard error of the mean difference, you should be able to use it in calculating the *t*-test. Consequently, the pooled variance model *t*-test is as follows:

CD-ROM link 8.6

Problem Generator: The t-Test
To practice hypothesis testing using a pooled variance model *t*-test, select *t*-test from the Problem Generator Menu on the CD-ROM. The Problem Generator will create as many practice problems as you need and will demonstrate each step in their solution so that you can check your work.

Equation 8.10: $t = \dfrac{\overline{Y}_{A1} - \overline{Y}_{A2}}{\sqrt{\dfrac{s_p^2}{n_{A1}} + \dfrac{s_p^2}{n_{A2}}}}$

$$df = n_{A1} + n_{A2} - 2$$

This is the same as:

$$t = \frac{\overline{Y}_{A1} - \overline{Y}_{A2}}{s_{PD}}$$

Note that the numerator and degrees of freedom are identical to the separate variance model *t*-test. Only the manner of estimating the standard errors are different.

Confidence Intervals Based on the Pooled Variance Approach

Finding confidence intervals for the pooled variance approach is very similar to the separate variance approach except that one substitutes s_{PD} for s_D.

The two-sided confidence interval for a nondirectional two-tailed alternative hypothesis is as follows:

Equation 8.11: $\overline{Y}_D - t_{1-\alpha/2} s_{PD}$ and $\overline{Y}_D + t_{1-\alpha/2} s_{PD}$

The one-sided confidence interval for a one-tailed *positive* direction alternative hypothesis is as follows:

Equation 8.12: $\overline{Y}_D - t_{1-\alpha} s_{PD}$

The one-sided confidence interval for a one-tailed *negative* direction alternative hypothesis is as follows:

Equation 8.13: $\overline{Y}_D + t_{1-\alpha} s_{PD}$

Effect Size Calculations Based on the Pooled Variance Approach

The formula for estimating the population effect size using the pooled variance method is as follows:

Equation 8.14: $d = \dfrac{\overline{Y}_{A1} - \overline{Y}_{A2}}{s_P}$

Comparison of Two Approaches

We will conclude this section by illustrating in Textbox 8.8 the application of both the separate variance model *t*-test and the pooled variance model *t*-test to the unequal sample size data for the Drill Press scenario with the addition of the single participant used in Textbox 8.7.

Textbox 8.8

Comparison of Separate Variance Model *t*-Test and Pooled Variance Model *t*-Test

Hypotheses

$$H_0: \mu_{A1} = \mu_{A2} \text{ or } \mu_D = 0 \text{ (null hypothesis)}$$

$$H_a: \mu_{A1} \neq \mu_{A2} \text{ or } \mu_D \neq 0 \text{ (nondirectional, or two-tailed, alternative hypothesis)}$$

Significance level

$$\alpha = .05 \text{ (probability value for significance testing)}$$

Test statistic

Either separate variance model or pooled variance model *t*-test.

Separate Variance Model t-Test

$$t = \frac{\overline{Y}_{A1} - \overline{Y}_{A2}}{\sqrt{\dfrac{s_{A1}^2}{n_{A1}} + \dfrac{s_{A2}^2}{n_{A2}}}} = \frac{70.00 - 80.00}{\sqrt{\dfrac{7.91^2}{5} + \dfrac{7.07^2}{6}}} = \frac{-10.00}{4.57} = -2.19$$

Critical value

For $\alpha = 05.05$ (two-tailed) and df $= (n_1 - 1) + (n_2 - 1) = (5 - 1) + (6 - 1) = 9$, tabled value of *t* is ± 2.26.

Exact Probability

Using a computer program, you find that $p = .060$ is the exact probability associated with a calculated value of ± 2.19 and df $= 9$.

Confidence Interval

$$\overline{Y}_D - t_{1-a/2}s_D = -10.00 - (2.26)(4.57) \text{ and } \overline{Y}_D + t_{1-a/2}s_D = -10.00 + (2.26)(4.57) = -20.33$$
$$\text{and } .33 \text{ or } -20.33 \leq \mu_D \leq 0.33.$$

Effect Size

$$d = \frac{\overline{Y}_{A1} - \overline{Y}_{A2}}{s} = \frac{70.00 - 80.00}{7.91} = -1.26 \text{ Using } s \text{ from the drill and practice group}$$

Decision

The calculated value (-2.19) fails to exceed the critical value (± 2.26). You fail to reject the null hypothesis and cannot accept the alternative hypothesis. You cannot conclude that the two methods of teaching cartography produce different examination results.

---

continued

Textbox 8.8 (Continued)

Possible Decision Error

You may have committed a Type II error. You failed to reject the null hypothesis when it may have been false.

Other

The confidence interval and the effect size are both fairly large.

Pooled Variance Model t-Test

Calculated value:

$$t = \frac{\overline{Y}_{A1} - \overline{Y}_{A2}}{\sqrt{\frac{s_P^2}{n_{A1}} + \frac{s_P^2}{n_{A2}}}} = \frac{70.00 - 80.00}{\sqrt{\frac{7.46^2}{5} + \frac{7.46^2}{6}}} = \frac{-10.00}{4.52} = -2.21$$

Critical Value

For $\alpha = .05$ (two-tailed) and df $= (n_1 - 1) + (n_2 - 1) = (5 - 1) + (6 - 1) = 9$, tabled value of t is: ± 2.26.

Exact Probability

Using a computer program, you find that $p = .054$ is the exact probability associated with a calculated value of ± 2.21 and df $= 9$.

Confidence Interval

$$\overline{Y}_D - t_{1-\alpha/2} s_{PD} = -10.00 - (2.26)(4.52) \text{ and } \overline{Y}_D + t_{1-\alpha/2} s_{PD} = -10.00 + (2.26)(4.52) = -20.22$$
$$\text{and } 0.22 \text{ or } -20.22 \leq \mu_D \leq 0.22.$$

Effect Size

$$d = \frac{\overline{Y}_{A1} - \overline{Y}_{A2}}{s_p} = \frac{-10.00}{7.46} = -1.34$$

Decision

The calculated value (-2.21) fails to exceed the critical value (± 2.26). You fail to reject the null hypothesis and cannot accept the alternative hypothesis. You cannot conclude that the two methods of teaching cartography produce different examination results.

Possible Decision Error

You may have committed a Type II error. You failed to reject the null hypothesis when it may have been false.

Other

The confidence interval and the effect size are both fairly large.

The calculations in Textbox 8.8 illustrate that the separate variance and pooled variance model *t*-tests do not result in the same calculated value of *t* when both sample sizes and variances differ between the two groups. In the example, there was only a single difference in sample sizes between the groups (i.e., 5 versus 6) and the group variances appear similar. With larger differences between the groups in sample sizes and variances, the two models might yield very different results. Therefore, we need guidelines for choosing between them. Before we offer these guidelines, we need to review the assumptions underlying the *t*-test.

UNDERLYING ASSUMPTIONS

The *t*-test is based on several underlying assumptions about the data used for analysis. Fortunately, the *t*-test is generally robust to **assumption violations** and can be used even when the following conditions are not strictly met:

- The variability within each group should be normally distributed.
- Each data point, or score, should be independent of every other data point.
- The variances of the two groups should be equal, or homogeneous.

What can you do when these assumptions are not met? In the first instance, you want to try and understand why the assumptions have not been met to determine better the nature of the problem. In the second instance, you can select among a variety of alternatives, depending on the nature and degree of the assumption violation. In extreme cases, you may even go so far as to suspend the use of data analysis because you judge the data to be of poor quality.

The Variability Within Each Group Should Be Normally Distributed

The population from which each group is sampled is assumed to be normally distributed. Fortunately, this is only a problem for the *t*-test when sample sizes are small and the departure from normality is extreme. To overcome problems of non-normality one could do the following:

- Discard outliers (i.e., extreme scores) in skewed distributions.
- Convert the original scores, or "normalize" them, and then apply the *t*-test.
- Use a nonparametric test, covered later in this book, which makes no or fewer assumptions about the nature of the data (but which is likely to be a less sensitive or less powerful statistical test, increasing the risk of making Type II errors).

Each Data Point, or Score, Should Be Independent of Every Other Data Point

When the data *between* the two groups are related to each other (e.g., test scores on the same individual taken both before and after the treatment), the correlated samples or dependent samples *t*-test is used in place of the independent samples *t*-test.

We will cover this statistical technique when we cover repeated measures designs in Chapter 12.

When the data *within* each group are related to each other (e.g., individual test scores for participants who studied with teammates and learned together):

- Use a different unit of analysis (e.g., the mean of each small team).
- Use a more sophisticated parametric statistical test (e.g., randomized block design).
- Perform a more conservative test by lowering *alpha* (e.g., test at .01 instead of .05).
- Use a nonparametric procedure that does not assume independence of scores.

The Variances of the Two Groups Should Be Equal or Homogeneous

The population variances from which the two samples were drawn should be equal. Variance heterogeneity (i.e., when variances are not homogeneous) is especially a problem when sample sizes are both small *and* unequal. Otherwise, the *t*-test is generally *robust* to this assumption violation. The effect of this assumption violation with unequal and small sample sizes is to make the *t*-test too liberal, leading to an increase in the likelihood of making Type I errors beyond the nominal alpha level.

Two solutions to this problem are as follows:

- Use samples of the same size.
- When equal sample sizes are not possible, use the separate variance model *t*-test but reduce the degrees of freedom used to find the critical value (see below).

Evaluating Homogeneity of Variance There are several procedures for evaluating **homogeneity of variance.** We will briefly cover three of these—F_{max}, Levene's test, and Bartlett's test—since you may encounter one or more of them, especially if you conduct data analysis using a computer package.

The popular opinion among statisticians suggests that conducting these tests is of limited value. In circumstances in which they are needed most (e.g., small, unequal sample sizes), the tests are poorest. In contrast, for samples about equal in size, relatively big differences in the population variances seem to have only small consequences for the conclusions derived from the *t*-test.

F_{max} A simple procedure, F_{max}, is recommended by Keppel et al. (1992). Form a ratio of variances of the two groups:

$$\text{Equation 8.15: } F_{max} = \frac{s^2_{largest}}{s^2_{smallest}}$$

CD-ROM link 8.7

Problem Generator: The t-Test
To practice making the decision between separate and pooled variance model *t*-tests, select *t*-test from the Problem Generator Menu on the CD-ROM. The Problem Generator will create as many practice problems as you need and will tell you which model is correct for each example using the F_{max} test.

Textbox 8.9

F_{max} for the Drill Press Scenario

In the Drill Press scenario with equal sample sizes (see Textbox 8.1), the group variances are also equal. Therefore, $F_{max} = (7.91)^2/(7.91)^2 = 1.0$. Clearly, the assumption of variance homogeneity is met, because the group variances are equal.

When a case was added to the example (see Textbox 8.7), the variances were no longer identical. Are they heterogeneous?

$$F_{max} = \frac{s^2_{largest}}{s^2_{smallest}} = \frac{(7.91)^2}{(7.07)^2} = 1.25$$

The difference between the variances of the two groups is not very large. Therefore, you can be reasonably assured that the assumption of variance homogeneity has been met.

If the ratio is larger than 3.0, the homogeneity of variance assumption is not met. See Textbox 8.9 for an example using the Drill Press scenario.

Levene's and Bartlett's Tests   Two other procedures exist for determining variance heterogeneity that generally require the use of statistical software: Levene's test and Bartlett's test. Levene's test for homogeneity of variance is the preferred method when the data come from continuous, but not necessarily normal, distributions. The computations involve finding, for each case, the absolute difference from the group mean and then performing an analysis of variance on these differences. (See Chapter 10, which covers the Oneway Analysis of Variance.) When the test statistic is significant, the homogeneity of variance assumption is not met.

Another test is Bartlett's test for homogeneity of variance. Bartlett's test is used when the data come from normal distributions; the test is not robust to departures from normality, making it less preferable than Levene's test.

CHOOSING BETWEEN THE SEPARATE AND POOLED VARIANCE MODELS

Computationally, a choice between the two models is needed only when both the group sample sizes and the group variances are not identical. When sufficient evidence exists to conclude that the variances are heterogeneous, use the separate variance model with reduced degrees of freedom. When sufficient evidence does not exist to conclude that the variances are heterogeneous, use the pooled variance model.

Reduced Degrees of Freedom   To reduce the effects of variance heterogeneity, which makes the *t*-test too powerful and too sensitive to mean differences between groups, reduce the degrees of freedom[3] used to find the critical value of *t* for the separate variance model *only*. A simple manual calculation approach to reducing degrees of freedom exists:

$$\textbf{Equation 8.16: } \text{Reduced df} = (n_{A1} + n_{A2} - 2)/2$$

Use the reduced df instead of $n_{A1} + n_{A2} - 2$.

This procedure effectively cuts in half the degrees of freedom used to determine the critical value of *t* for the separate variance model, reducing the degrees of freedom results in a higher critical value of *t* being identified. This, in turn, makes the test more conservative and is a procedure that should be applied when variance heterogeneity is a problem.

The approach taken in computer programs such as Minitab and SPSS is also to reduce the degrees of freedom, but the procedure is more complicated, more exact, and often results in a fractional degree of freedom (Minitab truncates this to an integer):

$$\text{df} = \frac{1}{z_{A1} + z_{A2}} \qquad \text{where } z_k = \left[\frac{\dfrac{s_k^2}{n_k}}{\dfrac{s_{A1}^2}{n_{A1}} + \dfrac{s_{A1}^2}{n_{A1}}} \right]^2 \Big/ (n_k - 1)$$

Guidelines for Choosing Between the Two Models

When should you use the separate variance model *t*-test and when should you use the pooled variance model *t*-test? Textbox 8.10 contains some simple guidelines for choosing between the two models.

PUTTING IT ALL TOGETHER

We have tried to emphasize here why the *t*-test is superior to the *z*-test for making inferences about differences between the means of two groups. The family of *t*-distributions allows one to find the appropriate critical value even when testing small sample sizes. When sample sizes are small, the critical value for the *t*-test is larger than the critical value for the *z*-test. In addition, the family of *t*-distributions allows one to find the appropriate critical value when sample sizes are large. When sample sizes are large, the critical value for the *t*-test is similar to the critical value for the *z*-test.

---

[3]This reduction in degrees of freedom applies to finding the critical value only. It has no bearing on the procedures used to compute the calculated value.

Textbox 8.10

Guidelines for Using the Separate and Pooled Variance *t*-Tests

When sample sizes are identical and variances are identical; when sample sizes are not identical but variances are identical

- The calculated values of both procedures are the same.
- The degrees of freedom, and hence the critical values for both procedures, are the same.
- Therefore, both procedures lead to the identical conclusions; either one may be used.

When sample sizes are identical but variances are not identical

- The calculated values of both procedures are the same.
- Because variances are not identical, statistical packages (e.g., Minitab, SPSS, SYSTAT) will adjust the degrees of freedom for the separate variance model downward. Therefore, the critical values of both procedures will not be the same.
- If the variances are different, use the reduced degrees of freedom approach of the separate variance model to find the critical value.
- If the variances are not different, use the complete degrees of freedom approach of the pooled degrees of freedom model.

When sample sizes are not identical and variances are not identical

- The calculated values of the two procedures are different.
- Because variances are not identical, statistical packages (e.g., Minitab, SPSS, SYSTAT) will adjust the degrees of freedom for the separate variance downward. Therefore, the critical values of both procedures will also not be the same.
- If the variances are different, use the separate variance model to find both the calculated value and the critical value with reduced degrees of freedom.
- If the variances are not different, use the pooled variance model to find both the calculated value and the critical value with full degrees of freedom.

We also showed how other statistical procedures were or were not affected by the use of the *t*-test. The procedures included confidence intervals, effect size calculations, and power.

Finally, we discussed the differences between the separate variance model *t*-test and the pooled variance model *t*-test in terms of estimating the standard error of the mean difference. We discussed assumption violations and the critical problem created by variance heterogeneity. We concluded with a set of guidelines for choosing between the two models and deciding when to use reduced degrees of freedom and why.

The Separate Variance Model t-Test   The calculated value of t is the same as the calculated value of z:

$$\text{Equation 8.1: } t = \frac{\overline{Y}_{A1} - \overline{Y}_{A2}}{s_D}$$

$$\text{Equation 8.2: } t = \frac{\overline{Y}_{A1} - \overline{Y}_{A2}}{\sqrt{\dfrac{s_{A1}^2}{n_{A1}} + \dfrac{s_{A2}^2}{n_{A2}}}}$$

$$\text{Equation 8.3: } t = \frac{\overline{Y}_{A1} - \overline{Y}_{A2}}{\sqrt{\dfrac{\dfrac{\sum (Y_{iA1} - \overline{Y}_{A1})^2}{(n_{A1} - 1)}}{n_{A1}} + \dfrac{\dfrac{\sum (Y_{iA2} - \overline{Y}_{A2})^2}{(n_{A2} - 1)}}{n_{A2}}}}$$

As sample size decreases, the critical value of the t-test increases. The degrees of freedom for finding the critical value of t is as follows:

$$\text{Equation 8.4: } df = (n_1 - 1) + (n_2 - 1) = (n_1 + n_2) - 2 = N - 2$$

Confidence Intervals (Separate Variance Model)   The two-sided confidence interval for a nondirectional two-tailed alternative hypothesis is as follows:

$$\text{Equation 8.5: } \overline{Y}_D - t_{1-\alpha/2}s_D \text{ and } \overline{Y}_D + t_{1-\alpha/2}s_D$$

The one-sided confidence interval for a one-tailed *positive* direction alternative hypothesis is as follows:

$$\text{Equation 8.6: } \overline{Y}_D - t_{1-\alpha}s_D$$

The one-sided confidence interval for a one-tailed *negative* direction alternative hypothesis is as follows:

$$\text{Equation 8.7: } \overline{Y}_D + t_{1-\alpha}s_D$$

Effect Sizes (Separate Variance Approach)   We compute effect sizes as before:

$$\text{(Equation 7.4) } d = \frac{\overline{Y}_{A1} - \overline{Y}_{A2}}{s}$$

For all but the smallest sample sizes, the steps for estimating power given in Chapter 7 may be used.

In addition, the formula for determining the appropriate group sample size given in Chapter 7 may be used whenever the expected sample sizes are moderate in size.

The Pooled Variance Model t-Test   The formula for the standard error using the pooled variance approach is given below. The pooling procedure is relatively straightforward. It is the weighted average of the estimates from the two samples.
First you need to find the pooled variance (s_P^2):

$$\text{Equation 8.8: } s_P^2 = \frac{(n_{A1} - 1)s_{A1}^2 + (n_{A2} - 1)s_{A2}^2}{n_{A1} + n_{A2} - 2}$$

Next, use the pooled variance (s_P^2) to find the standard error of the mean difference (s_{PD}):

$$\text{Equation 8.9: } s_{PD} = \sqrt{\frac{s_P^2}{n_{A1}} + \frac{s_P^2}{n_{A2}}}$$

The pooled variance model *t*-test is as follows:

$$\text{Equation 8.10: } t = \frac{\overline{Y}_{A1} - \overline{Y}_{A2}}{\sqrt{\frac{s_P^2}{n_{A1}} + \frac{s_P^2}{n_{A2}}}} \qquad df = n_{A1} + n_{A2} - 2$$

Confidence Intervals (Pooled Variance Approach)   The two-sided confidence interval for a nondirectional two-tailed alternative hypothesis is as follows:

$$\text{Equation 8.11: } \overline{Y}_D - t_{1-\alpha/2}s_{PD} \text{ and } \overline{Y}_D + t_{1-\alpha/2}s_{PD}$$

The one-sided confidence interval for a one-tailed *positive* direction alternative hypothesis is as follows:

$$\text{Equation 8.12: } \overline{Y}_D - t_{1-\alpha}s_{PD}$$

The one-sided confidence interval for a one-tailed *negative* direction alternative hypothesis is as follows:

$$\text{Equation 8.13: } \overline{Y}_D + t_{1-\alpha}s_{PD}$$

Effect Size (Pooled Variance Approach)   The formula for estimating the population effect size using the pooled variance method is as follows:

$$\text{Equation 8.14: } d = \frac{\overline{Y}_{A1} - \overline{Y}_{A2}}{s_P}$$

Underlying Assumptions

- The variability within each group should be normally distributed.
- Each data point, or score, should be independent of every other data point.
- The variances of the two groups should be equal or homogeneous.

A simple procedure exists for testing the homogeneity of variance assumption, but it is not always useful:

$$\textbf{Equation 8.15: } F_{max} = \frac{s^2_{largest}}{s^2_{smallest}}$$

In order to reduce the effects of variance heterogeneity, reduce the degrees of freedom used to find the critical value for the separate variance model *t*-test:

$$\textbf{Equation 8.16: } \text{Reduced df} = (n_{A1} + n_{A2} - 2)/2.$$

Use the reduced df instead of $n_{A1} + n_{A2} - 2$.

When variances are heterogeneous, it is not advisable to use the pooled variance model *t*-test.

Textbox 8.11

A Study of Laughter and Dissociation

People laugh during play, trauma, exhilaration, aggressive encounters, and even to express superiority. But why do people laugh during bereavement? Keltner and Bonanno (1997) studied 39 adults who had lost their spouses six months previously.

Using a bereavement interview and the results of self-report and other measures, participants were classified as either Laughers ($n = 21$) or Nonlaughers ($n = 18$). Laughers and Nonlaughers differed significantly on several emotion self-report indices. Laughers compared to Nonlaughers expressed less anger, $t(37) = -3.77$, $p < .001$; less distress, $t(37) = -2.61$, $p < .01$; and less overall negative emotion, $t(37) = -3.49$, $p < .001$. Laughers also showed reduced awareness of distress, $t(37) = 2.46$, $p < .05$. Finally, Laughers exhibited enhanced interpersonal relations compared to Nonlaughers based on their scores on the Dyadic Adjustment Scale; $t(37) = 2.10$, $p < .05$.

Keltner and Bonanno (1997) used these and other study findings to support their hypotheses concerning the benefits of laughter during bereavement. Specifically, laughter facilitates the adaptive response to stress by increasing the psychological distance from distress and by enhancing social relations.

KEY TERMS

Separate variance model *t*-test

Critical value

Degrees of freedom

Deviation score

N, n, n_1, n_{A1}

Exact probability

Estimated standard deviation

Pooled variance model *t*-test

Assumption violations

Homogeneity of variance

F_{max}

REFERENCES

Cohen, J. (1988). *Statistical power analysis for the behavioral sciences* (2nd ed.). Hillsdale, NJ: Lawrence Erlbaum Associates.

Hays, W. J. (1994). *Statistics*. (5th ed.). Fort Worth, TX: Harcourt Brace College Publishing.

Kelter, D., & Bonanno, G. A. (1997). A study of laughter and dissociation: Distinct correlates of laughter and smiling during bereavement. *Journal of Personality and Social Psychology, 73*, 687–702.

Keppel, G., Saufley, W. H., & Tokunaga, H. (1992). *Introduction to design and analysis: A student's handbook* (2nd ed.). New York: W. H. Freeman and Co.

PROBLEMS

Questions

Section 1   Conceptual/Definition

8.1. What happens to the shape of the population sampling distribution when sample sizes are small?

8.2. What is the separate variance model *t*-test, and how is this related to the *z*-test?

8.3. How are the *t*-test and the *z*-test different?

8.4. Define the term *degrees of freedom*.

8.5. What information is required to determine the critical value of *t*?

8.6. What assumption must be met in order to use the pooled variance model *t*-test?

8.7. What is the major advantage of the pooled variance model *t*-test over the separate variance model *t*-test?

8.8. Under what conditions will the pooled and separate models produce the same calculated value of *t*?

8.9. What assumptions underlie the use of the *t*-test?

8.10. How can homogeneity of variance be assessed?

Section 2   Numerical

8.11. What is the critical value of t for a nondirectional hypothesis for $\alpha = .05$ when the sample size of both groups is 8 (assuming that homogeneity of variance has not been violated)?

8.12. How would the answer to question 8.11 above change if homogeneity of variance had been violated?

The following data exists for both the experimental and control groups in a given experiment. Use it to answer questions 8.13 to 8.18.

Control: 23, 29, 32, 24, 27, 28

Experimental   36, 39, 43, 37, 40, 41, 38

8.13. Use the F_{max} procedure to assess homogeneity of variance.

8.14. Perform a nondirectional pooled variance t-test using $p = .05$.

8.15. Perform a directional separate variance t-test using $p = .05$ (assuming that the experimental group will produce a higher mean than the control group). Perform this calculation even though the results of the F_{max} indicate otherwise.

8.16. Determine the two-sided confidence interval for the estimated mean difference.

8.17. Determine the one-sided confidence interval for the estimated mean difference (for a negative direction alternative hypothesis).

8.18. Determine the effect size for this experiment.

The following information exists for a given study:

Group	n	Mean	SD	Standard Error of the Mean
1	6	12.33	2.34	0.95
2	6	17.50	1.87	0.76
$t = -4.23$		p-value $= .0018$		

The assumption of homogeneity of variance was not violated.

Answer the following questions:

8.19. Construct the 95% confidence interval for the mean difference (using the t-test approach).

8.20. Prove, using the F_{max} test, why the assumption of homogeneity of variance was not violated.

Testing the Difference Between Two or More Independent Groups

The Oneway between-Groups Analysis of Variance

OVERVIEW

Now that we have explored the possibilities involved in the analysis of data from two independent groups, it is time to take on the challenge of explaining the variability in the dependent variable when the independent variable has more than two values or levels. The Oneway Analysis of Variance is an inferential statistical procedure for testing the difference between two or more independent groups.

As you will see, the greater the number of independent groups involved in the analysis, the greater the analytical choices. We will begin by examining some of these choices, in particular the reasons for exploring general hypotheses about the treatment versus specific hypotheses.

We will then examine the computational procedures involved in the Oneway Analysis of Variance, especially how the total variability can be divided into additive components. You will also learn about the family of sampling distributions used for hypothesis testing.

We will look at assumptions underlying the Oneway Analysis of Variance and what to do about assumption violations. In addition, we will consider effect sizes and how to estimate a general effect size. Finally, we will cover the calculation of power and the use of power tables.

More specifically, we will address these questions:

1. What are omnibus hypotheses and what are the advantages of exploring them?
2. What are multiple comparisons and when should they be used?
3. What are some key concepts in the partitioning of variability and why is the partitioning of variability important?
4. How is the logic of the t-test extended to more than two groups?
5. What is the general linear model?
6. How does the Oneway Analysis of Variance partition the total variability in the dependent variable into two additive components?
7. Why is the calculated value considered a ratio of variances?
8. Why is the sampling distribution used for hypothesis testing skewed?
9. What are the alternative ways of computing effect sizes?
10. How can Cohen's power tables be used?

We begin with the scenario described in Textbox 9.1.

Textbox 9.1

Scenario: Rewarding Interest

A behavioral psychologist introduces a program of token rewards to inner city schoolchildren to help motivate them to learn and enhance their achievement in, and appreciation of, reading. The program seems to work fine until a cognitive psychologist comes along and remarks that once the rewards stop, the children will be less motivated than ever to read. The behavioral psychologist and the cognitive psychologist argue over the best way to explore the controversy. Eventually they agree to study whether the *type of reward* students receive affects subsequent task interest. In particular, they want to make comparisons among three groups: (1) a *no reward* group, (2) a group that receives rewards merely for borrowing books (*controlling reward*), and (3) a group that receives rewards only when they have demonstrated they have read and understood the borrowed books (*informational reward*).

As an expert in research and data analysis, you are asked to conduct a modest experiment to evaluate the effects of extrinsic rewards on intrinsic motivation. You take a representative sample of schoolchildren and randomly assign those whose parents have provided informed consent to one of the three groups. The children participate in the research for several months. At the end of the treatment, you measure the intrinsic interest of the students in a novel way. You merely count the number of library books students sign out from the school library in a two-month period. The data are presented in Table 9.1. Now you wish to proceed to analyze the data and test whether the treatment had an effect, using $\alpha = .05$ as the probability value for significance testing.

What are the steps and procedures you will follow to determine whether there is a significant difference among the three reward conditions? What are the null and alternative hypotheses? What is the alpha level you will use for significance testing? What test statistic and computational procedure will you employ? What is the calculated value? What is the critical value? What is your decision about the null and alternative hypotheses, and what type of decision error might you have made?

OMNIBUS TESTS OF SIGNIFICANCE

In this section, we provide a brief and generally nonmathematical rationale for the Oneway *Analysis of Variance* (**ANOVA**). We hope this rationale helps you to understand why the Oneway ANOVA exists as a general statistical tool for analyzing research situations in which the independent variable has multiple levels.

Multilevel Independent Variables

When referring to research design in previous chapters, we often simplified things by talking about *experimental* and *control* groups or *treatment* and *no treatment* groups. This is, however, a fairly restrictive way to do research. There are many situations in which you would want to examine simultaneously more than two levels of an independent variable, some of which are listed below:

TABLE 9.1   Library Books Borrowed by Controlling Reward (A_1), Informational Reward (A_2), and No Reward (A_3) Students

Controlling Rewards (A_1)	Informational Rewards (A_2)	No Rewards (A_3)
11	10	6
3	11	4
5	12	7
9	13	12
9	13	14
8	14	11
5	9	10
6	9	9
7	8	8
$n_{A1} = 9$	$n_{A2} = 9$	$n_{A3} = 9$
$\overline{Y}_{A1} = 7.00$	$\overline{Y}_{A2} = 11.00$	$\overline{Y}_{A3} = 9.00$
$s^2_{A1} = 6.25$	$s^2_{A2} = 4.50$	$s^2_{A3} = 9.73$

$N = 27$

$\overline{Y} = 9.00$

$s^2 = 9.08$

Quantitative differences among levels of the independent variable:

- Dosage level of drugs
- Length of stay in therapy
- Number of hours studied

Qualitative differences among levels of the independent variable:

- Classroom goal structures
- Feedback procedures
- Presentation media

The Oneway ANOVA is a statistical technique designed to deal with situations in which the independent variable has multiple levels. It is called *Oneway* to signify that there is only a single independent variable. Unlike the z-test and t-test it is not limited to the special case of an independent variable with only two values but can be applied to analysis situations in which the independent variable has more than two values.

In situations in which there are more than two levels of the independent variable, the Oneway ANOVA becomes a general, or omnibus, test of hypotheses. In other words, the ANOVA helps answer the question, "Are there any differences among the groups?" rather than more specific questions such as "Where were the specific differences among groups?" or "Is the mean of one group significantly different from the mean of another group?"

In situations in which there are only two levels of the independent variable, the Oneway ANOVA may also be used, but conclusions about the null and alternative hypotheses will be identical to those reached with the *t*-test. In fact, there is a precise mathematical relationship between the calculated value of *t* and the calculated value, *F*, of the Oneway ANOVA. For an independent variable with two levels or groups: $t^2 = F$. (A mathematical proof of the relationship between *t* and *F* can be found in Appendix 9.1 at the end of this chapter.)

SPECIFIC OR GENERAL HYPOTHESES?

Let's see how the Oneway ANOVA can help you to analyze the data from the Rewarding Interest scenario of Textbox 9.1. Your first challenge is to decide on the null and alternative hypotheses. To this point, only the simplest type of experimental design has been considered: a single independent variable with the smallest number of values (i.e., two) and a single dependent variable. That is not the situation in the Reward Interest scenario. The independent variable in the Reward Interest scenario has three values: Controlling Reward (A_1), Informational Reward (A_2), and No Reward (A_3).

Exploring Specific Hypotheses   How does one deal with the complication of having an independent variable with three levels? With the logic and techniques covered thus far, you might be inclined to follow the steps used when you conducted a *t*-test to compare two groups. Doing so, you might propose several sets of null and alternative hypotheses:

Set 1:

$$H_0: \mu_{A1} = \mu_{A2}$$
$$H_a: \mu_{A1} \neq \mu_{A2}$$

Set 1 compares controlling rewards and informational rewards.

Set 2:

$$H_0: \mu_{A1} = \mu_{A3}$$
$$H_a: \mu_{A1} \neq \mu_{A3}$$

Set 2 compares controlling rewards and no rewards.

Set 3:

$$H_0: \mu_{A2} = \mu_{A3}$$
$$H_a: \mu_{A2} \neq \mu_{A3}$$

Set 3 compares informational rewards and no rewards.

Each of the three sets contains a null and an alternative hypothesis about the equivalence of two population means. In each set, therefore, the third population mean is excluded. Using what you have learned thus far you would conduct a *t*-test making a **comparison or contrast** between the means implicated in each set. The results of each comparison would allow you to decide between the null and alternative hypotheses.

Because any one set omits the third mean entirely, you might be tempted to evaluate more than one set of hypotheses. If you did, you would then conduct more than one comparison between means. Although there are situations in which **multiple comparisons** should be undertaken, there are other situations in which multiple comparisons should be avoided.

When Multiple Comparisons Should Be Avoided
There are both practical and theoretical reasons against conducting multiple comparisons when the independent variable has more than two levels.

- There can be a large number of comparisons to evaluate and statistical calculations to perform. This means additional computational labor for you. The results of multiple statistical tests are certainly less parsimonious than a single statistical test asking whether the independent variable worked "in general."
- Evaluating all possible comparisons among groups requires that the same data be used repeatedly. There is some statistical redundancy in doing so.
- Doing multiple *t*-tests, each based on only a subset of the data (i.e., only two of the groups at a time), may result in a loss in power compared to using all the data for analysis.
- The likelihood of committing a Type I error somewhere in the collection of comparisons grows higher as the number of comparisons increases.

One of the inadequacies of multiple *t*-tests for exploring data from several groups is the time-consuming and cumbersome nature of the analyses. When the number of levels of the independent variable is large, the number of *t*-tests is also large. This procedure is rather cumbersome compared to a single, omnibus test. For example, imagine an independent variable with five levels labeled $A_1, A_2, A_3, A_4,$ and A_5. If one conducted all possible comparisons among pairs of groups, there would be 10 *t*-tests to perform:

$$A_1-A_2, A_1-A_3, A_1-A_4, A_1-A_5,$$
$$A_2-A_3, A_2-A_4, A_2-A_5,$$
$$A_3-A_4, A_3-A_5,$$
$$A_4-A_5$$

The individual *t*-tests give specific bits of information but do not answer the general question about the overall effect of the independent variable. Furthermore, using only subsets of the data can make each *t*-test less powerful because the sample size for each *t*-test, which is based on only two groups, is less than the sample size for all the groups combined.

Finally, with so many tests, there is an increased likelihood of a Type I error somewhere in the collection of tests. For example, imagine that you set $\alpha = .05$ for each individual comparison in your collection of tests. As the number of comparisons grows, the likelihood increases beyond .05 that one comparison in the collection will result in a false rejection of the null hypothesis.

When Multiple Comparisons Are Appropriate   In Chapter 10 we will return to consider in detail those situations in which it is appropriate to conduct a series of two-group (and other) comparisons, either in place of the omnibus Oneway ANOVA or in addition to the omnibus Oneway ANOVA. The use of a series of comparisons in place of the omnibus Oneway ANOVA is appropriate when the researcher has very specific hypotheses about differences among levels of the independent variable *and* when the set of comparisons is independent. One uses **planned multiple comparisons** to explore specific hypotheses in lieu of the omnibus test. In contrast, one uses **post hoc multiple comparisons** to probe for specific differences after one has found that the omnibus test is significant.

Exploring General Hypotheses   The null hypothesis for a Oneway ANOVA is that there are no significant differences among the means of the various treatment groups. It can be expressed as follows:

$$H_0: \mu_{A1} = \mu_{A2} = \mu_{A3} = \mu_{Ak} \text{ where } k \text{ is the number of treatment levels}$$

Or equivalently it could be expressed as follows:

$$H_0: \text{ all } \mu_A\text{'s are equal}$$

The alternate hypothesis is as follows:

$$H_a: \text{ not all } \mu_A\text{'s are equal}$$

The null hypothesis is readily understandable. It says that there are no significant differences among the group means. The alternative hypothesis is harder to understand. It says that there is at least one significant difference among the group means. The alternate hypothesis H_a cannot be interpreted to mean that the treatment means are all different from one another, only that at least one difference exists in the set of means. As will become clear, the Oneway ANOVA actually computes the average variability among group means as a way to address the **omnibus hypothesis**. Additionally, accepting H_a does not in any way indicate where the difference(s) exist(s) between the group means. To find this out, you will want to use post hoc multiple comparisons, which are covered in Chapter 10.

Partitioning Variability

In the Rewarding Interest scenario of Textbox 9.1, there are a total of 27 participants, and for each of them you know how many books were borrowed in a two-month period. For each participant, you also know to which Reward Type they were exposed. The omnibus, or general, question concerns whether there is a significant relationship between the independent variable, Reward Type, and the dependent variable, Books Borrowed. Put another way, the omnibus question asks whether the amount of variability in the dependent variable, Books Borrowed, explained by the independent variable, Reward Type, is so large that it is unlikely to have occurred merely as a function of chance.

Key Concepts in the Partitioning of Variability   A few key concepts are embedded in the prior paragraph. One key concept concerns the overall variability in the dependent variable, Books Borrowed, that is, the general fluctuation among participants in their book borrowing. What is responsible for this behavior?

CD-ROM link 9.1

Activity 9.1: The Oneway ANOVA and the Calculated F-Value
In Activity 9.1, you can explore key concepts associated with the Oneway ANOVA by varying the between-groups variability and within-groups variability of three groups of data. This will help you to understand how the Oneway ANOVA partitions the total variability in a data set.

Another key concept concerns the variability in the dependent variable, Books Borrowed, and whether it may be explained by fluctuations in the independent variable, Reward Type. More specifically, the alternative hypothesis says that not all group means are equal. In contrast, the null hypothesis says that none of the variability in the dependent variable may be explained by fluctuations in the independent variable.

A final key concept concerns the supposition that some variability in the dependent variable is due to chance fluctuation among the participants. That is, there are differences in book-borrowing behavior that cannot be explained and that one attributes to random variability or error.

You have now arrived at a critical point in your understanding of Oneway ANOVA. You should have an intuitive appreciation that the **total variability** in the dependent variable can be partitioned into two additive components: **between-groups variability** (including variability in the dependent variable, which may be attributed to fluctuations in the independent variable) and **within-groups variability** (including variability in the dependent variable, which may be attributable to chance fluctuations among the participants).

In other words:

Total variability = between-groups variability + within-groups variability

Illustrating the Partitioning of Total Variability   Imagine that you conducted a very large study of book borrowing instead of just the small investigation described in the Rewarding Interest scenario of Textbox 9.1. Furthermore, imagine that you chose initially to ignore the experimental condition to which participants belonged. Instead, you decided to "lump" all the data together.

Total Variability   If you then decided to construct a frequency distribution of books borrowed, it should look something like the normal distribution illustrated in Figure 9.1. You should find that the mean of all the book-borrowing scores is the most frequently occurring score and that there are fewer students who borrow less than the average and fewer students who borrow more than the average. Very little borrowing will be rare, while a great deal of borrowing will also be rare. Finally, total variability is represented by the area under the normal curve.

Between-Groups Variability   Now imagine that you decided to create a frequency distribution for each of the groups in the experiments: Controlling Reward (A_1), Informational Reward (A_2), and No Reward (A_3). Each of the three separate frequency distributions should also be normal in shape, as illustrated in Figure 9.2.

Remember that even if the null hypothesis is true and the treatment had no effect, you would not expect the three group means to be identical. Chance fluctuation, or more precisely, sampling error, will result in some fluctuation in the group means. On the other hand, if the treatment was effective, there would also be differences among the means attributable to the effect of the independent variable: type of reward.

Between-groups variability is represented by the differences among the group means. Between-groups variability is *not* represented by the fluctuation in scores within each of the groups.

Within-Groups Variability   What represents the fluctuation of scores within the groups? Look at Figure 9.3 and consider each group distribution separately. Within-groups variability is represented by the area under each of the normal curves.

When only the total variability in book borrowing is represented, one arrives at the single frequency distribution shown in Figure 9.1. When the *same* variability in book borrowing between and within groups is represented, one arrives at the three frequency distributions shown in Figures 9.2 and 9.3.

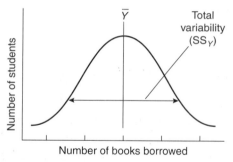

Figure 9.1 Frequency distribution of total variability in book borrowing

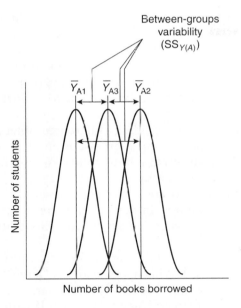

Figure 9.2 Three frequency distributions used to illustrate between-groups variability in book borrowing

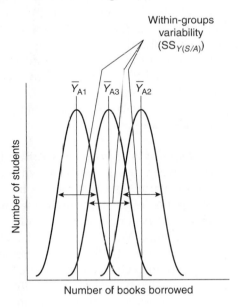

Figure 9.3 Three frequency distributions used to illustrate within-groups variability in book borrowing

The Importance of Partitioning Variability   Why is partitioning total variability important? Because you will eventually use the partitioned variability as the basis of your next statistical test: the *F*-test. If you can show that the average variability among groups is much larger than the average variability within

groups, you will be inclined to reject the null hypothesis and conclude that the treatment created a difference among groups beyond the influence of chance fluctuation or sampling error.

In other words, you cannot judge whether the treatment was effective only from an examination of the magnitude of the differences among the groups. You must judge the differences among the groups relative to the differences within the groups.

Extending the Logic of the t-Test   Understanding differences among several groups relative to differences within each group is an extension of the approach we took concerning the mean difference between two groups. We use the *t*-test to analyze the mean differences between two groups.

The *t*-test is a ratio. In the numerator of the *t*-ratio is the mean difference, an indication of variability between two groups. In the denominator of the *t*-ratio is the standard error, an indication of average within-groups variability further adjusted by sample size.

Clearly, the *t*-test is designed to assess the mean difference relative to both within-groups variability and sample size. What appears to be a "large" mean difference may not be unusual if within-groups variability is also large. Conversely, what appears to be a "small" mean difference may be unusual if within-groups variability is small.

For an independent variable with more than two values, the logic of the Oneway ANOVA is similar; the *F*-test, which is the statistical test you will use, is also a ratio like the *t*-test. In the numerator of the *F*-ratio is the average between-groups variability. This represents chance fluctuation or sampling error plus any effects of the treatment. In the denominator of the *F*-ratio is the average within-groups variability. This represents only chance fluctuation or error because one cannot explain statistically why individual scores fluctuate. Therefore, what appears to be a "large" average between-groups variability may not be unusual if the average within-groups variability is also large.

Judging Between-Groups Variability in Light of Within-Groups Variability   Figure 9.4 illustrates the same degree of between-groups variability as Figure 9.3. However, the magnitude of within-groups variability is increased in Figure 9.4; there is greater fluctuation among participants in Book Borrowing within each of the three treatment groups. Within each group the amount of book borrowing fluctuated a great deal from the mean of that group. With the increased variability in book borrowing among the participants, it is harder to determine whether the differences between the groups represents more than chance fluctuation.

In which situation would you be more likely to judge that Reward Type affects Book Borrowing? The consistency of student responses within each of the groups as illustrated in Figure 9.3 should increase your subjective confidence that there was a treatment effect compared to the inconsistency illustrated in Figure 9.4. The Oneway ANOVA is based on this logic, that judging differences among the groups depends on knowing the consistency of scores within the groups.

The General Linear Model   If you have conducted a proper, true experiment and assigned participants randomly to treatment conditions, you should be able to

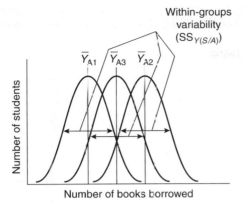

Figure 9.4 Three frequency distributions used to illustrate *increased* within-groups variability in book borrowing

make an important assumption. Before exposing participants to the experimental treatment, you assume that the distributions of each of the groups are equivalent and representative of the population from which they were drawn. Any difference in means among groups is a function of sampling error. Furthermore, the variability among subjects within each group is assumed to be random due to undistinguished individual differences and unsystematic influences.

Thus, any participant's score (Y) *before* introducing the treatment is a function of the overall or grand mean of the base population from which the sample was drawn and random error. This score can be estimated as follows:

$$Y_i = \overline{Y} + E_i$$

where:

Y_i = score for the ith individual

$\overline{Y}$ = estimated base population mean

E_i = estimate of random error for the ith individual

In the experiment which follows, the participants in each of the groups are exposed to a specific level of the independent variable. The estimated effect of the treatment (A) may be equal to or greater than zero.

Thus, any participant's score at the *conclusion* of the investigation is a function of the overall or grand mean, the effect of the treatment, and random error. You can estimate this score as follows:

$$Y_{ij} = \overline{Y} + A_j + E_{ij}$$

where:

Y_{ij} = score for the ith individual in the jth group

$\overline{Y}$ = estimated base population mean

A_j = estimated treatment effect for group j

E_{ij} = estimate of random error for the ith individual in the jth group

TABLE 9.2 Hypothetical Estimates of Influences on Information Rewards Group			
Y_{ij}	$\bar{Y}$	A_j	E_{ij}
10	9	2	−1
11	9	2	0
12	9	2	1
13	9	2	2
13	9	2	2
14	9	2	3
9	9	2	−2
9	9	2	−2
8	9	2	−3

In Table 9.2 we give a hypothetical breakdown of subjects' scores for the Informational Reward Condition from the Rewarding Interest scenario.

Furthermore, you may wish to represent these influences in the population. Thus, any participant's score at the conclusion of the investigation is as follows:

$$\text{Equation 9.1: } Y_{ij} = \mu + \alpha_j + \varepsilon_{ij}$$

where:

Y_{ij} = score for the *i*th individual in the *j*th group

μ = base population mean

α_j = treatment effect for group *j* (not to be confused with α, the probability value for significance testing)

ε_{ij} = random error for the *i*th individual in the *j*th group

Equation 9.1 is known as the **general linear model.** The model may be taken to mean that any individual score is the sum of the mean of the base population, the effect of the treatment, and random error.

THE SIMPLE MATHEMATICS OF VARIANCE PARTITIONING

It is crucial to understand the concepts and mathematical procedures of partitioning total variability into two additive components, between-groups variability and within-groups variability, as they are the first building block in the Oneway ANOVA. We will take a closer look at each of these components in turn. Then we will consider the *F*-test as a ratio of two variances or mean squares: mean squares between-groups in the numerator and mean squares within-groups in the denominator.

We want first to show how it is possible to divide the total variability in the dependent measure into two additive components. In order to do so, one needs to remember a basic descriptive statistic.

What procedure has already been covered for determining the variability in a sample set of scores? The unbiased variance (s^2) is a procedure for estimating *average* variability:

$$\textbf{(Equation 4.13)}\ s^2 = \frac{\sum\limits_{1}^{N}(Y_i - \overline{Y})^2}{N-1}$$

In other words, one finds the sum of the squared deviations and then divides by $N - 1$ to find the estimated variance (s^2).

Total Variability

To estimate *total* variability, on the other hand, one would not divide the sum of squared deviations by $N - 1$. This total variability is called the *total sum of squares for the dependent variable* (Y), or SS_Y for short.[1] More precisely, total variability in the dependent variable (SS_Y) represents the sum of squared deviations from the overall, or grand, mean:

$$\textbf{Equation 9.2:}\ SS_Y = \sum\limits_{1}^{N}(Y_i - \overline{Y})^2$$

For the total variability in the Rewarding Interest scenario, you would find the 27 deviations about the grand mean (9.00), square each deviation, and then sum the squared deviation scores:

$$SS_Y = (11 - 9)^2 + (3 - 9)^2 + \cdots + (8 - 9)^2 = 236.00$$

But the scores for the participants in the Rewarding Interest scenario are not merely lumped together in a long list. As indicated in Table 9.1, the data are organized according to which reward type participants were exposed. The data are organized into columns, which correspond to levels of the treatment. You can compute SS_Y in a fashion that recognizes the organization of the data into these columns:

$$\textbf{Equation 9.3:}\ SS_Y = \sum\limits_{1}^{A}\sum\limits_{1}^{n}(Y_i - \overline{Y})^2 = \sum\limits_{1}^{N}(Y_i - \overline{Y})^2$$

The double summation signs tell you to sum the squared deviation scores for all the individuals in group A_1, then go on and sum the squared deviation scores for all the individuals in group A_2, and finally sum the squared deviations scores for all the individuals in group A_3. The sum of the deviation scores for groups $A_1 + A_2 + A_3$ is SS_Y.

Let's look more closely at how we do this. See Table 9.3.

---

[1]Also abbreviated as SS_{TOT} or SS_T.

TABLE 9.3 Calculating SS$_Y$ for Rewarding Interest Data

	A_1			A_2			A_3	
Y_i	$(Y_i - \overline{Y})$	$(Y_i - \overline{Y})^2$	Y_i	$(Y_i - \overline{Y})$	$(Y_i - \overline{Y})^2$	Y_i	$(Y_i - \overline{Y})$	$(Y_i - \overline{Y})^2$
11	2	4	10	1	1	6	−3	9
3	−6	36	11	2	4	4	−5	25
5	−4	16	12	3	9	7	−2	4
9	0	0	13	4	16	12	3	9
9	0	0	13	4	16	14	5	25
8	−1	1	14	5	25	11	2	4
5	−4	16	9	0	0	10	1	1
6	−3	9	9	0	0	9	0	0
7	−2	4	8	−1	1	8	−1	1

$$\text{SS}_Y \text{ for } A_1 = \sum_1^n (Y_i - \overline{Y})^2 = 86 \qquad \text{SS}_Y \text{ for } A_2 = \sum_1^n (Y_i - \overline{Y})^2 = 72 \qquad \text{SS}_Y \text{ for } A_3 = \sum_1^n (Y_i - \overline{Y})^2 = 78$$

$$\text{SS}_Y = 86 + 72 + 78 = 236$$

$$\text{SS}_Y = \sum_1^A \sum_1^n (Y_i - \overline{Y})^2 = 236$$

The total variability, or SS$_Y$, represents the sum of the squared deviations about the overall mean of the dependent variable, which in the Rewarding Interest scenario is Books Borrowed. The total variability in the dependent variable is what you hope to explain further. In particular, you want to know how much variability is attributable to the treatment and how much is a function of influences you cannot explain or that are due to chance. To do so, you need to know how to partition SS$_Y$.

BETWEEN-GROUPS VARIABILITY

How can you determine the variability that exists among the groups? To this point, variability has always been considered in terms of deviations from a mean. This idea will be used here also. You will once again calculate deviations from the grand mean, but the deviations will be of the *group mean* from the grand mean. You will use the term SS$_{Y(A)}$ to symbolize the variability in the dependent variable which is attributable to variability among treatment groups.[2] SS$_{Y(A)}$ is the sum of the weighted squared deviations of each group mean from the grand mean:

$$\textbf{Equation 9.4: } \text{SS}_{Y(A)} = \sum_1^A n_A (\overline{Y}_A - \overline{Y})^2$$

[2]Also abbreviated as SS$_{BG}$.

Textbox 9.2

Computing Variability Between-Groups ($SS_{Y(A)}$)

For the Rewarding Interest scenario:

$$SS_{Y(A)} = [9(7.00 - 9.00)^2] + [9(11.00 - 9.00)^2] + [9(9.00 - 9.00)^2] = 72.00$$

See Textbox 9.2 for an illustration using the data from the Rewarding Interest scenario.

Why weight or multiply each group mean deviation score by n? What you are actually doing is finding group mean deviation scores for every participant and then summing them. Because the group mean deviation scores from the grand mean are the same for every participant in a group, you only need to find the deviation score once per group and then multiply it by n, the number of participants in the group. $SS_{Y(A)}$, therefore, is the sum of the deviations of the group mean from the grand mean for every participant.

What Does $SS_{Y(A)}$ Represent?   If the independent variable had *no* effect on the dependent variable, the group means would be similar to one another but not necessarily identical. Any differences between the means would be a function of chance fluctuation or sampling error. The grand mean represents the mean of means. If the independent variable had no effect on the dependent variable, the group means would vary only slightly from the grand mean.

If, on the other hand, the independent variable had a *significant* effect on the dependent variable, the group means would not be expected to be similar to one another and, therefore, the group means would vary "substantially" from the grand mean, especially relative to the variability among participants.

Of course, researchers do statistical analyses to determine whether the independent variable had a significant effect on the dependent variable. Thus, between-groups variability ($SS_{Y(A)}$) always represents some fluctuation among the groups, which is a function of chance, and may also represent some fluctuation among the groups due to the treatment:

$$SS_{Y(A)} = \text{error variability} + \text{treatment variability}$$

Within-Groups Variability

To determine the likelihood that the between-groups variability represents more than sampling error, you must be able to compare between-groups variability to within-groups variability. How can you determine the variability that exists within the groups?

Here, too, you will consider variability in terms of deviations from a mean. However, you will *not* compute the deviations from the grand mean to find within-groups variability. Instead, for each group you will find the individual deviation of each subject (S) from the group mean. More precisely, within-groups variability $(SS_{Y(S/A)})$ is the sum of the squared individual deviation scores from the respective group mean.[3] Note that the subscript S/A means subjects within groups A.

$$\textbf{Equation 9.5: } SS_{Y(S/A)} = \sum_{1}^{A} \sum_{1}^{n} (Y_i - \overline{Y}_A)^2$$

For example, in the Rewarding Interest scenario:

$$\begin{aligned} SS_{Y(S/A)} &= (11 - 7)^2 + \cdots + (7 - 7)^2 + (10 - 11)^2 \\ &\quad + \cdots + (8 - 11)^2 + (6 - 9)^2 + \cdots + (8 - 9)^2 \\ &= 164.00 \end{aligned}$$

Let's look more closely at how to do this by examining Table 9.4.

What Does $SS_{Y(S/A)}$ Represent?   The variability within groups cannot be explained statistically by any variable under investigation. Because the research includes only a single independent variable—in the scenario, it is Reward Type— it cannot be used to explain why scores vary from individual to individual *within* any one group. All the individuals within a group are exposed to the same level

---

TABLE 9.4 Calculating $SS_{Y(S/A)}$ for Rewarding Interest Data

A_1			A_2			A_3		
Y_i	$(Y_i - \overline{Y}_{A1})$	$(Y_i - \overline{Y}_{A1})^2$	Y_i	$(Y_i - \overline{Y}_{A2})$	$(Y_i - \overline{Y}_{A2})^2$	Y_i	$(Y_i - \overline{Y}_{A3})$	$(Y_i - \overline{Y}_{A3})^2$
11	4	16	10	−1	1	6	−3	9
3	−4	16	11	0	0	4	−5	25
5	−2	4	12	1	1	7	−2	4
9	2	4	13	2	4	12	3	9
9	2	4	13	2	4	14	5	25
8	1	1	14	3	9	11	2	4
5	−2	4	9	−2	4	10	1	1
6	−1	1	9	−2	4	9	0	0
7	0	0	8	−3	9	8	−1	1

$$SS_{Y(S/A)} \text{ for } A_1 = \sum_{1}^{n} (Y_i - \overline{Y}_{A1})^2 \qquad SS_{Y(S/A)} \text{ for } A_2 = \sum_{1}^{n} (Y_i - \overline{Y}_{A2})^2 \qquad SS_{Y(S/A)} \text{ for } A_3 = \sum_{1}^{n} (Y_i - \overline{Y}_{A3})^2$$
$$= 50.00 \qquad\qquad\qquad = 36.00 \qquad\qquad\qquad = 78.00$$

$$SS_{Y(S/A)} = 50.00 + 36.00 + 78.00 = 164.00$$

$$SS_{Y(S/A)} = \sum_{1}^{A} \sum_{1}^{n} (Y_i - \overline{Y}_A)^2 = 164.00$$

---

[3]Also abbreviated SS_{WG}.

of the treatment. No other variable is included in the research design, which may explain why scores within groups vary on the dependent variable, Books Borrowed. Thus, in the absence of another variable in the design, one assumes that the fluctuation in scores within groups is a function of chance or error variability. In other words, the fluctuation within groups is due to reasons that cannot be explained under the present circumstances.

Nevertheless, there may indeed be one or more variables that explain the variability within groups. For example, perhaps reading ability explains why some students within a group borrow more books than others. But remember that you have not actually measured or otherwise controlled for reading ability in the experiment. It is not a variable in the experiment as designed. You cannot know which students within a group had different reading abilities and certainly cannot know whether, in the current investigation, there was any relationship between reading ability and the tendency to borrow books.

Let's take a closer look at the books borrowed by a couple of students in the Controlling Reward condition. The first student, Mary, borrowed 11 books, and the second student, John, borrowed only 3 books. Clearly the difference in Mary's and John's book borrowing cannot be explained by Reward Type, because they were both exposed to the same reward. No other variable has been measured or manipulated. The difference in their book borrowing cannot be explained or accounted for by you. Thus, within-groups variability ($SS_{Y(S/A)}$) always represents some fluctuation within the groups that is a function of chance:

$$SS_{Y(S/A)} = \text{error variability}$$

Finally, notice that within-groups variability ($SS_{Y(S/A)} = 164.00$) is smaller than total variability ($SS_Y = 236.00$). Is this always the case? Yes! Within-groups variability is always smaller than total variability. Total variability includes variability within the groups and between the groups.

The Subdivision of Total Variability   We have shown how one can compute three sums of squares: the total sums of squares for the dependent variable, the sums of squares for the dependent variable attributable to the treatment and sampling error, and the sums of squares for the dependent variable due to subject-to-subject variability. These sums of squares are related:

Total variability = within-groups variability + between-groups variability

$$SS_Y = SS_{Y(S/A)} + SS_{Y(A)}$$

For the Rewarding Interest scenario:

$$236.00 = 164.00 + 72.00$$

Interested readers should consult Ferguson (1981) for a simple mathematical proof that total variability can be partitioned into two additive components: within-groups variability and between-groups variability.

THE *F*-TEST

CD-ROM link 9.2

Problem Generator: Oneway ANOVA

To practice hypothesis testing using a Oneway ANOVA, select Oneway ANOVA from the Problem Generator Menu on the CD-ROM. The Problem Generator will create as many practice problems as you need, and will demonstrate each step in their solution so that you can check your work.

We now have three sums of squares. While these sums of squares are important measures of variability, they are not variances and lack an important feature of variances. The next step in computing the Oneway ANOVA is to convert each of the sums of squares to a **mean square,** or variance. The ratio of mean squares will be the calculated value of the *F*-test. Finding the critical value of *F* will allow you to make a decision concerning the null and alternative hypotheses.

From Sums of Squares to Variances

Variances are measures of mean variability. Because a variance is an average, one can, for example, compare the variability of one set of scores to another set of scores irrespective of the number of scores making up each set. Being able to compare variances is critical in ANOVA, as you will shortly see. Therefore, you have to convert each sum of squares to an average or mean square (MS). You already know each numerator term, or SS; you now have to find each appropriate denominator term.

Converting SS_Y ***to*** MS_Y You want to find the mean square from the sum of squares for Y. Recall the formula for the (unbiased) variance:

$$\text{(Equation 4.13)} \quad s^2 = \frac{\sum\limits_{1}^{N} (Y_i - \bar{Y})^2}{N - 1}$$

You can rewrite this as follows:

Equation 9.6: $MS_Y = SS_Y / df_Y$

Where MS_Y refers to the total mean square, SS_Y refers to the total sums of squares, and df_Y is an abbreviation for the total degrees of freedom, or $N - 1$.

For the Reward Type scenario:

$$MS_Y = 236/26 = 9.08$$

In other words, MS_Y is simply s^2.

Partitioning the Total Degrees of Freedom   How does one determine the average variability for the between-groups and within-groups terms? The key is finding the appropriate degrees of freedom for each term. The degrees of freedom associated with the between-groups term is defined as the number of levels for the independent variable (the number of treatment conditions) minus 1 and is expressed mathematically as

$$df_A = A - 1$$

For the Rewarding Interest scenario, $df_A = 3 - 1 = 2$.

The degrees of freedom associated with the within-groups term is the degrees of freedom for *each* treatment group multiplied by the number of treatment conditions. The degrees of freedom for each treatment group is the number of subjects in the group minus 1. Therefore, one can express mathematically the degrees of freedom for the entire within-group term as

$$df_{S/A} = A(n - 1)$$

For the Rewarding Interest scenario, $df_{S/A} = 3(9 - 1) = 24$.

Additivity of Degrees of Freedom   We were able to show that the total sums of squares (SS_Y) can be partitioned into two additive components: the between-groups sum of squares ($SS_{Y(A)}$) and the within-groups sum of squares ($SS_{Y(S/A)}$). It is also the case that the total degrees of freedom (df_Y) can also be partitioned into two additive components: the between-groups degrees of freedom (df_A) and the within-groups degrees of freedom ($df_{S/A}$).

$$df_Y = df_A + df_{S/A}$$

Which also means

$$N - 1 = (A - 1) + A(n - 1)$$

For the Rewarding Interest scenario:

$$27 - 1 = (3 - 1) + [3(9 - 1)]$$

Mean Squares

Now that we have determined the appropriate degrees of freedom for each sums of squares, it is relatively straightforward to find the correct mean squares.

The average variability between groups is as follows:

$$\textbf{Equation 9.7: } MS_{Y(A)} = SS_{Y(A)}/df_A$$

For the Rewarding Interest scenario:

$$MS_{Y(A)} = 72.00/(3 - 1) = 36.00$$

The average variability within the groups is as follows:

Equation 9.8: $MS_{S/A} = SS_{S/A}/df_{S/A}$

For the Rewarding Interest scenario:

$$MS_{S/A} = 164.00/[3(9-1)] = 164.00/24 = 6.83$$

Nonadditivity of Mean Squares You might be tempted to think that because both the sums of squares and the degrees of freedom each have additive properties, that the mean squares would be additive too. Unfortunately, the mean squares are *not* additive:

$$MS_Y \neq MS_{Y(A)} + MS_{Y(S/A)}$$

For the Rewarding Interest scenario:

$$9.08 \neq 36.00 + 6.83$$

F as a Ratio of Variances

Each mean square represents a different measure of average variability. In the case of $MS_{Y(A)}$, the mean square reflects variability attributable to chance fluctuation or sampling error and perhaps some influence of the treatment. In the case of $MS_{Y(S/A)}$, the mean square reflects only variability attributable to chance.

What the Mean Squares Mean Imagine for the moment that the treatment did not work. That is, imagine that you knew that Reward Type truly had no effect on Book Borrowing. If the treatment did not work, then the two averages—$MS_{Y(A)}$ and $MS_{Y(S/A)}$—should be about equal, because they both represent only error variability.

In other words, if the null hypothesis is correct:

$$MS_{Y(A)} \approx MS_{Y(S/A)} \quad \text{and also} \quad MS_{Y(A)}/MS_{Y(S/A)} \approx 1.0$$

Now imagine for the moment that the treatment did work. That is, imagine that you knew that Reward Type truly had an effect on Book Borrowing. If the treatment did work, then the two averages—$MS_{Y(A)}$ and $MS_{Y(S/A)}$—should be unequal since $MS_{Y(A)}$ represents the effect of the treatment plus error variability while $MS_{Y(S/A)}$ represents only error variability.

In other words, if the alternative hypothesis is correct:

$$MS_{Y(A)} > MS_{Y(S/A)} \quad \text{and also} \quad MS_{Y(A)}/MS_{Y(S/A)} > 1.0$$

Inferential statistics are used to help one make decisions about the null and alternative hypotheses when it isn't known whether the treatment worked and one wants to make an informed guess about whether it did. How does one do this?

The Calculated Value as a Ratio of Variances   The answer lies in comparing $MS_{Y(A)}$ and $MS_{Y(S/A)}$ by computing the ratio $MS_{Y(A)}/MS_{Y(S/A)}$. If this calculated value of the ratio is close to 1.00, you can reasonably assume the treatment did not work and fail to reject the null hypothesis. In contrast, if the calculated value is much larger than 1.00, you can reasonably assume that the treatment did work and reject the null hypothesis. This ratio is called the F-ratio in honor of the statistician who developed it, Sir Ronald A. Fisher:

$$\text{Equation 9.9: } F = MS_{Y(A)}/MS_{Y(S/A)}$$

We have just described the gist of hypothesis testing for the Oneway ANOVA. You find the **calculated value,** which is the ratio $MS_{Y(A)}/MS_{Y(S/A)}$, and compare it to some **critical or tabled value** for a particular value of alpha, the probability value for significance testing. When the calculated value exceeds the critical value, you reject the null hypothesis; when the calculated value is not larger than the critical value, you fail to reject the null hypothesis.

What is the calculated value for the Rewarding Interest scenario?

$$MS_A/MS_{S/A} = 36.00/6.83 = 5.27$$

Is this calculated value very large? Should you reject the null hypothesis? What is the likelihood this calculated value occurred as a function of chance? You need to know the critical value in order to know what decision to take about the null and alternative hypotheses.

CD-ROM link 9.3

Activity 9.2: F-Distributions and the Critical F-Value
Activity 9.2 allows you to vary both numerator and denominator degrees of freedom and see their effects on the shape of an *F*-distribution. You can also learn how a critical *F*-value is determined by an area under an *F*-distribution.

The Critical Value of the F-Ratio   How do you find the critical value for the Oneway ANOVA? The family of t-distributions is not appropriate because, among other reasons, it is not designed for situations in which the treatment has more than two levels. Fortunately, you can turn to the family of F-distributions to find the critical value. See Appendix D.

In order to find a critical or tabled value, you need to have three pieces of information:

1. Alpha (α), the probability value for significance testing
2. The degrees of freedom for the numerator (df_A), which is $A - 1$
3. The degrees of freedom for the denominator ($df_{S/A}$), which is $A(n - 1)$

See Textbox 9.3 for an illustration using the Rewarding Interest scenario.

Taking a Closer Look F is a ratio of two variances. Because variances must always be positive numbers (or zero), it follows that the critical value of F cannot be a negative number. This is one way in which F is different from z and t, both of which can be negative or positive. This fact also helps to explain why the shapes of the corresponding sampling distributions of F tend to be positively skewed, because negative values of F are not possible.

Textbox 9.3

The Critical Value for the Rewarding Interest Scenario

For the Rewarding Interest scenario, use $\alpha = .05$ as the probability value for significance testing. Numerator degrees of freedom equal 2; denominator degrees of freedom equal 24. The tabled value of F is 3.40. To reject the null hypothesis, the average variability between groups ($MS_{Y(A)}$) must be almost 3.5 times as large as the average variability within groups ($MS_{Y(S/A)}$).

Since $5.27 > 3.40$, you reject the null hypothesis. Reward Type had a significant ($p < .05$) influence on book borrowing. Between-groups variance was more than five times the size of within-groups variance.

More precisely, if the estimate of the variance between groups in the numerator is smaller than the estimate of variance within groups in the denominator, the calculated value of F will be less than 1.0 but greater than zero. It will never be negative. If the opposite is the case and the estimate of variance between groups in the numerator is larger than the estimate of variance within groups in the denominator, the calculated value of F will be greater than 1. Here too the calculated value of F will never be negative and may occasionally be much greater than 1.0.

$$\text{If } MS_{Y(A)} < MS_{Y(S/A)}, \; 0.0 < F < 1.0$$
$$\text{If } MS_{Y(A)} > MS_{Y(S/A)}, \; F > 1.0$$

Therefore, the null hypothesis of equality of population means will be rejected only if the calculated value of F is *larger* than that expected through random sampling if the null hypothesis is true. Consequently, the region of rejection is entirely in the upper tail of the F-distribution.

See Figure 9.5 for an illustration of one sampling distribution of F.

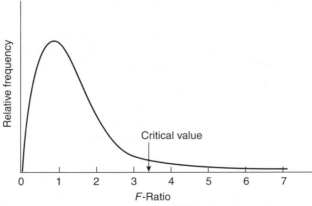

Figure 9.5 An illustration of an F-distribution

Interval Estimation   There is one unfortunate consequence of the sampling distributions of *F* being positively skewed. Because the distributions are not symmetrical, it is difficult to calculate a confidence interval or to use interval estimation. Generally speaking, one side of the confidence interval would need to be much larger than the other side. This is one reason why confidence intervals using *F* are not reported. In addition, the parameter for interval estimation is not a mean or a mean difference but something more complicated and less intuitive.

The Family of Sampling Distributions   Just as Gosset, writing under the pen name "Student," developed a family of sampling distributions for the *t*-ratio, Fisher developed a family of sampling distributions for the *F*-ratio. The concept of the sampling distribution for the *F*-ratio is the same as for other sampling distributions. The sampling distribution provides the probabilities associated with various *F*-ratios when the null hypothesis is true. As is the case with other sampling distributions, no matter how large the calculated value there is still some likelihood it may represent the operation of chance fluctuation.

As the numerator and denominator degrees of freedom vary, the shape of the sampling distribution also varies. That is why the critical value changes as the degrees of freedom change.

Furthermore, the parameters of the particular sampling distribution of *F* are estimated from the data from a single experiment. That is, one uses the results of one investigation to estimate where on the particular *F*-distribution the critical value lies associated with a specific value of alpha (e.g., .05, .01, .001). The accuracy of the estimate depends on meeting the test's assumptions, which will be discussed shortly.

Factors that Influence the Critical Value   We said that if the treatment failed to have an effect, the ratio of between-groups and within-groups variances or mean squares used to form the calculated value of *F* should be approximately 1.00. If so, it is reasonable not to reject the null hypothesis. The tabled values let one know how much larger this ratio needs to be in order to reject the null hypothesis. Note that when both the numerator and denominator degrees of freedom are infinitely large, the critical value is 1.00. Even a calculated value as small as 1.01 would result in a decision to reject the null hypothesis.

In contrast, when both the numerator and denominator degrees of freedom are small, the size of the critical value is large. That means that the calculated value of *F* must be quite large if one is to reject the null hypothesis.

As the number of participants in each of the groups grows larger, the size of the critical value decreases. Scan down any column of the tabled values in Appendix D to verify this.

Similarly, as the number of treatment groups grows large, the size of the critical value also decreases. Scan across any row of the tabled values in Appendix D to verify this.

Finally, various computer programs report the exact probability associated with the calculated value of *F*. If you use the exact probability for decision making, remember that it must be smaller than alpha, the probability value you selected, in advance, for hypothesis testing.

Reporting ANOVA Results

When reporting the calculated value in the text of a report, the convention is to list both the numerator and denominator degrees of freedom along with whether the calculated value is significant. For example, $F(2, 24) = 5.27$, $p < .05$.

A more complete report of a key analysis can also be presented in tabular form as an ANOVA Summary Table. The basic form of an ANOVA Summary Table is shown in Table 9.5. Table 9.6 is the ANOVA Summary Table for the Rewarding Interest scenario.

UNDERLYING ASSUMPTIONS

As a parametric statistical procedure, the F-test relies on numerous assumptions about the data being analyzed for the results of hypothesis testing to be accurate. We briefly review these assumptions and then discuss the effects of assumption violations on the accuracy of the test results.

In general, researchers are concerned with whether the actual rate of Type I error is close to the nominal rate of Type I error or the alpha value selected for

TABLE 9.5 Oneway ANOVA Summary Table (General Form)

Source	SS	df	MS	F	p
Treatment (Between Groups)	$SS_{Y(A)}$	$A-1$	$MS_{Y(A)}$	$MS_{Y(A)}/MS_{Y(S/A)}$	
Error (Within Groups)	$SS_{Y(S/A)}$	$A(n-1)$	$MS_{Y(S/A)}$		
Total	SS_Y	$N-1$			

*Elements in the ANOVA Summary Table:

Source:	Source of variability
SS:	Sums of squares
df:	Degrees of freedom
MS:	Mean square
F:	Calculate value of F
p:	Either an indication of whether the probability value has been exceeded *or* the exact probability associated with the calculated value

TABLE 9.6 Oneway ANOVA Summary Table

Effect of Reward Type on Book Borrowing

Source	SS	df	MS	F	p
Reward Type	72.00	2	36.00	5.27	*
Error	164.00	24	6.83		
Total	236.00	26			

*$p < .05$.

hypothesis testing. That is, with certain assumption violations, might the chance of falsely rejecting the null hypothesis be many times larger than assumed?

Assumptions

The ANOVA model makes certain assumptions regarding the nature of the data. They are as follows:

- There is a normal distribution to the scores within each treatment group. This is the assumption of *normality.*
- The scores are independent of one another, both within each treatment group as well as across the different treatment groups. This is the assumption of *independence.*
- The scores show the same degree of variability from treatment group to treatment group. This is the assumption of *homogeneity of variance.*

Effects of Assumption Violations

Statisticians (e.g., Rogan & Keselman, 1977) have studied the effects of assumption violations on the ANOVA *F*-test. While modest violations are often not worrisome, severe violations can be problematic. It is always advisable to examine the data for assumption violations and to proceed cautiously when in doubt. In extreme cases, it may be necessary to suspend data analysis if the data are of poor quality.

Normality   The effects of violating the assumption of normality are of little consequence for large sample sizes (e.g., $n \geq 30$), even when the violation is severe. Even for small sample sizes, the problem is seldom worth worrying about. It is best solved by increasing sample sizes when it is practical to do so. Otherwise, one could discard outliers, convert the original scores to normalize them, or use a less powerful nonparametric test such as those covered later in this book.

Nonindependence   Nonindependence of scores can have large effects on the results of the Oneway ANOVA. Consequently, the Repeated Measures ANOVA (see Chapter 12) should be used when the data *between* the groups are related to one another (e.g., the same participants are exposed to each of the treatments and measured on multiple occasions).

The data *within* the groups may also be related. For example, students in a classroom may form friendship groups and influence one another in ways that impact the research. High degrees of within-group dependence may be overcome by changing the unit of analysis (e.g., from individuals to groups), performing a more conservative *F*-test by lowering alpha (e.g., from .05 to .01), using a parametric test that takes the dependency within groups into account, or using a less powerful nonparametric test.

Homogeneity of Variance   The variance homogeneity assumption can be violated without serious risk as long as group sample sizes (*n*) are approximately equal, with the ratio of the largest to the smallest being no more than 1.5.

Homogeneity of variance can be assessed using the following tests so long as the normality assumption is met:

> Bartlett-Box F
>
> Cochran's C
>
> Levene's Test (use when the normality assumption is not met)
>
> Hartley's F_{max}

F_{max} can be computed easily by hand; it is simply the ratio of the largest to the smallest group variances (i.e., $s^2_{largest}/s^2_{smallest}$). F_{max} less than 3.0 means that it is generally safe to proceed. However, as we noted in Chapter 8, the popular opinion among statisticians suggests that conducting these tests is of limited value. In circumstances in which they are needed most (e.g., small, unequal sample sizes), the tests are poorest.

When the variance homogeneity assumption has been violated, the following procedures should be considered:

- Reduce the probability value for significance testing downward (e.g., from .05 to .01). This makes the Oneway ANOVA *F*-test more conservative, which counters the potential effects of the assumption violation.
- Use an equivalent nonparametric statistical test with fewer assumptions but with lower statistical power.
- Transform the observations on the dependent variable so that the variance homogeneity assumption is no longer violated. This means that any conclusions made as a result of the analysis must be made on the transformed dependent variable and not on the original dependent variable.

EFFECT SIZE CALCULATIONS AND POWER

In this section we will review procedures for calculating the effect size and present alternatives. We will also discuss procedures for estimating power.

Effect Size Calculations for Two Groups

One of three methods may be chosen for computing an effect size for two groups: **single-group standard deviation effect size, pooled two-group standard deviation effect size,** and **average group standard deviation effect size.** These methods will yield similar results if within-group variances are homogeneous. For an independent variable with three levels, three effect sizes may be calculated. For an independent variable with five levels, 10 effect sizes may be calculated.

When group variances are heterogeneous, the method of computing an effect size will yield different results. You will compute the most conservative estimate of the effect size when the largest value of *s* is used in the denominator. When group variances are approximately homogeneous, it may be preferable to base the effect size calculation on the average group standard deviation, because it is based on all the participants in the study.

Single-Group Standard Deviation Effect Size   Recall that one formula for calculating the effect size for two groups is as follows:

$$\text{(Equation 7.4)} \quad d = \frac{\overline{Y}_{A1} - \overline{Y}_{A2}}{s}$$

where s = standard deviation of a single group

Pooled Two-Group Standard Deviation Effect Size   In Chapter 8, we provided a second formula for computing effect sizes based on the standard deviation pooled across two groups:

$$\text{(Equation 8.14)} \quad d = \frac{\overline{Y}_{A1} - \overline{Y}_{A2}}{s_p}$$

where s_p = standard deviation pooled for two groups

Average Group Standard Deviation Effect Size   Finally, one may calculate an effect size based on the mean difference between two groups divided by the average standard deviation within groups. Remember that $MS_{Y(S/A)}$ is the average variability within all the groups. More precisely:

$$\text{Equation 9.10:} \quad d = \frac{\overline{Y}_{A1} - \overline{Y}_{A2}}{\sqrt{MS_{Y(S/A)}}}$$

See Textbox 9.4 for an illustration comparing the three calculation methods. Note that when group standard deviations are identical, the effect sizes calculated by each of the methods is identical.

Using R^2 and f to Estimate the General Effect Size

The problem with effect size calculations, as we have described them so far, is that they are limited to those situations in which you are concerned with only two groups at a time. In the context of the Oneway ANOVA, however, there can be more than two groups under investigation. Under these circumstances you may also wish to know about the overall size of the effect. In other words, you might want to know what effect the treatment as a whole had on the dependent variable.

Estimating the general effect size is advantageous when the researcher is interested in considering the influence of the treatment variable overall. However, there is some loss of information compared to two-group effect sizes. Although the sign of the effect size can be determined and is meaningful when one is dealing with two groups, general effect sizes only yield positive values, because it is illogical to do otherwise.

A straightforward method for estimating the general effect of a treatment is to use R^2, or the squared multiple correlation coefficient. We will cover the correlation

---

Textbox 9.4

Comparison of Three Methods for Computing the Two-Group Effect Size

Compute effect sizes for the Controlling Reward and Informational Reward groups from the Rewarding Interest scenario:

Single-group standard deviation effect size:

$$d = \frac{7.00 - 11.00}{2.50} = -1.60 \text{ (using } s \text{ for } A_1\text{, Controlling Rewards)}$$

Pooled two-group standard deviation effect size:

$$d = \frac{7:00 - 11.00}{2.32} = -1.72$$

Average group standard deviation effect size:

$$d = \frac{7.00 - 11.00}{\sqrt{6.83}} = -1.53$$

---

coefficient in greater detail starting in Chapter 13 and show how it can be used for other purposes.

$$\textbf{Equation 9.11: } R^2 = \frac{SS_{Y(A)}}{SS_Y}$$

Remember that SS_Y represents all the variability in the dependent variable; it can be divided into two additive components ($SS_{Y(A)}$ and $SS_{Y(S/A)}$). Thus, R^2 represents primarily that proportion of variability in the dependent variable attributed to differences among the treatment groups. The larger the proportion, the stronger are the treatment effects observed in the experiment.

Note that there is an old tradition of representing the proportion R^2 by the symbol η^2 (eta squared) and referring to this proportion as the correlation ratio. Both R^2 and η^2 are conceptually and numerically identical.

Cohen (1988) developed a measure of general effect size (f) for the F-ratio based on R^2. The general effect size (f) is interpreted in the same way that d is interpreted for the two-group effect size:

$$\textbf{Equation 9.12: } f = \sqrt{\frac{R^2}{1 - R^2}}$$

According to Cohen (1988), effect sizes for the Oneway ANOVA can be classified into one of three categories:

- An f of .10 is a small effect size.
- An f of .25 is a medium effect size.
- An f of .40 is a large effect size.

See Textbox 9.5 for an illustration of R^2 and f using the Rewarding Interest scenario.

Another Method for Estimating General Effect Sizes: ω^2

While R^2 and η^2 are good descriptive statistics for judging the magnitude of treatment effects, Hays (1994) argues that they are overly optimistic estimates of the true population strength of association. Hays suggests using ω^2 (omega squared) to estimate the population effect size:

$$\textbf{Equation 9.13: } \omega^2 = \frac{SS_{Y(A)} - (A-1)MS_{Y(S/A)}}{SS_Y + MS_{Y(S/A)}}$$

According to Cohen (1988):

- An ω^2 of .01 is a small effect.
- An ω^2 of .06 is a medium effect.
- An ω^2 of .15 is a large effect.

See Textbox 9.6 for an illustration.

Textbox 9.5

General Effect Size Calculation (R^2 and f)

For the Rewarding Interest scenario:

$$R^2 = \frac{72.00}{236.00} = .31$$

$$f = \sqrt{\frac{.31}{1-.31}} = .67$$

According to Cohen, an f of .67 is a large effect.

Textbox 9.6

General Effect Size Calculation (ω^2)

For the Rewarding Interest scenario:

$$\omega^2 = \frac{72.00 - (3.00 - 1.00)6.83}{236.00 + 6.83} = \frac{58.34}{242.83} = .24$$

An omega squared of .24 would be considered a large effect by Cohen (1988).

Power

Cohen (1988) provides power tables for the ANOVA using f.[4] A condensed version of these tables is given in Appendix E. Each section represents the degrees of freedom for the numerator (i.e., the degrees of freedom from 1 though 8 for the independent variable, $A - 1$). Power is presented for *group,* not total, sample sizes (n) of 5 to 100. Three probability values for significance testing are included (i.e., $\alpha = .01, .05, .10$). The F_c column represents the critical, or tabled, value of F required to reject the null hypothesis. There are three columns for effect sizes (i.e., $f = .10$, or a small effect; $f = .25$, or a medium effect; and $f = .40$, or a large effect). The values for power beyond .99 are represented as **.

You may use Appendix E in several ways. First, you may want to determine the sample size you will need to achieve a desired power given your guess as to the effect size you will obtain. Second, you may want to determine the power you might expect given a certain sample size and estimated effect size. Remember from Chapter 8 that the larger the estimated effect size, the higher the power of the statistical test. Third, you may want to determine the effect size you might expect given a certain sample size and estimated power. In other words, you can use the power tables to determine expected power, sample size, or effect size when you can take an informed guess as to two of these three factors. Results from prior studies and/or pilot investigations are useful in helping you with these estimates. Textbox 9.7 illustrates the use of the ANOVA power tables for the Rewarding Interest scenario.

Textbox 9.7

Use of Power Tables for the Rewarding Interest scenario

Imagine that you wanted to treat the data from the Rewarding Interest scenario as a pilot study. First, what was the power of the statistical test to reject the null hypothesis in this study? To answer this question, note the following:

$$n = 9$$

$$F_c(2, 24) = 3.40 \text{ (critical value)}$$

$$f = .67$$

$$\alpha = .05$$

The tabled values do not list $n = 9$ or $f = .67$. The closest approximation is $n = 10$ and $f = .40$, with $F_c = 3.354$. Using these values, you estimate power as only .45. By extrapolation, for $f = .67$, you might conservatively guess that power was closer to .70.

What group sample size is desirable for $\beta = .80$? If you use $f = .40$ (large effect), you should have 20 participants per group (n), or a total of 60 subjects (N), to achieve a power of .78. If you use $f = .67$, by extrapolation you might guess that you should have approximately 15 participants per group (n), or a total of 45 subjects (N), to achieve a power of approximately .80.

---

[4]Similar tables of power are provided by Hays (1994) for ω^2.

PUTTING IT ALL TOGETHER

This chapter provided an opportunity to expand your statistical tools to include situations in which the independent variable has more than two levels. The Oneway Analysis of Variance (ANOVA) was introduced as a general tool for the statistical analysis of data from experiments in which a single independent variable could have multiple values, or levels. Thus the Oneway ANOVA is more flexible than the t-test, which is restricted to pairwise comparisons.

We noted that the Oneway ANOVA asks general, or omnibus, questions about the effect of the treatment and is not useful for exploring specific hypotheses concerning group differences, which are reserved for multiple comparisons. We also noted that one key to the Oneway ANOVA lay in its ability to partition the total variability in the dependent variable into two additive components: between-groups variability and within-groups variability. Next, we noted that the F-test associated with the Oneway ANOVA is a ratio of two variances. If this ratio is large enough, it suggests the treatment worked and you can reasonably reject the null hypothesis. We also discussed the assumptions of the Oneway ANOVA and ways to deal with assumption violations. Finally, we noted how to compute estimates of effect size and power for the Oneway ANOVA.

Exploring General Hypotheses

$$H_0: \text{all } \mu\text{'s are equal}$$

$$H_a: \text{not all } \mu\text{'s are equal}$$

Partitioning the Total Y Variability

Total variability = between-groups variability + within-groups variability

Equation 9.3: $SS_Y = \displaystyle\sum_1^A \sum_1^n (Y_i - \overline{Y})^2 = \sum_1^N (Y_i - \overline{Y})^2$

Equation 9.4: $SS_{Y(A)} = \displaystyle\sum_1^A n_A(\overline{Y}_A - \overline{Y})^2$

Equation 9.5: $SS_{Y(S/A)} = \displaystyle\sum_1^A \sum_1^n (Y_i - \overline{Y}_A)^2$

The Degrees of Freedom

Total $df_Y = N - 1$

Between-groups $df_A = A - 1$

Within-groups $df_{S/A} = A(n - 1)$

$df_Y = df_A + df_{S/A}$

Mean Squares   The average variability between-groups is as follows:

$$\text{Equation 9.7: } MS_{Y(A)} = SS_{Y(A)}/df_A$$

The average variability within the groups is as follows:

$$\text{Equation 9.8: } MS_{Y(S/A)} = SS_{Y(S/A)}/df_{S/A}$$

Unfortunately, the mean squares are *not* additive:

$$MS_Y \neq MS_{Y(A)} + MS_{Y(S/A)}$$

The F-Ratio

$$\text{Equation 9.9: } F = MS_{Y(A)}/MS_{Y(S/A)}$$

Assumptions Underlying the Oneway ANOVA

- There is a normal distribution to the scores within each treatment group. This is the assumption of *normality*.
- The scores are independent of one another both within each treatment group as well as across the treatment groups. This is the assumption of *independence*.
- The scores show the same degree of variability from treatment group to treatment group. This is the assumption of *homogeneity of variance*.

Although modest violations are often not worrisome, severe violations can be problematic. It is always advisable to examine the data for assumption violations and to proceed cautiously when in doubt. In extreme cases, it may be necessary to suspend data analysis if the data are of poor quality.

Effect Size Calculations for Two Groups   Single-group standard deviation effect size:

$$\textbf{(Equation 8.4) } d = \frac{\overline{Y}_{A1} - \overline{Y}_{A2}}{s}$$

where s = standard deviation of a single group

Pooled two-group standard deviation effect size:

$$\textbf{(Equation 8.14) } d = \frac{\overline{Y}_{A1} - \overline{Y}_{A2}}{s_p}$$

where s_p = standard deviation pooled across groups A_1 and A_2.

Average group standard deviation effect size:

$$\text{Equation 9.10: } d = \frac{\overline{Y}_{A1} - \overline{Y}_{A2}}{\sqrt{MS_{Y(S/A)}}}$$

Using R^2, f, and ω^2 to Estimate the General Effect Size A straightforward method for estimating the general effect of a treatment is to use R^2, or the squared multiple correlation coefficient:

$$\text{Equation 9.11: } R^2 = \frac{SS_{Y(A)}}{SS_Y}$$

Cohen (1988) developed a measure of general effect size (f) for the F-ratio based on R^2. The general effect size (f) is interpreted in the same way that d is interpreted for the two-group effect size:

$$\text{Equation 9.12: } f = \sqrt{\frac{R^2}{1 - R^2}}$$

Hays suggests using ω^2 (omega squared) to estimate the population effect size:

$$\text{Equation 9.13: } \omega^2 = \frac{SS_{Y(A)} - (a - 1)MS_{Y(S/A)}}{SS_Y + MS_{Y(S/A)}}$$

Cohen's power tables may be used to estimate the sample size you need, the power you might expect, and the effect size you might obtain.

Textbox 9.8

Real Time: Oneway ANOVA

Crime is more frequent on television than in the real world, and shows featuring crime are ubiquitous. How do children interpret such material? One way to find out is to investigate the types of scripts, or schemes, children have of such shows. Low and Durkin (1997), investigated whether children understood the representation of crime and legal process on television, whether their understanding changed with age, and whether they understood the relationship of the parts of the program to the whole. Children, 20 each from grades 1, 3, 5, and 7, and 20 undergraduates, were the participants in the study. All subjects were interviewed about what happens on police shows, and the responses were coded into propositions.

A Oneway ANOVA on the total number of propositions was conducted. A significant effect of Age, $F(4, 95) = 33.21$, $p < .001$ was found. Propositions were then coded into one of four categories: action (any type of specific action), description (what people or things looked like), reactions (reference to internal thoughts, emotions, or physical state), elaborations (additional information or clarification to the above). Significant effects for Age were found for the action propositions and for elaboration. (Multiple comparisons were conducted to probe age effects and will be reported at the conclusion of Chapter 10.)

The authors also examined how young children, older children, and adults understood the criminal justice system by analyzing whether participants mentioned pursuit of the criminals, crime control actions of the police, and due process after apprehension. A Oneway ANOVA using the three age groups revealed a significant effect on the complexity of participants' criminal justice models, $F(2, 95) = 23.94$, $p < .001$. (The results of these multiple comparisons will also be reported at the end of Chapter 10.)

KEY TERMS

ANOVA

Comparison or contrast

Multiple comparison

Planned multiple comparisons

Post hoc multiple comparisons

Omnibus hypothesis

Total variability

Between-groups variability

Within-groups variability

General linear model

F-ratio

Mean squares

Calculated value

Critical or tabled value

Single-group standard deviation effect size

Pooled two-group standard deviation effect size

Average group standard deviation effect size

REFERENCES

Cohen, J. (1988). *Statistical power analysis for the behavioral sciences.* (2nd ed.). Hillsdale, NJ: Lawrence Erlbaum Associates.

Ferguson, G. A. (1981). *Statistical analysis in psychology and education.* (5th ed.). New York: McGraw-Hill Book Co.

Hays, W. L. (1994). *Statistics.* (5th ed.). Orlando, FL: Harcourt Brace College Publishers.

Kirk, R. E. (1982). *Experimental design: Procedures for the behavioral sciences.* (2nd ed.). Monterey, CA: Brooks/Cole.

Low, J., & Durkin, K. (1997). Children's understanding of events and criminal justice process in police programs. *Journal of Applied Developmental Psychology, 18,* 179–205.

Rogan, J. C., & Keselman, H. J. (1977). Is the Anova *F*-test robust to variance heterogeneity when sample sizes are equal?: An investigation via a coefficient of variation. *American Educational Research Journal, 14,* 493–498.

PROBLEMS

Questions

Section 1   Conceptual/Definition

9.1. What is the difference between a qualitative independent variable and a quantitative independent variable?

9.2. What are the primary differences between F and t as inferential statistical procedures?

9.3. List the reasons against conducting multiple comparisons when the independent variable has more than two levels.

9.4. The null hypothesis for the F-test, in the general case is $H_0: \mu_1 = \mu_2 = \mu_3 = \mu_a$. The alternate hypotheses is H_a: all μ's are not equal. Why is the alternate hypothesis not written as $H_a: \mu_1 \neq \mu_2 \neq \mu_3 \neq \mu_k$?

9.5. To what does the term *partitioning of variability* refer?

9.6. What does $SS_{Y(A)}$ represent? What does $SS_{Y(S/A)}$ represent? What does the addition of these two components of variability represent?

9.7. What is the *General Linear Model*?

9.8. The intersection of the MS column and the Total row is often left blank in ANOVA Summary Tables. Why is this the case? What does this intersection represent?

9.9. Why must the critical value of F always be a positive number?

9.10. In order to find a critical or tabled value of F what information is required?

9.11. Why is it more difficult to calculate a confidence interval for an F-test than a z-test or t-test?

9.12. What are the underlying assumptions of the F-test?

Section 2   Numerical

9.13. In a given experiment, 32 subjects are randomly assigned (equally) to one of three treatment conditions. The data are as follows:

A_1	A_2	A_3
12	17	19
14	19	23
15	21	28
12	22	27
13	23	26
15	21	28
16	25	24

Prepare a completed ANOVA Summary Table and evaluate the obtained (calculated) omnibus F.

9.14. In a given experiment, 32 subjects are randomly assigned (equally) to one of four treatment conditions. The data are as follows

A_1	A_2	A_3	A_4
55	54	75	78
57	46	68	49
59	66	63	75
67	65	50	67
45	59	66	81
49	67	69	58
52	62	72	73
50	58	69	65

Prepare a completed ANOVA Summary Table and evaluate the obtained (calculated) omnibus F.

9.15. In a given experiment, 32 subjects are randomly assigned (equally) to one of three treatment conditions. The data are as follows:

A_1	A_2	A_3
5	8	8
4	4	7
6	6	6
7	5	5
8	7	4

Evaluate the obtained (calculated) omnibus F. (*Hint:* You do not need to perform any serious calculations in order to answer this question.)

9.16. Given the dataset in question 9.13, determine the effect size using R^2 and ω^2.

9.17. Given the dataset in question 9.14, determine the effect size using R^2 and ω^2.

9.18. Given the dataset in question 9.13, determine the general effect size f (Cohen, 1988).

9.19. Given the dataset in question 9.14, determine the general effect size f (Cohen, 1988).

9.20. In a given experiment, 24 subjects are randomly assigned (equally) to one of four treatment conditions. The data are as follows:

A_1	A_2	A_3	A_4
88	94	91	92
92	91	89	94
93	89	88	93
87	90	92	90
90	88	91	89
91	92	93	88

Prepare a completed ANOVA Summary Table and evaluate the obtained (calculated) omnibus F.

9.21. Given the dataset in question 9.20, determine the effect size using R^2 and ω^2.

9.22. Given the dataset in question 9.20, determine the general effect size f (Cohen, 1988).

APPENDIX 9.1: A PROOF THAT $t^2 = F$

$$t = \frac{\overline{Y}_{A1} - \overline{Y}_{A2}}{s_D} = \frac{\overline{Y}_{A1} - \overline{Y}_{A2}}{\sqrt{\dfrac{s_{A1}^2}{n_{A1}} + \dfrac{s_{A2}^2}{n_{A2}}}}$$

separate variance formula t-test; assume equal ns.

$$t^2 = \frac{(\overline{Y}_{A1} - \overline{Y}_{A2})^2}{\dfrac{s_{A1}^2}{n_{A1}} + \dfrac{s_{A2}^2}{n_{A2}}}$$

square both sides of the equation

$$t^2 = \frac{(\overline{Y}_{A1} - \overline{Y}_{A2})^2}{\dfrac{s_{A1}^2 + s_{A2}^2}{n}}$$

using certain rules of algebra

We will first show the equivalence of the denominator of the F-ratio ($MS_{Y(S/A)}$) and the denominator of t^2

1. $SS_{Y(S/A)} = \sum\limits_{1}^{A} \sum\limits_{1}^{n} (Y_i - \overline{Y}_A)^2$

2. $MS_{Y(S/A)} = SS_{Y(S/A)}/df_{S/A}$

3. $MS_{Y(S/A)} = \dfrac{\sum\limits_{1}^{A} \sum\limits_{1}^{n} (Y_i - \overline{Y}_A)^2}{A(n-1)}$

4. What does the formula look like when you examine the within-groups variance for each of the two groups separately?

$$MS_{Y(S/A1)} = \frac{\sum\limits_{1}^{n} (Y_i - \overline{Y}_{A1})^2}{(n-1)} = s_{A1}^2$$

$$MS_{Y(S/A2)} = \frac{\sum\limits_{1}^{n} (Y_i - \overline{Y}_{A2})^2}{(n-1)} = s_{A2}^2$$

5. These formulas are the formulas for the unbiased variance of each group taken separately. Therefore the mean square error term ($MS_{Y(S/A)}$) is merely the average of these two terms:

$$MS_{Y(S/A)} = \frac{s_{A1}^2 + s_{A2}^2}{2}$$

6. Now you can proceed to make some substitutions:

$$\frac{s_{A1}^2 + s_{A2}^2}{n} = \frac{MS_{Y(S/A)}}{n} + \frac{MS_{Y(S/A)}}{n} = \frac{2MS_{Y(S/A)}}{n}$$

We will next show the equivalence of the numerator of the F-ratio (MS_A) and the numerator of t^2.

1. $SS_{Y(A)} = \sum\limits_{1}^{A} n_A(\overline{Y}_A - \overline{Y})^2$

2. $MS_{Y(A)} = \dfrac{\sum\limits_{1}^{A} n_A(\overline{Y}_A - \overline{Y})^2}{A-1}$

3. Because $A = 2$, $A - 1 = 1$. Therefore, for two groups $SS_{Y(A)} = MS_{Y(A)}$.

4. Let us expand $SS_{Y(A)}$:

$$MS_{Y(A)} = SS_{Y(A)} = n[(\overline{Y}_{A1} - \overline{Y}) + (\overline{Y}_{A2} - \overline{Y})]^2$$

5. The difference between each group mean and the grand mean is *twice* the size of the difference between the two group means. Therefore:

$$2MS_{Y(A)} = 2SS_{Y(A)} = 2n[(\overline{Y}_{A1} - \overline{Y}) + (\overline{Y}_{A2} - \overline{Y})]^2 = n(\overline{Y}_{A1} - \overline{Y}_{A2})^2$$

6. Dividing both sides by n yields:

$$(\overline{Y}_{A1} - \overline{Y}_{A2})^2 = \frac{2MS_{Y(A)}}{n}$$

Now you are ready to put the denominator and numerator together:

$$t^2 = \frac{(\overline{Y}_{A1} - \overline{Y}_{A2})^2}{\dfrac{s_{A1}^2 + s_{A2}^2}{n}} = \frac{\dfrac{2MS_{Y(A)}}{n}}{\dfrac{2MS_{Y(S/A)}}{n}} = \frac{MS_{Y(A)}}{MS_{Y(S/A)}} = F$$

chapter 10

Testing the Difference Between Two or More Independent Groups

Multiple Comparisons

OVERVIEW

In Chapter 9, we examined the use of the Oneway Analysis of Variance (ANOVA) for testing differences between groups when the single independent variable has two or more levels. In situations in which there are more than two levels of the independent variable, the Oneway ANOVA becomes an omnibus test of hypotheses. In other words, the ANOVA helps answer the question "Are there any differences among the groups?" rather than more specific questions such as "Where were the specific differences among the groups?" or "Is the mean of one group significantly different from the mean of another group?"

We now turn our attention to situations in which more specific information is required about the treatment effects via the use of multiple comparisons. In particular, we will consider *planned* multiple comparison procedures used to explore specific hypotheses about mean differences *instead of* the omnibus hypothesis tested in the Oneway ANOVA. In addition, we will consider *post hoc* multiple comparison procedures used to identify where there are differences between groups *after* the omnibus test is found to be significant.

In exploring multiple comparisons, we will address the following questions:

1. What are simple and complex comparisons?
2. What are the rules for using planned comparisons? For post hoc comparisons?
3. Why shouldn't one do both planned and post hoc comparisons?
4. What makes a planned comparison valid and independent?
5. How does a set of independent comparisons partition between-groups variability?
6. How does one statistically evaluate a planned comparison?
7. What are important conceptual units for error rate?
8. What are the important differences between Tukey's HSD method and Scheffé's S method?
9. How does one find the critical values for each post hoc method?

We will draw on the Rewarding Interest scenario from Chapter 9 (see Textbox 9.1) to illustrate key points and computational procedures. Although we will use the data here for both planned and post hoc comparisons, we do so only as a way to illustrate the similarities and differences between the techniques. A researcher chooses to conduct either planned comparisons in lieu of the omnibus *F*-test or post hoc comparisons if the *F*-test is significant. A researcher *does not* conduct both planned and post hoc comparisons on the same data. This is an important point and we will repeat it again in this chapter.

MULTIPLE COMPARISONS BASICS

Let's begin with a nontechnical definition of a comparison. We will also briefly review the situations in which multiple comparisons should be avoided as well as the situations in which their use is desirable. Finally, we will give a brief overview of the different guidelines and rules for using planned comparisons and post hoc comparisons.

What Is a Comparison?

A **comparison or contrast** among means is a difference among means. A **simple comparison** is a difference between two group means. For example, in the Rewarding Interest scenario of Textbox 9.1, the difference between book borrowing for informational versus controlling rewards is a simple comparison. A **complex comparison** is a difference among more than two group means. For example, in the Rewarding Interest scenario, the difference in book borrowing for controlling and informational rewards together versus no rewards is a complex comparison.

When Multiple Comparisons Should Be Avoided

There are several reasons against conducting multiple comparisons when the independent variable has more than two levels.

- There can be a large number of comparisons to evaluate and statistical calculations to perform. Having these many tasks means additional computational labor for you. And the results are certainly less parsimonious than exploring in one test whether the independent variable worked "in general."
- Evaluating all possible comparisons between groups requires that the same data be used repeatedly. There is some statistical redundancy in doing so.
- Doing multiple *t*-tests, each based on only a subset of the data (i.e., only two of the groups at a time), may result in a loss in power compared to using all the data for analysis.
- The likelihood of committing a Type I error somewhere in the collection of comparisons grows higher as the number of comparisons increases.

Why Use Multiple Comparisons?

The Oneway ANOVA explores the *omnibus*, or general, hypothesis that concerns whether all treatment group means are equal. Exploring this omnibus hypothesis can be advantageous. But there are two situations in which the reliance on only the omnibus procedure is either inappropriate or insufficient.

The omnibus procedure is inappropriate when the researcher is able to specify *in advance* a set of more specific hypotheses than the general hypothesis. In these situations a set of planned comparisons should be used *instead of* the omnibus *F*-test.

The omnibus procedure is insufficient when the researcher wishes to further analyze the data *following* the discovery of a significant *F*-test. The *F*-test indicates only that not all the treatment group means were equal. In these situations a set of post hoc comparisons should be used *in addition to* the omnibus *F*-test. Post hoc comparisons identify where there are significant differences among the groups.

Finally, no comparisons are necessary when the independent variable has only two levels; when only two groups are involved there is nothing to differentiate an omnibus test from a comparison.

Planned Comparisons (Also Known as A Priori Comparisons)

Imagine that the experimenter has, in advance of any statistical analysis, posed two or more specific hypotheses about differences among the means. For example, instead of wondering whether the omnibus alternative hypothesis was correct, the researcher was interested in testing specific hypotheses about the means. In such a case, the researcher is correct to use planned comparisons instead of the omnibus Oneway ANOVA.

The following rules apply to the use of planned comparisons:

1. They must be specified in advance of data analysis.
2. They are used in place of the omnibus *F*-test.
3. The probability value for significance testing is based on the individual comparison and not the collection or family of comparisons.
4. The set of planned comparisons should normally be independent to avoid statistical redundancy in the analyses.

Post Hoc Comparisons (Also Known as A Posteriori Comparisons)

Now imagine that the experimenter has, at the outset, no particular questions to answer separately but is initially interested only in whether the omnibus hypothesis is correct. If the general, omnibus alternative hypothesis is correct, the researcher now wishes to explore further where the differences among groups lie.

The following rules apply to the use of post hoc comparisons:

1. They are not specified in advance of data analysis.
2. The omnibus *F*-test must first be found to be significant. If it is not significant, no post hoc tests should be performed.
3. The probability value for significance testing is based on the collection or family of comparisons and not on the individual comparison.
4. The set of post hoc comparisons need not be independent.

There are several alternative statistical tests available for post hoc comparisons. We will consider two of the most popular: Tukey's HSD and Scheffé's *S* method.

PLANNED COMPARISONS

Recall that the *F*-test for the Oneway ANOVA is a procedure that helps one decide between the omnibus null and alternative hypotheses:

$$H_0: \text{all } \mu_A\text{'s are equal}$$

$$H_a: \text{not all } \mu_A\text{'s are equal}$$

Specific Hypotheses

There may be circumstances in which the researcher *begins* data analysis with more specific hypotheses than evaluated by the omnibus *F*-test. For example, consider the Rewarding Interest scenario of Textbox 9.1. Imagine in the first instance that the researcher was interested, not in whether there were *any* differences among the groups, but in something more specific. The researcher wishes to assess whether there is a difference between informational rewards (A_2) versus no rewards (A_3). The researcher is also interested in whether there is a difference between controlling rewards (A_1) versus informational and no rewards (A_2 and A_3). How might we specify these concerns as two sets of null and alternative hypotheses?

Informational Rewards versus No Rewards

$$H_0: \mu_{A2} = \mu_{A3}$$

$$H_a: \mu_{A2} \neq \mu_{A3}$$

A **pairwise** or simple **comparison** will be used to help the researcher choose between null and alternative hypotheses.

*Controlling Rewards versus Informational
and No Rewards*

$$H_0: \mu_{A1} = (\mu_{A2} + \mu_{A3})/2$$

$$H_a: \mu_{A1} \neq (\mu_{A2} + \mu_{A3})/2$$

Put another way:

$$H_0: \mu_{A1} = .5\mu_{A2} + .5\mu_{A3}$$

$$H_a: \mu_{A1} \neq .5\mu_{A2} + .5\mu_{A3}$$

Note that we are contrasting the group mean for controlling rewards with the average or equally weighted combination of group means for informational and no rewards. Therefore, a **nonpairwise** or complex **comparison** will be used to help the researcher choose between null and alternative hypotheses.

Whether the null and alternative hypotheses are simple (e.g., one group versus another group) or complex (e.g., two groups versus one other group), there is always a "duality" or "two-sidedness" to them. That is, one expresses each comparison as the difference between one mean (or means) and another mean (or means). In other words, the underlying logic of a planned comparison is similar to that of a *t*-test wherein one evaluates the difference between two groups.

Rules for Evaluating Planned Comparisons

In order to evaluate planned comparisons, researchers must do the following:

1. Ensure that the comparison weights are valid and independent.
2. Apply the weights to the respective group means.
3. Find the sum of squares and mean squares for each comparison.
4. Calculate an *F*-ratio for each comparison and compare it to the critical value.

Symbol System

The symbol for representing the population value of a planned comparison is the Greek letter ψ (psi). The symbol for representing the *estimated* population value of a planned comparison is *p*.

A planned comparison is a difference between means. It can be expressed as a sum of the *weighted* means, where *c* is the **weight** or **comparison coefficient**:

$$p = (c_{A1})(\overline{Y}_{A1}) + (c_{A2})(\overline{Y}_{A2}) + (c_{A3})(\overline{Y}_{A3}) + \cdots$$

The more general form of this equation is as follows:

Equation 10.1: $p = \sum_{1}^{A} (c_A)(\overline{Y}_A)$

See Textbox 10.1 for an example.

Textbox 10.1

Planned Comparisons for the Rewarding Interest Scenario

For the first planned comparison in the Rewarding Interest scenario from Textbox 9.1 (A_2 versus A_3):

$$(0)(7.00) + (+1)(11.00) + (-1)(9.00) = -2.00$$

Notice that one "gets rid of" the mean of the Controlling Reward group (A_1) by assigning a weight of zero.

For the next planned comparison (A_1 versus A_2 and A_3):

$$(1)(7.00) + (-.5)(11.00) + (-.5)(9.00) = -3.00$$

Valid Planned Comparisons

A comparison is **valid** if the sum of the comparison weights is zero.

Equation 10.2: For each p: $\sum c_A = 0.0$

Textbox 10.2 gives an example.

Independence of Planned Comparisons

In creating a set of planned comparisons, you want to be sure that each comparison in the set asks something unique. Given that it is possible to create both simple comparisons between two groups and complex comparisons, the number of possible comparisons can be very large.

Possible Comparisons For example, given an independent variable with four levels, there are many comparisons possible:

1. All possible single means versus single means (i.e., pairwise comparisons)
2. All possible pairs of means versus single means
3. All possible pairs of means versus pairs of means
4. All possible triads of means versus single means

CD-ROM link 10.1

Activity 10.1: Planned Comparisons
Activity 10.1 allows you to select sets of planned comparisons and see how variability in the dependent variable is partitioned through these comparisons. Try verifying Equation 10.3 by experimenting with both dependent and independent comparisons!

Each and every one of these comparisons will not add something new—most of the comparisons will be redundant. What does this redundancy mean? Mathematically, it means that the explained variability associated with a comparison overlaps with (is correlated with) the explained variability associated with one or more other comparisons.

Independent Comparisons Here we have a very important concept about the nature of planned comparisons and their relationship to the Oneway ANOVA. Remember that the Oneway ANOVA divides total variability into two components: variability between groups and variability within groups. The between-groups variability from the ANOVA with more than two groups can be further subdivided into additive components.

Textbox 10.2

Checking the Validity of Rewarding Interest Scenario Comparisons

Is the first comparison valid? Yes, the weights sum to zero: $(0 - 1 + 1) = 0.0$.

Is the second comparison valid? Yes, the weights sum to zero. $(+1 - .5 - .5) = 0.0$.

These additive components are planned comparisons. The maximum number of **independent planned comparisons** in a set is equal to $A - 1$ (i.e., the number of levels of the independent variable less 1; also known as the df_A).

Each planned comparison corresponds to a single degree of freedom of the $A - 1$ degrees of freedom. Thus, the number of independent planned comparisons is $A - 1$. Furthermore, a set of independent planned comparisons among the levels of A has the following property:

$$\textbf{Equation 10.3: } SS_{Y(A)} = \sum_1^A SS_{Y(p)}$$

In other words, the between-groups sums of squares can be further subdivided into the sums of squares for the set of independent planned comparisons.

Finally, mathematically there can be more than one set of independent planned comparisons for a group of means. It is up to the researcher to find the one set appropriate for the investigation. Table 10.1 provides seven sets of independent comparisons when there are four groups.

TABLE 10.1 Sets of Independent Comparisons among Four Means

Set	c_1	c_2	c_3	c_4
1	1 0 1/2	−1 0 1/2	0 1 −1/2	0 −1 −1/2
2	1 0 1/2	0 1 −1/2	−1 0 1/2	0 −1 −1/2
3	1 0 1/2	0 1 −1/2	0 −1 −1/2	−1 0 1/2
4	1 1/2 1/3	−1 1/2 1/3	0 −1 1/3	0 0 −1
5	1/2 1/2 −1/2	1/2 −1/2 1/2	−1/2 −1/2 −1/2	−1/2 1/2 1/2
6	1/2 2/3 −1/3	1/2 −2/3 1/3	−1/2 1/3 2/3	−1/2 −1/3 −2/3
7	1/2 3/4 −1/4	1/2 −3/4 1/4	−1/2 1/4 3/4	−1/2 −1/4 −3/4

Source: Table 10.1 is taken from Roger E. Kirk's (1995) *Experimental Design: Procedures for the Behavioral Sciences,* p. 130 and is reproduced with the kind permission of the author and publisher.

The difficulty of creating a complete set of independent comparisons increases with the number of groups. You should not have difficulty creating a set of two comparisons when you are working with three groups. You will probably find it a more formidable chore to write a set of four independent comparisons when you are working with five groups.

Determining Whether Comparisons Are Independent　Two planned comparisons are *independent* if the product of the weights assigned to each mean sum to zero. Mathematically, independence exists in the following situation:

$$\text{Equation 10.4: } \sum_{1}^{A} c_{1A}c_{2A} = 0.0$$

where:

c_{1A} = coefficient for group A in the first comparison

c_{2A} = coefficient for group A in the second comparison

See Textbox 10.3 for an example.

Avoid One Occasional Mistake　On occasion, some students erroneously sum the entire set of comparison weights as a means to assess their independence. Doing so is certainly fast and easy but, unfortunately, is often incorrect. The only way to determine whether comparisons are independent is to compute the sum of the crossproducts of weights for each of the possible pairs in a set, making sure that each sum is zero.

In the two sets of comparisons, shown in Textbox 10.4, you will notice that the comparison weights in both sets sum to zero. However, both sets are not composed of independent comparisons. Only the first set A contains three comparisons where each is independent of the other two.

Statistically Evaluating Planned Comparisons

So far you have determined how to find valid and independent comparison weights and how to apply these weights to their respective group means. It is now

---

Textbox 10.3

Checking the Independence of the Rewarding Interest Comparisons

You can determine if the two planned comparisons for the Rewarding Interest scenario (see Textbox 9.1) are independent:

$$c_{1A1}c_{2A1} + c_{1A2}c_{2A2} + c_{1A3}c_{2A3} = 0.0$$

For comparisons 1 and 2:

$$(0)(+1) + (+1)(-.5) + (-1)(-1) = 0.0 - .5 + .5 = 0.0$$

Textbox 10.4

Why Summing the Weights to Test the Independence of Comparisons Doesn't "Add Up"

A. Three comparisons among four groups

1	−1	0	0	
0	0	1	−1	A set of three independent comparisons
.5	.5	−.5	−.5	
1.5	−.5	.5	−1.5	The sum of the comparison weights is zero.

B. Three comparisons among four groups

1	−1	0	0	
0	0	1	−1	A set of three nonindependent comparisons
.5	−.5	.5	−.5	(Comparison 3 is not independent of either 1 or 2.)
1.5	−1.5	1.5	−1.5	The sum of the comparison weights is zero.

CD-ROM link 10.2

Problem Generator: Planned Comparisons
To practice evaluating a planned comparison, select planned comparisons from the Problem Generator Menu on the CD-ROM. The Problem Generator will create as many practice problems as you need and will demonstrate each step in their solution so that you can check your work.

time to take these weighted means and compute the sums of squares, mean squares, and *F*-ratio for each comparison.

The sum of squares for a comparison is as follows:

$$\text{Equation 10.5: } SS_{Y(p)} = \frac{n(p)^2}{\displaystyle\sum_{1}^{A} c_A^2}$$

$$\text{where } p = \sum_{1}^{A} c_A \bar{Y}_A$$

The mean square for a comparison is as follows:

$$\text{Equation 10.6: } MS_{Y(p)} = SS_{Y(p)}/df_p = SS_{Y(p)}$$

(Remember that each comparison has only one numerator: df.)
The calculated value of *F* is as follows:

$$\text{Equation 10.7: } F_p = MS_{Y(p)}/MS_{Y(S/A)} \qquad df_p = 1, df_{S/A} = A(n-1)$$

Textbox 10.5 provides an illustration of the use of simple and complex comparisons. Textbox 10.6 shows that a set of independent, valid planned comparisons partitions between-groups variability into additive components.

Textbox 10.5

Statistically Evaluating the Rewarding Interest Planned Comparisons

For the first planned comparison (A_2 versus A_3):

1. *Find the calculated value:*

$$SS_{Y(p1)} = \frac{9[(0)7.00 + (+1)11.00 + (-1)(9.00)]^2}{(0)^2 + (1)^2 + (-1)^2} = \frac{9[2.00]^2}{2} = 18.00$$

$$MS_{Y(p1)} = 18.00/1.00 = 18.00$$

$$F_{p1} = 18.00/6.83 = 2.640$$

You compute the $MS_{Y(S/A)}$ in exactly the same fashion you do for the omnibus F-test. (See Table 9.6). If a computer program is handy, you would run the standard Oneway ANOVA to obtain this value. You would, not, however, examine the results of the omnibus F-test to see if there was an overall effect, because the research question is different.

2. *Compare calculated and critical values:*

What is the critical (tabled) value?
For df = 1,24, α = .05, the critical value is 4.26.
Note that the denominator degrees of freedom is 24, not 16, because the data from all the participants were used to calculate the within-groups variance ($MS_{Y(S/A)}$). Therefore, this procedure is more powerful than a t-test that uses the data for only two groups to form the error term.
The calculated value, 2.64, is smaller than the critical value, 4.26.
You fail to reject the null hypothesis for this comparison. You cannot conclude that there is a significant difference between informational rewards and no rewards with regard to children's book-borrowing behavior.

For the second planned comparison (A_1 versus A_2 and A_3):

1. *Find the calculated value:*

$$SS_{Y(p2)} = \frac{9[(+1)7.00 + (-.5)11.00 + (-.5)(9.00)]^2}{(1)^2 + (-.5)^2 + (-.5)^2} = \frac{9[3.00]^2}{1.50} = 54.00$$

$$MS_{Y(p2)} = 54.00/1.00 = 54.00$$

$$F_{p2} = 54.00/6.83 = 7.910$$

2. *Compare calculated and critical values:*

The calculated value, 7.91, is larger than the critical value, 4.26.
You reject the null hypothesis for this comparison. There is a significant difference in the book borrowing of children when they are offered controlling rewards compared to informational rewards and no rewards.

Textbox 10.6

Planned Comparisons and the Partitioning of Variance

Do the planned comparisons really divide the between-groups variability into additive components?

$$SS_{Y(A)} = \sum_{1}^{A} SS_{Y(p)}$$

$$SS_{Y(A)} = SS_{Y(p1)} + SS_{Y(p2)}$$

From Table 9.6, $SS_{Y(A)} = 72.00$

$$SS_{Y(p1)} = 18.00$$

$$SS_{Y(p2)} = 54.00$$

$$72.00 = 18.00 + 54.00$$

If one were to add a third comparison to this set of two comparisons, for example, controlling rewards versus informational rewards (i.e., A_1 versus A_3), the third comparison would add further variability. Therefore, the sums of squares for the third comparison would not necessarily be independent of the other two. Because of this loss of independence, $SS_{Y(A)}$ would no longer be equal to the sums of squares for the three comparisons.

Dealing with Variance Heterogeneity

There are actually two related statistical tests for evaluating planned comparisons: the *t*-test and the *F*-test. When variances are homogeneous (and group sample sizes are equal), the *t*-test and the *F*-test for a comparison produce related computed values because $t^2 = F$.

However, when there is **variance heterogeneity,** the *t*-test and the *F*-test for a comparison may produce different conclusions. When variances are heterogeneous, do not use the *F*-test to evaluate planned comparison. Instead, use the separate variance model *t*-test with reduced dfs.

Why is this so? When the variances of all of the groups are equal, an error term based on all the groups, as in the *F*-test, will be the same as an error term based only on a subset of the groups, as in the *t*-test. In contrast, when the variances of all of the groups are not equal, an error term based on all the groups will not be the same as an error term based only on a subset of the groups.

POST HOC COMPARISONS

Even though tests for planned comparisons form a useful technique in experimentation, it is common for the experimenter to have no specific questions to begin with. The initial concern is to establish only whether (some aspect of) the treatment worked. Given a significant overall test, the task is then to explore the data to find the source of these effects.

Post hoc comparisons are for those situations in which the researcher does not have specific hypotheses decided in advance. In those situations, the researcher clearly lacks a firm idea of the precise nature of the differences among groups. (A firm idea of the precise nature of the differences would be evidenced by the researcher actually doing planned comparisons in lieu of the omnibus test.)

The techniques for comparisons to be introduced now are strictly applicable only to the situation in which a preliminary Oneway ANOVA has shown overall significance. After the overall F has been found significant, then any comparisons may be made. Unlike planned comparisons there is never a requirement that such post hoc comparisons be independent. Although there are a variety of post hoc multiple comparison procedures, we will concentrate on the two most widely used: Tukey's HSD method and Scheffé's S method.

After finding a significant omnibus effect in the Oneway ANOVA, the researcher is likely to want to explore for any and all possible differences among the groups and not restrict the probes to a small number of independent comparisons. That's fine, but it creates two difficulties that have to be addressed. First, there are often a large number of significance tests to be performed. Second, the post hoc comparisons that make up a set are not restricted to those that are independent and, consequently, there is redundancy in the analyses. Adding the sums of squares for each of the post hoc comparisons in a set results in a sum of squares often much larger than the between-groups sum of squares ($SS_{Y(A)}$).

Because of the large number of comparisons and their nonindependence, post hoc procedures avoid using a probability value for significance testing, and hence a critical value, determined solely for each comparison. Instead the probability value and critical value are determined according to the number and nature of the comparisons undertaken in the set or family. This is a critical feature of post hoc comparisons, and we address it first before examining the two post hoc procedures in greater detail.

Conceptual Unit for Error Rate

If an experiment contains two treatment levels, and therefore only one comparison among the means is possible, the probability of committing a Type I error if the null hypothesis is true is determined by the significance level adopted. Although the interpretation of a significance level is unambiguous for experiments with two levels of the independent variable, it becomes confusing for multilevel variables involving several simultaneous comparisons.

The confusion arises in the case of **multiple comparisons** because a significance level can be specified for a number of different conceptual units. That is, we can redefine our error rate depending on the conceptual unit employed. Although there are several more, we will restrict our discussion to two of the most widely used conceptual units for error rate: error rate per comparison and familywise error rate.

Type I Error Rate for a Collection of Comparisons   Hays (1994, p. 450) provides the following formula for estimating the likelihood of one or more Type I errors occurring in a collection of independent comparisons:

$$\textbf{Equation 10.8: } 1 - (1 - \alpha)^c$$

where:

$\alpha =$ alpha level

$c =$ number of comparisons

Imagine you had a collection of 10 independent comparisons and wanted to evaluate each one using $\alpha = .05$. If so,

$$1 - (1 - .05)^{10} = 1 - .60 = .40$$

By doing multiple *t*-tests and setting α at .05 for *each* comparison, the likelihood of a Type I error somewhere in the *set* of comparisons is much higher (.40) than for any one comparison.

Error Rate per Comparison   An **error rate per comparison** is defined as the probability that any one of C comparisons will be falsely declared significant. Error rate per comparison is the error rate that is controlled when planned multiple comparisons are performed and alpha is the level of significance for each comparison.

$$\text{Error rate per comparison} = \frac{\text{Number of comparisons falsely declared significant}}{\text{Total number of comparisons}}$$

Error rate per comparison is the probability of making a Type I error on any given comparison. This error rate treats each comparison as if it were the only one being made.

Familywise Error Rate   **Familywise error rate** is the probability that one or more erroneous statements will be made in a collection of associated statistical tests (e.g., simple and complex comparisons among the group means of a multilevel independent variable). Setting familywise error rate is used to guard against making any erroneous statements in a family of comparisons.

In post hoc comparisons, this is the error rate that is controlled by using Tukey's or Scheffé's method. The use of familywise error rate is based on the premise that it is just as serious to make one erroneous statement in a collection as it is to make, say, five.

$$\text{Familywise error rate} = \frac{\text{Number of families with at least one contrast falsely declared significant}}{\text{Total number of families}}$$

Textbox 10.7

Per Comparison versus Familywise Error Rates

Suppose there were 1000 experiments and for each experiment eight contrasts were each subjected to a test of significance. Thus, each experiment would be evaluated by a family of eight comparisons. For the total 8000 tests of significance, 800 are truly false and these false tests are contained within just 200 experiments.

$$\text{Error rate per comparison} = 800/8000 = .10$$

$$\text{Familywise error rate} = 200/1000 = .20$$

Familywise error rate is the probability of making a Type I error anywhere in a collection or family of comparisons. For example, when a family contains five comparisons, the familywise error rate is the probability that the collection of comparisons will contain at least one false rejection of the null hypothesis.

Textbox 10.7 contains another example for both error rates.

Since post hoc comparisons need to control for familywise error rate and planned comparisons do not, one might reasonably ask what effect this has on the evaluation of each comparison. When comparisons are looked at one at a time, it is much easier to reject the null hypothesis when a comparison is planned rather than post hoc. Specifically, the critical value one needs to exceed to reject the null hypothesis is smaller for a planned comparison than it is for a post hoc comparison. We will demonstrate this principle on the Rewarding Interest dataset after examining the procedures for post hoc comparisons.

Tukey's HSD

Tukey's HSD (honestly significant difference) test is for testing all pairwise comparisons among means. It is best to use this method when sample sizes are approximately the same for all the groups.

In this approach you need to find the calculated value of each pairwise contrast you wish to evaluate. You then need to find the critical value for evaluating each contrast. You must compare each calculated value against the critical value to judge whether each contrast is significant.

Finding the Calculated Value   Finding the calculated value is a straightforward procedure. It is the same one used to find the calculated value of a planned contrast.

Computational formula for post hoc (ph) comparisons:

$$\textbf{Equation 10.5: } SS_{Y(ph)} = \frac{n(p)^2}{\sum\limits_{1}^{A} c_A^2} \qquad \text{where } p = \sum\limits_{1}^{A} c_A \bar{Y}_A$$

$$\text{Equation 10.6: } MS_{Y(ph)} = SS_{Y(ph)}/df_{ph}$$

(Remember that each comparison has only one numerator df.)

$$\text{Equation 10.7: } F_{ph} = MS_{Y(ph)}/MS_{Y(S/A)} \qquad df_{ph} = 1, df_{S/A} = A(n-1)$$

Finding the Critical Value It should be obvious that if the computational procedures for the calculated value of planned and post hoc comparisons are the same, then the critical values of the two procedures must be different, given that they attempt to control different error rates.

To find the critical value for the Tukey test (F_T) for making *all* pairwise comparisons among means:

$$\text{Equation 10.8: } F_T = \frac{(q_T)^2}{2}$$

where q_T is an entry in the Studentized range distribution. See Appendix F. To find the correct value of q_T you need:

1. $df_{S/A}$, which is $N - A$ or $(n-1)A$
2. k, the number of treatment means ($k = A$)
3. α_{FW}, alpha for the familywise Type I error selected, which is usually .05 or .01.

We will once again use the Rewarding Interest scenario to illustrate the computations for the Tukey test. See Textbox 10.8. However, it bears repeating that no researcher ever undertakes both planned and post hoc comparisons on the same dataset. We do so here for computational simplicity and to show the similarities and differences between approaches.

Scheffé's *S* Method

If the omnibus *F*-test is significant, **Scheffé's** *S* method can be used to make all possible comparisons among means, both pairwise comparisons and nonpairwise comparisons. This method is less powerful than Tukey's for pairwise comparisons and is generally recommended only when nonpairwise comparisons are also included. Error rate is set familywise. Unlike Tukey's HSD, cell sizes (n) can be unequal for Scheffé's *S* method.

While Scheffé's *S* method affords the opportunity to examine a larger number of comparisons, there is a cost to pay. Controlling for familywise error rate when one plans to examine both simple, pairwise comparisons and complex, nonpairwise comparisons means the number of comparisons in the family is larger than when only pairwise comparisons are examined. As a result, the critical value used to evaluate any one comparison is larger for the *S* method than the HSD method. All other things equal, it is harder to reject the null hypothesis for Scheffé's *S* method than Tukey's HSD method. The Scheffé *S* method is not a very powerful procedure. Because it is not, sometimes comparisons that would have been judged significant with use of the HSD approach fail to reach significance with use of the *S* method.

Finally, one does not conduct both Scheffé and Tukey tests on the same data. Conducting multiple tests of this sort is an unacceptable form of data snooping. If

---

<table>
<tr><td align="center">Textbox 10.8</td></tr>
</table>

Tukey Post Hoc Comparisons for the Rewarding Interest Scenario

Imagine that for the Reward Interest scenario, (see Textbox 9.1) you had no specific a priori questions to ask but had merely computed an *F*-ratio and determined that there was an overall effect ($p < .05$). See Table 9.6 for the Oneway ANOVA summary table. Now you want to look further into the data and test all possible pairwise comparisons (A_1 versus A_2, A_1 versus A_3, and A_2 versus A_3).

As you can readily see, the number of possible pairwise comparisons (three) to be evaluated for the post hoc analysis is only slightly larger than the two independent comparisons evaluated for the planned analysis.

For one post hoc comparison (A_2 versus A_3):

1. *Find the calculated value:*

$$SS_{Y(ph1)} = \frac{9[(0)7.00 + (+1)11.00 + (-1)(9.00)]^2}{(0)^2 + (1)^2 + (-1)^2} = \frac{9[2.00]^2}{2} = 18.00$$

$$MS_{Y(ph1)} = 18.00/1.00 = 18.00$$

$$F_{ph1} = 18.00/6.83 = 2.640$$

You compute the $MS_{Y(S/A)}$ in exactly the same fashion you do for the omnibus *F*-test. (See Table 9.6.)

2. *Compare calculated and critical values:*

What is the critical (tabled) value?

$$F_T = \frac{(q_T)^2}{2}$$

To find q_T:

$$df_{S/A} = N - A \text{ or } (n-1)A = 24$$

$$k = A = 3$$

$$\alpha_{FW} = .05$$

$$q_T = 3.53$$

$$F_T = \frac{(q_T)^2}{2} = \frac{(3.53)^2}{2} = 6.23$$

The calculated value, 2.64, is smaller than the critical value, 6.23.

You fail to reject the null hypothesis for this comparison. You cannot conclude that there is a significant difference between informational rewards and no rewards with regard to children's book-borrowing behavior.

---

continued

Textbox 10.8 (Continued)

For another post hoc comparison (A_1 versus A_2):

1. *Find the calculated value:*

$$SS_{Y(ph2)} = \frac{9[(+1)7.00 + (-1)11.00 + (0)(9.00)]^2}{(1)^2 + (-1)^2 + (0)^2} = \frac{9[-4.00]^2}{2} = 72.00$$

$$MS_{Y(ph2)} = 72.00/1.00 = 72.00$$

$$F_{ph2} = 72.00/6.83 = 10.540$$

2. *Compare calculated and critical values:*

What is the critical (tabled) value?

$$F_T = \frac{(q_T)^2}{2} = \frac{(3.53)^2}{2} = 6.23$$

The calculated value, 10.54, is larger than the critical value, 6.23.

You reject the null hypothesis for this comparison. You conclude that there is a significant difference between informational rewards and controlling rewards with regard to children's book-borrowing behavior.

For a third post hoc comparison (A_1 versus A_3):

1. *Find the calculated value:*

$$SS_{Y(ph3)} = \frac{9[(+1)7.00 + (0)11.00 + (-1)(9.00)]^2}{(1)^2 + (0)^2 + (-1)^2} = \frac{9[-2.00]^2}{2} = 18.00$$

$$MS_{Y(ph3)} = 18.00/1.00 = 18.00$$

$$F_{ph3} = 18.00/6.83 = 2.64$$

2. *Compare calculated and critical values:*

What is the critical (tabled) value?

$$F_T = \frac{(q_T)^2}{2} = \frac{(3.53)^2}{2} = 6.23$$

The calculated value, 2.64, is smaller than the critical value, 6.23.

You fail to reject the null hypothesis for this comparison. You cannot conclude that there is a significant difference between no rewards and controlling rewards with regard to children's book-borrowing behavior.

---

you wish only to conduct pairwise comparisons, and if cell sizes are equal, use Tukey's HSD. If you wish to conduct both simple and complex comparisons, or if cell sizes are unequal, use only the Scheffé S method.

Finding the Calculated Value   Finding the calculated value with the Scheffé S method is a straightforward procedure. It is the same procedure you used to find the calculated value of a planned contrast. It is also the same as the computational procedure for Tukey's HSD except one is no longer restricted to exploring only pairwise comparisons.

The computational formula for post hoc (ph) comparisons is as follows:

To find the sum of squares:

$$\textbf{Equation 10.5: } SS_{Y(ph)} = \frac{n(p)^2}{\displaystyle\sum_{1}^{A} c_A^2} \qquad \text{where } p = \sum_{1}^{A} c_A \overline{Y}_A$$

To find the mean squares:

$$\textbf{Equation 10.6: } MS_{Y(ph)} = SS_{Y(ph)} / df_{ph}$$

(Remember that each comparison has only one numerator: df.)

To find the calculated value of F:

$$\textbf{Equation 10.7: } F_{ph} = MS_{Y(ph)} / MS_{Y(S/A)} \qquad df_{ph} = 1. \; df_{S/A} = A(n-1)$$

Finding the Critical Value Because the computational formulas are the same for Tukey's HSD and Scheffé's S methods, the critical values must be different given that Scheffé's S method allows for the evaluation of both pairwise and non-pairwise comparisons.

To find the critical value for Scheffé's S method (F_S) for making *all possible* comparisons among means:

$$\textbf{Equation 10.9: } F_S = (a - 1)F(df_A, df_{S/A})$$

See examples in Textbox 10.9 for the Rewarding Interest scenario.

Comparison of Planned and Post Hoc Comparisons As you saw, it is possible to use the contrast approach to conduct planned and post hoc comparisons (either Tukey or Scheffé). The calculated values of the contrasts do not change, whether the comparisons are planned or post hoc. However, the critical values do change depending on the comparison method used.

On a per-comparison basis it is harder to reject the null hypothesis when using the Scheffé method than when using the Tukey method than when doing a planned comparison via the F-test.

Notice that the critical value of Scheffé > Tukey > F-test.

In our example dataset the critical values were

Planned comparisons (F) = 3.40

Tukey (F_T) = 6.23

Scheffé (F_S) = 6.80

Textbox 10.9

Scheffé's *S* Post Hoc Comparison for the Rewarding Interest Scenario

Having first established the overall significant effect of Reward Type on Book Borrowing, we now wish to probe the omnibus effect by conducting all possible comparisons between the means. What are all the possible simple and complex comparisons?

1. A_1 versus A_2
2. A_1 versus A_3
3. A_2 versus A_3
4. A_1 and A_2 versus A_3
5. A_1 and A_3 versus A_2
6. A_1 versus A_2 and A_3

Calculated values. We have previously computed the calculated values for four of six of these comparisons in illustrating planned or pairwise post hoc comparisons:

1. A_1 versus A_2: $F_{ph1} = 10.54$
2. A_1 versus A_3: $F_{ph2} = 2.64$
3. A_2 versus A_3: $F_{ph3} = 2.64$
6. A_1 versus A_2 and A_3: $F_{ph6} = 7.91$

Computing the remaining critical values reveals:

4. A_1 and A_2 versus A_3: $F_{ph4} = 0.00$
5. A_1 and A_3 versus A_2: $F_{ph5} = 7.91$

Comparing calculated and critical values. What is the critical (tabled value)?

$$F_S = (a - 1)F (\mathrm{df}_A, \mathrm{df}_{S/A}) = (3 - 1)3.40 = 6.80.$$

Only three calculated values exceed this critical value: (1) A_1 versus A_2, (5) A_1 and A_3 versus A_2, and (6) A_1 and A_2 versus A_3.

PUTTING IT ALL TOGETHER

We offered that planned comparisons should be undertaken by the researcher as an alternative to the omnibus Oneway ANOVA only when the researcher has specific hypotheses about differences between the treatment groups. Furthermore, the $A - 1$ planned comparisons should be independent and should further partition the between-groups variability into additive components.

Post hoc comparisons are undertaken following a significant omnibus test. We recommended the Tukey HSD when simple, pairwise comparisons are undertaken and when group sample sizes are equal. For all possible comparisons or when group sample sizes are unequal, we recommended Scheffé's *S* method.

Planned Comparisons

A planned comparison is a difference between means. It can be expressed as a sum of the *weighted* means, where c is the weight or comparison coefficient:

$$\text{Equation 10.1: } p = \sum_1^A (c_A)(\overline{Y}_A)$$

A comparison is valid if the sum of the comparison weights is zero.

$$\text{Equation 10.2: For each } p: \sum c_A = 0.0$$

A set of independent planned comparisons among the levels of A has the following property:

$$\text{Equation 10.3: } SS_{Y(A)} = \sum_1^A SS_{Y(p)}$$

Two planned comparisons are independent if the product of the weights assigned to each mean sum to zero. Mathematically, independence exists in the following situation:

$$\text{Equation 10.4: } \sum_1^A c_{1A}c_{2A} = 0.0$$

where:

c_{1A} = coefficient for group A in the first comparison

c_{2A} = coefficient for group A in the second comparison

Evaluating Planned Comparisons In order to evaluate planned comparisons, you must do the following:

1. Ensure that the comparison weights are valid and independent.
2. Apply the weights to the respective group means.
3. Find the sum of squares and mean squares for each comparison.
4. Calculate an F-ratio for each comparison and compare it to the critical value.

To statistically evaluate a planned comparison:

The Sum of Squares for a comparison is as follows:

$$\text{Equation 10.5: } SS_{Y(p)} = \frac{n(p)^2}{\sum_1^A c_A^2} \qquad \text{where } p = \sum_1^A c_A\overline{Y}_A$$

The Mean Square for a comparison is as follows:

$$\text{Equation 10.6: } MS_{Y(p)} = SS_{Y(p)}/df_p = SS_{Y(p)}$$

(Remember that each comparison has only one numerator df.)

The calculated value of F is as follows:

Equation 10.7: $F_p = \text{MS}_{Y(p)}/\text{MS}_{Y(S/A)}$ $\qquad$ $\text{df}_p = 1, \text{df}_{S/A} = A(n-1)$

Post Hoc Comparisons

Computational formulas for post hoc (ph) comparisons are the same as for planned comparisons. However, the critical values are different.

To find the critical value for the Tukey test (F_T) for making *all* pairwise comparisons among means:

$$\textbf{Equation 10.8: } F_T = \frac{(q_T)^2}{2}$$

where q_T is an entry in the Studentized range distribution. See Appendix F.

Textbox 10.10

Real Time: Post Hoc Comparisons

In Chapter 9 we reported the omnibus Oneway ANOVA results of a study examining children's understanding of the content of television police shows (Low & Durkin, 1997). In this section we will report the results of the post hoc comparisons that probed the significant effects for specific age-related differences.

Low and Durkin reported that there was an overall main effect of Age on the number of propositions reported, $F(4, 95) = 33.21$, $p < .05$. Post hoc Tukey tests indicated that both Grade 1 and Grade 3 had significantly lower mean numbers of propositions ($M = 2.15$ and 2.85, respectively) than Grade 5 ($M = 5.70$), Grade 7 ($M = 8.80$), and Adults ($M = 9.40$) ($p < .05$). Post hoc tests also revealed that Grade 5 students had a lower number of propositions than Grade 7 and Adults ($p < .05$).

Grade and Propositions were coded into one of four categories—action, description, reactions, elaborations—but there were significant omnibus effects for action and elaboration propositions only. Tukey tests indicated that Grade 3 students had a higher mean proportion of action propositions ($M = .93$) than Grade 5 ($M = .49$), Grade 7 ($M = .50$), and Adults ($M = .33$) ($p < .05$). Tukey tests revealed that the mean proportion of elaboration propositions for Grade 3 children ($M = .03$) was significantly lower than the means for Grade 5 ($M = .33$), Grade 7 ($M = .34$), and Adults ($M = .49$) ($p < .05$). In addition, adults had a higher mean proportion than Grade 5 or 7 children ($p < .05$).

Tukey tests on the analysis of the criminal justice system indicated that Grade 1 children had simpler scripts ($M = 1.45$) than Grade 3 ($M = 1.95$), Grade 5 ($M = 2.20$), Grade 7 ($M = 2.75$), and Adults ($M = 2.45$) ($p < .05$). Grade 3 children had less complex scripts than Grade 7 and Adults, and Grade 5 children had less complex scripts than Grade 7 or Adults ($p < .05$).

The results of the analyses conducted by Low and Durkin supported their hypothesis that, with age, scripts become more elaborate and hierarchical. By Grade 7 more abstract variations on the basic script appeared. A developmental trend of increasing complexity in the understanding of the criminal justice system was also evident with the models progressing from the simple Pursuit Model to the more complex and abstract Due Process Model.

To find the correct value of q_T you need:

1. $\text{df}_{S/A}$, which is $N - A$ or $(n-1)A$
2. k, the number of treatment means $(k = A)$
3. α_{FW}, alpha for the familywise Type I error selected, which is usually .05 or .01.

To find the critical value for Scheffé's S method (F_S) for making *all possible* comparisons among means:

Equation 10.9: $F_S = (a-1)F(\text{df}_A, \text{df}_{S/A})$

Notice that the critical value of Scheffé > Tukey > F-test.

KEY TERMS

Comparison or contrast

Simple comparison or Pairwise comparison

Complex comparison or Nonpairwise comparison

Weight or comparison coefficient

Valid planned comparison

Independent planned comparison

Variance heterogeneity

Multiple comparisons

Error rate per comparison

Familywise error rate

Tukey's HSD

Scheffé's S

REFERENCES

Hays, W. L. (1994). *Statistics.* (5th ed.). Orlando, FL: Harcourt Brace College Publishers.

Kirk, R. E. (1995). *Experimental design: Procedures for the behavioral sciences.* (3rd ed.). Pacific Grove, CA: Brooks/Cole.

Low, J., & Durkin, K. (1997). Children's understanding of events and criminal justice process in police programs. *Journal of Applied Developmental Psychology, 18,* 179–205.

PROBLEMS

Questions

Section 1   Conceptual/Definition

10.1. What are simple and complex comparisons?

10.2. When are multiple comparisons used?

10.3. Under what condition(s) are an omnibus test and a comparison equivalent?

10.4. What are the rules for using planned comparisons?

10.5. What are the rules for using post hoc comparisons?

10.6. What is the criterion for determining when a comparison is valid?

10.7. Define independence both mathematically and conceptually. Why is the requirement of independence essential in conducting planned comparisons?

10.8. Comparisons can be evaluated using either a *t*-test or an *F*-test. Under what condition(s) will the tests produce different results?

10.9. Discuss the similarities and differences between planned and post hoc comparisons.

10.10. Should both Scheffé and Tukey tests be conducted on the same data?

Section 2   Numerical

10.11. How many *t*-tests would be required to test all possible combinations among pairs of means in a situation where four levels of an independent variable were being tested? Given this number of tests what would be the effective alpha (error rate) given the family of tests conducted if each test was conducted using $\alpha = .05$?

10.12. How many *t*-tests would be required to test all possible combinations among pairs of means in a situation in which three levels of an independent variable were being tested? Given this number of tests what would be the effective alpha (error rate) given the family of tests conducted if each test was conducted using $\alpha = .05$?

10.13. What per-comparison alpha would have to be used in order to evaluate five pairwise comparisons in order to keep the error rate for the study as a whole at the .05 level?

10.14. What per-comparison alpha would have to be used in order to evaluate two pairwise comparisons in order to keep the error rate for the study as a whole at the .05 level?

10.15. A study in which there were an equal number of subjects per group has produced the following results:

$$\text{Sums: } A_1 = 97, A_2 = 148, A_3 = 175$$

$$\text{Means: } A_1 = 13.86, A_2 = 21.14, A_3 = 25$$

$$SS_{Y(A)} = 448.29, df_{Y(A)} = 2, MS_{Y(A)} = 224.15$$

$$SS_{Y(S/A)} = 119.71, df_{Y(S/A)} = 18, MS_{Y(S/A)} = 6.65$$

$$SS_Y = 568, df_Y = 20, F = 33.70$$

Use the Tukey method to test all possible pairwise comparisons.

Use the following information to answer questions 10.16 to 10.19: A study in which there were an equal number of subjects per group has produced the following results:

$$\text{Sums: } A_1 = 434, A_2 = 477, A_3 = 532, A_4 = 546$$

$$\text{Means: } A_1 = 54.25, A_2 = 59.6, A_3 = 66.5, A_4 = 68.25$$

$$SS_{Y(A)} = 999.30, df_{Y(A)} = 3, MS_{Y(A)} = 331.10$$

$$SS_{Y(S/A)} = 1894.90, df_{Y(S/A)} = 28, MS_{Y(S/A)} = 67.70$$

$$SS_Y = 2894.20, df_Y = 31, F = 4.92$$

10.16. Use the Tukey method to test all possible pairwise comparisons.

10.17. What critical value would be used for the Scheffé method?

10.18. What critical value of F would be used to evaluate planned comparisons? What is the maximum number of comparisons in a complete set of independent comparisons for this data?

10.19. Conduct a complete set of planned comparisons using Set 1 from Table 10.1.

10.20. A study in which there were an equal number of subjects per group has produced the following results:

$$\text{Sums: } A_1 = 56, A_2 = 84, A_3 = 84, A_4 = 56$$

$$\text{Means: } A_1 = 8, A_2 = 12, A_3 = 12, A_4 = 8$$

$$SS_{Y(A)} = 112, df_{Y(A)} = 3, MS_{Y(A)} = 37.33$$

$$SS_{Y(S/A)} = 48, df_{Y(S/A)} = 24, MS_{Y(S/A)} = 2$$

$$SS_Y = 160, df_Y = 27, F = 18.67$$

(a) What critical value of F would be used to evaluate pairwise post hoc comparisons using the Tukey method?

(b) What critical value would be used for the Scheffé method?

(c) What critical value of F would be used to evaluate planned comparisons?

(d) What is the maximum number of comparisons in a complete set of independent comparisons for these data?

chapter 11

Analyzing More Than a Single Independent Variable

Factorial Between-Groups Analysis of Variance

OVERVIEW

Just when you were getting comfortable with analyzing the effect of a multilevel independent variable on the dependent variable, we are going to upset the apple cart again and stretch your understanding further. The new challenge you will face is how to analyze and understand the effects of more than a single independent variable. Specifically, we will explain how to use the Factorial Between-Groups Analysis of Variance for analyzing variability in the dependent variable that may have been caused by two or more independent variables.

Factorial designs are a great boon to researchers but they can present logical challenges that need to be overcome. Therefore, the first portion of this chapter is given over to a detailed understanding of Factorial designs. Believe it or not, the fanciest statistic you will see in this entire first section is a mean.

After we have developed your understanding of Factorial designs, we will cover the Factorial ANOVA as the statistical method for analyzing these designs. Like the Oneway ANOVA, the Factorial ANOVA also partitions variability into additive components. And like the Oneway ANOVA, with the Factorial ANOVA planned comparisons are used in lieu of omnibus tests and post hoc comparisons are used to probe significant omnibus effects, as we will show. Finally, we will explain something unique to Factorial ANOVA. We will show how to explore the significant interaction of two factors by using tests of simple effects.

Along the way, some of the questions we will answer include the following:

1. How does a researcher combine independent variables into a single study?
2. What is the difference between a main effect and an interaction effect?
3. How does the Factorial ANOVA partition variability into the additive components for main and interaction effects?
4. How does one compute effect sizes and power for the Factorial ANOVA?
5. What are the important assumptions underlying this statistical test?
6. When and how should one use planned comparisons?
7. When and how should one use post hoc comparisons?
8. What are the advantages and disadvantages of simple effect tests?
9. What are the decision rules for simple effects?
10. How does one probe a significant, omnibus simple effect?

Let us start with the scenario in Textbox 11.1.

We have introduced a new wrinkle and further complexity to the kind of investigation researchers are capable of analyzing statistically. As illustrated in the Speed Whiz scenario, it is possible to design experiments in which researchers can study the effects of multiple factors on a single dependent variable.

To fully appreciate the statistical analysis of Factorial designs, however, requires that one first take a more careful look at the logic of Factorial designs and especially the interpretation of various patterns of results. To ease you into this understanding, we begin with the presentation of a simpler Factorial design than the Speed Whiz scenario.

Textbox 11.1

Scenario: Speed Whiz*

You conduct an experiment to determine the effects of type of training (e.g., massed practice, spaced practice, no practice) and reward condition (e.g., small, none) on the speed with which students can correctly solve multiplication problems (measured in seconds). Participants in the small reward condition are given certificates for one of three results: (1) for studying for three hours one day (i.e., massed practice); (2) for studying for one hour each day for several days (i.e., spaced practice); or (3) merely reviewing the teacher's lesson (i.e., no practice). Participants in the no-reward condition receive no recognition for studying or reviewing. All participants complete a timed quiz to determine the average speed in seconds with which they correctly solved multiplication problems.

With eight subjects per experimental condition (i.e., cell), the following results were obtained (see Table 11.1):

*In the Speed Whiz scenario, the means are not whole numbers. Although this makes manual calulations a bit more cumbersome, it should help prevent mixing individual scores with mean scores when deviation scores are computed.

TABLE 11.1 3 × 2 Factorial Design: Effects of Type of Training and Reward Condition

		Type of Training					
		Massed Practice		Spaced Practice		No Practice	
Reward Condition	Small	26	14	41	82	36	87
		41	16	26	86	39	99
		28	29	19	45	59	126
		92	31	59	37	27	104
	None	51	35	39	114	42	133
		96	36	104	92	92	124
		97	28	130	87	156	68
		22	76	122	64	144	142

FACTORIAL DESIGNS

Factorial designs are used when a researcher is interested in investigating the effect of two or more independent variables (i.e., factors)—each by itself and also in interaction with one another—on a dependent variable. Each independent variable must have no less than two values or levels that differ either quantitatively or qualitatively.

The effect of each independent variable on the dependent variable, without consideration of the other factor(s), is called a **main effect.** A main effect is one averaged across levels of the other factor(s). The effect of the combination of two or more independent variables on the dependent variable is called an **interaction effect.** When an interaction effect is present, one knows that the effect of one independent variable on the dependent variable varies as a function of the values of another independent variable.

The simultaneous investigation of two or more independent variables is both important and common in social science research. Rarely do treatments operate uniformly in all circumstances or similarly with all participants. More often, researchers are faced with individual and setting factors that modify the effectiveness of these treatments. Thus, researchers are more often searching for the optimal conditions for use and deciding whether and to what extent the effectiveness of one factor, say, *A*, depends on the values of another factor, say, *B*.

For example, imagine you wanted to study the effects of classroom structures (cooperative, individualistic) on student achievement for boys and girls. Students and their teachers who agree to participate are randomly assigned to either the cooperative structure condition or the individualistic structure condition. At the end of several months all students are tested on a common examination.

An interaction effect would exist if classroom structures produced different achievement results for boys than girls (e.g., girls learned more from cooperative structures while boys learned more from individualistic ones). Put another way, one could conclude in this example that the effectiveness of classroom structures varies according to student gender. Knowledge of the effects of classroom structures alone is not sufficient to understand the circumstances under which all students learn best.

Note that the study just described includes a variable, classroom structures, which is manipulated by, and under the control of, the researcher. It also includes a second variable, student gender, which is neither manipulated by, nor under the control of, the researcher. A factorial design that includes both manipulated and nonmanipulated variables produces results that must be interpreted carefully when one attempts to make causal inferences.

In particular, a significant Structure × Gender interaction effect may not be interpreted as student gender causing the classroom structures to operate differently. For example, another factor such as student ability or subject matter preferences may differentiate the participants and explain why boys and girls react differently under cooperative structures compared to individualistic ones.

We discussed threats to internal validity more fully in Chapter 2. In general, rival explanations to a main effect or interaction effect are possible whenever the independent variables(s) are not manipulated by the researcher.

CD-ROM link 11.1

Activity 11.1: Main Effects and Interactions
In Activity 11.1, you can change the values of the four group means in a simple 2 × 2 Factorial design. As you manipulate the means, you will create main effects and interactions. By studying how main effects and interactions are represented in both a table and a graph, you will develop a better understanding of these fundamental concepts.

The Simplest Case: A 2 × 2 Factorial

Before we deal with the statistical analysis of Factorial designs, it is important that you understand how to represent the results of these designs and interpret the findings. We will take the simplest possible Factorial design, one involving two independent variables, each with only two values or levels, and a single dependent variable. See Textbox 11.2 for a brief synopsis of a hypothetical experiment concerning children's storybook preferences.

We will represent a variety of hypothetical outcomes of the experiment in two ways: (1) a Factorial design table, and (2) a graph. The **Factorial design table** is a particular form of contingency table (see Chapter 3) where mean scores on the dependent variable are recorded. In a Factorial design table with two independent variables, the columns represent different values of one independent variable (A). In contrast, the rows represent different values of the other independent variable (B).

The main effect of A may be examined by looking at the column means (i.e., A_1 [boys] versus A_2 [girls]). In contrast, the main effect of B may be examined by looking at the row means (i.e., B_1 [fantasy-based characters] versus B_2 [reality-based characters]). Finally, the $A \times B$ interaction effect may be examined by looking at the cell means (i.e., A_1B_1 [boys exposed to fantasy-based characters] and A_2B_2 [girls exposed to reality-based characters] versus A_1B_2 [boys exposed to reality-based characters] and A_2B_1 [girls exposed to fantasy-based characters]). A Factorial design table set up to input the mean preference scores (Y) is shown in Table 11.2.

A graph is a second, useful method for displaying the mean results of an experiment with two or more independent variables. Traditionally, the ordinate, or vertical y-axis, is reserved for the mean values of the dependent variable (Y). The abscissa, or horizontal x-axis, is reserved for the values of one of the independent variables (e.g., B). The values of the other independent variable (e.g., A) are repre-

---

Textbox 11.2

Storybook Preferences of Preschool Children

A child psychologist is interested in the storybook preferences of preschool children. She wonders whether children prefer stories with characters that are fantasy-based or reality-based. Furthermore, she is interested in the preferences of boys compared to girls. She conducts a simple study with 60 boys and 60 girls. Half of the children are read a story with fantasy-based characters. The other half are read the same story except the characters are reality-based. Following the stories, each child is asked to rate his or her enjoyment of the story on a 10-point scale, with a 1 (a sad face) being a low rating and a 10 (a happy face) being a high rating.

TABLE 11.2 2 × 2 Factorial Design Table: Identifying Row, Column, and Cell Means				
		Gender		
		Boys	Girls	
Character	Fantasy	A_1B_1	A_2B_1	B_1
Type	Reality	A_1B_2	A_2B_2	B_2
		A_1	A_2	

sented by use of separate lines with a legend to identify the values. A Factorial design graph set up to input the mean preference scores (Y) is shown in Figure 11.1.

The Factorial design tables and graphs that follow present fictitious results of several possible study outcomes: no effects, one main effect only, an interaction effect only, two main effects, one main effect and an interaction, and two main effects plus an interaction. Below each factorial is a brief verbal description of each outcome. For simplicity, assume that all mean differences not zero are significant. Note that there is a table and graph for representing each set of fictitious results. You may prefer the graphical form of data display to the table, or vice versa.

Outcome A: No Effects   Girls and boys (A_1 versus A_2) did not differ in their enjoyment of stories. No preference was shown for character type (B_1 versus B_2).

In Table 11.3 all cell, row, and column means are identical. In Figure 11.2, the line plotting the results for boys overlaps the line plotting the results for girls. Neither line has any slope.

Outcome B: One Main Effect   Girls preferred the stories more than boys (A_1 versus A_2). There were no differences in character type preferences (B_1 versus B_2).

In Table 11.4, the column means are higher for girls compared to boys. In Figure 11.3, the line plotting the results for girls is above the line plotting the results

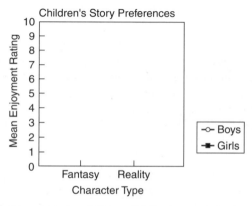

Figure 11.1 2 × 2 Factorial design graph

TABLE 11.3 2 × 2 Factorial Design Table: No Effects

		Gender		
		Boys	Girls	
Character	Fantasy	7.0	7.0	7.0
Type	Reality	7.0	7.0	7.0
		7.0	7.0	

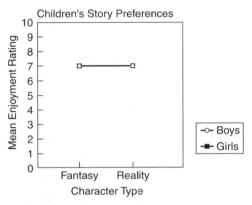

Figure 11.2 2 × 2 factorial design graph: No effects

TABLE 11.4 2 × 2 Factorial Design Table: One Main Effect

		Gender		
		Boys	Girls	
Character	Fantasy	7.0	8.0	7.5
Type	Reality	7.0	8.0	7.5
		7.0	8.0	

for boys. Note that the two line plots have identical zero slopes and are parallel to each other.

Imagine that you had placed the two values of gender on the horizontal *x*-axis and drawn separate lines for each character type. The appearance of the graph would change. The line for fantasy-based characters would overlap the line for reality-based characters. The overlapping lines would also have a slope indicating that the results were different for boys and girls.

Outcome C: An Interaction Only   Overall, there was no evidence suggesting a general preference for one type of character compared to another (B_1 versus B_2). Nor was there any overall evidence of a difference in preferences for boys com-

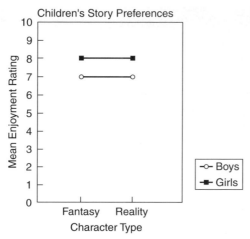

Figure 11.3 2×2 Factorial design graph: One main effect

pared to girls (A_1 versus A_2). However, boys preferred reality-based characters and girls preferred fantasy-based characters (A_1B_1 and A_2B_2 vs. A_1B_2 and A_2B_1).

In Table 11.5, there are no differences between the overall column means comparing boys and girls. Similarly, there are no differences between the overall row means comparing fantasy-based and reality-based character types. However, when you examine the cell means, differences among groups are apparent. Although girls rated fantasy-based characters (8.0) *higher* than reality-based characters (6.0), boys rated fantasy-based characters (6.0) *lower* than reality-based characters (8.0).

These data illustrate an interaction effect because the influence of Character Type is not uniform for all values of Gender. For girls, fantasy characters are preferred (change = +2.00); for boys, fantasy characters are not preferred (change = −2.00).

Evidence of the interaction of Character Type and Gender is also apparent in Figure 11.4. Note that the line plot for boys is not parallel to the line plot for girls. Nonparallel line plots are indicative of the presence of an interaction effect. In the current example, the plots cross each other, indicating that the Character Type treatment has the opposite effect on boys than girls. This type of interaction is called a **disordinal interaction.** The lines intersect or cross within the plot.

Another type of interaction effect occurs when the magnitude of the effect of one independent variable remains in the same direction but varies in size across

TABLE 11.5 2×2 Factorial Design Table: Interaction Effect

		Gender		
		Boys	Girls	
Character	Fantasy	6.0	8.0	7.0
Type	Reality	8.0	6.0	7.0
		7.0	7.0	

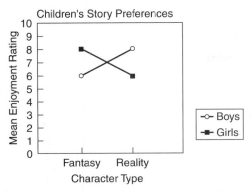

Figure 11.4 2 × 2 Factorial design graph: Interaction effect

levels of another independent variable. The plots of the two lines do not cross but they are not parallel. This type of interaction is called an **ordinal interaction** because the lines do not intersect or cross within the plot. (See Outcome E: One Main Effect and an Interaction for an example of an ordinal interaction.)

Outcome D: Two Main Effects   Girls preferred the stories more than boys (A_1 versus A_2) Fantasy-based characters were rated higher than reality-based ones (B_1 versus B_2).

In examining Table 11.6, note that there is a general preference for girls to rate the stories (8.0) higher than the boys rated the stories (7.0). The difference between the ratings of the girls compared to the ratings of the boys (change = +1.00) is the same whether the children were rating fantasy-based characters or reality-based characters.

Note also that there is a general preference for fantasy-based characters (8.5) compared to reality-based characters (6.5). The difference between the ratings of the fantasy-based characters compared to the ratings of the reality based characters (change = +2.00) is the same whether the ratings were gathered from boys or from girls.

Figure 11.5 illustrates the presence of two main effects. Note that the two line plots do not overlap and are sloped equally. The presence of identical slopes is indicative that the two treatment effects are *additive*. In other words, the effect of Character Type on storybook preferences does not vary according to the children's

TABLE 11.6 2 × 2 Factorial Design Table: Two Main Effects

		Gender		
		Boys	Girls	
Character	Fantasy	8.0	9.0	8.5
Type	Reality	6.0	7.0	6.5
		7.0	8.0	

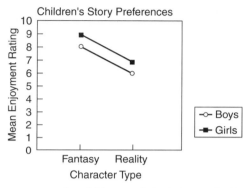

Figure 11.5 2 × 2 Factorial design graph: Two main effects

gender. Similarly, the relationship between Gender and Preference remains the same regardless of the type of stories to which children are exposed.

Outcome E: One Main Effect and an Interaction
Girls preferred fantasy-based characters more than boys (A_1B_1 and A_2B_2 versus A_1B_2 and A_2B_1).

The column means for Gender in Table 11.7 suggest that there is an overall difference in story preferences. However, when the cell means are examined, note that the gender differences are confined to fantasy-based characters. There are no rating differences between the sexes for reality-based characters. In other words, the overall difference between the ratings of boys and girls came about only because of how the children rated one type of storybook character. Thus, the effects of Character Type and Gender are *nonadditive*.

The presence of both an interaction effect and a main effect requires care in interpretation. It can be imprecise and misleading to conclude that a significant main effect means the treatment (*A*) worked uniformly across levels of a second variable (*B*).

Figure 11.6 also shows that the influence of Character Type and Gender are nonadditive. The line plots are not parallel but do not cross, indicating the presence of an ordinal interaction.

Outcome F: Two Main Effects and an Interaction
In general, girls liked the stories more than boys (A_1 versus A_2) and reality-based characters were somewhat preferred (B_1 versus B_2). More precisely, although girls preferred fantasy-

TABLE 11.7 2 × 2 Factorial Design Table: Main and Interaction Effects

		Gender		
		Boys	Girls	
Character	Fantasy	6.0	8.0	7.0
Type	Reality	7.0	7.0	7.0
		6.5	7.5	

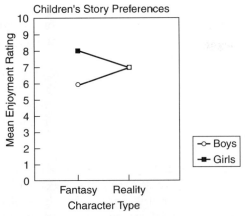

Figure 11.6 2 × 2 Factorial design graph: Main and interaction effects

based characters, boys liked reality-based ones (A_1B_1 and A_2B_2 versus A_1B_2 and A_2B_1).

Both Table 11.8 and Figure 11.7 show general differences between levels of the two variables (Character Type, Gender), which are more precisely understood by

TABLE 11.8   2 × 2 Factorial Design Table: Two Main Effects Plus Interaction

		Gender		
		Boys	Girls	
Character	Fantasy	5.0	9.0	7.5
Type	Reality	7.0	8.0	7.5
		6.0	8.5	

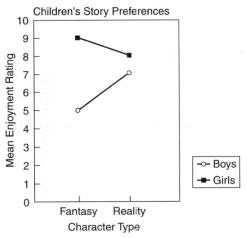

Figure 11.7 2 × 2 Factorial design graph: Two main effects plus interaction

examining individual cells in the Factorial design. For example, the magnitude of the difference in story preferences for boys and girls depends on the type of character used. Girls showed a preference for fantasy-based characters while boys showed a preference for reality-based characters.

If you were to choose a single story to read to a preschool class, these hypothetical findings suggest you should pick a story that uses reality-based characters. If, however, you were able to choose a story for individual children, you would be wiser to mix your selection, picking reality-based characters for boys and fantasy-based characters for girls.

Understanding Your Own Factorial Designs   Researchers employ Factorial designs because of the importance of investigating the effects of two or more independent variables on the dependent variable. Factorial designs are often more efficient than multiple experiments because it can be easier and cheaper to study independent variables simultaneously rather than successively.

Arguably more important, however, is the value of studying the combined influence of multiple independent variables on the dependent variable. Understanding the main and interaction effects can be important both theoretically and practically.

Along with the advantages of Factorial designs come certain disadvantages, mostly centering on the complexities of analysis and interpretation. Although we hope our detailed analyses of hypothetical outcomes from a 2×2 Factorial design help you understand these designs, there is one other important suggestion we would like to offer: Make your hypothesized results numerically explicit before you conduct the study.

Whether you are doing a course project, a thesis investigation, or a funded research study, you will find it useful if you input *hypothesized* means into a factorial design table and graph. In other words, work with the mean values you expect will result from your investigation. Doing so usually clarifies the nature of your hypotheses and avoids confusion later on. In particular, watch for initial inconsistencies between written main effect hypotheses and expected results that resemble interaction effects.

A Bit More on Main Effects and Interactions

You should now have an appreciation for the logic of Factorial designs and an understanding of how to interpret the data from studies that combine two or more independent variables. The explanations considered in the simple case of a 2×2 Factorial design can be extended to include treatment variables with more than two levels. Obviously, the greater the number of levels of each independent variable, the higher the likelihood of interpretive difficulties.

More Complex Two-Factor Designs   Table 11.9 represents a 3×4 Factorial design showing how the three levels of *A* combined with the four levels of *B*. Figure 11.8 shows two main effects but the absence of any interaction effect. The differences between the *A* means is the same for each level of *B*.

TABLE 11.9 Cells of a 3 × 4 Factorial Design		
A_1B_1	A_2B_1	A_3B_1
A_1B_2	A_2B_2	A_3B_2
A_1B_3	A_2B_3	A_2B_3
A_1B_4	A_2B_4	A_2B_4

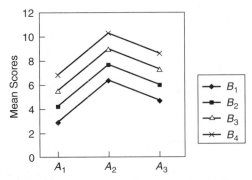

Figure 11.8 Two main effects in a 3 × 4 Factorial design

Designs with More than Two Factors

It is possible to study more than two independent variables in a single factorial experiment. Table 11.10 represents a 2 × 2 × 2 three-factor design with independent variables A, B and C.

The seven testable hypotheses here are

- A, B, C main effects
- AB, AC, BC interactions
- ABC interaction

Finding a significant ABC interaction means that all three independent variables in combination explain variability in the outcome measure (Y). For example, one might conclude that the effect of A depends on the particular values of both B and C.

Imagine that you added a third variable, Story Length (C), to the existing Gender (A) by Character Type (B) Factorial design. Story Length (C) has two levels: short (C_1) and long (C_2). One form of a three-way interaction of factors A, B, and C is illustrated in Figure 11.9.

TABLE 11.10 Cells of a 2 × 2 × 2 Factorial Design			
$A_1B_1C_1$	$A_2B_1C_1$	$A_1B_1C_2$	$A_2B_1C_2$
$A_1B_2C_1$	$A_2B_2C_1$	$A_1B_2C_2$	$A_2B_2C_2$

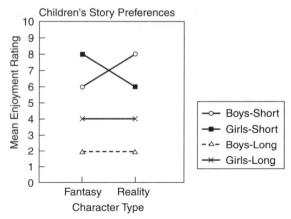

Figure 11.9 The three-way interaction of gender (*A*), character type (*B*), and story length (*C*)

For short stories, the character-type preferences of boys is different than the character-type preferences of girls. However, this same pattern is not apparent when long stories are used in place of short ones. Boys rated long stories low regardless of character-type. Girls rated the stories somewhat higher but also showed no preference for a character-type.

Dealing with More Complex Designs   In the case of multilevel independent variables, we suggest you begin the task of interpretation by considering only two values of each variable both in forming your preliminary hypotheses about main and interaction effects and in interpreting the results. As the design and findings become clearer, increase the complexity by adding levels into the Factorial design.

Similarly, Factorial designs that combine more than two independent variables should be approached carefully and treated incrementally. Begin with two variables and ignore the others. Then add a third variable by duplicating the Factorial design table and graph for each level of the third variable. In other words, don't try to deal with the complexity all at once. Build up to it by making the design simpler to begin with.

Finally, in the examples just covered the simplifying assumption was made that any mean difference was statistically significant. Of course, this is not always the case in reality. Therefore, one needs to find a statistical tool to help determine when main and interaction effects are significant. Such a tool is the Factorial Analysis of Variance.

FACTORIAL ANALYSIS OF VARIANCE

The Factorial Between-Groups Analysis of Variance (ANOVA) is for the analysis of data from research designs that simultaneously evaluate the effects of more than one independent variable on a single dependent variable and in which different participants are assigned to each of the groups in the Factorial design (i.e., between-groups). We will explore some of the challenges of within-groups designs, where participants may be exposed to more than one level of the treatment, in Chapter 12.

Subdividing Between-Groups Variability

The Factorial ANOVA operates in much the same way that the Oneway ANOVA operates: it partitions the total variability into additive components. These additive components are also:

Total variability = Between-groups variability + within-groups variability

But the Factorial ANOVA goes further than the Oneway ANOVA in that it *subdivides* between-groups variability. For example, in a design with two independent variables, A and B:

Between-groups variability = A variability + B variability + AB variability

This variability represents

- The main effect of A.
- The main effect of B.
- The interaction effect of $A \times B$.

Therefore, in a Twoway Factorial design:

$$\text{Total variability} =$$
$$A \text{ variability} + B \text{ variability} + AB \text{ variability} + \text{within-groups variability}$$

Omnibus Hypotheses

Given a Twoway Factorial design, the analysis of variance tests three general hypotheses, or *omnibus hypotheses*, about group differences. The first omnibus hypothesis concerns mean differences among the levels of factor A, independent of any influence of factor B.

The null hypothesis for the A main effect is

$$H_{A0}: \text{all } \mu_A\text{'s are equal}$$

The alternative hypothesis for the A main effect is

$$H_{Aa}: \text{not all } \mu_A\text{'s are equal}$$

For the Speed Whiz scenario of Textbox 11.1, we will determine whether there is a main effect of Type of Training on Response Time.

The second omnibus hypothesis concerns mean differences among the levels of factor *B*, independent of any influence of factor *A*.

The null hypothesis for the *B* main effect is

$$H_{B0}: \text{all } \mu_B\text{'s are equal}$$

The alternative hypothesis for the *B* main effect is

$$H_{Ba}: \text{not all } \mu_B\text{'s are equal}$$

For the Speed Whiz scenario, we will determine whether there is a main effect of Reward Condition on Response Time.

The third omnibus hypothesis concerns mean differences among the levels of factor *A* and *B* considered together.

The null hypothesis for the $A \times B$ interaction effect is

$$H_{AB0}: \text{all } \mu_{AB}\text{'s are equal}$$

The alternative hypothesis for the $A \times B$ interaction effect is

$$H_{ABa}: \text{not all } \mu_{AB}\text{'s are equal}$$

For the Speed Whiz scenario, we will determine whether there is an interaction effect of Type of Training and Reward Condition on Response Time. A significant interaction says the effect of Type of Training varies with Reward Condition. Alternately, a significant interaction also says the effect of Reward Condition varies with Type of Training.

Each null hypothesis says that there are no significant differences among the appropriate means. Each alternative hypothesis says that there is at least one significant difference between the appropriate means. Each alternative hypothesis cannot be interpreted as the appropriate means are all different from one another, only that at least one difference exists in the set of means. Additionally, accepting an alternative hypothesis does not in any way indicate where the difference(s) exist(s) among the appropriate means.

Later in this chapter, we will present procedures for analyzing specific differences among means. We will explain planned and post hoc comparison procedures for Factorial ANOVA. In addition, we will deal with the special case of significant interactions and the use of tests of simple effects.

The General Linear Model

In Chapter 10, we introduced the idea of the general linear model and showed how one could partition an individual's score into several components. We now want to extend this idea from a single treatment to two treatments and their interaction.

In a Twoway Between-Groups ANOVA, any participant's score at the *conclusion* of the investigation is a function of the overall or grand mean, the effect of the treatment *A*, the effect of the treatment *B*, the interaction effect of $A \times B$, and random error. One can estimate this score as

$$Y_{ijk} = \overline{Y} + A_j + B_k + AB_{jk} + E_{ijk}$$

where:

Y_{ijk} = score for the *i*th individual in the *jk*th group

$\overline{Y}$ = estimated base population mean

A_j = estimated main effect for row *j*

B_k = estimated main effect for column *k*

AB_{jk} = estimated interaction effect for cell *jk*

E_{ijk} = estimate of random error for the *i*th individual in the *jk*th group

In Table 11.11 we give a hypothetical breakdown of some participants' scores from the Speed Whiz scenario. The participants are those who received massed practice and a small reward.

How did we arrive at the values in Table 11.11? The row, column, and cell means are given in Table 11.12. The column labeled $\overline{Y}$ is the overall, or grand, mean for all participants, which is 69.95. The column labeled A_j is the difference between the column mean for the Massed Practice conditions and the grand mean, or −25.07. The column labeled B_k is the difference between the row mean for the Small Reward conditions and the grand mean, or −17.91. The column labeled AB_{jk} is the difference between the cell mean for Massed Practice, Small Reward condition and the grand mean, or −35.32. The last column labeled E_{ijk} is the difference between the participant's actual score and the sum of the four influences.

TABLE 11.11   Hypothetical Estimates of Influences on Massed Practice, Small Reward Group

Y_{ijk}	$\overline{Y}$	A_j	B_k	AB_{jk}	E_{ijk}
26	69.95	−25.07	−17.91	−35.32	34.35
41	69.95	−25.07	−17.91	−35.32	49.35
28	69.95	−25.07	−17.91	−35.32	36.35
92	69.95	−25.07	−17.91	−35.32	100.35
14	69.95	−25.07	−17.91	−35.32	22.35
16	69.95	−25.07	−17.91	−35.32	24.35
29	69.95	−25.07	−17.91	−35.32	37.37
31	69.95	−25.07	−17.91	−35.32	39.35

TABLE 11.12 3 × 2 Factorial Design Table of Means for the Effects of Type of Training (*A*) and Reward Condition (*B*) on Average Response Speed (*Y*)

		Type of Training (A)*			
		MP	SP	NP	
Reward	Small	$\overline{Y}_{A1B1} = 34.63$	$\overline{Y}_{A2B1} = 49.38$	$\overline{Y}_{A3B1} = 72.13$	$\overline{Y}_{B1} = 52.04$
Condition (B)	None	$\overline{Y}_{A1B2} = 55.13$	$\overline{Y}_{A2B2} = 94.00$	$\overline{Y}_{A3B2} = 112.63$	$\overline{Y}_{B2} = 87.25$
		$\overline{Y}_{A1} = 44.88$	$\overline{Y}_{A2} = 71.69$	$\overline{Y}_{A3} = 92.38$	$\overline{Y} = 69.95$

*MP = massed practice, SP = spaced practice, NP = no practice.

Furthermore, one may wish to represent these influences in the population. Thus, any participant's score at the conclusion of the investigation is

Equation 11.1: $Y_{ijk} = \mu + \alpha_j + \beta_k + \alpha\beta_{jk} + \varepsilon_{ijk}$

where:

Y_{ijk} = score for the *i*th individual in the *jk*th group

μ = base population mean

α_j = main effect for row *j*

β_k = main effect for column *k*

$\alpha\beta_{jk}$ = estimated interaction effect for cell *jk*

e_{ijk} = random error for the *i*th individual in the *jk*th group

Equation 11.1 is known as the *general linear model.* The model may be taken to mean that any individual score is the sum of the mean of the base population, the effects of the treatments, and random error.

Partitioning Variability in Twoway ANOVA

For the Oneway ANOVA, you saw that total variability, between-groups variability, and within-groups variability were each the sum of squared deviations from some mean. You can extend this thinking to Factorial ANOVA—in particular, for the Twoway ANOVA.

Total variability is the sum of the squared deviations of individual scores from the grand mean:

(Equation 9.2) $SS_Y = \sum_{1}^{N} (Y_i - \overline{Y})^2$

For a twoway Factorial design you can rewrite this as follows:

Equation 11.2: $SS_y = \sum_{1}^{A} \sum_{1}^{B} \sum_{1}^{n} (Y_i - \overline{Y})^2 = \sum_{1}^{N} (Y_i - \overline{Y})^2$

The leftmost equation for SS$_Y$ is the sum of the squared individual deviation scores from the grand mean added together in the following order:

The values of *A* are the slowest moving.

The values of *n* are the fastest moving

In other words, the triple summation notation merely specifies the order in which the squared deviation scores are added together. When $A = 3, B = 2$, and $n = 8$ the 48 deviation scores (i.e., $3 \times 2 \times 8 = 48$) are summed in the following order:

1. For the lowest value of *A* (1) and the low value of *B* (1), you sum the squared deviations from the grand mean for cases 1 to *n* in this cell.
2. For the lowest value of *A* (1) and the high value of *B* (2), you next sum the squared deviations from the grand mean for cases 1 to *n* in this cell.
3. For the middle value of *A* (2) and the low value of *B* (1), you next sum the squared deviations from the grand mean for cases 1 to *n* in this cell.
4. For the middle value of *A* (2) and the high value of *B* (2), you next sum the squared deviations from the grand mean for cases 1 to *n* in this cell.
5. For the highest value of *A* (3) and the low value of *B* (1), you next sum the squared deviations from the grand mean for cases 1 to *n* in this cell.
6. For the highest value of *A* (3) and the high value of *B* (2), you next sum the squared deviations from the grand mean for cases 1 to *n* in this cell.

For the Twoway ANOVA, between-groups variability consists of three additive components: $SS_{Y(A)} + SS_{Y(B)} + SS_{Y(AB)}$. Therefore,

$$\textbf{Equation 11.3: } SS_{Y(A)} = nB \sum_{1}^{A} (\overline{Y}_A - \overline{Y})^2$$

where $SS_{Y(A)}$ includes the sum of the squared group mean deviations for *A* from the grand mean.

$$\textbf{Equation 11.4: } SS_{Y(B)} = nA \sum_{1}^{B} (\overline{Y}_B - \overline{Y})^2$$

where $SS_{Y(B)}$ includes the sum of the squared group mean deviations for *B* from the grand mean.

$$\textbf{Equation 11.5: } SS_{Y(AB)} = n \sum_{1}^{A} \sum_{1}^{B} (\overline{Y}_{AB} - \overline{Y}_A - \overline{Y}_B + \overline{Y})^2$$

where $SS_{Y(AB)}$ includes the sum of the squared deviations of the *AB* cell means from the grand mean but excludes the sum of the squared deviations for *A* from the grand mean and for *B* from the grand mean.

In addition, the total between-groups variability ($SS_{Y(bet)}$) can be found as follows:

$$\textbf{Equation 11.6: } SS_{Y(bet)} = n \sum_{1}^{A} \sum_{1}^{B} (\overline{Y}_{AB} - \overline{Y})^2$$

where $SS_{Y(bet)} = SS_{Y(A)} + SS_{Y(B)} + SS_{Y(AB)}$. Note that $SS_{Y(bet)}$ serves as a computational check.

One can also find the within-groups variability:

$$\text{Equation 11.7: } SS_{Y(S/AB)} = \sum_1^A \sum_1^B \sum_1^n (Y_i - \overline{Y}_{AB})^2$$

where $SS_{Y(S/AB)}$ includes the sum of the individual deviations from their respective cell means.

Finally, one also knows that $SS_{Y(bet)} + SS_{Y(S/AB)} = SS_Y$ and serves as another computational check.

A complete mathematical proof of the partitioning of the total variability into additive components for a Twoway ANOVA can be found in Ferguson (1981). The logic of the proof is an extension of the logic used for the Oneway ANOVA.

From SS to MS to *F*

Once the sums of squares are calculated correctly, you find the appropriate degrees of freedom to compute the mean squares. The calculated values of *F* are *ratios of mean squares.*

Deriving the Degrees of Freedom

$$df_A = A - 1$$

$$df_B = B - 1$$

$$df_{AB} = (A - 1)(B - 1)$$

(Also $df_{bet} = AB - 1$ or $df_A + df_B + df_{AB}$

Within Group df ⟶ $df_{S/AB} = AB(n - 1)$

$df_Y = N - 1$ or $nAB - 1$ (also $df_Y = df_{S/AB} + df_{bet} = df_{S/AB} + df_A + df_B + df_{AB}$)

Deriving the Mean Squares

$$\text{Equation 11.8: } MS_{Y(A)} = SS_{Y(A)}/df_A$$

$$\text{Equation 11.9: } MS_{Y(B)} = SS_{Y(B)}/df_B$$

$$\text{Equation 11.10: } MS_{Y(AB)} = SS_{Y(AB)}/df_{AB}$$

$$\text{Equation 11.11: } MS_{Y(S/AB)} = SS_{Y(S/AB)}/df_{S/AB}$$

Deriving the Calculated Values of F

$$\text{Equation 11.12: } F_A = MS_{Y(A)}/MS_{Y(S/AB)}$$

$$\text{Equation 11.13: } F_B = MS_{Y(B)}/MS_{Y(S/AB)}$$

$$\text{Equation 11.14: } F_{AB} = MS_{Y(AB)}/MS_{Y(S/AB)}$$

CD-ROM link 11.2

Activity 11.2: Partitioning of Variability in Factorial ANOVA
This activity builds on the Activity 11.1 by introducing the calculated *F*-values for Main Effects and Interactions in a Factorial ANOVA. As before, you will be changing the values of group means in a simple 2 × 2 Factorial design. As the group means change, you will be able to observe the effect this has on the calculated *F*-value for each Main Effect and for the Interaction.

Twoway Factorial ANOVA: Computational Example

Use the data from the Speed Whiz scenario in Table 11.1 to perform the calculations for a 3 × 2 Factorial ANOVA. The first step in these calculations is to compute the cell, row, column, and grand means (see Table 11.12). Working with the individual scores in Table 11.1 and the Table of Means, compute the sum of squares, mean squares, and *F*-ratios. Use $\alpha = .05$ as the probability value for significance testing. See Textbox 11.3 for the computations.

Other Issues in Factorial ANOVA

In Chapter 9 we covered a variety of other issues and techniques that are applicable to Factorial ANOVA,

---

Textbox 11.3

Twoway Factorial ANOVA: Speed Whiz Scenario

The first step of the statistical analysis is the computation of means on *Y*, the dependent variable, which in the scenario is average speed in seconds to answer multiplication problems correctly. Specifically, one will want column means for Type of Training (*A*), row means for Reward Condition (*B*), cell means for *AB*, and the overall or grand mean. (See Table 11.12 on page 330 for the means also illustrated in Figure 11.10.)

The second step in computing the analysis of variance is to find the sum of squares, mean squares, and *F*-ratios.

---

continued

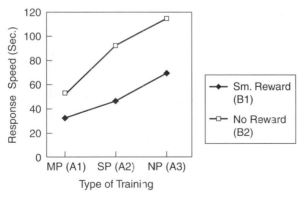

Figure 11.10 3 × 2 Factorial design graph of the means for the effects of type of training (*A*) and reward condition (*B*) on average response speed (*Y*)

Textbox 11.3 (Continued)

Between-Groups Sums of Squares

Using the means in Table 11.12, compute the sums of squares for the A main effect, the B main effect, and the AB interaction:

$$SS_{Y(A)} = nB \sum_{1}^{A} (\overline{Y}_A - \overline{Y})^2$$

$$= (8)(2)[(44.88 - 69.65)^2 + (71.69 - 69.65)^2 + (92.38 - 69.65)^2]$$

$$= 18{,}150.04$$

$$SS_{Y(B)} = nA \sum_{1}^{B} (\overline{Y}_B - \overline{Y})^2$$

$$= (8)(3)[(52.04 - 69.65)^2 + (87.25 - 69.65)^2] = 14{,}876.93$$

$$SS_{Y(AB)} = n \sum_{1}^{A} \sum_{1}^{B} (\overline{Y}_{AB} - \overline{Y}_A - \overline{Y}_B + \overline{Y})^2$$

$$= (8)[(34.63 - 44.88 - 52.04 + 69.65)^2$$

$$+ \cdots + (112.63 - 92.38 - 87.25 + 69.65)^2]$$

$$= 1332.04$$

Between-Groups Sums of Squares Computational Check

$$SS_{Y(\text{bet})} = n \sum_{1}^{A} \sum_{1}^{B} (\overline{Y}_{AB} - \overline{Y})^2$$

$$= (8)[(34.63 - 69.65)^2 + (55.13 - 69.65)^2 + \cdots + (112.63 - 69 - 65)^2$$

$$= 34{,}359.01$$

$$SS_{Y(\text{bet})} = SS_{Y(A)} + SS_{Y(B)} + SS_{Y(AB)}$$

$$= 18{,}150.04 + 14{,}876.93 + 1332.04.$$

Within-Groups Sum of Squares

$$SS_{Y(S/AB)} = \sum_{1}^{A} \sum_{1}^{B} \sum_{1}^{n} (Y_i - \overline{Y}_{AB})^2$$

$$= [(26 - 34.63)^2 + (41 - 34.63)^2 + \cdots + (68 - 112.63)^2 + (142 - 112.63)^2$$

$$= 42{,}667.38$$

Total Sum of Squares

Using the individual scores in Table 11.1 at the beginning of the chapter and the grand mean, compute the total variability in Y:

$$SS_Y = \sum_{1}^{A} \sum_{1}^{B} \sum_{1}^{n} (Y_i - \overline{Y})^2 = \sum_{1}^{N} (Y_i - \overline{Y})^2$$

$$= [(26 - 69.65)^2 + (41 - 69.65)^2 + \cdots + (68 - 69.65)^2 + (142 - 69.65)^2]$$

$$= 77{,}024.98$$

continued

Textbox 11.3 (Continued)

Total Sums of Squares Computational Check

$$SS_Y = SS_{Y(bet)} + SS_{Y(S/AB)}$$
$$= 77{,}024.98 \approx 34{,}359.01 + 42{,}667.38 \text{ (Allowing for rounding error)}$$

Degrees of Freedom

$$df_A = A - 1 = 3 - 1 = 2$$
$$df_B = B - 1 = 2 - 1 = 1$$
$$df_{AB} = (A - 1)(B - 1)(3 - 1)(2 - 1) = 2$$
$$\text{(Also } df_{bet} = AB - 1 \text{ or } df_A + df_B + df_{AB} = (3)(2) - 1 = 5 \text{ or } 2 + 1 + 2$$
$$df_{S/AB} = AB(n - 1) = (3)(2)(8 - 1) = 42$$
$$df_Y = N - 1 \text{ or } nAB - 1 \text{ (also } df_Y = df_{S/AB} + df_{bet} = df_{S/AB} + df_A + df_B + df_{AB})$$
$$df_Y = 48 - 1 = 47 \text{ or } (8)(3)(2) - 1 = 47 \text{ (also} = 2 + 1 + 2 + 42)$$

Mean Squares

$$MS_{Y(A)} = SS_{Y(A)}/df_A = 18{,}150.04/2 = 9075.02$$
$$MS_{Y(B)} = SS_{Y(B)}/df_B = 14{,}876.93/1 = 14{,}876.93$$
$$MS_{Y(AB)} = SS_{Y(AB)}/df_{AB} = 1332.04/2 = 666.02$$
$$MS_{Y(S/AB)} = SS_{Y(S/AB)}/df_{S/AB} = 42{,}667.38/42 = 1015.89$$

Calculated Values of F

$$F_A = MS_{Y(A)}/MS_{Y(S/AB)} = 8.93$$

The calculated value 8.93 exceeds the critical value $F(2, 42) = 3.22$ ($\alpha = .05$).

$$F_B = MS_{Y(B)}/MS_{Y(S/AB)} = 14.64$$

The calculated value 14.64 exceeds the critical value $F(1, 42) = 4.07$ ($\alpha = .05$).

$$F_{AB} = MS_{Y(AB)}/MS_{Y(S/AB)} = 0.66$$

The calculated value .66 fails to exceed the critical value $F(2, 42) = 3.22$ ($\alpha = .05$).

The Factorial ANOVA for the data from the Speed Whiz scenario is summarized in Table 11.13.

Conclusion

Training had a significant effect on average response speed. Mass, spaced, and no practice response times were not all uniform. Reward condition also affected response speed. The fastest times were given by those participants who received a small reward. However, we failed to find sufficient evidence that the type of training interacted with whether participants were offered a reward or not.

TABLE 11.13   Twoway ANOVA Summary Table: Effects of Type of Training (A) and Reward Condition (B) on Average Response Speed

Source of Variation	Sums of Squares	Degrees of Freedom	Mean Squares	F-Ratio
Training (A)	18,150.04	2	9075.02	8.93*
Reward (B)	14,876.93	1	14,876.93	14.64*
Interaction (AB)	1332.04	2	666.02	0.66
Subjects within groups (S/AB)	42,667.38	42	1015.89	

*$p < .05$

CD-ROM link 11.3

Problem Generator: Factorial ANOVA

To practice hypothesis testing using a Factorial ANOVA, select Factorial ANOVA from the Problem Generator Menu on the CD-ROM. The Problem Generator will create as many practice problems as you need, and will demonstrate each step in their solution so that you can check your work.

including effect sizes, power, and assumption violations. You will see that these applications are fairly straightforward.

Effect Sizes   In Chapter 9, we described three methods for computing the effect size for two groups: single-group standard deviation effect size, pooled two-group standard deviation effect size, and average group standard deviation effect size. These methods will yield similar results if within-groups variances are homogeneous.

In Factorial ANOVA, the researcher may choose to compute effect sizes for two groups across levels of a treatment variable (i.e., the rows or columns means from a Factorial design table) or across cells of the combined treatments if interaction effects are of interest.

From Chapter 9, the formula for the average group standard deviation effect size is as follows:

$$\textbf{(Equation 9.10)}\; d = \frac{\overline{Y}_{A1} - \overline{Y}_{A2}}{\sqrt{\mathrm{MS}_{Y(S/A)}}}$$

You can adapt it for Factorial ANOVA by substituting the correct Factorial ANOVA error term and using * *in lieu of the label for any one term.*

$$\textbf{Equation 11.15:}\; d = \frac{\overline{Y}_{*1} - \overline{Y}_{*2}}{\sqrt{\mathrm{MS}_{Y(S/AB)}}}$$

See Textbox 11.4 for an illustration.

Textbox 11.4

Effect Sizes from Speed Whiz Scenario

Use the average group standard deviation method to compute two effect sizes, one comparing the effects of massed versus spaced practice (ES_1), the second comparing the effects of massed versus spaced practice when participants were offered a small reward (ES_2).

For ES_1:

$$d = \frac{\overline{Y}_{A1} - \overline{Y}_{A2}}{\sqrt{MS_{Y(S/AB)}}} = \frac{44.88 - 71.59}{\sqrt{1015.89}} = -.84$$

For ES_2:

$$d = \frac{\overline{Y}_{A1B1} - \overline{Y}_{A2B1}}{\sqrt{MS_{Y(S/AB)}}} = \frac{34.63 - 49.38}{\sqrt{1015.89}} = -.46$$

Use the general effect size (f) to compute the effect size for the interaction of Type of Training and Reward Condition:

$$R^2 = \frac{SS_{Y(AB)}}{SS_Y} = \frac{1332.04}{42,667.38} = .03$$

$$f = \sqrt{\frac{R^2}{1 - R^2}} = \sqrt{\frac{.03}{1 - .03}} = .18$$

In Chapter 9 we also covered three methods for estimating the general effect size: R^2, f, and ω^2. These methods may also be used for Factorial ANOVA to estimate the size of main and interaction effects.

From Chapter 9, the formula for R^2 is as follows:

$$\textbf{(Equation 9.11)}\ R^2 = \frac{SS_{Y(A)}}{SS_Y}$$

You can readily adapt this formula by using * in lieu of the label for any one term:

$$\textbf{Equation 11.16:}\ R^2 = \frac{SS_{Y(*)}}{SS_Y}$$

Also

$$\textbf{(Equation 9.12)}\ f = \sqrt{\frac{R^2}{1 - R^2}}$$

See Textbox 11.4 for an illustration.

Textbox 11.5

Use of Power Tables for the Speed Whiz Scenario

Imagine that you wish to determine the power of the *F*-test to reject the null hypothesis that there is no interaction of Type of Training and Reward Condition. To solve this problem, note the following:

$$n = 8$$

$$F_c (2, 42) = 3.22 \text{ (critical value)}$$

$$f = .18$$

$$\alpha = .05$$

The tabled values do not list $n = 8$ or $f = .18$. The closest approximation is $n = 10$ and $f = .25$, with $F_c = 5.488$. Using these values, you estimate that power is a lowly .06. By extrapolation, for $f = .18$, you might guess that power is .04 or lower.

Power   Once you have computed *f* you may proceed to use the procedures outlined in Chapter 9 for the calculation of power and the use of Cohen's (1988) power tables given in Appendix E. For example, Textbox 11.5 illustrates the estimation of power for the $A \times B$ interaction effect.

Underlying Assumptions   The Factorial ANOVA model makes the same assumptions as the Oneway ANOVA model regarding the nature of the data. The assumptions are as follows:

1. There is a normal distribution to the scores within each treatment group. This is the assumption of *normality*.
2. The scores are independent of one another both within each treatment group as well as across the different treatment groups. This is the assumption of *independence*.
3. The scores show the same degree of variability from treatment group to treatment group. This is the assumption of *homogeneity of variance*.

Procedures for evaluating and dealing with assumption violations are covered in Chapter 9.

MULTIPLE COMPARISON AND SIMPLE EFFECT TESTS

The Factorial ANOVA provides several omnibus tests. In the case of a design with two independent variables, there are three tests of significance:

1. Main effect of factor *A*
2. Main effect of factor *B*
3. Interaction effect of $A \times B$

As with the Oneway ANOVA, it is often reasonable to examine these general treatment effects more closely. In this section we will consider planned and post hoc multiple comparison procedures for Factorial ANOVA as well as tests of simple effects when the $A \times B$ interaction is significant.

Overview

In Chapter 10, we consider planned comparisons as an alternative to the omnibus test of significance for the Oneway ANOVA. In Factorial ANOVA, you can also use planned comparisons. The basic logic is similar although the calculations seem more complex.

Planned comparisons may be used to explore specific hypotheses *instead of* the omnibus main and interaction tests in Factorial ANOVA when treatment factors have more than a single degree of freedom. The planned comparisons should be valid and independent so that the variance components are additive.

In Chapter 10, we presented post hoc comparisons as an adjunct following the discovery of a significant omnibus test of the treatment variable. Post hoc comparisons may be used *following significant omnibus main or interaction tests* in Factorial ANOVA. Only the omnibus effects found to be significant are explored. You may wish to undertake only simple pairwise comparisons or also analyze complex comparisons.

Finally, when one finds a **significant interaction effect** many statisticians recommend computing tests of *simple effects*. A significant interaction means that the two independent variables should be considered in combination, because the effect of one independent variable changes with variation in the second independent variable. Therefore, simple effect tests explore the general effects of one independent variable at *each* level of another independent variable.

Planned Orthogonal Comparisons Procedures for Factorial ANOVA

The logic and computational form of planned comparisons for Factorial ANOVA follows what was developed in Chapter 10 for the Oneway ANOVA. Each comparison needs to be valid, and each set needs to be composed of independent comparisons. However, in a Twoway Factorial design you will have three sets of planned comparisons: (1) a set exploring the levels of A; (2) a set exploring the levels of B; and (3) a set exploring the levels of $A \times B$.

Review of Planned Comparisons The logic and basic techniques for planned comparisons in Factorial ANOVA follow closely what we provided in Chapter 10 for the Oneway ANOVA. We have, therefore, made appropriate, minor substitutions below to the equations from Chapter 10. In particular, we use a $*$ to stand for any one of the A, B, and $A \times B$ factors in the Twoway Factorial ANOVA.

A planned comparison is a difference between means. It can be expressed as a sum of the *weighted* means, where c is the weight, or comparison, coefficient:

$$p = (c_{*1})(\overline{Y}_{*1}) + (c_{*2})(\overline{Y}_{*2}) + (c_{*3})(\overline{Y}_{*3}) + \cdots$$

The more general form of this equation is as follows:

$$\textbf{Equation 11.17: } p = \sum_{1}^{*} (c*)(\overline{Y}*)$$

A comparison is valid if the sum of the comparison weights is zero:

$$\textbf{Equation 11.18: For each } p\text{: } \sum c* = 0.0$$

Each planned comparison corresponds to a single degree of freedom of the $* - 1$ degrees of freedom. Thus, the number of independent planned comparisons in a set is $* - 1$. Furthermore, a set of independent planned comparisons among the levels of * has the following property:

$$\textbf{Equation 11.19: } \mathrm{SS}_{Y(*)} = \sum_{1}^{*} \mathrm{SS}_{Y(p)}$$

Two planned comparisons are independent if the product of the weights assigned to each mean sum to zero. Mathematically, independence exists in the following situation:

$$\textbf{Equation 11.20: } \sum_{1}^{*} c_{1*}c_{2*} = 0.0$$

To statistically evaluate each planned comparison, compute the SS, MS, and *F*-ratio:

$$\textbf{Equation 11.21: } \mathrm{SS}_{Y(p)} = \frac{n(p)^2}{\displaystyle\sum_{1}^{A} c_{*}^{2}} \qquad \text{where} \qquad p = \sum_{1}^{A} c*\overline{Y}*$$

$$\textbf{(Equation 10.6) } \mathrm{MS}_{Y(p)} = \mathrm{SS}_{Y(p)}/\mathrm{df}_p = \mathrm{SS}_{Y(p)}$$

(Remember that each comparison has only one numerator df.)

$$\textbf{Equation 11.22: } F_p = \mathrm{MS}_{Y(p)}/\mathrm{MS}_{Y(S/AB)} \qquad \mathrm{df}_p = 1, \ \mathrm{df}_{S/AB} = AB(n-1)$$

Valid Comparison Weights for Factorial Designs   In factorial designs, finding a set of valid, independent comparisons for exploring specific differences among the levels of each treatment variable is no more difficult than doing so in Oneway ANOVA in which only a single treatment variable is being studied. However, finding a set of valid, independent comparisons for exploring specific differences among the means of two or more treatment variables *in combination* is not as readily apparent. Fortunately, Hays (1994) offers useful guidelines for creating these comparisons.

To begin with, a set of valid, independent comparisons needs to be created for each treatment variable. In the Speed Whiz scenario of Textbox 11.1, for example, one might want to explore the following two specific (null and alternative) hypotheses about the three different *levels* of Type of Training:

Massed Practice versus Spaced Practice:

$$H_0: \mu_{A1} = \mu_{A2}$$
$$H_a: \mu_{A1} \neq \mu_{A2}$$

No Practice versus Massed Practice and Spaced Practice:

$$H_0: \mu_{A3} = .5\mu_{A1} + .5\mu_{A2}$$
$$H_a: \mu_{A3} \neq .5\mu_{A1} + .5\mu_{A2}$$

One may also want to explore the null and alternative hypotheses concerning the two *levels* of Reward Condition:

Small Reward versus No Reward:

$$H_0: \mu_{B1} = \mu_{B2}$$
$$H_a: \mu_{B1} \neq \mu_{B2}$$

What about the planned comparisons concerning the Type of Training by Reward interaction? Use a comparison table to help specify them.

Creating a Comparison Table   In a Factorial design, each of the comparisons among *levels* involves more than two *groups*, or cells. Therefore, one needs to take each of the groups into account when assigning **comparison weights.** To do so, create a comparison table of columns and rows in which each of the columns represents particular combinations of the levels of the treatments and each of the rows represents the weights assigned to each group according to the specific hypotheses you wish to explore. See Table 11.14.

TABLE 11.14 Comparison Table for 3 × 2 Speed Whiz Factorial Design

		A_1B_1	A_1B_2	A_2B_1	A_2B_2	A_3B_1	A_3B_2
		34.63	55.13	49.38	94.00	72.13	112.63
	Comparison						
A	1. p_{A1}	$1/2$	$1/2$	$-1/2$	$-1/2$	0	0
	2. p_{A2}	$1/4$	$1/4$	$1/4$	$1/4$	$-1/2$	$-1/2$
B	3. p_{B1}	$1/3$	$-1/3$	$1/3$	$-1/3$	$1/3$	$-1/3$
$A \times B$	4. p_{AB1}	$1/6$	$-1/6$	$-1/6$	$1/6$	0	0
	5. p_{AB2}	$1/12$	$-1/12$	$1/12$	$-1/12$	$-1/6$	$1/6$

Group Means and Comparison Weights

For example, to compare Massed (A_1) versus Spaced Practice (A_2), assign contrast weights to each of the six groups in the Factorial design. Groups A_1B_1 and A_1B_2 will each be assigned positive weights (1/2). Groups A_2B_1 and A_2B_2 will each be assigned negative weights ($-1/2$). And groups A_3B_1 and A_3B_2 will be assigned zero weights (0).

For the Speed Whiz scenario of Textbox 11.1, the comparison table will have six columns representing the 3×2 cells in the Factorial design. There will be $A - 1$, or two rows for the contrast weights for comparisons among the levels of Type of Training; $B - 1$, or one row for the comparison among the levels of Reward Condition; and $A - 1 \times B - 1$, or two rows for the comparisons exploring the combination of Type of Training and Reward Condition. Also add a row of cell means.

Using the Comparison Table   With the comparison table, it is much easier to find a set of valid, independent comparisons for exploring specific differences among the means of two or more treatment variables in combination. To do so, multiply the comparison weights for each comparison in A with the comparison weights for each comparison in B. For the Speed Whiz scenario, the products of these weights appear as the last two rows to the comparison table. Note that the total number (5) of rows for comparisons in the table equals the total between-groups degrees of freedom (i.e., $[A \times B] - 1$, or $[3 \times 2] - 1$). Comparison 4 (p_{AB1}) uses the products of the weights for comparisons 1 and 3. Comparison 5 (p_{AB2}) uses the products of the weights for comparisons 2 and 3. Note that the weights for each comparison (4 and 5) in the $A \times B$ combination are valid because they sum to zero even though the sum of their absolute values is not 1.0. These last two rows are the weights for the two planned comparisons concerning the Type of Training by Reward interaction.

The statistical evaluation of planned comparisons uses the same procedures as presented in Chapter 10. See Textbox 11.6 for an illustration for the first and fifth planned comparisons that use the weights in Table 11.14 for the Speed Whiz scenario.

Post Hoc Comparisons for Factorial ANOVA

In Chapter 10, we presented two of the most widely used post hoc comparison procedures. We recommended Tukey's HSD for all possible pairwise comparisons and Scheffé's S method for both pairwise and nonpairwise comparisons.

The logic and basic techniques for post hoc comparisons in Factorial ANOVA follow closely what we provided for the Oneway ANOVA. We have, therefore, made appropriate, minor substitutions below in the equations from Chapter 10. In particular, we use a * as a general symbol to stand for any one of the factors in the Factorial ANOVA.

Tukey's HSD   Tukey's HSD (honestly significant difference) test is for evaluating all pairwise comparisons among means.

Finding the Calculated Value   This is the same procedure used to find the calculated value of a planned contrast except that contrasts should be limited to

---

Textbox 11.6

Speed Whiz Planned Comparisons

For the First Planned Comparison:

1. *Find the calculated value:*

$$SS_{Y(pA1)} = \frac{8[(1/2)34.63 + (1/2)55.13 + (-1/2)(49.38) + (-1/2)(94.00) + (0)(72.13) + (0)(112.63)]^2}{(1/2)^2 + (1/2)^2 + (-1/2)^2 + (-1/2)^2 + (0)^2 + (0)^2}$$

$$= \frac{8(26.81)^2}{.25 + .25 + .25 + .25 + 0 + 0} = 5750.21$$

$$MS_{Y(pA1)} = 5750.21/1.00 = 5750.21$$

$$F_{pA1} = 5750.21/1015.89 = 5.66$$

2. *Find the critical value:*

For df = 1, 42 and α = .05, the critical value is 4.07.

3. *Compare calculated and critical values:*

The calculated value, 5.66, is larger than the critical value, 4.07.
You reject the null hypothesis for this comparison. You conclude that there is a significant difference between massed and spaced practice on the average response speed to multiplication problems.

For the Fifth Planned Comparison:

1. *Find the calculated value:*

$$SS_{Y(pAB2)} = \frac{8[(1/12)34.63 + (-1/12)55.13 + (1/12)(49.38) \\ + (-1/12)(94.00) + (-1/6)(72.13) + (1/6)(112.63)]^2}{(1/12)^2 + (-1/12)^2 + (-1/12)^2 + (-1/12)^2 + (-1/6)^2 + (1/6)^2}$$

$$= \frac{8(1.32)^2}{.01 + .01 + .01 + .01 + .03 + .03} \approx 174.24$$

$$MS_{Y(pAB2)} = 174.24/1.00 = 174.24$$

$$F_{pAB2} = 174.24/1015.89 = 0.17$$

2. *Find the critical value:*

For df = 1, 42 and α = .05, the critical value is 4.07.

3. *Compare calculated and critical values:*

The calculated value, 0.17, is smaller than the critical value, 4.07.
You cannot reject the null hypothesis for this comparison.

probing significant effects. In addition, use cell means instead of row and column means to find the calculated value. For example, see comparison 1 in Table 11.14.

Computational formula for post hoc (ph) comparisons:

$$\textbf{Equation 11.23: } SS_{Y(ph)} = \frac{n(p)^2}{\sum\limits_{1}^{*} c_*^2} \qquad \text{where } p = \sum\limits_{1}^{A} c_* \overline{Y}_*$$

$$\textbf{(Equation 10.6) } MS_{Y(ph)} = SS_{Y(ph)} / df_{ph}$$

(Remember that each comparison has only one numerator df.)

$$\textbf{Equation 11:24: } F_{ph} = MS_{Y(ph)} / MS_{Y(S/AB)} \qquad df_{ph} = 1, \ df_{S/AB} = AB(n-1)$$

Finding the Critical Value   To find the critical value for the Tukey test (F_T) for making *all* pairwise comparisons among row, column, or cell means to probe a significant effect, use the same equation provided in Chapter 10:

$$\textbf{(Equation 10.9) } F_T = \frac{(q_T)^2}{2}$$

where q_T is an entry in the Studentized range distribution. See Appendix F.

However, to find the correct value of q_T you need the following:

1. $df_{S/AB}$, which is $N - AB$ or $(n-1)AB$
2. k, the number of treatment levels ($k = A$ for exploring a significant A main effect; $k = B$ for exploring a significant B main effect and $k = AB$ for exploring a significant AB interaction effect).
3. α_{FW}, alpha for the familywise Type I error selected, which is usually .05 or .01.

In Textbox 11.7 we illustrate the calculation of the Tukey HSD test for the Speed Whiz scenario.

Scheffé's S Method   If the omnibus *F*-test is significant, Scheffé's *S* method can be used to make all possible comparisons among means, both pairwise comparisons and nonpairwise comparisons.

Finding the Calculated Value   This is the same procedure used to find the calculated value of a planned contrast except that contrasts should be limited to probing significant effects. See also the section on Tukey's HSD in this chapter.

Finding the Critical Value   Make slight modifications to the procedure in Chapter 10 to find the critical value for Scheffé's *S* method (F_S) for making *all possible* comparisons among means:

$$\textbf{Equation 11.25: } F_S = (* - 1)F(df_*, \ df_{S/AB})$$

Textbox 11.7

Tukey HSD Post Hoc Comparisons for Speed Whiz Scenario

After computing the omnibus *F*-tests for the Type of Training (3) by Reward Condition (2) Factorial ANOVA, you can proceed to explore further the significant effects. Both main effects were significant, but the interaction was not significant. Because the Reward Condition factor has only two levels, there is no point in conducting post hoc comparisons. You already know there is a significant difference in average response time for the rewarded participants compared to the participants who did not receive a reward. Thus, differences among the three levels of Type of Training will be probed.

The first of three possible pairwise comparisons is illustrated below in which massed and spaced practice are compared. The means and the comparison weights are as follows:

A_1B_1	A_1B_2	A_2B_1	A_2B_2	A_3B_1	A_3B_2
34.63	55.13	49.38	94.00	72.13	112.63
1/2	1/2	−1/2	−1/2	0	0

1. *Find the calculated value for a pairwise comparison:*

$$SS_{Y(pA1)} = \frac{8[(1/2)34.63 + (1/2)55.13 + (-1/2)(49.38) + (-1/2)(94.00) + (0)(72.13) + (0)(112.63)]^2}{(1/2)^2 + (1/2)^2 + (-1/2)^2 + (-1/2)^2 + (0)^2 + (0)^2}$$

$$= \frac{8(-26.81)^2}{.25 + .25 + .25 + .25 + 0 + 0} = 5750.21$$

$$MS_{Y(pA1)} = 5750.21/1.00 = 5750.21$$

$$F_{pA1} = 5750.21/1015.89 = 5.66$$

2. *Find the critical value for a pairwise comparison*

$$F_T = \frac{(q_T)^2}{2}$$

$$df_{S/AB} = N - AB \qquad \text{or } 48 - 6 = 42$$

$$k = A = 3$$

$$\alpha_{FW} = .05$$

$$F_T = (3.44)^2/2 = 5.92$$

3. *Compare calculated and critical values*

The calculated value, 5.66, is smaller than the critical value, 5.92.

You fail to reject the null hypothesis regarding a difference in response time for massed versus spaced practice. (Note that this difference was significant as a planned comparison. As noted in Chapter 10, post hoc comparisons control for familywise error rate and, consequently, are more conservative tests.)

We invite you to compute the two other pairwise comparisons to find where there is a significant difference among the levels of Type of Training.

Textbox 11.8

Scheffé's Post Hoc Comparisons for Speed Whiz Scenario

You decide to use Scheffé's S method to probe the significant main effect of Type of Training. This method allows you to examine not only the simple pairwise comparisons among levels of a factor but also the complex, nonpairwise comparisons. Because the method for computing the calculated values is no different than for either planned comparisons or the Tukey HSD approach, it will not be repeated here. Only one comparison will be evaluated, although others are possible and would need to be performed.

1. *Find the calculated value for a comparison:*

$$F_{pA1} = 5750.21/1015.89 = 5.66$$

2. *Find the critical value for a comparison:*

$$F_S = (* - 1)F(\text{df}_*, \text{df}_{S/AB}) \qquad \text{where } * = A$$
$$F_S = (2)(3.23) = 6.46$$

3. *Compare calculated and critical values:*

The calculated value, 5.66, is smaller than the critical value, 6.46.

You fail to reject the null hypothesis regarding a difference in response time for massed versus spaced practice. (Note that the critical value for Scheffé's method is larger than for Tukey's method, which is larger than the critical value for a planned comparison.)

We invite you to compute the other comparisons to find where there is a significant difference among the levels of Type of Training.

Remember that you use a $*$ to stand for any one of the factors A or B or their interaction ($A \times B$) in the Factorial ANOVA as appropriate. For example, to probe the significant effect of Type of Training, $* = A$.

In Textbox 11.8 we illustrate the calculation of Scheffé's S method for the Speed Whiz scenario.

Tests of Simple Effects

When one finds a significant interaction effect, many statisticians recommend computing tests of *simple effects*. A significant interaction means that the two independent variables should be considered in combination, because the effect of one independent variable changes with variation in the second independent variable. Therefore, **simple effect tests** explore the general effects of one independent variable at *each* level of another independent variable.

Advantages of Simple Effect Tests When the interaction is significant, it usually means that exploring the main effects is of less interest because one has already discovered that the effects of one variable depend on the effects of another variable. That is, the two variables should be understood in combination.

Therefore, some statisticians suggest that the main effect tests can be ignored by following up on significant interaction effects with tests of simple effects. (What actually happens in simple effect tests is that the variability due to the interaction is added to the variability attributed to *each* main effect.) To proceed with tests of simple effects there is a requirement that the interaction effect be significant; however, there is no requirement that the main effects be significant.

Simple effect tests explore the general effects of one independent variable at each level of another independent variable. This is similar to what one would do if one conducted separate experiments of the effect of a variable repeatedly over different levels of another variable (e.g., A at B_1, A at B_2). For example, in one experiment you explore the effects of Type of Training when participants are offered a small reward for participating. In a second experiment you explore the effects of Type of Training when participants are offered no reward for participating. See Textbox 11.9.

Disadvantages of Simple Effect Tests   Each set of simple effect tests combines variability due to the main effect with variability due to the interaction. Herein lies a possible problem. In an $A \times B$ factorial design, there are two sets of simple effects: (1) the simple effects of A at all levels of B, and (2) the simple effects of B at all levels of A. Each set of simple effect tests combine the appropriate main effect variability with the variability attributable to the interaction:

1. $SS_{Y(A)\text{ at all }B} = SS_{Y(A)} + SS_{Y(AB)}$
2. $SS_{Y(B)\text{ at all }A} = SS_{Y(B)} + SS_{Y(AB)}$

Textbox 11.9

Simple Effects in the Speed Whiz Scenario

The interaction of Type of Training and Reward Condition failed to reach significance with the data from the Speed Whiz scenario. Therefore, tests of simple effects are not appropriate to use. But if the interaction was significant, what would be the simple effects that should have been examined?

There are the two simple effects of Training at both levels of Reward:

1. Simple effect of Training at Small Rewards (A at B_1) compares cells A_1B_1, A_2B_1, and A_3B_1.
2. Simple effect of Training at No Rewards (A at B_2) compares cells A_1B_2, A_2B_2, and A_3B_2.

There are also the three simple effects of Rewards for each level of Training:

1. Simple effect of Reward at Massed Practice (B at A_1) compares cells A_1B_1 and A_1B_2.
2. Simple effect of Reward at Spaced Practice (B at A_2) compares cells A_2B_1 and A_2B_2.
3. Simple effect of Reward at No Practice (B at A_3) compares cells A_3B_1 with A_3B_2.

Note that the two sets of simple effects are *not* independent. Each set has the variability due to the interaction term. In other words, conducting the two sets of simple effects in a Twoway Factorial ANOVA means that the variability attributable to the interaction of the two factors gets used twice. The fact that the two sets of simple effects contain some of the same variability means that the total variability in the dependent variable is not partitioned into separate, additive components. Some of the variability explained by the simple effects of factor A at levels of B is also explained by the simple effects of factor B at levels of A.

We recommend the use of simple effect tests as another tool in your arsenal for understanding the data from Factorial designs. However, we urge you to be mindful of the issue of nonindependence of the sets of simple effects.

Strategy for Using Simple Effects   Table 11.15 offers a strategy for using simple effect tests. Note that when a simple effect is significant, post hoc comparisons may subsequently be used.

Partitioning Variability for Simple Effect Tests   In a Twoway $A \times B$ Factorial ANOVA, there are two sets of simple effects: (1) the set of simple effects of A at each level of B, and (2) the set of simple effects of B at each level of A. Start by computing the sum of squares for each simple effect in a set.

Compute the Sum of Squares for the Simple Effects of A   The sum of squares for the simple effects of A is computed as follows:

$$SS_{Y(A \, \text{at} \, B_1)} = n \sum_1^A (\overline{Y}_{AB_1} - \overline{Y}_{B_1})^2$$

$$SS_{Y(A \, \text{at} \, B_2)} = n \sum_1^A (\overline{Y}_{AB_2} - \overline{Y}_{B_2})^2$$

TABLE 11.15   A Recommended Post Hoc Analysis Strategy for Factorial Designs

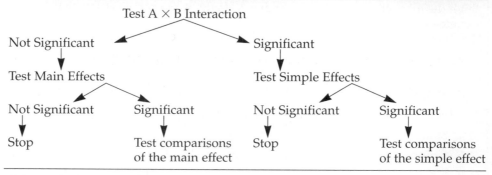

(Adapted from Keppel et al., 1992, p. 300.)

Or more generally, for each level of B find the following:

Equation 11.26: $SS_{Y(A\,at\,B_*)} = n \sum_{1}^{A} (\overline{Y}_{AB_*} - \overline{Y}_{B_*})^2$

Computational check:

The sum of the sum of squares for the simple effects of A at all levels of B is equal to the sum of squares for the main effect of A plus the sum of squares for the $A \times B$ interaction.

$$\sum_{1}^{B} SS_{Y(A\,at\,B_*)} = SS_{Y(A)} + SS_{Y(AB)}$$

Compute the Sum of Squares for the Simple Effects of B   The sum of squares for the simple effects of B is computed as follows:

$$SS_{Y(B\,at\,A_1)} = n \sum_{1}^{B} (\overline{Y}_{A_1B} - \overline{Y}_{A_1})^2$$

$$SS_{Y(B\,at\,A_2)} = n \sum_{1}^{B} (\overline{Y}_{A_2B} - \overline{Y}_{A_2})^2$$

Or more generally, for each level of A find the following:

Equation 11.27: $SS_{Y(B\,at\,A_*)} = n \sum_{1}^{B} (\overline{Y}_{A_*B} - \overline{Y}_{A_*})^2$

Computational check:

The sum of the sum of squares for the simple effects of B at all levels of A is equal to the sum of squares for the main effect of B plus the sum of squares for the $A \times B$ interaction.

$$\sum_{1}^{A} SS_{Y(B\,at\,A_*)} = SS_{Y(B)} + SS_{Y(AB)}$$

Degrees of Freedom, Mean Squares and F-Ratios

Degrees of Freedom for the Simple Effects of B

$$df_{A\,at\,B_1} = A - 1, df_{Aa:B_2} = A - 1, \text{ and so on.}$$

More generally:

$$df_{A\,at\,B_*} = A - 1.$$

Degrees of Freedom for the Simple Effects of B

$$df_{B \, at \, A_1} = B - 1, \, df_{B \, at \, A_2} = B - 1, \text{ and so on.}$$

More generally:

$$df_{B \, at \, A_*} = B - 1$$

Mean Squares: All mean squares are respective: SS/df

F-Ratios: All F-ratios are *respective:* $MS/MS_{Y(S/AB)}$

Sample Problem: Behavioral Change
In order to illustrate the computation of simple effects we need a Twoway Factorial ANOVA design that includes a simple interaction effect. We found a simple example of a 3×2 Factorial design. In this design, the relative effectiveness of three drugs (factor A) on behavioral changes in two types of mental patients (factor B) were studied. (Problem adapted from Winer, 1971, pp. 436–441.)

The raw data are presented in Table 11.16 and the means are in Table 11.17. The results of a Twoway Factorial ANOVA are presented in Table 11.18. The calculations for the simple effect tests of A at both levels of B are given in Textbox 11.10. We ask that you try and compute the simple effects of B at all levels of A. A modified ANOVA Summary Table that includes the simple effect tests is presented in Table 11.19, where you can check your calculations.

TABLE 11.16   Behavioral Change Raw Data

		Type of Drug (A)		
		A_1	A_2	A_3
Patient (B)	Schizophrenic	8, 4, 0	10, 8, 6	8, 6, 4
	Depressive	14, 10, 6	4, 2, 0	15, 12, 9

TABLE 11.17   Behavioral Change Cell, Row, and Column Means

		Type of Drug (A)			
		A_1	A_2	A_3	
Patient (B)	Schizophrenic	4.0	8.0	6.0	6.0
	Depressive	10.0	2.0	12.0	8.0
		7.0	5.0	9.0	7.0

TABLE 11.18 ANOVA Summary Table for Behavioral Change

Source of Variation	Sums of Squares	Degrees of Freedom	Mean Squares	F-Ratio
Drug (A)	48.00	2	24.00	2.72
Patient (B)	18.00	1	18.00	2.04
Interaction (AB)	144.00	2	72.00	8.15*
Subjects within groups (S/AB)	106.00	12	8.83	

*$p < .05$.

Textbox 11.10

Simple Effects Tests of A at Both Levels of B for the Behavioral Change Data

Sum of squares:

$$SS_{Y(A\,at\,B_1)} = n \sum_1^A (\overline{Y}_{AB_1} - \overline{Y}_{B_1})^2$$

$$(3)[(4.00 - 6.00)^2 + (8.00 - 6.00)^2 + (6.00 - 6.00)^2] = 24.00$$

$$SS_{Y(A\,at\,B_2)} = n \sum_1^A (\overline{Y}_{AB_2} - \overline{Y}_{B_2})^2$$

$$(3)[(10.00 - 8.00)^2 + (2.00 - 8.00)^2 + (12.00 - 8.00)^2] = 168.00$$

Computational check:

$$SS_{Y(A\,at\,all\,B)} = SS_{Y(A)} + SS_{Y(AB)}$$

$$24.00 + 168.00 = 48.00 + 144.00 = 192.00$$

Mean squares:

$$MS_{Y(A\,at\,B_1)} = 24.00/2 = 12.00$$

$$MS_{Y(A\,at\,B_2)} = 168.00/2 = 84.00$$

F-ratios:

$$F_{A\,at\,B_1} = 12.00/8.83 = 1.36$$

$$F_{A\,at\,B_2} = 84.00/8.83 = 9.51*$$

$$F_{crit}(2, 12) = 3.89, \alpha = .05. \text{ (This is the critical value.)}$$

*$p < .05$

TABLE 11.19 ANOVA Summary Table for Behavioral Change that Includes Simple Effects				
Source of Variation	*Sums of Squares*	*Degrees of Freedom*	*Mean Squares*	*F-Ratio*
Drug (A)	48.00	2	24.00	2.72
A at B_1	*24.00*	*2*	*12.00*	*1.36*
A at B_2	*168.00*	*2*	*84.00*	*9.51**
Patient (B)	18.00	1	18.00	2.04
B at A_1	*54.00*	*1*	*54.00*	*6.12**
B at A_2	*54.00*	*1*	*54.00*	*6.12**
B at A_3	*54.00*	*1*	*54.00*	*6.12**
Interaction (AB)	144.00	2	72.00	8.15*
Subjects within groups (S/AB)	106.00	12	8.83	

*$p < .05$.

Probing Significant Simple Effects

Tests of simple effects are omnibus tests. When a factor has more than two levels (i.e., df > 1), a significant simple effect does not provide sufficient information regarding which levels of the treatment vary. In order to gain a more precise understanding, post hoc comparisons of significant simple effects should be performed.

For the post hoc analysis of simple effects, we again recommend either the Tukey method for pairwise comparisons or the Scheffé S method for all possible comparisons. The procedures previously covered in this chapter are readily adapted to probes of simple effects. We illustrate their application on the Behavioral Change data in Textbox 11.11.

Textbox 11.11

Post Hoc Comparisons for Significant Simple Effects

According to Table 11.19, one of the two simple effects of A is significant and three of three simple effects of B are significant. But only the significant simple effect of A at B_2 requires followup post hoc comparisons. The three simple effects of B are single degree of freedom tests that cannot be further analyzed.

The three drugs had significantly different effects on the behavior of depressed patients. If you elect to explore only pairwise comparisons of this one significant simple effect, you will conduct three tests using Tukey's HSD method. If, however, you elect to explore all possible comparisons, you will conduct six tests of significance using Scheffé's S method.

We illustrate below the calculation of one of the pairwise comparisons comparing drugs A_1 and A_2 for depressed patients (B_2). Find the critical value for Tukey's HSD and the critical value for S, which will be larger. Remember that one does not normally use both HSD and S, just as one does not normally use both planned and post hoc comparisons.

---

continued

Textbox 11.11 (Continued)

The means and the comparison weights are as follows:

A_1B_1	A_1B_2	A_2B_1	A_2B_2	A_3B_1	A_3B_2
4.0	10.0	8.0	2.0	6.0	12.00
0	1	0	−1	0	0

1. *Find the calculated value for a pairwise comparison:*

$$SS_{Y(pA_1 \text{ at } B_2)} = \frac{3[(0)4.00 + (1)10.00 + (0)(8.00) + (-1)(2.00) + (0)(6\,0) + (0)(12.00)]^2}{(0)^2 + (1)^2 + (0)^2 + (-1)^2 + (0)^2 + (0^{-2}}$$

$$= \frac{3(8.00)^2}{.0 + 1^2 + 0 + 1^2 + 0 + 0} = 96.00$$

$$MS_{Y(pA_1 \text{ at } B_2)} = 96.00/1.0C = 96.00$$

$$F_{pA_1 \text{ at } B_2} = 96.00/8.83 = 10.87$$

2. *Find the critical value, F_T:*

$$F_T = \frac{(q_T)^2}{2}$$

- $df_{S/AB} = N - AB$ or $18 - 6 = 12$
- $k = A = 3$
- $\alpha_{FW} = .05$

$$F_T = (3.77)^2/2 = 7.11$$

3. *Find the critical value, F_S:*

$$F_S = (* - 1)F(df_*, df_{S/AB})\qquad \text{where } * = A$$

$$F_S = (2)(3.89) = 7.78$$

4. *Compare the calculated and critical values:*

If you were to undertake only pairwise comparisons of the significant simple effect of A at B_2 and, therefore, used the Tukey HSD test, the calculated value of the comparison of drugs A_1 and A_2 for depressed patients (10.97) would exceed the critical value, 7.11.

If you were to undertake both pairwise and complex comparisons of the significant simple effect of A at B_2 and, therefore, used the Scheffé S test, the calculated value of the comparison of drugs A_1 and A_2 for depressed patients (10.97) would exceed the critical value, 7.78.

Note yet again that the critical value of the Scheffé S method is larger than the critical value of Tukey's HSD method.

PUTTING IT ALL TOGETHER

Researchers frequently employ designs in which more than a single independent variable is manipulated and in which the influences of these factors on the dependent variable are analyzed. We concentrated on first explaining Factorial designs and then explaining the Factorial Analysis of Variance, the statistical tool to analyze the effects of two or more independent variables.

We took the simplest Factorial design involving two independent variables, each with only two levels, which we called a *2× 2 Factorial design*. A variety of different outcomes of this design based on a combination of main and interaction effects were shown. We defined an interaction effect as the effect of one independent variable modified by a second independent variable. We made a special point of differentiating main effects from an interaction effect. This section concluded with a discussion of more complex twoway designs and with the introduction of threeway designs.

We next extended your understanding of the concepts and techniques of Oneway ANOVA to the situation in which more than a single independent variable is present. The Twoway ANOVA was shown to partition total variability into between-groups and within-groups sources and also subdivides between-groups variability into three additive components: *A* variability, *B* variability, and $A \times B$ variability. From these sums of squares, mean squares, and three *F*-ratios were computed. We also dealt with the calculations of effect sizes and power and briefly covered assumptions underlying the tests.

The next challenge was multiple comparisons. Shown was the possibility of extending the logic used for the Oneway ANOVA to the Factorial ANOVA. In particular, planned comparisons should be undertaken when one is not interested in omnibus tests but has more specific questions about the data. Also shown was how to use a comparison weight table to ensure valid and independent comparisons among the levels of *A*, the levels of *B*, and the $A \times B$ interaction. We next showed how it was possible to use either Tukey HSD test or Scheffé *S* method to probe significant, omnibus main and interaction effects.

Finally, the advantages and disadvantages of simple effect tests to probe significant interaction effects were considered. We showed how to compute tests of simple effects for *A* at all levels of *B* and *B* at all levels of *A*. We concluded by covering post hoc procedures when simple effects are significant.

Partitioning Variability in Twoway ANOVA

Total variability =
A variability + *B* variability + *AB* variability + within-groups variability

Total variability is the sum of the squared deviations of individual scores from the grand mean:

Equation 11.2: $\displaystyle \mathrm{SS}_Y = \sum_{1}^{A} \sum_{1}^{B} \sum_{1}^{n} (Y_i - \overline{Y})^2 = \sum_{1}^{N} (Y_i - \overline{Y})^2$

For the Twoway ANOVA, between-groups variability consists of three additive components: $SS_{Y(A)} + SS_{Y(B)} + SS_{Y(AB)}$. Therefore,

$$\text{Equation 11.3: } SS_{Y(A)} = nB \sum_{1}^{A} (\overline{Y}_A - \overline{Y})^2$$

$$\text{Equation 11.4: } SS_{Y(B)} = nA \sum_{1}^{A} (\overline{Y}_B - \overline{Y})^2$$

$$\text{Equation 11.5: } SS_{Y(AB)} = n \sum_{1}^{A} \sum_{1}^{B} (\overline{Y}_{AB} - \overline{Y}_A - \overline{Y}_B + \overline{Y})^2$$

One also finds within-groups variability:

$$\text{Equation 11.7: } SS_{Y(S/AB)} = \sum_{1}^{A} \sum_{1}^{B} \sum_{1}^{n} (Y_i - \overline{Y}_{AB})^2$$

The Degrees of Freedom

$$df_A = A - 1$$
$$df_B = B - 1$$
$$df_{AB} = (A - 1)(B - 1)$$

The Mean Squares

$$\text{Equation 11.8: } MS_{Y(A)} = SS_{Y(A)}/df_A$$

$$\text{Equation 11.9: } MS_{Y(B)} = SS_{Y(B)}/df_B$$

$$\text{Equation 11.10: } MS_{Y(AB)} = SS_{Y(AB)}/df_{AB}$$

$$\text{Equation 11.11: } MS_{Y(S/AB)} = SS_{Y(S/AB)}/df_{S/AB}$$

The Calculated Values of F

$$\text{Equation 11.12: } F_A = MS_{Y(A)}/MS_{Y(S/AB)}$$

$$\text{Equation 11.13: } F_B = MS_{Y(B)}/MS_{Y(S/AB)}$$

$$\text{Equation 11.14: } F_{AB} = MS_{Y(AB)}/MS_{Y(S/AB)}$$

Effect Sizes   The average group standard deviation effect size is as follows:

$$\textbf{Equation 11.15: } d = \frac{\overline{Y}_{*1} - \overline{Y}_{*2}}{\sqrt{\text{MS}_{Y(S/AB)}}}$$

Methods for estimating the general effect size are as follows:

$$\textbf{Equation 11.16: } R^2 = \frac{\text{SS}_{Y(*)}}{\text{SS}_Y}$$

also

$$\textbf{(Equation 9.12) } f = \sqrt{\frac{R^2}{1 - R^2}}$$

Power   See Chapter 9.

Planned Comparisons   The general form for the equation for a comparison is as follows:

$$\textbf{Equation 11.17: } p = \sum_1^A (c*)(\overline{Y}*)$$

A comparison is valid if the sum of the comparison weights is zero:

$$\textbf{Equation 11.18: For each } p\text{: } \sum c* = 0.0$$

A set of independent planned comparisons among the levels of * has the following property:

$$\textbf{Equation 11.19: } \text{SS}_{Y(*)} = \sum_1^* \text{SS}_{Y(p)}$$

Two planned comparisons are independent if the product of the weights assigned to each mean sum to zero. Mathematically, independence exists when

$$\textbf{Equation 11.20: } \sum_1^* c_{1*}c_{2*} = 0.0$$

To statistically evaluate each planned comparison, compute the SS, MS, and F-ratio:

$$\textbf{Equation 11.21: } \text{SS}_{Y(p)} = \frac{n(p)^2}{\sum_1^A c_*^2} \qquad \text{where } p = \sum_1^A c_* \overline{Y}*$$

$$\textbf{(Equation 10.6) } \text{MS}_{Y(p)} = \text{SS}_{Y(p)} / \text{df}_p = \text{SS}_{Y(p)}$$

(Remember that each comparison has only one numerator df.)

$$\textbf{Equation 11.22: } F_p = \text{MS}_{Y(p)} / \text{MS}_{Y(S/AB)} \qquad \text{df}_p = 1, \text{df}_{S/AB} = AB(n-1)$$

Post Hoc Comparisons   Computational formula for post hoc (ph) comparisons:

$$\text{Equation 11.23: } SS_{Y(ph)} = \frac{n(p)^2}{\sum\limits_{1}^{*} c_*^2} \qquad \text{where } p = \sum\limits_{1}^{A} c_* \overline{Y}_*$$

$$\text{(Equation 10.6) } MS_{Y(ph)} = SS_{Y(ph)}/df_{ph}$$

(Remember that each comparison has only one numerator df.)

$$\text{Equation 11:24: } F_{ph} = MS_{Y(ph)}/MS_{Y(S/AB)} \qquad df_{ph} = 1, df_{S/AB} = AB(n-1)$$

Find the critical value for the Tukey test (F_T) for making *all* pairwise comparisons as follows:

$$\text{(Equation 10.9) } F_T = \frac{(q_T)^2}{2}$$

where q_T is an entry in the Studentized range distribution. See Appendix F. To find the correct value of q_T you need:

1. $df_{S/AB}$, which is $N - AB$ or $(n-1)AB$
2. k, the number of treatment levels ($k = A$ for exploring a significant A main effect; $k = B$ for exploring a significant B main effect; and $k = AB$ for exploring an AB interaction effect)
3. α_{FW}, alpha for the familywise Type I error selected, which is usually .05 or .01.

Find the critical value for Scheffé's S method (F_S) as follows:

$$\text{Equation 11.25: } F_S = (* - 1)F(df_*, df_{S/AB})$$

Simple Effects   For each level of B, find:

$$\text{Equation 11.26: } SS_{Y(A \text{ at } B_*)} = n \sum\limits_{1}^{A} (\overline{Y}_{AB_*} - \overline{Y}_{B_*})^2$$

Computational check:

$$\sum\limits_{1}^{B} SS_{Y(A \text{ at } B_*)} = SS_{Y(A)} + SS_{Y(AE)}$$

For each level of A find:

$$\text{Equation 11.27: } SS_{Y(B \text{ at } A_*)} = n \sum\limits_{1}^{B} (\overline{Y}_{A_* B} - \overline{Y}_{A_*})^2$$

Computational check:

$$\sum_{1}^{A} SS_{Y(B \, at \, A_*)} = SS_{Y(B)} + SS_{Y(AB)}$$

Degrees of Freedom

$$df_{A \, at \, B_*} = A - 1$$
$$df_{B \, at \, A_*} = B - 1$$

Mean Squares   All mean squares are respective: SS/df

F-Ratios   All F-ratios are respective: $MS/MS_{Y(S/AB)}$

Textbox 11.12

Are Attractive People Really Rated More Favorably?
An Example of a Factorial Design

If you knew nothing about people except their gender and physical attractiveness, would that influence your perceptions of their academic performance, their need for achievement, their intelligence, and their initiative to achieve because of ability and effort? Chia, Alfred, Grossnickle, and Lee (1998) hypothesized that attractive people and men would be perceived more positively on the above characteristics when compared to unattractive people and women. They showed 144 undergraduate students (81 women and 63 men) photos of an attractive and unattractive male and an attractive and unattractive female. Each participant completed a questionnaire for each photo in which the photos were rated for academic traits necessary for success in college; on the influence of ability, effort, course difficulty, and luck on performance; and on physical attractiveness.

    An Attractiveness (high versus low attractiveness) by Gender (men versus women) Factorial design was carried out. Analysis of mean perceptions of academic performance yielded main effects for attractiveness $F(1,140) = 8.89$, $p < .01$; gender, $F(1,140) = 17.78$, $p < .001$; and an interaction $F(1,140) = 14.48$, $p < .001$, where the unattractive male was seen to be performing at the highest level, while the unattractive female was seen to be performing at the lowest level. Analysis of achievement-related traits yielded a main effect for attractiveness and gender ($F(1,140) = 51.55$, $p < .001$, and $F(1,140) = 5.27$, $p < .05$, respectively). Analysis of perceived intelligence yielded a main effect for gender, $F(1,140) = 23.35$, $p < .001$ and a significant interaction, $F(1,140) = 12.95$, $p < .001$, where unattractive men were seen as most intelligent and unattractive women were seen as least intelligent. All told, the basic assertion that, given only gender and physical attractiveness information, people draw inferences based on that information favoring males and attractiveness in females, was supported.

KEY TERMS

Factorial design

Main effect

Interaction effect

Factorial design table

Disordinal interaction

Ordinal interaction

Significant interaction effect

Comparison weights

Simple effects tests

REFERENCES

Chia, R. C., Alfred, L. J., Grossnickle, W. F., & Lee, G. W. (1998). Effects of attractiveness and gender on the perception of achievement-related variables. *The Journal of Social Psychology, 138* (4), 47.

Cohen, J. (1988). *Statistical power analysis.* (2nd ed.). Hillsdale, NJ: Lawrence Erlbaum Associates.

Ferguson, G. A. (1981). *Statistical analysis in psychology and education.* (5th ed.). New York: McGraw Hill Book Co.

Hays, W. L. (1994). *Statistics.* (5th ed.). Orlando, FL: Harcourt Brace College Publishers.

Keppel, G., Saufley, W. H., Jr, & Tokunaga, H. (1992). *Introduction to design and analysis: A student's handbook.* (2nd ed.). New York: W. H. Freeman & Co.

Winer, B. J. (1971). *Statistical principles in experimental design.* (2nd ed.). New York: McGraw Hill.

PROBLEMS

Questions

Section 1   Conceptual/Definition

11.1. When are Factorial designs useful to a researcher?

11.2. In Factorial ANOVA, the between-groups sums of squares is partitioned into three different components. Identify these three components.

11.3. How many omnibus hypotheses can be tested in a Twoway Factorial design?

11.4. What are the underlying assumptions in Factorial ANOVA?

11.5. What is the recommended procedure for follow-up analysis when a significant interaction is found in a Factorial ANOVA?

11.6. What is the major disadvantage of using simple effect tests?

11.7. One often sees the term *partitioning of sums of squares.* Are only sums of squares partitioned in Factorial ANOVA (or Oneway ANOVA)?

11.8. In a given study in which four treatment conditions were compared, would the error variance be different if the data were analyzed using a Oneway ANOVA or a Factorial (2×2) ANOVA?

11.9. Is a Factorial ANOVA an independent design?

11.10. Why is simple effect analysis used when a significant interaction exists in a Factorial design rather than going directly to post hoc comparisons?

Section 2   Numerical

11.11. For the dataset below prepare a Factorial ANOVA Summary Table. Prepare a simple effects analysis, if necessary. Also, determine the critical value of F_T and F_S that would be used for evaluating multiple comparisons for significant simple effects A at B_1 and B at A_1.

		Factor A			Factor A	
		A_1			A_2	
	B_1	5	6		5	8
		6	9		4	2
		2	4		4	3
		4	4		5	3
		2	8		6	4
		4	5		3	2
		1			8	
	B_2	5	7		9	8
		4	5		5	6
		3	7		3	8
Factor B		4	4		7	9
		5	3		3	6
		5	4		8	6
		6			5	
	B_3	4	5		5	3
		3	2		8	8
		6	3		9	6
		8	5		10	11
		2	3		10	6
		2	4		6	6
		2			7	

11.12. Prepare a Factorial ANOVA Summary Table for the Factorial design shown below.

		Factor A			Factor A	
		A_1			A_2	
	B_1	4	7		10	8
		5	5		9	9
		4	6		8	11
		6	5		8	12
		3	7		7	8
Factor B						
	B_2	5	8		9	8
		7	7		14	15
		8	6		13	11
		7	9		12	15
		9	8		14	13

11.13. The following ANOVA Table resulted from an analysis of a given set of data.

Oneway ANOVA Summary Table

Source	SS	df	MS	F	p
Treatment	590.34	3	196.78	10.08	< .05
Error	1483.65	76	19.52		
Total	2073.99	79			

Had the data been analyzed as a 2×2 Factorial design, complete a Factorial ANOVA Table given the following information: $SS_{Y(A)} = 101.76$, $SS_{Y(B)} = 103.24$.

11.14. For the dataset below prepare a Factorial ANOVA Summary Table. Use the general effect size (f) to compute the effect size for the interaction of factor A and factor B.

		Factor A					
		A_1		A_2		A_3	
Factor B	B_1	29	17	43	84	37	88
		40	18	29	88	37	97
		26	27	16	48	58	129
		95	32	55	65	29	112
	B_2	50	37	100	115	102	132
		92	34	109	99	98	129
		96	26	126	89	159	101
		24	79	128	90	143	142

11.15. For the dataset below prepare a Factorial ANOVA Summary Table. Prepare a simple effects analysis, if necessary.

		Factor A									
		A_1		A_2		A_3		A_4		A_5	
Factor B	B_1	6	4	5	5	8	9	13	14	15	17
		7	9	11	7	11	7	12	9	19	12
		3		6		13		10		13	
	B_2	14	13	12	14	11	17	14	12	15	18
		18	11	10	11	10	12	19	13	12	13
		12		15		15		17		16	
	B_3	15	13	14	11	16	13	16	11	17	14
		18	15	17	14	20	16	18	14	15	16
		14		15		17		19		19	

chapter 12 Within-Groups Designs

Analyzing Repeated Measures

OVERVIEW

In presenting the *t*-test and the analysis of variance for independent samples, statistical methods were covered for examining the effect(s) of a single independent variable with two levels, a single independent variable with more than two levels, and multiple independent variables. Common to each of these designs was the use of separate groups of participants assigned to each level of each treatment. In other words, it was assumed that the responses generated on the dependent variable by one group of participants were completely independent of the responses of other groups.

In exploring within-groups designs, this assumption will not be made. Instead, you will be dealing with the statistical methods to use when researchers take repeated measures of the dependent variable from the same subject or from subjects who are matched to one another.

There are many research situations in which repeated measures are used. In studies of learning, for example, researchers might want to track participants' behavior over time as new methods and techniques are introduced or to study persistence or extinction. As you will see, there are both advantages and disadvantages to within-groups designs. In designing a study, you will want to weigh the potential advantages of within-groups designs in your research situation against the potential disadvantages. In critiquing a study, you will want to give special consideration to whether and how the researcher using a within-groups design was able to overcome the design difficulties and whether the explanations she or he offers are credible.

In this chapter statistical methods will be covered that allow data to be analyzed from two dependent samples (correlated samples *t*-test), more than two dependent samples (Oneway Within-Groups ANOVA), and factorial designs that combine both a multilevel within-groups factor and a multilevel between-groups factor (Factorial ANOVA for Mixed Designs). Both the similarities and the differences with statistical methods for between-groups designs will be shown.

Some of the specific questions to be answered include the following:

1. What is the layout of a within-groups design?
2. What are the arguments in favor of using within-groups designs?
3. What are the arguments against using within-groups designs?
4. How does counterbalancing eliminate certain threats to internal validity?

5. How does the correlated samples *t*-test remove the dependency in the scores?
6. Is there a parallel between the correlated samples *t*-test and the Oneway Within-Groups ANOVA?
7. What about procedures for estimating effect sizes and power and doing multiple comparisons?
8. What is the circularity assumption, and why is it so important?
9. How does the mixed design partition variability into additive components, and why are there two error terms?

We begin with the scenario in Textbox 12.1 and the case of the three experiments of composition skill development.

To this point, we have presented designs in which different participants were assigned to each of the levels of the independent variable. Now we will present designs in which the same participants participate in multiple levels of the treatment variable.

Within-groups designs (also known as **repeated measures designs**) primarily employ the *same subjects* for *each* level of a treatment variable. That is, all subjects are exposed to all levels of the independent variable. The independent variable may have a minimum of two levels with no (theoretical) maximum number of levels.

Textbox 12.1

Phonics Tonics

With the advent of the whole language approach to instruction, schoolchildren in certain areas of the country no longer use basal readers, practice grammar intensively, or receive drill and practice in spelling. Parents, taught in the traditional manner, often expect their children to demonstrate mastery of the skills traditional activities promote. To fill the gap between parental expectations and school practice, commercial firms have sprung up that offer game-like products aimed at helping children acquire traditional skills in reading and writing.

One of these firms approaches you to help analyze the data from a series of three small experiments designed to determine how well their product improves composition skills. The dependent measure of composition skill provides a total composition skill score ranging from zero (undeveloped skill) to 25 (highly developed skill). In the first experiment, five children take the test prior to using the firm's product (pretest) and then are retested immediately after using the product at home for one month (posttest). In the second experiment, a group of five children are tested prior to using the product at home (pretest), immediately after using the product at home for one month (posttest), and then a month later with no further use of the product (delayed posttest). In the third and final experiment, two groups of five students each repeat the second experiment under different conditions. One group works with the product at home and the second group works with the product at school. The results of the three experiments are presented in Tables 12.1a–c.

Are there gains in composition skills over time? Do these skills maintain themselves? Does the context for learning impact on the findings?

TABLE 12.1*a* Pretest and Posttest Composition Skill Scores			
Student	*Pretest*	*Posttest*	*Gain*
Al	4	10	6
Famil	5	12	7
Jossee	8	13	5
Lin	10	17	7
Mo	13	18	5
$\overline{Y}$	8.00	14.00	6.00
s	3.67	3.39	1.00

TABLE 12.1*b* Pretest, Posttest, and Delayed Posttest Composition Skill Scores			
Student	*Pretest*	*Posttest*	*Delayed Posttest*
Lauren	14	19	15
Fazio	9	18	12
Leila	7	15	11
Dominic	5	11	8
Lee	5	12	4
$\overline{Y}$	8.00	15.00	10.00

BASICS OF WITHIN-GROUPS DESIGNS

Designs with a Single Treatment

When a single within-groups treatment has two levels, the data may be analyzed via the *t*-test for correlated or dependent samples. The One-Group Pretest–Posttest Design (see Chapter 2) is a classic example of a within-groups design in which the treatment variable has two levels: the absence of the treatment prior to pretesting and the presence of the treatment prior to posttesting. As we discussed in Chapter 2 and will summarize again below, such designs pose numerous threats to internal validity and raise concerns about whether differences between pretest and posttest scores represent treatment effects or alternative influences.

When a single within-groups treatment has more than two levels, one uses the *F*-test for within-groups designs. To better understand the difference between a multilevel within-groups treatment and a multilevel between-groups treatment, consider Table 12.2. Note that the there are three different subjects in each of the three levels of the between-groups design. In contrast, there are the same three subjects in each of the levels of the within-groups design.

TABLE 12.1c   Pretest, Posttest, and Delayed Posttest Composition Skill Scores: Homework versus Schoolwork

Homework

Student	Pretest	Posttest	Delayed Posttest
Jacob	14	18	15
Bill	9	17	12
Wilma	7	16	11
Sarah	5	13	8
Jane	5	11	4
$\overline{Y}$	8.00	15.00	10.00

Schoolwork

Student	Pretest	Posttest	Delayed Posttest
Alex	15	21	23
Jess	12	20	20
Ally	10	17	19
Fiona	7	13	16
Sam	6	14	12
$\overline{Y}$	10.00	17.00	18.00

TABLE 12.2   Comparison of Single Variable Between-Groups Design and Within-Groups Design

Between-Groups Design			Within-Groups Design		
A_1	A_2	A_3	A_1	A_2	A_3
S_1	S_4	S_7	S_1	S_1	S_1
S_2	S_5	S_8	S_2	S_2	S_2
S_3	S_6	S_9	S_3	S_3	S_3

Designs with More Than a Single Treatment

Research designs with more than a single treatment may include only between-groups factors, as covered in Chapter 11. Designs with multiple independent variables may also include only within-groups factors. That is, the same subjects are exposed to all levels of all the treatment combinations. Finally, designs with multiple independent variables may represent a mixture of within-groups factors and between-groups factors. That is, the same subjects are exposed to all the levels of the within-groups factor(s) but different subjects are exposed to each of the levels of the between-groups factor(s). An example of a mixed design, with one within-groups factor and one between-groups factor is illustrated in Table 12.1c. Here different students are assigned to study at home or at school. But each student takes the pretest, the posttest, and the delayed posttest.

In this chapter we will present only a sampling of possible within-groups and mixed designs. In particular, we will cover the *t*-test for two dependent samples, the Oneway Within-Groups ANOVA, and a mixed design with one within-groups factor and one between-groups factor.

Other Uses of Within-Groups Analyses

The most common use of the dependent samples *t*-test and within-groups ANOVA are for situations in which the same subjects are tested repeatedly. But there are other situations in which these statistical tests can and should be used. In fact, any design in which there is a degree of dependency among the observations is a candidate for the statistical approaches covered in this chapter. For example, research involving twins, each member of the pair assigned to different treatment conditions, would require the use of within-groups analyses because there is a natural dependency between the scores of each twin. In general, studies in which participants are matched on important characteristics and then assigned to different groups for study require the use of within-groups analyses. For example, you might want to match students on an aptitude measure and then assign them to experimental learning conditions.

Remember that an important assumption of the independent samples *t*-test and the Between-Groups ANOVA is that the observations are independent of one another. Failing to meet this assumption can have serious consequences, and thus the use of these tests is no longer recommended. Instead, the dependent samples *t*-test and the Within-Groups ANOVA are recommended alternatives.

The Advantages of Within-Groups Designs

The first advantage of within-groups designs is a practical one. The researcher does not need to engage additional subjects for each new treatment condition (i.e., level of the independent variable).

The second advantage is that error variability is reduced in the within-groups design compared to the between-groups design. Thus, the design has increased statistical power and, therefore, a reduced likelihood of making Type II errors. An example and more elaborate explanation will follow.

The Disadvantages of Within-Groups Designs

With the use of within-groups designs, there is the practical disadvantage of requiring a greater involvement of individual participants (i.e., they are each exposed to multiple treatments and multiple outcomes). Although you may use fewer participants, you are asking that they participate in each treatment condition and complete the dependent measure more than once. This disadvantage may be inconsequential when the treatment is of short duration and intensity and when measurement is brief and unobtrusive. In contrast, this disadvantage can be especially troublesome when treatments are especially time-consuming and measurement is difficult.

The most serious disadvantages to the within-groups design are threats to internal and external validity (Campbell & Stanley, 1966). Threats to internal validity may serve as rival explanations to a possible treatment effect. When the within-groups design has an independent variable with only two levels (e.g., One Group Pretest–Posttest Design), threats to internal validity may include the following:

- Maturation
- Regression
- Instrumentation
- Testing
- History

Consequently, researchers need to avoid using within-groups designs in situations in which there is some reasonable possibility that one or more of these threats to internal validity may operate. However, the probability of their occurrence can sometimes be controlled by carefully planning the research. For example, maturational influences can sometimes be controlled by shortening the test–retest interval.

Alternately, threats to internal validity can be controlled by making certain design modifications. One of these is the use of a technique called **counterbalancing,** which is discussed in the next section. Another is the use of the time series design, as discussed in Chapter 2.

When the within-groups design has more than two levels of the independent variable, especially multiple pretests and multiple posttests (e.g., Time Series Design), most threats to internal validity are reduced, although the influence of external events (i.e., history) may remain an especially viable alternative explanation of a treatment effect.

Unfortunately, when the within-groups design has more than two levels, a particular threat to external validity is likely: **multiple-x interference**. That is, the effects of the initial treatment may carry over to subsequent treatments.

Counterbalancing

You will recall that the passage of time is a prerequisite for the operation of threats to internal validity in the One-Group Pretest–Posttest Design and more generally in the within-groups design with more than two levels of the independent variable. For example, a change in time is a signal that maturation may have operated or that testing (practice) effects may have operated. In such a case, the difference between the data collected at, say, time 1 and time 2 may not be a function of the treatment but may be due to some rival influence.

But what if researchers did not present the different levels of the independent variable in the same order to all participants? For example, what if some subjects received treatment 1 first, others received treatment 2 first, and still others received treatment 3 first? This approach is called *counterbalancing* and is illustrated in Table 12.3. (See also Design 11 in Campbell & Stanley, 1966, pp. 50–52.)

TABLE 12.3	Within-Groups Design: Counterbalancing		
Subjects	*Time 1*	*Time 2*	*Time 3*
S_1	A_1	A_2	A_3
S_2	A_2	A_3	A_1
S_3	A_3	A_1	A_2

Of course, counterbalancing depends on the experimenter's ability to vary the order in which the treatments are introduced.

The effect of counterbalancing is to control for threats to internal validity by confounding them with the different orders of presenting the treatments. Thus every treatment (A_1, A_2, A_3) gets an equal amount of the operating threat(s) to internal validity.

There are two situations in which counterbalancing may be used. The simplest is when only one participant receives each order of the treatment. The second and more usual is when multiple participants receive each order of the treatment.

Single Subjects per Order To analyze counterbalanced designs, first reorganize the data into the subjects by treatment matrix shown previously (see Table 12.1*b*). In other words, once counterbalancing has been done as part of the study's design, you may forget about it for data analysis if you wish when using single subjects per order.

Multiple Subjects per Order It is often desirable to have more than a single subject per order of presentation in the counterbalanced design. For example, researchers might have five subjects complete order 1, five subjects complete order 2, and five subjects complete order 3. In such a case, there is no longer a completely within-groups design. Although each subject does receive all of the treatments, different groups of subjects receive the treatments in different orders. Thus, *treatments* are a within-groups factor and *order* is a between-groups factor. Such a design should be treated as a mixed design for analysis purposes.

The presence of **carryover** or multiple-*x* interference effects may be tested in this design. The presence of a significant Treatments × Order interaction is a signal of the presence of carryover effects, which makes the main effect test of the treatments mute. To eliminate carryover effects from the above design requires examining only those data in which each treatment is given first. This is the simple effect of Treatments at time 1. In effect, this becomes a between-groups design only, with all repeated testings discarded.

CORRELATED OR DEPENDENT SAMPLES *t*-TEST

Before proposing a solution to the challenge posed by repeated measures, we briefly review the independent samples *t*-test. We then present two methods that yield equivalent results for calculating the correlated samples *t*-test and confidence intervals: (1) the raw score method and (2) the individual difference score method. We conclude by showing how to compute effect sizes and power for two correlated groups.

Review of the Independent Samples t-Test

The independent samples t-test determines whether the difference between two group means are significantly different, if you have a nondirectional alternative hypothesis, or whether one mean is significantly larger than, or less than, a second group mean, if you have a directional alternative hypothesis. For the mean difference to be judged significant, it needs to be located on an appropriate "tail" of the estimated sampling distribution of mean differences. If the mean difference could occur rarely as a function of chance, one rejects the null hypothesis and accepts the alternative hypothesis. In other words, the calculated t-value needs to exceed the critical t-value for one to reject the null hypothesis and accept the alternative hypothesis.

In Chapter 8, we gave the formula for the separate variance model t-test for independent samples:

$$\text{(Equation 8.2) Estimated } t = \frac{\overline{Y}_{A1} - \overline{Y}_{A2}}{\sqrt{\dfrac{s^2_{A1}}{n_{A1}} + \dfrac{s^2_{A2}}{n_{A2}}}}$$

Researchers are drawn to apply similar logic and a similar test in the case of correlated or dependent samples. However, the dependency or consistency among the scores is problematic. Researchers have to find a way to remove the dependency among the scores in order to use the t-test. This dependency violates an important assumption of the t-test concerning the independence of the samples.

Correlated Samples t-Test: Raw Score Method

The dependency or consistency among the scores is the extent to which individual scores remain unchanged from one measurement to the second measurement (e.g., from pretest to posttest) except for the influence of the treatment. When there is complete dependency or consistency, the scores from one measurement would be expected to be perfectly correlated with the scores from the second measurement.[1] That is, if there was total dependency between the two sets of scores, there would be a perfect linear relationship between them which would appear as a straight line in a scatterplot of the two sets. When there are repeated measures, knowledge of the first set of scores taken at time 1 would allow one to predict without error the second set of scores taken at time 2.

Similarly, when there is a complete lack of dependency or consistency, the two sets of scores would be expected to be totally uncorrelated. Knowledge of the scores at time 1 would be of no use in trying to predict the scores at time 2.

---

[1]See Chapter 13 for a thorough explanation and computational examples of the Pearson product moment correlation coefficient (r).

Finally, when the scores exhibit only a degree of dependency or consistency, the scores from one measurement would be expected to be somewhat correlated with the scores from the second measurement. Time 1 scores predict time 2 scores, but there is error in the prediction.

For correlated samples, one could apply the same formula as the separate variance model *t*-test for independent samples, except that some portion of within-groups variability, attributable to the dependency or consistency of the scores, would have to be removed.

Computational Formula   Therefore, a formula for the dependent or correlated samples *t*-test is as follows:

$$\text{Equation 12.1: } t_C = \frac{\overline{Y}_{A1} - \overline{Y}_{A2}}{\sqrt{\dfrac{s_{A1}^2}{n_{A1}} + \dfrac{s_{A2}^2}{n_{A2}} - \left(2r \dfrac{s_{A1}}{\sqrt{n_{A1}}} \dfrac{s_{A2}}{\sqrt{n_{A2}}}\right)}}$$

where $r = \dfrac{\sum (Y_{iA1} - \overline{Y}_{A1})(Y_{iA2} - \overline{Y}_{A2})}{\sqrt{\sum (Y_{iA1} - \overline{Y}_{A1})^2}\sqrt{\sum (Y_{iA2} - \overline{Y}_{A2})^2}}$

This is equivalent to the following:

$$\text{Equation 12.2: } t_C = \frac{\overline{Y}_{A1} - \overline{Y}_{A2}}{\sqrt{\dfrac{\dfrac{\sum (Y_{iA1} - \overline{Y}_{A1})^2}{n_{A1} - 1}}{n_{A1}} + \dfrac{\dfrac{\sum (Y_{iA2} - \overline{Y}_{A2})^2}{n_{A2} - 1}}{n_{A2}} - \left(2r \dfrac{s_{A1}}{\sqrt{n_{A1}}} \dfrac{s_{A2}}{\sqrt{n_{A2}}}\right)}}$$

And also to the following:

$$\text{Equation 12.3: } t_C = \frac{\overline{Y}_{A1} - \overline{Y}_{A2}}{s_C} \qquad \text{where}$$

$$\text{Equation 12.4: } s_C = \sqrt{\dfrac{s_{A1}^2}{n_{A1}} + \dfrac{s_{A2}^2}{n_{A2}} - \left(2r \dfrac{s_{A1}}{\sqrt{n_{A1}}} \dfrac{s_{A2}}{\sqrt{n_{A2}}}\right)}$$

CD-ROM link 12.1

Activity 12.1: Comparison of Standard Errors
In Activity 12.1, you can adjust the dependency between two sets of scores and observe the effect it has on the calculated values for independent and dependent samples *t*-tests. As the degree of dependency increases, you will see that the magnitude of the correction to the standard error in the dependent samples *t*-test's calculated value.

Comparison of Standard Errors   You can see that the numerators of the independent samples *t*-test and the dependent samples *t*-test are identical. The denominators are similar. In the independent samples *t*-test, the denominator contains the standard error of the mean difference, s_D. In the dependent samples t-test, the denominator, s_C, contains the same standard error but corrected for the dependence between the two sets of scores. Therefore, as the dependence between the two sets grows larger, the denominator of the dependent samples t-test grows smaller. Conversely, as the dependence between the two sets of scores grows smaller, s_C grows larger. When there is absolutely no dependency between scores, the denominator of the independent samples t-test is identical to the denominator of the dependent samples t-test.

Note that to compute the dependent samples t-test, the sample sizes for both groups must be equal. In other words, participants must provide scores for both the first and second measurements. Missing observations at either time results in either the complete removal of the participant or the replacement of the missing score (e.g., mean substitution).

Degrees of Freedom The degrees of freedom for finding the critical value of the dependent samples t is as follows:

Equation 12.5: $df = n - 1$ where n is the number of paired observations.

Confidence Intervals The two-sided confidence interval for a nondirectional alternative hypothesis is as follows:

$$\text{Equation 12.6: } \overline{Y}_D - t_{1-\alpha/2}s_C \text{ and } \overline{Y}_D + t_{1-\alpha/2}s_C$$

This is identical to Equation 8.5 for the independent samples t-test except that in Equation 12.6 one uses the standard error of the correlated samples, s_C.

The one-sided confidence interval for a one-tailed *positive* direction alternative hypothesis is as follows:

$$\text{Equation 12.7: } \overline{Y}_D - t_{1-\alpha}s_C$$

The one-sided confidence interval for a one-tailed *negative* direction alternative hypothesis is as follows:

$$\text{Equation 12.8: } \overline{Y}_D + t_{1-\alpha}s_C$$

Application: Phonics Tonics Scenario Apply the correlated samples t-test to the data from the first experiment in the Phonics Tonics scenario (see Table 12.1a). Also use the independent samples t-test for the same data. This is *not* a correct application of the independent samples t-test but will help to illustrate why the correlated samples t-test is a more powerful statistic. See Textbox 12.2. Note the calculated value of the correlated samples t-test is -13.42, while the calculated value of the independent samples t-test is -2.68.

Textbox 12.2

Illustration of Correlated Samples *t*-test: Raw Score Method, Phonics Tonics Scenario

Correlated samples *t*-test:

$$t_C = \frac{\overline{Y}_{A1} - \overline{Y}_{A2}}{\sqrt{\frac{s_{A1}^2}{n_{A1}} + \frac{s_{A2}^2}{n_{A2}} - \left(2r \frac{s_{A1}}{\sqrt{n_{A1}}} \frac{s_{A2}}{\sqrt{n_{A2}}}\right)}} = \frac{8.00 - 14.00}{\sqrt{\frac{(3.67)^2}{5} + \frac{(3.39)^2}{5} - \left(2(.963)\left(\frac{3.67}{2.24}\right)\left(\frac{3.39}{2.24}\right)\right)}} \approx -13.42$$

$$df = n - 1 = 4$$

For a directional alternative hypothesis (i.e., one-tailed test) with $\alpha = .01$, the critical value is: 3.747. Therefore, you reject the null hypothesis.

Given the directional alternative hypothesis, that posttest scores will exceed pretest scores, you can also find the one-sided confidence interval for a negative mean difference:

$$\overline{Y}_D + t_{1-\alpha} s_c = -6 + (-3.47)(0.45) = -7.56.$$

You can be 99% confident that students will gain as much as 7.56 points on the composition skills test over time.

Now calculate the independent samples *t*-test *for illustration purposes only:*

$$t_C = \frac{\overline{Y}_{A1} - \overline{Y}_{A2}}{\sqrt{\frac{s_{A1}^2}{n_{A1}} + \frac{s_{A2}^2}{n_{A2}}}} = \frac{8.00 - 14.00}{\sqrt{\frac{(3.67)^2}{5} + \frac{(3.39)^2}{5}}} = -2.68$$

$$df = n_{A1} - 1 + n_{A2} - 1 = 8.$$

For a directional alternative hypothesis (i.e., one-tailed test) with $\alpha = .01$, the critical value is 2.896. Therefore, had these data been uncorrelated, you would *fail* to reject the null hypothesis.

The calculated value of the correlated samples *t*-test is larger than the calculated value of the independent samples *t*-test when both formulas are used on the same data. The effect of removing the dependency among the scores is to reduce the size of the denominator of the *t*-ratio.

Correlated Samples *t*-Test: Individual Difference Score Method

An alternative procedure to using the raw scores (i.e., the individual pretest scores and the individual posttest scores) for calculating the correlated samples *t*-test is to use individual **difference scores** or **gain scores**. Computing a difference scores has the effect of removing the dependency or consistency among the scores because what is consistent between the time 1 measurement and the time 2 measurement is removed by subtraction. A secondary benefit is that the manual calculations for finding the calculated value are easier to perform.

Each individual difference score (Y_{A1-A2}) is the difference between scores on the dependent variable at time 1 (A_1) and time 2 (A_2). Therefore, using the individual difference score approach, one has only a single group of scores with which to work.

The mean of the individual difference scores is

$$\overline{Y}_{A1-A2} = \frac{\sum Y_{A1-A2}}{n_{A1-A2}}$$

The mean of the individual difference scores is, of course, the same as the difference between the mean of the time 1 scores and the mean of the time 2 scores:

$$\overline{Y}_{A1-A2} = \overline{Y}_{A1} - \overline{Y}_{A2}$$

The unbiased standard deviation of the individual difference scores is

$$s_{A1-A2} = \sqrt{\frac{\sum (Y_{A1-A2} - \overline{Y}_{A1-A2})^2}{n_{A1-A2} - 1}}$$

The standard error of the individual difference score is

Equation 12.9: $s_{ID} = \dfrac{s_{A1-A2}}{\sqrt{n_{A1-A2}}} = \dfrac{\sqrt{\dfrac{\sum (Y_{A1-A2} - \overline{Y}_{A1-A2})^2}{n_{A1-A2} - 1}}}{\sqrt{n_{A1-A2}}}$

And the standard error of the individual difference scores is the same as the standard error for two correlated samples:

$$s_{ID} = s_C$$

Therefore, the *t*-tests for correlated samples, individual difference score method, is as follows:

Equation 12.10: $t_C = \dfrac{\overline{Y}_{A1-A2}}{s_{ID}}$

This is equivalent to

Equation 12.11: $t_C = \dfrac{\overline{Y}_{A1-A2}}{\dfrac{s_{A1-A2}}{\sqrt{n_{A1-A2}}}}$

and to

Equation 12.12: $t_C = \dfrac{\overline{Y}_{A1-A2}}{\dfrac{\sqrt{\dfrac{\sum (Y_{A1-A2} - \overline{Y}_{A1-A2})^2}{n_{A1-A2} - 1}}}{\sqrt{n_{A1-A2}}}}$

The degrees of freedom remain:

(Equation 12.5) df $= n - 1$ where n is the number of paired observations.

The gain scores in Table 12.1a are used to illustrate the calculation of the correlated samples t-test: individual difference score method. See Textbox 12.3. Note that the standard deviation of the gain score (1.00) is smaller than either the pretest or the posttest standard deviations (3.67 and 3.39, respectively).

Effect Size and Power

We will provide procedures for the estimation of effect sizes and power for two correlated samples. We will also show the similarities and differences between the procedures when the two samples are independent versus when the two samples are correlated.

Effect Size   For two independent samples, the basic formula for the calculation of the effect size is the following:

$$\textbf{(Equation 8.4)}\ d = \frac{\overline{Y}_{A1} - \overline{Y}_{A2}}{s}$$

Textbox 12.3

Illustration of Correlated Samples t-Test: Individual Difference Score Method, Phonics Tonics Scenario

$$\overline{Y}_{A1-A2} = \frac{\sum Y_{A1-A2}}{n_{A1-A2}} = \frac{-30}{5} = -6.00$$

$$s_{A1-A2} = \sqrt{\frac{\sum (Y_{A1-A2} - \overline{Y}_{A1-A2})^2}{n_{A1-A2} - 1}} = \sqrt{\frac{4.00}{4}} = 1.00$$

$$s_{ID} = \frac{s_{A1-A2}}{\sqrt{n_{A1-A2}}} = \frac{1.00}{2.24} = 0.45$$

$$t_C = \frac{\overline{Y}_{A1-A2}}{s_{ID}} = \frac{-6.00}{0.45} \approx -13.45$$

The calculated value of the correlated sample t-test does not depend on the method of calculation. Both the raw score method and the individual difference score method yield identical calculated values within rounding error. By calculating each individual difference score, one removes the dependency that exists between the time 1 scores and the time 2 scores.

For two correlated samples, the formula for the calculation of the effect size is as follows:

$$\textbf{Equation 12.13: } d_C = \frac{\overline{Y}_{A1} - \overline{Y}_{A2}}{s_{A1-A2}}$$

Because the standard deviation of the difference score is used in the denominator of the ratio, the effect size for correlated samples will be larger than the effect size had the two groups been treated as independent. If, however, a comparison of the effect sizes from two or more studies of different designs is desired, the researcher may account for design differences by either of the following methods:

- Compute all effect sizes as if the data were drawn from two independent samples, or
- If only difference scores are available, multiply d_C by $\sqrt{2(1-r)}$, where r is the correlation between measures 1 and 2, to get an approximation of d (Cohen, 1988).

See Textbox 12.4 for an illustration.

Power By substituting the standard error for correlated samples s_C for the standard error for independent samples s_D, you can use the steps in Textbox 7.6

Textbox 12.4

Effect Size Calculations for Dependent Sample: Phonics Tonics Scenario

You want to find the size of the effect for the two correlated samples in Table 12.1a:

$$d_C = \frac{\overline{Y}_{A1} - \overline{Y}_{A2}}{s_{A1-A2}} = \frac{-6.00}{1.00} = -6.00$$

Had you treated these samples as independent then:

$$d = \frac{\overline{Y}_{A1} - \overline{Y}_{A2}}{s} = \frac{-6.00}{3.67} = -1.63 \text{ (using the pretest standard deviation in the denominator).}$$

Or you might have corrected d_C to approximate d:

$$d = d_C [\sqrt{2(1-r)}] = -6.00(0.27) = -1.63.$$

In this example, when you remove the dependency, the estimates of effect size are especially large. Even when you do not remove the dependency, the effect size is large. Because the correlation between pretest and posttest scores is so large ($r = +.963$), there is a marked difference in the estimates (i.e., -6.00 versus -1.63).

and explained in Chapter 7 to estimate power when dealing with two dependent samples:

1. Estimate the population mean difference for the alternative sampling distribution ($\overline{Y}_{DA}$).
2. Estimate the standard error of the alternative sampling distribution (s_{CA}).
3. Find the critical value for the null sampling distribution and convert it to a raw score (CV_R).
4. Compute z_A from CV_R.
5. Find β and power $(1 - \beta)$ by finding the exact probability of z_A.

ONEWAY WITHIN-GROUPS ANOVA

We now want to extend the logic of the analysis for two correlated or dependent samples to the situation in which the independent variable has more than two values, or levels. In other words, we want you to be able to analyze data from designs in which the same or matched participants are tested on more than two occasions. We will use the data from Table 12.1*b* throughout this section as our example. In the second experiment of the Phonics Tonics scenario of Textbox 12.1, participants are pretested, posttested, and finally receive a delayed posttest.

Underlying Logic

Remember that in the between-groups design, differences between group means may come about due to chance, even when there is no effect of the treatment. Indeed, *when there is no treatment effect*, the *F*-ratio represents two estimates of the operation of chance:

$MS_{Y(A)}$, the average variability from group to group

$MS_{Y(S/A)}$, the average variability from subject to subject

Thus, in the between-groups design when there is *no* treatment effect (i.e., the null hypothesis is true), $MS_{Y(A)}$ equals (approximately) $MS_{Y(S/A)}$ and the *F*-ratio should be about 1.0. However, when there is a treatment effect, the *F*-ratio is greater than 1.0, signaling that $MS_{Y(A)}$ represents a treatment effect *plus* chance variability.

In contrast, when there are repeated measures, the same subjects serve in each of the treatment conditions. Thus, a major source of variability found in the between-groups design is not found in the within-groups design: variability from group to group due only to chance differences in subjects. This means that the average variability between treatment means when there is *no* treatment effect will not be the same as the average variability within groups (i.e., from subject to subject). In other words, there is a certain *consistency* or *dependency* among the scores for each subject—the scores across groups are no longer independent of one another. This also means that $MS_{Y(S/A)}$ *overrepresents* the operation of chance when compared to $MS_{Y(A)}$.

How to account for the dependency among the scores for each subject in the within-groups design? Partition the variability within groups ($SS_{Y(S/A)}$) into two additive components:

1. $SS_{Y(S)}$, or variability from subject to subject
2. $SS_{Y(AS)}$, or variability of each subject across treatment conditions

You will *not* account for the dependency among subjects by adjusting the between-groups term ($SS_{Y(A)}$).

Analyzing the Data With and Without the Dependencies

To get a better idea of what we mean, begin with the analysis of the data in Table 12.1*b* using the Oneway Between-Groups ANOVA. In other words, ignore the dependency among scores and proceed incorrectly to compute the sums of squares and partition the total variability. Then, remove the dependency among the scores and repeat the analysis.

If you incorrectly treated the data in Table 12.1*b* as a Oneway Between-Groups design, you would perform the following calculations, noting the following:

Total variability = between-groups variability + within-groups variability

From Chapter 9, the total sum of squares is

$$\textbf{(Equation 9.3) } SS_Y = \sum_1^A \sum_1^n (Y_i - \overline{Y})^2 = \sum_1^N (Y_i - \overline{Y})^2$$

$$= (14 - 11)^2 + (9 - 11)^2 + \cdots + (8 - 11)^2 + (4 - 11)^2$$

$$= 306.00$$

From Chapter 9, the between-groups sum of squares is:

$$\textbf{(Equation 9.4) } SS_{Y(A)} = \sum_1^A n_A(\overline{Y}_A - \overline{Y})^2$$

$$= (5)(8 - 11)^2 + (5)(15 - 11)^2 + (5)(10 - 11)^2 = 130.00$$

From Chapter 9, the within-groups sum of squares is:

$$\textbf{(Equation 9.5) } SS_{Y(S/A)} = \sum_1^A \sum_1^n (Y_i - \overline{Y}_A)^2$$

$$= (14 - 8)^2 + (9 - 8)^2 + \cdots + (8 - 10)^2 + (4 - 10)^2$$

$$= 176.00$$

Now notice what happens to the calculations when the effects of the dependency or consistency in subject's responses are removed. How is this done? By using each subject's mean score to represent the consistency and subtracting the (row) mean from the individual scores. (See Table 12.4.)

TABLE 12.4	Removing the Dependency among the Scores							
Student	A_1	A_2	A_3	$\overline{Y}_S$	$A_1 - \overline{Y}_S$	$A_2 - \overline{Y}_S$	$A_3 - \overline{Y}_S$	*Mean*
Lauren	14	19	15	16.00	−2	3	−1	0.0
Fazio	9	18	12	13.00	−4	5	−1	0.0
Leila	7	15	11	11.00	−4	4	0	0.0
Dominic	5	11	8	8.00	−3	3	0	0.0
Lee	5	12	4	7.00	−2	5	−3	0.0
$\overline{Y}_A$	8.00	15.00	10.00	11.00	−3.00	4.00	−1.00	0.0

Now compute a second Oneway Between-Groups ANOVA using participants' scores with the dependency removed:

From Chapter 9, the total sum of squares is:

$$\textbf{(Equation 9.3) } SS_Y = \sum_1^A \sum_1^n (Y_i - \overline{Y})^2 = \sum_1^N (Y_i - \overline{Y})^2$$

$$= (-2 - 0)^2 + (-4 - 0)^2 + \cdots + (0 - 0)^2 + (-3 - 0)^2$$

$$= 144.00$$

However, since this sum of squares is without the dependencies, label it as such.

$$SS_{YWD} = 144.00$$

From Chapter 9, the between-groups sum of squares is:

$$\textbf{(Equation 9.4) } SS_{Y(A)} = \sum_1^A n_A (\overline{Y}_A - \overline{Y})^2$$

$$= (5)(-3 - 0)^2 + (5)(4 - 0)^2 + (5)(-1 - 0)^2 = 130.00$$

However, since this sum of squares is without the dependencies also, label it as such.

$$SS_{Y(A)WD} = 130.00$$

From Chapter 9, the within-groups sum of squares is:

$$\textbf{(Equation 9.5) } SS_{Y(S/A)} = \sum_1^A \sum_1^n (Y_i - \overline{Y}_A)^2$$

$$= (-2 - 3)^2 + (-4 - 3)^2 + \cdots + (0 - 1)^2 + (-3 - 1)^2$$

$$= 14.00$$

Finally, since this sum of squares is without the dependencies, label it as such.

$$SS_{Y(S/A)WD} = 14.00$$

Note that the between-groups sum of squares, $SS_{Y(A)} = 130.00$, based on raw scores, is identical to the between-groups sum of squares, $SS_{Y(A)WD} = 130.00$, based on the scores with dependencies removed. Note also that the magnitude of the *differences* between the treatment means (e.g., A_1 versus A_2) remains unchanged whether you compare the raw score means or the means with dependencies removed.

However, the within-groups sum of squares, $SS_{Y(S/A)} = 176.00$, based on the raw scores, is much larger than within-groups sum of squares $SS_{Y(S/A)WD} = 14.00$, based on the scores with the dependencies removed. By removing the dependencies among subjects' scores, the size of within-groups variability is reduced.

$SS_{Y(S/A)WD}$ includes no overall deviation from subject to subject because each subject has a mean score of zero and the grand mean of all scores is also zero. These calculations illustrate that the within-groups sums of squares for the raw data can be made smaller by removing the consistency or dependency among individual subject's scores.

Therefore, it is possible to remove the dependency among subjects' scores when correlated or matched samples are used. The removal of the dependency can be accomplished in a way that reduces the size of within-groups variability but leaves between-groups variability unaffected.

But the procedure described is somewhat cumbersome. How can one do this without first computing difference scores?

Computational Procedures for the Oneway Within-Groups ANOVA

The computational formula for the Oneway Within-Groups ANOVA sums of squares for raw data allows the total variability to be further partitioned.

The basic terms remain unchanged from the Oneway Between-Groups ANOVA. Total variability is as follows:

(Equation 9.3) $SS_Y = \sum_1^A \sum_1^n (Y_i - \overline{Y})^2 = \sum_1^N (Y_i - \overline{Y})^2$

Between-groups variability is as follows:

(Equation 9.4) $SS_{Y(A)} = \sum_1^A n_A(\overline{Y}_A - \overline{Y})^2$

$$(5)(8-11)^2 + (5)(15-11)^2 + (5)(10-11)^2 = 130.00$$

Within-groups variability is as follows:

(Equation 9.5) $SS_{Y(S/A)} = \sum_1^A \sum_1^n (Y_i - \overline{Y}_A)^2$

$$(14-8)^2 + (9-8)^2 + \cdots + (8-10)^2 + (4-10)^2 = 176.00$$

However, you will partition $SS_{Y(S/A)}$ into two additive components:

1. $SS_{Y(S)}$, or variability from subject to subject
2. $SS_{Y(AS)}$, or variability of each subject across treatment conditions

$SS_{Y(AS)}$ is the sum of squares you will use to make up the error term for the significance test of the treatment effect for correlated or repeated measures. Therefore, you will not use $SS_{Y(S/A)}$ as your error term for this design.

$SS_{Y(AS)}$ is not an accidental symbol. It represents the interaction of subjects and the treatment. In other words, it represents the variability or inconsistency of individual subjects across different treatment conditions.

Partitioning $SS_{Y(S/A)}$

$$\text{Equation 12.14: } SS_{Y(S)} = A \sum_{1}^{n} (\overline{Y}_S - \overline{Y})^2$$

Using the raw data and means from Table 12.4:

$$SS_{Y(S)} = 3[(16 - 11)^2 + (13 - 11)^2 + (11 - 11)^2 + (8 - 11)^2 + (7 - 11)^2] = 162.00$$

$$\text{Equation 12.15: } SS_{Y(AS)} = \sum_{1}^{A} \sum_{1}^{n} (Y - \overline{Y}_S - \overline{Y}_A + \overline{Y})^2$$

$$SS_{Y(AS)} = (14 - 16 - 8 + 11)^2 + (9 - 13 - 8 + 11)^2$$
$$+ \cdots + (8 - 8 - 10 + 11)^2 + (4 - 7 - 10 + 11)^2 = 14.00$$

Partitioning SS_Y   You have now partitioned total variability into three additive components:

$$SS_Y = SS_{Y(A)} + SS_{Y(S)} + SS_{Y(AS)}$$

For the second experiment (see Table 12.1*b*) in the Phonics Tonics scenario of Textbox 12.1:

$$306.00 = 130.00 + 162.00 + 14.00$$

Degrees of Freedom   The familiar terms:

$$\text{Equation 12.16: For the treatment: } df_A = A - 1$$

$$\text{Equation 12.17: For subjects within groups: } df_{S/A} = (n - 1)A \text{ or } N - A$$

For the partitioning of subjects within groups:

$$\text{Equation 12.18: For subjects: } df_S = n - 1$$

$$\text{Equation 12.19: For the } AS \text{ interaction: } df_{AS} = (A - 1)(n - 1)$$

$$\text{Total variability} = An - 1 = (a - 1) + (n - 1) + (A - 1)(n - 1)$$

Mean Squares

$$\text{Equation 12.20: } MS_{Y(A)} = SS_{Y(A)}/df_A$$

$$\text{Equation 12.21: } MS_{Y(AS)} = SS_{Y(AS)}/df_{AS}$$

$$\text{And also: } MS_{Y(S)} = SS_{Y(S)}/df_S$$

F-ratio The *F*-test of the treatment *A* is:

$$\text{Equation 12.22: } MS_{Y(A)}/MS_{Y(AS)}$$

The test of the subjects is seldom reported. It is $MS_{Y(S)}/MS_{Y(AS)}$.

See Table 12.5 for the Oneway Within-Groups ANOVA Summary Table for the second experiment described in the Phonics Tonics scenario.

Assumptions and Assumption Violations

Within-groups designs involve correlated or matched samples. Therefore, the Oneway Within-Groups ANOVA model makes different assumptions regarding the nature of the data than the Oneway Between-Groups model. Although assumptions regarding normality and homogeneity of variance still hold, there is no longer the assumption that scores are independent across levels of the independent variable.

Circularity Assumption In place of the independence assumption, the Oneway Within-Groups ANOVA relies on the **circularity assumption** (also known as the *sphericity assumption*). The circularity assumption concerns the nature of the dependency among participants' scores across levels of the treatment (*A*) when there are more than two levels. Except for chance fluctuation, one would expect the correlation among participant scores for any two levels of the treatment to be equal.

When the circularity assumption is met, it means that the average error term, $MS_{Y(AS)}$, accurately reflects any two levels of the treatment, because the within-groups dependencies are approximately the same regardless of which levels of the treatment one considers. However, when the circularity assumption is not met, the average error term $MS_{Y(AS)}$ is based on different size dependencies among levels of the treatment. Consequently, the average may underrepresent the within-groups correlations among certain levels of the treatment and overrepresent other ones. Of course, when there are only two levels of the treatment, the circularity assumption must be met, because there is only a single correlation among subjects' scores to worry about. Therefore, the circularity assumption does not come into play for correlated or dependent samples *t*-tests.

Unfortunately, when there are more than two levels of the treatment, the consequences of failing to meet the circularity assumption are not trivial. The Oneway Within-Groups ANOVA is not robust to violations of the circularity assumption. When the assumption is not met, the omnibus test of the treatment is too liberal and the actual probability of making a Type I error is higher than the nominal probability value. In other words, violation of the circularity assumption leads to an increased likelihood of rejecting the null hypothesis when it is true.

TABLE 12.5 Oneway Within-Groups ANOVA Summary Table: Phonics Tonics Experiment 2					
Source	SS	df	MS	F	p
Tests (A)	130.00	2	65.00	23.14	<.01
Subjects (S)	162.00	4	40.50		
Error (AS)	14.00	8	1.75		
Total	306.00	14			

Dealing with Violations of the Circularity Assumption   There is a test for determining whether the circularity assumption has been met (Mauchley, 1940). However, the test is sensitive to departures from normality and can yield significant results even when the circularity assumption has been met. Therefore, it is not often recommended. Instead, a three-step strategy is recommended whenever repeated measures are involved.

There is a fairly simple, but conservative, correction (Geisser & Greenhouse, 1958) for dealing with possible problems associated with violations of the circularity assumption. The correction lowers both numerator and denominator degrees of freedom used to enter the *F*-table and find the critical value. These reduced degrees of freedom mean that the critical value is now increased in size, making it more difficult for one to reject the null hypothesis.

There is a more complex, and more precise, correction (Huynh & Feldt, 1970) that also lowers both numerator and denominator degrees of freedom. Fortunately, the Huynh-Feldt calculations for adjusted degrees of freedom are performed in some computer ANOVA programs.

The recommended procedure is to follow a three-step strategy:

1. Begin by analyzing the data in the regular manner. Find the critical *F*-value using the complete degrees of freedom. *Stop* if the calculated value of *F* is not significant. Do not proceed further. Proceed to step 2 only if the calculated value is significant.
2. Carry out the Geisser-Greenhouse (lower-bound) correction using reduced degrees of freedom where $df_A = 1.0$ and $df_{AS} = n - 1$. Find the critical *F*-value for df = 1, $n - 1$ at the alpha value you have selected. *Stop* if the calculated value is significant in this situation. There is no need to proceed further; the finding is significant. Proceed to step 3 only if the calculated value is now not significant.
3. Carry out the Huynh-Feldt (epsilon) correction using reduced degrees of freedom. Epsilon is usually a fraction less than 1, and so degrees of freedom are reduced.

$$df_A = \varepsilon(A - 1)$$

$$df_{AS} = \varepsilon(A - 1)(n - 1)$$

Textbox 12.5

Three-Step Strategy for Dealing with the Circularity Assumption: Experiment 2 of the Phonics Tonics Scenario

Step 1

In step 1 of the three-step strategy, you calculate the mean squares and F-ratio using the full degrees of freedom, that is $df_A = A - 1$; $df_{AS} = (A - 1)(n - 1)$. We also use these dfs to find the critical value. Consequently, our mean squares and F (see Table 12.5) are

$$MS_{Y(A)} = 130.00/2 = 65.00$$

$$MS_{Y(AS)} = 14.00/8 = 1.75$$

$$F(2, 8) = 65.00/1.75 = 37.14.$$

The critical value for $df = 2, 8$, and $\alpha = .01$ is 8.65.

The calculated value (37.14) is larger than the critical value (8.65). Therefore, you proceed to step 2.

Step 2 (If Step 1 is Significant)

In step 2, use the Geisser-Greenhouse reduced degrees of freedom, $df_A = 1$ and $df_{AS} = (n - 1)$ to find the critical value.

The critical value for $df = 1, 4$ and $\alpha = .01$ is 21.20. (Note the large increase in the critical value from step 1.)

The calculated value (37.14) is larger than the critical value (21.20). The treatment is significant even here, and you need proceed no further.

Step 3 (If Step 2 Is Not Significant)

Since the most conservative test revealed that the treatment was significant, step 3 is not necessary.

Find the critical F-value using the reduced degrees of freedom and compare it to the calculated value. Accept these results as *the* test of significance.

See Textbox 12.5 for an illustration of this three-step approach to dealing with the circularity assumption.

Multiple Comparisons

The procedures for planned and post hoc multiple comparisons for within-groups designs follow a similar logic to the procedures described for between-groups designs. A particular issue for within-groups designs is the appropriate error term for each comparison. When the researcher is confident that the circularity assumption is met, it is appropriate to use an error term based on the average of all levels of the treatment combined, namely $MS_{Y(AS)}$. However, when the researcher cannot be confident that the circularity assumption is met, it is appropriate to avoid the use of the average error term and use an error term specific to the levels of the treatment involved in the comparison.

We will illustrate the calculation of multiple comparisons when the circularity assumption is met, using the average error term $MS_{Y(AS)}$, and describe how to proceed when the circularity assumption is not met.

Computational Procedures for Planned Comparisons (Circularity Assumption Is Met)   When the circularity assumption is met, the logic and computational procedures for planned comparisons in within-groups designs is generally unchanged from planned comparisons in between-groups designs:

1. Planned comparisons are used instead of the omnibus test.
2. Contrasts must be valid and independent.
3. The sum of squares for the set of comparisons must equal the sum of squares for the omnibus test of the effect.
4. The numerator of the F-ratio is computed in an identical fashion to the between-groups design.

The sum of squares for a planned comparison is:

$$\textbf{(Equation 10.5) } SS_{Y(p)} = \frac{n(p)^2}{\sum\limits_{1}^{A} c_A^2} \qquad \text{where } p = \sum\limits_{1}^{A} c_A \overline{Y}_A$$

The mean squares for a planned comparison is:

$$\textbf{(Equation 10.6) } MS_{Y(p)} = SS_{Y(p)}/df_p = SS_{Y(p)}$$

(Remember that each comparison has only one numerator: df.)

5. However, the denominator of the F-ratio is not $MS_{Y(S/A)}$, but $MS_{Y(AS)}$. Therefore, the F-ratio for a planned comparison is:

$$\textbf{Equation 12.23: } F_p = MS_{Y(p)}/MS_{Y(AS)}, \ df_p = 1, \ df_{AS} = (A-1)(n-1)$$

Computational Procedures for Post Hoc Comparisons (Circularity Assumption Is Met)   When the circularity assumption is met, the logic and computational procedures for post hoc comparisons in within-groups designs is generally unchanged from post hoc comparisons in between-groups designs.

1. Post hoc comparisons are used following a significant omnibus test.
2. Contrasts must be valid, but they need not be independent.
3. The numerator of the F-ratio is computed in an identical fashion to the between-groups design.
4. However, the denominator of the F-ratio is $MS_{Y(AS)}$ (see Equation 12.23).
5. For pairwise comparisons use the Tukey HSD method; for all possible comparisons use the Scheffé S method.

6a. To find the critical value for Tukey's HSD for making all pairwise comparisons:

$$\textbf{(Equation 10.9)}\ F_T = \frac{(q_T)^2}{2}$$

where q_T is an entry in the Studentized range distribution. See Appendix F. To find the correct value of q_T you need the following:

$$\text{df}_{AS},\ \text{which is}\ (A-1)(n-1)$$

$$k,\ \text{the number of treatment means}\ (k = A)$$

$$\alpha_{FW},\ \text{alpha for the familywise Type I error selected,}$$
$$\text{which is usually .05 or .01.}$$

6b. To find the critical value for Scheffé's S method (F_S) for making all possible comparisons:

$$\text{Equation 12.24:}\ F_S = (a-1)F\,(\text{df}_A,\ \text{df}_{AS})$$

See Textbox 12.6 for an example of the three multiple comparison procedures.

Computational Procedures for Multiple Comparisons (Circularity Assumption Is Not Met)

When the circularity assumption is not met, it is not appropriate to use the average error term $\text{MS}_{Y(AS)}$. Instead, the error term should be based only on that subset of the data involved in the contrast. Doing so may result in a reduction of the power of the test compared to the use of the average error term because denominator degrees of freedom are smaller, but it will result in a potential increase in the accuracy with which error variance is estimated.

Other than computing an error term specific to each comparison, the rules for planned and post hoc comparisons still apply. Conduct planned comparisons instead of the omnibus test. They must be valid and independent. Conduct post hoc comparisons only after the omnibus test is significant. Control error rate familywise using either the Tukey or Scheffé procedures.

When the circularity assumption is not met, each simple or complex comparison will have its own error term, whether comparisons are planned or post hoc. To find each error term we compute the Oneway Within-Groups ANOVA for the data involved in the comparison only. For pairwise comparisons, this computation is straightforward. For complex comparisons the data should be combined according to the contrast weights assigned.

For example, imagine you wanted to compute the complex comparison of the second level of the treatment versus the first and third levels. You need do nothing to the values of A_2 but you need to find the average of the values of A_1 and A_3 before proceeding to compute the ANOVA. In other words, to find the correct error term for each comparison, the data are combined in such a way that every Oneway Within-Groups ANOVA has only two levels.

The specific error terms and reduced degrees of freedom can now be substituted for the general error term and full degrees of freedom described above.

Textbox 12.6

Within-Groups Multiple Comparisons: Experiment 2
of the Phonics Tonics Scenario

We will illustrate the steps in conducting planned and post hoc comparisons for experiment 2 of the Phonics Tonics scenario. It bears repeating that one would never conduct both planned and post hoc comparisons. And if one were doing only post hoc comparisons, one would not do both Tukey and Scheffé tests.

For each illustration, begin by computing the calculated value of the contrast. For the illustration, compare pretest scores (A_1) with posttest scores (A_2). Then find the critical value for each of the comparison procedures:

$$SS_{Y(p)} = \frac{n(p)^2}{\sum\limits_1^A c_A^2} \qquad \text{where } p = \sum\limits_1^A c_A \overline{Y}_A$$

$$\frac{5[(+1)8.00 + (-1)15.00 + (0)(10.00)]^2}{(-1)^2 + (1)^2 + (0)^2} = \frac{5[7.00]^2}{2} = 122.50$$

$$MS_{Y(p)} = SS_{Y(p)}/df_p = SS_{Y(p)} = 122.50/1 = 122.50$$

$$F_p = MS_{Y(p)}/MS_{Y(AS)} = 122.50/1.75 = 70.00$$

$$df_p = 1, \; df_{AS} = (A - 1)(n - 1)$$

Planned Comparisons: Critical Value

Use a conservative probability value of $\alpha = .01$. For df = 1, 8, the critical value of F is 11.30. The calculated value (70.00) exceeds the critical value (11.30) and the null hypothesis is rejected.

Post Hoc Comparisons: Tukey Critical Value

$$F_T = \frac{(q_T)^2}{2} = \frac{(5.64)^2}{2} = 15.90$$

$$df_{AS} = 8$$

$$k = 8$$

$$\alpha_{FW} = .01.$$

The calculated value (70.00) exceeds the critical value (15.90) and the null hypothesis is rejected.

Post Hoc Comparisons: Scheffé Critical Value

$$F_S = (a - 1)F \, (df_A, \, df_{AS}) = (2)(8.65) = 17.30.$$

The calculated value (70.00) exceeds the critical value (17.30), and the null hypothesis is rejected.

Effect Size and Power

Effect Size Calculations for Two Groups   In an earlier section of this chapter on the correlated samples *t*-test we gave formulas for computing effect sizes that either included or excluded variability attributable to subjects. To find the effect size for two correlated samples (see Equation 12.13) it is easiest to first find the individual difference scores and to compute the standard deviation of the individual difference scores. We demonstrate the calculation of the effect size for two correlated groups in Textbox 12.7. We also show the value of the effect size if these data came from independent samples.

General Effect Size Calculations   In Chapter 9 we gave the following indices of the general effect size: R^2, f, and ω^2. The first two measures require no adjustment for within-groups designs:

$$\text{(Equation 9.11) } R^2 = \frac{SS_{Y(A)}}{SS_Y}$$

$$\text{(Equation 9.12) } f = \sqrt{\frac{R^2}{1 - R^2}}$$

Textbox 12.7

Effect Size for Two Correlated Samples from Within-Groups Design: Experiment 2 of the Phonics Tonics Scenario

You want to estimate the size of the effect for the difference between pretest (A_1) and posttest (A_2) for experiment 2 of the Phonics Tonics scenario. Find the individual difference scores, compute the mean and the unbiased standard deviation, and then find d_C:

$$d_C = \frac{\overline{Y}_{A1} - \overline{Y}_{A2}}{s_{A1-A2}} = \frac{-7.00}{1.58} = -4.43$$

For comparison purposes you might wish to compute the effect size as if the groups were independent. Use the pretest standard deviation as the denominator, and find d:

$$d = \frac{\overline{Y}_{A1} - \overline{Y}_{A2}}{s} = \frac{-7.00}{3.74} = -1.87$$

By removing the dependency among scores, the standard deviation of d_C is much smaller than the standard deviation of d. Both effect sizes are large, but the effect size for correlated samples is larger. These fictitious data were created with small samples sizes but with a significant treatment effect. The consequence is effect sizes to yearn for!

Textbox 12.8

General Effect Size Calculations for Within-Groups Designs: Experiment 2 of the Phonics Tonics Scenario

Compute each of three general effect size measures for the within-groups factor using the ANOVA Summary Table (see Table 12.5):

$$R^2 = \frac{SS_{Y(A)}}{SS_Y} = \frac{130.00}{306.00} = .42$$

$$f = \sqrt{\frac{R^2}{1 - R^2}} = \sqrt{\frac{.42}{1 - .42}} = .86$$

$$\omega^2 = \frac{SS_{Y(A)} - (a - 1)MS_{Y(AS)}}{SS_Y + MS_{Y(AS)}} = \frac{130 - (3 - 1)1.75}{306.00 + 1.75} = .43$$

Regardless of the method of calculation, the general effect is found to be quite large.

The computational formula for ω^2 is modified slightly for within-groups designs:

Equation 12.25: $\omega^2 = \dfrac{SS_{Y(A)} - (a - 1)MS_{Y(AS)}}{SS_Y + MS_{Y(AS)}}$

Textbox 12.8 contains general effect size calculations for experiment 2 of the Phonics Tonics scenario in Textbox 12.1.

Power   Cohen (1988) provides power tables for the ANOVA using f. Remember that f is a measure of effect size based on the total variability in the design. A condensed version of these tables is given in Appendix E. Each section represents the degrees of freedom for the numerator (i.e., the degrees of freedom from 1 though 8 for the independent variable, $A - 1$). Power is presented for sample sizes (n) of 5 to 100. Three probability values for significance testing are included (i.e., $\alpha = .01$, .05, .10). The F_c column represents the critical or tabled value of F required to reject the null hypothesis. There are three columns for effect sizes (i.e., $f = .10$, or a small effect; $f = .25$, or a medium effect; and $f = .40$, or a large effect). The values for power beyond .99 are represented as **.

What is the effect of using f as a measure of effect size for within-groups designs? When the dependency among the within-groups scores is high, the use of f and the tables will provide a conservative estimate of power. That is, f provides the same estimate of power regardless of the correlation among the repeated measures.

MIXED DESIGNS

The correlated samples *t*-test and Oneway Within-Groups ANOVA share one thing in common. They are intended for those situations in which there are repeated measures for only a single independent variable. But what about more complex designs in which two or more variables are investigated simultaneously?

It is possible to employ Factorial designs with more than a single within-groups factor. For example, researchers might ask a single group of five participants to allow the researchers to take the participants' heart rates before, during, and after two types of physical activity: squash and racquetball. In other words, researchers would have created a time of testing (3) by type of activity (2) Factorial design. In total, a total of 30 heart rate measures would have been collected. And researchers would be able to explore the main effects of Testing, Activity, and the Testing × Activity interaction.

Mixed factorial designs can also be employed when there is a combination of between-groups and within-groups factors. Experiment 3 in the Phonics Tonics scenario is an example of a mixed design. It includes three levels of the testing (*A*) within-groups factor: Pretest, Posttest, and Delayed Posttest. It also includes two levels of the Setting (*B*) between-groups factor: Home and School. The design is a 3 × 2 mixed Factorial type composed of 10 students, each of whom completes the composition skills test three times. See Table 12.1c. One would be interested in testing the main effects of Testing and Setting as well as the Testing × Setting interaction.

Underlying Logic

We will explain the ANOVA calculations for a mixed design with one between-groups factor and one within-groups factor. You will thus be able to appreciate the logic of the calculations in even more complex designs. The "trick" in mixed designs is finding the correct error term to test each effect. The error term used to test the between-groups factors is not the same one used to test the within-groups factors, for reasons outlined earlier in this chapter, which means that you will have more than a single error term whenever you employ mixed designs. Nevertheless, you will still be partitioning the total variability in the dependent variable (*Y*) into additive components, just as you have done in all the other ANOVAs covered.

Review of Oneway Within-Groups ANOVA Remember that when we presented the Oneway Within-Groups ANOVA we said that total variability could be divided into additive components. These components were

$$SS_Y = SS_{Y(A)} + SS_{Y(S)} + SS_{Y(AS)}$$

In addition, we said that the error variability from a between-groups analysis was actually the sum of these latter two components. That is,

$$SS_{Y(S/A)} = SS_{Y(S)} + SS_{Y(AS)}$$

Finally, we noted that whether we computed a between-groups analysis or a within-groups analysis two terms remained unchanged: total variability (SS_Y) and treatment variability (SS_A).

Extension to Mixed Designs   Now we want to extend this logic to a mixed design with one within-groups and one between-groups factor. If one were to analyze this design incorrectly as a Twoway Between-Groups ANOVA, one would get the following additive components:

$$SS_Y = SS_{Y(A)} + SS_{Y(B)} + SS_{Y(AB)} + SS_{Y(S/AB)}.$$

What about the sums of squares in a mixed design?

In a factorial design, SS_Y is the same whether you treat the data correctly as a mixed design or incorrectly as only a between-groups design.

The treatment factors $SS_{Y(A)}$, $SS_{Y(B)}$, and $SS_{Y(AB)}$ are the same whether you treat the data correctly as a mixed design or incorrectly as only a between-groups design.

However, the error term from the between-groups design ($SS_{Y(S/AB)}$) is partitioned by the mixed design into two additive components:

$$SS_{Y(S/AB)} = SS_{Y(S/B)} + SS_{Y(AS/B)}$$

Use $SS_{Y(S/B)}$ to form the error term for testing the between-groups factor (B).
Use $SS_{Y(AS/B)}$ to form the error term for testing the within-groups factor A and the $A \times B$ interaction.

> **Between groups design:** $SS_Y = SS_{Y(A)} + SS_{Y(B)} + SS_{Y(AB)} + \mathbf{SS_{Y(S/AB)}}$
>
> **Mixed design:** $SS_Y = SS_{Y(A)} + SS_{Y(B)} + SS_{Y(AB)} + \mathbf{SS_{Y(S/B)}} + \mathbf{SS_{Y(AS/B)}}$

Why Two Error Terms?   One error term is needed in a mixed design for testing the between-groups factor where subjects are randomly assigned to the levels of factor B. In experiment 3 of the Phonics Tonics scenario, Factor B is Setting (Home, School). As in a purely between-groups design, an error term is needed in a mixed design that represents variability within groups averaged across levels of the between-groups factor.

A second error term is needed in a mixed design for testing the within-groups factor (and the interaction term) where subjects are tested repeatedly across levels of factor A. In experiment 3, Factor A is Testing (Pretest, Posttest, and Delayed Posttest). As in a purely within-groups design, an error term is needed in a mixed design that represents the variability of subjects across the levels of the within-groups factor. Furthermore, one also has to take into account that there are two groups of subjects.

Computational Procedures for the Twoway Mixed Design ANOVA

The computational formulas from Chapter 11 can be used to compute the total sums of squares and the sums of squares for the main effects and interaction in a twoway mixed design. To help you perform the calculations, two tables of means have been created. Table 12.6 contains the means for factors A and B in combination. See Figure 12.1 for a plot of these means. Table 12.7 contains the means for factor B and subjects (S) in combination. Each subject's mean score is the average of all three testings. Remember that the raw data are given in Table 12.1c.

The total sum of squares is the following:

(Equation 11.2) $$SS_Y = \sum_1^A \sum_1^B \sum_1^n (Y_i - \overline{Y})^2 = \sum_1^N (Y_i - \overline{Y})^2$$
$$= (14 - 13)^2 + (9 - 13)^2 + \cdots + (16 - 13)^2 + (12 - 13)^2$$
$$= 772.00$$

TABLE 12.6 Means for Testing (A) and Setting (B): AB Matrix

	Pretest (A_1)	Posttest (A_2)	Delayed Test (A_3)	Mean
Home (B_1)	8.00	15.00	10.00	11.00
School (B_2)	10.00	17.00	18.00	15.00
Mean	9.00	16.00	14.00	13.00

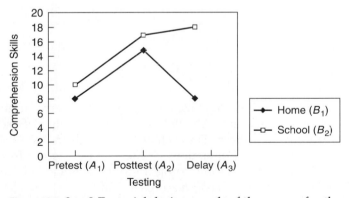

Figure 12.1 3×2 Factorial design graph of the means for the effects of testing (A) and setting (B) on composition skills (Y)

TABLE 12.7 Means for Setting (B) and Subjects (S): BS Matrix

	Subjects					Mean
Home (B_1)	$S_1 = 15.67$	$S_2 = 12.67$	$S_3 = 11.33$	$S_4 = 8.67$	$S_5 = 6.67$	11.00
School (B_2)	$S_6 = 19.67$	$S_7 = 17.33$	$S_8 = 15.33$	$S_9 = 12.00$	$S_{10} = 10.67$	15.00

The sum of squares for factor *A* is the following:

$$\textbf{(Equation 11.3) } SS_{Y(A)} = nB \sum_{1}^{A} (\overline{Y}_A - \overline{Y})^2$$

$$= (5)(2)[(9 - 13)^2 + (16 - 13)^2 + (14 - 13)^2] = 260.00$$

The sum of squares for factor *B* is the following:

$$\textbf{(Equation 11.4) } SS_{Y(B)} = nA \sum_{1}^{B} (\overline{Y}_B - \overline{Y})^2$$

$$= (5)(3)[(11 - 13)^2 + (15 - 13)^2] = 120.00$$

The sum of squares for *A* × *B* interaction is the following:

$$\textbf{(Equation 11.5) } SS_{Y(AB)} = n \sum_{1}^{A} \sum_{1}^{B} (\overline{Y}_{AB} - \overline{Y}_A - \overline{Y}_B + \overline{Y})^2$$

$$= (5)[(8 - 11 - 9 + 13)^2 + (10 - 15 - 9 + 13)^2$$

$$+ \cdots + (10 - 11 - 14 + 13)^2 + (18 - 15 - 14 + 13)^2$$

$$= 60.00$$

However the error term from the Twoway Between-Groups ANOVA must be partitioned into two additive components. Each component will be an error term in the mixed design:

$$SS_{Y(S/AB)} = \sum_{1}^{A} \sum_{1}^{B} \sum_{1}^{n} (Y_i - \overline{Y}_{AB})^2 = ? + ?$$

Before we get to the partitioning, take a close look at the error term $SS_{Y(S/AB)}$ from the Factorial Between-Groups ANOVA. It is the variability of each subject from his or her respective cell mean. For each of the six cells in the 3 × 2 factorial design, find the sum of squared deviations of each subject's score from the cell mean. For each cell mean there are five subject scores. There are six cell means. There are, therefore, 30 squared deviation scores to sum:

$$SS_{Y(S/AB)} = [(14 - 8)^2 + (9 - 8)^2 + \cdots + (16 - 18)^2 + (12 - 18)^2] = 332.00$$

How does one partition this variability and calculate the two error terms for the mixed design?

The Between-Groups Error Term   You will need to find the error term for the between-groups factor *B* (Setting) where, across levels of the factor, scores are assumed to be *independent*. That is, you want to compute the variability between the subjects in each level of the between-groups treatment B (Setting), on the one hand, while ignoring the variability within the subjects as reflected in the levels of the within-groups treatment factor A (Testing), on the other hand.

But how can you "ignore" any variability across levels of the within-groups factor A (Testing)? Using each subject's mean response across levels of the within-groups factor A (Testing) excludes the unwanted variability. The BS matrix of means in Table 12.7 represents only variability *between* subjects and not variability *within* subjects.

You can, therefore, compute a **between-groups error term** using the BS matrix of means by doing the following:

1. Find the squared deviations of each subject's mean score from the group mean score of the appropriate level of the between-groups factor.
2. Add these deviation scores together, then multiply by A, the levels of the within-groups factor.

The between-groups error term is the following:

Equation 12.26:
$$SS_{Y(S/B)} = A \sum_{1}^{B} \sum_{1}^{n} (\overline{Y}_{BS} - \overline{Y}_B)^2$$

$$= 3[(15.67 - 11.00)^2 + (12.67 - 11.00)^2$$
$$+ \cdots + (12.00 - 15.00)^2 - (10.67 - 15.00)^2]$$
$$= 316.67$$

The Within-Groups Error Term

You now need to find the error term for the within-groups factor A (Testing) where, across levels of the factor, scores are assumed to be *dependent*. This will also be the error term for testing the $A \times B$ interaction.

Think back to how the dependency problem was handled when you were dealing with a within-groups factor alone. You "removed" the consistency among subjects across levels of the repeated factor and concentrated on the inconsistency. This inconsistency was the interaction of the within-groups treatment with the subjects.

The following is the error term for a Oneway Within-Groups ANOVA:

(Equation 12.15)
$$SS_{Y(AS)} = \sum_{1}^{A} \sum_{1}^{n} (Y - \overline{Y}_S - \overline{Y}_A + \overline{Y})^2$$

The sum of squares for the error term for the within-groups factor in a mixed design is very similar. One also computes the sum of squares for an interaction, but the calculation is somewhat more elaborate.

Think of the sum of squares as having two parts. In the first part, compute the sum of squares for the first level of the between-groups factor (B_1). In the second part, compute the sum of squares for the second level of the between-groups factor (B_2). Then add both parts together.

In effect, you are calculating a **within-groups error term** for each level of the between-groups factor B (Setting). (For example, note below that the mean of the appropriate level of B is added back into the deviation score.)

The within-groups error term is the following:

$$\text{Equation 12.27: } SS_{Y(AS/B)} = \sum_1^A \sum_1^B \sum_1^n (Y - \overline{Y}_{AB} - \overline{Y}_{BS} + \overline{Y}_B)^2$$

$$= (14.00 - 8.00 - 15.67 + 11.00)^2$$
$$+ (9.00 - 8.00 - 12.67 + 11.00)^2$$
$$+ \cdots + (16.00 - 18.00 - 12.00 + 15.00)^2$$
$$+ (12.00 - 18.00 - 10.67 + 15.00)^2$$
$$= 15.33$$

Computational check:

$$SS_{Y(S/AB)} = SS_{Y(S/B)} + SS_{Y(AS/B)}$$
$$332.00 = 316.67 + 15.33$$

Degrees of Freedom

Equation 12.28: For the within-groups treatment: $\text{df}_A = A - 1$

Equation 12:29: For the between-groups treatment: $\text{df}_B = B - 1$

Equation 12.30: For the $A \times B$ interaction: $\text{df}_{AB} = (A - 1)(B - 1)$

Equation 12.31: For the between-groups error term: $\text{df}_{(S/B)} = B(n - 1)$

Equation 12.32: For the within-groups error term: $\text{df}_{(AS/B)} = B(A - 1)(n - 1)$

Total $\text{df} = ABn - 1$

Mean Squares

Equation 12.33: $MS_{Y(A)} = SS_{Y(A)}/\text{df}_A$

Equation 12.34: $MS_{Y(B)} = SS_{Y(B)}/\text{df}_B$

Equation 12.35: $MS_{Y(AB)} = SS_{Y(AB)}/\text{df}_{AB}$

Equation 12.36: $MS_{Y(S/B)} = SS_{Y(S/B)}/\text{df}_{S/B}$

Equation 12.37: $MS_{Y(AS/B)} = SS_{Y(AS/B)}/\text{df}_{AS/B}$

TABLE 12.8 3 × 2 Mixed Design ANOVA Summary Table: Phonics Tonics Experiment 3					
Source	SS	df	MS	F	p
Seting (B)	120.00	1	120.00	3.03	.120
Error (S/B)	316.67	8	39.58		
Tests (A)	260.00	2	130.00	135.65	<.01
Tests (A) × Set (B)	60.00	2	30.00	31.30	<.01
Error (AS/B)	15.33	16	0.96		
Total	772.00	29			

F-Ratios

$$\text{Equation 12.38: } MS_{Y(A)}/MS_{Y(AS/B)}$$

$$\text{Equation 12.39: } MS_{Y(B)}/MS_{Y(S/B)}$$

$$\text{Equation 12.40: } MS_{Y(AB)}/MS_{Y(AS/B)}$$

See Table 12.8 for an example of the Mixed-Design ANOVA Summary Table.

The results of the analysis of experiment 3 (see Table 12.8) reveal that there is a significant main effect of Testing. Composition scores vary, depending on the time students completed the tests. While the Setting main effect failed to reach significance, there was a significant Setting by Testing interaction. Differences in Skill scores over time varied according to whether students studied at home or at school.

PUTTING IT ALL TOGETHER

This chapter showed how to analyze data from correlated or matched samples. Most frequently, these designs involve repeated measures in which the same participants provide a response on the dependent variable on more than one occasion. By comparing a simple between-groups design with a simple within-groups design, the similarities and differences between the two were shown.

The advantages of within-groups designs are both practical and statistical. The researcher does not need to engage additional subjects for each new treatment condition. Error variability is reduced in within-groups designs, and statistical power is increased.

There is, under certain circumstances, the practical disadvantage of requiring more of individual participants. The most serious disadvantage lies in the weaknesses of the design to control for threats to internal and external validity. However, under certain circumstances, counterbalancing may be used to reduce threats to internal validity.

The correlated samples *t*-test removes the dependency in subjects' scores, thereby reducing the size of the standard error used in the denominator of the *t*-ratio. Two ways were presented of computing the correlated samples *t*-test: the raw score method and the difference score method. Ways to compute effect sizes for two correlated samples were shown with a correction to make the effects comparable to those from between-groups designs, where appropriate.

It is also important to remove the dependency among scores in a Oneway Within-Groups ANOVA. The partitioning of total variability into three additive components was illustrated: (1) variability explained by the treatment, (2) variability explained by subjects, and (3) variability explained by the interaction of the treatment and subjects. Treatment variability is identical to what one would encounter in a between-groups design. However, the error term for the between-groups design is now subdivided for the within-groups design. Only the variability explained by the interaction of subjects and the treatment is used to test the treatment effect.

The circularity assumption in within-groups designs was considered. One assumes that the degree of the dependency among subjects does not change over levels of the within-groups treatment. This is a critical assumption, and so a three-stage approach was offered to test the omnibus effect of the treatment. Also presented were procedures for multiple comparisons when the assumption was met and when it was violated.

The final section of the chapter looked at two-way Factorial designs in which one factor was a within-groups factor and the other factor was a between-groups one. In this section it was shown how the two main effect and interaction sums of squares were computed just like a factorial between-groups ANOVA. The difference is in the way the between-groups error term is partitioned into additive components. For the mixed design, one error term is computed for the between-groups factor and a second error term is computed for the within-groups factor and the interaction.

Correlated Samples *t*-Test

Raw Score Method   The raw score formula for computing the correlated samples *t*-test is

$$\text{Equation 12.1: } t_C = \frac{\overline{Y}_{A1} - \overline{Y}_{A2}}{\sqrt{\dfrac{s_{A1}^2}{n_{A1}} + \dfrac{s_{A2}^2}{n_{A2}} - \left(2r\dfrac{s_{A1}}{\sqrt{n_{A1}}}\dfrac{s_{A2}}{\sqrt{n_{A2}}}\right)}}$$

This is equivalent to

$$\text{Equation 12.2: } t_C = \frac{\overline{Y}_{A1} - \overline{Y}_{A2}}{\sqrt{\dfrac{\dfrac{\sum (Y_{iA1} - \overline{Y}_{A1})^2}{(n_{A1} - 1)}}{n_{A1}} + \dfrac{\dfrac{\sum (Y_{iA2} - \overline{Y}_{A2})^2}{(n_{A2} - 1)}}{n_{A2}} - \left(2r\dfrac{s_{A1}}{\sqrt{n_{A1}}}\dfrac{s_{A2}}{\sqrt{n_{A2}}}\right)}}$$

and also to

$$\text{Equation 12.3: } t_C = \frac{\overline{Y}_{A1} - \overline{Y}_{A2}}{s_C} \quad \text{where}$$

$$\text{Equation 12.4: } s_C = \sqrt{\frac{s_{A1}^2}{n_{A1}} + \frac{s_{A2}^2}{n_{A2}} - \left(2r\frac{s_{A1}}{\sqrt{n_{A1}}}\frac{s_{A2}}{\sqrt{n_{A2}}}\right)}$$

Equation 12.5: $\text{df} = n - 1$ where n is the number of paired observations.

The two-sided confidence interval for a nondirectional alternative hypothesis is

$$\text{Equation 12.6: } \overline{Y}_D - t_{1-\alpha/2}s_C \text{ and } \overline{Y}_D + t_{1-\alpha/2}s_C$$

The one-sided confidence interval for a one-tailed *positive* direction alternative hypothesis is

$$\text{Equation 12.7: } \overline{Y}_D - t_{1-\alpha}s_C$$

The one-sided confidence interval for a one-tailed *negative* direction alternative hypothesis is

$$\text{Equation 12.8: } \overline{Y}_D + t_{1-\alpha}s_C$$

Difference Score Method The standard error of the individual difference score is

$$\text{Equation 12.9: } s_{\text{ID}} = \frac{s_{A1-A2}}{\sqrt{n_{A1-A2}}} = \frac{\sqrt{\dfrac{\sum (Y_{A1-A2} - \overline{Y}_{A1-A2})^2}{n_{A1-A2} - 1}}}{\sqrt{n_{A1-A2}}}$$

The *t*-tests for correlated samples individual difference score method is

$$\text{Equation 12.10: } t_C = \frac{\overline{Y}_{A1-A2}}{s_{\text{ID}}}$$

This is equivalent to

$$\text{Equation 12.11: } t_C = \frac{\overline{Y}_{A1-A2}}{\dfrac{s_{A1-A2}}{\sqrt{n_{A1-A2}}}}$$

and to

$$\text{Equation 12.12: } t_C = \frac{\overline{Y}_{A1-A2}}{\dfrac{\sqrt{\sum (Y_{A1-A2} - \overline{Y}_{A1-A2})^2}}{\dfrac{n_{A1-A2} - 1}{\sqrt{n_{A1-A2}}}}}$$

The degrees of freedom for both methods is

Equation 12.5: df $= n - 1$,   where n is the number of paired observations.

Effect Size and Power   For two correlated samples, the formula for the calculation of the effect size is

$$\text{Equation 12.13: } d_C = \frac{\overline{Y}_{A1} - \overline{Y}_{A2}}{s_{A1-A2}}$$

If a comparison of the effect sizes from two or more studies of different designs is desired, the researcher may account for design differences by either of the following methods:

1. Compute all effect sizes as if the data were drawn from two independent samples.
2. If only difference scores are available, multiply d_C by $\sqrt{2(1 - r)}$, where r is the correlation between measures 1 and 2, to get an approximation of d (Cohen, 1988).

Power   By substituting s_C for s_D, you can use the steps in Textbox 7.6 and explained in Chapter 7 to estimate power when dealing with two dependent samples:

1. Estimate the population mean difference for the alternative sampling distribution $(\overline{Y}_{DA})$.
2. Estimate the standard error of the alternative sampling distribution (s_{CA}).
3. Find the critical value for the null sampling distribution and convert it to a raw score (CV_R).
4. Compute z_A from CV_R.
5. Find β and power $(1 - \beta)$ by finding the exact probability of z_A.

Oneway Within-Groups ANOVA

Computational Procedures   Total variability is

$$\text{(Equation 9.3) } SS_Y = \sum_{1}^{A} \sum_{1}^{n} (Y_i - \overline{Y})^2 = \sum_{1}^{N} (Y_i - \overline{Y})^2$$

Between-groups variability is

$$\text{(Equation 9.4) } SS_{Y(A)} = \sum_{1}^{A} n_A (\bar{Y}_A - \bar{Y})^2$$

Subject variability is

$$\text{Equation 12.14: } SS_{Y(S)} = A \sum_{1}^{n} (\bar{Y}_S - \bar{Y})^2$$

Interaction of subjects and treatment variability (error term) is

$$\text{Equation 12.15: } SS_{Y(AS)} = \sum_{1}^{A} \sum_{1}^{n} (Y - \bar{Y}_S - \bar{Y}_\ell + \bar{Y})^2$$

Degrees of Freedom

Equation 12.16: For the treatment: $df_A = A - 1$

Equation 12.17: For subjects within groups: $df_{S/A} = (n - 1)A$ or $N - A$

Equation 12.18: For subjects: $df_S = n - 1$

Equation 12.19: For the AS interaction: $df_{AS} = (A - 1)(n - 1)$

Mean Squares

Equation 12.20: $MS_{Y(A)} = SS_{Y(A)} / df_A$

Equation 12.21: $MS_{Y(AS)} = SS_{Y(AS)} / df_{AS}$

F-Ratio

Equation 12.22: $MS_{Y(A)} / MS_{Y(AS)}$

Dealing with Violations of the Circularity Assumption The recommended procedure is to follow a three-step strategy:

1. Begin by analyzing the data in the regular manner. Find the critical *F*-value using the complete degrees of freedom. *Stop* if the calculated value of *F* is not significant. Do not proceed further. Proceed to step 2 only if the calculated value is significant.
2. Carry out the Geisser-Greenhouse (lower-bound) correction using reduced degrees of freedom where $df_A = 1.0$ and $df_{AS} = n - 1$. Find the critical *F*-value for $df = 1$, $n - 1$ at the alpha value you have selected. *Stop* if the calculated value is significant in this situation. There is no need to proceed further; the

finding is significant. Proceed to step 3 only if the calculated value is now not significant.

3. Carry out the Huynh-Feldt (epsilon) correction using reduced degrees of freedom. Epsilon is usually a fraction less than 1, and so degrees of freedom are reduced.

$$df_A = \varepsilon(A - 1)$$

$$df_{AS} = \varepsilon(A - 1)(n - 1)$$

Find the critical F-value using the reduced degrees of freedom and compare it to the calculated value. Accept these results as *the* test of significance.

Computational Procedures for Planned Comparisons (Circularity Assumption Is Met)   The sum of squares for a planned comparison is

$$\textbf{(Equation 10.5) } SS_{Y(p)} = \frac{n(p)^2}{\sum\limits_{1}^{A} c_A^2} \qquad \text{where } p = \sum\limits_{1}^{A} c_A \overline{Y}_A$$

The mean squares for a planned comparison is

$$\textbf{(Equation 10.6) } MS_{Y(p)} = SS_{Y(p)}/df_p = SS_{Y(p)}$$

(Remember that each comparison has only one numerator df.)

However, the denominator of the F-ratio is not $MS_{Y(S/A)}$, but $MS_{Y(AS)}$. Therefore, the F-ratio for a planned comparison is:

$$\textbf{Equation 12.23: } F_p = MS_{Y(p)}/MS_{Y(AS)}, \; df_p = 1, \; df_{AS} = (A - 1)(n - 1)$$

Computational Procedures for Post Hoc Comparisons (Circularity Assumption Is Met)   The *calculated* values for each comparison are computed as above (see Equation 12.23).

To find the critical value for Tukey's HSD method for making all pairwise comparisons:

$$\textbf{(Equation 10.9) } F_T = \frac{(q_T)^2}{2}$$

where q_T is an entry in the Studentized range distribution. See Appendix F.

To find the correct value of q_T you need the following:

df_{AS}, which is $(A - 1)(n - 1)$

k, the number of treatment means ($k = A$)

α_{FW}, alpha for the familywise Type I error selected, which is usually .05 or .01

To find the critical value for Scheffé's S method (F_S) for making all possible comparisons:

Equation 12.24: $F_S = (a - 1)F (\text{df}_A, \text{df}_{AS})$

Computational Procedures for Multiple Comparisons (Circularity Assumption Is Not Met)
When the circularity assumption is not met, each simple or complex comparison will have its own error term, whether comparisons are planned or post hoc. To find each error term, compute the Oneway Within-Groups ANOVA for the data involved in the comparison only. For pairwise comparisons, this computation is straightforward. For complex comparisons, the data should be combined according to the contrast weights assigned.

Effect Size and Power
Effect sizes for two groups:

To find the effect size for two correlated samples (see Equation 12.13), it is easiest to first find the individual difference scores and to compute the standard deviation of the individual difference scores.

For general effect sizes:

$$\textbf{(Equation 9.11) } R^2 = \frac{SS_{Y(A)}}{SS_Y}$$

$$\textbf{(Equation 9.12) } f = \sqrt{\frac{R^2}{1 - R^2}}$$

$$\textbf{Equation 12.25: } \omega^2 = \frac{SS_{Y(A)} - (a - 1)MS_{Y(AS)}}{SS_Y + MS_{Y(AS)}}$$

Power
Cohen (1988) provides power tables for the ANOVA using f. When the dependency among the within-groups scores is high, the use of f provides a conservative estimate of power.

Mixed Designs

Total variability is

$$\textbf{(Equation 11.2) } SS_Y = \sum_1^A \sum_1^B \sum_1^n (Y_i - \overline{Y})^2 = \sum_1^N (Y_i - \overline{Y})^2$$

Variability due to A is

$$\textbf{(Equation 11.3) } SS_{Y(A)} = nB \sum_1^A (\overline{Y}_A - \overline{Y})^2$$

Variability due to B is

$$\textbf{(Equation 11.4) } SS_{Y(B)} = nA \sum_1^B (\overline{Y}_B - \overline{Y})^2$$

Variability due to the *AB* interaction is

$$\text{(Equation 11.5) } SS_{Y(AB)} = n \sum_1^A \sum_1^B (\overline{Y}_{AB} - \overline{Y}_A - \overline{Y}_B + \overline{Y})^2$$

Variability due to subjects within *B* is

$$\text{Equation 12.26: } SS_{Y(S/B)} = A \sum_1^B \sum_1^n (\overline{Y}_{BS} - \overline{Y}_B)^2$$

Variability for the *AS* interaction within *B* is

$$\text{Equation 12.27: } SS_{Y(AS/B)} = \sum_1^A \sum_1^B \sum_1^n (Y - \overline{Y}_{AB} - \overline{Y}_{BS} + \overline{Y}_B)^2$$

Degrees of Freedom

Equation 12.28: For the within-groups treatment: $df_A = A - 1$

Equation 12.29: For the between-groups treatment: $df_B = B - 1$

Equation 12.30: For the $A \times B$ interaction: $df_{AB} = (A - 1)(B - 1)$

Equation 12.31: For the between-groups error term: $df_{(S/B)} = B(n - 1)$

Equation 12.32: For the within-groups error term: $df_{(AS/B)} = B(A - 1)(n - 1)$

Mean Squares

Equation 12.33: $MS_{Y(A)} = SS_{Y(A)}/df_A$

Equation 12.34: $MS_{Y(B)} = SS_{Y(B)}/df_B$

Equation 12.35: $MS_{Y(AB)} = SS_{Y(AB)}/df_{AB}$

Equation 12.36: $MS_{Y(S/B)} = SS_{Y(S/B)}/df_{S/B}$

Equation 12.37: $MS_{Y(AS/B)} = SS_{Y(AS/B)}/df_{AS/B}$

F-Ratios

Equation 12.38: $MS_{Y(A)}/MS_{Y(AS/B)}$

Equation 12.39: $MS_{Y(B)}/MS_{Y(S/B)}$

Equation 12.40: $MS_{Y(AB)}/MS_{Y(AS/B)}$

Textbox 12.9

Mixed ANOVA: Cooperation and Dominance between Girls and Boys

From preschool age, gender influences the social behavior of children. Girls prefer to play with girls and boys prefer to play with boys. Neppl and Murray (1997) investigated social dominance and play patterns among female dyad, mixed dyad (boys tasks), and mixed dyad (girls tasks) preschool children. Children were given free play with stereotypically masculine play materials or stereotypically feminine play materials. Participants were 48 children who were between four and five years of age. Children's play was coded for Social Dominance, Social Play Level, and Cognitive Play Level (Functional, Constructive, Dramatic, and Nonplay).

The researchers conducted a Groups (3) × Task (2) mixed ANOVA on several outcomes. There was a significant Groups × Task interaction effect, $F(2, 45) = 6.60$, $p < .05$, for aspects of social dominance. In mixed-gender dyads, girls refused to follow boys' leads when engaged in feminine tasks, while boys in mixed-sex dyads refused to follow girls' leads during masculine activities.

For social play there was a significant main effect for Group, $F(2, 45) = 21.01$, $p < .001$. Post hoc comparisons showed that female dyad groups had the highest levels of cooperative play. There was also more cooperative play during feminine tasks compared to masculine tasks for all three groups: $F(1, 45) = 5.23$, $p < .05$.

Three of the four measures of cognitive play level had significant Group effects: Functional Play Levels, $F(2, 45) = 3.79$, $p < .05$; Constructive Play Levels, $F(2, 45) = 4.73$, $p < .05$; and Dramatic Play Levels, $F(2, 45) = 4.65$, $p < .05$. The Group × Task Interaction effect was also significant for Functional Play Levels, $F(2, 45) = 3.63$, $p < .05$, and for Dramatic Play Levels, $F(2, 45) = 3.85$, $p < .05$. Post hoc comparisons showed that boys had higher levels of functional play during feminine activities and that boys sometimes engaged in less constructive play than girls. Finally, girls were more likely to engage in dramatic play in the feminine activities while boys exhibited more dramatic play in the masculine activities.

Neppl and Murray (1997) offer several implications of the findings for classroom settings. For example, if more cooperative play is desired, it will most likely come from same-sex dyads. If more dramatic play is desired, it will be seen for girls during feminine activities and for boys during masculine activities.

KEY TERMS

Within-groups designs

Repeated measures designs

Counterbalancing

Multiple-x interference

Carryover effects

Difference or gain scores

Circularity assumption

Between-groups error term

Within-groups error term

Mixed designs

REFERENCES

Campbell, D. T., & Stanley, J. C. (1966). *Experimental and quasi-experimental designs for research*. Chicago, IL: Rand McNally. (First appeared in: Gage, N. L. (ed.). *Handbook of research on teaching*. 1963. Chicago, IL: Rand McNally).

Cohen, J., (1988). *Statistical power analysis for the behavioral sciences.* (2nd ed.). Hillsdale, NJ: Lawrence Erlbaum Associates.

Geisser, S., & Greenhouse, S. W. (1958). An extension of Box's results on the use of the *F* distribution in multivariate analysis. *Annals of Mathematical Statistics, 29,* 891–995.

Huynh, H., & Feldt, L. S. (1970). Conditions under which mean square ratios in repeated measures have exact *F* distributions. *Journal of the American Statistical Association, 65,* 1582–1589.

Mauchley, J. W. (1940). Significance tests for sphericity of a normal *n*-variate distribution. *Annals of Mathematical Science, 11,* 204–209.

Neppl, T. K., & Murray, A. D. (1997). Social dominance and play patterns among preschoolers: Gender comparisons. *Sex Roles: A Journal of Research, 36,* 5–6, 381–394.

PROBLEMS

Questions

Section 1   Conceptual

12.1. How do within-groups designs primarily differ from the between-groups designs covered in the text?

12.2. What assumption of between-groups designs is not an assumption of within-groups designs? What assumption of within-groups designs is not an assumption of between-groups designs?

12.3. What are the primary advantages of within-groups designs over between-groups designs?

12.4. What are the primary disadvantages of within-groups designs over between-groups designs?

12.5. What is counterbalancing and why is it used?

12.6. What is a mixed design? Provide a simple example of a mixed design.

12.7. Under what condition will an independent samples *t*-test and a dependent samples *t*-test provide the same results for a given set of data?

12.8. In a Oneway between-groups design, total variability = between-groups variability + within-groups variability. How does this change in a Oneway within-groups design?

12.9. The procedures for dealing with violations of the circularity assumption involve reducing the degrees of freedom associated with the test. Why is this the case?

12.10. Mixed designs are considered to be complex. Why is this the case?

Section 2   Numerical

12.11. Five subjects were involved in a pretest–posttest study. Their respective scores were as follows (starting with the first subject):

Pretest: 72, 81, 69, 75, 79

Posttest: 76, 85, 74, 80, 84

Use the raw-score method for the correlated samples *t*-test to determine if there is a significant difference between the pretest and posttest scores at

$\alpha = .05$. Use the individual difference score method for the correlated samples t-test to determine if there is a significant difference between the pretest and posttest scores at $\alpha = .05$.

12.12. Six subjects were involved in a pretest–posttest study. Their respective scores were as follows (starting with the first subject):

Pretest: 16, 14, 17, 19, 21, 15

Posttest: 12, 19, 18, 19, 22, 13

Use the raw-score method for the correlated samples t-test to determine if there is a significant difference between the pretest and posttest scores at $\alpha = .05$. Determine the two-sided 95% confidence interval for the estimated mean difference.

12.13. Seven subjects are exposed to three different cognitive development strategies. After each strategy the subjects are asked to complete a task. The time, in minutes, to complete the task is measured. The tasks are equivalent. The time in minutes for each subject on each task was as follows:

Strategy 1: 9, 10, 10, 12, 8, 9, 7

Strategy 2: 8, 11, 11, 12, 9, 11, 9

Strategy 3: 11, 13, 9, 13, 10, 10, 12

Assume that circularity is not a problem. Test the null hypothesis H_0: $\mu_{A1} = \mu_{A2} = \mu_{A3}$ at $\alpha = .05$. If appropriate, conduct a post hoc comparison to determine whether or not a difference exists between strategy 1 and strategy 2 at $\alpha = .05$.

12.14. Eight subjects are part of a given study where a pretest, posttest, and delayed posttest are measured. The measurement is a score on a test. The test scores for each subject on each task were as follows:

Pretest: 26, 28, 29, 32, 24, 30, 33, 37

Posttest: 25, 33, 31, 38, 23, 34, 36, 39

Delayed posttest: 22, 27, 30, 36, 23, 31, 29, 33

Assume that circularity is not a problem. Test the null hypothesis H_0: $\mu_{A1} = \mu_{A2} = \mu_{A3}$ at $\alpha = .05$. If appropriate, conduct a post hoc comparison to determine whether or not a difference exists between the pretest and the combination of the posttest and delayed posttest at $\alpha = .05$.

12.15. Fifteen subjects are part of a study in which three different teaching strategies are examined. The 15 subjects are randomly assigned to each of the three groups. Each subject is given an immediate and delayed posttest. The scores for each subject are shown below. Prepare an ANOVA Summary Table for the above data. Assume that circularity is not a problem.

Immediate posttest:

Strategy 1: 11, 13, 16, 10, 14

Strategy 2: 10, 14, 16, 11, 17

Strategy 3: 14, 19, 21, 22, 23

Delayed posttest:

Strategy 1: 9, 11, 13, 13, 12

Strategy 2: 10, 13, 13, 11, 12

Strategy 3: 13, 18, 19, 20, 24

12.16. Ten subjects are part of a study in which two different drugs are being tested. The 10 subjects are randomly assigned to the two groups. Each subject's reactions to the drug are measured with a blood test right after the drug is taken and again 24 hours later. The blood test measures for each subject are shown below. Prepare an ANOVA Summary Table for the data. Assume that circularity is not a problem.

Immediate:

Drug 1: 107, 118, 98, 124, 115

Drug 2: 98, 95, 103, 111, 92

24-hour delay:

Drug 1: 118, 125, 112, 133, 142

Drug 2: 110, 121, 116, 121, 103

12.17. The following Within-Groups ANOVA Summary Table was generated from a correlated dataset. Assuming that the dataset was not correlated, prepare the Between-Groups ANOVA Summary Table that would be generated from the same data.

Source	SS	df	MS	F	p
Treatments (A)	100.00	2	50.00	35.98	$<.05$
Subjects (S)	120.00	9	13.33		
Error (AS)	25.00	18	1.39		
Total	245.00	29			

13
chapter

Determining the Relationship Between Two Variables

Correlation

OVERVIEW

In the last several chapters, various forms of the Analysis of Variance (ANOVA) were highlighted. The ANOVA statistical techniques all have in common the analysis of the variability in a single dependent measure. But they vary in terms of the number (one or more) and the nature (between groups or within groups) of the independent variable(s) used to explain the variability. Furthermore, ANOVA techniques are often associated with experimental designs in which the researcher manipulates or varies the values of the independent variable.

In this chapter, the correlation coefficient will be examined as a statistical tool to summarize the extent to which two variables are related. It can be used to measure the degree to which two outcome measures, two predictor variables, or a predictor and an outcome measure are related. Yes, a correlation coefficient is a descriptive statistic. But it can be more. It can also be used for inferential purposes, as in, "Is this correlation significant?"

We will be taking a close look at some of the basic issues in correlation. Addressed will be questions such as the following:

1. What are different ways to interpret the correlation between two variables?
2. How does one distinguish between a Oneway ANOVA and a correlation?
3. What do different size correlations look like when the data are plotted?
4. What is the difference between the z-score and covariation methods?
5. What are the inferential uses of the correlation coefficient?
6. How does one find the strength of association for r?
7. What are important cautions and limitations?

As usual, the chapter begins with a brief scenario. See Textbox 13.1 for the description of a study exploring the relationship between parental involvement and children's reading achievement.

Textbox 13.1

Scenario: Parental Performance

There are great demands placed on families these days. In two-parent families, it is not unusual for both parents to be working. In one-parent families, it is seldom that a single parent does not work. More than ever, parents appear to be occupied with earning a living to support themselves and their children. In doing so, they often do not have ample time to spend with their offspring. For this and other reasons, researchers have become increasingly interested in the relationship between parental involvement with children and performance at school.

To begin exploring this issue, you conduct a small pilot study to investigate the relationship between parental involvement and the reading achievement of young children. To do so, you ask a group of five single mothers with children in first grade to record the number of hours spent reading and doing homework with their child in the past month. Each parent and the school also permits you to record for analysis the results of the end-of-month reading test that summarizes for each child the number of key concepts understood. The results are found in Table 13.1.

TABLE 13.1 Monthly Concept Attainment Scores (*Y*) and Hours of Parental Involvement (*A*)

Student	Parental Involvement (A) (Hours Spent)	Concept Attainment (Y) (Reading Test Score)
John	3	11
Mary	1	7
Jessica	4	15
Allison	5	13
Burt	2	9

CORRELATION BASICS

You will use a statistical technique called the **Pearson product moment correlation** to summarize the **degree of linear relationship** between two variables, such as hours of parental involvement (*A*) and monthly concept attainment scores (*Y*). You will also want to know whether the relationship between *A* and *Y* is significant.

There are many situations in which it is useful to know the extent to which two variables are linearly related. Questions about the correlation between two variables include: Is the amount of television viewing among children negatively related to academic test scores? Is self-concept correlated with school success? Which personality traits are correlated with job satisfaction? Are economic indices related to stock market trends?

Similarities with Other Research Situations

In the Parental Performance scenario, you probably noticed some things that make the scenario similar to research situations that have already been covered and some things that make the scenario different. What are the important similarities? There is an outcome measure here (Concept Attainment), and participants' scores on it have been measured. More importantly, there is an attempt to explain the variability in Concept Attainment scores by seeing whether the fluctuation or variability in Parental Involvement is related in any way. In other words, a rudimentary hypothesis has been formed that says that changes in one variable (Parental Involvement) are related to changes in a second variable (Concept Attainment Score).

Differences from Other Research Situations

What are the important differences? It should be clear that this scenario departs from others previously covered by not being a true experiment. There is no treatment under the control of the experimenter.

Variables Are Not Manipulated In particular, what you might like to describe as the independent variable—parental involvement—is not manipulated. It is merely a measured variable. Your hypothesis, then, should not be a *causal* hypothesis. You cannot know whether parental involvement causes a child's concept attainment to change. However, you can know whether parental involvement and concept attainment are related to each other. In other words, you can answer the question, "What is the *co-relation* between parental involvement and concept attainment?"

Right now, this may seem like a subtle distinction but it can be far from that, as you soon will understand more thoroughly. This distinction is so important, in fact, that researchers often do not use the same terms to refer to variables in experiments and variables in correlational investigations. These different terms help remind one of the important differences between these two research designs. For experiments, researchers are accustomed to using the terms *independent variable* and *dependent variable*. In correlational investigations the terms **predictor variable** and **outcome variable,** respectively, are used instead. In the Parental Performance scenario of Textbox 13.1, the predictor variable is Parental Involvement and the outcome variable is Concept Attainment.

Continuous Predictors Another important difference has to do with the values of the predictor variable in a correlational investigation as compared to the values of the independent variable in an experiment. In a correlational investigation, the predictor variable is a measured variable. It is often possible to measure many values of a predictor variable but usually quite impractical to manipulate more than just a few values of an independent variable. Thus, it is common to see a predictor variable that is continuous and an independent variable that is discrete. It is also common for the predictor variable to be on an interval, or ratio, scale of measurement.[1]

Naturalistic Inquiry   Correlational investigations are used in situations in which experimentation is impractical or impossible. For example, it may be impractical to conduct a true experiment when the treatment of interest is supposed to last for years or is highly disruptive to the participants' regular routines. It may be impossible to conduct a true experiment when the treatment of interest is expected to have a deleterious effect on participants' well-being. Because variables are not manipulated, only measured, correlational investigations can be more naturalistic forms of inquiry compared to experiments. They are often higher in external validity than experiments, and experiments are often higher in internal validity.

What We Call the Variables Is Not Important   In the Parental Performance scenario of Textbox 13.1, Parental Involvement (*A*) is the predictor variable and Concept Attainment (*Y*) is the outcome measure. But the use of the correlation coefficient is not limited to variables categorized in this way. It can be used to describe the relationship between any two continuous variables when measured on interval scales. It bears emphasizing that one can describe the correlation between two predictor variables, two outcome measures, and a predictor variable and an outcome measure.

A researcher, for example, might be interested in measuring the degree to which the frequency of physical exertion is related to overall psychological well-being. Or a researcher might need to know whether school achievement tests are correlated with standardized tests. Or a researcher might want to know whether drug dosage levels are related to the speed of patient recovery. In each of these examples, a correlation coefficient can be computed to describe the degree of linear relationship between two variables.

Making Causal Inferences   Remember, the statistical procedures that you employ do not "know" whether the numerical data available for analysis come from a true experiment, a quasi-experiment, or a correlational investigation. The inferential statistical tests only allow you to conclude with a certain degree of certainty whether the hypothesized relationship is a function of chance. The statistical tests do not themselves allow one to judge whether a causal inference is warranted.

Correlation and Causation

The major difference between an experimental study and a correlational study has to do especially with causal explanation. Because subjects are randomly assigned

---

[1]There are adaptations of the basic correlation to include predictor and outcome measures which are not continuous or use ordinal scales of measurement.

to conditions and the researcher controls what subjects are exposed to (e.g., experimental versus control conditions), extraneous influences are eliminated. In a true experiment, threats to internal validity do not operate as rival explanations to the influence of the treatment. This is the essence of experimental control.

Alternative Explanations   In a correlational study one knows that because variables are only measured and not manipulated, reverse variable and third-variable explanations of a phenomenon are possible. A **reverse variable explanation** reverses the direction of causal relationship. A **third-variable** or **rival explanation** means that an additional variable may be responsible for the relationship established between the two variables of interest.

For example, imagine you found that there was a correlation between the predictor variable, Parental Involvement (*A*), and the outcome variable, Concept Attainment (*Y*). How might this relationship be explained?

You might suspect that there was a causal link such that parental involvement helped children to improve their reading. Schematically, this can be represented as

$A \longrightarrow Y$ (the arrow indicates the direction of causality).

Reverse Variable Explanations   Possibly, parental involvement and a child's reading ability are related to each other in different ways. For example, a *reverse variable* explanation suggests the opposite direction for a causal relationship. Children with good reading ability prompt parents to spend more time reading with them, while children who struggle tend not to want, or encourage, parental involvement. Schematically, this *reverse variable* explanation can be represented as

Third-Variable Explanations   Yet another explanation of the relationship between parental involvement and a child's reading ability focuses on a *third variable* as the causal agent. For example, explicit encouragement from teachers (*B*) may cause *both* greater parental involvement and greater concept attainment by students. Schematically, this *third-variable* explanation can be represented as

Uncertain Conclusions   In a basic correlational study, a researcher may be frustrated in her quest to get at the underlying nature of the phenomenon because she cannot know with certainty how the relationship came about. The Parental Performance scenario is an example in which a definitive conclusion about causality is not possible.

As we will see in the chapters that follow, it is possible to move toward a better understanding of the phenomenon by measuring the many other variables that may influence the relationship between the two major variables of interest and especially those few that theory says are important. Then, the researcher can begin to examine whether the relationship she is interested in establishing exists when the influence of other variables is removed. This is the essence of statistical control.

Oneway ANOVA versus Correlation: What Is the Difference?

Both the Oneway ANOVA and the correlation coefficient can be used to determine whether there is a significant relationship between two variables. For the Oneway ANOVA, the basic question is, "Does the independent variable explain a significant degree of variability in the dependent variable?"

If a significant relationship is found, and the data came from a true experiment, the researcher might wish to conclude that the treatment *caused* some of the variability in the dependent measure. If the data did not come from a true experiment, a causal explanation is generally unwarranted, but the Oneway ANOVA might still be used for analysis. Furthermore, the independent variable *must* be a categorical variable (e.g., experimental versus control), usually limited to only a few values, or "levels." The dependent variable is a continuous variable on an interval or ratio scale of measurement. Finally, the Oneway ANOVA determines the extent of both the linear and curvilinear relationship between variables when the predictor variable has two or more values.

For the Pearson correlation, the basic question is, "What is the degree to which two variables are linearly related?" and secondly, "Is the relationship significant?"

For a simple correlational investigation, it is often possible to identify one variable as the predictor variable and another as the outcome variable and thus to explore the degree to which the predictor variable *explains* some of the variability in the outcome measure. Furthermore, the predictor variable does not have to be a categorical variable but may be a continuous variable *not* limited to only a few values, or levels. The outcome variable is a continuous variable on an interval or ratio scale of measurement. But the Pearson correlation determines only the extent to which two variables are linearly related.

CORRELATION: SCATTERPLOTS

"One picture is worth a thousand words." For coming to an understanding of the degree of correlation between two variables, we heartily agree. We will use graphical means, specifically the **scatterplot,** to develop your understanding of the correlation coefficient as a statistical tool for summarizing the relationship between two variables.

Creating a Scatterplot

A scatterplot is a graphical means for displaying bivariate data. **Bivariate data** are generally data from two variables collected from the same participants. The data from the Parental Performance scenario are an example of bivariate data because there are scores for each child on both Parental Involvement (A) and Concept Attainment (Y).

The Axes   To represent bivariate data in a scatterplot requires that each of the variables become axes on the graph. Traditionally, the vertical axis is used to represent values of the outcome variable (Y), and the horizontal axis is used to represent values of the predictor variable (A).

Range of Values   To make the graphical representation clear requires some forethought. For example, you should ensure that the range of values for each axis is sufficiently broad to include all the measured values of the variable. However, the range of values should not be so broad that the measured values represent only a small portion of the range you selected. For example, in the pilot study of the Parental Performance scenario, the measured values of concept attainment (Y) range from 7 to 15. The range of values for Y should be no less than 7 to 15. But how large should they be? A range as large as 0 to 500 would be too great. It would make the graphical representation of the data difficult to see.

In deciding on a range of values, give particular consideration to making the graphical display effective and easy to understand. Also consider the theoretical limit of the variables under study and whether you wish to compare your current results to those previously obtained or those likely to be obtained in future investigations.

Illustration   For the purposes of illustration, we will use the range 0 to 20 for Concept Attainment (Y) and 0 to 10 for Parental Involvement (A). For each student, find their score on the Concept Attainment (Y) axis and on the Parental Involvement (A) axis. Each student will have one point on the scatterplot corresponding to where their Y and A scores meet. For example, John's point is located where $Y = 11$ and $A = 3$ meet. See Figure 13.1.

Interpreting a Scatterplot

The scatterplot in Figure 13.1 illustrates what appears to be a positive, but imperfect, relationship between Parental Involvement and Concept Attainment. As the hours of Parental Involvement increase, there is a tendency for children's Concept Attainment to increase. At least that's the case for Mary, Burt, and John.

There's an exception to this tendency, which you notice when comparing Jessica and Allison. Allison's mother spent five hours reading with her and Allison scored 13 on the concept attainment test. In contrast, Jessica's mother spent only four hours reading with her daughter yet Jessica had the highest test score (15).

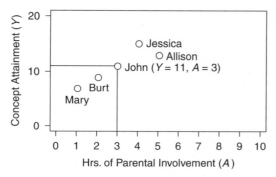

Figure 13.1 Annotated scatterplot of Parental Involvement and Concept Attainment

Different Datasets and Their Scatterplots   Look at more fictitious datasets and the scatterplots they produce. Each of the eight datasets in Table 13.2 contains the Concept Attainment scores (Y) and Parental Involvement time (A) for 10 children. The scores are the same for each set of A and Y scores. Furthermore, the order of the A scores is the same for all eight sets. Only the order of the Y scores varies from set to set. The first set of fictitious scores for 10 children is A_1 and Y_1.

Perfect Positive Relationship   The scatterplot in Figure 13.2a illustrates a perfect **positive linear relationship** between A_1 scores and Y_1 scores. As scores on A_1 increase, scores on Y_1 increase. Note that all the points in the scatterplot fall along a straight line.

Perfect Negative Relationship   The scatterplot in Figure 13.2b also illustrates a perfect linear relationship but in this case it is a **negative linear relationship.** As scores on A_2 increase, scores on Y_2 decrease. Here too, all the points in the scatterplot fall along a straight line.

Strong Positive Relationship   The scatterplot in Figure 13.2c illustrates a strong positive linear relationship between A_3 scores and Y_3 scores. As scores on A_3 increase, scores on Y_3 generally increase. But the relationship between A_3 and Y_3 is not perfect. Not all the points fall along a straight line.

Strong Negative Relationship   The scatterplot in Figure 13.2d illustrates a strong negative linear relationship between A_4 scores and Y_4 scores.

Moderate Positive Relationship   The scatterplot in Figure 13.2e illustrates a moderate positive linear relationship between A_5 scores and Y_5 scores. As scores

TABLE 13.2 Eight Fictitious Datasets for Parental Involvement (*A*) and Concept Attainment (*Y*)

	A_1	Y_1		A_2	Y_2		A_3	Y_3		A_4	Y_4
Jay	1	1	Innes	1	19	Al	1	1	Donna	1	17
Mike	2	3	Tom	2	17	Quito	2	5	Bif	2	19
Ralph	3	5	Bob	3	15	Jose	3	9	Jim	3	13
Ron	4	7	Rick	4	13	Jack	4	3	Ted	4	15
Sally	5	9	Ida	5	11	Tod	5	7	Nan	5	11
Bill	6	11	Lola	6	9	Lucy	6	11	Fram	6	7
Luka	7	13	Bo	7	7	Ibar	7	15	Deb	7	3
Hal	8	15	Alf	8	5	Nono	8	13	Dot	8	9
Pierre	9	17	Sue	9	3	Bobi	9	19	Vera	9	5
Louis	10	19	Sep	10	1	Jill	10	17	Elmo	10	1

	A_5	Y_5		A_6	Y_6		A_7	Y_7		A_8	Y_8
Al	1	3	Terri	1	17	Pam	1	17	Jim	1	19
Sam	2	1	Ho	2	9	Val	2	3	Bette	2	5
Bjorn	3	11	Jason	3	13	Les	3	9	Al	3	1
Mike	4	7	Joey	4	19	Jere	4	7	Tom	4	11
Jeff	5	15	Alan	5	5	Phil	5	13	Jan	5	15
Timmy	6	5	Sally	6	15	Brian	6	15	Carol	6	13
Lou	7	19	Ven	7	7	Steve	7	11	Cy	7	7
Sue	8	13	Gilles	8	11	Tony	8	1	Jon	8	9
Candi	9	9	Pedro	9	1	Roe	9	5	Bob	9	3
Alice	10	17	Alain	10	3	Alex	10	19	Jan	10	17

on A_5 increase, there is a discernible tendency for scores on Y_5 to increase. But the relationship between A_5 and Y_5 is far from perfect. Many of the points fall far from a straight line.

Moderate Negative Relationship   The scatterplot in Figure 13.2*f* illustrates a moderate negative linear relationship between A_6 scores and Y_6 scores.

Lack of a Relationship   The scatterplots in Figures 13.2*g* and 13.2*h* illustrate the lack of a detectable relationship between *A* scores and *Y* scores. In these last two fictitious datasets, there is no way of predicting how a child with a high level of parental involvement will perform on the reading test at month's end.

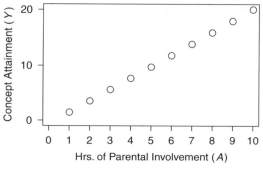

Figure 13.2a Scatterplot of dataset 1

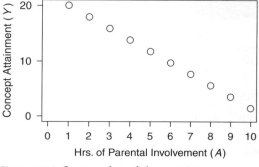

Figure 13.2b Scatterplot of dataset 2

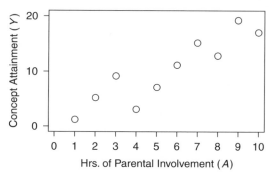

Figure 13.2c Scatterplot of dataset 3

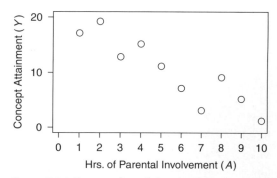

Figure 13.2d Scatterplot of dataset 4

THE PEARSON PRODUCT MOMENT CORRELATION

If one picture can be worth a thousand words, then maybe one number can do likewise. We have emphasized the importance of descriptive statistics in terms of their ability to summarize the important characteristics of a set of numbers. The correlation coefficient is another descriptive statistic because it usefully summarizes. However, it is unique in comparison to other descriptive statistics in that it summarizes the degree to which two sets of scores vary together or are co-related.

The Pearson product moment correlation, named after its developer, Karl Pearson, provides a single numerical index of the degree to which paired observations vary together. Like all descriptive statistics, the correlation coefficient grows increasingly useful as the number of paired observations increases in size (unlike most of the datasets we use for examples).

Describing Linear Relationships

Correlations are most often used to describe the **degree of linear relationship** between two variables or paired observations, normally for the same participants or dependent participants:

- Two different variables, same participants (e.g., correlate height and weight).

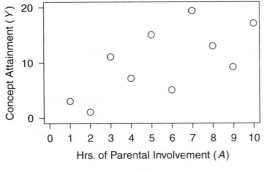

Figure 13.2e Scatterplot of dataset 5

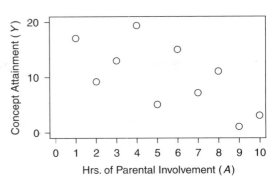

Figure 13.2f Scatterplot of dataset 6

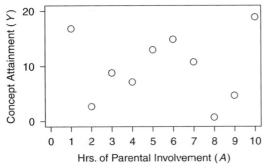

Figure 13.2g Scatterplot of dataset 7

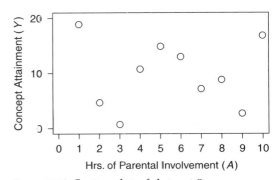

Figure 13.2h Scatterplot of dataset 8

- The same variables measured on two separate occasions, same participants (e.g., correlate personality scores at age 10 with personality scores at age 15).
- The same variable measured for each member of dependent pairs (e.g., correlate IQ scores of twins A with the IQ scores of twins B).

Although it is mathematically possible to correlate virtually any two sets of scores so long as the number of scores in each case is equal, it is not always conceptually meaningful to do so. For this reason it is generally considered inappropriate to correlate the scores of different, independent participants on different variables.

Range of Values

The range of values for the correlation coefficient is from -1 (a perfect negative or inverse linear relationship) through 0 to $+1$ (a perfect positive linear relationship).

1. A correlation of -1.00 means that two variables (A, Y) are perfectly related. As the values of A increase, the values of Y decrease. Knowledge of A is sufficient to predict values of Y without error. (See Figure 13.2b.)
2. A correlation between -1.00 and 0.0 (e.g., $-.50$) means that there is a relationship between two variables, but it is not perfect. As the values of A increase, there is a tendency for the values of Y to decrease. But knowledge

of *A* is not sufficient to predict values of *Y* without error. (See Figures 13.2*d* and 13.2*f*.)

3. A correlation of 0.0 means that two variables are completely unrelated. As the values of *A* change, there is no way to predict or explain the values of *Y*. In other words, *A* and *Y* are independent of each other. (See Figures 13.2*g* and *h*.)

4. A correlation between 0.0 and +1.00 (e.g., +.50) means that there is a relationship between two variables, but it is not perfect. As the values of *A* increase, there is a tendency for the values of *Y* to increase. But knowledge of *A* is not sufficient to predict values of *Y* without error. (See Figures 13.2*c* and 13.2*e*.)

5. A correlation of +1.00 means that two variables (*A*, *Y*) are perfectly related. As the values of *A* increase, the values of *Y* increase. Knowledge of *A* is sufficient to predict values of *Y* without error. (See Figure 13.2*a*.)

The Contribution of Karl Pearson

One of the major tenets of Charles Darwin's theory of evolution was the existence of individual differences among organisms in a species. To verify Darwin's theory, it was important to identify traits on which organisms of a species differed and then to explore whether those traits were influenced by heredity.

Darwin's cousin, Francis Galton, was intrigued with these problems and his research on them founded the study of individual differences. For example, Galton was interested in the heritability of human height, so he explored the relationship between the height of parents and their offspring. Initially, Galton used the scatterplot to determine whether there were discernible relationships between traits—such as parental height and offspring height—suggesting an influence of heredity.

CD-ROM link 13.1

Activity 13.1: The Pearson Product Moment Correlation
Activity 13.1 visually demonstrates how the Pearson product moment correlation coefficient expresses the linear relationship between two variables. By changing the direction of the relationship from positive to negative, you can practice interpreting a numerical correlation coefficient and relating it to different scatterplots.

Galton realized that he could often summarize these relationships with a single straight line through the data. However, it was not until 1896 that the scientist Karl Pearson, associated with Galton's laboratory, developed the mathematical treatment of these matters that resulted in the computational procedures we use today.

Computing the Pearson Product Moment Correlation

It may have occurred to you that there are certain problems in assessing the degree of linear relationship between any two variables:

1. The forms of measurement of the variables may be different (e.g., height in inches vs. weight in pounds; hours of parental involvement vs. numbers of concepts learned).

2. The variances of the measures may be different (e.g., participants' heights may vary only a little, while participants' weights may vary a lot; the number of hours of parental involvement may vary somewhat, while students' concept attainment may vary greatly).

Pearson's technique accounts for these anomalies in computing the correlation coefficient.

There are two methods for computing the correlation between two variables. These methods are related and always yield exactly the same result:

- z-score method
- Covariation method

The basic idea behind the correlation coefficient is quite simple and like many of the statistical techniques discussed so far, it has a lot to do with the variability of each variable (A, Y). However, instead of examining only the variability of the two variables separately, one also examines their variability together, or their covariability.

Remember that variability reflects the degree to which scores fluctuate about a mean. Therefore, covariability reflects the degree to which scores on A fluctuate about the mean of A *in relation to* the degree to which scores on Y fluctuate about the mean of Y.

The *z*-Score Method

The z-score method is especially easy to compute and easy to understand as long as the data are already in the form of z-scores. Each set of A and Y scores to be correlated must first be converted to z-scores (i.e., the mean of the z-scores for each set will be zero and the standard deviation will be 1.0).

For the sample (N) of Y scores:

$$\textbf{(from Equation 5.2) } z_{Yi} = \frac{Y_i - \overline{Y}}{s_Y}$$

Remember, s is the unbiased standard deviation of the Y scores.

Use the same formula but now compute z_{Ai} for the sample (N) of A scores. Thus, both sets of scores are converted to the same metric with equal variability.

The formula for r is then merely

$$\textbf{Equation 13.1: } r = \frac{\sum (z_{Ai}z_{Yi})}{N - 1}$$

where $N - 1$ is the number of pairs of A and Y scores.

Note that the numerator for r contains the *sum of the products* and that r is merely the (unbiased) average of those products. Therefore, the correlation coefficient measures the average degree to which paired observations in a set deviate together from their respective means.

Parental Performance Example   Here is an example of the z-score method based on the five paired observations of parental involvement (*A*) and concept attainment (*Y*) given in Table 13.1 and illustrated in Figure 13.1. Table 13.3 reproduces the paired observations and shows the intermediate calculations.

Another Example: A Perfect Relationship   You can use the same values as those in Table 13.3 but in a slightly different order to see what happens when there is a perfect relationship between *A* and *Y*. To show this perfect relationship, reverse the concept attainment scores for Jessica and Allison and repeat the calculations.[2] See Table 13.4.

TABLE 13.3   Correlation (*z*-Score Method) of Concept Attainment (*Y*) and Hours of Parental Involvement (*A*)

Student	A	z_{Ai}	Y	z_{Yi}	$z_{Ai}z_{Yi}$
John	3	0.00	11	0.00	0.00
Mary	1	−1.27	7	−1.27	1.60
Jessica	4	0.63	15	1.27	0.80
Allison	5	1.27	13	0.63	0.80
Burt	2	−0.63	9	−0.63	0.40
Mean	3.00	0.00	11.00	0.00	—
Std. Dev.	1.58	1.00	3.16	1.00	—

$$r = \frac{\sum (z_{Ai}z_{Yi})}{N-1} = \frac{3.60}{4} = +0.90$$

TABLE 13.4   Perfect Correlation (*z*-Score Method) of Concept Attainment (*Y*) and Hours of Parental Involvement (*A*)

Student	A	z_{Ai}	Y	z_{Yi}	$z_{Ai}z_{Yi}$
John	3	0.00	11	0.00	0.00
Mary	1	−1.27	7	−1.27	1.60
Jessica	4	0.63	13	0.63	0.40
Allison	5	1.27	15	1.27	1.60
Burt	2	−0.63	9	−0.63	0.40
Mean	3.00	0.00	11.00	0.00	—
Std. Dev.	1.58	1.00	3.16	1.00	—

$$r = \frac{\sum (z_{Ai}z_{Yi})}{N-1} = \frac{4.00}{4} = +1.00$$

[2]In case you were wondering, merely changing the order of the value of variables does not always guarantee a perfect relationship. Why? Because the Pearson product moment correlation is used for interval data; both the order of values and the magnitude of deviations from the mean is important.

Notes on the z-Score Method   When there is a perfect relationship between two variables (A, Y) that have been converted to z-scores, the sum of the products is the largest it can be given any other order of the values of each of the variables. Furthermore, the sum of the products is equal to the number of paired observations.

1. When $r = \pm 1.00$, $\sum z_{Ai}z_{Yi}$ is maximum.
2. When $r = \pm 1.00$, $\sum z_{Ai}z_{Yi}$ (disregarding sign or valence) is equal to $N - 1$.
3. r, computed via the z-score method, is merely the (unbiased) *average* of the products $z_{Ai}z_{Yi}$.
4. Remember that z-scores are really deviation scores. When A and Y deviate equally and consistently, the correlation between A and Y has to be high. Conversely, when $r = 0.0$, $\sum z_{Ai}z_{Yi} = 0.0$.

The Covariation Method

You may want to use the **covariation method** to compute r when the data are in "raw" score form and have not been converted to z-scores. The covariation method for computing r is the covariance between two variables divided by the product of the square root of the variances of each variable as in Equation 13.2. The results for r will be identical whether you use the covariation method or the z-score method.

$$\textbf{Equation 13.2: } r = \frac{\dfrac{\sum (A_i - \overline{A})(Y_i - \overline{Y})}{N - 1}}{\dfrac{\sqrt{\sum (A_i - \overline{A})^2}\sqrt{\sum (Y_i - \overline{Y})^2}}{N - 1}}$$

This is the same as

$$r = \frac{AY \text{ covariance}}{\sqrt{A \text{ variance}}\sqrt{Y \text{ variance}}}$$

Covariance   The numerator of Equation 13.2 contains the formula known as the **covariance**. Like the variance, the covariance is an average. Specifically, the covariance is the average of the cross products of the A and Y deviations.

The greater the strength of the relationship between A and Y, the larger the absolute value of the sum of the cross products. Moreover, the largest cross product occurs if the largest A deviation score is paired with the largest Y deviation score, the second largest cross product occurs if the second-largest A deviation score is paired with the second-largest Y deviation score, and so on. Thus, the more the A deviations vary consistently with the Y deviations the larger the sum of the cross products will be.

CD-ROM link 13.2

Activity 13.2: The Meaning of Covariance
By varying the deviation of a data point from its mean, you can see how the covariation formula for correlation represents the shared variability between the variables.

In addition, the sum of the cross products is affected by the number of paired A and Y scores. Dividing the sum by $N-1$ and finding the unbiased average of the cross products means that the covariance does not increase in size as sample size increases.

The denominator of Equation 13.2 contains the square root of the variances or the standard deviations of both A and Y. If you divide the covariance by the standard deviations of A and Y, you obtain a measure of the degree of the relationship between two variables that is independent of the dispersion of the two variables.

Covariation   You can simplify Equation 13.2 by the cancellation of $N-1$ from both numerator and denominator. This simpler calculation, therefore, contains the sum of cross products in the numerator (SS_{AY}) also known as the covariation of A and Y. The denominator contains the square root of the sum of squares for A (SS_A) times the sum of squares for Y (SS_Y).

The formula may be rewritten using these simpler terms:

$$\textbf{Equation 13.3: } r = \frac{\sum (A_i - \bar{A})(Y_i - \bar{Y})}{\sqrt{\sum (A_i - \bar{A})^2}\sqrt{\sum (Y_i - \bar{Y})^2}} = \frac{SS_{AY}}{\sqrt{SS_A SS_Y}}$$

This is the same as

$$r = \frac{AY \text{ covariation}}{\sqrt{A \text{ variation}}\sqrt{Y \text{ variation}}}$$

When doing the calculations for the covariation (i.e., numerator) term, be careful to note the sign of the product. Multiplication of the A and Y deviation scores does not necessarily result in a positive number.

Parental Performance Example   Here is an example of the covariation method based on the five paired observations of Parental Involvement (A) and Concepts Attainment (Y) given in Table 13.1 and illustrated in Figure 13.1. Table 13.5 reproduces the paired observations and shows the intermediate calculations.

Why Is It Called the "Product Moment" Correlation?   In physics, "moment" is a function of the distance of an object from the center of gravity. With any set of scores, the mean may be considered the center of gravity, while the individual deviation scores from the mean are the moments. As you can see by examining the covariation formula, Pearson's r is obtained by taking the products of the paired moments about the mean.

INFERENTIAL USES

The correlation coefficient is a descriptive or summary statistic that describes the extent to which two sets of numbers are related, or covary. Although this single

| | | | | TABLE 13.5 Correlation (Covariation Method) of Concept Attainment (Y) and Hours of Parental Involvement (A) | | | |

Student	A	$A_i - \overline{A}$	$(A_i - \overline{A})^2$	Y	$Y_i - \overline{Y}$	$(Y_i - \overline{Y})^2$	$(A_i - \overline{A})(Y_i - \overline{Y})$
John	3	0	0	11	0	0	0
Mary	1	−2	4	7	−4	16	8
Jessica	4	1	1	15	4	16	4
Allison	5	2	4	13	2	4	4
Burt	2	−1	1	9	−2	4	2
Mean	3.00			11.00			
Std. Dev.	1.58			3.16			
Sum			10			40	18

$$r = \frac{\sum (A_i - \overline{A})(Y_i - \overline{Y})}{\sqrt{\sum (A_i - \overline{A})^2}\sqrt{\sum (Y_i - \overline{Y})^2}} = \frac{SS_{AY}}{\sqrt{SS_A SS_Y}} = \frac{18}{\sqrt{10}\sqrt{40}} = \frac{18}{20} = +0.90$$

numerical summary is a descriptive statistic, the information it contains can be used to ask an inferential question: "What is the likelihood that the value of the correlation obtained on this sample of participants could have come about due to chance?" In other words, it is possible to ask whether the obtained correlation coefficient is significant.

Hypothesis Testing

The underlying logic for testing hypotheses about correlations is similar to the logic employed for testing hypotheses about means. Researchers employ a sample of data in order to make an inference, or best guess, about the population. The choice is between two alternative hypotheses: the null hypothesis, which often says that there is no correlation in the population, and the alternative hypothesis, which often says that there is a correlation in the population. (Less frequently, researchers are interested in knowing whether the population correlation is a particular size.) Finally, it must be recognized that sampling error can affect a sample estimate of the population correlation. Even when the true population correlation is zero, a sample estimate can be obtained that is not zero merely as a function of chance. What one wishes to determine is the likelihood that the obtained, sample estimate could have come about due to sampling error when the true population correlation is zero. If the likelihood that the obtained sample estimate could have come about very rarely as a function of chance alone, then the null hypothesis will be rejected and the alternative hypothesis accepted.

Null and Alternative Hypotheses Use the correlation computed from the sample data (r) to decide between the null and alternative hypotheses concerning the population parameter. The population parameter for a correlation is indicated by the Greek letter ρ, pronounced "**rho.**"

Nondirectional

H_0: ρ = 0 (null hypothesis)

H_a: ρ ≠ 0 (nondirectional, or "two-tailed," alternative hypothesis)

Positive directional

H_0: ρ ≤ 0 (null hypothesis)

H_a: ρ > 0 (positive directional, or "one-tailed," alternative hypothesis)

Negative directional

H_0: ρ ≥ 0 (null hypothesis)

H_a: ρ < 0 (negative directional, or "one-tailed," alternative hypothesis)

To decide between the null and alternative hypotheses, compare the calculated value and the critical (i.e., tabled) value. If the calculated value exceeds the critical value, reject the null hypothesis and accept the alternative hypothesis. Whether you reject the null hypothesis or not, it is possible you may have committed a decision error. If you rejected the null hypothesis and the null hypothesis was correct, you committed a Type I error. If, however, you failed to reject the null hypothesis and it was incorrect, you committed a Type II error.

Calculated and Critical Values

The critical values for the *t*-distribution and the *F*-distribution can be used to determine whether the calculated value of *r* is significant. First, however, the calculated value of *r* must be converted to a *t*-statistic or an *F*-statistic.

Converting r to t   The formula for converting the calculated value of *r* to a calculated value of *t* is as follows:

Equation 13.4: $t = \dfrac{r}{\sqrt{(1 - r^2)/(N - 2)}}$

where degrees of freedom (df) equals $N - 2$.

CD-ROM link 13.3

Problem Generator: Correlation
To practice hypothesis testing with correlation coefficients, select Correlation from the Problem Generator Menu on the CD-ROM. The Problem Generator will create as many practice problems as you need and will demonstrate each step in their solution so that you can check your work.

The formula will be explained more fully in Chapter 14 where procedures for converting *r* to an *F*-statistic are also shown.

Tabled Critical Values of r   At times converting *r* to a calculated *t*-statistic or *F*-statistic and then finding the tabled, critical value may be advantageous. A simpler and sometimes more convenient alternative is to use *r* directly, without converting to *t*, and finding the tabled, critical value of r. Tabled values of r are provided in Appendix G. The decision you arrive at using this direct method will be identical to the decision you arrive at using the t or F methods.

To use the table of critical values requires that you know: whether the alternative hypothesis is directional or not, alpha or the probability value for significance testing, and the degrees of freedom. The degrees of freedom is $N - 2$ (i.e., the number of paired observations minus 2).

Parental Performance Example

Textbox 13.2 is an example of hypothesis testing based on the five paired observations of Parental Involvement (A) and Concepts Attainment (Y) given in Table 13.1 and illustrated in Figure 13.1.

Textbox 13.2

Is the Correlation Between Concept Attainment and Parental Involvement Significant?

The null hypothesis is clear in the Parental Performance scenario of Textbox 13.1 but the wording leaves some room for interpretation with regard to the alternative hypothesis. Because there is no explicit statement predicting a positive relationship between parental involvement and concept attainment, treat the alternative hypothesis as nondirectional. Use $\alpha = .05$ for significance testing.

What is the critical value?
Degrees of freedom (df) $= N - 2 = 3$
Alpha, the probability value for significance testing $= .05$
Alternative hypothesis (H_a) $=$ nondirectional, or two-tailed
Critical r value $= \pm.88$
Critical t value $= \pm3.182$

What is the calculated value?
Using either the z-score or covariation methods, you have already calculated the correlation between concept attainment and parental involvement:
Calculated value (r) $= +0.90$.
You can also use the t-test approach:

Calculated value (t) $= t = \dfrac{r}{\sqrt{(1 - r^2)/(N - 2)}} = \dfrac{.9}{.25} = +3.60$

What is your decision about the null and alternative hypotheses?
The calculated r-value ($+.90$) exceeds the critical r value ($\pm .88$) Similarly, the calculated t-value ($+3.60$) exceeds the critical t-value (±3.182). Therefore, you reject the null hypothesis in favor of the alternative hypothesis. There is a significant relationship between hours of involvement by parents and number of concepts attained by their children.

Furthermore, there is the chance that your best guess may be incorrect and you may have committed a Type I error.

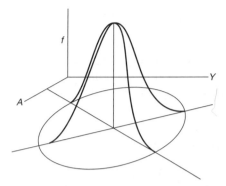

Figure 13.3 Geometric model of a bivariate normal distribution

Underlying Assumptions

One key assumption that underlies the Pearson product moment correlation is that the paired observations are assumed to be *independent* from one another. Each pair of A and Y scores should be independent of all the other pairs of A and Y scores.

Another key assumption is that the values of the predictor variable (A) and the outcome variable (Y) are each expected to be distributed normally. In particular, it is assumed that A and Y have a joint **bivariate normal distribution.** Figure 13.3 illustrates a particular bivariate normal distribution where the variances of A and Y are equal and the correlation between the two variables is zero.

CONFIDENCE INTERVALS

A confidence interval is a range of values in which a population parameter (e.g., ρ) is included with a certain degree of confidence. For example, you might want to know what range of values around the estimated correlation is 95% certain to include the population correlation.

To estimate the confidence interval requires that one uses the appropriate sampling distribution. Doing so ensures that the size of the estimated confidence interval will be related to sample size. The smaller the sample size, the larger the estimated confidence interval. This means that when the number of paired observations is small, the estimated confidence interval for the correlation coefficient will be large. As the number of paired observations increases, the width of the estimated confidence interval decreases (all other things equal).

Skewed Distribution of *r*

Unfortunately, straightforward methods for estimating the confidence interval for the correlation coefficient require that the sampling distribution be normally distributed. When the population correlation is zero, the sampling distribution is normally distributed. However, when the population correlation is not zero, and especially as it approaches ± 1.00, the sampling distribution is not normally distributed but heavily skewed. A **skewed sampling distribution** may adversely affect the accuracy of the confidence interval.

Why is the sampling distribution of the correlation coefficient skewed? Because there are maximum values for the correlation coefficient of ± 1.00 that put limits on the range of scores. For example, imagine that the true population correlation $\rho = +.90$. If one were to take repeated random samples from the population and compute correlations, scores below $+.90$ would range widely while scores above $+.90$ would not range widely because the maximum score is $+1.00$. In other words, scores below $+.90$ will be more widely distributed than scores above $+.90$, and the distribution of scores would not be symmetrical as in a normal distribution. In general, the greater the population correlation deviates from zero, the more the sampling distribution is skewed.

Fisher's Transformation

The problem of skewness in the sampling distribution of the correlation coefficient was addressed by Ronald Fisher. Fisher's solution was to convert logarithmically the values of r so that they would not be restricted to maximum values of ± 1.00. Fisher called this transformation z, but it is *not* the same z as the standard score formula presented in prior chapters. Therefore, we will call **Fisher's transformation** z_F.

The formula for transforming r to Fisher's z_F is as follows:

$$\textbf{Equation 13.5: } z_F = \frac{1}{2} \left[\log_e(1 + r) - \log_e(1 - r) \right]$$

Instead of computing the transformation yourself, you may wish to use the table for converting r to z_F in Appendix H. Note that the values of r and z_F are quite close when r is close to zero. As r deviates from zero, the discrepancy between r and z_F increases. As r gets closer to its maximum value, the value of z_F is quite discrepant from the value of r.

Estimating Confidence Intervals

The estimation of the confidence interval for the correlation coefficient is now reasonably straightforward. First, convert r to z_F. Second, find the confidence interval for z_F. Third, transform the two endpoints of the confidence interval for z_F back to values of r.

The formula for estimating the two-sided confidence interval for z_F is as follows:

$$\textbf{Equation 13.6: } z_F - z_{1-\alpha/2} s_{z_F} \text{ and } z_F - z_{1-\alpha/2} s_{z_F}$$

where s_{z_F} is the standard error of z_F and is given by

$$\textbf{Equation 13.7: } s_{z_F} = \frac{1}{\sqrt{N - 3}}$$

Textbox 13.3

Confidence Interval for the Correlation of Concept Attainment and Parental Involvement

1. You will need to find z_F for $r = .90$. From Appendix H, $z_F = 1.472$.
2. Find the confidence interval for z_F as follows:
    a. Find $z_{.95/2}$. The tabled value of z equals ± 1.96.
    b. Find the standard error:

    $$s_{z_F} = \frac{1}{\sqrt{N-3}} = \frac{1}{\sqrt{2}} = .71$$

    c. $z_F - z_{1-\alpha/2}s_{z_F}$ and $z_F + z_{1-\alpha/2}s_{z_F} = 1.47 - 1.39$ and $1.47 + 1.39 = +.08$ and $+2.86$.
3. Now that a confidence interval has been expressed as values of z_F, use Appendix H to convert these values back to r.

    $$\text{For } z_F = +.08, r = +.08$$

    $$\text{For } z_F = +2.86, r = +.99$$

    Your estimate of the 95% confidence interval is $+.08 \leq \rho \leq +.99$.

Parental Performance Example   Textbox 13.3 shows the estimation of the 95% confidence interval based on the five paired observations of Parental Involvement (A) and Concept Attainment (Y) given in Table 13.1 and illustrated in Figure 13.1 and for which the correlation was previously computed, $r = +.90$.

The Value of Confidence Intervals

The Parental Performance scenario of Textbox 13.1 illustrates the advantage of estimating confidence intervals in addition to computing the correlation coefficient. As the example shows, small sample sizes mean that the estimated confidence interval for the correlation coefficient will be large, regardless of the size of r. In the example, the value of r is $+.90$, almost a perfect relationship, but the confidence interval reminds one that for a sample of this size, the true population correlation may range anywhere from near zero ($+.08$) to near perfect ($+.99$).

STRENGTH OF ASSOCIATION

In previous chapters the analysis of data from experimental designs was discussed, and procedures were presented for determining effect sizes for treatments. There is an analogous procedure for correlational designs. However, because correlational designs do not lend themselves to establishing causal relationships, the term *effect size* is inappropriate. For correlational designs, the term **strength of association** is more appropriate because it indicates only that two variables are related to each other.

Coefficient of Determination

The square of the correlation coefficient (r^2), known as the **coefficient of determination,** is a measure of strength of association. The square of the correlation coefficient equals the proportion of the total variability in the outcome variable (Y) that can be accounted for, explained by, or is associated with variability in the predictor variable (A). Note that the strength of association is always positive regardless of the sign of the correlation coefficient.

Strength of association measures, like effect size measures, are not substitutes for significance tests. Significance tests for correlations determine whether relationships are a function of chance. Strength of association measures estimate the size of the relationship between two variables.

Finally, the coefficient of determination (r^2), unlike the correlation coefficient (r), is on a ratio scale of measurement. Therefore, it *is* appropriate to use the coefficient of determination to compare directly two strengths of association. For example, $r^2 = .40$ is twice the size of $r^2 = .20$. In contrast, it is *not* appropriate to directly compare two correlation coefficients. For example, one cannot conclude that $r = +.70$ is twice the size of $r = +.35$, only that $r = +.70$ is larger than $r = +.35$.

Parental Performance Example

The correlation for the five paired observations of Parental Involvement (A) and Concept Attainment (Y) given in Table 13.1 and illustrated in Figure 13.1 was previously computed and resulted in $r = +.90$.

For $r = +.90$, $r^2 = +.81$.

Eighty-one percent of the variance in Concept Attainment can be explained by variability in Parental Involvement.

DERIVATIVES OF THE PEARSON PRODUCT MOMENT CORRELATION

The Pearson product moment correlation was intended to measure the degree of association between two variables when both of those variables are measured continuously and quantitatively. There are other statistics, derived from Pearson's correlation, to deal with other circumstances. We briefly describe some of these below.

Biserial Correlation The **biserial correlation** is used when one variable is continuous and quantitative and the second variable is reduced to a dichotomous variable from a continuous and quantitative one. For example, imagine you wished to correlate scores on an IQ test with final examination results in Chemistry, where each student's exam results were simplified to Pass or Fail.

Point Biserial Correlation   The **point biserial correlation** is used when one variable is continuous and quantitative and the second variable is a true dichotomy. For example, imagine you wished to correlate scores on an IQ test with Gender (i.e., male, female).

Tetrachoric Correlation   The **tetrachoric correlation** is used when both variables are continuous and quantitative and both variables are reduced to dichotomous ones. For example, imagine you wished to correlate IQ scores, expressed as the dichotomy "Above Average" and "Below Average," with passing or failing the Chemistry final.

Phi-Coefficient   The **phi-coefficient** is used when both variables are true dichotomies. For example, imagine you wished to correlate Gender (i.e., male, female) with Handedness (i.e., left-handed, right-handed).

Rank-Order Correlation   The **rank-order correlation** is used when the variables are on an ordinal scale of measurement. For example, imagine one wished to correlate final order of finish in a foot race with a pretest which ranked the competitors in order of cardiovascular fitness. Spearman's rho (ρ) to compute rank-order correlations will be discussed in Chapter 16.

SOME CAUTIONS AND LIMITATIONS

There are several important cautions and limitations to note regarding the Pearson product moment correlation. We will discuss the following: restriction of range, attenuation due to measurement error, departures from linearity, outliers, and dealing with missing values.

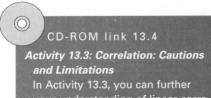

CD-ROM link 13.4

Activity 13.3: Correlation: Cautions and Limitations
In Activity 13.3, you can further your understanding of linear correlation by exploring the effect of outliers and nonlinear relationships on the correlation coefficient.

Restriction of Range

The correlation coefficient is affected by the **restriction of range** of the variables under investigation. The effect of the range restriction is to reduce the size of the correlation coefficient. The greater the restriction of range in either A or Y, the lower the correlation will be. This is not an infrequent problem in situations in which, for example, a convenient sample of participants is selected for study and the sample is more homogeneous on the traits under investigation than the population as a whole.

Example of Range Restriction   Variants of the data used in Table 13.2 and Figure 13.2*g* can be used to illustrate the problem of range restriction. Imagine that the concept attainment scores (Y_7) and parental involvement scores (A_7) for dataset 7 were from a single elementary school, Smith School. The scatterplot illustrated in Figure 13.2g shows that there is virtually no relationship between parental involvement and reading scores for the 10 children tested in this school. Indeed, the correlation between the scores is almost zero ($r = +.02$).

We will now add data for children from two other schools: Turner School and Leslie School. Each child from the two additional schools reads with his or her mother and completes the same test of concept attainment at the end of a month. However, there is an important difference in the emphasis placed on reading and parent involvement among the three schools. Smith School places virtually no emphasis on either reading or parental involvement. Turner School places moderate emphasis on both reading and parental involvement Students have greater parental involvement and better reading performance at this school. Leslie School places high emphasis on both reading and parental involvement. This school has the highest level of parental involvement and concept attainment of the three schools. The Concept Attainment (Y) and Parental Involvement (A) scores for children at the three schools are given in Table 13.6, and the scatterplots are illustrated in Figures 13.4a–d.

Note especially, that within any school dataset the range of Concept Attainment (Y) scores is 18.00 and the range of hours of Parental Involvement (A) is 9.00. However, when the data for the three schools are combined, the range of Concept Attainment (Y) scores is 38.00 and the range of hours of Parental Involvement (A) is 29.00. In any one dataset the range of values of both variables is restricted when compared to the range of values for both variables when the datasets are combined.

When one examines the relationship between Concept Attainment (Y) and Parental Involvement (A) one school at a time (see Figures 13.4a–c), the scatterplots fail to show a discernible relationship. Indeed the correlation between Concept Attainment (Y) and Parental Involvement (A) is almost nil at each school ($r = +.02$).

TABLE 13.6 Concept Attainment (Y) and Parental Involvement (A) at Three Schools

Smith School			Turner School			Leslie School		
Name	A	Y	Name	A	Y	Name	A	Y
Pam	1	17	Missy	11	27	Louis	21	37
Val	2	3	Alan	12	13	Lan	22	23
Les	3	9	Greg	13	19	Curt	23	29
Jere	4	7	Tyler	14	17	Jif	24	27
Phil	5	13	Pat	15	23	Tim	25	33
Brian	6	15	Gord	16	25	Bette	26	35
Steve	7	11	Frank	17	21	Anne	27	31
Tony	8	1	Salli	18	11	Eva	28	21
Roe	9	5	Fran	19	15	Dana	29	25
Alex	10	19	Ollie	20	29	Hal	30	39

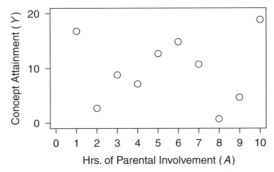

Figure 13.4a Scatterplot of Parental Involvement (*A*) and Concept Attainment (*Y*) at Smith School

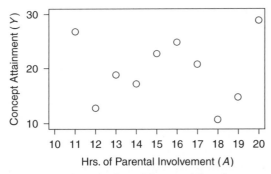

Figure 13.4b Scatterplot of Parental Involvement (*A*) and Concept Attainment (*Y*) at Turner School

However, when one combines the data for all 30 children from the three schools, a different picture emerges. From the combined scatterplot (see Figure 13.4*d*) it is now apparent that Concept Attainment (*Y*) and Parental Involvement (*A*) are positively related; the correlation is fairly large ($r = +.78$).[3]

Attenuation Due to Measurement Error

It is rarely the case that a researcher can measure predictor and outcome variables without measurement error. In the instance of some standardized tests, the degree of measurement error may be small. However, in the case of many locally developed instruments, the degree of measurement error may be large. For example, in the Parental Performance scenario there is some chance that parents will not report time spent reading with their children accurately or will give different estimates when asked on separate occasions. Similarly, scores on the test of concept

---

[3]This example illustrates mathematically the effect of range restriction on the correlation coefficient. It also illustrates the influence of a third variable (School Emphasis) on the relationship between two others (Concept Attainment, Parental Involvement).

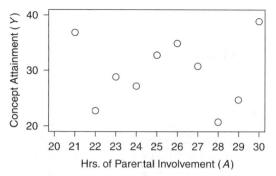

Figure 13.4c Scatterplot of Parental Involvement (*A*) and Concept Attainment (*Y*) at Leslie School

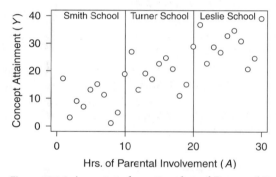

Figure 13.4d Annotated scatterplot of Parental Involvement (*A*) and Concept Attainment (*Y*) at three schools

attainment may partly reflect a child's mood that day, or his or her guessing correctly on a few test items, or the idiosyncratic way each teacher scores the test.

Correction for Attenuation   The effect of measurement error is always to reduce or attenuate the size of the correlation coefficient. Fortunately, it is possible to estimate what the correlation coefficient would be if measurement error were not present. However, the correction for attenuation formula (Nunnally, 1978, pp. 219–220) requires that one know the reliability (rel) of each measure.[4] If one knows, or can make a reasonable, informed estimate, then correcting the correlation for attenuation (*r**) is reasonably straightforward:

$$\text{Equation 13.8: } r^* = \frac{r}{\sqrt{\text{rel}_A}\sqrt{\text{rel}_Y}}$$

[4]In Chapter 2 we defined reliability as the degree a test is free from measurement error or how precise, consistent, or stable a participant's test score is over different testing and time spans. Reliabilities are correlation coefficients except the range of scores is from zero (no reliability) to +1 (perfect reliability). Reliabilities around .9 are considered excellent; reliabilities below .6 are considered marginal.

Note that the degree of correction depends on the extent of measurement error. When the predictor and outcome variables are perfectly reliable ($\text{rel}_A = \text{rel}_Y = 1.00$), there is no correction to the correlation ($r^* = r$). However, when there is considerable error in the measures, the formula may substantially increase the size of the correlation (r^*).

Example of Correction   Imagine you found the correlation between Parental Involvement and Concept Attainment was $r = +.50$. In addition, you knew the reliability of the Parental Involvement measure ($\text{rel}_A = .70$) and the Concept Attainment measure ($\text{rel}_Y = .80$). What would be the corrected correlation (r^*) you estimated?

$$r^* = \frac{r}{\sqrt{\text{rel}_A}\sqrt{\text{rel}_Y}} = \frac{+.50}{\sqrt{.70}\sqrt{.80}} = +.67$$

Departures from Linearity

The Pearson product moment correlation is used to describe the degree of *linear* relationship between two variables (paired observations). **Curvilinear relationships** are not accurately measured by simple correlational techniques. To the extent the relationship is curvilinear, the resulting statistic will misrepresent the true nature of the relationship.

Anxiety and Performance Example   The easiest way to detect departures from linearity is by visually inspecting a scatterplot of the data. One of the most famous examples of a curvilinear relationship in the social sciences is the inverted U-shaped relationship between personal anxiety and task performance. It is now well known that "moderate" levels of anxiety optimize task performance (i.e., the asymptote). When anxiety is either "low" or "high," performance suffers. See Figure 13.5.

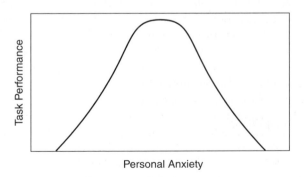

Figure 13.5 Curvilinear relationship between personal anxiety and task performance

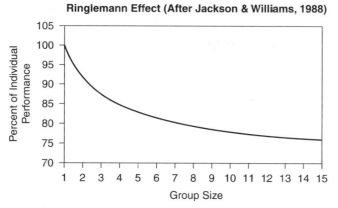

Figure 13.6 The curvilinear Ringlemann effect

The Ringlemann Effect   Another example of a curvilinear relationship is that between group size and personal productivity. The curvilinear Ringlemann effect is illustrated in Figure 13.6.

Transforming Variables   Curvilinear relationships can also be determined by transforming variables (e.g., raising variables to powers, expressing variables as logarithms, or taking square roots of variables) and then computing r. For example, squaring the predictor variable allows one to determine whether a curve with a single bend best fits the data. Cubing the predictor allows one to determine whether a curve with two bends best fits the data, and so on. In addition, the values of the variables may be converted to ranks and the rank-order correlation computed. See Chapter 16.

Outliers

Outliers are extreme values of a predictor or outcome variable that appear discrepant from the other values. Especially when the number of paired observations is small, outliers can have a strong influence on the calculated value of the correlation coefficient.

Detection   A simple way to detect outliers is to examine a scatterplot of the data and look for unusually large or small scores relative to the others. For example, consider the Parental Involvement and Concept Attainment data for the Smith School given in Table 13.3 and illustrated in Figure 13.4a with a correlation near zero ($r = +.02$). But now imagine you had erroneously included the data for an eleventh student, Hal ($A = 30$, $Y = 39$), from the Leslie School.

The inclusion of Hal's paired observations are illustrated in Figure 13.7. It is apparent that his data are discrepant from the other scores and that they change the appearance of the relationship between predictor (A) and outcome (Y)

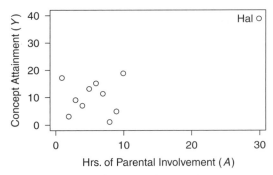

Figure 13.7 The influence of an outlier

measures. The calculated value of the correlation coefficient has changed dramatically too; now $r = +.78$. This is not an accurate representation of the relationship between Parental Involvement and Concept Attainment for the students at the Smith School.

Correction Outliers may be indicative of problems with the data, including faulty recording of results or careless responding on the part of research participants. If you suspect that data are incorrect, you should first attempt to verify your recording or check with participants about their responses. Discard data only as a last resort and mention your reason for doing so in your research report.

Statistical methods for detecting outliers are given in Chapter 14. You may want to examine standardized residuals greater than ±2.00 and consider whether to discard or recode these data.

Dealing with Missing Values

Remember that to compute a correlation, the two sets of scores to be correlated must both contain scores on the same participants. Missing scores are not allowed; at the least, a substituted value should be used or the case should be entirely eliminated from consideration (i.e., deleted from both variables being correlated). Separate calculations of z-scores and other statistics should be computed for each variable only when problems with missing values have been resolved, *never* before.

Solutions

1. Delete the participant entirely.
2. Substitute the mean score for the missing value.
3. Substitute other averages (mode, median).
4. Use a random number generator to create missing value substitutes that have the same mean and variance as the obtained values.
5. Use regression methods (see Chapter 14) to predict the missing score from knowledge of nonmissing values.

PUTTING IT ALL TOGETHER

The Pearson product moment correlation was described as a way to summarize the degree of linear relationship between two continuous variables measured on interval or ratio scales. The similarities and differences were highlighted in the situations in which the correlation is used compared with other statistical techniques such as the Oneway ANOVA. The limitations of correlational research for making causal inferences were discussed, because reverse variable and third-variable or rival explanations are possible. Scatterplots were used to illustrate a variety of correlations ranging from −1 through 0 to +1.

Computational Procedures

Three formulas were presented for the computation of the correlation coefficient.
z-score method:

$$\text{Equation 13.1: } r = \frac{\sum (z_{Ai} z_{Yi})}{N - 1}$$

Covariation methods:

$$\text{Equation 13.2: } r = \frac{\dfrac{\sum (A_i - \overline{A})(Y_i - \overline{Y})}{N - 1}}{\dfrac{\sqrt{\sum (A_i - \overline{A})^2} \sqrt{\sum (Y_i - \overline{Y})^2}}{N - 1}}$$

$$\text{Equation 13.3: } r = \frac{\sum (A_i - \overline{A})(Y_i - \overline{Y})}{\sqrt{\sum (A_i - \overline{A})^2} \sqrt{\sum (Y_i - \overline{Y})^2}} = \frac{SS_{AY}}{\sqrt{SS_A SS_Y}}$$

Two alternatives were provided to determine the significance of a correlation using either tabled values to find the critical value of r (see Appendix G) or the t-test to find the critical value:

$$\text{Equation 13.4: } t = \frac{r}{\sqrt{(1 - r^2)/(N - 2)}}$$

Because the sampling distribution of r tends to be skewed, a way was presented to determine the confidence interval via Fisher's transformation:

$$\text{Equation 13.5: } z_F = \frac{1}{2} [\log_e (1 + r) - \log_e (1 - r)]$$

The formula for the confidence interval for z_F is as follows:

$$\textbf{Equation 13.6: } z_F - z_{1-\alpha/2}s_{z_F} \text{ and } z_F + z_{1-\alpha/2}s_{z_F}$$

where s_{z_F} is the standard error of z_F:

$$\textbf{Equation 13.7: } s_{z_F} = \frac{1}{\sqrt{N-3}}$$

Transform the two endpoints of the confidence interval for z_F back to values of r.

Finally, the coefficient of determination, or measure of strength of association, is simply r^2.

Cautions and Limitations

There are several important cautions and limitations to note regarding Pearson's product moment correlation. The following were discussed: restriction of range, attenuation due to measurement error, departures from linearity, outliers, and dealing with missing values. The formula for correction due to attenuation is as follows:

$$\textbf{Equation 13.8: } r^* = \frac{r}{\sqrt{\text{rel}_A}\sqrt{\text{rel}_Y}}$$

Textbox 13.4

Correlation: Correlates of Test Anxiety

Is there a correlation between anxiety and neuroticism? Schmidt and Riniolo (1999) examined whether neuroticism was related to anxiety. They studied undergraduates who were just about to write a cumulative final examination in an introductory psychology statistics course. They asked the student volunteers (20 males, 27 females) to complete several questionnaires before taking their exams. These included a short version of a personality questionnaire with extraversion and neuroticism subscales, a shyness questionnaire, and a test anxiety questionnaire. Pearson's product-moment correlations were computed among the four measures. Neuroticism was significantly related to test anxiety, $r = +.27$, $p = .03$, and according to the authors, modestly related to shyness, $r = +.22$, $p < .07$ (but not if you use a more traditional alpha value for significance testing). There was an inverse relationship reported between shyness and extraversion, $r = -.27$, $p = .03$. The authors concluded that undergraduate students who reported higher levels of shyness were low on extraversion. Those who reported high amounts of neuroticism also reported a higher degree of anxiety, both in general and in a particular testing situation, indicating that neuroticism may underlie the anxiety that occurs for some adults when they expect to be evaluated.

KEY TERMS

Pearson product-moment correlation

Degree of linear relationship

Predictor variable

Outcome variable

Reverse variable explanation

Third variable or rival explanation

Scatterplot

Bivariate data

Positive linear relationship

Negative linear relationship

Covariation method

Covariance

Rho

Independence of paired observations

Bivariate normal distribution

Skewed sampling distribution

Fisher's transformation

Strength of association

Coefficient of determination

Biserial correlation

Point biserial correlation

Tetrachoric correlation

Phi-coefficient

Rank-order correlation

Restriction of range

Curvilinear relationships

Outliers

REFERENCES

Jackson, J., & Williams, K. (1988). *A review and theoretical analysis of social loafing*. Bronx, NY: Fordham University.

Nunnally, J. C. (1978). *Psychometric theory*. (2nd ed.). New York: McGraw-Hill.

Schmidt, L. A., & Riniolo, T. C. (1999) The role of neuroticism in test and social anxiety. *Journal of Social Psychology, 139*, 394.

PROBLEMS

Questions

Section 1   Conceptual/Definition

13.1. Is correlation a descriptive or an inferential statistic?

13.2. Do correlational studies allow for causal inference? Why or why not?

13.3. How does one distinguish between situations in which to use a Oneway ANOVA versus a correlation?

13.4. What is the range of possible values for the correlation coefficient?

13.5. Why is the correlation coefficient called the *product moment correlation*?

13.6. What are the key assumptions made in using the Pearson product moment correlation?

13.7. What is the coefficient of determination?

13.8. Why is restriction of range a problem in correlation?

13.9. The Pearson product moment correlation is sometimes referred to as the *linear correlation coefficient*. Why?

13.10. What is a simple method of detecting outliers in a bivariate dataset?

Section 2   Numerical

The following dataset exists for a correlational study. Use it to answer questions 13.11 to 13.13.

Subject	Education Level (Years), X	Reading Score, Y
1	12	82
2	13	71
3	12	54
4	12	86
5	14	74
6	16	46
7	16	55
8	13	53
9	12	55
10	12	57
11	12	64
12	12	56
13	13	59
14	14	63
15	14	66
16	12	53

13.11. Use the z-score method to determine the correlation (Pearson's *r*) between Education Level and Reading Score.

13.12. Use the covariation method to determine the correlation (Pearson's *r*) between Education Level and Reading Score.

13.13. Determine the null and alternate hypotheses, test the significance of *r* ($\alpha = .05$), and state your conclusion.

The following dataset exists for a correlational study. Use it to answer questions 13.14 to 13.16.

An instructor in a statistics course is interested in investigating the relationship between results on a Take-Home test (the midterm) and an In-Class test (the final).

Student	Take-Home Test	In-Class Test
1	12	82
2	13	71
3	12	54
4	12	86
5	14	74
6	16	46
7	16	55
8	13	53
9	12	55
10	12	57
11	12	64
12	12	56
13	13	59
14	14	63
15	14	66

13.14. Use the z-score method to determine the correlation (Pearson's r) between Take-Home and In-Class results.

13.15. Use the covariation method to determine the correlation (Pearson's r) between Take-Home and In-Class results.

13.16. Determine the null and alternate hypotheses, test the significance of r ($\alpha = .05$), and state your conclusion.

Use the following data set to answer questions 13.17 to 13.18.

Subject	A	Y	Y_1
1	5	13	30
2	8	19	69
3	4	11	21
4	12	27	149
5	16	35	261
6	9	21	86
7	18	39	329
8	10	23	105
9	13	29	174
10	3	9	14

13.17. Determine the correlation (Pearson's r) between A and Y using the z-score method. Comment on the results you find.

13.18. Determine the correlation (Pearson's r) between A and Y_1 using the covariation method. Is there a problem?

13.19. Use the following dataset to determine, using the covariation method, the correlation (Pearson's r) between A and Y.

Subject	A	Y
1	3	28
2	6	27
3	3	21
4	9	31
5	12	46

13.20. Use the following dataset to determine, using the covariation method, the correlation (Pearson's r) between A and Y.

Subject	A	Y
1	32	87
2	48	93
3	37	99
4	21	75
5	56	56
6	49	81

Determining the Relationship Between Two Variables

Simple Linear Regression

OVERVIEW

You can use the Pearson product moment correlation (r) to describe the degree of relationship between two variables and then evaluate whether this relationship is significant. But how can you use the knowledge of the relationship between two variables for prediction? Specifically, how can you use the knowledge of a relationship between predictor and outcome variables to predict scores on the outcome variable from knowledge of the predictor variable alone?

Being able to make predictions would be of practical and scientific value. As you might guess, prediction of this sort depends on first conducting a study where both predictor and outcome variables are measured and found to be related meaningfully. Then, in the future, one only needs to measure the predictor variable alone to gain some insight into what scores on the outcome variables are expected to be.

This type of prediction is used for college placement and employee selection, for example. Scores on college entrance examinations are used to make decisions about admissions, scholarships, and the applicants' likelihood of achieving success. Screening tests help identify candidates most likely to perform well on the job.

We will explore issues surrounding simple linear regression in the following pages. We will address questions such as the following:

1. What is the difference between correlation and regression?
2. How does one find the slope and intercept for the regression line when prediction is perfect?
3. How does one find the slope and intercept when prediction is imperfect?
4. Can variability be partitioned into additive components and a test of significance performed?
5. What are confidence intervals, strength of association, and power for simple regression?
6. What are the underlying assumptions in simple linear regression and how does one examine the data for assumption violations?

As usual, we begin the chapter with a small scenario and set of data. But unlike other chapters, neither the scenario nor the data are new ones. We repeat the Parental Performance scenario from Chapter 13 but add a new wrinkle. See Textbox 14.1.

Textbox 14.1

More on Parental Performance

In Chapter 13, which dealt with correlation, the Parental Performance scenario was presented. In that scenario, in Textbox 13.1, we asked you to imagine conducting a small pilot study to investigate the relationship between parental involvement and the reading achievement (Concept Attainment) of young children. To do so you asked a group of five single mothers to record the number of hours spent reading and doing homework with their children in first grade during the past month. Each parent and the school also permitted you to record for analysis the results of the end-of-month reading test, which summarizes for each child the number of key concepts understood.

The results (see Table 14.1) were as follows:

TABLE 14.1   Monthly Concept Attainment Scores (*Y*) and Hours of Parental Involvement (*A*)

Student	Parental Involvement (A) (Hours Spent)	Concept Attainment (Y) (Reading Test Score)
John	3	11
Mary	1	7
Jessica	4	15
Allison	5	13
Burt	2	9

You now face a new challenge. You would like to use the results from the five students in the Parental Performance scenario as the basis for estimating how *other* children will score on the Concept Attainment reading test (*Y*) when you know only the degree of Parental Involvement (*A*) for the other children. In other words, how can you predict values of *Y* from knowledge of *A*?

SOME SIMPLE REGRESSION BASICS

In this section some similarities and differences between correlation and regression are pointed out. Some basic concepts in simple regression are examined using the case of perfect prediction for illustration purposes.

What Is the Difference Between Correlation and Regression?

In Chapter 13, several issues were explored regarding the relationship between two variables:

- What is the correlation (*r*) between *A* and *Y*?
- Is the correlation significant?
- What is the confidence interval in which the population correlation lies?
- What is the strength of the association (r^2) between *A* and *Y*?

We will now extend your understanding of the relationship between two variables by concentrating on prediction. Specifically, what are the estimated values of Concept Attainment (Y) that can be predicted from the actual values of Parental Involvement (A)? We will use techniques of linear regression for this purpose. We will also explain ways to use regression techniques to conduct tests of significance, find confidence intervals, compute strength of association, and estimate power.

Researchers often conduct studies in which data on both predictor (A) and outcome measures (Y) are collected on a sample of participants to address other situations in which one has only measured a second sample's scores on the predictor variable (A) and wishes to estimate performance on the outcome variable (Y). For example, college admission committees may use performance on the Scholastic Aptitude Test to predict cumulative college grade point average. Or someone might want to predict the voting behavior of elected officials based on the attitudes of each official's constituents.

How then, can you succinctly distinguish between linear correlation and linear regression? **Linear correlation** refers to describing the degree of linear relationship between two variables (A and Y). The degree of the relationship is summarized in a single number, the correlation coefficient (r).

Linear regression refers to fitting a straight line through the scatterplot of A and Y scores. The regression equation can then be used to predict a subject's score on the outcome variable, Y, from knowledge of that subject's score on the predictor variable, A.

Regression and correlation are logically and mathematically related. For example, there is a mathematical relationship between the correlation coefficient and the regression coefficient (as we will show later).

In advanced textbooks, you will find that a major distinction between correlation and regression is in the nature of A, the predictor variable. In the regression model, there is a true predictor variable (A) and a true outcome variable (Y). In the correlation model, there is no firm distinction between the two variables A and Y. Furthermore, in the regression model, A is assumed to be fixed and measured without error. In contrast, in the correlation model no such assumptions are made about A.

Lines and Plots

In the preceding chapter on correlation (Chapter 13), the scatterplot was introduced as a way to illustrate the bivariate relationship between two variables. The scatterplots in Figure 13.2*a–h* illustrate a variety of bivariate relationships ranging from perfect to near zero. In the case of a perfect positive relationship (Figure 13.2*a*) and a perfect negative relationship (Figure 13.2*b*), obviously the relationship between A and Y can best be described by a single straight line. In the case of imperfect relationships, however, it is less obvious that the relationship between A and Y can best be described by a single straight line. The critical questions are, Which is the best straight line? How does one find that line?

In developing an explanation for simple linear regression, we will begin with the situation in which there is a perfect relationship between the predictor variable (*A*) and the outcome variable (*Y*). We will then consider the more usual case in which there is an imperfect relationship between *A* and *Y*.

Perfect Prediction

Imagine a situation in which the predictor variable (*A*) and the outcome measure (*Y*) are perfectly related (e.g., $r = +1.00$).[1] For example, imagine the data for the Parental Performance are as in Table 14.2.

Now imagine that a straight line is fitted to the data points and extends them to include the intersection with the *y*-axis. See Figure 14.1.

The line fitted to the data in Figure 14.1 can be described by two characteristics: slope and intercept.

TABLE 14.2 Data for Perfect Correlation of Concept Attainment (*Y*) and Hours of Parental Involvement (*A*)		
Student	A	Y
John	3	11
Mary	1	7
Jessica	4	13
Allison	5	15
Burt	2	9
Mean	3.00	11.00
Std. Dev.	1.58	3.16

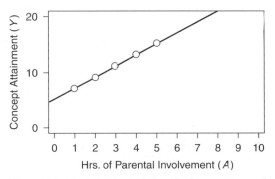

Figure 14.1 Straight line through data points when $r = +1.00$

[1] To simplify this initial explanation, let us also assume that you do not wish to use these sample values to make any inferences about population parameters.

Slope

The rate of change of one variable relative to another is known as the **slope** (also known as *rise over run*). The slope (*b*) is also the angle of the line's "tilt" relative to one of the axes:

CD-ROM link 14.1

Activity 14.1: Describing Linear Relationships
In Activity 14.1, you can vary the slope of a line and see how it represents the rate of change between two variables that have a perfect linear relationship with each other.

$$\textbf{Equation 14.1:} \ \text{Slope} \ (b) = \frac{\text{change in } Y}{\text{change in } A}$$

The appearance of a relationship between two variables (scatterplot) is affected by the variance of each variable. When a variable has a large variance, its **rate of change** is large. When a variable has a small variance, its rate of change is small.

Given two related variables, except that one variable (*Y*) has a large variance and the other variable (*A*) has a small variance, then large changes in *Y* will predict only small changes in *A*. Conversely, if *Y* has a small variance and *A* has a large variance, then only small changes in *Y* will predict large changes in *A*.

Example Values of the Slope

1. +1.0 (*Y* and *A* change equally; as *Y* increases, *A* increases at the same rate)
2. +.5 (*Y* changes half as quickly as *A*)
3. +3.0 (*Y* changes three times more quickly than *A*)
4. −1.0 (*Y* and *A* change equally; as *Y* increases, *A* decreases at the same rate)
5. −.5 (as *Y* increases, *A* decreases twice as fast)
6. −3.0 (*Y* increases three times as fast as *A* decreases)

Calculating the Slope   Finding the slope when there is a perfect relationship between *A* and *Y* is relatively straightforward. Calculate the difference between any two *Y*-scores. This is the change in *Y*. Now calculate the difference between the corresponding two *A* scores. This is the change in *A*.

For example, the change in *Y* for Burt and John is +2.00. Meanwhile, the change in *A* for Burt and John is +1.00.

$$\text{Slope} \ (b) = 2.00/1.00 = +2.00$$

See Figure 14.2.

Scatterplots and Slopes   Figure 14.2 illustrates a slope of +2.00. Yet it may not appear in the scatterplot as if the rate of change of *Y* is twice the rate of change of *A*. As you can see in the illustrations that follow, the appearance of the slope in a scatterplot is partly a function of the range of values used to graph both *Y* and *A*. Figures 14.3*a* and *b* illustrate the same data and the same slope (+2.00) but with a different range of *Y*-values in each case. In Figure 14.3*a*, the range of *Y*-values is restricted to 7 and 15. In Figure 14.3*b*, the range of *Y*-values extends from 0 to 100. In both cases the numerical value of the slope remains unchanged (+2.00). In gen-

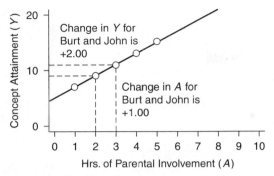

Figure 14.2 Finding the slope

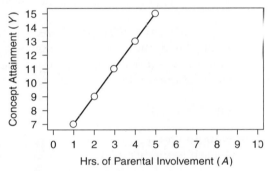

Figure 14.3a Scatterplot with restricted Y-range

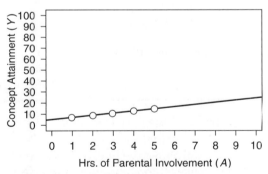

Figure 14.3b Scatterplot with extended Y-range

eral, it is only possible to detect the "true" slope visually when the allowable ranges of predictor scores (A) and outcome scores (Y) are identical.

Intercept

The **y-intercept** (a) of a straight line is the point at which the line crosses the y-axis at $A = 0.0$. The y-intercept can be either positive or negative, depending on whether the line intersects the y-axis above zero or below it.

CD-ROM link 14.2

Activity 14.1: Describing Linear Relationships
In addition to varying the slope, Activity 14.1 also allows you to vary the intercept for two variables that have a perfect linear relationship with one another. While changing the intercept value, note the corresponding changes in both the scatterplot and the equation for the intercept.

Finding the intercept mathematically requires that one know the mean values of both predictor and outcome variables as well as the slope:

Equation 14.2: Intercept $a = \overline{Y} - b\overline{A}$

If, for example, Y and A changed at the same rate (slope = 1.0), the intercept would be that value which when added to each A score would be a sum equal to its respective Y-score.

In the example of perfect prediction the intercept is

$$a = 11.00 - (+2.00)(3.00) = +5.00$$

The Formula for a Straight Line Now that you have calculated the slope and intercept, you can write a simple mathematical equation that expresses the values of the outcome variable (Y) as a function of the values of the predictor variable (A):

Equation 14.3: $Y = a + (b)(A)$

This is called the **regression equation** for a straight line.

The regression equation can be used to predict values of Y from knowledge of A:

$$Y = +5.00 - (+2.00)(A)$$

For example, for John's score on A (3.00) the Y value is 11.00:

$$Y = +5.00 - (+2.00)(3.00) = 11.00$$

IMPERFECT PREDICTION

In virtually all research situations, the predictor variable (A) and the outcome variable (Y) will not be perfectly related; the actual values of A and Y will not *all* fit onto a straight line—some values will fall above the line, others below. As the relationship between A and Y becomes weaker (more and more imperfect), visualization of the single straight line that fits the data best becomes difficult. See Figures 13.2*c–h* in Chapter 13. And in many research situations researchers might wish to use sample values to make inferences about population parameters.

Now consider the imperfect relationship between Parental Performance and Concept Attainment from the Parental Performance data in Table 14.1. These data are plotted in Figures 14.4*a–d*. In each figure, a different line is fit to the data. Which line fits the data best, and why? What are the differences among the fitted lines?

The straight line that fits the data best is illustrated in Figure 14.4*a*. The lines shown in the remaining figures (Figures 14.4*b–d*) fit the data less well. These alternatives to the **best fit line** (Figure 14.4*a*) are three of an endless number of lines that might be drawn.

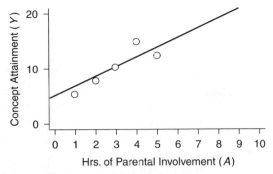

Figure 14.4a Best-fit straight line

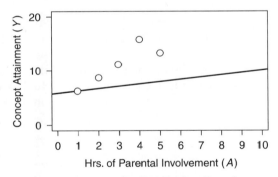

Figure 14.4b Fit straight line with offset intercept

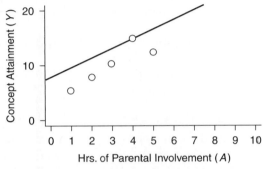

Figure 14.4c Fit straight line with offset slope

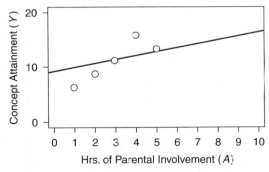

Figure 14.4d Fit straight line with offset intercept and slope

The Best-Fit Straight Line

Why is Figure 14.4*a* the best line? It is the one line that matches the data points most closely. Overall, this line is the one line where deviations of the data points from the line are smallest. The line in Figure 14.4*b* has the same slope or angle as the best-fit line but a different intercept or point at which the line crosses the *y*-axis. This change in intercept means there is less of a good match between the data points and the line. The line in Figure 14.4*c* has the same intercept as the best-fit line but a different slope. This change in slope means there is less of a good match between the data points and the line. Finally, the line in Figure 14.4*d* has both a different intercept and a different slope than the best-fit line. The changes in intercept and slope mean there is a poor match between the data points and the line.

The same slope can have many intercepts. Figures 14.4*a* and14.4*b* show two lines that have the same slope but different intercepts.

The same intercept can have many slopes. Figures 14.4*a* and 14.4*c* show two lines that have the same intercept but different slopes.

The Method of Least Squares   The "best"-fitting straight line is that line that reduces the sum of the squared deviations of the actual data points from the line to the smallest amount. This method of line fitting is called the **method of least squares**. Put another way, the method of least squares fits the line in such a way that the sum of the squared "distances" from the actual data points to the line is minimum.

Consider the lines previously fit to the data for the Parental Performance scenario in Table 14.1 and further illustrated below in Figures 14.5*a* and *b*. The line in Figure 14.5*a* fits the data better than the line in Figure 14.5*b* because the squared deviations[2] of the actual data points from the fit line is overall smaller in *a* than in *b*.

The best-fit line illustrated in Figure 14.5*a* does not fit the actual or obtained data perfectly. For example, the actual concept attainment (*Y*) score is +15.00 for

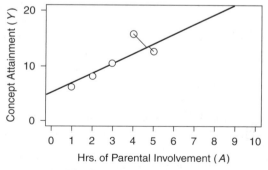

Figure 14.5*a* The best-fit straight line minimizes squared deviations

[2]Why squared deviations? Remember that the sum of the deviations about the mean is zero, because the positive deviations cancel the negative deviations. Squaring deviations scores allows one to detect the magnitude of the deviations irrespective of their sign.

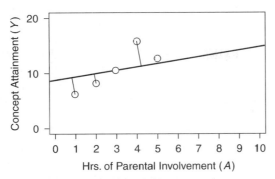

Figure 14.5*b* Other straight lines have larger squared deviations

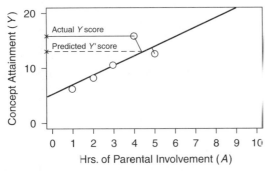

Figure 14.6 The predicted Y'-score does not always equal the actual Y-score

Jessica whose Parental Performance (A) score is +4.00. However, according to the best fit line, the predicted Concept Attainment score (Y') is slightly less than +14.00. Thus, you will need to distinguish between **actual, or obtained, scores (Y)** and **predicted, or estimated, scores (Y')**.

CD-ROM link 14.3

Activity 14.2: Imperfect Prediction
How good is your eye for estimating a line of best fit? In Activity 14.2, you can generate small sets of data, and try to adjust a line on the scatterplot so that it best represents the linear relationship between the two variables. As you learn how to make better visual estimates, you will see that the line of best fit is the one that reduces the sum of the squared deviations to their smallest amount.

What Is the Difference Between Y' and Y?

When there is a perfect relationship between the actual values of Y and A, the scatterplot will show that all the data fit exactly onto a straight line and the correlation between Y and A will be either +1.00 or −1.00. When all the data fit exactly onto a straight line and the correlation between variables is perfect, the predicted or estimated values (Y') are identical to the actual values (Y).

When the relationship between Y and A is not perfect, however, the scatterplot will show that all of the data *do not* fit exactly onto a straight line. The predicted, or estimated, values (Y') derived from the best-fit straight line will not always be the same as the actual values (Y). As the correlation between variables decreases, the discrepancy between actual values (Y) and estimated values (Y') increases. This discrepancy is known as the **residual.**

We can now refine our point about the method of least squares and the best-fit straight line. The best-fit straight line is that line in which $\sum (Y - Y')^2$ is at its minimum.

It should also be clear that one must also estimate the slope and intercept components used in the **regression equation** for a straight line:

$$\text{Equation 14.4: } Y' = a' + b'(A)$$

where:

$Y' = $ the estimated value of the outcome variable

$a' = $ estimated intercept also known as the regression constant

$b' = $ estimated slope also known as the regression coefficient

$A = $ actual value of the predictor variable

This equation can also be expressed in terms of actual Y-values instead of estimated Y'-values. When you do this, you need to add an estimate of error (E). Using Y instead of Y', you get:

$$Y = a' + b'(A) + E$$

where E is the difference between Y and Y' (also referred to as the *residual*).

Finally, you will once again use Greek symbols to signify the population parameters you are trying to estimate:

$$\text{Equation 14.5: } Y = \alpha + \beta(A) + \varepsilon$$

where:

α (alpha) $= $ population intercept

β (beta) $= $ population slope[3]

ε (epsilon) $= $ random error

Equation 14.5 is the *general linear model* for simple regression. Note the similarities between the general linear model for simple regression and the general linear model for the Oneway ANOVA given in Chapter 9.

Estimating the Slope (b′)   To estimate the slope (b'), you will use the covariance (see Chapter 13) between the predictor (A) and outcome (Y) variables divided by the variance of the predictor (A):

$$\text{Equation 14.6: The regression coefficient, } b' = \frac{\text{covariance}(A, Y)}{\text{variance}(A)}$$

---

[3]Do not confuse the use of β as the population slope with the use of β as the probability of making a Type II error. Similarly, α is the population intercept, not the probability value for significance testing.

The slope of the regression equation to predict Y from A depends on the degree of variability in the predictor *and* the degree of covariability between predictor and outcome variables. The larger the variance in A, the smaller the estimated slope (b'). On the other hand, the larger the covariance between Y and A, the larger the estimated slope (b').

If the variance of the predictor variable is large, the A-scores vary widely about the mean of A. When the predictor scores vary widely about their mean, the estimated slope (i.e., "rise" over "run") will be smaller than when the predictor scores vary slightly about their mean.

If the deviations scores of the predictor variable tend to be largest when the deviations scores of the outcome variable are largest, then the covariance will be high. If the relationship between the two sets of deviation scores is inconsistent (e.g., large A deviations associated with various size Y deviations), then the covariance will be small.

Recall from Chapter 13 that the covariance is the unbiased average of the cross products between predictor and outcome variables. Therefore, the estimated regression coefficient can be expressed as follows:

$$\text{Equation 14.7: } b' = \frac{\dfrac{\sum (A_i - \overline{A})(Y_i - \overline{Y})}{N - 1}}{\dfrac{\sum (A_i - \overline{A})^2}{N - 1}} = \frac{\sum (A_i - \overline{A})(Y_i - \overline{Y})}{\sum (A_i - \overline{A})^2}$$

Note that the $N - 1$ in both the numerator and denominator cancel each other out. Equation 14.7 can also be rewritten using simpler sums of squares (SS) notation:

$$\text{Equation 14.8: } b' = \frac{SS_{AY}}{SS_A}$$

Estimating the Intercept (a')

$$\text{Equation 14.9: } a' = \overline{Y} - b'(\overline{A})$$

This estimate ensures that the regression line passes through the point on the scatterplot where the mean of A and the mean of Y intersect.

See Textbox 14.2 for an example of estimating the slope, intercept and regression equation for the Parental Performance scenario. In the example, the estimated Y'-scores and the actual Y-scores are not always identical. As the correlation between predictor and outcome variables increases, the closer the estimated Y'-scores come to the actual Y-scores. As the correlation between predictor and outcome variables decreases, the further the estimated Y'-scores come to the actual Y-scores and the larger the residual scores.

The mean of the estimated scores ($\overline{Y}'$), however, will always equal the mean of the actual scores ($\overline{Y}$). Furthermore, the correlation between the actual Y-scores and A will always be identical to the correlation between the estimated Y'-scores and A. This is so because the values of the estimated Y'-scores are determined by the values of A.

Textbox 14.2

Imperfect Prediction and the Parental Performance Scenario

Use the data in Table 14.1 to estimate the regression coefficient (slope) and regression constant (intercept). Then use the regression equation to find the estimated values Y'. The calculated values are given in Table 14.3a.

Estimating the slope (b')

$$b' = \frac{\sum (A_i - \overline{A})(Y_i - \overline{Y})}{\sum (A_i - \overline{A})^2} = \frac{18.00}{10.00} = 1.80$$

Estimating the intercept (a')

$$a' = \overline{Y} - b'(\overline{A}) = 11.00 - 1.80(3.00) = 5.60$$

Estimating Y'

$$Y' = a' + b'(A)$$

Using the regression equation, find the estimated Y'-score for Mary ($A = 1$):

$$Y' = 5.60 + 1.80(1.00) = 7.40$$

The last column of Table 14.3a gives the estimated Y'-scores for each participant.

Now go on and use the regression equation to predict the reading test scores of a new group of students based only on the information you are able to gather about hours of parental involvement. To do so, for each child "plug" values of A into the regression equation:

$$Y' = 5.60 + 1.80(A)$$

Table 14.3b is an example of the regression equation in use for three students.

TABLE 14.3a Calculations for Regression of Concept Attainment (Y) on Hours of Parental Involvement (A)

Student	(A)	$A_i - \overline{A}$	$(A_i - \overline{A})^2$	Y	$Y_i - \overline{Y}$	$(Y_i - \overline{Y})^2$	$(A_i - \overline{A})(Y_i - \overline{Y})$	Y'
John	3	0	0	11	0	0	0	**11.00**
Mary	1	−2	4	7	−4	16	8	**7.40**
Jessica	4	1	1	15	4	16	4	**12.80**
Allison	5	2	4	13	2	4	4	**14.60**
Burt	2	−1	1	9	−2	4	2	**9.20**
Mean	3.00			11.00				**11.00**
Sum			10			40	18	

TABLE 14.3*b* Predicting Children's Concept Attainment (*Y'*) from Knowledge of Parental Involvement (*A*)		
Student	Actual Hours of Parental Involvement (A)	Estimated Concept Attainment Scores (Y')
Tom	2.0	9.20
Millie	3.5	11.90
Greg	6.0	16.40

Relationship Between the Correlation Coefficient (*r*) and the Regression Coefficient (*b'*)

We want to show the close relationship between the correlation coefficient and the regression coefficient. If two regression equations are computed—one in which Y is regressed on A, another in which A is regressed on Y—the mathematical relationship can be shown.

Consider the formulas for r and b' (for predicting Y' from A):

$$\text{(Equation 13.3)}\ r = \frac{SS_{AY}}{\sqrt{SS_A SS_Y}}$$

$$\text{Equation 14.8: } b' = \frac{SS_{AY}}{SS_A}$$

Notice that both formulas depend on the covariance of A and Y.

Now imagine that computation of two regression equations was attempted. In the first equation, estimate Y' from A (adding subscripts for clarification):

$$Y' = a_{Y'} + (b_{Y'})(A)$$

For the Parental Performance data:

$$Y' = 5.60 + 1.80(A)$$

In the second equation reverse things and estimate A' from the actual Y-scores:

$$A' = a_{A'} + (b_{A'})(Y)$$

For the Parental Performance data:

$$A' = -1.90 + 0.45(Y)$$

The two intercepts (a') are not identical nor are the two slopes (b'). Given that now there are two slopes, $b_{Y'}$ and $b_{A'}$, the following can be shown:

Equation 14.10: $r = \sqrt{(b_{Y'})(b_{A'})} = \sqrt{\dfrac{SS_{AY}}{SS_A}\dfrac{SS_{AY}}{SS_Y}} = \dfrac{SS_{AY}}{\sqrt{SS_A SS_Y}}$

For the Parental Performance example:

$$r = \sqrt{(1.80)(.45)} = \sqrt{\dfrac{18.00}{10.00}\dfrac{18.00}{40.00}} = \dfrac{18.00}{\sqrt{(10.00)(40.00)}} = +.90$$

The correlation coefficient (r) is simply the square root of the product of the two regression coefficients.

The z-Score Method for Determining the Regression Equation

When the obtained values of both A and Y have already been converted to z-scores, the converted scores can be used to determine the regression equation and the estimated scores will be in standard score form:

$$z_{Y'} = rz_A$$

where:

$z_{Y'}$ = estimated value of Y' expressed in standard score form

r = correlation between A- and Y-scores

z_A = actual value of A expressed in standard score form

There is no need to include an estimated value of the intercept in the z-score method for determining the regression equation because the intercept is always zero (0.0). The conversion of raw scores to standard scores results in both predicted and outcomes variables with means of zero (and standard deviations of 1.0).

STATISTICAL TESTS FOR SIMPLE REGRESSION

Now that we have used the regression equation to estimate Y' scores, we can explain how to partition variability and eventually conduct an F-test of significance. There are very close parallels between the partitioning of variability in simple regression and the partitioning of variability in the Oneway ANOVA (see Chapter 9). Once the total sum of squares has been divided into additive components, the appropriate mean squares can be found, and an F-ratio calculated. We also show how to compute the t-test.

Partitioning Variability

The partitioning of the total variability in simple regression is similar to the partitioning of total variability in the Oneway ANOVA.

For the Oneway ANOVA, total variability was partitioned into two additive components:

- Total variability = between-groups variability + within-groups (unexplained) variability

$$SS_Y = SS_{Y(A)} + SS_{Y(S/A)}$$

For simple regression, total variability can also be partitioned into two additive components:

- Total variability = variability explained by the predictor A (variability due to regression) + residual (unexplained) variability

$$SS_Y = SS_{Y(A)} - SS_{Y(RE)}$$

The **variability due to regression** $SS_{Y(A)}$ is the variability in the outcome measure (Y) that can be explained by the predictor (A).

Residual variability ($SS_{Y(RE)}$) is the variability in the outcome measure (Y) that cannot be explained.

To better understand how the total variability (SS_Y) for the outcome measure (Y) can be divided into two additive components, consider the identity for a single deviation score from the mean of Y:

$$Y - \overline{Y} = (Y' - \overline{Y}) + (Y - Y')$$

Figure 14.7 illustrates this equation graphically based on the Parental Performance data for one participant (Jessica).

Now square and sum both sides of the identity, which yields

$$\sum (Y - \overline{Y})^2 = \sum (Y' - \overline{Y})^2 + \sum (Y - Y')^2$$

You can now state the equations for each variability component:

$$\textbf{(Equation 9.3)} \ SS_Y = \sum (Y - \overline{Y})^2$$

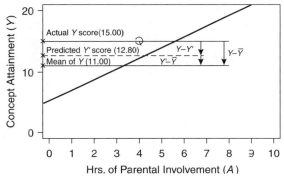

Figure 14.7 Partitioning of single deviation score

CD-ROM link 14.4

Activity 14.3: Test of Significance for Linear Regression

How is the total variability between two variables partitioned into variability explained by the predictor variable and residual variability? By varying the values of one data point, you can increase or decrease the linear correlation between the predictor variable and the outcome measure. As you change the degree of correlation between these two variables, notice how the *F*-ratio is affected.

SS_Y is the variability in *actual* Y-scores from the mean $\overline{Y}$, or *total variability*.

Equation 14.11: $SS_{Y(A)} = \sum (Y' - \overline{Y})^2$

$SS_{Y(A)}$ is the variability in *estimated* Y'-scores from the mean $\overline{Y}$, or *explained* variability. Because the estimated Y'-scores are based on the values of A, $SS_{Y(A)}$ also represents variability in actual Y-scores which can be explained by the predictor variable A.

Equation 14.12: $SS_{Y(RE)} = \sum (Y - Y')^2$

$SS_{Y(RE)}$ is the variability in *actual* Y-scores from *estimated* Y'-scores, or *unexplained* variability. Since $Y - Y'$ is the residual, Equation 14.12 is also known as **residual variability.**

These formula can be applied to the Parental Performance data (see Table 14.1) to arrive at the values shown in Table 14.4. Note that $SS_Y = SS_{Y(A)} + SS_{Y(RE)}$ (40.00 = 32.40 + 7.60).

From Sums of Squares to the *F*-Test

Now that the total variability in the outcome measure (Y) has been partitioned into additive components, the mean squares can be determined and an *F*-ratio formed. Before they are, we want to further elaborate on the similarities between simple regression and Oneway ANOVA as well as point out one important difference.

TABLE 14.4 Parental Performance Data Illustrating the Partitioning of Variability into Additive Components

Student	A	Y	Y'	$Y - \overline{Y}$	$(Y - \overline{Y})^2$ SS_Y	$Y' - \overline{Y}$	$(Y' - \overline{Y})^2$ $SS_{Y(A)}$	$Y - Y'$	$(Y - Y')^2$ $SS_{Y(RE)}$
John	3	11	11.00	0	0	0.00	0.00	0.00	0.00
Mary	1	7	7.40	−4	16	−3.60	12.96	−0.40	0.16
Jessica	4	15	12.80	4	16	1.80	3.24	2.20	4.84
Allison	5	13	14.60	2	4	3.60	12.96	−1.60	2.56
Burt	2	9	9.20	−2	4	−1.80	3.24	−0.20	0.40
Mean	3.00	11.00	11.00						
Sum of Squares					40		32.40		7.60

Similarities with Oneway ANOVA   In Chapter 9 on the Oneway Between-Groups ANOVA, we showed how the total variability (SS_Y) of the dependent variable could be partitioned into two additive components between-groups variability ($SS_{Y(A)}$) and within-groups variability ($SS_{Y(S/A)}$). The partitioning of variability in simple regression is analogous to variance partitioning in Oneway ANOVA. In simple regression total variability (SS_Y) is also partitioned into two additive components: variability due to regression (or explained variability, $SS_{Y(A)}$) and residual variability (or unexplained variability, $SS_{Y(RE)}$).

For the Oneway ANOVA, one calculates a ratio of variances ($MS_{Y(A)}/MS_{Y(SA)}$) to determine whether the numerator, the between-groups variance ($MS_{Y(A)}$), is significantly larger than the denominator, the within-groups variance ($MS_{Y(S/A)}$). This ratio of variances is the F-ratio. The calculated value of F is then compared to the tabled or critical value of F so that one can make a decision concerning the null and alternative hypotheses.

For the Oneway ANOVA, it was argued that the F-ratio should be approximately 1.0 when the null hypothesis is correct and the treatment has no effect. In this case, both the numerator, the between-groups variance $MS_{Y(A)}$ and the denominator, the within-groups variance $MS_{Y(S/A)}$, estimate the same thing: variance due to chance.

In contrast, it was argued that the F-ratio should be greater than 1.0 when the alternative hypothesis is correct and the treatment does have an effect. In this case, the numerator, the between-groups variance $MS_{Y(A)}$, estimates both chance fluctuation and the influence of the treatment, whereas the denominator, the within-groups variance $MS_{Y(S/A)}$, estimates only variance due to chance.

For simple regression, you will proceed in a similar fashion. Mean squares will be calculated to find both the variance explained by the predictor ($MS_{Y(A)}$) and the residual or unexplained variance ($MS_{Y(RE)}$). The ratio of these two variances ($MS_{Y(A)}/MS_{Y(RE)}$) is the calculated value of F which one then compares to the tabled or critical value in order to choose between the null and alternative hypotheses.

Differences from Oneway ANOVA   There is one important difference between the Oneway ANOVA and simple regression. In Oneway ANOVA, one explores whether there is *any* significant relationship between the independent variable and the dependent variable. In simple regression, one explores whether there is a significant *linear* relationship between the predictor variable and the outcome variable.

Determining Significance Using the F-Ratio in Simple Regression
Using the F-ratio to test the significance of a predictor requires that the following steps be followed:

1. Compute the sum of squares.
2. Find the degrees of freedom.
3. Compute the mean squares.
4. Calculate the F-ratio.
5. Compare the calculated value of F with the critical value of F.

Sums of Squares

$$\text{(Equation 10.3) } SS_Y = \sum (Y - \overline{Y})^2$$

$$\text{Equation 14.11: } SS_{Y(A)} = \sum (Y' - \overline{Y})^2$$

$$\text{Equation 14.12: } SS_{Y(RE)} = \sum (Y - Y')^2$$

The Sums of Squares Are Additive:

$$SS_Y = SS_{Y(A)} + SS_{Y(RE)}$$

$$\sum (Y - \overline{Y})^2 = \sum (Y' - \overline{Y})^2 + \sum (Y - Y')^2$$

Degrees of Freedom

$$df_Y = N - 1$$

$$df_A = A = 1 \text{ (since there is a single, continuous predictor)}$$

$$df_{RE} = N - A - 1$$

The degrees of freedom are additive:

$$df_Y = df_A + df_{RE}$$

Mean Squares

$$\text{Equation 14.13: } MS_{Y(A)} = SS_{Y(A)}/df_A$$

$$\text{Equation 14.14: } MS_{Y(RE)} = SS_{Y(RE)}/df_{RE}$$

$$\text{Equation 14.15: } MS_Y = SS_Y/df_Y$$

The mean squares are *not* additive:

$$MS_Y \neq MS_{Y(A)} + MS_{Y(RE)}$$

More on Mean Squares $MS_{Y(RE)}$ is also known as the **variance of estimate**; it is the variance of the residuals.

$\sqrt{MS_{Y(RE)}}$ is the **standard error of estimate**; it is the standard deviation of the residuals.

CD-ROM link 14.5

Problem Generator: Simple Linear Regression
To practice hypothesis testing using simple linear regression, select Simple Linear Regression from the Problem Generator Menu on the CD-ROM. The Problem Generator will create as many practice problems as you need and will demonstrate each step in their solution so that you can check your work.

The variance and standard deviation of the outcome variable can also be expressed as mean squares:

$$MS_Y = \frac{\sum (Y - \overline{Y})^2}{N - 1} = s^2$$

= the (unbiased) variance of the set of observed Y-scores.

$$\sqrt{MS_Y} = \sqrt{\frac{\sum (Y - \overline{Y})^2}{N - 1}} = s$$

= the (unbiased) standard deviation of the set of observed Y-scores.

The Calculated Value of F   The calculated value of F is a ratio of two mean squares:

Equation 14.16: $F = MS_{Y(A)}/MS_{Y(RE)}$

See Textbox 14.3 for an illustration using the Parental Performance scenario.

Regression Summary Table   The calculations can now be put into a Summary Table, which is useful for reporting the findings. See Table 14.5 which is a Regression Summary Table for the Parental Performance scenario.

Textbox 14.3

The Simple Regression of Concept Attainment (Y) on Parental Involvement (A)

The Parental Performance scenario will be used to show how you can calculate an F-ratio to determine whether Parental Involvement (A) significantly ($p < .05$) predicts variability in Concept Attainment (Y). See Table 14.3a for the individual squared deviation scores.

$$SS_{Y(A)} = \sum (Y' - \overline{Y})^2 = 32.40$$

$$SS_{Y(RE)} = \sum (Y - Y')^2 = 7.60$$

$$SS_Y = \sum (Y - \overline{Y})^2 = 40.00$$

$$MS_{Y(A)} = SS_{Y(A)}/df_A = 32.40$$

$$MS_{Y(RE)} = SS_{Y(RE)}/df_{RE} = 7.60/3 = 2.53$$

$$MS_Y = SS_Y/df_Y = 40.00/4 = 10.00$$

$$F_{calc} = 32.40/2.53 = 12.79$$

$$F_{crit} = 10.10 \text{ (for } df_A = 1, df_{RE} = 3, \text{ and alpha} = .05)$$

Because F_{calc} is greater than F_{crit}, reject the null hypothesis and accept the alternative hypothesis. Hours of parental involvement is a significant predictor of the reading achievement of young children.

TABLE 14.5 Summary Table: Regression of Concept Attainment (*Y*) on Hours of Parental Involvement (*A*)

Source	SS	df	MS	F
Parental Involvement (*A*) (Regression)	32.40	1	32.40	12.79*
Residual	7.60	3	2.53	
Total	40.00	4	10.00	

*$p < .05$

Testing Significance Using the *t*-Test

As just shown, one alternative to evaluating the significance of a predictor in simple regression is to use the *F*-test. In Chapter 13, another means was presented for evaluating the significance of one predictor via the *t*-test, which we used to test the significance of *r*. We now want to elaborate further on the uses of the *t*-test in simple regression. Keep in mind that both the *F*-test and two-tailed *t*-test will lead to identical conclusions in the case of simple regression, that is, where there is only a single predictor variable involved.[4]

In Chapter 13 this formula was given for testing the significance of *r*:

$$\textbf{(Equation 13.4)}\ t = \frac{r}{\sqrt{(1 - r^2)/(N - 2)}} \qquad \text{where degrees of free-dom (df) equals } N - 2.$$

It is possible to convert the *t*-test for correlation into the *t*-test for regression:

$$\textbf{Equation 14.17: } t = \frac{b'}{s_{b'}} = \frac{\dfrac{SS_{AY}}{SS_A}}{\sqrt{\dfrac{MS_{Y(RE)}}{SS_A}}}$$

where:

b' = estimated regression coefficient

$s_{b'}$ = estimated standard error of the regression coefficient

degrees of freedom (df) = $N - A - 1$ (or $N - 2$)

Also remember that for a single predictor (i.e., when numerator df = 1) $t^2 = F$. Therefore, squaring Equation 13.4 yields:

$$\textbf{Equation 14.18: } F = \frac{r^2}{(1 - r^2)/(N - 2)}$$

Textbox 14.4 illustrates the four methods of testing the significance of a single predictor.

---

[4]The equivalence of various significance tests in simple regression, where only a single predictor is involved, does not necessarily extend to multiple regression, where two or more predictors are involved.

Textbox 14.4

Four Ways of Testing the Significance of a Single Predictor

Four ways to test the significance of a single predictor are shown below: the *t*-test based on the correlation coefficient, the *t*-test based on the regression coefficient, the mean squares *F*-test, and the correlation method *F*-test. For each method, the data from the Parental Performance scenario will be used to show that you can arrive at results that are numerically equivalent.

Correlation Method *t*-Test

The calculated value is:

$$t = \frac{r}{\sqrt{(1-r^2)/(n-2)}} = \frac{0.90}{\sqrt{(1-(.90)^2/(5-2)}} = \frac{.90}{.25} = +3.58 \text{ (allowing for rounding error)}.$$

The critical value for a nondirectional alternative hypothesis for $\alpha = .05$, with df $= 3$, is 3.18. Since 3.58 is greater than 3.18, you reject the null hypothesis and accept the alternative hypothesis that there is a relationship between hours of parental involvement and number of concepts attained by children.

Regression Method *t*-Test

The calculated value is:

$$t = \frac{\dfrac{SS_{AY}}{SS_A}}{\sqrt{\dfrac{MS_{Y(RE)}}{SS_A}}} = \frac{\dfrac{18.00}{10.00}}{\sqrt{\dfrac{2.53}{10.00}}} = \frac{1.80}{.50} = +3.58$$

$$t = \frac{b'}{s_{b'}} = \frac{1.80}{.50} = +3.58$$

The critical value is 3.18, as above, and you also reject the null hypothesis.

Mean Squares *F*-Test

$$F_{calc} = MS_{Y(A)}/MS_{Y(RE)} = 32.40/2.53 = 12.79$$

$$F_{crit} = 10.10 \text{ (for df}_A = 1, \text{ df}_{RE} = 3, \text{ and } \alpha = .05)$$

Because 12.79 is greater than 10.10, you reject the null hypothesis. Furthermore, does $t^2 = F$?

$$(3.58)^2 = 12.79.$$

Correlation Method *F*-Test

The calculated value is

$$F = \frac{r^2}{\sqrt{(1-r^2)/(N-2)}} = \frac{.90^2}{\sqrt{(1-.90^2)/(5-2)}} = 12.79$$

This calculated value is identical to the value computed using the mean squares method. Since 12.79 is greater than 10.10, you reject the null hypothesis.

OTHER ISSUES IN SIMPLE LINEAR REGRESSION

This section covers a few other issues that simple regression holds in common with other inferential statistical procedures. These issues include confidence intervals, strength of association, power, and assumption violations.

Confidence Intervals

In Chapter 13 a means to compute the confidence interval for the correlation coefficient (r) was presented. Because the sampling distributions of the correlation coefficient can be skewed, a correlation coefficient must first be transformed before the confidence interval can be found.

As noted in Chapter 9, the sampling distributions for the F-ratio can also be skewed. This is the major reason why confidence intervals for the F-ratio are seldom reported.

Fortunately, the sampling distributions for the t-test are symmetrical. Thus, it is relatively straightforward to set confidence intervals around the regression coefficient (b'). Another advantage of the t-test is that one can evaluate directional, or one-tailed, hypotheses in addition to nondirectional, or two-tailed, hypotheses.

Confidence Interval for the Regression Coefficient (b') The estimated two-sided confidence interval for a nondirectional, two-tailed alternative hypothesis is as follows:

$$\textbf{Equation 14.19: } b' - t_{1-\alpha/2}s_{b'} \text{ and } b' + t_{1-\alpha/2}s_{b'}$$

where:

> b' = estimated regression coefficient;
>
> t = critical value for a particular probability value, degrees of freedom, and for a two-tailed test $(1 - \alpha/2)$; and
>
> $s_{b'}$ = estimated standard error of the regression coefficient.

Textbox 14.5 provides an example in which the Parental Performance scenario is used.

Strength of Association

The square of the correlation coefficient (r^2) or the square of the multiple correlation coefficient (R^2), both known as the *coefficient of determination,* is a measure of strength of association.[5] As mentioned in Chapter 13, the square of the correlation

---

[5]Note that we use the symbol r to refer to the correlation between a single predictor variable and an outcome variable; we use the symbol R to refer to the multiple correlation between one or more predictor variables and an outcome variable. Therefore, when there is only a single predictor, r and R are mathematically identical and may be used interchangeably; when there is more than a single predictor only R should be used.

> ### Textbox 14.5
>
> ### Confidence Interval for the Regression Coefficient
>
> Find the confidence interval for the regression coefficient from the Parental Performance scenario by testing a nondirectional alternative hypothesis with $\alpha = .05$.
>
> $$b' - t_{1-\alpha/2} s_{b'} \text{ and } b' + t_{1-\alpha/2} s_{b'} =$$
> $$1.80 - (3.18).50 \text{ and } 1.80 + (3.18).50$$
> $$.21 \leq \beta \leq 3.39$$
>
> The 95% confidence interval for β ranges from .21 to 3.39.
> Note that the confidence interval does not contain zero. Because it does not, you know that the regression coefficient for the predictor variable, Parental Involvement (A), is significantly different from zero.

---

coefficient (r^2) equals the proportion of total variability in the outcome measure (Y) that can be accounted for by the predictor variable (A).

As shown in Chapter 9, the coefficient of determination can be computed directly from the sums of squares:

$$\textbf{(Equation 9.11) } R^2 = \frac{SS_A}{SS_Y}$$

Finally, as also shown in Chapter 9, Cohen (1988) developed a measure of general effect size (f) for the F-ratio based on R^2:

$$\textbf{(Equation 9.12) } f = \sqrt{\frac{R^2}{1 - R^2}}$$

Use the same effect size classifications as done previously (see Chapter 9). That is:

- An f of .10 is a small effect size.
- An f of .25 is a medium effect size.
- An f of .40 is a large effect size.

However, be mindful that the term *effect size* is not preferred terminology for correlational investigations because causal influences cannot readily be established. *Strength of association* is the preferred term in this situation. Furthermore, the descriptions "small," "medium," and "large" are somewhat arbitrary and Cohen neither recommends their uniform application nor uses the same numerical values consistently for all statistical procedures.

See Textbox 14.6 for an illustration of R^2 and f using the Parental Performance scenario.

Textbox 14.6

Strength of Association and *f* for the Parental Performance Scenario

Estimate the strength of association between Parental Involvement (*A*) and Concept Attainment (*Y*) using both *r* and SS.

From the calculations in Chapter 13:

$$r = +.90 \qquad r^2 = .81$$

From Table 14.5, $SS_{Y(A)} = 32.40$ and $SS_Y = 40.00$

$$SS_{Y(A)}/SS_Y = 32.40/40.00 = .81$$

$$f = \sqrt{\frac{R^2}{1 - R^2}} = \sqrt{\frac{.81}{.19}} = 2.06$$

You conclude that an *f* of 2.06 is indicative of a large strength of association.

Power

In Chapter 9, we illustrated the use of Cohen's (1988) power tables for the ANOVA using *f*. A condensed version of these tables is given in Appendix E. Recall that each section represents the degrees of freedom for the numerator. Therefore, for simple regression for a single predictor, use numerator df = 1.0. Also recall that power is presented for *group*, not total, sample sizes (*n*) of 5 to 100. Therefore, total sample size for regression will be approximately double the group sample sizes shown for ANOVA with numerator df = 1.0 (i.e., when there are two groups df = 1.0).

In addition, three probability values for significance testing are included (i.e., $\alpha = .01, .05, .10$). The F_c column represents the critical or tabled value of *F* required to reject the null hypothesis. There are three columns for effect sizes (i.e., $f = .10$, or a small effect; $f = .25$, or a medium effect; and $f = .40$, or a large effect). The values for power beyond .99 are represented as **.

Appendix E may be used in several ways: (1) to determine the sample size you will need to achieve a desired power given your guess as to the strength of association you will obtain; (2) to determine the power you might expect given a certain sample size and estimated strength of association; and (3) to determine the strength of association you might expect given a certain sample size and estimated power. Textbox 14.7 illustrates the use of the power tables for the Parental Performance scenario and a second example.

Underlying Assumptions

The first assumption in simple linear regression concerns **normality.** The values of the predictor variable (*A*) and the outcome variable (*Y*) are each expected to be distributed normally.

The second assumption concerns **independence.** Each pair of *A*- and *Y*-scores should be independent of all the other pairs of *A* and *Y* scores.

Textbox 14.7

Use of Power Tables for the Parental Performance Scenario

Imagine that you wanted to treat the data from the Parental Performance scenario as a pilot study. How well could you use the tables to determine the power of the statistical test to reject the null hypothesis in this study? To answer this question, note the following:

$$N = 5 \text{ (therefore } n \approx 3)$$

$$F_{\text{crit}}(1, 3) = 10.10, p < .05$$

$$f = 2.06$$

You cannot use the power tables very accurately in this situation for two reasons: (1) the sample size is especially small and (2) f is very large. However, the trend in the tables suggests that power might be somewhat below .80. For a precise answer, you would be better off consulting the unabridged version of Cohen's tables.

Imagine a second study involving $N = 50$ participants and $r = +.25$ with $\alpha = .05$. Therefore,

$$N = 50 \text{ (therefore } n = 25)$$

$$F_{\text{crit}}(1, 48) = 4.04$$

$$f = \sqrt{\frac{R^2}{1 - R^2}} = \sqrt{\frac{(.25)^2}{1 - (.25)^2}} = .26 \text{ or approximately } .25$$

$$1 - \beta = .42 \text{ (power)}$$

If you were to conduct a further investigation, what sample size would you estimate would be needed for a desired power of .80?

Given $f \approx .25$, and $\alpha = .05$, you would need double the group sample size of approximately 75 participants extracted from the table, or a total sample size of 150 participants.

Finally, the third assumption concerns **homoscedasticity.** For every value of A the variances of Y are supposed to be equal, allowing for sampling error. See Figure 14.8. Note how the arrangement of the normal distributions takes on the appearance of a loaf of bread indicative of the uniformity in the size and shape of the Y-variances.

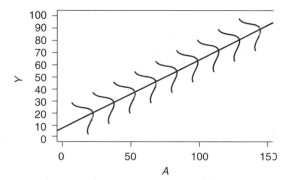

Figure 14.8 Illustration of homoscedasticity

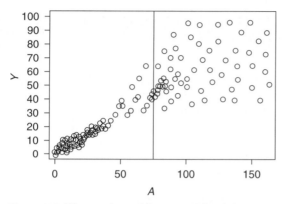

Figure 14.9 Illustration of heteroscedasticity

What might the data look like when the assumption of homoscedasticity is not met? The scatterplot shown in Figure 14.9 is a display of a fan-shaped spread of scores. The variability in the *Y*-scores for lower values of *A* is clearly smaller than the variability in the *Y*-scores for higher values of *A*. It is one example of **heteroscedasticity.**

In Figure 14.9, it is clear that the correlation between *Y* and *A* is not the same across all portions of the scatterplot. For values of *A* below 75, there is a fairly strong relationship between *Y* and *A*. In contrast, for values of *A* above 75, there is only a modest relationship between *Y* and *A*. Thus the correlation computed for all values of *Y* and *A* does not adequately represent the relationship. For a subset of the *A* and *Y* scores it underrepresents the relationship, while for another subset of *A* and *Y* scores it overrepresents it.

Using Standardized Residuals to Check the Data

In Chapter 13, we suggested that a careful examination of a scatterplot is useful in identifying problems with the data such as departures from linearity and heteroscedasticity. Another very useful approach is the plotting and study of **standardized residuals,** in particular, where standardized residuals are plotted against the predicted scores (Y').

The formula for obtaining standardized residuals (z_r) is as follows:

$$\text{Equation 14.20: } z_r = \frac{Y - Y'}{\sqrt{\text{MS}_{Y(RE)}}}$$

where:

$Y - Y'$ = deviation of an actual score (Y) from a predicted score (Y') and

$\sqrt{\text{MS}_{Y(RE)}}$ = standard deviation of the residuals (standard error of estimate).

The scatterplot of standardized residuals should reveal that the points appear to scatter randomly about the line originating from the mean of the residuals. If, however, the points describe a curve, it suggests that the regression is curvilinear. On the other hand, if the points are not evenly scattered about the line, heteroscedasticity is possible. Finally, are there extreme residuals or outliers that may distort the results? As a general rule, standardized residuals greater than ±2.00 should be considered as extreme and deserve special attention. See Textbox 14.8.

Textbox 14.8

Standardized Residuals and the Parental Performance Scenario

Use the data from the Parental Performance scenario to find and plot the standardized residuals. The general form of the regression equation is

$$Y' = a' + b'(A)$$

Using the regression equation for the Parental Performance data, you can find the estimated Y' score for Jessica ($A = 4$):

$$Y' = 5.60 + 1.80(4.00) = 12.80$$

Now find z_r for Jessica:

$$z_r = \frac{Y - Y'}{\sqrt{MS_{Y(RE)}}} = \frac{15.00 - 12.80}{\sqrt{2.53}} = \frac{2.20}{1.59} = 1.38$$

If you repeat these calculations for each of the four remaining students, you can then create a scatterplot like the one illustrated in Figure 14.10. Note that there are no extreme residuals. The small sample size prevents you from judging whether nonlinearity or heteroscedasticity are concerns.

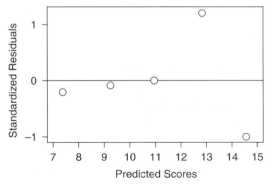

Figure 14.10 Scatterplot of standardized residuals

PUTTING IT ALL TOGETHER

Chapter 13 developed your fundamental understanding of the strengths and weaknesses of correlational designs in general and the statistical technique known as Pearson's product-moment correlation (r) in particular. This chapter picked up where you left off with correlation, extending your understanding to simple linear regression.

Linear correlation refers to the degree of linear relationship between two variables (A and Y). The degree of the relationship is summarized in a single statistic, the correlation coefficient (r).

Linear regression refers to fitting a straight line through the scatterplot of A- and Y-scores. The regression equation can then be used to predict a subject's score on the outcome variable Y from knowledge of that subject's score on the predictor variable A.

The case of perfect prediction was dealt with first. Slope was defined as:

$$\textbf{Equation 14.1: slope } (b) = \frac{\text{change in } Y}{\text{change in } A}$$

Intercept was defined as:

$$\textbf{Equation 14.2: Intercept } a = \overline{Y} - b\overline{A}$$

Finally, the formula for a straight line was given as:

$$\textbf{Equation 14.3: } Y = a + (b)(A)$$

This was called the *regression equation* for a straight line.

Next situations were considered in which there was imperfect prediction of the outcome variable from knowledge of the predictor variable. In such situations, one must estimate the slope and intercept components used in the regression equation for a straight line:

$$\textbf{Equation 14.4: } Y' = a' + b'(A)$$

where:

Y' = estimated value of the outcome variable.

a' = estimated intercept (also known as the regression constant).

b' = estimated slope (also known as the regression coefficient).

A = actual value of the predictor variable.

You can express the estimated regression coefficient as

$$\textbf{Equation 14.7: } \frac{\dfrac{\sum (A_i - \overline{A})(Y_i - \overline{Y})}{N - 1}}{\dfrac{\sum (A_i - \overline{A})^2}{N - 1}} = \frac{\sum (A_i - \overline{A})(Y_i - \overline{Y})}{\sum (A_i - \overline{A})^2}$$

$$\text{Equation 14.8: } b' = \frac{SS_{AY}}{SS_A}$$

You can also estimate the intercept

$$\text{Equation 14.9: } a' = \overline{Y} - b'(\overline{A})$$

This estimate ensures that the regression lines passes through the point on the scatterplot where the mean of A and the mean of Y intersect.

The concept of variance partitioning that was introduced in considering the Oneway ANOVA can also be used in simple linear regression. From this understanding, the formulas were presented for sums of squares, degrees of freedom, mean squares, and the calculated value of the F-ratio.

$$\text{(Equation 9.3) } SS_Y = \sum (Y - \overline{Y})^2$$

$$\text{Equation 14.11: } SS_{Y(A)} = \sum (Y' - \overline{Y})^2$$

$$\text{Equation 14.12: } SS_{Y(RE)} = \sum (Y - Y')^2$$

The sums of squares are additive:

$$SS_Y = SS_{Y(A)} + SS_{Y(RE)}$$

$$\sum (Y - \overline{Y})^2 = \sum (Y' - \overline{Y})^2 + \sum (Y - Y')^2$$

$$df_Y = N - 1$$

$$df_A = A \text{ (since there is a single, continuous predictor)}$$

$$df_{RE} = N - A - 1$$

The degrees of freedom are additive:

$$df_Y = df_A + df_{RE}$$

$$\text{Equation 14.13: } MS_{Y(A)} = SS_{Y(A)}/df_A$$

$$\text{Equation 14.14: } MS_{Y(RE)} = SS_{Y(RE)}/df_{RE}$$

$$\text{Equation 14.15: } MS_Y = SS_Y/df_Y$$

The mean squares are *not* additive:

$$MS_Y \neq MS_{Y(A)} + MS_{Y(RE)}$$

Finally, the calculated value of F is a ratio of two mean squares:

$$\text{Equation 14.16: } F = MS_{Y(A)}/MS_{Y(RE)}$$

The confidence interval for the regression coefficient (b') is:

Equation 14.19: $b' - t_{1-\alpha/2} s_{b'}$ and $b' + t_{1-\alpha/2} s_{b'}$

where:

b' = estimated regression coefficient;

t = critical value for a particular probability value, degrees of freedom, and for a two-tailed test $(1 - \alpha/2)$; and

$s_{b'}$ = estimated standard error of the regression coefficient.

The square of the correlation coefficient (r^2) or the square of multiple correlation coefficient (R^2), both known as the *coefficient of determination,* is a measure of strength of association. Therefore:

$$\textbf{(Equation 9.11) } R^2 = \frac{SS_A}{SS_Y}$$

$$\textbf{(Equation 9.12) } f = \sqrt{\frac{R^2}{1 - R^2}}$$

In Chapter 9, the use of Cohen (1988) power tables was illustrated for the ANOVA using f. A condensed version of these tables is given in Appendix E. For simple regression for a single predictor, use numerator df = 1.0. Furthermore, total sample size for regression will be approximately double the group sample sizes shown for ANOVA.

Textbox 14.9

Simple Linear Regression: Mental Chronometry

How much time does it take to think about a problem and then respond? Information processing research in this area is called *mental chronometry.* The Stroop interference effect is the phenomenon that occurs when an individual is asked to say the word for a color when it is printed in another color; for example, saying "green" when the color being printed is red. Individuals take longer to process and respond under such conditions. Similar interference phenomena occur for number naming, direction naming, and picture naming (Chen, 1997). Where does the interference occur? Chen (1997) was interested in analyzing whether the interference occurred at a particular stage of processing (stage approach) or whether it was a continuous interaction and accumulated throughout the naming process (interaction approach). Chen suggested that simple linear regression (SLR) would allow one to determine whether the stage approach or the interaction approach was operating. The stage approach would be reflected in the intercept of the regression function while the interaction approach would be reflected in the slope of the regression function.

To test the ability of the SLR to detect differences in interference effects, Stroop effect tasks that were known to be stage-related interference tasks were used. In one experiment, subjects were shown pairs of geometric figures on a computer with one member of the pair rotated 0, 60, 120, or 180 degrees. They were asked to compare these figures and indicate if they were identical (a positive response) or mirror images (a negative response). Chen hypothesized that

continued

Textbox 14.9 (Continued)

the angular disparity should affect the rotation process only and that the effect should be reflected in the intercept and not the slope of the regression function (a stage approach). Each subject's mean response times for the 60, 120, and 180 degrees were regressed on the mean response times for the 0 degrees disparity condition. In one experiment, the regression of 60 degrees gave an intercept of 221.36 (SE [standard error] = 96.33; $t = 2.30, p < .05$) and a slope of 1.11 (SE = .08, $t = 1.32, p > .09$); the regression of 120 degrees yielded an intercept of 397.67, (SE = 108.06, $t = 3.68, p < .001$) and a slope of 1.12 (SE = .09, $t = 1.26, p > .10$); the regression of 180 degrees yielded an intercept of 325.66 (SE = 106.05, $t = 3.07, p < .01$) and a slope of 1.22 (SE = .09, $t = 2.36, p < .05$). For the regressions R^2 was .83, .79, and .83, respectively.

The results of this experiment showed that for the 60- and 120-degree disparity condition, the intercepts, but not the slopes of the regression function, were affected. The results of the simple linear regression showed that stage effect interference was operating for these conditions as predicted. For the 180-degree disparity condition both intercept and slope were affected. This suggested to Chen that mental processes under the final condition may have been different from those in the other conditions and that perhaps both stage and interaction influences were operating.

KEY TERMS

Linear correlation

Linear regression

Slope

Rate of change

Y-intercept

Regression equation

Best-fit line

Method of least squares

Actual, or obtained, scores

Predicted, or estimated, scores

Residual

Regression equation

Regression constant

Regression coefficient

Variability due to regression

Residual variability

Variance of estimate

Standard error of estimate

Normality

Independence

Homoscedasticity

Heteroscedasticity

Standardized residuals

REFERENCES

Chen, J-Y. (1997) Mental chronometry with simple linear regression. *Perceptual and Motor Skills, 85*, 499–513.

Cohen, J. (1988). *Statistical power analysis for the behavioral sciences.* (2nd ed.). Hillsdale, NJ: Lawrence Erlbaum.

PROBLEMS

Questions

Section 1   Conceptual/Definition

14.1. What is the difference between correlation and regression?

14.2. Define *slope.*

14.3. When two variables are perfectly related (Pearson's $r = \pm 1$), what will be the slope of the regression line?

14.4. When two variables are perfectly related (Pearson's $r = \pm 1$), what does the associated scatterplot look like?

14.5. What is the *line of best fit*?

14.6. How is the estimated slope b' calculated?

14.7. When the z-score method for determining the regression equation is used, the regression line always passes through the origin. Why?

14.8. What is an important difference between Oneway ANOVA and simple linear regression?

14.9. Identify four different methods for testing the significance of a single predictor.

14.10. What assumptions underlie the use of the simple linear regression model?

Section 2   Numerical

Use the following data to answer questions 14.11 to 14.12:

A	Y
12	26
14	29
11	28
9	23
6	21

14.11. Prepare a Regression Summary Table. Is *A* a significant linear predictor of *Y*?

14.12. Determine the linear regression equation. Based upon this equation, determine the residual for each value of *Y*.

Use the following data to answer questions 14.13 to 14.14

A	Y
73	83
68	72
66	72
56	56
66	68
78	86
57	49
56	64
64	69
56	52
61	55
51	50
68	49
79	66
59	66

14.13. Test the significance of *A* as a linear predictor of *Y* using the regression method *t*-test.

14.14. Determine the linear regression equation and calculate the 95% confidence interval for b'.

14.15. For the dataset below, a perfect nonlinear relationship between A and Y exists ($Y = A_2 + 1$). There is no error in prediction. Prepare a Regression Summary Table and comment upon the results.

A	Y
5	26
8	65
4	17
12	145
16	257
9	82
18	325
10	101
13	169
3	10

14.16. For a given dataset, the coefficient of determination is 81.4%. The variance for the predicted variable (MS_Y) is 15.77, and there are six pairs of data in total. Prepare a Regression Summary Table.

14.17. Using the data in the table below prepare a Regression Summary Table.

A	Y
65	69
77	76
82	80
56	64
61	67
90	84
84	63
77	79
76	58
71	66

Use the following dataset to answer questions 14.18 to 14.19.

Subject	A	Y
1	8	28
2	6	27
3	3	21
4	9	31
5	12	46

14.18. Use the correlational method t-test to test the significance of A.

14.19. Use the correlational method F-test to test the significance of A.

14.20. Calculate b' for the dataset below.

Subject	A	Y
1	32	87
2	48	93
3	37	99
4	21	75
5	56	56
6	49	81

Dealing with More Than a Single Predictor Variable

Multiple Linear Regression

OVERVIEW

Whoever said that statistics was only for ivory-tower academics never had a chance to understand and use multiple linear regression. Why do we say that? Because multiple linear regression allows you to incorporate more than a single predictor into the analysis and explanation of the outcome measure. With it you can look at as few or as many of the factors considered to be important influences, especially if you can measure these predictors well. (The sky's the limit, if you need to go that high.)

Many researchers have read research reports where, while the investigator studied a variable carefully, it was one of little consequence. At the same time, researchers have all felt that other, more important or more interesting factors should have been included but weren't. Even when researchers read studies judged important, they have sometimes wondered how the influential variables from studies combine together.

Multiple linear regression is a correlational method of data analysis in which more than one predictor variable can be statistically analyzed, either simultaneously or successively. Although we concentrate here on the statistical procedures involved in the regression of a single outcome measure on two predictor variables, what you learn should be transferable to situations in which more than two predictors are involved. As you will see, you will also use what you learned about simple linear regression as the building blocks for the new concepts and techniques you will learn here.

These are some of the questions we hope to answer in this chapter:

1. What is the difference between simple and multiple regression when predictors are correlated with one another versus uncorrelated with one another?
2. How does one find the multiple regression equation for predicting scores on the outcome variable, taking into account two (or more) predictor variables?
3. What are the tests of significance for multiple linear regression, and in what important ways do they differ from the tests of significance for simple linear regression?
4. What is the difference between unique and shared variability?

5. What are the advantages of the incremental approach to multiple linear regression?
6. Is there necessarily a clear-cut answer to "which predictor is most important"?

To get things started, please read the Common Allies scenario in Textbox 15.1.

Textbox 15.1

Common Allies

Two graduate students, enrolled in a multidisciplinary course on marriage and the family, are having an academic argument at the local college watering hole. They are debating the factors that explain variability in marital happiness. The psychology graduate student insists that perceived partner sensitivity is a significant predictor of marital happiness. The sociology graduate student, on the other hand, is equally adamant that the cultural similarity between partners is the key to a successful marriage.

The two students agree to conduct a small study to settle their differences and to serve as the basis for a joint final paper in the course. The two students contact 10 married couples and get their agreement to be participants in the students' investigation. Each couple completes a measure of marital happiness, completes a joint measure of partner sensitivity, and fills in a questionnaire about their cultural similarity. The results are reported in Table 15.1.

Which of the two graduate students is correct? Do both partner sensitivity and cultural similarity predict marital happiness? Which of the two predictors is more important?

TABLE 15.1   Marital Happiness (Y), Partner Sensitivity (A), and Cultural Similarity (B)

Couple	Marital Happiness (Y)	Partner Sensitivity (A)	Cultural Similarity (B)
Jones	5	2	20
Smith	8	4	30
Pambookian	26	5	60
Abrams	25	9	55
Lou	18	8	45
Simard	15	5	30
Took	10	4	10
O'Leary	11	5	15
Brecht	18	7	20
Nadia	14	6	15

THE LOGIC OF MULTIPLE LINEAR REGRESSION

In Chapter 11, the statistical analysis of data for a single dependent variable and two (or more) independent variables was presented. There are situations in correlational research in which one wishes to study the relationship between the outcome variable and more than one predictor variable at the same time. In these situations, the statistical tool of choice is multiple linear regression (MLR) (Pedhazur, 1997). With more than a single predictor, the kinds of questions one might ask include:

- Is predictor *A* a significant predictor of variability in *Y*, the outcome variable? Predictor *B*? Predictor *C*? And so on.
- Does predictor *A* explain a meaningful amount of variability in *Y*, the outcome variable? Predictor *B*? Predictor *C*? And so on.

Both sets of questions above treat the predictors separately. The questions below treat the predictors together.

- Does the explanation of variability in the outcome variable (*Y*) significantly increase when more than one predictor is used?
- What are the fewest predictors one can use to explain variability in the outcome variable (*Y*)?

The use of correlational research is widespread. In conducting correlational studies, the investigator is not restricted to studying a single predictor variable and a single outcome variable. Indeed, the researcher is often interested in trying to explain as much of the variability in the outcome variable as possible. In order to do so, the investigator often collects data on more than a single predictor variable. A few examples of research situations that take advantage of multiple predictor variables are given in Textbox 15.2.

Textbox 15.2

Examples of Multiple Prediction

To what extent are final grades in a statistics course explained by undergraduate grade point average, verbal ability, math ability, and math anxiety?

To what degree can student's self-concept be predicted from academic achievement, socioeconomic status, and physical attractiveness?

How well can computer programming proficiency be explained by two variables: ability at logic and personal style of approaching problems?

Blue chip stock prices are important indices of the health of the national economy. What social, industrial, and political factors help explain these stock prices?

Which of the following factors explains why young children become at risk for school failure: parental education, early literacy, social support, school attendance, and socioeconomic factors?

The Multiple Regression Equation

When dealing with a single outcome measure (Y) and a single predictor variable (A), one expresses the regression equation for a straight line as

$$\textbf{(Equation 14.4) } Y' = a' + b'(A)$$

where:

Y' = estimated value of the outcome variable

a' = estimated intercept

b' = estimated regression coefficient

A = actual value of the predictor variable

At some point, you will want to determine a regression equation that takes advantage of multiple predictors. Such a regression equation is as follows:

$$\textbf{Equation 15.1: } Y' = a' + b'_A(A) + b'_B(B) + \cdots + b'_Z(Z)$$

where:

Y' = estimated value of the outcome variable

a' = estimated intercept

b'_A = estimated regression coefficient for predictor variable A

A = actual value of the first predictor variable

b'_B = estimated regression coefficient for predictor variable B

B = actual value of the second predictor variable

b'_Z = estimated regression coefficient for predictor variable Z

Z = actual value of the last predictor variable

You can also express this equation in terms of actual Y-values instead of estimated Y'-values. When you do this, you need to add an estimate of error (E). Using Y instead of Y', you get

$$Y = a' + b'_A(A) + b'_B(B) + \cdots + b'_Z(Z) + E$$

E is the difference between Y and Y' and is also referred to as the **residual**.

Finally, once again use Greek symbols to signify the population parameters you are trying to estimate:

$$Y = \alpha + \beta_A(A) + \beta_B(B) + \cdots + \beta_Z(Z) + \varepsilon$$

where:

α (alpha) = population intercept

β (beta) = population regression coefficient for each predictor

ε (epsilon) = random error

This equation represents the *general linear model* for multiple linear regression.

In a multiple linear regression equation, the contribution of more than one predictor variable is used to maximize the extent to which variability in the outcome measure (Y) can be explained. A multiple regression equation combines all the information about the predictors into a single mathematical statement. By combining the information from all the predictors together, the correlation is maximized between the predicted scores on the outcome measure (Y') and the actual scores on the outcome measure (Y). No simple regression equation, based on only a single predictor variable, can explain more variability in the outcome measure than a multiple regression equation that includes that single predictor variable and other predictor variables.

Uncorrelated versus Correlated Predictors

The calculation of regression statistics is a relatively straightforward matter when the predictor variables (A, B, etc.) are not correlated. But it is more complicated when the predictor variables are correlated with one another, especially when they share explained variability in the outcome measure (Y).

The **shared variability** in the outcome measure (Y) means that the predictors provide a certain amount of redundant information. Furthermore, this redundancy represents a fairly typical state of affairs. It is almost always the case that predictors that are measured, rather than manipulated, are correlated with one another.

This redundancy, or nonindependence, is illustrated via two three-ring ballantines (Venn diagrams) shown in Figure 15.1. Please note that the illustrations are used here for instructional purposes only, because it is not always possible to use Venn diagrams to represent all the complexities of possible relations among variables. We have also squared the correlations to make it clearer that we are representing the proportions of variance explained.

Uncorrelated Predictors Look closely at the leftmost diagram of Figure 15.1 where the two predictors are not correlated and, therefore, there is no variability in A explained by B ($r^2_{AB} = .00$). There is, however, variability in Y, which is explained by A ($r^2_{YA} = .20$), and variability in Y, which is explained by B ($r^2_{YB} = .20$). But what is the total variability in Y that is explained by the two predictors?

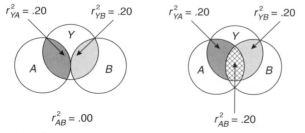

Figure 15.1 Venn diagrams illustrating uncorrelated (left) and correlated (right) predictor variables (not to scale)

Because the two predictors are uncorrelated, the total variability in Y explained by the two predictors (R^2_{YAB}) is merely the sum of the variability explained by each predictor separately:

$$R^2_{YAB} = r^2_{YA} + r^2_{YB} = .20 + .20 = .40^1$$

Correlated Predictors   Now try to deal with the more difficult case as represented in the rightmost diagram of Figure 15.1 where the two predictors are correlated and there is some variability in A explained by B $(r^2_{AB} = .20)$. In this case the total explained variability in Y is *not* merely the sum of the total variability explained by each predictor separately:

$$R^2_{YAB} \neq r^2_{YA} + r^2_{YB} \neq .20 + .20 \neq .40$$

Why? Because the two predictor variables in the rightmost diagram do not uniquely explain variability in the outcome variable Y. There is an overlap of prediction. If you were merely to add the Y-variability explained by each predictor separately, there would be a certain amount of explained variability added twice. In the rightmost diagram of Figure 15.1, this is the cross-hatched area where the Y-variability explained by A overlaps with the Y-variability explained by B.

You want a set of calculations for multiple regression that will compute the total variability in Y explained by the predictors but where the redundant explained variability among the predictors is counted only once, not repeatedly. Therefore, for two predictors the formula for the squared multiple correlation is as follows:

Equation 15.2: $R^2_{YAB} = \dfrac{r^2_{YA} + r^2_{YB} - 2r_{YA}r_{YB}r_{AB}}{1 - r^2_{AB}}$

CD-ROM link 15.1

Activity 15.1: Correlated Predictor Variables
What happens when predictor variables are correlated with one another as well as with the outcome measure? In Activity 15.1, you can vary the amount of variability explained by the predictor variables in the outcome measure, as well as the amount of variability shared among the predictor variables. As you change these values, you will see how the changes are represented in the three-ring ballantines. Is the total amount of variability explained in the outcome measure always equal to the sum of the variability explained by each individual predictor?

Notice that the formula takes into account both the correlation between each predictor and the outcome as well as the correlation between the predictors.

Use the formula to find R^2 for the rightmost diagram where the predictors are correlated:

$$R^2_{YAB} = \frac{r^2_{YA} + r^2_{YB} - 2r_{YA}r_{YB}r_{AB}}{1 - r^2_{AB}} = \frac{.20 + .20 - 2(.45)(.45)(.45)}{.80} = .28$$

---

[1]R^2_{YAB} is the squared multiple correlation coefficient where two predictors, A and B, are used to explain some of the variability in the outcome measure (Y). r^2_{YA} is the squared simple correlation coefficient between the predictor variable (A) and the outcome variable (Y).

Textbox 15.3

The Squared Multiple Correlation for the Common Allies Scenario

Use the formula to find R^2 for the data from the Common Allies scenario.
    Begin by finding the three simple correlations and their squares:

$$r_{YA} = +0.75 \quad r_{YA}^2 = .56$$

$$r_{YB} = +0.79 \quad r_{YB}^2 = .62$$

$$r_{AB} = +0.49 \quad r_{AB}^2 = .24$$

Now you can find the squared multiple correlation and the multiple correlation:

$$R_{YAB}^2 = \frac{r_{YA}^2 + r_{YB}^2 - 2r_{YA}r_{YB}r_{AB}}{1 - r_{AB}^2} = \frac{(.75)^2 + (.79)^2 - 2(.75)(.79)(.49)}{1 - (.49)^2} = .80$$

$$R_{YAB} = .89$$

Taken together, Partner Sensitivity (A) and Cultural Similarity (B) are highly correlated with Marital Happiness (Y). The two predictors explain 80% of the variance in the outcome measure.

Note that if you had incorrectly tried to add r_{YA}^2 and r_{YB}^2 (.56 + .62), you would have a resultant R_{YAB}^2 of 1.18. In other words, you would have arrived at the inconceivable conclusion that you had explained more than 100% of the variance in Marital Happiness, the outcome variable (Y).

Note also that R_{YAB}^2 is larger than either r_{YA}^2 or r_{YB}^2. The two predictors together explain more variability in Y than either predictor alone.

Now use the formula to find R^2 for the leftmost diagram in which the predictors are uncorrelated:

$$R_{YAB}^2 = \frac{r_{YA}^2 + r_{YB}^2 - 2r_{YA}r_{YB}r_{AB}}{1 - r_{AB}^2} = \frac{.20 + .20 - 2(.45)(.45)(.00)}{1.00} = .40$$

Notice that whenever the correlation between A and B is zero ($r_{AB} = .00$) the formula reduces to $R_{YAB}^2 = r_{YA}^2 + r_{YB}^2$.

See Textbox 15.3 for an illustration of the application of the formula to find the squared multiple correlation coefficient for two predictors using the Common Allies scenario.

THE MULTIPLE REGRESSION EQUATION AND TESTS OF SIGNIFICANCE

Given the possibility that two predictors are correlated, how does one find the regression equation? And how does one compute tests of significance for R^2 and each regression coefficient?

Components of the Multiple Regression Equation

One of the important uses of simple linear regression is the application of the regression equation to estimate values of the outcome variable from knowledge of the values of the predictor variable. This idea can readily be extended to multiple linear regression in which one uses more than a single predictor.

CD-ROM link 15.2

Problem Generator: Multiple Linear Regression
To practice calculating regression equations with two predictor variables, select Multiple Linear Regression from the Problem Generator Menu on the CD-ROM. The Problem Generator will create as many practice problems as you need and will demonstrate each step in their solution so that you can check your work.

Of course, there is little point to estimating the values of the outcome variable when the actual values are known. So it is worth repeating that one develops a regression equation based on a sample when both predictor and outcome variables can be measured in order to then use the results in situations in which the values of the outcome variable are not known and must be estimated.

Multiple Regression Coefficients In simple regression when there is only a single predictor, the regression coefficient is as follows:

$$\textbf{(Equation 14.6)} \; b' = \frac{\text{covariance}(A, Y)}{\text{variance}(A)}$$

The computational form of the regression coefficient is shown below:

$$\textbf{(Equation 14.7)} \; b' = \frac{\dfrac{\sum (A_i - \overline{A})(Y_i - \overline{Y})}{N-1}}{\dfrac{\sum (A_i - \overline{A})^2}{N-1}} = \frac{\sum (A_i - \overline{A})(Y_i - \overline{Y})}{\sum (A_i - \overline{A})^2}$$

The regression coefficient can also be rewritten in simpler sums of squares (SS) notation as follows:

$$\textbf{(Equation 14.8)} \; b' = \frac{SS_{AY}}{SS_A}$$

In multiple regression, you cannot use so simple a formula as Equation 14.8 to find the regression coefficient for each predictor. Instead you use formulas that also take into account any possible relationship between the predictors. Therefore, given two predictors, there are two regression coefficients:

$$\textbf{Equation 15.3:} \; b'_A = \frac{(SS_B)(SS_{YA}) - (SS_{AB})(SS_{YB})}{(SS_A)(SS_B) - (SS_{AB})^2}$$

$$\textbf{Equation 15.4:} \; b'_B = \frac{(SS_A)(SS_{YB}) - (SS_{AB})(SS_{YA})}{(SS_A)(SS_B) - (SS_{AB})^2}$$

Note that the denominator of both equations is the same.

Intercept In simple regression when there is only a single predictor, the formula for the intercept is as follows:

$$\text{(Equation 14.9) } a' = \overline{Y} - b'_A(\overline{A})$$

In multiple regression, given two predictors, the formula for the intercept is as follows:

$$\text{Equation 15.5: } a' = \overline{Y} - b'_A(\overline{A}) - b'_B(\overline{B})$$

Note that the **estimated intercept** for two predictors is similar *in form* to the estimated intercept for a single predictor with the inclusion of the product of the regression coefficient for the second predictor times the mean of the second predictor.[2]

Textbox 15.4 provides an illustration of estimating the multiple regression equation and its components based on the data from the Common Allies scenario:

Textbox 15.4

The Multiple Regression of Marital Happiness (Y) on Partner Sensitivity (A) and Cultural Similarity (B)

The Common Allies scenario will be used to illustrate the multiple regression equation for two predictors. As a preliminary step, find the means and sums of squares for calculating the regression coefficients and for finding the intercept:

$$\overline{Y} = 15.00$$
$$\overline{A} = 5.50$$
$$\overline{B} = 30.00$$

TABLE 15.2 Deriving the Multiple Regression Sums of Squares

Couple	$(Y - 15.00)^2$	$(A - 5.50)^2$	$(B - 30.00)^2$	$(Y - 15.00) \times (A - 5.50)$	$(Y - 15) \times (B - 30.00)$	$(A - 5.50) \times (B - 30.00)$
Jones	100.00	12.25	100.00	35.00	100.00	35.00
Smith	49.00	2.25	0.00	10.50	0.00	0.00
Pambookian	121.00	.25	900.00	−5.50	330.00	−15.00
Abrams	100.00	12.25	625.00	35.00	250.00	87.50
Lou	9.00	6.25	225.00	7.50	45.00	37.50
Simard	0.00	.25	0.00	0.00	0.00	0.00
Took	25.00	2.25	400.00	7.50	100.00	30.00
O'Leary	16.00	.25	225.00	2.00	60.00	7.50
Brecht	9.00	2.25	100.00	4.50	−30.00	−15.00
Nadia	1.00	.25	225.00	−.50	15.00	−7.50
SS	430.00	38.50	2800.00	96.00	870.00	160.00

continued

[2]The regression coefficient for *A* as a single predictor will not necessarily be the same as the regression coefficient for *A* when it is not a single predictor because the degree of relationship between predictors is taken into account in the second case only.

Textbox 15.4 (continued)

Use the sums of squares to compute the regression coefficients for the two predictors:

$$b_A' = \frac{(SS_B)(SS_{YA}) - (SS_{AB})(SS_{YB})}{(SS_A)(SS_B) - (SS_{AB})^2} = \frac{(2800.00)(96.00) - (160.00)(870.00)}{(38.50)(2800.00) - (160.00)^2} = \frac{129,600.00}{82,200.00} = +1.58$$

$$b_B' = \frac{(SS_A)(SS_{YB}) - (SS_{AB})(SS_{YA})}{(SS_A)(SS_B) - (SS_{AB})^2} = \frac{(38.50)(870.00) - (160.00)(96.00)}{(38.50)(2800.00) - (160.00)^2} = \frac{18,135.00}{82,200.00} = +.22$$

Now find the intercept:

$$a' = \overline{Y} - b_A'(\overline{A}) - b_B'(\overline{B}) = 15.00 - 1.58(5.50) - .22(30.00) \approx -.29$$

Using the intercept and the two regression coefficients, you can write the regression equation as follows:

$$Y' = a' + b_A'(A) + b_B'(B) = -.29 + 1.58(A) + .22(B)$$

Now use the regression equation to predict the value of Marital Happiness (Y') from knowledge of Partner Sensitivity ($A = 5$) and Cultural Similarity ($B = 40$) for a new couple, Mr. and Mrs. Getalife:

$$Y' = -.29 + 1.58(5) + .22(40) = 16.41$$

Mr. and Mrs. Getalife would have a slightly higher than average Marital Happiness score (16.41) given the sample mean Marital Happiness results (15.00).

Tests of Significance

In Chapter 14 four methods of testing the significance of a single predictor were shown. The methods—correlation method t-test, regression method t-test, correlation method F-test, and mean squares F-test—were mathematically related and resulted in identical hypothesis-testing decisions.

When more than a single predictor is present, however, these methods are neither equally applicable nor interchangeable. More specifically, we will show that the multiple correlation F-test and mean squares F-test can be used to test overall whether the **collection of predictors** explains a significant amount of variability in the outcome measure. In contrast, we will show that the appropriate regression method t-test can be used to test the significance of a *single* predictor while the correlation method t-test is only appropriate for uncorrelated predictors. The reason for the differences is explained below.

Testing the Significance of a Collection of Predictors: Simultaneous Approach

Two different computational methods for testing the significance of a collection of predictors will be examined. The first method is based on the multiple regression coefficient (R). The second method is based on the mean squares method. Testing a collection of predictors as a set is also called the **simultaneous approach** to multiple regression because all of the predictors are included at the same time.

Multiple Correlation Method   In Chapter 14 we explained that for a single predictor variable you could use the squared correlation coefficient to compute F:

$$\textbf{(Equation 14.18)}\ F = \frac{r^2}{(1 - r^2)/(N - 2)} \qquad \text{where df} = 1, N - 2$$

For multiple predictors, it is also possible, with a slight adjustment, to compute the F-ratio. For example, for two predictors the computation is as follows:

$$\textbf{Equation 15.6:}\ F = \frac{R^2_{YAB}/k}{(1 - R^2_{YAB})/(N - k - 1)}$$

where:

$\quad$ df $= k$ and $N - k - 1$

$\quad k =$ number of predictors. (In the Common Allies scenario, there are two predictors.)

The numerator is the average proportion of variance explained by the predictors. In other words, it is the total proportion of explained variability (R^2) divided by the number of predictors (k). The denominator is the average proportion of variance that is not explained.

Mean Squares Method   Recall from Chapter 9 that an F-ratio is a ratio of two variances, called *mean squares*. Each mean squares, in turn, is a sum of squares divided by the appropriate degrees of freedom. In Chapter 14 some of the concepts from analysis of variance were applied to simple linear regression. In particular, the total variability in the outcome variable (Y) was partitioned into two additive components: (1) variability explained by the predictor (A) and (2) residual or unexplained variability. In other words, for a single predictor[3]

$$SS_Y = SS_{Y(A)} + SS_{Y(RE)}$$

This same logic can be extended to multiple linear regression in which more than a single predictor is present. For example, when there are two predictors

$$SS_Y = SS_{Y(AB)} + SS_{Y(RE)}$$

But how to find the two additive components, $SS_{Y(AB)}$ and $SS_{Y(RE)}$? You know that R^2_{YAB} is the proportion of total variability in Y explained by the set of predictors. Therefore, you can use the proportion R^2 to find the sum of squares explained by A and B:

$$\textbf{Equation 15.7:}\ SS_{Y(AB)} = (R^2_{YAB})(SS_Y)$$

---

[3]$SS_{Y(A)}$ is the variability in Y explained by A. Do not confuse this with SS_{YA} which is the covariability of Y and A.

CD-ROM link 15.3

Problem Generator: Multiple Linear Regression
To practice hypothesis testing using multiple linear regression (multiple correlation method), select Multiple Linear Regression from the Problem Generator Menu on the CD-ROM. The Problem Generator will create as many practice problems as you need and will demonstrate each step in their solution so that you can check your work.

Similarly, $1 - R^2_{YAB}$ is the proportion of total variability in Y *not* explained by A and B. Therefore, you can use the proportion $1 - R^2$ to find the sum of squares *not* explained by A and B or the residual sum of squares:

Equation 15.8: $SS_{Y(RE)} = (1 - R^2_{YAB})(SS_Y)$

Now you can find the mean squares:

Equation 15.9: $MS_{Y(AB)} = SS_{Y(AB)}/k$ where k is the number of predictors.

Equation 15.10: $MS_{Y(RE)} = SS_{Y(RE)}/N - k - 1$

The *F*-ratio to test the significance of the set of two predictors is a ratio of two mean squares. The calculated value is as follows:

Equation 15.11: $F = MS_{Y(AB)}/MS_{Y(RE)}$ where $df = (k, N - k - 1)$

Textbox 15.5 illustrates the use of the multiple correlation and mean squares methods for determining whether a set of two predictors—Partner Sensitivity (A) and Cultural Similarity (B)—significantly explains variability in a single outcome measure—Marital Happiness (Y).

Testing a Set ≠ Testing One Predictor   It should be emphasized that a test of the multiple correlation coefficient using the simultaneous approach tells you whether the set of predictors explains a significant amount of variability in the outcome measure. Because this is a general test, when it is significant you know only that at least one predictor in the set explains a significant amount of unique variability in the outcome variable *unless* the degree of shared variability among the predictors is high. If the shared variability among predictors is high, possibly none of the predictors may explain a significant amount of unique variability in the outcome measure. This inability to explain can happen even when the test of the multiple correlation coefficient is significant.

Conversely, when a test of the multiple correlation coefficient is not significant, it does not imply that none of the individual predictors is significant. The omnibus test of all predictors can be less sensitive than a test of a single predictor. To explore which of the predictors is significant, other methods will be used, such as tests of the individual regression coefficients.

Test of Significance for the Regression Coefficients   The test of individual regression coefficients evaluates whether *each* coefficient differs from chance; it is not a test to be performed on the coefficients taken together. The test of significance, therefore, allows you to determine whether each predictor contributes a significant and unique amount to the explanation of the outcome variable (Y).

Textbox 15.5

Two Ways of Testing the Significance of a Set of Multiple Predictors

The data from the Common Allies scenario will be used to show how to calculate an *F*-test for the simultaneous analysis of a set of two predictors. This test will be illustrated using both the multiple correlation method and the mean squares method.

Multiple Correlation Method

$$F = \frac{R^2_{YAB}/k}{(1 - R^2_{YAB})/(N - k - 1)} = \frac{(.80)/2}{(1 - .80)/(10 - 2 - 1)} \approx 13.86$$

The critical value, for df = 2, 7 and α = .05, is 4.74.

Because the calculated value (13.86) exceeds the critical value (4.74), one rejects the null hypothesis. Taken together, Partner Sensitivity (*A*) and Cultural Similarity (*B*) explain a significant degree of variability in Marital Happiness (*Y*).

Mean Square Method*

$$SS_{Y(AB)} = (R^2_{YAB})(SS_Y) = (.80)(430.00) \approx 343.30$$

$$SS_{Y(RE)} = (1 - R^2_{YAB})(SS_Y) = (.20)(430.00) \approx 86.70$$

$$MS_{Y(AB)} = SS_{Y(AB)}/k = 343.30/2 \approx 171.65$$

$$MS_{Y(RE)} = SS_{Y(RE)}/N - k - 1 = 86.70/7 \approx 12.39$$

$$F = MS_{Y(AB)}/MS_{Y(RE)} = 171.65/12.39 \approx 13.86$$

The multiple correlation and mean square methods both yield the identical results mathematically. A summary table can also be created (see Table 15.3).

Note that the exact probability associated with a calculated value of $F = 13.86$ when degrees of freedom equal 2 and 7 is .004.

*Calculations done to greater precision yield the results reported here. Calculations done to two decimal points will vary slightly due to rounding error.

TABLE 15.3   Multiple Regression Summary Table for Common Allies Scenario

Source	SS	df	MS	F	p
Explained (*A* and *B*)	343.30	2	171.65	13.86	.004
Unexplained	86.70	7	12.39		
Total	430.00	9			

Shared Variability and the Problem of Collinearity   In undertaking the test of each regression coefficient, the shared, explained variability in *Y* among the predictors is *excluded* from consideration. Consider the rightmost Venn diagram in Figure 15.1. Note the cross-hatched area indicating the overlap in predicting the outcome variable *Y* based on predictors *A* and *B*. In the test of significance for each coefficient, this crosshatched area is not attributed to either predictor. In other words, the test of the regression coefficient evaluates the *unique* contribution of the predictor variable in explaining variability in the outcome variable.

When the correlations among predictors are high, a situation referred to as **collinearity** (see below) exists and the amount of explained variability in the outcome unique to any one predictor can be small. Under such a circumstance, the value of R^2 can be large, but if the overlap among the predictors is also great, it is conceivable that each test of significance for the individual predictors will be nonsignificant.

Such a finding can be disconcerting, to say the least. How can R^2 be large and significant yet none of the individual predictors be significant? Now that you have multiple predictors, and quite unlike the situation you faced with simple regression (see Chapter 14), the test of significance for R^2 is not the same as the test of individual regression coefficients.

The test of significance for R^2 evaluates whether *all* the outcome variability explained by the predictors, both shared and unique, is significant. The test of significance for each regression coefficient evaluates whether the outcome variability explained *uniquely* by a predictor is significant. Any variability shared among predictors is excluded from the tests of the regression coefficients.

CD-ROM link 15.4

Activity 15.2: Prediction with Multiple Predictor Variables
Activity 15.2 builds on what you learned in Activity 15.1 (correlated predictor variables). If two predictor variables explain a significant amount of variability in an outcome measure, does that also necessarily mean that each individual predictor uniquely explains a significant amount of variability? By manipulating the correlations between the two predictor variables and the outcome measure, you can see how these correlations affect the statistical significance of the predictors.

t-Test In general form, the test of significance for each regression coefficient is a *t*-test based on the regression coefficient (b') and the standard error of the regression coefficient ($s_{b'}$).

For simple linear regression, where only a single predictor is involved, we gave the following formula in Chapter 14 for the predictor A:

(Equation 14.17) $$t = \frac{b'}{s_{b'}} = \frac{\dfrac{SS_{AY}}{SS_A}}{\sqrt{\dfrac{MS_{Y(RE)}}{SS_A}}}$$

where:

b' = the estimated regression coefficient,

$s_{b'}$ = the estimated standard error of the estimated regression coefficient,

and degrees of freedom (df) equals $N - A - 1$ (or $N - 2$).

For multiple linear regression, where two predictors are involved, two regression coefficients need to be tested, one for predictor A and one for predictor B. Furthermore, in view of the use of multiple predictors, the appropriate regression coefficient needs to be found for the numerator and standard error for the denominator of each of two *t*-tests.

The regression coefficient for A is as follows:

(Equation 15.3) $$b'_A = \frac{(SS_B)(SS_{YA}) - (SS_{AB})(SS_{YB})}{(SS_A)(SS_B) - (SS_{AB})^2}$$

The regression coefficient for B is as follows:

$$\text{(Equation 15.4) } b'_B = \frac{(SS_A)(SS_{YB}) - (SS_{AB})(SS_{YA})}{(SS_A)(SS_B) - (SS_{AB})^2}$$

Recall that each regression coefficient takes into account the correlation between the two predictors. Likewise when one finds the standard error for each predictor for the denominator of the t-tests, one takes into account the correlation between predictors. Therefore, the standard error for predictor A is as follows:

$$\text{Equation 15.12: } s_{b'_A} = \sqrt{\frac{MS_{Y(RE)}}{SS_A(1 - r^2_{AB})}}$$

The standard error for predictor B is shown below:

$$\text{Equation 15.13: } s_{b'_B} = \sqrt{\frac{MS_{Y(RE)}}{SS_B(1 - r^2_{AB})}}$$

Putting these together we get the following equations for computing the t-tests to test the significance of each regression coefficient.

For predictor A:

$$\text{Equation 15.14: } t_A = \frac{b'_A}{s_{b'_A}} = \frac{\dfrac{(SS_B)(SS_{YA}) - (SS_{AB})(SS_{YB})}{(SS_A)(SS_B) - (SS_{AB})^2}}{\sqrt{\dfrac{MS_{Y(RE)}}{SS_A(1 - r^2_{AB})}}} \qquad \text{where df} = N - k - 1$$

For predictor B:

$$\text{Equation 15.15: } t_B = \frac{b'_B}{s_{b'_B}} = \frac{\dfrac{(SS_A)(SS_{YB}) - (SS_{AB})(SS_{YA})}{(SS_A)(SS_B) - (SS_{AB})^2}}{\sqrt{\dfrac{MS_{Y(RE)}}{SS_B(1 - r^2_{AB})}}} \qquad \text{where df} = N - k - 1$$

Confidence Intervals   You can use the general formula for a confidence interval given in Chapter 14. The two-sided confidence interval for a nondirectional two-tailed alternative hypothesis is as follows:

$$\text{(Equation 14.19) } b' - t_{1-\alpha/2} s_{b'} \text{ and } b' + t_{1-\alpha/2} s_{b'}$$

where:

b' = estimated regression coefficient

t = critical value for a particular probability value, degrees of freedom, and for a two-tailed test $(1 - \alpha/2)$

$s_{b'}$ = estimated standard error of the regression coefficient

In Textbox 15.6, Equations 15.14 and 15.15 are used to test the significance of each predictor's unique contribution to explaining variability in the outcome measure (Y). The 95% confidence intervals are also found.

Textbox 15.6

Using the *t*-Test to Test the Significance of Each Predictor

Use the data from the Common Allies scenario to answer several questions about the predictors: Is the unique contribution of Partner Sensitivity (A) to the explanation of variability in Marital Happiness (Y) significant? What is the 95% confidence interval? And is the unique contribution of Cultural Sensitivity (B) to the explanation of variability in Marital Happiness (Y) significant? What is the 95% confidence interval?

For Partner Sensitivity (A):

$$t_A = \frac{b'_A}{s_{b'_A}} = \frac{\dfrac{(SS_B)(SS_{YA}) - (SS_{AB})(SS_{YB})}{(SS_A)(SS_B) - (SS_{AB})^2}}{\sqrt{\dfrac{MS_{Y(RE)}}{SS_A(1 - r^2_{AB})}}} = \frac{1.58}{\sqrt{\dfrac{12.39}{38.50(1 - .49^2)}}} = \frac{1.58}{.65} \approx 2.43$$

$$CI = b' \pm t_{1-\alpha/2}s_{b'} = 1.58 \pm 2.37(.65) \approx +.04, \ +3.12$$

$$.04 \le \beta_A \le 3.12$$

For Cultural Similarity (B):

$$t_A = \frac{b'_B}{s_{b'_B}} = \frac{\dfrac{(SS_A)(SS_{YB}) - (SS_{AB})(SS_{YA})}{(SS_A)(SS_B) - (SS_{AB})^2}}{\sqrt{\dfrac{MS_{Y(RE)}}{SS_B(1 - r^2_{AB})}}} = \frac{.22}{\sqrt{\dfrac{12.39}{2800.00(1 - .49^2)}}} = \frac{.22}{.08} \approx 2.90$$

$$CI = b' \pm t_{1-\alpha/2}s_{b'} = .22 \pm 2.37(.08) \approx +.04, \ +.40$$

$$.04 \le \beta_B \le .40$$

For each *t*-test, the critical value for df $= N - k - 1$ (7) and $\alpha = .05$ is ± 2.365. Therefore, because the calculated value for each predictor exceeds the critical value, you can conclude that both Partner Sensitivity (A) and Cultural Sensitivity (B) contribute uniquely to the explanation of variability in Marital Happiness (Y). Therefore, both the Sociology major and the Psychology major are correct; each of the predictors explains a significant amount of variability in the outcome measure.

Finally, note the width of the confidence interval for each regression coefficient, which indicates a lack of precision in estimating the population parameter. The large width of the intervals is partly a function of the small sample size used in the investigation.

THE INCREMENTAL APPROACH TO MULTIPLE LINEAR REGRESSION

The simultaneous approach to multiple regression allows researchers to test the significance of the predictors as a set and then to determine whether each predictor contributes uniquely to the explanation of variability in the outcome measure. When the predictors are highly correlated, the set of predictors may significantly explain variability in the outcome variable but no one predictor may significantly explain a unique amount of variability in Y.

Incremental approaches to multiple linear regression allow other options for dealing with shared variability. Incremental approaches enter variables successively into a series of multiple regressions rather than simultaneously into a single regression. In **hierarchical regression,** the researcher decides on the order of entry of predictor variables. In **stepwise regression,** the order of entry is determined statistically. Both of these incremental approaches allow for shared variability to be assigned to a predictor variable.

Hierarchical Regression

In hierarchical regression, the researcher decides on the order of entry of predictors in a series of regression analyses. The researcher may elect to enter variables according to theoretical guidelines, for example, or according to the temporal sequence of factors, or some other criterion. Using the temporal sequence of factors, the researcher might decide that the influence of Cultural Similarity (B) on Marital Happiness (Y) occurs before the influence of Partner Sensitivity (A). Therefore, the researcher decides to enter Cultural Similarity (B) on step 1 of a hierarchical regression and Partner Sensitivity (A) on step 2.

The first step of a hierarchical regression is a simple linear regression because only a single predictor is involved. The second step of a hierarchical regression is a multiple linear regression because two predictors are involved.

The number of steps in a hierarchical regression is limited by the number of predictor variables and often by whether there is a significant increment in the amount of variability in the outcome measure explained on that step. In other words, the maximum number of steps is equal to the number of predictors. But there can be fewer steps if the remaining predictors do not add significantly to the prediction of Y. To understand incremental approaches to regression, it is important to consider further the partitioning of variability in the outcome measure.

Partitioning Variability Incrementally   Remember that in simple regression total variability in Y can be partitioned into two additive components: variability explained by the predictor (B) and variability not explained by the predictor:

$$SS_Y = SS_{Y(B)} + SS_{Y(RE)}$$

In multiple regression one can also partition the total variability in Y into two additive components: variability explained by the set of predictors and variability not explained by the set:

$$SS_Y = SS_{Y(AB)} + SS_{Y(RE)}$$

Note that the total variability in the outcome (SS_Y) remains unchanged, whether one is undertaking a simple or a multiple regression. Furthermore, the amount of explained variability in the multiple regression is either (if the second predictor adds nothing) equal to or (if the second predictor adds something) larger than the explained variability in the simple regression. That is,

$$SS_{Y(AB)} \geq SS_{Y(B)}$$

Finally, the amount of unexplained variability in the multiple regression is either equal to (if the second predictor adds nothing) or smaller than the unexplained variability in the simple regression.

See Textbox 15.7 for an illustration using the Common Allies scenario. For the illustration, recall that r^2 is the proportion of total variability in Y explained by a single predictor while R^2 is the proportion of total variability in Y explained by multiple predictors. Therefore, you can use these proportions to find the sum of squares explained by the predictors individually and collectively:

(Equation 15.7) $SS_{Y(AB)} = (R^2_{YAB})(SS_Y)$

The Increment in SS The sum of squares for Y due to a single predictor (B) or $SS_{Y(B)}$ represents all the outcome measure variability that the predictor (B) can explain. $SS_{Y(B)}$ includes the Y-variability explained uniquely by B and the Y-variability that B explains in common with A.

The sum of squares for Y due to both predictors (A and B) or $SS_{Y(AB)}$ represents all the outcome measure variability that the two predictors together can explain. The increment in the sum of squares, or $SS_{Y(AB-B)}$, is the difference in the sum of squares for Y due to a single predictor (B) and both predictors (A and B) together. $SS_{Y(AB-B)}$ is also the Y-variability explained uniquely by A:

$$SS_{Y(AB-B)} = SS_{Y(AB)} - SS_{Y(B)}$$

From SS to MS to F For two predictors, the total variability can now be divided into three additive components:

Y-variability due to B uniquely and in common with A:

Equation 15.16: $SS_{Y(B)} = (r^2_{YB})(SS_Y)$

Y-variability due uniquely to A:

Equation 15.17: $SS_{Y(AB-B)} = SS_{Y(AB)} - SS_{Y(B)}$

Y-variability not explained by the two predictors (A and B):

(Equation 15.8) $SS_{Y(RE)} = (1 - R^2_{YAB})(SS_Y)$

Furthermore,

$$SS_{Y(AB)} = SS_{Y(B)} + SS_{Y(AB-B)}$$

Textbox 15.7

Partitioning Variability Incrementally Using the Common Allies Scenario

Shown below is how to partition variability into additive components when either simple linear regression or multiple linear regression is used. Also shown is how the amount of explained variability in the Common Allies scenario is larger when two predictors are used than when a single predictor is used. Conversely, notice also that the amount of unexplained variability in the Common Allies scenario is smaller when two predictors are used than when a single predictor is used.

From Textbox 15.3:

$$r^2_{YA} = .56$$

$$r^2_{YB} = .62$$

$$R^2_{YAB} = .80$$

From Textbox 15.4:

$$SS_Y = 430.00$$

Now you can find the total variability in Y explained by each predictor individually and by the set of two predictors:

$$SS_{Y(A)} = (r^2_{YA})(SS_Y) = (.56)(430.00) \approx 239.38$$

$$\text{For } A, SS_{Y(RE)} = 430.00 - 239.38 = 190.62$$

$$SS_{Y(B)} = (r^2_{YB})(SS_Y) = (.62)(430.00) \approx 270.32$$

$$\text{For } B, SS_{Y(RE)} = 430.00 - 270.32 = 159.68$$

$$SS_{Y(AB)} = (R^2_{YAB})(SS_Y) = (.80)(430.00) \approx 343.30$$

$$\text{For the set of } A \text{ and } B, SS_{Y(RE)} = 430.00 - 343.30 = 86.70$$

The variability in Y explained by the set of A and B predictors ($SS_{Y(AB)} = 343.30$) is greater than the variability in Y explained by either predictor alone ($SS_{Y(A)} = 239.38$, $SS_{Y(B)} = 270.32$). The unexplained variability in Y is smaller for the set of A and B predictors compared to the unexplained variability for each predictor alone.

The mean squares are as follows:

Equation 15.18: $MS_{Y(B)} = SS_{Y(B)}/df_B$

Equation 15.19: $MS_{Y(AB-B)} = SS_{Y(AB-B)}/df_A$

Equation 15.20: $MS_{Y(RE)} = SS_{Y(RE)}/df_{N-k-1}$

The F-ratios are as follows:

Equation 15.21: $F = \text{MS}_{Y(B)}/\text{MS}_{Y(RE)}$, where $df = B, N - k - 1$

Equation 15.22: $F = \text{MS}_{Y(AB-B)}/\text{MS}_{Y(RE)}$, where $df = A, N - k - 1$

See Textbox 15.8 for an illustration of a hierarchical regression based on the data from the Common Allies scenario.

Which Predictor Is More Important?   Normally, researchers use the proportion of variance explained to answer questions about the importance of a predictor from a statistical perspective. However, when predictors are correlated,

---

Textbox 15.8

Hierarchical Regression of Marital Happiness (Y) on Cultural Sensitivity (B) and Partner Sensitivity (A)

Begin by finding the appropriate sums of squares:

$$\text{SS}_{Y(B)} = (r_{YB}^2)(\text{SS}_Y) = (.62)(430.00) \approx 270.32$$

$$\text{SS}_{Y(AB-B)} = \text{SS}_{Y(AB)} - \text{SS}_{Y(B)} = 343.30 - 270.32 = 72.98$$

$$\text{SS}_{Y(RE)} = (1 - R_{YAB}^2)(\text{SS}_Y) \approx 86.70$$

$$\text{Check: } \text{SS}_{Y(B)} + \text{SS}_{Y(AB-B)} + \text{SS}_{Y(RE)} = \text{SS}_Y$$

$$270.32 + 72.98 + 86.70 = 430.00$$

Next find the mean squares:

$$\text{MS}_{Y(B)} = \text{SS}_{Y(B)}/df_B = 270.32/1 = 270.32$$

$$\text{MS}_{Y(AB-B)} = \text{SS}_{Y(AB-B)}/df_A = 72.98/1 = 72.98$$

$$\text{MS}_{Y(RE)} = \text{SS}_{Y(RE)}/df_{N-k-1} = 86.70/7 = 12.39$$

The calculated values of F are as follows:

$$F = \text{MS}_{Y(B)}/\text{MS}_{Y(RE)} = 270.32/12.39 = 21.82$$

$$F = \text{MS}_{Y(AB-B)}/\text{MS}_{Y(RE)} = 72.98/12.39 = 5.89$$

The critical value of F for $df = 1, 7$ and $\alpha = .05$ is 5.59. Therefore, Cultural Similarity explains a significant amount of variability in Marital Happiness. In addition, Partner Sensitivity adds significantly to the prediction of Marital Happiness.

Finally, because Partner Sensitivity was entered last, the variance it explains is unique. Therefore, the square of the t-test for the regression coefficient for A from the simultaneous multiple regression should equal the F-test for A from the hierarchical regression:

$$t^2 = 2.43^2 = 5.89$$

which they almost always are, there is not always a single, clear-cut answer to such questions. That is because one may elect to look at the squared simple correlation, the unique variability explained by each predictor, or the hierarchical regression results to answer these questions. Textbox 15.9 provides an explanation and illustration.

In Chapter 14 the use of R^2, or the coefficient of determination, was presented as a measure of strength of association. And we also showed how to convert R^2 to f, another measure of strength of association. In some research situations, researchers might want to determine the strength of association for a collection of predictors. When several predictors are involved, Cohen (1988) recommends that guidelines for "small," "medium," and "large" strengths of association should be greater than those given for a single predictor.

- An f of .14 is a small strength of association.
- An f of .39 is a medium strength of association.
- An f of .59 is a large strength of association.

How Is Power Calculated?   Cohen (1988) gives the procedures for determining power for a collection of predictors in multiple linear regression. An approximation may be obtained by use of the procedures described in Chapter 14 but adjusted for more than one predictor.

Stepwise Regression

Stepwise regression is a second incremental regression procedure. It allows predictors to be entered in steps in the regression equation according to the magni-

---

Textbox 15.9

Explained Variance When Predictors Are Correlated

In the Common Allies scenario, the Psychology major believed that Partner Sensitivity was the most important predictor while the Sociology major believed that Cultural Similarity was the most important predictor. This issue might be addressed in several ways.

Examine r^2; notice that there is little to choose between the predictors. The proportion of variance explained by Partner Sensitivity is .56, while the proportion of variance explained by Cultural Similarity is .63. Because they are based on simple correlations, these proportions include variability in Y shared with the other predictor.

When the variability explained uniquely by each predictor is examined, there is also a small difference between the two predictors. The sum of squares in Y uniquely attributable to Partner Sensitivity is 72.98; the sum of squares in Y uniquely attributable to Cultural Sensitivity is 103.98.

However, when the shared variability in Y is assigned to only one predictor, the picture changes dramatically. Giving the shared variability in Y explained by both A and B only to B results in a sum of squares in Y attributable to Cultural Similarity of 270.32 and a sum of squares in Y attributable to Partner Sensitivity of only 72.98.

tude of their contribution to explaining additional variability in the outcome variable. Thus, shared variability is decided statistically, not theoretically.

In step 1, the predictor that explains the greatest variability enters the model. Normally, a minimum value called **F-to-enter** is specified (e.g., F-to-enter $= 3.00$) or the predictor cannot be used in the regression equation. In step 2, an F-statistic is calculated for each predictor not yet in the model. The predictor with the highest F-statistic enters on the second step if it exceeds the F-to-enter value. These steps are repeated until no variables meet the criterion for addition. Furthermore, researchers may also specify an F-to-remove value for discarding predictors that fail to explain sufficient variability on subsequent steps. Thus, when there are multiple predictors, stepwise regression allows the researcher not only to partition shared variability according to statistical criteria but also to identify the subset of predictors, each of which contributes significantly to the explanation of outcome variability.

SPECIAL ISSUES IN MULTIPLE LINEAR REGRESSION

There are several issues that require special consideration when multiple linear regression is used. These include outliers, ill-conditioned data, and the adjusted square correlation coefficient (adjusted R^2).

Outliers

In Chapter 14 we suggested that a useful diagnostic procedure is the plot of standardized residuals (z_r) against the predicted scores (Y').

The formula for obtaining standardized residuals (z_r) in multiple linear regression is also shown below:

$$\textbf{(Equation 14.20)}\ z_r = \frac{Y - Y'}{\sqrt{MS_{Y(RE)}}}$$

where:

$Y - Y' =$ deviation of an actual score (Y) from a predicted score (Y')

$\sqrt{MS_{(RE)}} =$ standard deviation of the residuals (standard error of estimate)

The scatterplot of standardized residuals should reveal that the points appear to scatter randomly about the line originating from the mean of the residuals. As a general rule, standardized residuals greater than ± 2.00 should be considered as extreme and deserve special attention. In Textbox 15.10 the identification and removal of an outlier from the Common Allies scenario substantially changes the findings in this small dataset.

Ill-Conditioned Data

Ill-conditioned data can cause both statistical and computational difficulties. We deal with two sources of ill-conditioning: multicollinearity and small coefficients of variation.

Plot of Residuals and Identification and Removal of an Outlier in the Common Allies Scenario

To find the standardized residuals, first find the predicted values of the outcome variable:

$$Y' = a' + b'_A(A) + b'_B(B) = -.29 + 1.58(A) + .22(B)$$

Next find the standard deviation of the residuals:

$$\sqrt{MS_{Y(RE)}} = \sqrt{12.39} = 3.52$$

The standardized residuals can now be computed for the 10 couples participating in the Common Allies scenario. For example, the standardized residual for the Jones couple is

$$z_r = \frac{Y - Y'}{\sqrt{MS_{Y(RE)}}} = \frac{5.00 - 7.27}{3.52} \approx -.85$$

Note that the standardized residual for the Pambookian couple is 2.25. Also see Figure 15.2. If the data for the Pambookians are removed, the squared multiple correlation based on data from nine couples becomes

$$R^2 = .93$$

The multiple regression equation becomes

$$Y' = -1.10 + 2.52(A) + .0319(B)$$

Furthermore, the regression coefficient for the Cultural Similarity predictor is no longer significant.

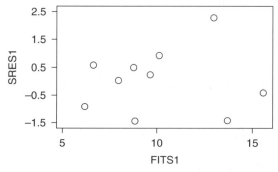

Figure 15.2 Plot of Predicted Scores (FITS1) and Standardized Residuals (SRES1)

Multicollinearity   In regression, **multicollinearity** occurs when the predictor variables are highly correlated among themselves. Multicollinearity is sometimes indicated when a predictor's tolerance is exceeded. Tolerance is

$1 - R^2$, where R^2 is the value resulting from regressing the
suspect predictor on the remaining predictors.

Computer programs use a default value for tolerance as small as 0.0001, meaning that the suspect predictor is almost perfectly predicted by the remaining predictors.

When multicollinearity occurs, the predicted values and residuals will be computed with high accuracy, but the regression coefficients will have very large standard deviations and may be numerically inaccurate. Possible solutions are: (1) eliminate predictors from the equation, especially if deleting them has little effect on the R^2 value, and (2) change predictors by taking linear combinations of them.

Small Coefficient of Variation In regression, the data are considered ill-conditioned if a predictor has a small coefficient of variation (i.e., the standard deviation divided by the mean of the predictor). In other words, a problem occurs if the predictor values are nearly constant. One possible solution is to subtract a constant from the data.

Adjusted R^2

If a variable is added to a regression equation, R^2 sometimes will get larger even if the added variable is of no real value. To compensate for this inflation, the squared correlation coefficient is adjusted by the degrees of freedom. This is an approximately unbiased estimate of the population R^2, and is calculated by the following formula:

$$\text{Equation 15.23: } R_{adj}^2 = \frac{(N-k)R^2 - 1}{(N-k) - R^2}$$

When the sample size is small and the number of predictors is large, the adjustment or **shrinkage** will be substantial. For large sample sizes and a small number of predictors, the shrinkage will be negligible. Calculations for the adjusted R^2 based on the Common Allies scenario are given in Textbox 15.11.

Textbox 15.11

Adjusted or Shrunken R^2 Calculations

For the Common Allies scenario:

$$R^2 = .80$$

$$N = 10$$

$$k = 2$$

$$R_{adj}^2 = \frac{(N-k)R^2 - 1}{(N-k) - R^2} = \frac{(10.00 - 8.00).80 - 1.00}{(10.00 - 8.00) - .80} \approx .74$$

PUTTING IT ALL TOGETHER

The computational and application issues in multiple linear regression were explored. Multiple regression is a data analysis technique for analyzing the variability in a single outcome measure by using more than one predictor variable. Important parallels were shown between multiple linear regression and simple linear regression. Ways in which the techniques are different were also illustrated, especially with regard to dealing with shared variability.

The simultaneous approach is useful for estimating the regression coefficients and the intercept in order to form the regression equation for multiple predictors. The squared multiple correlation coefficient is the proportion of total variability explained by the set of predictors, whereas the test of each regression coefficient evaluates the unique contribution of a predictor to explaining variability in the outcome measure.

The incremental approach to multiple linear regression allows predictors to enter the regression equation in successive steps. One advantage is in identifying the smallest subset of predictors that each significantly explain variability in the outcome variable. A second advantage is that shared variability may be assigned either theoretically (i.e., hierarchical regression) or statistically (i.e., stepwise regression) to predictors.

Finally, diagnostic procedures and special issues were covered, including the problem of outliers and ways to recognize and treat ill-conditioned data arising from multicollinearity and small coefficients of variation. The formula for adjusting R^2 was given which has a noticeable effect when there are a large number of predictors and a small sample size.

The Multiple Regression Equation

The regression equation for multiple predictors is as follows:

$$\text{Equation 15.1: } Y' = a' + b'_A(A) + b'_B(B) + \cdots + b'_Z(Z)$$

where:

Y' = estimated value of the outcome variable

a' = estimated intercept

b'_A = estimated regression coefficient for predictor variable A

A = actual value of the first predictor variable

b'_B = estimated regression coefficient for predictor variable B

B = actual value of the second predictor variable

b'_Z = estimated regression coefficient for predictor variable Z

Z = actual value of the last predictor variable

For two predictors, the formula for the squared multiple correlation is as follows:

$$\text{Equation 15.2: } R^2_{YAB} = \frac{r^2_{YA} + r^2_{YB} - 2r_{YA}r_{YB}r_{AB}}{1 - r^2_{AB}}$$

Given two predictors, there are two regression coefficients:

$$\text{Equation 15.3: } b'_A = \frac{(SS_B)(SS_{YA}) - (SS_{AB})(SS_{YB})}{(SS_A)(SS_B) - (SS_{AB})^2}$$

$$\text{Equation 15.4: } b'_B = \frac{(SS_A)(SS_{YB}) - (SS_{AB})(SS_{YA})}{(SS_A)(SS_B) - (SS_{AB})^2}$$

Given two predictors, the formula for the intercept is as follows:

$$\text{Equation 15.5: } a' = \overline{Y} - b'_A(\overline{A}) - b'_B(\overline{B})$$

Tests of Significance: Simultaneous Approach

There are two methods for determining the significance of the set of predictors. The multiple correlation method and the mean square method yield the identical calculated value.

Multiple Correlation Method

$$\text{Equation 15.6: } F = \frac{R^2_{YAB}/k}{(1 - R^2_{YAB})/(N - k - 1)}$$

where:

    df $= k$ and $N - k - 1$

     $k =$ the number of predictors

Mean Squares Method

$$\text{Equation 15.7: } SS_{Y(AB)} = (R^2_{YAB})(SS_Y)$$

$$\text{Equation 15.8: } SS_{Y(RE)} = (1 - R^2_{YAB})(SS_Y)$$

$$\text{Equation 15.9: } MS_{Y(AB)} = SS_{Y(AB)}/k \qquad \text{where } k = \text{the number of predictors}$$

$$\text{Equation 15.10: } MS_{Y(RE)} = SS_{Y(R)}/N - k - 1$$

$$\text{Equation 15.11: } F = MS_{Y(AB)}/MS_{Y(RE)} \qquad \text{where df} = (k, N - k - 1)$$

Tests of Significance for the Regression Coefficients
Each test determines whether the variance explained uniquely by a predictor is significant.

For predictor A:

Equation 15.14: $t_A = \dfrac{b'_A}{s_{b'_A}} = \dfrac{\dfrac{(SS_B)(SS_{YA}) - (SS_{AB})(SS_{YB})}{(SS_A)(SS_B) - (SS_{AB})^2}}{\sqrt{\dfrac{MS_{Y(RE)}}{SS_A(1 - r^2_{AB})}}}$ where df $= N - k - 1$

For predictor B:

Equation 15.15: $t_B = \dfrac{b'_B}{s_{b'_B}} = \dfrac{\dfrac{(SS_A)(SS_{YB}) - (SS_{AB})(SS_{YA})}{(SS_A)(SS_B) - (SS_{AB})^2}}{\sqrt{\dfrac{MS_{Y(RE)}}{SS_B(1 - r^2_{AB})}}}$ where df $= N - k - 1$

Confidence Intervals   The two-sided confidence interval for a nondirectional two-tailed alternative hypothesis is as follows:

$$\textbf{(Equation 14.19)} \ b' - t_{1-\alpha/2}s_{b'} \text{ and } b' + t_{1-\alpha/2}s_{b'}$$

where:

b' = estimated regression coefficient

t = critical value for a particular probability value, degrees of freedom, and for a two-tailed test $(1 - \alpha/2)$

$s_{b'}$ = estimated standard error of the regression coefficient

Incremental Approach to Multiple Regression

Incremental approaches to multiple linear regression allow other options for dealing with shared variability. In hierarchical regression, the researcher decides on the order of entry of predictor variables. In stepwise regression, the order of entry is determined statistically.

Hierarchical Regression   For two predictors, divide the total variability into three additive components:

1. Y-variability due to B uniquely and in common with A:

$$\textbf{Equation 15.16: } SS_{Y(B)} = (r^2_{YB})(SS_Y)$$

2. Y-variability due uniquely to A:

$$\textbf{Equation 15.17: } SS_{Y(AB-B)} = SS_{Y(AB)} - SS_{Y(B)}$$

3. *Y*-variability not explained by the two predictors (*A* and *B*):

$$\textbf{(Equation 15.8)}\ SS_{Y(RE)} = (1 - R^2_{YAB})(SS_Y)$$

The mean squares:

$$\textbf{Equation 15.18:}\ MS_{Y(B)} = SS_{Y(B)}/df_B$$

$$\textbf{Equation 15.19:}\ MS_{Y(AB-E)} = SS_{Y(AB-B)}/df_A$$

$$\textbf{Equation 15.20:}\ MS_{Y(RE)} = SS_{Y(RE)}/df_{N-k-1}$$

The *F*-ratios:

$$\textbf{Equation 15.21:}\ F = MS_{Y(B)}/MS_{Y(RE)},\ df = B, N - k - 1$$

$$\textbf{Equation 15.22:}\ F = MS_{Y(AB-B)}/MS_{Y(RE)},\ df = A, N - k - 1$$

Stepwise Regression Stepwise regression is a second incremental regression procedure. It allows predictors to be entered in steps in the regression equation according to the magnitude of their contribution to explaining additional variability in the outcome variable. Thus, shared variability is decided statistically, not theoretically.

Special Issues in Multiple Linear Regression

Several issues require special consideration when multiple linear regression is used. These include outliers, ill-conditioned data, and the adjusted square correlation coefficient (adjusted R^2).

To detect outliers, a useful diagnostic procedure is the plot of standardized residuals (z_r) against the predicted scores (Y'). The formula for obtaining standardized residuals (z_r) in multiple linear regression is as follows:

$$\textbf{(Equation 14.20)}\ z_r = \frac{Y - Y'}{\sqrt{MS_{Y(RE)}}}$$

where:

$$Y - Y' = \text{deviation of an actual score } (Y) \text{ from a predicted score } (Y')$$

$$\sqrt{MS_{Y(RE)}} = \text{standard deviation of the residuals (standard error of estimate)}$$

Multicollinearity is sometimes indicated when a predictor's tolerance is exceeded. Tolerance is

$1 - R^2$ where R^2 = the value resulting from regressing the suspect predictor on the remaining predictors

Furthermore, the data are considered ill-conditioned if a predictor has a small coefficient of variation (the standard deviation divided by the mean of the predictor).

Finally, an approximately unbiased estimate of the population R^2 is calculated by the following formula:

$$\text{Equation 15.23: } R^2_{\text{adj}} = \frac{(N-k)R^2 - 1}{(N-k) - R^2}$$

Textbox 15.12

Multiple Linear Regression: Children, Mothers, Stressful Events and the Development of Locus of Control

Locus of control is the perception of control a person feels he or she can exert over the environment. Those people considered to be externals perceive little relationship between their own actions and the events in the environment. Internals see the world as responsive to their actions. Externals tend to have lower self-esteem, while internals have higher self-esteem.

Carton and Nowicki (1996) examined the relationship among maternal warmth, maternal control, stressful events, and the development of locus of control in young children. Participants were second-grade children (28 boys and 27 girls) and their mothers. Each child completed a children's locus of control scale. The mothers completed a life-events scale, which looked at the number and type of stressful events in the family and assigned numerical value for amount of stress. Warmth and control were assessed by videotaping the interactions between mother and child during the completion of jigsaw puzzles.

Data were analyzed with multiple regression; children's Locus of Control score was the outcome measure. Total Frequency of Life Stressors, Total Stress Unit Value, Maternal Control, and Warmth were entered as predictors into the first equation. The four variables accounted for 53% of the variance in children's locus of control, $F(4, 50) = 14.12$, $p = .001$. Analyses to determine each variable's unique contribution indicated that Stress Unit Values [$t(50) = 2.62$, $p = .012$], Maternal Control [$t(50) = 3.21$, $p = .002$], and Maternal Warmth [$t(50) = -5.31$, $p = .001$] were significant and independent predictors of locus of control. Total Frequency of Life Stressors was not significant, [$t(50) = -1.05$, $p = .297$]. A second analysis looked at the influence of preschool versus elementary school stress on children's locus of control. Predictor variables were Preschool Stress Unit Values, Elementary Stress Unit Values, Maternal Warmth, and Maternal Control. The variables again accounted for 53% of the variability in the children's locus of control, $F(4, 50) = 14.13$, $p = .001$. Significant and independent predictors of locus of control were Maternal Control [$t(50) = 3.41$, $p = .001$], Maternal Warmth [$t(50) = -5.63$, $p = .001$], and Elementary Stress Unit Values [$t(50) = 3.07$, $p = .004$]. Preschool Stress Unit Values were not significant [$t(50) = .62$, $p = .541$].

Results suggest that internal locus of control is associated with less maternal control, more maternal warmth, and less stress during the child's recent past. Events that occurred in the child's early development had less impact than later stress events.

KEY TERMS

Shared variability	Collinearity	F-to-enter
Estimated intercept	Incremental approach	Ill-conditioned data
Collection of predictors	Hierarchical regression	Multicollinearity
Simultaneous approach	Stepwise regression	Shrinkage

REFERENCES

Carton, J. S., & Norwicki, S., Jr. (1996). Origins of generalized control expectancies: Reported child stress and observed maternal control and warmth. *The Journal of Social Psychology, 136* (6), 753.

Cohen, J. (1988). *Statistical power analysis for the behavioral sciences.* (2nd ed.). Hillsdale, NJ: Lawrence Erlbaum.

Pedhazur, E. J. (1997). *Multiple regression in behavioral research: Explanation and prediction.* (3rd ed.). Orlando, FL: Harcourt Brace College Publishers.

PROBLEMS

Questions

Section 1   Conceptual/Definition

15.1. Why does the calculation of regression statistics become more complicated when the predictor variables are correlated with one another, especially when they share explained variability in the outcome measure (Y)?

15.2. When the predictor variables in a regression model are uncorrelated, how is the total explained variability in Y determined? How does this change when the predictor variables are correlated?

15.3. In simple linear regression, four methods for testing the significance of a single predictor have been identified Each of the methods produces the same results. Is this the case for multiple linear regression as well?

15.4. The multiple correlation F-test and mean squares F-test are sometimes used for *simultaneous approaches* to multiple regression. Why?

15.5. What is *collinearity*? Why and when is it a problem?

15.6. What is an *incremental approach* to multiple linear regression, and how is it different from a *simultaneous approach*?

15.7. What is hierarchical regression, and how does it work?

15.8. What is stepwise regression, and how does it work?

15.9. Explain the term *ill-conditioned data*.

15.10. Many researchers prefer to use the adjusted R^2 figure rather than R^2 in building regression models. Why?

Section 2   Numerical

15.11. In a given study, two predictor variables are regressed on an outcome variable:

$$r_{YA} = .45, r_{YB} = .30, r_{AB} = 0$$

Determine R^2_{YAB}.

15.12. In a given study, two predictor variables are regressed on an outcome variable:

$$r_{YA} = .45, r_{YB} = .30, r_{AB} = .5$$

Determine R^2_{YAB}.

Use the following data to answer questions 15.13 to 15.14:

A	B	Y
69	14	71
90	16	84
75	11	69
84	14	76
71	17	73
87	12	69
80	16	82
93	19	90
74	17	70
78	13	75

15.13. Determine the estimated regression coefficients (b'_A) and (b'_B). Determine the regression equation.

15.14. Test the significance of the simultaneous effect of both A and B using the multiple correlation method ($\alpha = .05$).

Use the following data to answer questions 15.15 to 15.17:

A	B	Y
15	332	61
16	199	22
17	466	35
13	197	18
16	386	40
12	114	22
16	415	43
16	276	27
16	506	70
19	555	37

15.15. Test the significance of the simultaneous effect of both A and B using the mean squares method.

15.16. Test the significance of b'_A using the *t*-test method.
15.17. Determine the 95% confidence interval for b'_A.

Use the following data to answer questions 15.18 to 15.20:

A	B	Y
284	14	7.8
591	16	11.8
345	16	10.4
240	15	9.3
416	17	8.8
181	15	6.1
185	15	7.0
132	14	4.3
154	14	5.1
573	16	12.9

15.18. Test the significance of the simultaneous effect of both *A* and *B* using the mean squares method.
15.19. Test the significance of b'_B using the *t*-test method.
15.20. Determine the 95% confidence interval for b'_B.

chapter 16 Nonparametric Statistical Tests

OVERVIEW

We have dealt with what must seem like a vast array of statistical tests to analyze data in a host of different forms. We have considered the *t*-test to compare the data from two independent groups, the Oneway ANOVA for a single independent variable with two or more levels, and so on. Our presentation has covered inferential statistical techniques appropriate for and widely used for the analysis of experimental research as well as techniques appropriate for and widely used for correlational investigations.

While we have covered what seems like a wide and powerful range of statistical techniques, we have primarily limited ourselves to analysis methods for a single dependent or outcome variable. That is not the only important limitation. For all the inferential statistics covered so far, we have assumed that the dependent variable was measured on either an *interval or ratio scale*.

But what does one do when measurement is not that refined or precise? In this chapter we will cover a set of statistical techniques that are useful when measurement is nominal or ordinal. And we will include here those situations in which the assumptions of the parametric tests we have covered so far have been seriously violated and the use of alternative procedure(s) is desirable.

This chapter, then, is about a whole class of statistical techniques called *nonparametric* or *distribution-free tests.* It will add to your arsenal of choices for analyzing data. And just so you don't feel you will need a map to guide you through the maze of techniques, we have organized them to match up as closely as possible with their parametric counterparts. More specifically, we will cover the following issues:

1. What's a nonparametric test, and why would anyone want to use one?
2. How does one analyze nominal data?
3. What are the choices when the data are ordinal?
4. What are the nonparametric equivalents to the independent and dependent samples *t*-test, Oneway ANOVA, and the Pearson product moment correlation?
5. How does the rank-order correlation detect relationships between two variables that the Pearson product moment correlation is not able to find?

The scenario in Textbox 16.1 gets you started.

Scenario: The Golden Years

You decide to conduct a confidential survey of retirement-age pensioners in order to learn something about their political orientation, health concerns, economic situation, and so on. You are able to interview a random sample of 20 senior citizens of both sexes. The first questions you explore concern their orientation toward politics. You are able to categorize each of their replies into one of three categories: liberal (L), conservative (C), and no clear orientation (?). You also ask questions about their health and physical well-being. You establish that some have had major surgery and complain of ill-health and/or are taking medication for a variety of ailments (category = 1), and others are generally in good health with few, if any ailments (category = 2). In the next portion of the interview, you ask each of the seniors to complete an attitude inventory of physical and emotional intimacy. From the scores, you are able to rank each respondent from well-adjusted (1) to poorly adjusted (20). Another area explored is generosity. You ask each of the pensioners to tell you the approximate amount of her or his annual contributions to charitable causes and level of volunteer work from which you are able to rank the respondents from most generous (1) to least generous (20). See Table 16.1.

On closer examination, you notice that the data are in a strange form. Some of the responses are nonnumeric, but *all* of the responses are not on an interval scale of measurement. Trouble! What do you do now? Are there ways to analyze these data and come to a better understanding of your pensioners?

TABLE 16.1 Golden Years Scenario Dataset

Name	Gender	Married	Political Orientation	Health	Intimacy Rank	Generosity Rank
John	M	W	L	1	4	9
Sally	F	M	C	2	6	13
Dot	F	W	C	2	1	12
Joe	M	S	C	1	18	19
Syl	F	W	?	2	8	4
Jan	F	M	L	2	12	1
Pierre	M	M	C	1	19	14
Marc	M	S	L	2	7	2
Tambour	M	M	?	1	13	10
Esther	F	M	C	2	2	11
Vera	F	W	?	2	16	15
Dolores	F	W	C	1	17	20
Mike	M	M	C	1	14	18
Wayne	M	S	L	2	15	3
Wenda	F	M	?	2	11	17
Bill	M	S	C	2	20	5
Alice	F	M	L	2	10	8
Anne	F	S	C	2	3	7
Evelyne	F	W	C	2	9	16
Valerie	F	M	?	2	5	6

WHY NONPARAMETRIC STATISTICAL TESTS?

All the statistical tests you have studied so far are designed to test hypotheses about population parameters. For example, the *t*-test is used to choose between null and alternative hypotheses concerning two population means, μ_{A1} and μ_{A2}. Similarly, the Pearson product moment correlation is used to help choose between null and alternative hypotheses concerning the population correlation, ρ.

Assumptions and Assumption Violations

The statistical tests you have learned about rest on certain assumptions about population parameters. For example, important assumptions underlying the *t*-test include normality and homogeneity of variance. Because these tests all concern parameters and require assumptions about those parameters, they are called **parametric tests.**

The parametric tests covered in this book are generally robust to assumption violations. That means that even though these tests make certain assumptions, they are not greatly affected when the assumptions are not entirely met.

As we discussed in Chapter 7, the effects of assumption violations can be to modify the rate of both Type I and Type II errors from what the researcher expected. When the assumptions of the statistical test are completely met, the actual or empirical probability of Type I (and Type II) errors is the same as the nominal probability of Type I (and Type II) errors. However, when the assumptions of the statistical tests are not met, and especially when they are strongly violated, the actual or empirical probability of Type I (and Type II) errors will be different from the nominal probability of Type I (and Type II) errors.

Under these circumstances, an attractive alternative to parametric tests are tests that are not always designed to make inferences about population parameters and make fewer or no assumptions about those parameters. These alternatives are called either **nonparametric tests** or **distribution-free tests**.

This is not to suggest that there are no assumptions at all associated with nonparametric statistical tests. They may be better described as "assumption-freer" tests. For example, assumptions about the independence of observations are made for chi-square tests.

Scales of Measurement

Another characteristic of parametric tests is that they require data from an interval or ratio scale of measurement because the data being analyzed are subject to arithmetic operations such as adding, squaring, and averaging. This requirement does not apply to nonparametric tests.

In Chapter 2, we described the scales of measurement used by social scientists. There are four scales and they have different properties. Use of the **nominal scale** allows only for data categorization. Use of the **ordinal scale** allows for both data categorization and ordering. Use of the **interval scale** allows for data categorization, ordering, and equal intervals. Finally, use of the **ratio scale** allows for data categorization, ordering, equal intervals, and a true zero point.

There are situations in which the dependent or outcome variable is not measured on an interval or ratio scale of measurement. For example, researchers might ask participants to categorize candidates for governor as most clearly supporting one of several economic initiatives (i.e., new roads, industrial parks, technical colleges, or business tax rebates) and then analyze gender differences in the categorizations. Or researchers might ask participants to rank-order cereal preferences and then see whether the preferences vary as a function of age. In the former case, the perceived orientations of political candidates are categorized on a nominal scale of measurement. In the latter case, cereal preferences have been collected on an ordinal scale of measurement. In either case, researchers would be unable to use parametric statistical tests to analyze the data.[1]

Advantages and Disadvantages

Deciding to use a nonparametric test does not mean that your data are automatically correlational, just as deciding to use a parametric test does not mean that your data are automatically experimental. Data from either experimental or correlational designs may be analyzed with either type of test. Unfortunately, some students associate nonparametric tests with uncontrolled research and assume that these tests may not be used to analyze experiments properly. Not true.

The main advantage of nonparametric statistical tests is their flexibility. They can be used accurately without making assumptions about population parameters and without the data for the dependent or outcome measure being on an interval or ratio scale of measurement.

Consequently, researchers often turn to nonparametric statistical tests when they are concerned that the assumptions of parametric tests might have been seriously violated. They will also turn to nonparametric tests when they are concerned that the data might fail to meet the requirements for an interval scale of measurement (e.g., when the scale on a questionnaire does not appear to contain equal intervals among the response alternatives).

Given the flexibility of nonparametric tests, why would anyone choose to use parametric tests? The answer lies in the greater statistical power of parametric tests compared to nonparametric tests and the

> **CD-ROM link 16.1**
>
> *Activity 16.1: Comparing Parametric and Nonparametric Tests*
> Why do parametric tests have more power than nonparametric tests? In Activity 16.1, you can analyze the same dataset using both the *t*-test and the Mann-Whitney *U*-test. By changing data values within the dataset, you will see the effect of an ordinal scale of measurement on the sensitivity of the Mann-Whitney *U*-statistic.

[1]How might you redesign these studies to use parametric tests? In the political example, you might have participants use a Likert scale to rate the strength of each candidate's commitment to each type of economic initiative. In the cereal example, you might also have participants use a Likert scale to rate several cereals for taste and enjoyment. By changing the scale of measurement, you learn more about both gubernatorial and gustatorial preferences.

finding that most parametric tests are reasonably robust to assumption violations. This increase in power coupled with the robustness of parametric tests are why most researchers select these tests whenever they can reasonably use them.

There are, of course, situations in which nonparametric tests need to be used because of the nature of the research question, the quality of the instrument used for data collection, or otherwise because of the properties of the data. We will cover several of the more popular nonparametric tests including the ones listed below.

For outcome data on a nominal scale:

- Chi-square test of goodness of fit
- Chi-square test of association (or independence)

For outcome data on an ordinal scale:

1. Mann-Whitney *U*-test for two independent samples
2. Kruskal-Wallis Oneway ANOVA
3. Wilcoxon signed-ranks *T*-test for two dependent samples
4. Friedman ANOVA for two or more dependent samples
5. Spearman rank-order correlation

CHI-SQUARE AND THE ANALYSIS OF NOMINAL DATA

The chi-square (χ^2, pronounced "kye-square") statistic was developed by Karl Pearson in 1900. It can be used even when the data for the dependent or outcome measure to be analyzed are on a *nominal* scale of measurement (i.e., scores are qualitatively different).

When there is only a single variable of interest, the chi-square test is used to test **goodness of fit.** That is, how well do the sample values correspond to (hypothesized) population parameters? When there are two variables of interest, the chi-square test is used as a **test of independence**. That is, are the values of one variable related to or dependent on the values of a second variable?

Requirements for Using Chi-Square

The chi-square statistic is one of the most popular nonparametric statistics. It is safe to use because it requires so few assumptions and those assumptions are easily met. The test "works" even when distributions are skewed, variability is dramatically different among samples, and scale points are far from equal intervals. This is why chi-square is so widely used even though it is not a very powerful test.

Chi-square is called a nonparametric test because it makes no assumptions about either the population's mean or its shape. As you will see, the size of the sample is irrelevant for calculating the degrees of freedom. The only information necessary for finding the degrees of freedom is the number of categories or levels of one variable (goodness of fit) or two variables (test of independence).

The assumption of the chi-square test are threefold:

1. The samples have been randomly selected.
2. The observations are independent.
3. Group sample sizes are sufficiently large.

The sample size of each group can affect Type I and Type II error rates. In certain situations, five is the minimum group sample size.

Frequencies and Categories

Throughout the presentation of chi-square, the values of variables will be given in terms of frequencies. More precisely, the **expected frequencies** and **observed frequencies** of a value or category of a variable will be highlighted. For example, one can talk about the variable Gender, which has two values or categories: male and female. In a sample of 1000 people, one would expect the frequency of males and females to be equal: 500 and 500. But suppose one observes more males (525) than females (475). Is this difference between expected and observed frequencies significant? You can use the chi-square test to answer this question.

Similarly, one can talk about the variable Natural Hair Color and its values or categories: brown, black, red, blonde. In a sample of 1000 people one might expect 500 with brown hair, 250 with black hair, 75 with red hair, and 175 with blonde hair; but suppose a higher number of blondes (250) and a smaller number of brunettes (425) were observed. Here, too, you can ask whether there are significant differences between observed and expected frequencies.

Finally, one can explore whether there is a relationship between two variables also by examining expected and observed frequencies. For example, one might expect the number of excellent (A) and good grades (B) in mathematics to be about the same for male students as for female students. Suppose that 20 females earned As and 40 females earned Bs while 25 males earned As and 15 males earned Bs. Is there a significant discrepancy between expected and observed grades for females compared to males? The chi-square test helps you find the answer.

The chi-square test then, either goodness of fit (one variable) or test of independence (two variables), is based on a comparison between expected frequencies and observed frequencies.

When using the chi-square statistic, one converts the raw data into frequencies before it is analyzed further. In Chapter 3, we discussed grouped frequency distributions using class intervals. This technique is useful when the raw data are on an ordinal scale of measurement or higher and need to be organized into fewer, discrete categories. When data are nominal, as in the gender or hair color examples, reorganization is seldom necessary unless the number of discrete categories is too large or the sample size in any category is too small.

About Chi-Square

The chi-square statistic will be used to help determine the likelihood that the observed frequencies are the same (null hypothesis) or different (alternative hypothesis) from the expected frequencies. The null and alternative hypotheses are, therefore,

$$H_0: f_0 = f_e$$
$$H_a: f_0 \neq f_e$$

where f_o is the observed population frequency and f_e is the expected population frequency.

Calculated Value   The formula for the calculated value of the chi-square statistic is as follows:

$$\text{Equation 16.1: } \chi^2 = \sum \frac{(O_k - E_k)^2}{E_k}$$

where:

E_k = expected frequency for the category
O_k = observed frequency for the category
k = number of categories (values of the variable(s))

As the formula indicates, the computed value of chi-square is obtained by taking the following steps:

1. Find the difference between the observed and expected frequency for each of the k categories.
2. Square the difference so that all values are positive.
3. Divide each squared difference by the expected frequency to obtain an indication of the *relative* magnitude of the discrepancy.
4. Sum the values for all the k categories.

Critical Value   As the formula for the calculated value indicates, the value of chi-square is a measure of the discrepancy between observed and expected frequencies. When these discrepancies are large, the calculated value of chi-square will be large. When these discrepancies are small, the calculated value of chi-square will be small.

As we have said repeatedly throughout this text, you can expect some fluctuation in samples of scores drawn from a population merely as a function of chance. So you would not expect every random sample from a population to yield identical observed frequencies. Therefore, an important question is how much of a discrepancy can exist between observed and expected frequencies before you are prepared to say that you reject the null hypothesis.

The critical value of chi-square is the value you need to exceed to reject the null hypothesis and conclude with a degree of confidence that observed and expected frequencies represent different population parameters. How do you find the critical value? You need to know both alpha, the probability value for significance testing (e.g., .05 and .01), and the degrees of freedom.

Like other theoretical distributions (e.g., *t*-distributions and *F*-distributions), chi-square is a *family of distributions*. The shape of each chi-square distribution

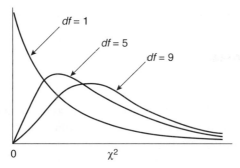

Figure 16.1 The shape of the chi-square distribution for different degrees of freedom

varies as a function of the degrees of freedom, which is *not* a function of sample size but is a function of the number of categories. Figure 16.1 illustrates the shape of the chi-square distribution for different values of degrees of freedom.

Note that the typical chi-square distribution is positively skewed. That means that near-zero differences in the magnitude between expected and observed frequencies should occur commonly when the null hypothesis is true. In contrast, large differences in the magnitude between expected and observed frequencies should occur rarely when the null hypothesis is true.

Although the typical chi-square distribution is positively skewed, note also that the degrees of freedom affect the shape of the distribution. Larger degrees of freedom are associated with a larger number of categories. The more categories you have, the more likely it is that you will obtain a large sum for the calculated value. On average, you should expect that the calculated value will be larger when you are summing over 10 categories than when you are summing over 6 categories, even when the null hypothesis is true. Therefore, for a particular probability value, the critical value of chi-square grows larger as the degrees of freedom increase. Critical values of chi-square are given in Appendix I for probability values ranging from .10 to .005.

Degrees of Freedom When dealing with the observed and expected frequencies of the categories of a single variable, use the chi-square statistic to test the goodness of fit. Here the degrees of freedom is simply the number of categories or values of the dependent or outcome variable (Y) minus 1 (i.e., $Y - 1$).

When dealing with the observed and expected frequencies for two variables, use the chi-square statistic as a test of independence. Here the degrees of freedom is the product of two things: (1) one less then the categories of the first variable and (2) one less than the categories of the second variable. The observed and expected frequencies of the variables should be organized by using a twoway contingency table, where the categories of the dependent or outcome variable will form the rows (Y) and the categories of the independent or predictor variable will form the columns (A). Therefore, the degrees of freedom for the test of independence are $(Y - 1)(A - 1)$. To reiterate:

1. Degrees of freedom for goodness of fit: $Y - 1$
2. Degrees of freedom for test of independence: $(Y - 1)(A - 1)$

We are now ready to look at the two major uses of chi-square: goodness of fit and tests of independence.

Goodness of Fit

The chi-square goodness of fit is a one-variable test to determine whether a significant difference exists between expected and observed frequencies. The expected frequencies are based on theory, prior research, or speculative arguments regarding the proportion of cases falling into each category of a variable. Occasionally, these expectations are based on the belief that the proportion of cases in each category will be the same.

To find the expected frequencies, begin with the **expected proportion** of the total responses for each value or category of the variable to be analyzed. The total of the value or category proportions should add to 1.00. Then multiply the expected proportion for each value or category by the total number of responses to find each expected frequency. The total of the expected frequencies should equal the total number of responses.

For example, imagine that retirement-age pensioners were expected to be equally divided on their political orientations. Therefore, the proportion of total responses should be equally distributed among liberal, conservative, and no clear orientation (i.e., 1/3, 1/3, and 1/3). Because there are 20 seniors who were surveyed (i.e., $N = 20$), the expected frequency for each category is $(.33) \times 20 = 7.33$.

We find it handy to use a table like the one shown in Table 16.2 to help compute the calculated value of chi-square. The columns of the table represent the steps in computing the calculated value. The rows of the table represent the categories or values of the variable being analyzed. See Textbox 16.2 for an illustration of the analysis of the political orientation data from the Golden Years scenario using the chi-square goodness-of-fit test.

Test of Independence

The chi-square test of independence is used to determine whether two variables are significantly related. The test of independence calculates the difference between observed and expected frequencies. The null hypothesis is that the two variables are unrelated; the alternative hypothesis is that the two variables are related. The

TABLE 16.2   Worktable for Computing Chi-Square

Values	O	E	$O - E$	$(O - E)^2$	$(O - E)^2/E$
A					
B					
C					
D					
Total	$N =$	$N =$	—	—	

Textbox 16.2

Chi-Square Goodness of Fit: Seniors' Political Orientation

You are interested in learning whether seniors have a particular political orientation. Therefore, your null hypothesis is that their choice of political orientations will be equally distributed across each of the categories. (.33 for each category). Your alternative hypothesis is that their choices will *not* be equally distributed across each of the categories. Given 20 respondents, the expected frequency in each category under the null hypothesis would be .33 × 20 = 7.33.

You can now use Equation 16.1 and the worktable introduced in Table 16.2 to find the calculated value of chi-square. See Table 16.3 for the intermediate calculations.

$$\chi^2 = \sum \frac{(O_k - E_k)^2}{E_k}$$

Degrees of freedom for goodness of fit: $Y - 1 = 2$.

The calculated value of chi-square is 2.45.

For $\alpha = .05$ and df = 2, the critical value of chi-square is 5.99 from Appendix I.

Therefore, you fail to reject the null hypothesis. You are unable to conclude that seniors hold a particular political orientation.

TABLE 16.3 Computing the Goodness-of-Fit Calculated Value: Seniors' Political Orientation

Values	O	E	O − E	(O − E)²	(O − E)²/E
Liberal	5	7.33	−2.33	5.43	0.74
Cons.	10	7.33	2.67	7.13	0.97
Uncertain	5	7.33	−2.33	5.43	0.74
Total	N = 20	N = 20	—	—	2.45

challenge of using the test of independence is first finding the expected frequencies, assuming that the variables are not related. We will explain how this is done via the example of gender and grades in mathematics.

It was suggested earlier that you might expect that the number of excellent (*A*) and good grades (*B*) in mathematics to be about the same for male students as for female students. To verify this you sample 100 students: 40 males and 60 females. You find that there are slightly more *B* grades (55) than *A* grades (45). Examining the data more closely, you find that 20 females earn *A*s and 40 females earn *B*s while 25 males earn *A*s and 15 males earn *B*s. Is there a significant discrepancy between expected and observed grades for females compared to males?

Begin by creating a contingency table (see Table 16.4) much like the Factorial design tables used in Chapter 11. The rows of the table will be the categories of the dependent or outcome variable which, in the example, is Math Grades. The columns of the table will be the categories of the independent or predictor variable which, in the example, is Gender.

TABLE 16.4 Recording Observed Frequencies			

		Gender		
		Males	Females	
Math	As	25	20	$n = 45$
Grades	Bs	15	40	$n = 55$
		$n = 40$	$n = 60$	$N = 100$

Finding the Expected Frequencies   In this example, you have the problem of an unequal number of males and females and an unequal number of *A* and *B* grades. This inequality makes determining the expected frequencies less obvious but not impossible.

You know that of 100 grades assigned, 45/100, or .45, are *A*s. Therefore, if there is no relationship between grades and gender, .45 of the 60 females (i.e., 27) should earn *A*s and .55 of the 60 females (i.e., 33) should earn *B*s. Similarly, you expect that .45 of the 40 males (i.e., 18) should earn *A*s and .55 of the 40 males (i.e., 22) should earn *B*s.

You need to express this logic mathematically and use the contingency table to record the expected frequencies. The mathematical formula for determining the expected frequencies for each combination of the two variables is as follows:

$$\text{Equation 16.2: } E_{YA} = n_Y n_A / N$$

In other words, the frequency (*n*) of a row, which represents a category of the dependent variable *Y*, times the frequency (*n*) of a column, which represents a value of the independent variable *A*, divided by the total sample size gives the expected frequencies for each cell of the contingency table. Note the computations in Table 16.5. As a computational check, make sure the sum of cell frequencies in each column and row are correct.

The Calculated and Critical Values   Now that there is both a table of expected frequencies and a table of observed frequencies, you can proceed to use the chi-square worktable (see Table 16.2) to help compute the calculated value. The completed worktable is reproduced in Table 16.6.

TABLE 16.5 Computing Expected Frequencies			

		Gender		
		Males	Females	
Math	As	$(45 \times 40)/100 = 18$	$(45 \times 60)/100 = 27$	$n = 45$
Grades	Bs	$(55 \times 40)/100 = 22$	$(55 \times 60)/100 = 33$	$n = 55$
		$n = 40$	$n = 60$	$N = 100$

TABLE 16.6 Computing Chi-Square Test of Independence: Grades × Gender

Values	O	E	O − E	(O − E)²	(O − E)²/E
Males *A*	25	18	7	49	2.72
Males *B*	15	22	−7	49	2.23
Females *A*	20	27	−7	49	1.81
Females *B*	40	33	7	49	1.48
Total	N = 100	N = 100	—	—	8.24

Is the calculated value (8.24) so large that it exceeds the critical value? For $\alpha = .05$ and df = 1 (i.e., $Y - 1 \times A - 1 = 2 - 1 \times 2 - 1 = 1$), the critical value given in Appendix I is 3.84. There is, therefore, a significant difference in mathematics grades for male students compared to females.

CD-ROM link 16.2

Problem Generator: Chi-Square
To practice hypothesis testing using the chi-square test of independence, select chi-square from the Problem Generator Menu on the CD-ROM. The Problem Generator will create as many practice problems as you need and will demonstrate each step in their solution so that you can check your work.

Golden Years Scenario In the Golden Years scenario of Textbox 16.1, you asked about the health of seniors. You now wonder if there is a difference in physical well-being related to gender. Using the data from the Golden Years scenario and the chi-square test of independence, you should get the answer shown in Textbox 16.3.

Dealing with Small Sample Sizes

The chi-square statistic may be inaccurate when the expected frequencies for any category or cell are 5 or lower. More precisely, for single degree-of-freedom tests, the expected cell frequencies should be 10. For

---

Textbox 16.3

Test of Independence: Golden Years Scenario

Using the data from Table 16.1, you are able to construct a 2×2 contingency table (see Table 16.7) showing the observed frequencies for health broken down by gender.

From the contingency table of observed frequencies (see Table 16.7), go on and construct a table of expected frequencies (see Table 16.8), using Equation 16.2.

Use the worktable (Table 16.2) to compute the chi-square calculated value. See Table 16.9 for the intermediate calculations.

The critical value for df = 1 and $\alpha = .05$ is 3.84. (See Appendix I.) Because the calculated value (6.71) exceeds the critical value, you reject the null hypothesis and conclude that elder women are in better health than elder men.

TABLE 16.7   Observed Frequencies: Health × Gender

		Gender			
		Males	Females		
Health	Poor	5	1	$n = 6$	
	Good	3	11	$n = 14$	
		$n = 8$	$n = 12$	$N = 20$	

TABLE 16.8   Expected Frequencies: Health × Gender

		Gender		
		Males	Females	
Health	Poor	$(6 \times 8)/20 = 2.40$	$(6 \times 12)/20 = 3.60$	$n = 6$
	Good	$(14 \times 8)/20 = 5.60$	$(14 \times 12)/20 = 8.40$	$n = 14$
		$n = 8$	$n = 12$	$N = 20$

TABLE 16.9   Computing Chi-Square Test of Independence: Golden Years Scenario

Values	O	E	O − E	$(O - E)^2$	$(O - E)^2/E$
Males Poor	5	2.40	2.60	6.76	2.82
Males Good	3	5.60	−2.60	6.76	1.21
Females Poor	1	3.60	−2.60	6.76	1.88
Females Good	11	8.40	2.60	6.76	.80
Total	$N = 20$	$N = 20$	—	—	$6.71 = \chi^2$

other situations, the expected cell frequency should be 5. There are various approaches to dealing with this problem:

- Yates Correction for Continuity
- Fisher's Exact Test
- Kolmogorov-Smirnov Goodness-of-Fit Test
- Collapsing categories

The Yates correction is discussed below. Otherwise proceed cautiously when sample sizes are so low that you are tempted to reduce the values of variables in order to conduct the chi-square analysis. When categories are pooled after the data have been examined, the random nature of the sample is questionable because you have tampered with it. Furthermore, the hypothesis now explored may be quite different from what was originally intended given how one or more variables have been redefined.

Yates Correction for Continuity   Whenever a chi-square has only a single degree of freedom (when for goodness of fit there are only two categories or when for the test of independence *each* variable has two categories) you may wish to apply **Yates correction for continuity** if the expected frequency in any cell is less than 10. The correction is designed to reduce the calculated value of chi-square, making the test more conservative:

$$\text{Equation 16.3: } \chi^2 = \sum \frac{\left(|O_k - E_k| - .5\right)^2}{E_k}$$

As you can see, you find the absolute value of the difference between observed and expected frequencies from which you then deduct .5. This reduction represents the correction and explains why the calculated value is smaller.

The Yates correction for continuity is correctly applied to the test of independence performed on data from the Golden Years scenario. In this example, expected cell frequencies are below 10 and the test needs to be made more conservative. Note the adjustments on the calculated value as shown in Table 16 10. The corrected calculated value is 4.39. You are still able to reject the null hypothesis using α = .05. However, had you used α = .01, the corrected calculated value would not exceed the critical value (6.63) and you would fail to reject the null hypothesis.

Multiple Comparisons

The chi-square test of independence is an *omnibus test* when the independent variable has more than two categories or values. It says that two variables are associated but does not specify the exact nature of the association. Like an ANOVA, it is possible to ask precise questions about where treatment differences lie by conducting a series of multiple comparisons.

TABLE 16.10 Using Yates Correction on Chi-Square Test of Independence: Golden Years Scenario

Values	O	E	$O - E$	$(|O - E| - .5)^2$	$(|O - E| - .5)^2/E$
Males Poor	5	2.40	2.60	4.41	1.84
Males Good	3	5.60	−2.60	4.41	.79
Females Poor	1	3.60	−2.60	4.41	1.23
Females Good	11	8.40	2.60	4.41	.53
Total	$N = 20$	$N = 20$	—	—	4.39

In order to undertake multiple comparisons among cells in a twoway contingency table, you must first identify which of the variables is the independent or predictor variable and which of the variables is the dependent or outcome variable. You should proceed only by conducting comparisons among levels of the independent variable.

The procedure for conducting pairwise comparisons is relatively straightforward. The following steps should be followed:

1. Select the data that pertain to the levels of the independent variable you are interested in contrasting.
2. Form a separate contingency table for these *observed* frequencies.
3. Find the expected cell frequencies.
4. Compute the calculated value of chi-square and compare it with the critical value.

To conduct complex comparisons, proceed as for simple comparisons except modify step 2 as follows: Combine the observed data for the levels of the independent variable you wish to contrast (e.g., $A_1 + A_2$ versus $A_3 + A_4$).

Measures of Association or Effect Size

By itself, the chi-square test of independence informs you only as to whether a relationship is significant but not the magnitude or size of the relationship. Importantly, the calculated value of chi-square, like other calculated values (e.g., t and F), does not unambiguously reflect the size of treatment effects for the simple reason that the calculated value is influenced by sample size. The larger the sample size, the larger the value of the test statistic. Indeed, if you were to take the data from the Golden Years scenario on Health and Gender and re-enter all the values a second time, so that you doubled the size of the dataset, you would find that the calculated value of chi-square would increase.

What is wanted is an index of relationship that is not so influenced by sample size. To simplify the discussion, we will limit you to situations in which the outcome or dependent variables have only two categories. In these situations, what can be used is a measure of effect size is called the **phi-coefficient (φ).** And as you might have guessed or hoped, it is based on two factors: (1) the calculated value of chi-square and (2) overall sample size, or N.

$$\text{Equation 16.4: } \varphi = \sqrt{\frac{\chi^2}{N}}$$

To help interpret the meaning of a given value of the phi-coefficient, Cohen (1988) has assigned the labels "small," "medium," and "large" to the following values:

.10 = small effect

.30 = medium effect

.50 = large effect

Textbox 16.4

Phi-coefficient: Golden Years Scenario

The chi-square statistic was computed to determine whether there was a relationship between Gender and Health. Whether you used the traditional chi-square calculated value or the Yates correction for continuity, you rejected the null hypotheses and concluded that older females had fewer health problems then older males.

But how strong is the relationship between Gender and Health? You can use the phi-coefficient to find out:

$$\varphi = \sqrt{\frac{\chi^2}{N}} = \sqrt{\frac{6.71}{20}} = .58 \text{ (uncorrected)}$$

$$\varphi = \sqrt{\frac{\chi^2}{N}} = \sqrt{\frac{4.39}{20}} = .47 \text{(corrected)}$$

There is a reasonably large relationship between Gender and Health among seniors.

The calculation and interpretation of the phi-coefficient is illustrated in Textbox 16.4.

THE ANALYSIS OF ORDINAL DATA

We will cover a few of the nonparametric tests available for analyzing data when the dependent or outcome measure is on an ordinal scale of measurement. These tests are: the Mann-Whitney U-test for two independent samples; the Kruskal-Wallis Oneway ANOVA; the Wilcoxon signed-ranks T-test for two dependent samples; the Friedman ANOVA for two or more dependent samples; and the Spearman rank correlation.

Mann-Whitney *U*-Test

The **Mann-Whitney *U*-test** is a nonparametric statistical test commonly used as an alternative to Student's t-test when the dependent or outcome variable is measured on an ordinal scale or when the assumptions of the t-test are seriously violated. The samples that make up the two groups must be independent. The U-test is used to choose between null and alternative hypotheses. The null hypothesis states that there is no difference in the scores of the population from which the two samples were selected. As in the t-test, in the U-test, the alternative hypothesis may be either directional (i.e., greater than, less than) or nondirectional (i.e., not equal). Either form of the alternative hypothesis states that sample scores arose from two different populations.

There are two computational procedures for the *U*-test. The computational procedure for small samples is used when both group sample sizes are 20 or less. The computational procedure for large samples is used when one or both group sample sizes exceed 20.

Calculated Value for Small Sample Sizes   The first step in calculating *U* is to place all the data, regardless of group membership, in rank order, with the smallest score receiving a rank of 1 and the largest score receiving a rank of *N*. If two or more observations have the same value (i.e., tied ranks), they are assigned the mean of the ranks they would have occupied. When there are a large number of tied ranks, the use of the *U*-test is questionable.

The second step is to split the rank scores into two groups according to the levels of the independent variable (e.g., experimental and control group).

The third step is to compute *U* for each of the two groups and pick whichever value is smaller:

$$\text{Equation 16.5: } U = \text{Smaller of} \begin{bmatrix} n_1 n_2 + \dfrac{n_1(n_1 + 1)}{2} - \sum R_1 \\[2ex] n_1 n_2 + \dfrac{n_2(n_2 + 1)}{2} - \sum R_2 \end{bmatrix}$$

where:

n = the group sample size

$\sum R$ = the sum of the rankings for one group

Critical Value for Small Sample Sizes   The critical values for the Mann-Whitney *U*-test are tabled in Appendix J. The table lists critical values for one- and two-tailed alternative hypotheses at several different significance levels. It also lists the critical values for sample sizes of each group ranging up to 20. Of great importance is to recognize that unlike other tests we have covered, a calculated value of *U* is significant when it is *equal to or less than* the tabled or critical value.

In Textbox 16.5 the Mann-Whitney *U*-test is used to analyze some of the ordinal data from the Golden Years scenario.

Calculated Value for Large Samples   When either of the samples contains more than 20 scores, a normal approximation procedure (*z*-test) should be used. The calculated value is determined as follows:

$$\text{Equation 16.6: } z = \frac{(U + .5) - n_1 n_2/2}{\sqrt{(n_1 n_2/12)(n_1 + n_2 + 1)}}$$

where U = the smaller value as defined in Equation 16.5

| Textbox 16.5 |

Mann Whitney *U*-Test: Golden Years Scenario

You asked each of the seniors to complete an attitude inventory of physical and emotional intimacy. From the scores you are able to rank each respondent from well-adjusted to poorly-adjusted. You want to know whether there are gender differences in intimacy rankings, so the alternative hypothesis is that there are differences between males and females. You decide to test for differences at the .05 level of significance. Use the overall rankings in Table 16.1 and then subdivide them into two groups according to gender. The sum of the ranks for the eight males is 110. The sum of the ranks for the 12 females is 100. Next compute *U*:

$$U = \text{Smaller of} \begin{bmatrix} n_1 n_2 + \dfrac{n_1(n_1+1)}{2} - \sum R_1 \\[2mm] n_1 n_2 + \dfrac{n_2(n_2+1)}{2} - \sum R_2 \end{bmatrix} = \begin{bmatrix} (8)(12) + \dfrac{8(8+1)}{2} - 110 = 22 \\[2mm] (8)(12) + \dfrac{12(12+1)}{2} - 100 = 74 \end{bmatrix} = 22$$

From Appendix J you find that the critical value of *U* is equal to 22 for a two-tailed test when $\alpha = .05$.

Because the calculated value (i.e., 22) is *equal to or less than* the critical value (i.e., 22), you reject the null hypothesis and conclude that there are gender differences in intimacy for seniors.

Critical Value for Large Samples   The critical value for z is found in Appendix A. Because of the way U is defined, the critical region is always in the lower tail of the normal distribution regardless of whether the test is one-tailed or two-tailed. To be significant, the z calculated value must be less than or equal to $-z_{\alpha/2}$ for a two-tailed test or less than or equal to $-z_c$ for a one-tailed test.

Kruskal-Wallis Oneway ANOVA *H*-Test

The **Kruskal-Wallis Oneway ANOVA *H*-test** is applicable when the dependent or outcome variable is measured on an ordinal scale or when the assumptions of the *F*-test are seriously violated and when the independent or predictor variable has two or more levels. The samples must be independent. The test is used to choose between null and alternative hypotheses. Like the *F*-test, this is an omnibus test when there are more than two groups. The null hypothesis states that there is no difference in the scores of the population from which the group samples were selected. The alternative hypothesis states that the sample scores arose from different populations. Sample sizes per group should be 6 or larger.

Calculated Value   The first step in calculating the *H*-test is to place all the data, regardless of group membership, in rank order, with the smallest score receiving a rank of 1 and the largest score receiving a rank of N. If two or more observations have the same value (i.e., tied ranks), they are assigned the mean of the ranks they would have occupied. When there are a large number of tied ranks, the use of the H-test is questionable.

The second step is to split the rank scores into groups according to the levels of the independent variable.

The third step is to compute H as follows:

$$\text{Equation 16.7: } H = \left[\frac{12}{N(N+1)}\right]\left[\sum_{1}^{A}\frac{(\sum R)^2}{n}\right] - 3(N+1)$$

where:

N = the total sample size

n = the group sample size

A = the number of groups (levels of the independent variable)

$\sum R$ = the sum of the ranks in each group

Critical Value   The critical values for the H-test is the chi-square distribution with $A-1$ degrees of freedom.

In Textbox 16.6 the Kruskal-Wallis Oneway ANOVA H-test is used to analyze some of the ordinal data from the Golden Years scenario.

Textbox 16.6

Kruskal-Wallis Oneway ANOVA *H*-test: Golden Years Scenario

Use the data in Table 16.1 to determine whether there is a relationship between Political Orientation and Generosity. Organize the rankings for Generosity according to Political Orientation, as shown in Table 16.11.

$$H = \left[\frac{12}{N(N+1)}\right]\left[\sum_{1}^{A}\frac{(\sum R)^2}{n}\right] - 3(N+1)$$

$$H = \left[\frac{12}{20(20+1)}\right]\left[\frac{(23)^2}{5} + \frac{(135)^2}{10} + \frac{(52)^2}{5}\right] - 3(20+1) = 7.55$$

The critical value for the H-test can be found by examining the chi-square distribution with 2 degrees of freedom. For $\alpha = .05$, the critical value you need to exceed is 5.99. Therefore, you reject the null hypothesis and conclude that there is a significant relationship between Political Orientation and Generosity.

Note that for two of the groups, sample sizes (5) are slightly suboptimal.

TABLE 16.11	Generosity Rankings Arranged by Political Orientation	
Liberal	Conservative	Uncertain
9	13	4
1	12	10
2	19	15
3	14	17
8	11	6
	20	
	18	
	5	
	7	
	16	
$\sum R = 23$	$\sum R = 135$	$\sum R = 52$

Correlated Samples

When the data for the dependent variable have been measured on an interval or ratio scale, and the assumptions of the test are met, the correlated samples t-test is the appropriate statistical tool for comparing two dependent samples and the Within-Groups or Repeated Measures ANOVA is the appropriate statistical tool for comparing two or more dependent samples. However, when the data for the dependent variable is only ordinal or the assumptions of the parametric test have been seriously violated, nonparametric tests should be used. The **Wilcoxon signed-ranks T-test** is the nonparametric equivalent to the correlated samples t-test. The **Friedman ANOVA** is the nonparametric equivalent to the Within-Groups ANOVA.

Wilcoxon Signed-Ranks T-Test   Because only two correlated samples are involved, it is possible to use the T-test to evaluate both directional and nondirectional alternative hypotheses. To compute the calculated value of the Wilcoxon signed-ranks T-test when N is 50 or less, do the following:

1. Rank-order the data for each of the two correlated samples *separately*.
2. Compute the difference between the ranks for the two correlated samples, noting the sign $(+/-)$. Drop from further consideration all zero differences. For each discarded score, reduce the sample size (N) by one.
3. Rank-order the differences but disregard their sign. For tied ranks, assign the mean of the ranks they would have occupied.
4. Sign the ranks again by noting the direction $(+/-)$ of the differences.
5. Sum the ranks associated with a positive difference. Sum the absolute value of the ranks associated with a negative difference.
6. T is the smaller of the two sums.

Appendix K gives one- and two-tailed critical values of the *T*-test for sample sizes ranging from 5 to 50 and for several levels of significance. Of great importance is to recognize that unlike other tests we have covered, a calculated value of *T* is significant when it is *equal to or less than* the tabled or critical value.

When *N* is larger than 50, a normal approximation procedure can be used. The calculated value is given by the following:

$$\textbf{Equation 16.8: } z = \frac{(T + .5) - N(N + 1)/4}{\sqrt{N(N + 1)(2N + 1)/24}}$$

Friedman ANOVA   The Friedman ANOVA is a nonparametric equivalent to the Within-Groups ANOVA. Because the critical value is dependent on the chi-square distribution, sample sizes should be no less than 5 per sample when there are only three repeated measures and at least 10 per sample when there are more than three repeated measures.

Preliminary to computing the calculated value, the scores for each measurement opportunity should be ranked and summed.

Then the calculated value (*FR*) should be computed:

$$\textbf{Equation 16.9: } FR = \left[\frac{12}{NA(A + 1)} \right] \left[\sum_{1}^{A} \frac{(\sum R)^2}{N} \right] - 3N(A + 1)$$

where:

　　N = the total sample size (number of participants)
　　A = the number of levels of the repeated measure
　　R = the rank score for each repeated measure

To find the critical chi-square value, refer to Appendix I for $A - 1$ degrees of freedom and for the alpha value you selected.

Spearman Rank-Order Correlation   The **Spearman rank-order correlation** coefficient (r_S) is used to describe the degree of relationship between a predictor and outcome variable when they have both been measured on ordinal scales. The rank-order correlation was first used by Sir Francis Galton but was named after the British psychologist Charles Spearman who used it extensively. The presence of tied ranks violates the assumptions underlying the rank correlation and it should not be used when ties in the data are frequent.

Mathematically, there is no difference between the Spearman rank-order correlation and the Pearson product moment correlation when the data to be correlated are in the form of ranks. When the data are measured on interval or ratio scales, the Pearson product moment correlation measures the degree of linear relationship between variables only. However, variables may be related in a nonlinear fashion. The Spearman rank-order correlation, because it measures the consistency of a relationship between variables measured on ordinal scales, is not affected by the form of that relationship.

Consider the data in Table 16.12. It shows the scores for five participants on two variables (Y, A); it also shows each set of scores converted to ranks (YR, AR). The scatterplot of Y and A is shown in Figure 16.2; the scatterplot for YR and AR is shown in Figure 16.3.

It is apparent that there is a perfect curvilinear relationship between Y and A. But the Pearson product moment correlation would not detect the perfect

TABLE 16.12 Interval Data Pairs and Their Ranked Counterparts

Y	A	YR	AR
1	1	1	1
10	10	2	2
15	30	3	3
16	50	4	4
17	70	5	5

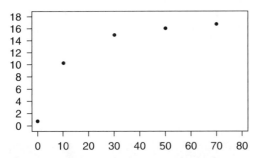

Figure 16.2 Scatterplot of paired interval data

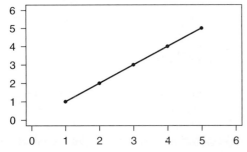

Figure 16.3 Scatterplot of paired ranked data

relationship because it is not a linear relationship. Variable Y does not change monotonically or consistently with variable A. However, the Spearman rank correlation would detect the perfect consistent relationship between YR and AR.

The range of the Spearman rank-order correlation is -1.0 to $+1.0$. A perfectly consistent inverse relationship between Y and A is equal to -1.0. A perfectly consistent positive relationship between Y and A is equal to $+1.0$. Varying degrees of relationship fall between these two extremes. A correlation of 0.0 indicates no relationship between Y and A.

The formula for calculating r_S is as follows:

$$\text{Equation 16.10: } r_S = 1 - \frac{6 \sum (R_Y - R_A)^2}{N(N^2 - 1)}$$

where:

$R_Y - R_A$ = the difference in ranks for each paired observation

N = the total number of paired observations.

As a computational check, you may use the formula for the Pearson product moment correlation given in Chapter 13 (see Equation 13.2). As long as you use the scores for both variables in their rank-order form, the two formulas yield identical results.

To determine whether a rank-order correlation is significant, use the critical values for the Pearson product moment correlation in Appendix G. Remember that the degrees of freedom equals the number of paired observations less 2 (i.e., $N - 2$).

The calculation of the Spearman rank-order correlation is illustrated in Textbox 16.7.

Textbox 16.7

Spearman Rank-Order Correlation: Golden Years Scenario

You wish to know whether there is a relationship between Intimacy and Generosity. Use the rank-order data from Table 16.1 to determine the extent to which there is a rank-order correlation between these two variables.

$$r_S = 1 - \frac{6 \sum (R_Y - R_A)^2}{N(N^2 - 1)} = \frac{(6)(974)}{(20)(20^2 - 1)} = +.27$$

The critical value for a nondirectional test of the correlation coefficient when $df = 18$ and $\alpha = .05$ is .444. You fail to reject the null hypothesis and therefore cannot conclude that intimacy and generosity are significantly related.

Putting It All Together

The majority of the inferential statistical tests presented in this text have been parametric statistical tests. Parametric statistical tests make a variety of assumptions about the characteristics of the population distribution from which samples are drawn. For many variables, such assumptions are warranted. But there are occasions where it appears that the assumptions underlying the parametric statistical tests are substantially violated, affecting the rate of Type I and Type II errors.

Although parametric statistical tests are robust to many assumption violations, they are not robust to all assumption violations under all conditions. In such circumstances it is appropriate to use nonparametric or distribution-free tests even though the researcher sacrifices some statistical power in the process.

A second, important use of nonparametric statistics is when the scale of measurement of the dependent variable is not an interval or ratio scale of measurement. Nonparametric procedures may also be used when the dependent or outcome variable is measured nominally or ordinally.

Two classes of nonparametric tests were covered: procedures for nominal data and procedures for ordinal data. For nominal data, we examined the chi-square goodness of fit, a one-variable test to determine whether a significant difference exists between expected and observed frequencies. The chi-square test of independence is used to determine whether two variables are significantly related.

For ordinal data, several nonparametric tests were examined. The Mann-Whitney *U*-test is a nonparametric statistical test commonly used as an alternative to Student's *t*-test. The Kruskal-Wallis Oneway ANOVA *H*-test is applicable when the independent or predictor variable has two or more levels. The Wilcoxon signed-ranks *T*-test is the nonparametric equivalent to the correlated samples *t*-test. The Friedman ANOVA is the nonparametric equivalent to the Within-Groups ANOVA. The Spearman rank correlation coefficient (r_S) is used to describe the degree of relationship between a predictor and outcome variable when they have both been measured on ordinal scales.

Chi-Square and the Analysis of Nominal Data

The assumption of the chi-square test are as follows:

- The samples have been randomly selected.
- The observations must be independent.
- Group sample sizes are sufficiently large.

The sample size of the group can affect Type I and Type II error rates. In certain situations, 5 is the minimum group sample size.

Calculated Value   The following is the formula for the calculated value of the chi-square statistic:

$$\text{Equation 16.1: } \chi^2 = \sum \frac{(O_k - E_k)^2}{E_k}$$

where:

O_k = observed frequency for the category

E_k = expected frequency for the category

k = number of categories (values of the variable(s))

The degrees of freedom are

- df for goodness of fit: $Y - 1$
- df for test of independence: $(Y - 1)(A - 1)$

The following is the mathematical formula for determining the expected frequencies for each combination of the two variables:

$$\text{Equation 16.2: } E_{YA} = n_Y n_A / N$$

Yates correction for continuity:

$$\text{Equation 16.3: } \chi^2 = \sum \frac{(|O_k - E_k| - .5)^2}{E_k}$$

Multiple Comparisons   The steps to follow for conducting pairwise comparisons are as follows:

- Select the data columns that pertain to the levels of the independent variable you are interested in contrasting.
- Form a separate contingency table for these *observed* frequencies.
- Find the expected cell frequencies.
- Compute the calculated value of chi-square and compare it to the critical value.

Measures of Association or Effect Size   The phi-coefficient is a measure of effect size based on chi-square :

$$\text{Equation 16.4: } \varphi = \sqrt{\frac{\chi^2}{N}}$$

To help interpret the meaning of a given value of the phi-coefficient, Cohen (1988) has assigned the labels "small," "medium," and "large" to the following values:

.10 = small effect

.30 = medium effect

.50 = large effect

The Analysis of Ordinal Data

Mann-Whitney U-Test For comparing two independent samples.

For small sample sizes:

$$\textbf{Equation 16.5: } U = \text{smaller of} \begin{bmatrix} n_1 n_2 + \dfrac{n_1(n_1+1)}{2} - \sum R_1 \\ n_1 n_2 + \dfrac{n_2(n_2+1)}{2} - \sum R_2 \end{bmatrix}$$

where:

n = the group sample size

$\sum R$ = the sum of the ranks for one group

Of great importance is to recognize that unlike other tests we have covered, a calculated value of U is significant when it is *equal to or less than* the tabled or critical value.

For large sample sizes: The calculated value is determined according to Equation 16.6:

$$\textbf{Equation 16.6: } z = \frac{(U + .5) - n_1 n_2 / 2}{\sqrt{(n_1 n_2 / 12)(n_1 + n_2 + 1)}}$$

where:

U = the smaller value as defined in Equation 16.5.

Kruskal-Wallis Oneway ANOVA H-Test

$$\textbf{Equation 16.7: } H = \left[\frac{12}{N(N+1)} \right] \left[\sum_{1}^{A} \frac{(\sum R)^2}{n} \right] - 3(N+1)$$

where:

N = the total sample size

n = the group sample size

A = the number of groups (levels of the independent variable)

$\sum R$ = the sum of the ranks in each group

Wilcoxon Signed-Ranks T-Test

1. Rank-order the data for each of the two correlated samples *separately*.
2. Compute the difference between the ranks for the two correlated samples noting the sign $(+/-)$. Drop from further consideration all zero differences. For each discarded score, reduce the sample size (N) by 1.
3. Rank-order the differences but disregard their sign. For tied ranks, assign the mean of the ranks they would have occupied.
4. Sign the ranks again by noting the direction $(+/-)$ of the differences.
5. Sum the ranks associated with a positive difference. Sum the absolute value of the ranks associated with a negative difference.
6. T is the smaller of the two sums.

A calculated value of T is significant when it is *equal to or less than* the tabled or critical value.

When N is larger than 50, a normal approximation procedure can be used. The calculated value is given by the following:

$$\textbf{Equation 16.8: } z = \frac{(T + .5) - N(N + 1)/4}{\sqrt{N(N + 1)(2N + 1)/24}}$$

Friedman ANOVA

$$\textbf{Equation 16.9: } FR = \left[\frac{12}{NA(A + 1)} \right] \left[\sum_{1}^{A} \frac{(\sum R)^2}{N} \right] - 3N(A + 1)$$

where:

N = the total sample size (number of participants)
A = the number of levels of the repeated measure
R = the rank score for each repeated measure

Spearman Rank-Order Correlation

$$\textbf{Equation 16.10: } r_S = 1 - \frac{6 \sum (R_Y - R_A)^2}{N(N^2 - 1)}$$

where:

$R_Y - R_A$ = the difference in ranks for each paired observation
N = the total number of paired observations

Textbox 16.8

Chi-Square: Gender Stereotypes?

Gender stereotyping is a common phenomenon in our society. Cross-cultural studies suggest that males are judged more negatively than females. Fiebert and Meyer (1997) examined lay descriptions of gender stereotypes. Thirty-eight undergraduates (18 male, 20 female) divided into five equivalent groups were instructed to respond to the phrase "A man (or woman) is _____." Groups were asked to fill in the blanks with a cultural stereotype. The groups first completed the responses for one gender and then did the remaining gender. The exercise ended when participants had difficulty producing novel responses. Responses were then compiled into two nonoverlapping lists of stereotypes for men and women. Judges then evaluated the responses as positive, negative, or neutral.

Seventy-nine responses were retained for the women, with 39 judged to be positive, 16 negative, and 24 neutral. Eighty-four responses were retained for the men, with 23 judged to be positive, 48 negative, and 13 neutral. A chi-square analysis revealed that significantly more negative stereotypes were produced for males than females $\chi^2(2) = 23.34$, $p < .001$.

The researchers report that these results are consistent with other findings, although there were more negative stereotypes generated in this study than in other studies.

KEY TERMS

Parametric tests

Nonparametric or distribution-free tests

Nominal scale

Ordinal scale

Interval scale

Ratio scale

Goodness of fit

Test of independence

Observed frequencies

Expected frequencies

Expected proportions

Yates correction for continuity

phi-coefficient (φ)

Mann-Whitney U-test

Kruskal-Wallis Oneway ANOVA H-test

Wilcoxon signed-ranks T-test

Friedman ANOVA

Spearman rank-order correlation

REFERENCES

Cohen, J. (1988). *Statistical power analysis.* (2nd ed.). Hillsdale, NJ: Lawrence Erlbaum Associates.

Fiebert, M. S., & Meyer, M. W. (1997). Gender stereotypes: a bias against men. *The Journal of Psychology, 131* (4), 407–411.

PROBLEMS

Questions

Section 1   Conceptual/Definition

16.1. What is a nonparametric test?

16.2. How do parametric and nonparametric tests differ with respect to scales of measurement?

16.3. Discuss the main advantages and disadvantages of nonparametric tests.

16.4. How is the chi-square goodness-of-fit test different from the chi-square test of independence?

16.5. The critical value of chi-square increases as the degrees of freedom are increased. Why?

16.6. What assumptions underlie the use of the chi-square test?

16.7. The Mann-Whitney U-test and Wilcoxon signed-ranks T-test are examples of nonparametric tests in which the null hypothesis is rejected when the calculated value is less than (or equal to) the critical value. Why?

16.8. What tests exist to examine data that are ordinal in nature?

16.9. What are the nonparametric equivalents to the independent and dependent samples t-test, Oneway ANOVA, and the Pearson product moment correlation?

16.10. The Mann-Whitney U-test and Kruskal-Wallis Oneway ANOVA are nonparametric equivalents of a t-test and Oneway ANOVA, respectively. Are these nonparametric statistics tests of mean differences? Why or why not?

Section 2   Numerical

16.11. As a high school principal, you have recently received data from your school board indicating that 82% of students entering high school (across the school district) graduate. You believe that your school has a higher graduation rate. This year, of the 1089 students that entered, 969 have graduated. Can you conclude that your school is performing better than the district average with respect to graduation rates?

16.12. You are interested in determining the existence of a significant interaction between three Preferred Instructional Strategies and Gender. Six hundred students in a large undergraduate introductory psychology course were asked about their preference regarding instructional strategies. The results are shown below. Perform a chi-square test of independence.

	Female	Male
Computer-based Technology	75	25
Video	150	50
Lecture	175	125

16.13. Use the appropriate nonparametric test to determine the effect of a treatment that produced the following rankings on a dependent variable:

Group A		Group B	
Subject	Rank	Subject	Rank
1	6	7	9
2	2	8	12
3	3	9	11
4	5	10	4
5	8	11	10
6	1	12	7
	$\sum R_A = 25$		$\sum R_B = 53$

16.14. Use the appropriate nonparametric test to determine the effect of a treatment that produced the following rankings on a dependent variable:

Group A		Group B	
Subject	Rank	Subject	Rank
1	4	8	12
2	3	9	5
3	8	10	14
4	7	11	1
5	10	12	6
6	13	13	11
7	9	14	2

16.15. Use the appropriate nonparametric test to determine the effect of a treatment that produced the following rankings on a dependent variable (17 subjects in total):

	Ranks					
Treatment Group 1	3.0	4	2.0	5.0	6.5	1.0
Treatment Group 2	8.5	10	6.5	8.5	11.0	12
Treatment Group 3	15.0	14	13.0	16.0	17.0	

16.16. Use the appropriate nonparametric test to determine the effect of a treatment that produced the following rankings on a dependent variable (12 subjects in total):

	Ranks			
Treatment Group 1	4	6	3	11
Treatment Group 2	2	7	10	8
Treatment Group 3	12	1	5	9

16.17. Use the appropriate nonparametric test to determine the effect of a treatment that produced the following scores on a dependent variable. Assume that there is reason to believe that the posttest score should produce better results than the pretest scores.

Subject	Pretest Score	Posttest Score
1	20	25
2	16	20
3	18	27
4	23	21
5	22	28
6	23	23
7	20	19
8	25	23
9	19	22
10	21	23
11	22	23
12	19	27

16.18. Use the appropriate nonparametric test to determine the effect of a treatment that produced the following rankings on a dependent variable (4 subjects in total):

	Ranks			
Treatment Group 1	4	6	3	11
Treatment Group 2	2	7	10	8
Treatment Group 3	12	1	5	9

16.19. A student was asked to rate the performance of five of her fellow classmates. Her teacher also rated each of the students and the results are shown below. Does a significant relationship exist?

Student	Student Rating	Teacher Rating
1	2	3
2	5	5
3	1	4
4	3	1
5	4	2

Areas Under the Standard Normal Curve Corresponding to Given Values of *z*

appendix A

Column 2 gives the proportion of the area under the entire curve that is between the mean ($z = 0$) and the positive value of *z*. Areas for negative values of *z* are the same as for positive values, because the curve is symmetrical.

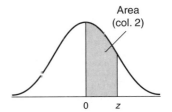

Area (col. 2)

Column 3 gives the proportion of the area under the entire curve that falls beyond the stated positive value of *z*. Areas for negative values of *z* are the same, because the curve is symmetrical.

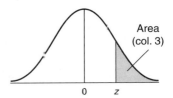

Area (col. 3)

z 1	Area between Mean and *z* 2	Area beyond *z* 3	*z* 1	Area between Mean and *z* 2	Area beyond *z* 3
.00	.0000	.5000	09	.0359	.4641
.01	.0040	.4960	.10	.0398	.4602
.02	.0080	.4920	.11	.0438	.4562
.03	.0120	.4880	.12	.0478	.4522
.04	.0160	.4840	.13	.0517	.4483
.05	.0199	.4801	.14	.0557	.4443
.06	.0239	.4761	.15	.0596	.4404
.07	.0279	.4721	.16	.0636	.4364
.08	.0319	.4681	.17	.0675	.4325

Source: From Table lli of R. A. Fisher & F. Yates (1974). *Statistical Tables for Biological, Agricultural and Medical Research.* 6th ed., published by Addison-Wesley Longman, London (previously published by Oliver and Boyd Ltd., Edinburgh). Reprinted by permission of the authors and publishers.

(continued)

z 1	Area between Mean and z 2	Area beyond z 3	z 1	Area between Mean and z 2	Area beyond z 3
.18	.0714	.4286	.52	.1985	.3015
.19	.0753	.4247	.53	.2019	.2981
.20	.0793	.4207	.54	.2054	.2946
.21	.0832	.4168	.55	.2088	.2912
.22	.0871	.4129	.56	.2123	.2877
.23	.0910	.4090	.57	.2157	.2843
.24	.0948	.4052	.58	.2190	.2810
.25	.0987	.4013	.59	.2224	.2776
.26	.1026	.3974	.60	.2257	.2743
.27	.1064	.3936	.61	.2291	.2709
.28	.1103	.3897	.62	.2324	.2676
.29	.1141	.3859	.63	.2357	.2643
.30	.1179	.3821	.64	.2389	.2611
.31	.1217	.3783	.65	.2422	.2578
.32	.1255	.3745	.66	.2454	.2546
.33	.1293	.3707	.67	.2486	.2514
.34	.1331	.3669	.68	.2517	.2483
.35	.1368	.3632	.69	.2549	.2451
.36	.1406	.3594	.70	.2580	.2420
.37	.1443	.3557	.71	.2611	.2389
.38	.1480	.3520	.72	.2642	.2358
.39	.1517	.3483	.73	.2673	.2327
.40	.1554	.3446	.74	.2704	.2296
.41	.1591	.3409	.75	.2734	.2266
.42	.1628	.3372	.76	.2764	.2236
.43	.1664	.3336	.77	.2794	.2206
.44	.1700	.3300	.78	.2823	.2177
.45	.1736	.3264	.79	.2852	.2148
.46	.1772	.3228	.80	.2881	.2119
.47	.1808	.3192	.81	.2910	.2090
.48	.1844	.3156	.82	.2939	.2061
.49	.1879	.3121	.83	.2967	.2033
.50	.1915	.3085	.84	.2995	.2005
.51	.1950	.3050	.85	.3023	.1977

z 1	Area between Mean and z 2	Area beyond z 3	z 1	Area between Mean and z 2	Area beyond z 3
.86	.3051	.1949	1.20	.3849	.1151
.87	.3078	.1922	1.21	.3869	.1131
.88	.3106	.1894	1.22	.3888	.1112
.89	.3133	.1867	1.23	.3907	.1093
.90	.3159	.1841	1.24	.3925	.1075
.91	.3186	.1814	1.25	.3944	.1056
.92	.3212	.1788	1.26	.3962	.1038
.93	.3238	.1762	1.27	.3980	.1020
.94	.3264	.1736	1.28	.3997	.1003
.95	.3289	.1711	1.29	.4015	.0985
.96	.3315	.1685	1.30	.4032	.0968
.97	.3340	.1660	1.31	.4049	.0951
.98	.3365	.1635	1.32	.4066	.0934
.99	.3389	.1611	1.33	.4082	.0918
1.00	.3413	.1587	1.34	.4099	.0901
1.01	.3438	.1562	1.35	.4115	.0885
1.02	.3461	.1539	1.36	.4131	.0869
1.03	.3485	.1515	1.37	.4147	.0853
1.04	.3508	.1492	1.38	.4162	.0838
1.05	.3531	.1469	1.39	.4177	.0823
1.06	.3554	.1446	1.40	.4192	.0808
1.07	.3577	.1423	1.41	.4207	.0793
1.08	.3599	.1401	1.42	.4222	.0778
1.09	.3621	.1379	1.43	.4236	.0764
1.10	.3643	.1357	1.44	.4251	.0749
1.11	.3665	.1335	1.45	.4265	.0735
1.12	.3686	.1314	1.46	.4279	.0721
1.13	.3708	.1292	1.47	.4292	.0708
1.14	.3729	.1271	1.48	.4306	.0694
1.15	.3749	.1251	1.49	.4319	.0681
1.16	.3770	.1230	1.50	.4332	.0668
1.17	.3790	.1210	1.51	.4345	.0655
1.18	.3810	.1190	1.52	.4357	.0643
1.19	.3830	.1170	1.53	.4370	.0630

(continued)

Appendix A *(continued)*

z 1	Area between Mean and z 2	Area beyond z 3	z 1	Area between Mean and z 2	Area beyond z 3
1.54	.4382	.0618	1.88	.4699	.0301
1.55	.4394	.0606	1.89	.4706	.0294
1.56	.4406	.0594	1.90	.4713	.0287
1.57	.4418	.0582	1.91	.4719	.0281
1.58	.4429	.0571	1.92	.4726	.0274
1.59	.4441	.0559	1.93	.4732	.0268
1.60	.4452	.0548	1.94	.4738	.0262
1.61	.4463	.0537	1.95	.4744	.0256
1.62	.4474	.0526	1.96	.4750	.0250
1.63	.4484	.0516	1.97	.4756	.0244
1.64	.4495	.0505	1.98	.4761	.0239
1.65	.4505	.0495	1.99	.4767	.0233
1.66	.4515	.0485	2.00	.4772	.0228
1.67	.4525	.0475	2.01	.4778	.0222
1.68	.4535	.0465	2.02	.4783	.0217
1.69	.4545	.0455	2.03	.4788	.0212
1.70	.4554	.0446	2.04	.4793	.0207
1.71	.4564	.0436	2.05	.4798	.0202
1.72	.4573	.0427	2.06	.4803	.0197
1.73	.4582	.0418	2.07	.4808	.0192
1.74	.4591	.0409	2.08	.4812	.0188
1.75	.4599	.0401	2.09	.4817	.0183
1.76	.4608	.0392	2.10	.4821	.0179
1.77	.4616	.0384	2.11	.4826	.0174
1.78	.4625	.0375	2.12	.4830	.0170
1.79	.4633	.0367	2.13	.4834	.0166
1.80	.4641	.0359	2.14	.4838	.0162
1.81	.4649	.0351	2.15	.4842	.0158
1.82	.4656	.0344	2.16	.4846	.0154
1.83	.4664	.0336	2.17	.4850	.0150
1.84	.4671	.0329	2.18	.4854	.0146
1.85	.4678	.0322	2.19	.4857	.0143
1.86	.4686	.0314	2.20	.4861	.0139
1.87	.4693	.0307	2.21	.4864	.0136

Appendix A *(continued)*					
z 1	Area between Mean and z 2	Area beyond z 3	z 1	Area between Mean and z 2	Area beyond z 3
2.22	.4868	.0132	2.56	.4948	.0052
2.23	.4871	.0129	2.57	.4949	.0051
2.24	.4875	.0125	2.58	.4951	.0049
2.25	.4878	.0122	2.59	.4952	.0048
2.26	.4881	.0119	2.60	.4953	.0047
2.27	.4884	.0116	2.61	.4955	.0045
2.28	.4887	.0113	2.62	.4956	.0044
2.29	.4890	.0110	2.63	.4957	.0043
2.30	.4893	.0107	2.64	.4959	.0041
2.31	.4896	.0104	2.65	.4960	.0040
2.32	.4898	.0102	2.66	.4961	.0039
2.33	.4901	.0099	2.67	.4962	.0038
2.34	.4904	.0096	2.68	.4963	.0037
2.35	.4906	.0094	2.69	.4964	.0036
2.36	.4909	.0091	2.70	.4965	.0035
2.37	.4911	.0089	2.71	.4966	.0034
2.38	.4913	.0087	2.72	.4967	.0033
2.39	.4916	.0084	2.73	.4968	.0032
2.40	.4918	.0082	2.74	.4969	.0031
2.41	.4920	.0080	2.75	.4970	.0030
2.42	.4922	.0078	2.76	.4971	.0029
2.43	.4925	.0075	2.77	.4972	.0028
2.44	.4927	.0073	2.78	.4973	.0027
2.45	.4929	.0071	2.79	.4974	.0026
2.46	.4931	.0069	2.80	.4974	.0026
2.47	.4932	.0068	2.81	.4975	.0025
2.48	.4934	.0066	2.82	.4976	.0024
2.49	.4936	.0064	2.83	.4977	.0023
2.50	.4938	.0062	2.84	.4977	.0023
2.51	.4940	.0060	2.85	.4978	.0022
2.52	.4941	.0059	2.86	.4979	.0021
2.53	.4943	.0057	2.87	.4979	.0021
2.54	.4945	.0055	2.88	.4980	.0020
2.55	.4946	.0054	2.89	.4981	.0019

(continued)

Appendix A *(continued)*

z 1	Area between Mean and z 2	Area beyond z 3	z 1	Area between Mean and z 2	Area beyond z 3
2.90	.4981	.0019	3.10	.4990	.0010
2.91	.4982	.0018	3.11	.4991	.0009
2.92	.4982	.0018	3.12	.4991	.0009
2.93	.4983	.0017	3.13	.4991	.0009
2.94	.4984	.0016	3.14	.4992	.0008
2.95	.4984	.0016	3.15	.4992	.0008
2.96	.4985	.0015	3.16	.4992	.0008
2.97	.4985	.0015	3.17	.4992	.0008
2.98	.4986	.0014	3.18	.4993	.0007
2.99	.4986	.0014	3.19	.4993	.0007
3.00	.4987	.0013	3.20	.4993	.0007
3.01	.4987	.0013	3.21	.4993	.0007
3.02	.4987	.0013	3.22	.4994	.0006
3.03	.4988	.0012	3.23	.4994	.0006
3.04	.4988	.0012	3.24	.4994	.0006
3.05	.4989	.0011	3.30	.4995	.0005
3.06	.4989	.0011	3.40	.4997	.0003
3.07	.4989	.0011	3.50	.4998	.0002
3.08	.4990	.0010	3.60	.4998	.0002
3.09	.4990	.0010	3.70	.4999	.0001

a p p e n d i x Table of Random Numbers

Column Number

Row	1	2	3	4	5	6	7	8	9	10	11	12	13	14	15	16	17	18	19	20	21
1	9	8	9	6	9	9	0	9	6	3	2	3	3	8	6	8	4	4	2	0	9
2	3	5	6	1	7	4	1	3	2	6	8	6	0	4	7	5	2	0	3	8	3
3	4	0	6	1	6	9	6	1	5	9	5	4	5	4	8	6	7	4	0	2	5
4	6	5	6	3	1	6	8	6	7	2	0	7	2	3	2	1	5	0	9	4	7
5	2	4	9	7	9	1	0	3	9	6	7	4	1	5	4	9	6	9	8	0	9
6	7	6	1	2	7	5	6	9	4	8	4	2	8	5	2	4	1	8	0	5	1
7	8	2	1	3	4	7	4	6	3	0	7	5	0	9	2	9	0	6	1	1	3
8	6	9	5	6	5	6	0	9	0	7	7	1	4	1	8	3	1	9	3	5	9
9	7	2	1	9	9	8	0	1	6	1	6	2	3	6	9	5	5	8	4	2	2
10	2	9	0	7	3	0	8	9	6	3	3	8	5	5	6	5	2	0	9	1	3
11	9	3	5	4	5	7	4	0	3	0	1	0	4	3	3	9	5	3	2	2	6
12	9	7	5	7	9	4	8	6	8	7	6	1	6	8	2	5	5	5	3	8	6
13	4	1	7	8	6	8	1	0	5	8	8	6	1	6	8	2	9	0	4	9	5
14	5	0	8	3	3	4	5	4	4	2	5	3	0	4	9	6	1	2	3	2	2
15	3	5	0	2	9	4	1	0	0	3	9	0	5	8	6	0	9	9	6	2	4
16	0	3	8	2	3	5	1	0	1	0	6	8	5	2	4	8	0	3	8	6	3
17	1	7	2	9	1	2	7	8	4	7	0	3	3	1	5	8	2	7	3	9	0
18	5	0	5	7	9	5	8	7	8	9	3	5	3	4	4	6	1	1	3	3	6
19	7	7	3	3	5	3	6	1	3	2	8	5	4	1	4	8	3	9	0	4	3
20	1	0	9	1	3	8	2	5	3	0	3	8	0	9	3	3	0	4	5	1	0
21	1	3	8	5	1	8	5	9	4	1	9	3	9	3	6	5	9	8	4	9	1
22	8	6	4	7	8	7	5	9	4	1	9	3	9	3	6	5	9	8	4	6	4
23	0	6	9	6	5	1	0	3	2	6	7	7	4	9	6	0	3	4	0	7	2
24	7	6	7	4	7	0	8	3	8	7	3	2	5	1	2	4	2	9	7	8	2
25	3	2	3	8	1	3	1	8	7	4	5	9	0	0	2	4	1	2	1	7	3
26	9	2	1	6	4	2	3	8	7	6	2	6	2	6	4	8	1	0	1	0	6
27	3	7	4	2	2	8	1	7	8	0	6	0	0	0	3	2	2	9	7	4	2
28	0	7	8	0	8	5	1	5	2	6	5	8	7	5	3	0	5	9	6	2	9
29	7	4	2	3	3	2	6	0	0	6	5	2	2	3	6	3	9	0	4	0	8
30	1	8	2	7	5	9	5	3	6	5	2	9	9	1	1	7	3	4	3	0	1
31	4	3	1	8	7	0	6	0	8	6	5	0	1	0	4	0	6	1	5	5	1
32	8	5	8	0	6	1	4	1	2	0	4	4	1	4	7	6	3	5	1	0	3
33	4	5	8	5	0	4	5	8	3	9	2	8	7	3	9	0	8	4	3	5	0
34	5	0	2	5	4	9	2	2	1	1	0	0	5	4	8	7	6	4	0	1	9
35	0	8	1	7	0	6	3	3	4	7	6	2	6	8	9	3	4	1	4	0	0
36	2	5	9	3	4	6	0	7	5	2	0	0	9	6	0	8	2	2	5	6	2
37	2	1	3	1	3	7	8	9	8	4	9	3	8	0	2	2	1	8	1	6	3
38	3	8	8	6	8	5	1	3	3	4	6	7	2	6	3	4	8	6	7	9	7
39	0	9	9	8	5	9	8	4	4	2	2	1	1	0	1	7	6	1	3	1	9
40	2	2	3	5	3	9	7	4	4	2	1	4	0	5	8	2	3	0	8	5	9

(continued)

Appendix B *(continued)*

Column Number

22	23	24	25	26	27	28	29	30	31	32	33	34	35	36	37	38	39	40	Row
7	1	1	9	1	2	7	3	5	1	8	4	0	4	1	0	6	0	3	1
7	7	9	1	4	9	9	5	9	2	0	1	6	1	2	6	6	7	0	2
6	3	7	8	3	3	8	4	3	9	3	9	0	0	9	8	3	5	2	3
0	8	6	6	5	9	6	2	7	3	5	9	0	1	8	0	9	6	9	4
8	7	3	5	6	8	8	1	2	0	2	3	2	6	4	3	1	9	7	5
8	8	4	7	0	1	7	6	8	2	1	6	3	2	1	8	1	8	3	6
7	2	6	9	5	4	1	7	3	8	7	1	5	6	5	6	4	3	6	7
0	1	5	2	8	6	5	5	7	8	1	8	7	1	2	4	0	4	1	8
5	5	2	1	8	6	9	8	9	8	0	5	8	9	9	4	1	3	4	9
4	2	8	5	0	7	9	8	4	3	5	8	0	9	4	6	6	0	5	10
8	6	6	4	7	1	5	1	6	4	6	7	6	0	8	7	3	5	2	11
0	1	4	2	9	8	6	8	0	7	6	5	1	9	1	3	7	0	3	12
7	0	9	8	7	6	9	0	6	5	4	0	3	6	5	6	3	5	0	13
3	4	7	8	0	2	0	8	0	3	4	9	2	5	7	7	8	6	4	14
6	1	0	5	0	6	1	4	9	4	7	3	9	1	7	6	4	5	8	15
4	8	1	6	9	5	6	2	0	4	6	1	6	8	1	9	9	1	1	16
5	1	3	6	1	9	5	4	1	2	5	4	2	9	5	6	2	4	0	17
7	0	3	5	3	7	4	1	7	5	4	8	3	7	4	8	5	7	2	18
6	6	3	6	3	0	0	9	4	2	2	5	1	8	9	·5	1	9	7	19
6	9	0	2	7	3	9	8	4	0	6	9	8	2	3	2	8	0	4	20
3	5	7	9	6	2	4	3	4	6	4	9	1	3	1	7	5	2	2	21
2	2	2	1	4	5	2	2	8	3	2	1	2	6	6	0	1	8	9	22
6	9	0	7	5	3	2	5	6	2	7	6	3	8	1	4	1	5	1	23
8	2	4	4	4	2	9	1	9	8	3	4	4	1	0	4	6	9	6	24
1	4	3	0	4	7	1	3	7	4	8	6	7	3	2	6	6	2	0	25
4	5	8	3	1	4	8	1	8	3	1	6	4	3	0	2	8	7	3	26
2	8	3	2	1	9	3	0	1	7	5	9	0	9	1	2	5	8	2	27
8	7	2	0	6	4	0	2	7	1	3	1	6	8	7	0	9	2	5	28
0	5	6	8	2	4	3	6	1	3	5	2	3	5	9	8	6	2	1	29
7	6	1	5	7	9	0	3	5	3	4	2	4	8	5	6	4	0	6	30
9	8	5	2	4	5	1	7	5	3	2	4	6	7	9	9	6	7	2	31
6	6	3	7	8	6	9	7	2	8	9	0	7	2	9	4	0	8	6	32
0	0	2	0	8	9	0	1	0	6	2	0	4	6	9	6	5	4	9	33
4	4	2	6	4	2	4	1	0	2	7	9	6	8	7	5	6	9	3	34
5	3	8	3	2	7	5	0	4	7	6	4	6	3	0	4	7	5	3	35
6	2	0	6	0	1	4	8	9	6	5	9	7	3	6	7	6	5	4	36
9	0	3	5	0	9	1	2	0	5	9	7	3	2	5	9	3	0	2	37
3	3	5	4	0	6	4	9	4	7	9	1	4	3	9	7	7	1	8	38
6	2	9	4	2	9	7	0	3	8	9	5	7	0	6	9	7	2	5	39
4	5	8	6	2	3	0	6	2	9	8	6	3	0	4	1	0	7	6	40

C Critical Values of the *t*-Distribution

	Critical Values for One-Tailed Test					
Alpha	.25	.10	.05	.025	.01	.005
	Critical Values for Two-Tailed Test					
df	.50	.20	.10	.05	.02	.01
1	1.000	3.078	6.314	12.706	31.821	63.657
2	.816	1.886	2.920	4.303	6.965	9.925
3	.765	1.638	2.353	3.182	4.541	5.841
4	.741	1.533	2.132	2.776	3.747	4.604
5	.727	1.476	2.015	2.571	3.365	4.032
6	.718	1.440	1.943	2.447	3.143	3.707
7	.711	1.415	1.895	2.365	2.998	3.499
8	.706	1.397	1.860	2.306	2.896	3.355
9	.703	1.383	1.833	2.262	2.821	3.250
10	.700	1.372	1.812	2.228	2.764	3.169
11	.697	1.363	1.796	2.201	2.718	3.106
12	.695	1.356	1.782	2.179	2.681	3.055
13	.694	1.350	1.771	2.160	2.650	3.012
14	.692	1.345	1.761	2.145	2.624	2.977
15	.691	1.341	1.753	2.131	2.602	2.947
16	.690	1.337	1.746	2.120	2.583	2.921
17	.689	1.333	1.740	2.110	2.567	2.898
18	.688	1.330	1.734	2.101	2.552	2.878
19	.688	1.328	1.729	2.093	2.539	2.861
20	.687	1.325	1.725	2.086	2.528	2.845

Source: From Table III of R. A. Fisher & F. Yates (1974). *Statistical Tables for Biological, Agricultural, and Medical Research.* 6th ed. Published by Addison-Wesley Longman: London. (Previously published by Oliver and Boyd Ltd., Edinburgh). Reprinted by permission of the authors and publishers.

(continued)

	Critical Values for One-Tailed Test					
	.25	.10	.05	.025	.01	.005
	Critical Values for Two-Tailed Test					
df	.50	.20	.10	.05	.02	.01
21	.686	1.323	1.721	2.080	2.518	2.831
22	.686	1.321	1.717	2.074	2.508	2.819
23	.685	1.319	1.714	2.069	2.500	2.807
24	.685	1.318	1.711	2.064	2.492	2.797
25	.684	1.316	1.708	2.060	2.485	2.787
26	.684	1.315	1.706	2.056	2.479	2.779
27	.684	1.314	1.703	2.052	2.473	2.771
28	.683	1.313	1.701	2.048	2.467	2.763
29	.683	1.311	1.699	2.045	2.462	2.756
30	.683	1.310	1.697	2.042	2.457	2.750
40	.681	1.303	1.684	2.021	2.423	2.704
60	.679	1.296	1.671	2.000	2.390	2.660
120	.677	1.289	1.658	1.980	2.358	2.617
∞	.674	1.282	1.645	1.960	2.326	2.576

appendix D Critical Values of the F Distribution

For each denominator degree of freedom, the first line represents $\alpha = .05$, the second $\alpha = .01$.

Degrees of Freedom: Denominator

Degrees of Freedom: Numerator

	1	2	3	4	5	6	7	8	9	10	11	12	14	16	20	24	30	40	50	75	100	200	500	∞
1	161	200	216	225	230	234	237	239	241	242	243	244	245	246	248	249	250	241	252	253	253	254	254	254
	4052	4999	5403	5625	5764	5859	5928	5981	6022	6056	6082	6106	6142	6169	6208	6234	6258	6286	6302	6323	6334	6352	6361	6366
2	18.51	19.00	19.16	19.25	19.30	1933	19.36	19.37	19.38	19.39	19.40	19.41	19.42	19.43	19.44	19.45	19.46	19.4/	19.47	19.48	19.49	19.49	19.50	19.50
	98.49	99.00	99.17	99.25	99.30	99.33	99.34	99.36	99.38	99.40	99.41	99.42	99.43	99.44	99.45	99.46	99.47	99.48	99.48	99.49	99.49	99.49	99.50	99.50
3	10.13	9.55	9.28	9.12	9.01	8.94	8.88	8.84	8.81	8.78	8.76	8.74	8.71	8.69	8.66	8.64	8.62	8.60	8.58	8.57	8.56	8.54	8.54	8.53
	34.12	30.82	29.46	28.71	28.24	27.91	27.67	27.49	27.34	27.23	27.13	27.05	26.92	26.83	26.69	26.60	26.50	26.41	26.35	26.27	26.23	26.18	26.14	26.12
4	7.71	6.94	6.59	6.39	6.26	6.16	6.09	6.04	6.00	5.96	5.93	5.91	5.87	5.84	5.80	5.77	5.74	5.71	5.70	5.68	5.66	5.65	5.64	5.63
	21.20	18.00	16.69	15.98	15.52	15.21	14.98	14.80	14.66	14.54	14.45	14.37	14.24	14.15	14.02	13.93	13.83	13.74	13.69	13.61	13.57	13.52	13.48	13.46
5	6.61	5.79	5.41	5.19	5.05	4.95	4.88	4.82	4.78	4.74	4.70	4.68	4.64	4.60	4.56	4.53	4.50	4.46	4.44	4.42	4.40	4.38	4.37	4.36
	16.26	13.27	12.06	11.39	10.97	10.67	10.45	10.27	10.15	10.05	9.96	9.89	9.77	9.68	9.55	9.47	9.38	9.29	9.24	9.17	9.13	9.07	9.04	9.02
6	5.99	5.14	4.76	4.53	4.39	4.28	4.21	4.15	4.10	4.06	4.03	4.00	3.96	3.92	3.87	3.84	3.81	3.77	3.75	3.72	3.71	3.69	3.68	3.67
	13.74	10.92	9.78	9.15	8.75	8.47	8.26	8.10	7.98	7.87	7.79	7.72	7.60	7.52	7.39	7.31	7.23	7.14	7.09	7.02	6.99	6.94	6.90	6.88
7	5.59	4.47	4.35	4.12	3.97	3.87	3.79	3.73	3.68	3.63	3.60	3.57	3.52	3.49	3.44	3.41	3.38	3.34	3.32	3.29	3.28	3.25	3.24	3.23
	12.25	9.55	8.45	7.85	7.46	7.19	7.00	6.84	6.71	6.62	6.54	6.47	6.35	6.27	6.15	6.07	5.98	5.90	5.85	5.78	5.75	5.70	5.67	5.65
8	5.32	4.46	4.07	3.84	3.69	3.58	3.50	3.44	3.39	3.34	3.31	3.28	3.23	3.20	3.15	3.12	3.08	3.05	3.03	3.00	2.98	2.96	2.94	2.93
	11.26	8.65	7.59	7.01	6.63	6.37	6.19	6.03	5.91	5.82	5.74	5.67	5.56	5.48	5.36	5.28	5.20	5.11	5.06	5.00	4.96	4.91	4.88	4.86
9	5.12	4.26	3.86	3.63	3.48	3.37	3.29	3.23	3.18	3.13	3.10	3.07	3.02	2.98	2.93	2.90	2.86	2.82	2.80	2.77	2.76	2.73	2.72	2.71
	10.56	8.02	6.99	6.42	6.06	5.80	5.62	5.47	5.35	5.26	5.18	5.11	5.00	4.92	4.80	4.73	4.64	4.56	4.51	4.45	4.41	4.36	4.33	4.31
10	4.96	4.10	3.71	3.48	3.33	3.22	3.14	3.07	3.02	2.97	2.94	2.91	2.86	2.82	2.77	2.74	2.70	2.67	2.64	2.61	2.59	2.56	2.55	2.54
	10.04	7.56	6.55	5.99	5.64	5.39	5.21	5.06	4.95	4.85	4.78	4.71	4.60	4.52	4.41	4.33	4.25	4.17	4.12	4.05	4.01	3.96	3.93	3.91

Source: Reproduced by permission from George W. Snedecor (1986). *Statistical Methods*. 8th ed. Copyright 1986 by The Iowa State University Press.

Degrees of Freedom: Denominator

Degrees of Freedom: Numerator

	1	2	3	4	5	6	7	8	9	10	11	12	14	16	20	24	30	40	50	75	100	200	500	∞
11	4.84	3.98	3.59	3.36	3.20	3.09	3.01	2.95	2.90	2.86	2.82	2.79	2.74	2.70	2.65	2.61	2.57	2.53	2.50	2.47	2.45	2.42	2.41	2.40
	9.65	7.20	6.22	5.67	5.32	5.07	4.88	4.74	4.63	4.54	4.46	4.40	4.29	4.21	4.10	4.02	3.94	3.86	3.80	3.74	3.70	3.66	3.62	3.60
12	4.75	3.88	3.49	3.26	3.11	3.00	2.92	2.85	2.80	2.76	2.72	2.69	2.64	2.60	2.54	2.50	2.46	2.42	2.40	2.36	2.35	2.32	2.31	2.30
	9.33	6.93	5.95	5.41	5.06	4.82	4.65	4.50	4.39	4.30	4.22	4.16	4.05	3.98	3.86	3.78	3.70	3.61	3.56	3.49	3.46	3.41	3.38	3.36
13	4.67	3.80	3.41	3.18	3.02	2.92	2.84	2.77	2.72	2.67	2.63	2.60	2.55	2.51	2.46	2.42	2.38	2.34	2.32	2.28	2.26	2.24	2.22	2.21
	9.07	6.70	5.74	5.20	4.86	4.62	4.44	4.30	4.19	4.10	4.02	3.96	3.85	3.78	3.67	3.59	3.51	3.42	3.37	3.30	3.27	3.21	3.18	3.16
14	4.60	3.74	3.34	3.11	2.96	2.85	2.77	2.70	2.65	2.60	2.56	2.53	2.48	2.44	2.39	2.35	2.31	2.27	2.24	2.21	2.19	2.16	2.14	2.13
	8.86	6.51	5.56	5.03	4.69	4.46	4.28	4.14	4.03	3.94	3.86	3.80	3.70	3.62	3.51	3.43	3.34	3.26	3.21	3.14	3.11	3.06	3.02	3.00
15	4.54	3.68	3.29	3.06	2.90	2.79	2.70	2.64	2.59	2.55	2.51	2.48	2.43	2.39	2.33	2.29	2.25	2.21	2.18	2.15	2.12	2.10	2.08	2.07
	8.68	6.36	5.42	4.89	4.56	4.32	4.14	4.00	3.89	3.80	3.73	3.67	3.56	3.48	3.36	3.29	3.20	3.12	3.07	3.00	2.97	2.92	2.89	2.87
16	4.49	3.63	3.24	3.01	2.85	2.74	2.66	2.59	2.54	2.49	2.45	2.42	2.37	2.33	2.28	2.24	2.20	2.16	2.13	2.09	2.07	2.04	2.02	2.01
	8.53	6.23	5.29	4.77	4.44	4.20	4.03	3.89	3.78	3.69	3.61	3.55	3.45	3.37	3.25	3.18	3.10	3.01	2.96	2.89	2.86	2.80	2.77	2.75
17	4.45	3.59	3.20	2.96	2.81	2.70	2.62	2.55	2.50	2.45	2.41	2.38	2.33	2.29	2.23	2.19	2.15	2.11	2.08	2.04	2.02	1.99	1.97	1.96
	8.40	6.11	5.18	4.67	4.34	4.10	3.93	3.79	3.68	3.59	3.52	3.45	3.35	3.27	3.16	3.08	3.00	2.92	2.86	2.79	2.76	2.70	2.67	2.65
18	4.41	3.55	3.16	2.93	2.77	2.66	2.58	2.51	2.46	2.41	2.37	2.34	2.29	2.25	2.19	2.15	2.11	2.07	2.04	2.00	1.98	1.95	1.93	1.92
	8.28	6.01	5.09	4.58	4.25	4.01	3.85	3.71	3.60	3.51	3.44	3.37	3.27	3.19	3.07	3.00	2.91	2.83	2.78	2.71	2.68	2.62	2.59	2.57
19	4.38	3.52	3.13	2.90	2.74	2.63	2.55	2.48	2.43	2.38	2.34	2.31	2.26	2.21	2.15	2.11	2.07	2.02	2.00	1.96	1.94	1.91	1.90	1.88
	8.18	5.93	5.01	4.50	4.17	3.94	3.77	3.63	3.52	3.43	3.36	3.30	3.19	3.12	3.00	2.92	2.84	2.76	2.70	2.63	2.60	2.54	2.51	2.49
20	4.35	3.49	3.10	2.87	2.71	2.60	2.52	2.45	2.40	2.35	2.31	2.28	2.23	2.18	2.12	2.08	2.04	1.99	1.96	1.92	1.90	1.87	1.85	1.84
	8.10	5.85	4.94	4.43	4.10	3.87	3.71	3.56	3.45	3.37	3.30	3.23	3.13	3.05	2.94	2.86	2.77	2.69	2.63	2.56	2.53	2.47	2.44	2.42
21	4.32	3.47	3.07	2.84	2.68	2.57	2.49	2.42	2.37	2.32	2.28	2.25	2.20	2.15	2.09	2.05	2.00	1.96	1.93	1.89	1.87	1.84	1.82	1.81
	8.02	5.78	4.87	4.37	4.04	3.81	3.65	3.51	3.40	3.31	3.24	3.17	3.07	2.99	2.88	2.80	2.72	2.63	2.58	2.51	2.47	2.42	2.38	2.36
22	4.30	3.44	3.05	2.82	2.66	2.55	2.47	2.40	2.35	2.30	2.26	2.23	2.18	2.13	2.07	2.03	1.98	1.93	1.91	1.87	1.84	1.81	1.80	1.78
	7.94	5.72	4.82	4.31	3.99	3.76	3.59	3.45	3.35	3.26	3.18	3.12	3.02	2.94	2.83	2.75	2.67	2.58	2.53	2.46	2.42	2.37	2.33	2.31
23	4.28	3.42	3.03	2.80	2.64	2.53	2.45	2.38	2.32	2.28	2.24	2.20	2.14	2.10	2.04	2.00	1.96	1.91	1.88	1.84	1.82	1.79	1.77	1.76
	7.88	5.66	4.76	4.26	3.94	3.71	3.54	3.41	3.30	3.21	3.14	3.07	2.97	2.89	2.78	2.70	2.62	2.53	2.48	2.41	2.37	2.32	2.28	2.26
24	4.26	3.40	3.01	2.78	2.62	2.51	2.43	2.36	2.30	2.26	2.22	2.18	2.13	2.09	2.02	1.98	1.94	1.89	1.86	1.82	1.80	1.76	1.74	1.73
	7.82	5.61	4.72	4.22	3.90	3.67	3.50	3.36	3.25	3.17	3.09	3.03	2.93	2.85	2.74	2.66	2.58	2.49	2.44	2.36	2.33	2.27	2.23	2.21

Degrees of Freedom: Numerator

	1	2	3	4	5	6	7	8	9	10	11	12	14	16	20	24	30	40	50	75	100	200	500	∞
25	4.24	3.38	2.99	2.76	2.60	2.49	2.41	2.34	2.28	2.24	2.20	2.16	2.11	2.06	2.00	1.96	1.92	1.87	1.84	1.80	1.77	1.74	1.72	1.71
	7.77	5.57	4.68	4.18	3.86	3.63	3.46	3.32	3.21	3.13	3.05	2.99	2.89	2.81	2.70	2.62	2.54	2.45	2.40	2.32	2.29	2.23	2.19	2.17
26	4.22	3.37	2.98	2.74	2.59	2.47	2.39	2.32	2.27	2.22	2.18	2.15	2.10	2.05	1.99	1.95	1.90	1.85	1.82	1.78	1.76	1.72	1.70	1.69
	7.72	5.53	4.64	4.14	3.82	3.59	3.42	3.29	3.17	3.09	3.02	2.96	2.86	2.77	2.66	2.58	2.50	2.41	2.36	2.28	2.25	2.19	2.15	2.13
27	4.21	3.35	2.96	2.73	2.57	2.46	2.37	2.30	2.25	2.20	2.16	2.13	2.08	2.03	1.97	1.93	1.88	1.84	1.80	1.76	1.74	1.71	1.68	1.67
	7.68	5.49	4.60	4.11	3.79	3.56	3.39	3.26	3.14	3.06	2.98	2.93	2.83	2.74	2.63	2.55	2.47	2.38	2.33	2.25	2.21	2.16	2.12	2.10
28	4.20	3.34	2.95	2.71	2.56	2.44	2.36	2.29	2.24	2.19	2.15	2.12	2.06	2.02	1.96	1.91	1.87	1.81	1.78	1.75	1.72	1.69	1.67	1.65
	7.64	5.45	4.57	4.07	3.76	3.53	3.36	3.23	3.11	3.03	2.95	2.90	2.80	2.71	2.60	2.52	2.44	2.35	2.30	2.22	2.18	2.13	2.09	2.06
29	4.18	3.33	2.93	2.70	2.54	2.43	2.35	2.28	2.22	2.18	2.14	2.10	2.05	2.00	1.94	1.90	1.85	1.80	1.77	1.73	1.71	1.68	1.65	1.64
	7.60	5.42	4.54	4.04	3.73	3.50	3.33	3.20	3.08	3.00	2.92	2.87	2.77	2.68	2.57	2.49	2.41	2.32	2.27	2.19	2.15	2.10	2.06	2.03
30	4.17	3.32	2.92	2.69	2.53	2.42	2.34	2.27	2.21	2.16	2.12	2.09	2.04	1.99	1.93	1.89	1.84	1.79	1.76	1.72	1.69	1.66	1.64	1.62
	7.56	5.39	4.51	4.02	3.70	3.47	3.30	3.17	3.06	2.98	2.90	2.84	2.74	2.66	2.55	2.47	2.38	2.29	2.24	2.16	2.13	2.07	2.03	2.01
32	4.15	3.30	2.90	2.67	2.51	2.40	2.32	2.25	2.19	2.14	2.10	2.07	2.02	1.97	1.91	1.86	1.82	1.76	1.74	1.69	1.67	1.64	1.61	1.59
	7.50	5.34	4.46	3.97	3.66	3.42	3.25	3.12	3.01	2.94	2.86	2.80	2.70	2.62	2.51	2.42	2.34	2.25	2.20	2.12	2.08	2.02	1.98	1.96
34	4.13	3.28	2.88	2.65	2.49	2.38	2.30	2.23	2.17	2.12	2.08	2.05	2.00	1.95	1.89	1.84	1.80	1.74	1.71	1.67	1.64	1.61	1.59	1.57
	7.44	5.29	4.42	3.93	3.61	3.38	3.21	3.08	2.97	2.89	2.82	2.76	2.66	2.58	2.47	2.38	2.30	2.21	2.15	2.08	2.04	1.98	1.94	1.91
36	4.11	3.26	2.86	2.63	2.48	2.36	2.28	2.21	2.15	2.10	2.06	2.03	1.98	1.93	1.87	1.82	1.78	1.72	1.69	1.65	1.62	1.59	1.56	1.55
	7.39	5.25	4.38	3.89	3.58	3.35	3.18	3.04	2.94	2.86	2.78	2.72	2.62	2.54	2.43	2.35	2.26	2.17	2.12	2.04	2.00	1.94	1.90	1.87
38	4.10	3.25	2.85	2.62	2.46	2.35	2.26	2.19	2.14	2.09	2.05	2.02	1.96	1.92	1.85	1.80	1.76	1.71	1.67	1.63	1.60	1.57	1.54	1.53
	7.35	5.21	4.34	3.86	3.54	3.32	3.15	3.02	2.91	2.83	2.75	2.69	2.59	2.51	2.40	2.32	2.22	2.14	2.08	2.00	1.97	1.90	1.86	1.84
40	4.08	3.23	2.84	2.61	2.45	2.34	2.25	2.18	2.12	2.07	2.04	2.00	1.95	1.90	1.84	1.79	1.71	1.69	1.66	1.61	1.59	1.55	1.53	1.51
	7.31	5.18	4.31	3.83	3.51	3.29	3.12	2.99	2.88	2.80	2.73	2.66	2.56	2.49	2.37	2.29	2.20	2.11	2.05	1.97	1.94	1.88	1.84	1.81
42	4.07	3.22	2.83	2.59	2.44	2.32	2.24	2.17	2.11	2.06	2.02	1.99	1.94	1.89	1.82	1.78	1.73	1.68	1.64	1.60	1.57	1.54	1.51	1.49
	7.27	5.15	4.29	3.80	3.49	3.26	3.10	2.96	2.86	2.77	2.70	2.64	2.54	2.46	2.35	2.26	2.17	2.08	2.02	1.94	1.91	1.85	1.80	1.78
44	4.06	3.21	2.82	2.58	2.43	2.31	2.23	2.16	2.10	2.05	2.01	1.98	1.92	1.88	1.81	1.76	1.72	1.66	1.63	1.58	1.56	1.52	1.50	1.48
	7.24	5.12	4.26	3.78	3.46	3.24	3.07	2.94	2.84	2.75	2.68	2.62	2.52	2.44	2.32	2.24	2.15	2.06	2.00	1.92	1.88	1.82	1.78	1.75
46	4.05	3.20	2.81	2.57	2.42	2.30	2.22	2.14	2.09	2.04	2.00	1.97	1.91	1.87	1.80	1.75	1.71	1.65	1.62	1.57	1.54	1.51	1.48	1.46
	7.21	5.10	4.24	3.76	3.44	3.22	3.05	2.92	2.82	2.73	2.66	2.60	2.50	2.42	2.30	2.22	2.13	2.04	1.98	1.90	1.86	1.80	1.76	1.72

(continued)

Degrees of Freedom: Denominator

Degrees of Freedom: Numerator

	1	2	3	4	5	6	7	8	9	10	11	12	14	16	20	24	30	40	50	75	100	200	500	∞
48	4.04	3.19	2.80	2.56	2.41	2.30	2.21	2.14	2.08	2.03	1.99	1.96	1.90	1.86	1.79	1.74	1.70	1.64	1.61	1.56	1.53	1.50	1.47	1.45
	7.19	5.08	4.22	3.74	3.42	3.20	3.04	2.90	2.80	2.71	2.64	2.58	2.48	2.40	2.28	2.20	2.11	2.02	1.96	1.88	1.84	1.78	1.73	1.70
50	4.03	3.18	2.79	2.56	2.40	2.29	2.20	2.13	2.07	2.02	1.98	1.95	1.90	1.85	1.78	1.74	1.69	1.63	1.60	1.55	1.52	1.48	1.46	1.44
	7.17	5.06	4.20	3.72	3.41	3.18	3.02	2.88	2.78	2.70	2.62	2.56	2.46	2.39	2.26	2.18	2.10	2.00	1.94	1.86	1.82	1.76	1.71	1.68
55	4.02	3.17	2.78	2.54	2.38	2.27	2.18	2.11	2.05	2.00	1.97	1.93	1.88	1.83	1.76	1.72	1.67	1.61	1.58	1.52	1.50	1.46	1.43	1.41
	7.12	5.01	4.16	3.68	3.37	3.15	2.98	2.85	2.75	2.66	2.59	2.53	2.43	2.35	2.23	2.15	2.06	1.96	1.90	1.82	1.78	1.71	1.66	1.64
60	4.00	3.15	2.76	2.52	2.37	2.25	2.17	2.10	2.04	1.99	1.95	1.92	1.86	1.81	1.75	1.70	1.65	1.59	1.56	1.50	1.48	1.44	1.41	1.39
	7.08	4.98	4.13	3.65	3.34	3.12	2.95	2.82	2.72	2.63	2.56	2.50	2.40	2.32	2.20	2.12	2.03	1.93	1.87	1.79	1.74	1.68	1.63	1.60
65	3.99	3.14	2.75	2.51	2.36	2.24	2.15	2.08	2.02	1.98	1.94	1.90	1.85	1.80	1.73	1.68	1.63	1.57	1.54	1.49	1.46	1.42	1.39	1.37
	7.04	4.95	4.10	3.62	3.31	3.09	2.93	2.79	2.70	2.61	2.54	2.47	2.37	2.30	2.18	2.09	2.00	1.90	1.84	1.76	1.71	1.64	1.60	1.56
70	3.98	3.13	2.74	2.50	2.35	2.23	2.14	2.07	2.01	1.97	1.93	1.89	1.84	1.79	1.72	1.67	1.62	1.56	1.53	1.47	1.45	1.40	1.37	1.35
	7.01	4.92	4.08	3.60	3.29	3.07	2.91	2.77	2.67	2.59	2.51	2.45	2.35	2.28	2.15	2.07	1.98	1.88	1.82	1.74	1.69	1.62	1.56	1.53
80	3.96	3.11	2.72	2.48	2.33	2.21	2.12	2.05	1.99	1.95	1.91	1.88	1.82	1.77	1.70	1.65	1.60	1.54	1.51	1.45	1.42	1.38	1.35	1.32
	6.96	4.88	4.04	3.56	3.25	3.04	2.87	2.74	2.64	2.55	2.48	2.41	2.32	2.24	2.11	2.03	1.94	1.84	1.78	1.70	1.65	1.57	1.52	1.49
100	3.94	3.09	2.70	2.46	2.30	2.19	2.10	2.03	1.97	1.92	1.88	1.85	1.79	1.75	1.68	1.63	1.57	1.51	1.48	1.42	1.39	1.34	1.30	1.28
	6.90	4.82	3.98	3.51	3.20	2.99	2.82	2.69	2.59	2.51	2.43	2.36	2.26	2.19	2.06	1.98	1.89	1.79	1.73	1.64	1.59	1.51	1.46	1.43
125	3.92	3.07	2.68	2.44	2.29	2.17	2.08	2.01	1.95	1.90	1.86	1.83	1.77	1.72	1.65	1.60	1.55	1.49	1.45	1.39	1.36	1.31	1.27	1.25
	6.84	4.78	3.94	3.47	3.17	2.95	2.79	2.65	2.56	2.47	2.40	2.33	2.23	2.15	2.03	1.94	1.85	1.75	1.68	1.59	1.54	1.46	1.40	1.37
150	3.91	3.06	2.67	2.43	2.27	2.16	2.07	2.00	1.94	1.89	1.85	1.82	1.76	1.71	1.64	1.59	1.54	1.47	1.44	1.37	1.34	1.29	1.25	1.22
	6.81	4.75	3.91	3.44	3.14	2.92	2.76	2.62	2.53	2.44	2.37	2.30	2.20	2.12	2.00	1.91	1.83	1.72	1.66	1.56	1.51	1.43	1.37	1.33
200	3.89	3.04	2.65	2.41	2.26	2.14	2.05	1.98	1.92	1.87	1.83	1.80	1.74	1.69	1.62	1.57	1.52	1.45	1.42	1.35	1.32	1.26	1.22	1.19
	6.76	4.71	3.88	3.41	3.11	2.90	2.73	2.60	2.50	2.41	2.34	2.28	2.17	2.09	1.97	1.88	1.79	1.69	1.62	1.53	1.48	1.39	1.33	1.28
400	3.86	3.02	2.62	2.39	2.23	2.12	2.03	1.96	1.90	1.85	1.81	1.78	1.72	1.67	1.60	1.54	1.49	1.42	1.38	1.32	1.28	1.22	1.16	1.13
	6.70	4.66	3.83	3.36	3.06	2.85	2.69	2.55	2.46	2.37	2.29	2.23	2.12	2.04	1.92	1.84	1.74	1.64	1.57	1.47	1.42	1.32	1.24	1.19
1000	3.85	3.00	2.61	2.38	2.22	2.10	2.02	1.95	1.89	1.84	1.80	1.76	1.70	1.65	1.58	1.53	1.47	1.41	1.36	1.30	1.26	1.19	1.13	1.08
	6.66	4.62	3.80	3.34	3.04	2.82	2.66	2.53	2.43	2.34	2.26	2.20	2.09	2.01	1.89	1.81	1.71	1.61	1.54	1.44	1.38	1.28	1.19	1.11
∞	3.84	2.99	2.60	2.37	2.21	2.09	2.01	1.94	1.88	1.83	1.79	1.75	1.69	1.64	1.57	1.52	1.46	1.40	1.35	1.28	1.24	1.17	1.11	1.00
	6.64	4.60	3.78	3.32	3.02	2.80	2.64	2.51	2.41	2.32	2.24	2.18	2.07	1.99	1.87	1.79	1.69	1.59	1.52	1.41	1.36	1.25	1.15	1.00

Power Tables for the Analysis of Variance

Fc is the critical value of F.

Degrees of Freedom Numerator = 1

$\alpha = .01$		f			$\alpha = .05$		f			$\alpha = .10$		f		
n	Fc	.10	.25	.40	Fc	.10	.25	.40	Fc	.10	.25	.40
5	11.259	.01	.03	.06	5.318	.06	.11	.20	3.458	.11	.19	.33
10	8.285	.01	.05	.17	4.414	.06	.18	.40	3.007	.13	.30	.55
15	7.636	.01	.09	.30	4.196	.07	.26	.57	2.894	.15	.39	.70
20	7.353	.02	.14	.44	4.098	.09	.34	.70	2.842	.16	.48	.81
25	7.194	.02	.19	.57	4.043	.10	.42	.80	2.813	.18	.56	.88
30	7.093	.02	.24	.67	4.007	.11	.49	.87	2.794	.20	.62	.93
35	7.023	.03	.30	.76	3.982	.12	.55	.92	2.781	.22	.68	.96
40	6.971	.03	.35	.83	3.963	.14	.61	.95	2.771	.24	.73	.97
45	6.932	.04	.40	.88	3.949	.15	.66	.97	2.763	.25	.77	.98
50	6.901	.05	.46	.92	3.938	.16	.71	.98	2.757	.27	.81	.99
100	6.765	.11	.83	**	3.889	.29	.94	**	2.731	.42	.97	**

Degrees of Freedom Numerator = 2

$\alpha = .01$		f			$\alpha = .05$		f			$\alpha = .10$		f		
n	Fc	.10	.25	.40	Fc	.10	.25	.40	Fc	.10	.25	.40
5	6.927	.01	.03	.07	3.885	.06	.11	.22	2.807	.12	.20	.34
10	5.488	.01	.06	.21	3.354	.07	.20	.45	2.511	.13	.31	.59
15	5.149	.02	.11	.38	3.220	.08	.29	.64	2.434	.15	.42	.76
20	4.998	.02	.17	.55	3.159	.09	.38	.78	2.398	.17	.52	.87
25	4.913	.02	.23	.69	3.124	.10	.47	.87	2.378	.19	.60	.93
30	4.858	.03	.30	.80	3.101	.12	.55	.93	2.365	.21	.68	.96
35	4.819	.03	.37	.87	3.085	.13	.62	.96	2.355	.23	.74	.98
40	4.791	.04	.44	.92	3.074	.15	.68	.98	2.348	.25	.79	.99
45	4.770	.05	.50	.95	3.065	.16	.74	.99	2.343	.26	.83	**
50	4.752	.05	.56	.97	3.058	.18	.79	.99	2.339	.28	.87	**
100	4.677	.13	.92	**	3.026	.32	.98	**	2.321	.45	.99	**

Source: From Table R of R. P. Runyon, A. Haber, D. J. Pittenger, & K. A. Coleman (1996). *Fundamentals of Behavioral Statistics.* 8th ed. Reprinted with permission of the McGraw-Hill Companies.

(continued)

Appendix E *(continued)*

Degrees of Freedom Numerator = 3

$\alpha = .01$		f			$\alpha = .05$	f			$\alpha = .10$	f		
n	Fc	.10	.25	.40	Fc	.10	.25	.40	Fc	.10	.25	.40
5	5.292	.01	.03	.08	3.239	.06	.12	.24	2.462	.12	.20	.37
10	4.377	.01	.07	.25	2.866	.07	.21	.51	2.243	.14	.33	.64
15	4.152	.02	.13	.46	2.769	.08	.32	.71	2.184	.16	.45	.82
20	4.050	.02	.20	.65	2.725	.10	.43	.85	2.157	.18	.56	.91
25	3.992	.03	.28	.79	2.699	.11	.43	.93	2.142	.20	.65	.96
30	3.955	.03	.36	.88	2.683	.13	.61	.96	2.132	.22	.73	.98
35	3.929	.04	.45	.94	2.671	.14	.69	.98	2.124	.24	.79	.99
40	3.910	.04	.53	.97	2.663	.16	.76	.99	2.119	.26	.84	**
45	3.895	.05	.60	.98	2.656	.17	.81	**	2.115	.28	.88	**
50	3.883	.05	.67	.99	2.651	.19	.85	**	2.112	.30	.91	**
100	3.831	.16	.97	**	2.627	.36	.99	**	2.098	.49	**	**

Degrees of Freedom Numerator = 4

$\alpha = .01$		f			$\alpha = .05$	f			$\alpha = .10$	f		
n	Fc	.10	.25	.40	Fc	.10	.25	.40	Fc	.10	.25	.40
5	4.431	.01	.03	.09	2.866	.06	.12	.26	2.249	.12	.21	.39
10	3.767	.01	.08	.30	2.579	.07	.23	.56	2.074	.14	.36	.69
15	3.600	.02	.15	.54	2.503	.08	.36	.78	2.027	.16	.49	.86
20	3.523	.02	.24	.74	2.467	.10	.47	.90	2.005	.18	.61	.94
25	3.480	.03	.33	.86	2.447	.12	.58	.96	1.992	.21	.70	.98
30	3.451	.03	.43	.93	2.434	.13	.67	.98	1.984	.23	.78	.99
35	3.431	.04	.52	.97	2.425	.15	.75	.99	1.978	.25	.84	**
40	3.417	.05	.61	.99	2.418	.17	.81	**	1.974	.27	.89	**
45	3.406	.06	.68	**	2.413	.19	.86	**	1.971	.30	.92	**
50	3.397	.07	.75	**	2.408	.21	.90	**	1.968	.32	.94	**
100	3.357	.19	.99	**	2.390	.40	**	**	1.956	.53	**	**

Degrees of Freedom Numerator = 5

α = .01		f			α = .05		f			α = .10		f		
n	Fc	.10	.25	.40	Fc	.10	.25	.40	Fc	.10	.25	.40
5	3.895	.01	.03	.10	2.621	.06	.13	.29	2.103	.12	.22	.42
10	3.377	.01	.09	.35	2.386	.07	.25	.61	1.957	.14	.38	.73
15	3.243	.02	.17	.62	2.323	.09	.39	.83	1.917	.16	.52	.90
20	3.182	.02	.27	.81	2.294	.10	.52	.93	1.898	.19	.65	.96
25	3.147	.03	.38	.91	2.277	.12	.63	.98	1.888	.21	.75	.99
30	3.124	.04	.49	.97	2.266	.14	.73	.99	1.881	.24	.82	**
35	3.108	.05	.59	.99	2.258	.16	.80	**	1.876	.26	.88	**
40	3.096	.05	.68	**	2.253	.18	.86	**	1.872	.29	.92	**
45	3.087	.06	.75	**	2.248	.20	.90	**	1.869	.31	.95	**
50	3.080	.07	.81	**	2.245	.22	.93	**	1.867	.34	.96	**
100	3.048	.21	**	**	2.229	.44	**	**	1.857	.57	**	**

Degrees of Freedom Numerator = 6

α = .01		f			α = .05		f			α = .10		f		
n	Fc	.10	.25	.40	Fc	.10	.25	.40	Fc	.10	.25	.40
5	3.528	.01	.04	.12	2.445	.06	.13	.31	1.996	.12	.25	.45
10	3.103	.01	.10	.40	2.246	.07	.27	.66	1.870	.14	.23	.77
15	2.992	.02	.20	.68	2.193	.09	.42	.86	1.835	.17	.40	.92
20	2.94	.03	.31	.86	2.167	.11	.56	.95	1.819	.19	.56	.98
25	2.911	.03	.43	.95	2.153	.13	.68	.99	1.809	.22	.68	.99
30	2.892	.04	.55	.98	2.143	.15	.77	**	1.803	.25	.78	**
35	2.878	.05	.65	.99	2.137	.17	.84	**	1.799	.28	.86	**
40	2.868	.06	.74	**	2.132	.19	.89	**	1.796	.30	.91	**
45	2.861	.07	.81	**	2.128	.21	.93	**	1.793	.33	.94	**
50	2.855	.08	.87	**	2.125	.24	.96	**	1.791	.36	.96	**
100	2.828	.24	**	**	2.112	.47	**	**	1.783	.60	.98	**

Degrees of Freedom Numerator = 7

α = .01		*f*			α = .05		*f*			α = .10		*f*		
n	Fc	.10	.25	.40	Fc	.10	.25	.40	Fc	.10	.25	.40
5	3.258	.01	.04	.13	2.313	.06	.14	.33	1.913	.12	.24	.47
10	2.898	.02	.11	.45	2.140	.08	.29	.70	1.802	.14	.42	.80
15	2.803	.02	.22	.74	2.092	.09	.45	.90	1.771	.17	.59	.94
20	2.759	.03	.35	.90	2.070	.11	.60	.97	1.757	.20	.72	.99
25	2.734	.04	.48	.97	2.057	.13	.72	.99	1.748	.23	.82	**
30	2.717	.04	.60	.99	2.049	.16	.81	**	1.743	.26	.88	**
35	2.705	.05	.71	**	2.043	.18	.88	**	1.739	.29	.93	**
40	2.697	.07	.79	**	2.039	.20	.92	**	1.736	.32	.96	**
45	2.690	.08	.86	**	2.036	.23	.95	**	1.734	.35	.98	**
50	2.685	.09	.90	**	2.033	.25	.97	**	1.732	.37	.99	**
100	2.662	.27	**	**	2.021	.51	**	**	1.724	.63	**	**

Degrees of Freedom Numerator = 8

α = .01		*f*			α = .05		*f*			α = .10		*f*		
n	Fc	.10	.25	.40	Fc	.10	.25	.40	Fc	.10	.25	.40
5	3.052	.01	.04	.14	2.208	.06	.15	.35	1.847	.12	.25	.49
10	2.739	.02	.12	.49	2.055	.08	.31	.73	1.747	.15	.44	.83
15	2.655	.02	.24	.78	2.013	.10	.48	.92	1.719	.18	.61	.96
20	2.617	.03	.38	.93	1.993	.12	.63	.98	1.706	.21	.75	.99
25	2.594	.04	.53	.98	1.981	.14	.75	**	1.699	.24	.84	**
30	2.580	.05	.65	**	1.974	.16	.84	**	1.694	.27	.91	**
35	2.570	.06	.75	**	1.969	.19	.90	**	1.690	.30	.95	**
40	2.562	.07	.83	**	1.965	.21	.94	**	1.688	.33	.97	**
45	2.556	.08	.89	**	1.962	.24	**	**	1.686	.36	.98	**
50	2.552	.10	.93	**	1.959	.27	**	**	1.684	.39	.99	**
100	2.531	.30	**	**	1.949	.54	**	**	1.677	.66	**	**

Percentage Points of the Studentized Range Statistic

a p p e n d i x F

To find the critical area of q_T, locate the cell in the table formed by the intersection of the row containing the degrees of freedom associated with the error term and the column containing the number of means contributing to the analysis, and select the value of q_T listed for your choice of α_{FW}.

k = Number of Means (Tukey Test)

df_{error}	α_{FW}	2	3	4	5	6	7	8	9	10	11	12	13	14	15	16	17	18	19	20
5	.05	3.64	4.60	5.22	5.67	6.03	6.33	6.58	6.80	6.99	7.17	7.32	7.47	7.60	7.72	7.83	7.93	8.03	8.12	8.21
	.01	5.70	6.98	7.80	8.42	8.91	9.32	9.67	9.97	10.24	10.48	10.70	10.89	11.08	11.24	11.40	11.55	11.68	11.81	11.93
6	.05	3.46	4.34	4.90	5.30	5.63	5.90	6.12	6.32	6.49	6.65	6.79	6.92	7.03	7.14	7.24	7.34	7.43	7.51	7.59
	.01	5.24	6.33	7.03	7.56	7.97	8.32	8.61	8.87	9.10	9.30	9.48	9.65	9.81	9.95	10.08	10.21	10.32	10.43	10.54
7	.05	3.34	4.16	4.68	5.06	5.36	5.61	5.82	6.00	6.16	6.30	6.43	6.55	6.66	6.76	6.85	6.94	7.02	7.10	7.17
	.01	4.95	5.92	6.54	7.01	7.37	7.68	7.94	8.17	8.37	8.55	8.71	8.86	9.00	9.12	9.24	9.35	9.46	9.55	9.65
8	.05	3.26	4.04	4.53	4.89	5.17	5.4	5.60	5.77	5.92	6.05	6.18	6.29	6.39	6.48	6.57	6.65	6.73	6.80	6.87
	.01	4.75	5.64	6.2	6.62	6.96	7.24	7.47	7.68	7.86	8.03	8.18	8.31	8.44	8.55	8.66	8.76	8.85	8.94	9.03
9	.05	3.20	3.95	4.41	4.76	5.02	5.24	5.43	5.59	5.74	5.87	5.98	6.09	6.19	6.28	6.36	6.44	6.51	6.58	6.64
	.01	4.60	5.43	5.96	6.35	6.66	6.91	7.13	7.33	7.49	7.65	7.78	7.91	8.03	8.13	8.23	8.33	8.41	8.49	8.57
10	.05	3.15	3.88	4.33	4.65	4.91	5.12	5.30	5.46	5.60	5.72	5.83	5.93	6.03	6.11	6.19	6.27	6.34	6.40	6.47
	.01	4.48	5.27	5.77	6.14	6.43	6.67	6.87	7.05	7.21	7.36	7.49	7.60	7.71	7.81	7.91	7.99	8.08	8.15	8.23
11	.05	3.11	3.82	4.26	4.57	4.82	5.03	5.20	5.35	5.49	5.61	5.71	5.81	5.90	5.98	6.06	6.13	6.20	6.27	6.33
	.01	4.39	5.15	5.62	5.97	6.25	6.48	6.67	6.84	6.99	7.13	7.25	7.36	7.46	7.56	7.65	7.73	7.81	7.88	7.95
12	.05	3.08	3.77	4.20	4.51	4.75	4.95	5.12	5.27	5.39	5.51	5.61	5.71	5.80	5.88	5.95	6.02	6.09	6.15	6.21
	.01	4.32	5.05	5.50	5.84	6.10	6.32	6.51	6.67	6.81	6.94	7.06	7.17	7.26	7.36	7.44	7.52	7.59	7.66	7.73
13	.05	3.06	3.73	4.15	4.45	4.69	4.88	5.05	5.19	5.32	5.43	5.53	5.63	5.71	5.79	5.86	5.93	5.99	6.05	6.11
	.01	4.26	4.96	5.40	5.73	5.98	6.19	6.37	6.53	6.67	6.79	6.90	7.01	7.10	7.19	7.27	7.35	7.42	7.48	7.55

Source: From Table 29 of E. S. Pearson, & H. O. Hartley (eds.) (1966). *Biometrika Tables for Statisticians*, vol. 1. 3rd ed., New York: Cambridge University Press. Reprinted by permission of the Biometrika Trustees.

(continued)

k = Number of Means (Tukey Test)

df_{error}	α_{FW}	2	3	4	5	6	7	8	9	10	11	12	13	14	15	16	17	18	19	20
14	.05	3.03	3.70	4.11	4.41	4.64	4.83	4.99	5.13	5.25	5.36	5.46	5.55	5.64	5.71	5.79	5.85	5.91	5.97	6.03
	.01	4.21	4.89	5.32	5.63	5.88	6.08	6.26	6.41	6.54	6.66	6.77	6.87	6.96	7.05	7.13	7.20	7.27	7.33	7.39
15	.05	3.01	3.67	4.08	4.37	4.59	4.78	4.94	5.08	5.20	5.31	5.40	5.49	5.57	5.65	5.72	5.78	5.85	5.90	5.96
	.01	4.17	4.84	5.25	5.56	5.80	5.99	6.16	6.31	6.44	6.55	6.66	6.76	6.84	6.93	7.00	7.07	7.14	7.20	7.26
16	.05	3.00	3.65	4.05	4.33	4.56	4.74	4.90	5.03	5.15	5.26	5.35	5.44	5.52	5.59	5.66	5.73	5.79	5.84	5.90
	.01	4.13	4.79	5.19	5.49	5.72	5.92	6.08	6.22	6.35	6.46	6.56	6.66	6.74	6.82	6.90	6.97	7.03	7.09	7.15
17	.05	2.98	3.63	4.02	4.30	4.52	4.70	4.86	4.99	5.11	5.21	5.31	5.39	5.47	5.54	5.61	5.67	5.73	5.79	5.84
	.01	4.10	4.74	5.14	5.43	5.66	5.85	6.01	6.15	6.27	6.38	6.48	6.57	6.66	6.73	6.81	6.87	6.94	7.00	7.05
18	.05	2.97	3.61	4.00	4.28	4.49	4.67	4.82	4.96	5.07	5.17	5.27	5.35	5.43	5.50	5.57	5.63	5.69	5.74	5.79
	.01	4.07	4.70	5.09	5.38	5.60	5.79	5.94	6.08	6.20	6.31	6.41	6.50	6.58	6.65	6.73	6.79	6.85	6.91	6.97
19	.05	2.96	3.59	3.98	4.25	4.47	4.65	4.79	4.92	5.04	5.14	5.23	5.31	5.39	5.46	5.53	5.59	5.65	5.70	5.75
	.01	4.05	4.67	5.05	5.33	5.55	5.73	5.89	6.02	6.14	6.25	6.34	6.43	6.51	6.58	6.65	6.72	6.78	6.84	6.89
20	.05	2.95	3.58	3.96	4.23	4.45	4.62	4.77	4.90	5.01	5.11	5.20	5.28	5.36	5.43	5.49	5.55	5.61	5.66	5.71
	.01	4.02	4.64	5.02	5.29	5.51	5.69	5.84	5.97	6.09	6.19	6.28	6.37	6.45	6.52	6.59	6.65	6.71	6.77	6.82
24	.05	2.92	3.53	3.90	4.17	4.37	4.54	4.68	4.81	4.92	5.01	5.10	5.18	5.25	5.32	5.38	5.44	5.49	5.55	5.59
	.01	3.96	4.55	4.91	5.17	5.37	5.54	5.69	5.81	5.92	6.02	6.11	6.19	6.26	6.33	6.39	6.45	6.51	6.56	6.61
30	.05	2.89	3.49	3.85	4.10	4.30	4.46	4.60	4.72	4.82	4.92	5.00	5.08	5.15	5.21	5.27	5.33	5.38	5.43	5.47
	.01	3.89	4.45	4.80	5.05	5.24	5.40	5.54	5.65	5.76	5.85	5.93	6.01	6.08	6.14	6.20	6.26	6.31	6.36	6.41
40	.05	2.86	3.44	3.79	4.04	4.23	4.39	4.52	4.63	4.73	4.82	4.90	4.98	5.04	5.11	5.16	5.22	5.27	5.31	5.36
	.01	3.82	4.37	4.70	4.93	5.11	5.26	5.39	5.50	5.60	5.69	5.76	5.83	5.90	5.96	6.02	6.07	6.12	6.16	6.21
60	.05	2.83	3.40	3.74	3.98	4.16	4.31	4.44	4.55	4.65	4.73	4.81	4.88	4.94	5.00	5.06	5.11	5.15	5.20	5.24
	.01	3.76	4.28	4.59	4.82	4.99	5.13	5.25	5.36	5.45	5.53	5.60	5.67	5.73	5.78	5.84	5.89	5.93	5.97	6.01
120	.05	2.80	3.36	3.68	3.92	4.10	4.24	4.36	4.47	4.56	4.64	4.71	4.78	4.84	4.90	4.95	5.00	5.04	5.09	5.13
	.01	3.70	4.20	4.50	4.71	4.87	5.01	5.12	5.21	5.30	5.37	5.44	5.50	5.56	5.61	5.66	5.71	5.75	5.79	5.83
∞	.05	2.77	3.31	3.63	3.86	4.03	4.17	4.29	4.39	4.47	4.55	4.62	4.68	4.74	4.80	4.85	4.89	4.93	4.97	5.01
	.01	3.64	4.12	4.40	4.60	4.76	4.88	4.99	5.08	5.16	5.23	5.29	5.35	5.40	5.45	5.49	5.54	5.57	5.61	5.65

Values of the Correlation Coefficient Required for Different Levels of Significance When $H_0: \rho = 0$

a p p e n d i x G

	Levels of Significance for a One-Tailed Test			
	.05	.025	.01	.005
	Levels of Significance for a Two-Tailed Test			
df	.10	.05	.02	.01
1	.988	.977	.9995	.9999
2	.900	.950	.980	.990
3	.805	.878	.934	.959
4	.729	.811	.882	.917
5	.669	.754	.833	.874
6	.622	.707	.789	.834
7	.582	.666	.750	.798
8	.549	.632	.716	.765
9	.521	.602	.685	.735
10	.497	.576	.658	.708
11	.476	.553	.634	.684
12	.458	.532	.612	.661
13	.441	.514	.592	.641
14	.426	.497	.574	.623
15	.412	.482	.558	.606
16	.400	.468	.542	.590
17	.389	.456	.528	.575
18	.378	.444	.516	.561
19	.369	.433	.503	.549
20	.360	.423	.492	.537
21	.352	.413	.482	.526
22	.344	.404	.472	.515
23	.337	.396	.462	.505
24	.330	.388	.453	.496
25	.323	.381	.445	.487

(continued)

Source: © 1963 R. A. Fisher and F. Yates. Reprinted by permission of Addison-Wesley Longman Limited, Reprinted by permission of Pearson Education Limited. and From E. W. Minium, B. M. King, G. Bear (1993). *Statistical Reasoning in Psychology and Education.* 3rd ed. Copyright John Wiley & Sons, Inc., Reprinted by permission of [Wiley-Liss, Inc, subsidiary of] John Wiley & Sons, Inc.

	Levels of Significance for a One-Tailed Test			
	.05	.025	.01	.005
	Levels of Significance for a Two-Tailed Test			
df	.10	.05	.02	.01
26	.317	.374	.437	.479
27	.311	.367	.430	.471
28	.306	.361	.423	.463
29	.301	.355	.416	.456
30	.296	.349	.409	.349
32	.287	.339	.397	.436
34	.279	.329	.386	.424
36	.271	.320	.376	.413
38	.264	.312	.367	.403
40	.257	.304	.358	.393
42	.251	.297	.350	.384
44	.426	.291	.342	.376
46	.240	.285	.335	.368
48	.235	.279	.328	.361
50	.231	.273	.322	.354
55	.220	.261	.307	.339
60	.211	.250	.295	.325
65	.203	.240	.284	.313
70	.195	.232	.274	.302
75	.189	.224	.265	.292
80	.183	.217	.256	.283
85	.178	.211	.249	.275
90	.173	.205	.242	.267
95	.168	.200	.236	.260
100	.164	.195	.230	.254
120	.150	.178	.210	.232
150	.134	.159	.189	.208
200	.116	.138	.164	.181
300	.095	.113	.134	.148
400	.082	.098	.116	.128
500	.073	.088	.104	.115
1000	.052	.062	.073	.081

Values of Fisher's z_F for Values of r

r	z_F	r	z_F	r	z_F	r	z_F	r	z_F
.000	.000	.200	.203	.400	.424	.600	.693	.800	1.099
.005	.005	.205	.208	.405	.430	.605	.701	.805	1.113
.010	.010	.210	.213	.410	.436	.610	.709	.810	1.127
.015	.015	.215	.218	.415	.442	.615	.717	.815	1.142
.020	.020	.220	.224	.420	.448	.620	.725	.820	1.157
.025	.025	.225	.229	.425	.454	.625	.733	.825	1.172
.030	.030	.230	.234	.430	.460	.630	.741	.830	1.188
.035	.035	.235	.239	.435	.466	635	.750	.835	1.204
.040	.040	.240	.245	.440	.472	.640	.758	.840	1.221
.045	.045	.245	.250	.445	.478	.645	.767	.845	1.238
.050	.050	.250	.255	.450	.485	.650	.775	.850	1.256
.055	.055	.255	.261	.455	.491	.655	.784	.855	1.274
.060	.060	.260	.266	.460	.497	.660	.793	.860	1.293
.065	.065	.265	.271	.465	.504	.665	.802	.865	1.313
.070	.070	.270	.277	.470	.510	.670	.811	.870	1.333
.075	.075	.275	.282	.475	.517	.675	.820	.875	1.354
.080	.080	.280	.288	.480	.523	.680	.829	.880	1.376
.085	.085	.285	.293	.485	.530	.685	.838	.885	1.398
.090	.090	.290	.299	.490	.536	.690	.848	.890	1.422
.095	.095	.295	.304	.495	.543	.695	.858	.895	1.447
.100	.100	.300	.310	.500	.549	.700	.867	.900	1.472
.105	.105	.305	.315	.505	.556	.705	.877	.905	1.499
.110	.110	.310	.321	.510	.563	.710	.887	.910	1.528
.115	.116	.315	.326	.515	.570	.715	.897	.915	1.557
.120	.121	.320	.332	.520	.576	.720	.908	.920	1.589
.125	.126	.325	.337	.525	.583	.725	.918	.925	1.623
.130	.131	.330	.343	.530	.590	.730	.929	.930	1.658
.135	.156	.335	.348	.535	.597	.735	.940	.935	1.697
.140	.141	.340	.354	.540	.604	.740	.950	.940	1.738
.145	.146	.345	.360	.545	.611	.745	.962	.945	1.783
.150	.151	.350	.365	.550	.618	.750	.973	.950	1.832
.155	.156	.355	.371	.555	.626	.755	.984	.955	1.886
.160	.161	.360	.377	.560	.633	.760	.996	.960	1.946
.165	.167	.365	.383	.565	.640	.765	1.008	.965	2.014
.170	.172	.370	.388	.570	.648	.770	1.020	.970	2.092
.175	.177	.375	.394	.575	.655	.775	1.033	.975	2.185
.180	.182	.380	.400	.580	.662	.780	1.045	.980	2.298
.185	.187	.385	.406	.585	.670	.785	1.058	.985	2.443
.190	.192	.390	.412	.590	.678	.790	1.071	.990	2.647
.195	.198	.395	.418	.595	.685	.795	1.085	.995	2.994

Source: From Table VIII of R. A. Fisher & F. Yates (1974). *Statistical Tables for the Biological, Agricultural and Medical Research.* 6th ed. Published by Addison-Wesley Longman:London (previously published by Oliver & Boyd, Ltd. Edinburgh). Reprinted by permission of the authors and publishers.

Upper Percentage Points of the Chi-Square Distribution*

*The table entries are critical values of χ^2.

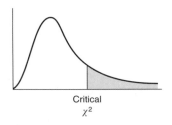

Critical
χ^2

	Proportion in Critical Region						Proportion in Critical Region				
df	.10	.05	.025	.01	.005	df	.10	.05	.025	.01	.005
1	2.71	3.84	5.02	6.63	7.88	20	28.41	31.41	34.17	37.57	40.00
2	4.61	5.99	7.38	9.21	10.60	21	29.62	32.67	35.48	38.93	41.40
3	6.25	7.81	9.35	11.34	12.84	22	30.81	33.92	36.78	40.29	42.80
4	7.78	9.49	11.14	13.28	14.86	23	32.01	35.17	38.08	41.64	44.18
5	9.24	11.07	12.83	15.09	16.75	24	33.20	36.42	39.36	42.98	45.56
6	10.64	12.59	14.45	16.81	18.55	25	34.38	37.65	40.65	44.31	46.93
7	12.02	14.07	16.01	18.48	20.28	26	35.56	38.89	41.92	45.64	48.29
8	13.36	15.51	17.53	20.09	21.96	27	36.74	40.11	43.19	46.96	49.64
9	14.68	16.92	19.02	21.67	23.59	28	37.92	41.34	44.46	48.28	50.99
10	15.99	18.31	20.48	23.21	25.19	29	39.09	42.56	45.72	49.59	52.34
11	17.28	19.68	21.92	24.72	26.76	30	40.26	43.77	46.98	50.89	53.67
12	18.55	21.03	23.34	26.22	28.30	40	51.81	55.76	59.34	63.69	66.77
13	19.81	22.36	24.74	27.69	29.82	50	63.17	67.50	71.42	76.15	79.49
14	21.06	23.68	26.12	29.14	31.32	60	74.40	79.08	83.30	88.38	91.95
15	22.31	25.00	27.49	30.58	32.80	70	85.53	90.53	95.02	100.42	104.22
16	23.54	26.30	28.85	32.00	34.27	80	96.58	101.88	106.63	112.33	116.32
17	24.77	27.59	30.19	33.41	35.72	90	107.56	113.14	118.14	124.12	128.30
18	25.99	28.87	31.53	34.81	37.16	100	118.50	124.34	129.56	135.81	140.17
19	27.20	30.14	32.85	36.19	38.58						

Source: From Table 8 of E. S. Pearson & H. O. Hartley (Eds.) (1966). *Biometrika Tables for Statisticians*, vol. 1, 3rd ed., New York: Cambridge University Press. Reprinted by permission of the Biometrika Trustees.

a p p e n d i x   **J** | # Critical Values of Mann-Whitney's U[a]

For a one-tailed test at α = .01 (roman type) and α = .005 (boldface type) and for two-tailed test at α = .02 (roman type) and α = .01 (boldface type)

n_2 \ n_1 →	1	2	3	4	5	6	7	8	9	10	11	12	13	14	15	16	17	18	19	20
1	—[b]	—	—	—	—	—	—	—	—	—	—	—	—	—	—	—	—	—	—	—
2	—	—	—	—	—	—	—	—	—	—	—	—	0	0	0	0	0	0	1	1
																		—	**0**	**0**
3	—	—	—	—	—	0	0	1	1	1	2	2	2	3	3	4	4	4	4	5
						—	**—**	**—**	**0**	**0**	**0**	**1**	**1**	**1**	**2**	**2**	**2**	**2**	**3**	**3**
4	—	—	—	—	0	1	1	2	3	3	4	5	5	6	7	7	8	9	9	10
					—	**0**	**0**	**1**	**1**	**2**	**2**	**3**	**3**	**4**	**5**	**5**	**6**	**6**	**7**	**8**
5	—	—	—	0	1	2	3	4	5	6	7	8	9	10	11	12	13	14	15	16
				—	**0**	**1**	**1**	**2**	**3**	**4**	**5**	**6**	**7**	**7**	**8**	**9**	**10**	**11**	**12**	**13**
6	—	—	—	1	2	3	4	6	7	8	9	11	12	13	15	16	18	19	20	22
				0	**1**	**2**	**3**	**4**	**5**	**6**	**7**	**9**	**10**	**11**	**12**	**13**	**15**	**16**	**17**	**18**
7	—	—	0	1	3	4	6	7	9	11	12	14	16	17	19	21	23	24	26	28
			—	**0**	**1**	**3**	**4**	**6**	**7**	**9**	**10**	**12**	**13**	**15**	**16**	**18**	**19**	**21**	**22**	**24**
8	—	—	0	2	4	6	7	9	11	13	15	17	20	22	24	26	28	30	32	34
			—	**1**	**2**	**4**	**6**	**7**	**9**	**11**	**13**	**15**	**17**	**18**	**20**	**22**	**24**	**26**	**28**	**30**
9	—	—	1	3	5	7	9	11	14	16	18	21	23	26	28	31	33	36	38	40
			0	**1**	**3**	**5**	**7**	**9**	**11**	**13**	**16**	**18**	**20**	**22**	**24**	**27**	**29**	**31**	**33**	**36**
10	—	—	1	3	6	8	11	13	16	19	22	24	27	30	33	36	38	41	44	47
			0	**2**	**4**	**6**	**9**	**11**	**13**	**16**	**18**	**21**	**24**	**26**	**29**	**31**	**34**	**37**	**39**	**42**
11	—	—	1	4	7	9	12	15	18	22	25	28	31	34	37	41	44	47	50	53
			0	**2**	**5**	**7**	**10**	**13**	**16**	**18**	**21**	**24**	**27**	**30**	**33**	**36**	**39**	**42**	**45**	**48**
12	—	—	2	5	8	11	14	17	21	24	28	31	35	38	42	46	49	53	56	60
			1	**3**	**6**	**9**	**12**	**15**	**18**	**21**	**24**	**27**	**31**	**34**	**37**	**41**	**44**	**47**	**51**	**54**
13	—	0	2	5	9	12	16	20	23	27	31	35	39	43	47	51	55	59	63	67
		—	**1**	**3**	**7**	**10**	**13**	**17**	**20**	**24**	**27**	**31**	**34**	**38**	**42**	**45**	**49**	**53**	**56**	**60**
14	—	0	2	6	10	13	17	22	26	30	34	38	43	47	51	56	60	65	69	73
		—	**1**	**4**	**7**	**11**	**15**	**18**	**22**	**26**	**30**	**34**	**38**	**42**	**46**	**50**	**54**	**58**	**63**	**67**
15	—	0	3	7	11	15	19	24	28	33	37	42	47	51	56	61	66	70	75	80
		—	**2**	**5**	**8**	**12**	**16**	**20**	**24**	**29**	**33**	**37**	**42**	**46**	**51**	**55**	**60**	**64**	**69**	**73**
16	—	0	3	7	12	16	21	26	31	36	41	46	51	56	61	66	71	76	82	87
		—	**2**	**5**	**9**	**13**	**18**	**22**	**27**	**31**	**36**	**41**	**45**	**50**	**55**	**60**	**65**	**70**	**74**	**79**
17	—	0	4	8	13	18	23	28	33	38	44	49	55	60	66	71	77	82	88	93
		—	**2**	**6**	**10**	**15**	**19**	**24**	**29**	**34**	**39**	**44**	**49**	**54**	**60**	**65**	**70**	**75**	**81**	**86**
18	—	0	4	9	14	19	24	30	36	41	47	53	59	65	70	76	82	88	94	100
		—	**2**	**6**	**11**	**16**	**21**	**26**	**31**	**37**	**42**	**47**	**53**	**58**	**64**	**70**	**75**	**81**	**87**	**92**
19	—	1	4	9	15	20	26	32	38	44	50	56	63	69	75	82	88	94	101	107
		0	**3**	**7**	**12**	**17**	**22**	**28**	**33**	**39**	**45**	**51**	**56**	**63**	**69**	**74**	**81**	**87**	**93**	**99**
20	—	1	5	10	16	22	28	34	40	47	53	60	67	73	80	87	93	100	107	114
		0	**3**	**8**	**13**	**18**	**24**	**30**	**36**	**42**	**48**	**54**	**60**	**67**	**73**	**79**	**86**	**92**	**99**	**105**

[a] To be significant for any given n_1 and n_2, the obtained U must be *equal to* or *less than* the value shown in the table.

[b] Dashes in the body of the table indicate that no decision is possible at the stated level of significance.

Source: From Table D.12 in R. E. Kirk (1990). *Statistics: An Introduction.* 3rd ed. p. 610. Copyright 1990 by Holt, Rinehart and Winston. Reproducd by permission of the publisher.

Critical values for a one-tailed test at α = .05 (roman type) and α = .025 (boldface type) and for two-tailed test at α = .10 (roman type) and α = .05 (boldface type)

n_2	1	2	3	4	5	6	7	8	9	10	11	12	13	14	15	16	17	18	19	20
1	—	—	—	—	—	—	—	—	—	—	—	—	—	—	—	—	—	—	0	0
																			—	—
2	—	—	—	—	0	0	0	1	1	1	1	2	2	2	3	3	3	4	4	4
	—	—	—	—	—	—	—	**0**	**0**	**0**	**0**	**1**	**1**	**1**	**1**	**1**	**2**	**2**	**2**	**2**
3	—	—	0	0	1	2	2	3	3	4	5	5	6	7	7	8	9	9	10	11
	—	—	—	—	**0**	**1**	**1**	**2**	**2**	**3**	**3**	**4**	**4**	**5**	**5**	**6**	**6**	**7**	**7**	**8**
4	—	—	0	1	2	3	4	5	6	7	8	9	10	11	12	14	15	16	17	18
	—	—	—	**0**	**1**	**2**	**3**	**4**	**4**	**5**	**6**	**7**	**8**	**9**	**10**	**11**	**11**	**12**	**13**	**13**
5	—	0	1	2	4	5	6	8	9	11	12	13	15	16	18	19	20	22	23	25
	—	—	**0**	**1**	**2**	**3**	**5**	**6**	**7**	**8**	**9**	**11**	**12**	**13**	**14**	**15**	**17**	**18**	**19**	**20**
6	—	0	2	3	5	7	8	10	12	14	16	17	19	21	23	25	26	28	30	32
	—	—	**1**	**2**	**3**	**5**	**6**	**8**	**10**	**11**	**13**	**14**	**16**	**17**	**19**	**21**	**22**	**24**	**25**	**27**
7	—	0	2	4	6	8	11	13	15	17	19	21	24	26	28	30	33	35	37	39
	—	—	**1**	**3**	**5**	**6**	**8**	**10**	**12**	**14**	**16**	**18**	**20**	**22**	**24**	**26**	**28**	**30**	**32**	**34**
8	—	1	3	5	8	10	13	15	18	20	23	26	28	31	33	36	39	41	44	47
	—	**0**	**2**	**4**	**6**	**8**	**10**	**13**	**15**	**17**	**19**	**22**	**24**	**26**	**29**	**31**	**34**	**36**	**38**	**41**
9	—	1	3	6	9	12	15	18	21	24	27	30	33	36	39	42	45	48	51	54
	—	**0**	**2**	**4**	**7**	**10**	**12**	**15**	**17**	**20**	**23**	**26**	**28**	**31**	**34**	**37**	**39**	**42**	**45**	**48**
10	—	1	4	7	11	14	17	20	24	27	31	34	37	41	44	48	51	55	58	62
	—	**0**	**3**	**5**	**8**	**11**	**14**	**17**	**20**	**23**	**26**	**29**	**33**	**36**	**39**	**42**	**45**	**48**	**52**	**55**
11	—	1	5	8	12	16	19	23	27	31	34	38	42	46	50	54	57	61	65	69
	—	**0**	**3**	**6**	**9**	**13**	**16**	**19**	**23**	**26**	**30**	**33**	**37**	**40**	**44**	**47**	**51**	**55**	**58**	**62**
12	—	2	5	9	13	17	21	26	30	34	38	42	47	51	55	60	64	68	72	77
	—	**1**	**4**	**7**	**11**	**14**	**18**	**22**	**26**	**29**	**33**	**37**	**41**	**45**	**49**	**53**	**57**	**61**	**65**	**69**
13	—	2	6	10	15	19	24	28	33	37	42	47	51	56	61	65	70	75	80	84
	—	**1**	**4**	**8**	**12**	**16**	**20**	**24**	**28**	**33**	**37**	**41**	**45**	**50**	**54**	**59**	**63**	**67**	**72**	**76**
14	—	2	7	11	16	21	26	31	36	41	46	51	56	61	66	71	77	82	87	92
	—	**1**	**5**	**9**	**13**	**17**	**22**	**26**	**31**	**36**	**40**	**45**	**50**	**55**	**59**	**64**	**67**	**74**	**78**	**83**
15	—	3	7	12	18	23	28	33	39	44	50	55	61	66	72	77	83	88	94	100
	—	**1**	**5**	**10**	**14**	**19**	**24**	**29**	**34**	**39**	**44**	**49**	**54**	**59**	**64**	**70**	**75**	**80**	**85**	**90**
16	—	3	8	14	19	25	30	36	42	48	54	60	65	71	77	83	89	95	101	107
	—	**1**	**6**	**11**	**15**	**21**	**26**	**31**	**37**	**42**	**47**	**53**	**59**	**64**	**70**	**75**	**81**	**86**	**92**	**98**
17	—	3	9	15	20	26	33	39	45	51	57	64	70	77	83	89	96	102	109	115
	—	**2**	**6**	**11**	**17**	**22**	**28**	**34**	**39**	**45**	**51**	**57**	**63**	**67**	**75**	**81**	**87**	**93**	**99**	**105**
18	—	4	9	16	22	28	35	41	48	55	61	68	75	82	88	95	102	109	116	123
	—	**2**	**7**	**12**	**18**	**24**	**30**	**36**	**42**	**48**	**55**	**61**	**67**	**74**	**80**	**86**	**93**	**99**	**106**	**112**
19	0	4	10	17	23	30	37	44	51	58	65	72	80	87	94	101	109	116	123	130
	—	**2**	**7**	**13**	**19**	**25**	**32**	**38**	**45**	**52**	**58**	**65**	**72**	**78**	**85**	**92**	**99**	**106**	**113**	**119**
20	0	4	11	18	25	32	39	47	54	62	69	77	84	92	100	107	115	123	130	138
	—	**2**	**8**	**13**	**20**	**27**	**34**	**41**	**48**	**55**	**62**	**69**	**76**	**83**	**90**	**98**	**105**	**112**	**119**	**127**

Critical Values of Wilcoxon's T^a

N	Level of Significance for a One-Tailed Test				N	Level of Significance for a One-Tailed Test			
	.05	.025	.01	.005		.05	.025	.01	.005
	Level of Significance for a Two-Tailed Test					Level of Significance for a Two-Tailed Test			
	.10	.05	.02	.01		.10	.05	.02	.01
5	0	—	—	—	28	130	116	101	91
6	2	0	—	—	29	140	126	110	100
7	3	2	0	—	30	151	137	120	109
8	5	3	1	0	31	163	147	130	118
9	8	5	3	1	32	175	159	140	128
10	10	8	5	3	33	187	170	151	138
11	13	10	7	5	34	200	182	162	148
12	17	13	9	7	35	213	195	173	159
13	21	17	12	9	36	227	208	185	171
14	25	21	15	12	37	241	221	198	182
15	30	25	19	15	38	256	235	211	194
16	35	29	23	19	39	271	249	224	207
17	41	34	27	23	40	286	264	238	220
18	47	40	32	27	41	302	279	252	233
19	53	46	37	32	42	319	294	266	247
20	60	52	43	37	43	336	310	281	261
21	67	58	49	42	44	353	327	296	276
22	75	65	55	48	45	371	343	312	291
23	83	73	62	54	46	389	361	328	307
24	91	81	69	61	47	407	378	345	322
25	100	89	76	68	48	426	396	362	339
26	110	98	84	75	49	446	415	379	355
27	119	107	92	83	50	466	434	397	373

[a]The symbol T denotes the smaller sum of ranks associated with differences that are all of the same sign. For any given N (number of ranked differences), the obtained T is significant at a given level if it is *equal to* or *less than* the value shown in the table.

Source: From Table J of R. P. Runyon, A. Haber, D. J. Pittenger, & K. A. Coleman (1996). *Fundamentals of Behavioral Statistics*, 8th ed. Reprinted with permission of the McGraw-Hill Companies. Also adapted from F. Wilcoxon, S. K. Kati, & R. A. Wilcox (1963), *Critical Values and Probability Levels of the Wilcoxon Rank-Sum Test and the Wilcoxon Signed-Rank Test*. Wayne, NJ: American Cyanimid Company.

Answers

CHAPTER 1

1.1. One major purpose of statistics is to summarize the important characteristics of a set of numbers (data). Measures of central tendency (e.g., the mean) and measures of variability (e.g., the standard deviation) are frequently used descriptive statistics. A second major purpose of statistics is to make inferences about population parameters from sample values. Statistical tests like the *t*-test and the Analysis of Variance F-test are two of many inferential statistical tests we will present in the text.

1.2. A *variable* is a characteristic that can take on different values for different members of a group or set being studied.

1.3. A *constant* is a characteristic that takes on the same value for all members of a group or set being studied.

1.4. A *qualitative variable* consists of attributes or non-quantitative characteristics of objects, people, or events. A *quantitative variable* consists of a count or numerical measurement of the characteristics of objects, people, or events.

1.5. Quantitative variables can be discrete or continuous. A *discrete variable* can assume only a finite number of values; it consists of separate, indivisible categories. No values can exist between two neighboring categories. A *continuous variable* can assume an infinite number of values; it is divisible into an infinite number of fractional parts. The speed of motor vehicles, the distance between stationary objects, and reaction time are examples of continuous quantitative variables.

1.6. An *independent variable* is the variable under the experimenter's control. It is the treatment or manipulation whose effects are being studied. A *dependent variable* is some form of measured behavior ranging from physiological responses, to think-aloud protocols, to standardized test results, to unobtrusive recordings of children's fantasy play.

1.7. A *predictor variable* is the variable that is hypothesized to explain variability in the outcome variable. An *outcome variable* in a correlational investigation is also some form of measured behavior. Outcome variables from correlational investigations are not fundamentally different from dependent variables used in experiments.

1.8. *Variability* is the degree of inconsistency in a set of numbers or distribution of scores. Measures of variability describe the extent to which scores in a distribution are clustered together or spread out.

1.9. A code sheet or book helps insure that coding is done consistently and that there are rules governing how to treat every type of response.

1.10. The values are mutually exclusive, which means that an element cannot be in more than one category, and they do not involve a count or numerical measurement. This is a qualitative variable.

1.11. The two different forms of storytelling are the independent variable. The recall measure is the dependent variable.

1.12. Since time-on-task is a numerical measurement of the characteristic time (as measured in hours), it is a quantitative variable. As time-on-task is a variable under the experimenter's control, it is the independent variable.

1.13. Since there is no manipulation of an independent variable, but two variables are measured and an attempt is made to determine the relationship between the two variables, this would be classified as a correlational investigation.

CHAPTER 2

2.1. The design of an empirical investigation includes all aspects of a study's methodology. Consideration of research design means that the researcher is attending to the details surrounding the exploration of the research questions or hypotheses of interest. This consideration is particularly important because inadequacies in the design of an investigation can seldom, if ever, be overcome by the use of sophisticated statistical techniques. "Garbage in, garbage out" is a tired but true expression that applies to consideration of the quality of the statistical conclusions arising from poorly designed studies.

2.2. Ethical guidelines help ensure that researchers respect the rights and dignity of every research participant. These guidelines recognize that participants need to be aware of the nature of their participation and assent to their role, be allowed to discontinue if they feel uncomfortable, and have their rights to privacy and confidentiality protected.

2.3. Experimental investigations attempt to establish a cause-and-effect relationship between two variables: the independent and dependent variables. Correlational investigations seek only to determine whether the measured relationship between predictor and outcome variables occurred as a function of chance.

2.4. One question is, Did the researcher really find what she or he claims to have found, or is there another way to explain the findings? This question focuses on the credibility of the conclusions drawn from the study. A second question is, Will the same results happen all the time with everyone, everywhere? These questions focus on the applicability or generalizability of the conclusions drawn from the study.

2.5. *Internal validity* exists when the experimental treatment has a noticeable impact on the specific experimental situation under consideration. Internal validity exists when it can be shown that the independent variable, as manipulated, produced a change in the dependent variable, as measured. Threats to internal validity are rival explanations to the effect of the treatment.

2.6. *External validity* exists to the extent the research findings can be generalized across people, settings, treatment variables, and measurement variables. For example, a variety of instruments, techniques, or manipulations may be deemed acceptable operational definitions of a construct with no certainty that a finding with one instrument generalizes to another. Therefore, threats to external validity are limiting conditions to the effect of the treatment, not rival explanations to the effect of the treatment.

2.7. Pre-experimental designs are attempts at experimentation that are so flawed that numerous probable threats to internal validity often disqualify the research as providing useful scientific evidence. Pre-experimental designs are among the most widely used research designs in use for applied research purposes. Pre-experimental designs include the One-Shot Case Study, the One-Group Pretest–Posttest Design, and the Static Group Comparison Design.

2.8. Experimental control is the extent to which various research designs control for threats to internal and external validity. Statistical control occurs when an extraneous variable is measured and its influence on the outcome variable removed before the influence of the predictor variable is examined. Although generally less effective and conclusive than experimental control, statistical control can be used to help reduce or eliminate certain threats to internal validity.

2.9. A true experimental design control for all threats to internal validity. The two most popular true experimental designs are the Pretest–Posttest Control Group Design and the Posttest-Only Control Group Design.

2.10. True experimental designs are distinguished primarily in terms of their ability to control for threats to external validity or those factors that define the limiting conditions of a treatment's effectiveness.

2.11. Quasi-experimental designs control for most of, but not all, the threats to internal validity. Compared to pre-experiments, quasi-experiments reduce the probability that a rival explanation is a viable alternative to a treatment effect. Thus, they represent realistic compromises when it is impractical, impossible, or undesirable to conduct a true experiment. Unfortunately, they sometimes require a greater number of groups to study and/or a greater number of observations of those groups than their true experimental counterparts.

2.12. *Measurement* is the process of assigning numbers to characteristics of people, objects, or events according to a set of rules. A *nominal* scale allows for the classification and labeling of elements or objects into mutually exclusive and exhaustive categories based on defined features. An *ordinal* scale allows for the classification and labeling of elements or objects into mutually exclusive and

exhaustive categories based on defined features that are numerically ranked or otherwise ordered with respect to one another. However, equal differences among numbers does not reflect equal magnitude differences among the corresponding categories. An *interval* scale allows for the classification and labeling of elements or objects into mutually exclusive and exhaustive categories based on defined features that are numerically ranked or otherwise ordered with respect to one another. In addition, equal differences among numbers reflect equal magnitude differences among the corresponding categories. A *ratio* scale is an interval scale with the added characteristic that the origin or zero point of the scale represents the absence of the measured characteristic.

2.13. Reliability is the degree to which a test is free from measurement error or how precise, consistent, or stable a participant's test score is over different testing and time spans. Reliabilities are reported like correlation coefficients are, except the range of scores is from 0 (no reliability) to +1 (perfect reliability). Reliabilities around .9 are considered excellent; reliabilities below .6 are considered marginal.

2.14. Validity is the degree to which a test measures what it purports to measure: a test's "truthfulness." Validity is concerned with the appropriateness, meaningfulness, and usefulness of the specific inferences made from test scores. The categories of validity are content validity, criterion-related validity, and construct validity.

2.15. COB officials hypothesize that interactive video displays will improve public attitudes toward banks. The independent variable is interactive video displays (presence, absence). The dependent variable is public attitudes toward banks.

2.16. Using the Posttest-Only Control Group Design we will randomly assign bank customers waiting in line to one of two queues. One queue will be shown the interactive video display, the second queue will have no display. Following their bank transactions, customers will be asked to complete a questionnaire about their attitude toward banks.

2.17. We can ask all the customers entering a branch of the COB bank to participate in a study for a chance at a prize drawing. The participants would first complete the questionnaire, then watch the interactive video, and then complete the questionnaire a second time. The possible rival explanations in this design are history, maturation, testing, instrumentation, and possibly regression. The likeliest threat is testing.

2.18. The Pretest–Posttest Control Group Design is superior to the Posttest-Only Control Group Design because it allows researchers to check on group equivalence and the adequacy of random assignment at the pretest. It is inferior because it allows pretest sensitization to operate and because it is inefficient, requiring an additional round of testing.

2.19. The interaction of testing and X is a threat to external validity if the pretest acts as a catalyst, thereby allowing the treatment to work. It is not a threat to internal validity because by itself it has no effect on the dependent variable.

2.20. Test stability measures the shift in scores over time but not whether the items on a test measure the same thing.

CHAPTER 3

Section 1: Conceptual/Definition

3.1. Having a large number of scores makes it difficult to understand the salient features of a dataset. Organizing and displaying the data is one way of summarizing data. Data that is organized and displayed visually can help researchers understand the data better.

3.2. Data screening is the process of examining the data for unusual or anomalous characteristics as well as to determine qualities of the shape of a distribution of scores. A good visual display is useful in allowing us both a means to comprehend the data as well as a means to ensure that the data have been properly scored and that the data conform to our assumptions and expectations.

3.3. One method (the popular method) deals with tied ranks by assigning the highest rank in the category to each tied score. In the mathematical method, the tied ranks are assigned the average rank for the scores which are tied.

3.4. A *percentile point* ($P_\%$), also called a *percentile* or *centile*, is a point on the original measurement scale at or below which a specified percentage of scores falls. In contrast, the *percentile rank* of a score (PR_Y) is a point on the percentile scale that gives the percentage of scores falling at or below the specified score. Note that a percentile or percentile rank is not a percentage correct.

3.5. Percentiles emanate from ranking the data. This ranking procedure converts the original measurement scale, even if it was interval or ratio, to an ordinal scale.

3.6. The determination of the interval size for a grouped frequency distribution is essentially a compromise between ease of understanding the results and the amount of detail provided. As the class intervals grow larger, the examination results are easier to comprehend but a certain degree of detail is lost.

3.7. The first assumption is that, in a class interval, the scores are uniformly distributed among the limits of the interval and not bunched together around a particular value or values. The second assumption is that whenever a single score must represent a class interval, the interval midpoint is the representative score. In other words, one assumes that all the scores within the interval can be represented adequately by its midpoint. For example, 64.5 is the midpoint for the class interval 60–69.

3.8. Although data often represent discrete values (i.e., whole numbers or integers) those dealing with the data may want to be able to interpret them as continuous variables that can take on fractional values. That is, although the scores were recorded as whole numbers, imagine that the recorded value actually represents a value that falls within certain limits, called the *exact limits*, or *real limits*. Thus, the values 79.5 and 80.5 represent the lower real limit and the upper real limit, respectively, for an examination score of 80. If individual scores can have exact limits, class intervals can be treated likewise. For example, the exact limits for the class interval 80–89 is 79.5 and 89.5, respectively. The use of exact limits is important when one wishes to estimate percentiles and percentile ranks from grouped data.

3.9. Crosstabulation, or the use of a contingency table, allows researchers to organize and display the values or levels of one variable according to the values or levels of a second variable. In experimental research, you might want to tabulate participants' reaction on the dependent variable separately for each value of the independent variable such as the treatment group and the control group. An examination of the crosstabulated data might help you begin to explore and understand whether the independent variable had an effect on the dependent variable.

3.10. A histogram is a graph that depicts the frequencies or percentages of individual scores, or grouped scores in class intervals, by the length of its bars. The scale of measurement on the vertical axis, the *y*-axis, is the frequency or percentage of scores. The scale of measurement on the horizontal axis, the *x*-axis, is the range of scores for the variable under consideration.

3.11. A bar graph is a graph that is used to illustrate data when the scale of measurement is nominal.

3.12. A pie chart is a circle divided into sectors that represent the proportionate frequency or percentage frequency of the class intervals.

3.13. A frequency polygon, also known as a *frequency curve* or *line graph*, is another means to depict a frequency distribution for individual or grouped scores. For the frequency polygon, assume that the scores in the class interval can be represented by the midpoint. For each interval, plot the frequency of scores at the midpoint and then connect the midpoints with straight lines. A cumulative frequency polygon may also be used to illustrate a cumulative frequency distribution for both individual and grouped scores. A cumulative frequency polygon is also known as an *ogive*. Line graphs may also be used to illustrate percentage and cumulative percentages for both individual and grouped data.

3.14. A stem-and-leaf plot (Tukey, 1977) is a means of visual display that allows for exploration of the data and its distribution while retaining the information of the original scores.

3.15. A box-and-whisker plot (Tukey, 1977) is a display that represents information about central tendency, dispersion, and the shape of a distribution all in a single, visual form. The "box" in a box-and-whisker plot refers to the rectangular portion of the display. The lower horizontal line of the box represents Q_1, the first interquartile, or the 25th percentile of the scores. The upper horizontal line of the box represents Q_3, the third interquartile, or the 75th percentile of the scores. When there is little overall variability in the scores, the height of the box will be small. When there is a great deal of overall variability in the scores, the height of the box will be large.

Section 2: Numerical

3.16.

Data	Sorted	Popular Method	Mathematical Method
5	7	5	5.0
6	6	4	4.0
4	5	2	2.5
7	5	2	2.5
5	4	1	1.0
		Sum = 14	Sum = 15

The two methods usually produce a different sum of the ranks. The mathematical method will always produce a sum that is equal to the sum of the ordered positions. The popular method will produce a sum that is less than the sum of the ordered positions.

3.17. $P_{20} = 55$, $P_{40} = 62$, $P_{60} = 64$, $P_{80} = 68$

3.18. $PR_{64} = 15$, $PR_{70} = 85$

3.19. $Q_1 = 56$, $Q_3 = 66$

3.20.

Class Interval	Frequency	Cumulative Frequency	Percent	Cumulative Percent
45–49	3	3	15	15
50–54	0	3	0	15
55–59	3	6	15	30
60–64	6	12	30	60
65–69	4	16	20	80
70–74	1	17	5	85
75–79	3	20	15	100

3.21.

Class Interval	Frequency	Cumulative Frequency	Percent	Cumulative Percent
44.5–49.5	3	3	15	15
49.5–54.5	0	3	0	15
54.5–59.5	3	6	15	30
59.5–64.5	6	12	30	60
64.5–69.5	4	16	20	80
69.5–74.5	1	17	5	85
74.5–79.5	3	20	15	100

$$Q_1 = 54.5 + \left(\frac{(20 \times .25) - 3}{3}\right)5 = 54.5 + 3.33 = 57.83$$

$$Q_3 = 64.5 + \left(\frac{(20 \times .75) - 12}{4}\right)5 = 64.5 + 3.75 = 68.25$$

$$PR_{70} = \left(\frac{12 + \left[\frac{(70 - 64.5)}{5}\right]4}{20}\right)100 = 82$$

3.22.

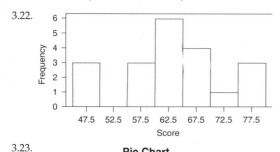

3.23.

Pie Chart

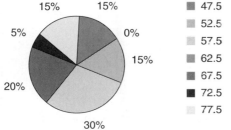

3.24.

Frequency Polygon

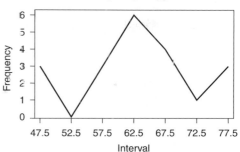

Cumulative Frequency Polygon

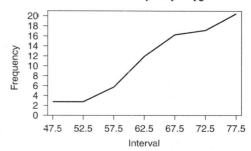

3.25.

Stem	Leaf	Frequency
4	789	3
5	569	3
6	1233445668	10
7	0779	4

3.26.

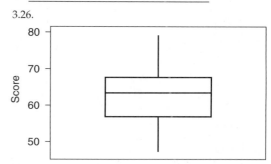

3.27.

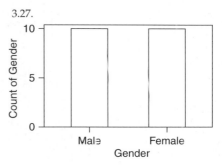

CHAPTER 4

Section 1: Conceptual/Definition

4.1. The *mean* is the arithmetic average of all the scores in a distribution. It is computed by adding together all the scores in the set and then dividing by N, the total number of scores. The *mode* is the most frequently occurring score in a set or distribution of scores. The *median* is the score that divides a distribution of scores exactly in half when the numerical values are arranged in order.

4.2. A *deviation about the mean* is an original score from a distribution of scores minus the mean score of that distribution. Each score in a distribution of scores will have an associated *deviation about the mean*. The sum of the deviations about the mean for a distribution must equal zero.

4.3. The mode is the most frequently occurring score in a set or distribution of scores. Unlike the mean, it is possible for a distribution to have more than one mode, or not to have a mode at all.

4.4. The mode is generally regarded as the easiest measure of central tendency to compute, and the mean is the most difficult. The mode has meaning for all scales of measurement. The mean and median have no real interpretation for nominal variables. The mode does not always produce a unique value as does the mean and median. The mode and median are not especially sensitive to extreme scores. The mean is the most dependable and stable measure of central tendency. It is, however, not useful for nominal or ordinal variables and is sensitive to extreme values.

4.5. When the mean and median do not result in the same value, the distribution of scores from which they are calculated is skewed. When the mean is less than the median, the distribution of scores will be negatively skewed. When the mean is greater than the median, the distribution of scores is positively skewed.

4.6. *Kurtosis* describes the extent to which a frequency distribution of scores is bunched around the center or spread toward the endpoints. The more the scores are bunched around the center, the less variability exists in the distribution and the distribution appears peaked. The more the scores are spread toward the endpoints, the more variability exists in the distribution and the distribution appears flat. A frequency distribution with bunched scores that give the appearance of peakedness is called *leptokurtic*. A frequency distribution with widely spread scores that give the appearance of flatness is called *platykurtic*. A frequency distribution with scores which are neither bunched or widely spread and that does not appear either peaked or flat is called *mesokurtic*.

4.7. Measures of central tendency are like balance points. They describe what is typical in a distribution of scores. Measures of dispersion describe the extent to which the scores in a distribution of scores vary from one another. Both measures of central tendency and measures of dispersion are required in order to understand the nature of a distribution of scores.

4.8. The *range* is the difference between the highest and lowest scores in a distribution of scores. Only the highest and lowest score is taken into account in the calculation of the range. The *variance* is the average squared deviation from the mean for a distribution of scores. Every score in the distribution is taken into account in the calculation of the variance. The *standard deviation* is simply the square root of the variance.

4.9. Division by the total number of scores (N) is the correct computational procedure when your intention is only to describe the dispersion in the set of scores with which you are presented. In other words, divide by N when you are not interested in making an inference from this set of scores, or sample, to a larger group, or population. When the variance and standard deviation are used strictly as a descriptive tool, division by N is proper. However, there are many times when one is interested in using the sample data set to make an inference or best guess about a much larger dataset or population. Under such circumstances $N-1$ should be used.

4.10. Average deviation (AD) is the first moment about the mean:

$$AD = \frac{\sum (Y - \bar{Y})}{N} = 0$$

Variance (S^2) is the second moment about the mean:

$$S^2 = \frac{\sum (Y_i - \bar{Y})^2}{N}$$

Skewness (S^3) is the third moment about the mean:

$$S^3 = \frac{\sum (Y_i - \bar{Y})^3}{N}$$

Kurtosis (S^4) is the fourth moment about the mean:

$$S^4 = \frac{\sum (Y_i - \bar{Y})^4}{N}$$

Section 2   Numerical

4.11. Mean $= 14$ Mode $= 14$ Median $= 14$

4.12. The distribution of scores is symmetric, because the mean, mode and median have the same value.

4.13.
$12 - 14 = -2$	$14 - 14 = 0$
$18 - 14 = 4$	$10 - 14 = -4$
$14 - 14 = 0$	$12 - 14 = -2$
$16 - 14 = 2$	$14 - 14 = 0$
$16 - 14 = 2$	Sum $= 0$

4.14. Range $= 18$ Variance $= 21.52$

Standard Deviation $= 4.64$

4.15.
Score	$(Y_i - \bar{Y})$	$(Y_i - \bar{Y})^2$	$(Y_i - \bar{Y})^3$	$(Y_i - \bar{Y})^4$
75	-3	9	-27	81
80	2	4	8	16
76	-2	4	-8	16
79	1	1	1	1
84	6	36	216	1296
69	-9	81	-729	6561
87	9	81	729	6561
81	3	9	27	81
76	-2	4	-8	16
78	0	0	0	0
80	2	4	8	16
82	4	16	64	256
77	-1	1	-1	1
72	-6	36	-216	1296
74	-4	16	-64	256
	$\sum = 0$	$\sum = 302$	$\sum = 0$	$\sum = 16454$

$$AD = \frac{\sum (Y - \overline{Y})}{N} = \frac{0}{15} = 0$$

$$S^2 = \frac{\sum (Y_i - \overline{Y})^2}{N} = \frac{302}{15} = 20.13$$

$$S^3 = \frac{\sum (Y_i - \overline{Y})^3}{N} = \frac{0}{16} = 0$$

$$S^4 = \frac{\sum (Y_i - \overline{Y})^4}{N} = \frac{16454}{15} = 1096.93$$

4.16. Mean = 9.25   Standard deviation = 1.803

4.17.

−1.25	−1.25	0.75	3.75	−2.25
−2.25	−0.25	−3.25	−0.25	−1.25
−0.25	2.75	−1.23	0.75	0.75
0.75	1.75	−0.25	2.75	−0.25
				$\sum = 0$

4.18. Group 1   Mean = 11.33
Standard Deviation = 1.581

Group 2   Mean = 7.25
Standard Deviation = 1.035

4.19. Mean = 9.412   Standard Deviation = 2.476

4.20. By adding all the scores together and dividing by N, you are calculating a weighted mean. You could have added the two means together and divided by 2 to produce a new unweighted mean of 9.29. The choice of weighted versus unweighted mean depends on the purpose to which the data are to be used. When one wishes the mean to represent all the individual scores equally, a weighted mean is the most appropriate choice. If, however, one wishes the mean to represent all the group scores equally, then an unweighted mean is the most appropriate choice.

CHAPTER 5

Section 1   Conceptual/Definition

5.1. *Descriptive statistics*, like the mean and standard deviation, numerically summarize the important characteristics of a distribution of scores. Descriptive statistics help you to understand the information contained in a large dataset. *Inferential statistics*, like the *t*-test and *F*-test, allow people to make inferences, or best guesses, about population parameters from sample values. Inferences are made about a population based upon results obtained from a sample selected from that population.

5.2. A subjective approach to probability is one in which intuition is used to determine the likelihood of events. In most situations, these best guesses about the likelihood of events are accurate and adaptive. An empirical approach to the probability of events would use far more careful and rigorous means than one applies in everyday life when one generates subjective probabilities of events. Some social scientists would attempt to estimate these probabilities via experimental methods using carefully controlled laboratory settings. Other social scientists would attempt to estimate these probabilities via correlational methods using naturalistic, unobtrusive settings. The objective approach to probability takes advantage of mathematical rules in order to determine the likelihood with which specific events will occur under known conditions.

5.3. The combination of the empirical and objective approaches lies at the core of inferential statistics. By comparing the evidence obtained from scientific observation with the mathematical probabilities associated with certain patterns of findings, one is are able to make an educated guess as to the likelihood or probability that her or his empirical findings occurred only as a function of chance.

5.4. Inferential statistics are never needed when the research conducted measures the entire population of interest. It is only when the entire population cannot be measured but only a sample is measured that inferential statistics are necessary.

5.5. *Error variability* is variability that cannot be explained. It can also be thought of as variability that occurs by chance or by random fluctuation.

5.6. When you ask about the outcome of a single event (e.g., the next toss of a coin), you are concerned about the outcome of a single independent event. In contrast, when you ask about a particular pattern of outcomes (e.g., several tosses of a coin), you are concerned about the multiple outcomes of several independent events. In other words, a single outcome is the result of a single action. A multiple outcome is result of a series of actions.

5.7. The single most important distribution in inferential statistics is the normal distribution, (also referred to as the *bell-shaped distribution*).

5.8. *Binomial* loosely means "two names." We use it here to refer to a variable that at any one time (trial) can take two, and only two, discrete values. The most famous example of the binomial distribution involves coin tosses and their associated probabilities.

5.9. The normal distribution is actually a family of distributions. Each distribution can have a different mean and standard deviation but the areas under the curve are always the same.

5.10. The *binomial distribution* is used for a variable with only two discrete values, whereas the normal distribution is used for variables with continuous (i.e., infinite) values.

5.11. (1) The normal distribution is symmetric about the mean. The left half of the distribution is a mirror image of the right half.

(2) Fifty percent of the values or scores fall at or below the mean, and 50% of the cases fall at or above the mean.

(3) The most likely outcome is represented by values in the center of the distribution (i.e., the mean), and the least likely outcomes are away from the center in the tails of the distribution.

(4) The normal distribution is actually a family of distributions. Each distribution can have a different mean and standard deviation but the areas under the curve are *always* the same.

(5) The normal distribution is unimodal and not skewed. Therefore, the mean, median, and mode of the normal distribution are the same value.

5.12. The area from one end, or tail, of the normal distribution to the mean, or midpoint, includes 50% of the cases or values.

$\overline{Y} \pm 1s = 68.26\%$, $\overline{Y} + 1s = 84.13\%$ile,
$\overline{Y} - 1s = 15.87\%$ile, $\overline{Y} \pm 1.96s = 95.00\%$,
$\overline{Y} + 1.96s = 97.50\%$ile, $\overline{Y} - 1.96s = 2.50\%$ile,
$\overline{Y} \pm 2.57s = 99.00\%$ile, $\overline{Y} + 2.57s = 99.50\%$ile,
$\overline{Y} - 2.57s = .50\%$ile.

5.13. *Standardizing a variable* means converting it to a new variable that has a mean of zero and a standard deviation of 1. The conversion is accomplished through the formula:

$$z_i = \frac{Y_i - \overline{Y}}{s}$$

5.14. Raw scores, when presented without their mean and standard deviation, contain less information than standardized scores (which are constructed around a particular mean and standard deviation).

5.15. In a normal distribution, percentiles are not on an interval scale of measurement. In contrast, standard scores are on an interval scale of measurement. In other words, percentiles are concentrated around the center of the normal distribution and spread around the tails of the distribution. Standard scores are neither concentrated nor spread.

5.16. All *T*-scores are raw scores converted to have any mean and any standard deviation, although they are most frequently used to have a mean of 50.00 and standard deviation of 10.00. The formula for conversion is

$$T_i = \overline{Y}_T + \frac{s_T(Y_i - \overline{Y})}{s}$$

where: $\overline{Y}_T$ is the transformed or desired mean

s_T is the transformed or desired standard deviation.

Section 2 Numerical

5.17. The formula is as follows:

$$P = \frac{7!}{(4!)(7-4)!} = .2734$$

There is a 27.34% probability of getting 4 heads when a coin is tossed 7 times.

5.18. The formula is as follows:

$$P = \frac{7!}{(5!)(7-5)!} = .1641$$

There is a 16.41% probability of getting 5 heads when a coin is tossed 7 times.

5.19. A score of 83 is the mean +1 standard deviation. You know that $\overline{Y} \pm 1s = 68.26\%$. From this you know that 31.74% $(1 - .6826 = .3174)$ of the scores will lie outside this range. Since the normal distribution is symmetrical, you can further conclude that one half of 31.74%, or 15.87%, of the exam scores will be above 83.

5.20. A score of 59 is the mean − 2 standard deviations. You know that $\overline{Y} \pm 2s$ is approximately 95%. From this, you know that 5% $(1 - .95 = .05)$ of the scores will lie outside this range. Since the normal distribution is symmetrical, you can further conclude that approximately one-half of 5%, or 2.5%, of the exam scores will be below 59.

5.21. Conversion to a z-score is as follows:

$$z_i = \frac{102 - 120}{12} = -1.5$$

The area between the mean and a z-score of −1.5 is .4332. When the positive half of the distribution is taken into account, this means that 93.32% of the observations are above 102. This represents 46.67 observations.

5.22. An area beyond z of .005 is associated with a z-score of −2.57 (from the table). To determine the actual observation associated with a z-score of 2.57, you can use the z-score formula:

$$-2.57 = \frac{Y - 120}{12}$$

In solving for Y, you find that .5% of observations will fall below 89.16.

5.23. $t_i = 50 + \frac{10(130 - 120)}{12} = 58.33$

5.24. $z_i = \frac{40 - 38}{8} = .25$. The area beyond z associated with a z-score of .25 is .4013. This means that 40.13% of the schools will have a dropout rate higher than 40%. Given 30 schools in the sample, this percentage corresponds to approximately 12 schools.

5.25. $z_i = \frac{50 - 38}{7} = 1.5$. The area beyond z associated with a z-score of 1.5 is .0668. This means that 6.68% of the schools will have a dropout rate higher than 50%. Given 30 schools in the sample, it is expected that approximately 2 schools will have to be investigated.

5.26. $z_i = \frac{25 - 38}{8} = -1.625$. The area beyond z associated with a z-score of −1.625 is .0526. This means that 5.26% of the schools will have a dropout rate lower than 25%. Given 30 schools in the sample, it is expected that approximately 2 schools will receive special recognition.

CHAPTER 6

Section 1 Conceptual/Definition

6.1. Yes, one can draw an incorrect conclusion. In making any inference about the population from a sample, one merely takes a best guess; there is always some likelihood that a best guess or inference is wrong. Inferential statistics allow you to make best guesses only based on the chance probability associated with the sample data. No matter your inference, there is always some likelihood that your guess is wrong and that you have made an incorrect generalization about population parameters from sample values.

6.2. No, statistical results do not guarantee meaningful results. Both sound research methodologies and statistical analyses are required to achieve meaningful results.

6.3. *Inferential statistics* is concerned with the procedures for taking sample findings and making generalizations to populations. To ensure they are distinguished from sample statistics, population parameters are represented by Greek symbols.

6.4. A *population*, or universe, is the entire group of persons, events, or objects having at least one trait in common. A *population parameter* is any measure obtained by having observed or recorded the entire population.

6.5. A *sample* is a subset of the population of interest. It is a smaller number of objects, events, or people taken from the total number making up the population. A *sample statistic* is any measure obtained by having observed or recorded some sample from the population of interest.

6.6. A *random sample* is one in which each individual or case in the defined population of interest has an equally likely chance of being included in the sample selected. A *convenience sample* is a sample selected based on availability or ease. Generalizeability is far better with random samples than with convenience samples.

6.7. Using random assignment of participants to treatment conditions (e.g., experimental and control groups) helps ensure that prior to the introduction of the treatment, the participants in the groups varied only as a function of chance. That is, random assignment helps ensure the initial equivalence of the groups at the beginning of research. Random assignment helps prevent selection bias and contributes to the internal validity of the investigation.

6.8. In point estimation, the value of a sample statistic, or point, such as the sample mean, is used to estimate, or infer, the value of a population parameter, such as the population mean. In interval estimation, the sample statistic, in combination with an estimate of how much error or imprecision might be associated with this estimate, is used to form a range of values or confidence interval.

6.9. A sampling distribution is a distribution of sample statistics, such as a collection of means, variances, or standard deviations, taken from the population of interest. Not all sample statistics yield the same value; therefore, sampling error is the extent to which a sample statistic is discrepant from the corresponding population parameter.

6.10. Maximum likelihood: The principle of maximum likelihood says that when one is faced with a choice of several population parameter values, the best choice is that value that makes the sample value have the highest probability among the possible population parameter values.

Unbiased: An unbiased estimator exists when it neither consistently overestimates nor consistently underestimates population parameter values.

Consistency: A consistent estimator is one that more closely approximates the value of the population parameter as sample size increases.

Relative efficiency: A relatively efficient estimator is one that has a small sampling error or confidence interval.

Sufficiency: A sufficient estimator is one that contains all the information about the population; estimation cannot be improved by considering any other aspect of the data.

6.11. If a population has a variance σ^2 and a mean μ, the distribution of sample means from samples of N independent observations approaches the form of a normal distribution, with variance σ^2/N and mean μ, as sample size N increases. The mean of the sampling distribution of means is the same as the population mean. The variance of the sampling distribution of means for samples of the same size is always the population variance divided by the sample size (which is the same for each sample). As sample size increases, the shape of the sampling distribution of means more closely approximates a normal distribution regardless of the shape of the population from which the samples were drawn.

6.12. So long as sample size is large, the sampling distribution is shaped like a normal distribution regardless of the shape of the population from which the samples were taken.

6.13. The variance (and standard deviation) of the sampling distribution are affected by sample size. The larger the sample size, the smaller the estimated variance (and estimated standard deviation) of the sampling distribution.

6.14. It is important to highlight the distinction between the standard deviation, s, and the standard error, s_M. The standard deviation, s, estimates the average distance between individual scores and the population mean. The standard error, s_M, estimates the average distance between sample statistics and the population mean of those statistics. The standard deviation, s, provides an estimate of variability for the individual scores in the population while the standard error, s_M, provides a measure of variability for the sample statistics drawn from the population.

6.15. A confidence interval is a range of values around a point estimate that defines a certain percentage or probability that the population parameter is within that range of values.

6.16. An alpha (α) level defines the probability of making an error in rejecting the null hypothesis. This is a subjective probability that is determined by the researcher at the outset of the research process. A p-value is an observed probability. It is a statement regarding the possibility of obtaining results through chance factors.

6.17. A critical value is the value of a statistic (i.e., parameter estimate) that the calculated value must need to exceed if one is to reject the null hypothesis.

Section 2   Numerical

6.18. $\bar{Y} = \dfrac{\sum Y_i}{N} = 26.1$ $s^2 = \dfrac{\sum (Y_i - \bar{Y})^2}{N-1} = 20.34$

$s = \sqrt{\dfrac{\sum (Y_i - \bar{Y})^2}{N-1}} = 4.51$

6.19. $s_M = \dfrac{s}{\sqrt{N}} = \dfrac{4.51}{\sqrt{10}} = 1.426$

6.20. $\bar{Y} \pm 1.96 s_M = 26.1 \pm 1.96\,(1.426) = 23.3 \leq \mu \leq 28.9$

6.21. $\bar{Y} = \dfrac{\sum Y}{N} = 38.8$ $s^2 = \dfrac{\sum (Y_i - \bar{Y})^2}{N-1} = 14.36$

$s = \sqrt{\dfrac{\sum (Y_i - \bar{Y})^2}{N-1}} = 3.79$

6.22. $s_M = \dfrac{s}{\sqrt{N}} = \dfrac{3.79}{\sqrt{10}} = 1.2$

6.23. $\bar{Y} \pm 1.96 s_M = 38.8 \pm 1.96\,(1.2) = 36.49 \leq \mu \leq 41.15$

6.24. Control: $\bar{Y} = \dfrac{\sum Y_i}{N} = 26.6$

$s^2 = \dfrac{\sum (Y_i - \bar{Y})^2}{N-1} = 11.29$

$s = \sqrt{\dfrac{\sum (Y_i - \bar{Y})^2}{N-1}} = 3.36$

Experimental: $\bar{Y} = \dfrac{\sum Y_i}{N} = 33.2$

$s^2 = \dfrac{\sum (Y_i - \bar{Y})^2}{N-1} = 10.18$

$s = \sqrt{\dfrac{\sum (Y_i - \bar{Y})^2}{N-1}} = 3.19$

6.25. Control: $s_M = \frac{s}{\sqrt{N}} = \frac{3.36}{\sqrt{5}} = 1.5$

Experimental: $s_M = \frac{s}{\sqrt{N}} = \frac{3.19}{5} = 1.43$

6.26. Control:
$\overline{Y} \pm 1.96 s_M = 26.6 \pm 1.96(1.5) = 23.66 \le \mu \le 29.54$

Experimental:
$\overline{Y} \pm 1.96 s_M = 33.2 \pm 1.96(1.43) = 30.4 \le \mu \le 36.0$

6.27. $s_D = \sqrt{\frac{s_{A1}^2}{n_{A1}} + \frac{s_{A2}^2}{n_{A2}}} = \sqrt{\frac{11.29}{5} + \frac{10.18}{5}} = 2.07$

$z_D = \frac{\overline{Y}_{A1} - \overline{Y}_{A2}}{s_D} = \frac{26.6 - 33.2}{2.07} = -3.19$

Since the calculated value (-3.19) is greater than the critical value (± 1.96), reject the null hypothesis and accept the alternative hypothesis. The means of the control and experimental groups are significantly different from one another.

CHAPTER 7

Section 1 Conceptual/Definition

7.1. State the null and alternative hypotheses.

Select the probability value for significance testing.

Select the appropriate test statistic.

Compute the calculated value of the test statistic.

Find the critical value of the test statistic.

Compare the calculated and critical values in order to make a decision about the null and alternative hypotheses.

7.2. A statistical hypothesis is a statement about the parameters of one or more population distributions. Scientific hypotheses are usually statements about phenomena and their underlying bases. Statistical hypotheses, on the other hand, are usually descriptions of population characteristics without explanation of why populations have these characteristics.

7.3. When the procedure of falsification is used, failing to reject the null hypothesis is not proof that the null hypothesis is correct. Although there may be insufficient or inconclusive evidence in support of the alternative hypothesis, one cannot use the lack of evidence as support for the null hypothesis.

7.4. A directional alternative hypothesis specifies the form of disagreement with the null hypothesis. For example, a directional alternative hypothesis may specify the direction of inequivalence of population parameters (e.g., $H_a: \mu_{A1} > \mu_{A2}$). Directional alternative hypotheses are also referred to as *one-tailed hypotheses;* nondirectional alternative hypotheses are also referred to as *two-tailed hypotheses.* The selection of directional or nondirectional alternative hypothesis affects the critical value used for significance testing. Directional alternative hypotheses will usually result in a critical value that is smaller than what would be obtained using a nondirectional hypothesis. As a result, a smaller calculated value is required to reject the null hypothesis.

7.5. A Type I error occurs when the null hypothesis is rejected but it is true.

A Type II error occurs when the null hypothesis is not rejected but it is false.

7.6. Beta (β) is the probability of making a Type II error or failing to reject the null hypothesis when it is false. The power of a statistical test is the probability of rejecting the null hypothesis when it is false. They are related in that power can be defined as $1 - \beta$.

7.7. The level of significance or alpha (α).

The size of the sample.

The size of within-groups variability.

The size of the expected (or actual) treatment effect.

Whether directional or nondirectional hypotheses are specified.

7.8. No, the null and alternative hypotheses do not have the same sampling distribution. It is easy to understand the sampling distribution for the null hypothesis. However, there is a sampling distribution under the alternative hypothesis that has an overall mean difference not equal to zero and a standard error.

7.9. The most critical step is in guessing the expected population mean difference for the alternative sampling distribution. This must be done carefully since guessing too small a mean difference artificially decreases the estimated power of the test, while guessing too large a mean difference artificially increases the estimated power of the test.

7.10. The calculated value of a statistic is compared with the critical value in order to make a decision about the null and alternative hypotheses. If the calculated value exceeds the critical value, reject the null hypothesis and accept the alternative hypothesis.

7.11. Effect size is a useful index of the strength of a treatment effect. It allows for ready comparison across contexts or multiple research findings where different measurement methods may be employed and differences in the degree of chance or unexplained variability may be operative. It can be computed using the following formula:

$$d = \frac{\overline{Y}_{A1} - \overline{Y}_{A2}}{s}$$

Section 2 Numerical

7.12. The critical value of z for a nondirectional test at $\alpha = .05$ is ± 1.96. For a directional test using the same level of alpha, the critical value is ± 1.65.

7.13. A critical value of z of ± 1.65 results in a larger region of rejection than a critical value of ± 1.96.

7.14. Type I error occurs when the null hypothesis is rejected but it is true. As alpha is increased from .05 to .10, Type I error also increases, as there is a greater chance of rejecting the null hypothesis when it is true.

7.15. Beta (β) is the probability of making a Type II error or failing to reject the null hypothesis when it is false. As alpha is increased from .05 to .10, beta (β) will decrease, as there is a greater chance of rejecting the null hypothesis when it is false.

7.16. $z_D = \dfrac{\overline{Y}_{A1} - \overline{Y}_{A2}}{\sqrt{\dfrac{s_{A1}^2}{n_{A1}} + \dfrac{s_{A2}^2}{n_{A2}}}}$

In examining the formula above, the within-groups variability is represented by group variances (s^2). As the variance increases, so does the denominator of z_D. This in turn decreases the value of z_D, which decreases the probability of rejecting the null hypothesis when it is wrong. This means that Type II error is increased.

7.17. $s_D = \sqrt{\dfrac{s_{A1}^2}{n_{A1}} + \dfrac{s_{A2}^2}{n_{A2}}} = \sqrt{\dfrac{5.29}{5} + \dfrac{6.5}{5}} = 1.54$

$z_D = \dfrac{\overline{Y}_{A1} - \overline{Y}_{A2}}{s_D} = \dfrac{14.4 - 18}{1.54} = -2.34$

Since the calculated value (-2.34) is greater than the critical value (± 1.96), one rejects the null hypothesis and accepts the alternative hypothesis. The means of the control and experimental groups are significantly different from one another.

7.18. $\overline{Y}_D \pm z_{1-a/2} s_D = (14.4 - 18) \pm 1.96\,(1.54)$

$\qquad\qquad\qquad = -6.62 \le \mu_D \le -.58$

7.19. $\overline{Y}_D + z_{1-a} s_D = (14.4 - 18) + 1.65\,(1.54)$

$\qquad\qquad\qquad = -3.6 \le \mu_D \le -1.06$

7.20. $d = \dfrac{\overline{Y}_{A1} - \overline{Y}_{A2}}{s} = \dfrac{14.4 - 18}{(2.3 + 2.55)/2} = -1.48$

7.21. $\overline{Y}_{DA} = +3.6$, $s_{DA} = 1.54$

$\mathrm{CV}_R = +z_{1-a}(s_D) = +1.65\,(1.54) = +2.54$

$z_A = [\mathrm{CV}_R - \overline{Y}_{DA}]/s_D = (+2.54 - 3.6)/1.54 = -.69$

$\beta = p\,(z_A = .69) = .50 + .2549 = .7549$

$1 - \beta = .2451.$

CHAPTER 8

Section 1   Conceptual/Definition

8.1. As sample size decreases, the shape of the population sampling distribution deviates from the shape of the standard normal distribution. The smaller the sample size, the less the standard normal distribution represents the actual shape of the population sampling distribution.

8.2. $t = \dfrac{\overline{Y}_{A1} - \overline{Y}_{A2}}{\sqrt{\dfrac{s_{A1}^2}{n_{A1}} + \dfrac{s_{A2}^2}{n_{A2}}}}$

In the denominator of the calculated value for the separate variance model t-test, the variance for each group is computed separately and then combined. The formula for the separate variance model t-test is exactly the same as the z-test for the difference between two means.

8.3. The z-test uses the normal distribution to determine critical values. The t-test uses the t-distribution to determine critical values. For sample sizes above 30, both t and z will have very similar critical values. However for sample sizes below 30, the critical value of t will be higher than the critical value of z.

8.4. In statistics, *degrees of freedom,* usually abbreviated as df or v (Greek nu), refers to the number of scores whose values are free to vary. The term comes from the physical sciences, where it refers to the number of planes or directions in which an object is free to move

8.5. To determine the critical value of t, one needs the following information: The degrees of freedom as calculated by the formula df $= (n_1 - 1) + (n_2 - 1) = (n_1 - n_2) - 2 = N - 2$; whether the alternative hypothesis is one-tailed or two-tailed; the α (alpha), or probability value for significance testing.

8.6. The assumption of homogeneity of variance must be met in order to use the pooled variance model t-test.

8.7. The advantage of using the pooled variance model t-test is that the standard error tends to be smaller in size than when the separate variance model is used. This results in a larger calculated value of t, which in turn increases the probability of rejecting the null hypothesis.

8.8. The pooled and separate models produce the same calculated value of t when the sample size of the two groups is the same and/or when the variances of the two groups are identical.

8.9. The following assumptions underlie the use of the t-test: Each data point, or score, should be independent of every other data point; the variability, s, within each group should be normally distributed; the variances of the two groups should be equal, or homogeneous.

8.10. A simple procedure, F_{max}, exists for evaluation of homogeneity of variance. It is calculated as

$$F_{max} = \dfrac{s_{largest}^2}{s_{smallest}^2}$$

If the ratio is larger than 3.0, the homogeneity of variance assumption is not met. Two other procedures exist for determining variance heterogeneity that generally require the use of statistical software: Levene's test and Bartlett's test.

Section 2   Numerical

8.11. df $= (n_1 - 1) + (n_2 - 1) = 7 + 7 = 14$

The critical value of t for 14 degrees of freedom at $\alpha = .05 = 2.145$

8.12. df $= [(n_1 - 1) + (n_2 - 1)]/2 = (7 + 7)/2 = 7$

The critical value of t for 7 degrees of freedom at $\alpha = .05 = 2.365$

8.13. $F_{max} = \dfrac{s_{largest}^2}{s_{smallest}^2} = \dfrac{10.96}{5.81} = 1.88$

Since $F_{max} < 3.0$, there is insufficient evidence to conclude that homogeneity of variance has been violated.

8.14. $t = \dfrac{\overline{Y}_{A1} - \overline{Y}_{A2}}{\sqrt{\dfrac{s_p^2}{n_{A1}} + \dfrac{s_p^2}{n_{A2}}}} = \dfrac{27.17 - 39.14}{\sqrt{\dfrac{2.86^2}{6} + \dfrac{2.86^2}{7}}}$

$\qquad = \dfrac{-11.97}{1.59} = -7.52$

The critical value for this test is 2.201 (11 df). Since the absolute value of t is greater than the critical value, one can conclude that the means of the two groups are significantly different

8.15. $s_D = \sqrt{\dfrac{s_{A1}^2}{n_{A1}} + \dfrac{s_{A2}^2}{n_{A2}}} = \sqrt{\dfrac{10.96}{6} + \dfrac{5.8}{7}} = 1.63$

$t = \dfrac{\overline{Y}_{A1} - \overline{Y}_{A2}}{s_D} = \dfrac{27.17 - 39.14}{1.63} = -7.34$

Since the absolute value of t (7.34) is greater than the one-tailed critical value (± 1.796), one rejects the null hypothesis and accepts the alternative hypothesis. The mean of the experimental group is significantly higher than that of the control group.

8.16. $\overline{Y}_D \pm t_{1-\alpha/2} s_D = (27.17 - 39.14) \pm 2.201\,(1.59)$

$= -15.47 \leq \mu_D \leq -8.47$

8.17. $\overline{Y}_D \pm t_{1-\alpha/2} s_D = (27.17 - 39.14) + 1.796\,(1.59)$

$= -11.97 \leq \mu_D \leq -9.11$

8.18. $d = \dfrac{\overline{Y}_{A1} - \overline{Y}_{A2}}{s} = \dfrac{27.17 - 39.14}{\dfrac{(3.31 + 2.41)}{2}} = -4.18$

8.19. $\text{CI} = \overline{Y}_D \pm t_{.95} s_D$

$= (12.33 - 17.50) \pm 2.23 \left(\sqrt{\dfrac{s_p^2}{n_{A1}} + \dfrac{s_p^2}{n_{A2}}} \right)$

$= (12.33 - 17.50) \pm 2.23 \left(\sqrt{\dfrac{4.50}{6} + \dfrac{4.50}{6}} \right)$

$= -7.9 \leq \mu_D \leq -2.24$

8.20. $F_{max} = \dfrac{s_{largest}^2}{s_{smallest}^2} = \dfrac{5.48}{3.5} = 1.57$

Since $F_{max} < 3.0$ there is insufficient evidence to conclude that homogeneity of variance has been violated.

CHAPTER 9

Section 1   Conceptual/Definition

9.1. The levels of a qualitative independent variable differ in kind. The levels of a quantitative variable differ in amount.

9.2. The F-test allows for the simultaneous testing of more than two levels of an independent variable whereas a t-test can test only two levels of an independent variable. Since the F-distribution contains only positive values, there is only one possible alternative hypothesis for an F-test. The t-distribution, which has both positive and negative values, can have both nondirectional and directional alternative hypotheses. The F-test is an omnibus test that answers the general question about the overall effect of the independent variable. The t-test is a more specific test that answers a direct question about two levels of an independent variable.

9.3. There can be a large number of comparisons to evaluate and statistical calculations to perform.

Evaluating all possible comparisons between groups requires that the same data be used repeatedly, which results in statistical redundancy.

Doing multiple t-tests, each based on only a subset of the data (i.e., only two of the groups at a time), may result in a loss in power compared to using all the data for analysis.

The likelihood of committing a Type I error somewhere in the collection of comparisons grows higher as the number of comparisons increases.

9.4. The null hypothesis is readily understandable. It says that there are no significant differences between the group means. The alternative hypothesis is harder to understand. It says that there is at least one significant difference between the group means. H_a cannot be interpreted as the treatment means are all different from one another, only that at least one difference exists in the set of means.

9.5. The term *partitioning of variability* refers to the fact that total variability in the dependent variable can be partitioned into two additive components: between-groups variability (including variability in the dependent variable, which may be attributed to or caused by fluctuations in the independent variable) and within-groups variability (including variability in the dependent variable, which may be attributable to fluctuations among the participants or chance fluctuation).

9.6. $SS_{Y(A)}$ = error variability + treatment variability. It is also known as *between-groups variability*.

$SS_{Y(S/A)}$ = error variability.

$SS_{Y(S/A)} + SS_{Y(A)}$ = total variability (SS_Y).

9.7. The *General Linear Model* is a mathematical model that may be taken to mean that any individual score (or observation) is the sum of the mean of the base population, the effects of the treatment, and random error.

9.8. It is left blank because mean squares are not additive in the same way that sums of squares are additive. The intersection of the total row and the MS column is the total variance for the dependent variable (MS_Y). It is not filled in because $MS_Y \neq MS_{Y(A)} + MS_{Y(S/A)}$.

9.9. F is a ratio of two variances. Because variances must always be positive numbers (or zero), it follows that the critical value of F cannot be a negative number. This is one way in which F is different from z and t, both of which can be negative or positive.

9.10. The following information is required to find a critical value of F:

Alpha, the probability value for significance testing.

The degrees of freedom for the numerator (df_A) which is $A - 1$, and the degrees of freedom for the denominator ($df_{S/A}$), which is $A(n - 1)$.

9.11. Sampling distributions of F are positively skewed. As such, the distributions are not symmetrical and calculating a confidence interval or using interval estimation is therefore difficult.

9.12. There are three main assumptions underlying the use of the F-test: (1) There is a normal distribution to the scores within each treatment group, which is the *assumption of normality*; (2) the scores are independent of one another, both within each treatment group as well as across the different treatment groups, which is the *assumption of independence*; (3) the scores show the same degree of variability from treatment group to treatment group, which is the *assumption of homogeneity of variance*.

Section 2 Numerical

9.13. $SS_{Y(A)} = 448.29$, $df_A = 2$, $MS_{Y(A)} = 224.15$

$SS_{Y(S/A)} = 119.71$, $df_{S/A} = 18$, $MS_{Y(S/A)} = 6.65$

$SS_Y = 568$, $df_Y = 20$, $F = 33.70$

Because the calculated value of F (33.70) is greater than the critical value of F (3.55), the null hypothesis is rejected in favor of the alternative hypothesis and it can be concluded that the means of the three treatment conditions are not all the same.

9.14. $SS_{Y(A)} = 999.3$, $df_A = 3$, $MS_{Y(A)} = 331.1$

$SS_{Y(S/A)} = 1894.9$, $df_{S/A} = 28$, $MS_{Y(S/A)} = 67.7$

$SS_Y = 2894.2$, $df_Y = 31$, $F = 4.92$

Because the calculated value of F (4.92) is greater than the critical value of F (2.90), the null hypothesis is rejected in favor of the alternative hypothesis and it can be concluded that the means of the four treatment conditions are not all the same.

9.15. The means for the three treatment groups are equal ($\mu = 6$). Because the means are all equal, there is no variability between groups and therefore $SS_{Y(A)} = 0$. It follows that $MS_{Y(A)}$ must also be equal to zero. This, in turn, will produce a calculated value of zero for F. A calculated value for F of 0 cannot be significant, and therefore there is insufficient evidence to reject the null hypothesis.

9.16. $R^2 = \dfrac{SS_{Y(A)}}{SS_Y} = \dfrac{448.29}{568.00} = 78.90\%$

$\omega^2 = \dfrac{SS_{Y(A)} - (a-1)MS_{Y(S/A)}}{SS_Y + MS_{Y(S/A)}}$

$= \dfrac{448.29 - (3.00 - 1.00)6.65}{568.00 + 6.65} = .76$

9.17. $R^2 = \dfrac{SS_{Y(A)}}{SS_Y} = \dfrac{999.30}{2894.20} = 34.50\%$

$\omega^2 = \dfrac{SS_{Y(A)} - (a-1)MS_{Y(S/A)}}{SS_Y - MS_{Y(S/A)}}$

$= \dfrac{999.30 - (4.00 - 1.00)67.70}{2894.20 + 67.70} = .27$

9.18. $f = \sqrt{\dfrac{R^2}{1 - R^2}} = \sqrt{\dfrac{.789}{1 - .789}} = 1.94$

9.19. $f = \sqrt{\dfrac{R^2}{1 - R^2}} = \sqrt{\dfrac{.345}{1.00 - .345}} = .73$

$F_S = (a-1)F(df_A, df_{S/A}) = (4-1)f(3, 24)$

$= 3(3.01) = 9.03$

9.20. $SS_{Y(A)} = 2.125$, $df_A = 3$, $MS_{Y(A)} = .708$

$SS_{Y(S/A)} = 95.5$, $df_{S/A} = 20$, $MS_{Y(S/A)} = 4.775$

$SS_Y = 97.625$, $df_Y = 23$, $F = .148$

Because the calculated value of F (.708) is less than the critical value of F (8.66), there is insufficient evidence to reject the null hypothesis.

9.21. $R^2 = \dfrac{SS_{Y(A)}}{SS_Y} = \dfrac{2.125}{97.625} = 2.18\%$

9.22. $f = \sqrt{\dfrac{R^2}{1 - R^2}} = \sqrt{\dfrac{.0218}{1.00 - .0218}} = .15$

CHAPTER 10

Section 1 Conceptual/Definition

10.1. A simple comparison (also referred to as a *pairwise comparison*) is a difference between two group means. A complex comparison is a difference between more than two group means.

10.2. Multiple comparisons are used when the researcher is able to specify, in advance, a set of more specific hypotheses than the general hypothesis. In these situations a set of planned comparisons should be used instead of the omnibus F-test. Multiple comparisons are also used when the researcher wishes to further analyze the data following the discovery of a significant F-test. The F-test indicates only that not all the treatment group means were equal. In these situations a set of post hoc comparisons should be used in addition to the omnibus F-test.

10.3. When only two groups are involved, there is nothing to differentiate an omnibus test from a comparison and they will produce equivalent results.

10.4. The following rules apply to the use of planned comparisons: (a) They must be specified in advance of data analysis; (b) they are used in place of the omnibus F-test; (c) the probability value for significance testing is based on the individual comparison and not the collection or family of comparisons; (d) the set of planned comparisons should normally be independent to avoid statistical redundancy in the analyses.

10.5. The following rules apply to the use of post hoc comparisons: (a) They are not specified in advance of data analysis; (b) The omnibus F-test must first be found to be significant; if it is not significant, no post hoc tests should be performed; (c) The probability value for significance testing is based on the collection or family of comparisons and not on the individual comparison; (d) The set of post hoc comparisons need not be independent.

10.6. A comparison is valid if the sum of the comparison weights is zero. Mathematically this can be expressed as $\sum c_A = 0.0$.

10.7. Mathematically, independence means that two vectors (representing the comparisons) occur at right angles to each other. This occurs when

$\displaystyle\sum_{1}^{A} c_{1A}c_{2A} = 0.0$. This requirement is important in

conducting planned comparisons because it allows for an entire set of comparisons to be conducted using only the information that is required to evaluate the omnibus F-test. As a result, the per-comparison alpha can be kept at the same level as would have been used to evaluate the omnibus test. It is also for this reason that planned comparisons can be used as an alternative to the omnibus F-test.

10.8. When variances are heterogeneous, the t-test and the F-test for a comparison may produce different conclusions. When variances are heterogeneous, do not use the F-test to evaluate planned comparison. Instead, use the separate variance model t-test with reduced degrees of freedom.

10.9. They are similar in that both use the same calculated value, because they share the same formula for the calculated value. They differ in that: (a) planned comparisons must be specified in advance of data collection; (b) they result in different critical values (the critical value for planned comparisons is lower than for post hoc comparisons); (c) planned comparisons must be independent.

10.10. No. Conducting multiple tests of this sort is an unacceptable form of data snooping. If you wish only to conduct pairwise comparisons and cell sizes are equal, you can use Tukey's HSD. If you wish to conduct both simple and complex comparisons, or if cell sizes are unequal, use only the Scheffé S method.

Section 2 Numerical

10.11. Six tests would be required (A_1–A_2, A_1–A_3, A_1–A_4, A_2–A_3, A_2–A_4, A_3–A_4). The effective rate of α could be calculated as follows: $1 - (1 - \alpha)^c = 1 - (1 - .05)^6 = .265$.

10.12. Three tests would be required (A_1–A_2, A_1–A_3, A_2–A_3). The effective rate of α could be calculated as follows: $1 - (1 - \alpha)^c = 1 - (1 - .05)^3 = .143$

10.13. $1 - (1 - \alpha)^5 = .05$. The per-comparison alpha would be .01

10.14. $1 - (1 - \alpha)^2 = .05$. The per-comparison alpha would be .025

10.15. $F_T = \dfrac{(q_T)^2}{2} = \dfrac{(3.61)^2}{2} = 6.52$

A_1 vs. A_2
$F_{ph1} = MS_{Y(ph1)}/MS_{y(S/A)} = 185.8/6.65 = 27.94$
therefore reject H_0

A_1 vs. A_3
$F_{ph2} = MS_{Y(ph2)}/MS_{y(S/A)} = 434.58/6.65 = 65.35$
therefore reject H_0

A_2 vs. A_3
$F_{ph3} = MS_{Y(ph3)}/MS_{y(S/A)} = 52.07/6.65 = 7.83$
therefore reject H_0

10.16. $F_T = \dfrac{(q_T)^2}{2} = \dfrac{(3.86)^2}{2} = 7.45$

A_1 vs. A_2
$F_{ph1} = MS_{Y(ph1)}/MS_{y(S/A)} = 115.56/67.67 = 1.71$
therefore fail to reject H_0

A_1 vs. A_3
$F_{ph2} = MS_{Y(ph2)}/MS_{y(S/A)} = 600.25/67.67 = 8.87$
therefore reject H_0

A_1 vs. A_4
$F_{ph3} = MS_{Y(ph3)}/MS_{y(S/A)} = 784.00/67.67 = 11.59$
therefore reject H_0

A_2 vs. A_3
$F_{ph4} = MS_{Y(ph4)}/MS_{y(S/A)} = 189.06/67.67 = 2.79$
therefore fail to reject H_0

A_2 vs. A_4
$F_{ph5} = MS_{Y(ph5)}/MS_{y(S/A)} = 297.56/67.67 = 4.40$
therefore fail to reject H_0

A_3 vs. A_4
$F_{ph6} = MS_{Y(ph6)}/MS_{y(S/A)} = 12.25/67.67 = .18$
therefore fail to reject H_0

10.17. $F_S = (A - 1)F \, (df_A, df_{S/A}) = (4 - 1)F \, (3, 28) = 8.85$

10.18. The critical value used to evaluate planned comparisons is 4.2 (df = 1,28). The maximum number of comparisons in a complete set of planned comparisons is $(a - 1)$ which is 3 in this example.

10.19. F_p, df $(1,28) = 4.2$

1, −1, 0, 0
$F_{p1} = MS_{Y(p1)}/MS_{Y(S/A)} = 115.56/67.67 = 1.71$
therefore fail to reject H_0

0, 0, 1, −1
$F_{p2} = MS_{Y(p2)}/MS_{Y(S/A)} = 12.25/67.67 = .18$
therefore fail to reject H_0

.5, .5, −.5, −.5
$F_{p3} = MS_{Y(p3)}/MS_{Y(S/A)} = 871.53/67.67 = 12.88$
therefore reject H_0

10.20. (a) $F_T = \dfrac{(q_T)^2}{2} = \dfrac{(3.86)^2}{2} = 7.45$

(b) $F_S = (A - 1)F \, (df_A, df_{S/A})$
$= (4 - 1)F \, (3, 28) = 8.85$

(c) F_p, df $(1,28) = 4.2$

(d) The maximum number of comparisons in a complete set of planned comparisons is $(a - 1)$, which is 3 in this example.

CHAPTER 11

Section 1 Conceptual/Definition

11.1. Factorial designs are used when a researcher is interested in investigating the effect of two or more independent variables (i.e., factors), each by itself and also in interaction with one another, on a dependent variable. Each independent variable must have no less than two values, or levels, which differ either quantitatively or qualitatively.

11.2. The between-groups sums of squares is partitioned into the main effect for factor A, the main effect for factor B and the interaction between factors A and B.

11.3. Three distinct omnibus hypotheses can be tested in a two-way Factorial design, one for each of the sources of between-groups variability. Therefore, there will be a hypothesis for the main effect for factor A, one for the main effect for factor B, and a third for the interaction between factors A and B.

11.4. The Factorial ANOVA model makes the same assumptions as the Oneway ANOVA model. The assumptions are as follows: there is a normal distribution to the scores within each treatment group (the assumption of normality); the scores are independent of one another both within each treatment group as well as across the different treatment groups (the assumption of independence); the scores show the same degree of variability from treatment group to treatment group (the assumption of homogeneity of variance).

11.5. When a significant interaction is found, many statisticians recommend computing tests of simple effects. A significant interaction means that the two independent variables should be considered in combination, because the effect of one independent variable changes with variation in the second independent variable. Therefore, simple effect tests explore the general effects of one independent variable at each level of another independent variable.

11.6. The two sets of simple effects that are conducted in a Twoway Factorial ANOVA are not independent. Each set has the variability due to the interaction term. In other words, conducting the two sets of simple effects in a Twoway Factorial ANOVA means that the variability attributable to the interaction of the two factors gets used twice. Simple effects analysis is therefore not an orthogonal procedure.

11.7. No, both sums of squares and their associated degrees of freedom are partitioned.

11.8. No, the error variance would be the same. Error variance is defined as average within-group variance, and this variance does not change when data is analyzed with use of a Oneway or Factorial ANOVA.

11.9. Yes, a Factorial ANOVA is an independent design. Each of the sources of variability for the main effects and interaction(s) are independent of one another.

11.10. One purpose of simple effect analysis is to reduce the number of post hoc comparisons that are ultimately conducted in a Factorial ANOVA. Post hoc comparisons are not conducted for simple effects that are not significant.

Section 2   Numerical

11.11.

Source	SS	df	MS	F
Factor A	52.51	1	52.51	13.36*
Factor B	19.41	2	9.71	2.47
Interaction	46.18	2	23.09	5.88*
Error	282.62	72		

*$p < .05$

Source of Variation	SS	df	MS	F
Factor A	52.51	1	52.51	13.36*
A at B_1	0.35	1	0.35	0.09
A at B_2	16.97	1	16.97	4.32*
A at B_3	81.38	1	81.38	20.70*
Factor B	19.41	2	9.71	2.47
B at A_1	7.54	2	3.77	0.96
B at A_2	58.05	2	29.03	7.39*
Interaction AB	46.18	2	72.00	5.88*
Subjects within groups (S/AB)	282.62	72	3.93	

*$p < .05$

A at B_1 $F_T = (2.83)^2/2 = 4.00$
$F_S = (2 - 1)F(1, 72) = 3.98$

B at A_1 $F_T = (3.4)^2/2 = 5.78$
$F_S = (2 - 1)F(2, 72) = 6.26$

11.12.

Source	SS	df	MS	F
Factor A	193.60	1	193.60	66.76*
Factor B	78.40	1	78.40	27.03*
Interaction	3.60	1	3.60	1.24
Error	104.40	36		

*$p < .05$

11.13.

Source	SS	df	MS	F
Factor A	101.76	1	101.76	5.21*
Factor B	103.24	1	103.24	5.29*
Interaction	385.34	1	385.34	19.75*
Error	1483.65	76	19.52	

*$p < .05$

11.14.

Source	SS	df	MS	F
Factor A	24096	2	12048	16.63*
Factor B	22145	1	22145	30.38*
Interaction	3420	2	1710	2.35
Error	30612	42	729	

*$p < .05$

$$R^2 = \frac{SS_{Y(AB)}}{SS_Y} = \frac{3420}{80.273} = 0.043$$

$$f = \sqrt{\frac{R^2}{1 - R^2}} = \sqrt{\frac{.043}{1 - .043}} = 0.21$$

11.15.

Source	SS	df	MS	F
Factor A	191.00	4	47.75	7.70*
Factor B	424.20	2	212.10	34.20*
Interaction	137.81	8	17.23	2.78*
Error	372.00	60	6.20	

*$p < .05$

Source of Variation	Sums of Squares	Degrees of Freedom	Mean Square	F-ratio
Factor A	191.00	4	47.75	7.7*
A at B_1	287.20	4	71.80	11.6*
A at B_2	25.36	4	6.34	1.0
A at B_3	16.24	4	4.06	0.7
Factor B	424.19	2	212.10	34.2*
B at A_1	245.73	2	122.89	19.8*
B at A_2	148.93	2	74.47	12.0*
B at A_3	115.60	2	57.80	9.3*
B at A_4	46.53	2	23.27	3.8*
B at A_5	5.20	2	2.60	0.4
Interaction AB	137.81	8	17.23	2.8*
Subjects within-groups S/AB	372.00	60	6.20	

*$p < .05$

CHAPTER 12

Section 1   Conceptual

12.1. Between-groups designs are characterized by different participants being assigned to each of the levels of the independent variable. Within-groups designs (also known as *repeated measures designs*) primarily employ the same subjects for each level of a treatment variable. That is, all subjects are exposed to all levels of the independent variable.

12.2. Because, by definition, the observations in within-groups designs are related, there is no assumption that observations are independent across levels of the independent variable. In place of the independence assumption, the Oneway Within-Groups

ANOVA relies on the circularity assumption (also known as the sphericity assumption). When there are only two levels of the treatment, the circularity assumption is not an issue.

12.3. The primary advantages of within-groups designs over between-groups designs are that fewer subjects are required and therefore the researcher does not need to engage additional subjects for each new treatment condition, and error variability is reduced in the within-groups designs, thereby increasing statistical power.

12.4. In practical terms, within-groups designs require more of individual participants. This requirement becomes particularly troublesome as the treatment and measurement become longer and more intensive. There may also be increased threats to internal and external validity.

12.5. Counterbalancing is used to control for threats to internal validity by confounding the threats with the different orders of presenting the treatments. It does not remove the threats but negates their effects by ensuring that each treatment gets an equal amount of the operating threats to internal validity.

12.6. A mixed design is a design in which both within-groups factors and between-groups factors exist. The simplest example of a mixed design is a 2×2 factorial in which for factor A the subjects are different across the two levels and for factor B the subjects are the same across the two levels.

12.7. An examination of the formula involved shows that an independent samples t-test and a dependent samples t-test will provide the same results for a given set of data when the correlation between the two sets of observations is zero.

12.8. In a Oneway within-groups design, total variability equals between-groups variability plus within-groups variability error, as is the case with the Oneway between-groups design. However, in a Oneway within-groups design, within-groups variability is further subdivided into two components: (1) variability from subject to subject and (2) variability of subjects across treatment conditions.

12.9. When the degrees of freedom are reduced, the critical value for the test is increased. This makes the test more conservative and decreases the chance of making a Type I error when the circularity assumption is violated.

12.10. Mixed designs are considered to be complex because they include more than one error term. The between-groups factor is associated with a between-groups error term. The within-groups error term has a different error term.

Section 2   Numerical

12.11. Raw scored method:

$$t_C = \frac{\overline{Y}_{A1} - \overline{Y}_{A2}}{\sqrt{\frac{s_{A1}^2}{n_{A1}} + \frac{s_{A2}^2}{n_{A2}} - \left(2r \frac{s_{A1}}{\sqrt{n_{A1}}} \frac{s_{A2}}{\sqrt{n_{A2}}}\right)}}$$

$$= \frac{75.2 - 79.8}{\sqrt{\frac{(4.92)^2}{5} + \frac{(4.82)^2}{5} - \left(2(.944)\left(\frac{4.92}{\sqrt{5}}\right)\left(\frac{4.82}{\sqrt{5}}\right)\right)}}$$

$$= -18.95$$

The critical value of t_C with 4 degrees of freedom is ± 2.776. Because the calculated value is larger than the absolute value of the critical value, you reject the null hypothesis. There is sufficient evidence to show a significant difference between the pretest and posttest.

Individual difference score method:

$$t_C = \frac{\overline{Y}_{A1-A2}}{\frac{s_{A1-A2}}{\sqrt{n_{A1-A2}}}} = \frac{-4.6}{\frac{.55}{2.24}} = 18.81$$

The critical value of t_C with 4 degrees of freedom is ± 2.776. Because the calculated value is larger than the absolute value of the critical value, you reject the null hypothesis. There is sufficient evidence to show a significant difference between the pretest and posttest. (Note that the two calculated values are identical except for rounding error.)

12.12.
$$t_C = \frac{\overline{Y}_{A1} - \overline{Y}_{A2}}{\sqrt{\frac{s_{A1}^2}{n_{A1}} + \frac{s_{A2}^2}{n_{A2}} - \left(2r \frac{s_{A1}}{\sqrt{n_{A1}}} \frac{s_{A2}}{\sqrt{n_{A2}}}\right)}}$$

$$= \frac{17 - 17.17}{\sqrt{\frac{(2.61)^2}{6} + \frac{(3.87)^2}{6} - \left(2(.615)\left(\frac{2.61}{\sqrt{6}}\right)\left(\frac{3.87}{\sqrt{6}}\right)\right)}}$$

$$= -.14$$

The critical value of t_C with 5 degrees of freedom is 2.571. Because the calcualted value is *not* larger than the absolute value of the critical value you fail to reject the null hypothesis. There is insufficient evidence to show a significant difference between the pretest and posttest.

$$\overline{Y}_D \pm t_{C1-\alpha/2} s_C = -.17 \pm 2.571 (1.25)$$

$$= -3.38 \le \mu_D \le 3.05$$

12.13.

Source	SS	df	MS	F	p
Strategy (A)	12.10	2	6.05	4.38	<.05
Subjects (S)	26.57	6	4.43		
Error (AS)	16.57	12	1.38		
Total	55.25	20			

The critical value of F is 3.88. Because this amount is lower than the calculated value of F, you reject the null hypothesis. There is sufficient evidence to show a significant difference among the three strategies.

The post hoc companion is:

$$F_p = MS_{Y(p)} / MS_{Y(AS)} = 2.53 / 1.38 = 1.83$$

$$F_T = \frac{(q_T)^2}{2} = \frac{(3.77)^2}{2} = 7.1$$

Because the critical value is higher than the calculated value, there is insufficient evidence to show that a significant difference exists between strategy 1 and strategy 2.

12.14.

Source	SS	df	MS	F	p
Tests (A)	52.00	2	26.00	7.18	<.05
Subjects (S)	462.96	7	66.14		
Error (AS)	50.67	14	3.62		
Total	565.62	23			

The critical value of F is 3.74. Because this amount is lower than the calculated value of F, you reject the null hypothesis. There is sufficient evidence to show a significant difference among the test times.

The post hoc comparison is:

$$F_p = MS_{Y(p)}/MS_{Y(AS)} = 2.96/3.62 = .82$$

$$F_S = (A-1)F (df_A, df_{AS}) = (2)(3.74) = 7.48$$

Because the critical value is higher than the calculated value, there is insufficient evidence to show that a significant difference exists between the pretest and the combination of the posttest and delayed posttest.

12.15. Strategy is a between-groups factor (i.e., subjects differ across the three strategies), and Time is a within-groups factor (i.e., subjects are the same for the immediate and delayed posttest).

Source	SS	df	MS	F	p
Strategy (B)	314.07	2	157.04	11.23	<.05
Error (S/B)	167.80	12	13.98		
Time (A)	13.34	1	13.34	6.74	<.05
Time ×					
Strategy B	.86	2	.43	.22	>.05
Error (AS/B)	23.80	12	1.98		
Total	519.87	29			

12.16. Drug is a between-groups factor (i.e., subjects differ across the two drugs), and Time is a within-groups factor (i.e., subjects are the same for the immediate and 24-hour delay measurements).

Source	SS	df	MS	F	p
Drug (B)	1125.00	1	1125.00	12.38	<.05
Error (S/B)	726.80	8	90.85		
Time (A)	871.20	1	871.20	13.67	<.05
Time ×					
Strategy B	1.80	1	1.80	.03	>.05
Error (AS/B)	510.00	8	63.75		
Total	3234.80	19			

12.17. The sum of squares due to Subjects (S) and the sum of squares due to $A \times S$ must be added together to form the between-groups error term when the study is analyzed as a Between-Groups ANOVA. $SS_{Y(S/A)} = SS_{Y(S)} + SS_{Y(AS)}$.

Source	SS	df	MS	F	p
Treatments					
(A)	100.00	2	50.00	9.31	<.05
Error (S/A)	145.00	27	5.37		
Total	245.00	29			

CHAPTER 13

Section 1 Conceptual/Definition

13.1. Correlation can be both a descriptive statistic and an inferential statistic. As a descriptive statistic it is a measure of the extent to which two variables are related. As an inferential statistic it is often used to determine whether the extent to which two variables are related is significantly different from zero.

13.2. No, correlational studies do not allow for causal inference. In correlational studies, because variables are only measured and not manipulated, reverse variable and third-variable explanations of a phenomenon are possible.

13.3. Oneway ANOVA is most often used for experiments when the independent variable is categorical. The correlation coefficient is most often used for nonexperiments when both variables are continuous.

13.4. The range of values for the correlation coefficient is from -1 (a perfect negative, or inverse, relationship) to $+1$ (a perfect positive relationship). A correlation coefficient of zero indicates the absence of a relationship.

13.5. In physics, "moment" is a function of the distance of an object from the center of gravity. With any set of scores, the mean may be considered the center of gravity while the individual deviation scores from the mean are the moments. As you can see by examining the covariation formula, Pearson's r is obtained by taking the products of the paired moments about the mean.

13.6. One key assumption which underlies Pearson's product-moment correlation is that the paired observations are assumed to be independent from one another. Each pair of A and Y scores should be independent of all the other pairs of A and Y scores. A second key assumption is that the values of the predictor variable (A) and the outcome variable (Y) are each expected to be distributed normally. In particular, it is assumed that A and Y have a joint distribution that is bivariate normal.

13.7. The coefficient of determination is the square of the correlation coefficient (r^2). The coefficient of determination equals the proportion of the total variability in the outcome variable (Y) that can be accounted for, explained by, or associated with variability in the predictor variable (A). Note that the strength of association is always positive regardless of the sign of the correlation coefficient.

13.8. The correlation coefficient is affected by the restriction of range of the variables under investigation. The effect of the range restriction is to reduce the size of the correlation coefficient. The greater the restriction of range in either A or Y, the lower the correlation will be.

13.9. The Pearson product moment correlation is used to describe the degree of linear relationship between two variables (paired observations). Curvilinear relationships are not accurately measured by simple correlational techniques. To the extent the relationship is curvilinear, r will misrepresent the true nature of the relationship.

13.10. A simple way to detect outliers is to examine a scatterplot of the data and look for unusually large or small scores relative to the others.

Section 2   Numerical

13.11. $r = \dfrac{\sum (z_{Ai} z_{Yi})}{N - 1} = \dfrac{-4.0685}{15} = -.271$

13.12. $r = \dfrac{SS_{AY}}{\sqrt{SS_A SS_Y}} = \dfrac{-63.13}{\sqrt{28.94 \times 1871.75}} = -.271$

13.13. $H_0: \rho = 0$ (null hypothesis)

$H_a: \rho \neq 0$ (nondirectional, or "two-tailed," alternative hypothesis)

The critical value of r (at $\alpha = .05$, two-tailed) with 14 degrees of freedom is .497. Because the absolute value of the calculated r value (.271) is less than the critical r value (.497), one accepts the null hypothesis and concludes that there is insufficient evidence to support a relationship between Education Level and Reading Score.

13.14. $r = \dfrac{\sum (z_{Ai} z_{Yi})}{N - 1} = \dfrac{9.7648}{14} = .697$

13.15. $r = \dfrac{SS_{AY}}{\sqrt{SS_A SS_Y}} = \dfrac{968.6}{\sqrt{985.74 \times 1956.4}} = .697$

13.16. $H_0: \rho \leq 0$ (null hypothesis)

$H_a: \rho > 0$ (directional positive "one-tailed" alternative hypothesis)

The critical value of r (at $\alpha = .05$, one-tailed) with 13 degrees of freedom is .441. Because the absolute value of the calculated r value (.697) is greater than the critical r value (.441), one rejects the null hypothesis in favor of the alternative hypothesis and concludes that there is sufficient evidence to support a significant positive relationship between Take-Home and In-Class results.

13.17. $r = \dfrac{SS_{AY}}{\sqrt{SS_A SS_Y}} = \dfrac{455.2}{\sqrt{227.6 \times 910.4}} = +1.00$

Pearson's correlation coefficient of +1.00 indicates that a perfect, positive relationship exists between A and Y. A closer inspection of the data reveals that in fact $Y = 2A + 3$. The Pearson product moment correlation is +1.00, because a linear equation was used to derive Y from A.

13.18. $r = \dfrac{SS_{AY}}{\sqrt{SS_A SS_Y}} = \dfrac{4667.6}{\sqrt{227.6 \times 100293.6}} = .977$

Yes, there is a small problem. If you created a scatterplot, you would see that the variables are related in a nonlinear way. In fact, in this example $Y = A^2 + 5$. This is a perfect relationship. Therefore, you would want Pearson's r to be equal to +1.00. However, remember that Pearson's r is a measure of the linear relationship between two variables. In this case, because the relationship is nonlinear, Pearson's r slightly underestimates the true relationship between the variables.

13.19. $r = \dfrac{SS_{AY}}{\sqrt{SS_A SS_Y}} = \dfrac{117.2}{\sqrt{45.2 \times 349.2}} = .933$

13.20. $r = \dfrac{SS_{AY}}{\sqrt{SS_A SS_Y}} = \dfrac{-294.5}{\sqrt{833.5 \times 1160.84}} = -.3$

CHAPTER 14

Section 1   Conceptual/Definition

14.1. Linear correlation refers to describing the degree of linear relationship between two variables (A and Y). The degree of the relationship is summarized in a single number, the correlation coefficient (r). Linear regression refers to fitting a straight line through the scatterplot of A-scores and Y-scores. The regression equation can then be used to estimate a subject's score on the outcome variable Y only from knowledge of that subject's score on the predictor variable A.

14.2. The slope of a line is defined as the rate of change of one variable relative to another. The slope (b) is also the angle of the line's tilt relative to one of the axes and is calculated as the change in Y divided by the change in A.

14.3. The slope of the regression line cannot be determined from the correlation coefficient alone. A perfect correlation between two variables can result in any nonzero value for the slope of the regression line.

14.4. When two variables are perfectly related, all the data points will form into a straight line.

14.5. The *line of best fit* is the straight line that reduces the sum of the squared deviations of the actual data points from the line to the smallest amount. This method of line fitting is called the *method of least squares*. Put another way, the method of least squares fits the line in such a way that the sum of the squared "distances" from the actual data points to the line is at its minimal value.

14.6. $b' = \dfrac{\text{covariance}(A, Y)}{\text{variance}(A)} = \dfrac{SS_{AY}}{SS_A}$

14.7. The point where the mean of A and the mean of Y intersect is always on the regression line. One of the properties of standardized variables is that they have a mean of zero. Given these two facts, when the z-score method for determining the regression equation is used, the regression line always passes through the origin.

14.8. In Oneway ANOVA, one explores whether there is any significant relationship between the independent variable and the dependent variable. In simple regression, one explores whether there is a significant *linear* relationship between the predictor variable and the outcome variable.

14.9. Four methods for testing the significance of a single predictor are as follows:

Correlation method t-test

Regression method t-test

Mean squares F-test

Correlation method F-test

14.10. There are three critical assumptions that must be met in using the simple linear regression model:

Normality. The values of the predictor variable (A) and the outcome variable (Y) are each expected to be distributed normally.

Independence. Each pair of A and Y scores should be independent of all the other pairs of A and Y scores.

Homoscedasticity. For every value of A the variances of Y are equal allowing for sampling error.

Section 2 Numerical

14.11.

Source	SS	df	MS	F	p
(A) (Regression)	39.23	1	39.23	19.7	<.05
Residual	5.97	3	1.99		
Total	45.20	4			

$F(1, 3) = 10.13$ is the critical value for $\alpha = .05$. Since $p < .05$, A is a significant linear predictor of Y.

14.12. $Y' = 14.7 + 1.03A$

Residuals $= -1.04, -0.1, 1.98, -0.96, .12$

14.13. $t = \dfrac{\dfrac{SS_{AY}}{SS_A}}{\sqrt{\dfrac{MS_{Y(RE)}}{SS_A}}} = \dfrac{\dfrac{968.6}{985.73}}{\sqrt{\dfrac{77.28}{985.73}}} = \dfrac{.98}{.28} = +3.51$

$t(1, 13) = 2.16$

Because the calculated value of t is greater than the critical value, you can conclude that A is a significant linear predictor of Y.

14.14. $Y' = 1.0 + .983A$

$CI = b' \pm t_{1-\alpha/2}s_{b'}$

$= .983 \pm (2.16 \times .28)$

$= .378 \leq \beta \leq 1.588$

14.15.

Source	SS	df	MS	F	p
(A) (Regression)	95,723	1	95,723	167.53	<.05
Residual	4,571	8	571		
Total	100,294	9			

$F(1, 8) = 5.32$ is the critical value for $\alpha = .05$. Therefore, although A would be considered a significant linear predictor of Y, there is still error when this dataset is examined by use of a linear regression model. However, one knows that the data is perfectly related but in a nonlinear way. This is evidence that a problem exists when a linear regression model is used to analyze nonlinear data.

14.16.

Source	SS	df	MS	F	p
(A) (Regression)	64.15	1	64.15	17.48	<.05
Residual	14.68	4	3.67		
Total	78.83	5			

$F(1, 4) = 7.71$ is the critical value for $\alpha = .05$.

14.17.

Source	SS	df	MS	F	p
(A) (Regression)	175.08	1	175.08	2.86	>.05
Residual	489.32	8	61.17		
Total	664.40	9			

$F(1, 8) = 5.32$ is the critical value for $\alpha = .05$.

14.18. $t = \dfrac{r}{\sqrt{(1-r^2)/(n-2)}}$

$= \dfrac{0.933}{\sqrt{(1-(.933)^2/(5-2)}}$

$= \dfrac{0.933}{0.25} = 4.49$

For $\alpha = .05$, the critical value of t with $df = 3$ is 3.18. Because the calculated value of t is greater than the critical value, sufficient evidence exists to show that A is a significant linear predictor of Y.

14.19. $F = \dfrac{r^2}{\sqrt{(1-r^2)/(n-2)}}$

$= \dfrac{.933^2}{(1-.933)^2/(5-2)} = 20.16$

For $\alpha = .05$, the critical value of F with $df = (1, 3)$ is 10.10. Because the calculated value of F is greater than the critical value, sufficient evidence exists to show that A is a significant linear predictor of Y.

14.20. $b' = \dfrac{SS_{AY}}{SS_A} = \dfrac{-294.5}{833.5} = -.35$

CHAPTER 15

Section 1 Conceptual/Definition

15.1. The shared variability in the outcome measure (Y) means that the predictors provide a certain amount of redundant information. Furthermore, this redundancy represents a fairly typical state of affairs because predictors that are measured, rather than manipulated, are rarely uncorrelated with one another. The difficulty occurs when decisions must be made as to how the shared variability will be attributed to individual predictor variables.

15.2. When the predictor variables are uncorrelated, the total explained variability in Y is the sum of the variability explained by each predictor separately. When the predictor variables are correlated, the total explained variability in Y is not the sum of the variability explained by each predictor separately. The total explained variability in Y is the sum of the unique contribution of each predictor plus variability in the outcome measure that is shared by predictors.

15.3. No, in multiple linear regression these methods are neither equally applicable nor interchangeable. The multiple correlation F-test and mean squares F-test can be used to test whether the collection of predictors together explain a significant amount of variability in the outcome measure. In contrast, the regression method t-test can be used to test the significance of a single predictor, and the correlation method t-test is only appropriate for uncorrelated predictors.

15.4. Both of these methods test the significance of a set of predictors as a collection. They do not attempt to examine the relative contribution of the predictors individually. In this sense they are general tests used to determine whether a set of predictors is related in a linear fashion with the outcome variable (Y).

15.5. When the correlations among predictors is high, a situation referred to as *collinearity* exists and the amount of explained variability in the outcome unique to any one predictor can be small. Under such a circumstance, the value of R^2 can be large, but if the overlap among the predictors is also great, it is conceivable that each test of significance for the individual predictors will be nonsignificant.

15.6. The *simultaneous approach* to multiple regression allows researchers to test the significance of the predictors as a set and then to determine whether each predictor contributes uniquely to the explanation of variability in the outcome measure. *Incremental approaches* to multiple linear regression allow other options for dealing with shared variability. Incremental approaches enter variables successively into a series of multiple regressions rather than simultaneously into a single regression.

15.7. Hierarchical regression is an example of an incremental approach to multiple linear regression. In hierarchical regression, the researcher decides on the order of entry of predictors in a series of regression analyses. The researcher may elect to enter variables according to theoretical guidelines, for example, according to the temporal sequence of factors, or some other criterion.

15.8. Stepwise regression is an example of an incremental regression procedure. It allows predictors to be entered in steps in the regression equation according to the magnitude of their contribution to explaining additional variability in the outcome variable. Thus, the assignment of shared variability is decided statistically, not theoretically.

15.9. Data are ill-conditioned when situations exist that can cause both statistical and computational difficulties. Two main sources of ill conditioning are multicollinearity and small coefficients of variation. Multicollinearity occurs when the predictor variables are highly correlated among themselves. Small coefficients of variation occur when predictor values are nearly constant.

15.10. If a variable is added to a regression equation, R^2 will get larger even if the added variable is of no real value. To compensate for this, the squared correlation coefficient is adjusted by the degrees of freedom. In this way an unbiased estimate of the population R-squared value is created.

Section 2   Numerical

15.11. $R_{YAB}^2 = \dfrac{r_{YA}^2 + r_{YB}^2 - 2r_{YA}r_{YB}r_{AB}}{1 - r_{AB}^2}$

$= \dfrac{.45^2 + .30^2 - 2(.45)(.30)(0)}{1.00 - 0^2} = .2925$

15.12. $R_{YAB}^2 = \dfrac{r_{YA}^2 + r_{YB}^2 - 2r_{YA}r_{YB}r_{AB}}{1 - r_{AB}^2}$

$= \dfrac{.45^2 + .30^2 - 2(.45)(.30)(.50)}{1 - .50^2} = .21$

15.13. $b_A' = \dfrac{(SS_B)(SS_{YA}) - (SS_{AB})(SS_{YB})}{(SS_A)(SS_B) - (SS_{AB})^2}$

$= \dfrac{(56.90)(368.10) - (42.10)(107.90)}{(600.90)(56.90) - (42.10)^2} = .506$

$b_A' = \dfrac{(SS_A)(SS_{YB}) - (SS_{AB})(SS_{YA})}{(SS_A)(SS_B) - (SS_{AB})^2}$

$= \dfrac{(600.90)(107.90) - (42.10)(368.10)}{(600.90)(56.90) - (42.10)^2} = 1.52$

$a' = \overline{Y} - b_A'(\overline{A}) - b_B'(\overline{B})$

$= 75.90 - .506(80.10) - 1.52(14.90) = 12.72$

$Y' = 12.72 + .506A + 1.52B$

15.14. $R_{YAB}^2 = \dfrac{r_{YA}^2 + r_{YB}^2 - 2r_{YA}r_{YB}r_{AB}}{1 - r_{AB}^2}$

$= \dfrac{.696^2 + .663^2 - 2(.696)(.663)(.228)}{1.00 - .228^2} = .754$

$F = \dfrac{R_{YAB}^2/k}{(1 - R_{YAB}^2)/(N - k - 1)}$

$= \dfrac{.745/2}{(1 - .754)/(10.00 - 2.00 - 1.00)} = 10.72$

The critical value for $\alpha = .05$ is $F(2, 7) = 4.47$. Since the calculated value is larger than the critical value, the combined effect of A and B is significant.

15.15. $R_{YAB}^2 = \dfrac{r_{YA}^2 + r_{YB}^2 - 2r_{YA}r_{YB}r_{AB}}{1 - r_{AB}^2}$

$= \dfrac{.31^2 + .643^2 - 2(.31)(.643)(.827)}{1.00 - .827^2} = .571$

$SS_{Y(AB)} = (R_{YAB}^2)(SS_Y) = .571 \times 2622.50 = 1497.45$

$MS_{Y(AB)} = SS_{Y(AB)}/k = 1497.45/2.00 = 748.73$

$SS_{Y(RE)} = (1 - R_{YAB}^2)(SS_Y) = .429 \times 2622.50 = 1125.05$

$MS_{Y(RE)} = SS_{Y(RE)}/N - k - 1 = 1125.05/7.00 = 160.72$

$F = MS_{Y(AB)}/MS_{Y(RE)} = 748.73/160.72 = 4.66$

For $\alpha = .05$, the critical value is $F(2, 7) = 4.47$. Since the calculated value exceeds the critical value, the combined effect of A and B is significant.

15.16. $b_A' = \dfrac{(SS_B)(SS_{YA}) - (SS_{AB})(SS_{YB})}{(SS_A)(SS_B) - (SS_{AB})^2}$

$= \dfrac{(192,752.40)(93.00) - (2130.40)(14,461.00)}{(34.40)(192,752.40) - (2130.40)^2}$

$= -6.16$

$SS_{Y(RE)} = (1 - R_{YAB}^2)(SS_Y) = .429 \times 2622.50 = 1125.05$

$MS_{Y(RE)} = SS_{Y(RE)}/N - k - 1 = 1125.05/7.00 = 160.72$

$s_{b_A'} = \sqrt{\dfrac{MS_{Y(RE)}}{SS_A(1 - r_{AB}^2)}} = \sqrt{\dfrac{160.72}{34.40(.316)}} = 3.85$

$t = \dfrac{b'}{s_{b'}} = \dfrac{-6.16}{3.85} = -1.60$

For $\alpha = .05$, $t_{crit} = 2.365$

Because the calculated value is less than the critical value, one can conclude that the unique contribution of A is not significant.

15.17. $\text{CI} = b' \pm t_{1-\alpha/2} s_{b'}$

$\text{CI} = -6.16 \pm 2.365 \times 3.85$

$\text{CI} = (-15.27, 2.95)$

$-15.27 \leq \beta_A \leq 2.95$

15.18. $R^2_{YAB} = \dfrac{r^2_{YA} + r^2_{YB} - 2r_{YA}r_{YB}r_{AB}}{1 - r^2_{AB}}$

$= \dfrac{.915^2 + .715^2 - 2.00(.915)(.715)(.736)}{1.00 - .736^2}$

$= .841$

$\text{SS}_{Y(AB)} = (R^2_{YAB})(\text{SS}_Y) = .841 \times 72.07 = 60.61$

$\text{MS}_{Y(AB)} = \text{SS}_{Y(AB)}/k = 60.61/2.00 = 30.31$

$\text{SS}_{Y(RE)} = (1 - R^2_{YAB})(\text{SS}_Y) = .159 \times 72.07 = 11.46$

$\text{MS}_{Y(RE)} = \text{SS}_{Y(RE)}/N - k - 1 = 11.46/7.00 = 1.64$

$F = \text{MS}_{Y(AB)}/\text{MS}_{Y(RE)} = 30.31/1.64 = 18.48$

For $\alpha = .05$, $F(2, 7) = 4.47$. Therefore, the combined effect of A and B is significant.

15.19. $b'_B = \dfrac{(\text{SS}_A)(\text{SS}_{YB}) - (\text{SS}_{AB})(\text{SS}_{YA})}{(\text{SS}_A)(\text{SS}_B) - (\text{SS}_{AB})^2}$

$= \dfrac{(254,452.91)(18.80) - (1150.80)(3920.25)}{(254,452.91)(9.60) - (1150.80)^2}$

$= .243$

$\text{SS}_{Y(RE)} = (1 - R^2_{YAB})(\text{SS}_Y) = .159 \times 72.07 = 11.46$

$\text{MS}_{Y(RE)} = \text{SS}_{Y(RE)}/N - k - 1 = 11.46/70 = 1.64$

$s_{b'_B} = \sqrt{\dfrac{\text{MS}_{Y(RE)}}{\text{SS}_B(1 - r^2_{AB})}} = \sqrt{\dfrac{1.64}{9.60(.458)}} = .61$

$t = \dfrac{b'}{s_{b'}} = \dfrac{.243}{.61} = .398$

For $\alpha = .05$, $t_{\text{crit}} = 2.365$

Because the calculated value is less than the critical value, one can conclude that the unique contribution of B is not significant.

15.20. $\text{CI} = b' \pm t_{1-\alpha/2} s_{b'}$

$\text{CI} = .243 \pm 2.365 \times .61$

$\text{CI} = (-1.20, 1.69)$

$-1.20 \leq \beta_B \leq 1.69$

CHAPTER 16

Section 1 Conceptual/Definition

16.1. A nonparametric test is a statistical test that is not designed to make inferences about population parameters and makes fewer or no assumptions about those parameters than parametric tests.

16.2. Parametric tests require data from interval or ratio scales of measurement, because the data being analyzed are subject to arithmetic operations such as adding, squaring, and averaging. This requirement does not apply to nonparametric tests, which can be used with ordinal and nominal scales of measurement.

16.3. The main advantage of nonparametric statistical tests is their flexibility. They can be used accurately without having to make assumptions about population parameters and without the data for the dependent or outcome measure being on an interval or ratio scale of measurement. The main disadvantage of nonparametric tests is their relative lack of power when compared to parametric equivalents.

16.4. The chi-square goodness-of-fit test is used with only one variable, whereas the chi-square test of independence is used with two variables.

16.5. $\chi^2 = \sum \dfrac{(O_k - E_k)^2}{E_k}$

An examination of this formula shows that as the number of categories increases so will the calculated value of chi-square (unless the observed and expected frequencies are identical). Even when the null hypothesis is true, the value of chi-square will increase by chance alone as the number of categories increases. The critical value of chi-square is based on the number of categories and therefore must increase as the number of categories increase.

16.6. The assumptions of the chi-square test are as follows: (1) samples have been randomly selected, (2) the observations are independent, (3) group sample sizes are sufficiently large.

16.7. Both tests determine a calculated value as the lower of two sums of the ranks. The lower this amount, the greater the separation between the two groups. Therefore, the calculated value that represents the greatest difference between two groups is zero. This means that a calculated value must be lower than (or equal to) a critical value to reject H_0.

16.8. The following tests can be used to examine data that is ordinal in nature:

Mann-Whitney U-test

Wilcoxon signed-ranks T-test

Kruskal-Wallis Oneway ANOVA H-test

Friedman ANOVA

Spearman rank-order correlation

16.9.

Parametric test	Nonparametric equivalent.
Independent samples t-test	Mann-Whitney U-test
Dependent samples t-test	Wilcoxon signed-ranks T-test
Oneway ANOVA	Kruskal-Wallis Oneway ANOVA H-test
Pearson product–moment correlation	Spearman rank-order correlation

16.10. These are not tests of mean differences. Both of these tests are applied to ordinal data and use rank sums. The ranks are determined by whether one score is higher than another score and do not take into account the magnitude of the difference. As a result, these tests are better described as tests of differences in the distributions of groups.

Section 2   Numerical

16.11. $\chi^2 = \sum \dfrac{(O_k - E_k)^2}{E_k}$

$= \dfrac{(969.00 - 892.98)^2}{892.98} + \dfrac{(120.00 - 189.02)^2}{189.02}$

$= 31.67$

$\chi^2_{crit}(df = 1) = 3.84$, $\alpha = .05$. Because the calculated value of chi-square is greater than the critical value chi-square, you can conclude that your school performed at a higher level than the school district average.

16.12. $\chi^2 = \sum \dfrac{(O_k - E_k)^2}{E_k}$

$= \dfrac{(75.00 - 66.67)^2}{66.67} + \dfrac{(25.00 - 33.33)^2}{33.33} +$

$\dfrac{(150.00 - 133.33)^2}{133.33} + \dfrac{(50.00 - 66.67)^2}{66.67}$

$+ \dfrac{(175.00 - 200.00)^2}{200.00} + \dfrac{(125.00 - 100.00)^2}{100.00}$

$= 18.75$

$\chi^2_{crit}(df = 2) = 5.99$, $\alpha = .05$. Because the calculated value of chi-square is greater than the critical value chi-square, we can conclude that Preferred Instructional Strategies and Gender are related.

16.13. $U =$ Smaller of

$\left[n_1 n_2 + \dfrac{n_1(n_1 + 1)}{2} - \sum R_1 = 6 \times 6 + \dfrac{6(6+1)}{2} - 25 = 32 \right.$

$\left. n_1 n_2 + \dfrac{n_2(n_2 + 1)}{2} - \sum R_2 = 6 \times 6 + \dfrac{6(6+1)}{2} - 53 = 4 \right]$

$= 4$

$U_{crit} = 5$. Because $U_{calc}(4)$ is less than $U_{crit}(5)$, you can conclude that the treatment has produced differential effects.

16.14. $U =$ Smaller of

$\left[n_1 n_2 + \dfrac{n_1(n_1 + 1)}{2} - \sum R_1 = 7 \times 7 + \dfrac{7(7+1)}{2} - 54 = 23 \right.$

$\left. n_1 n_2 + \dfrac{n_2(n_2 + 1)}{2} - \sum R_2 = 7 \times 7 + \dfrac{7(7+1)}{2} - 51 = 26 \right]$

$= 23$

$U_{crit} = 8$, $\alpha = .05$. Because $U_{calc}(23)$ is greater than $U_{crit}(8)$, there is insufficient evidence to show that the treatment has produced differential effects.

16.15. $H = \dfrac{12}{17(17 + 1)} \left[\dfrac{(21.5)^2}{6} + \dfrac{(56.5)^2}{6} + \cdots + \dfrac{(75)^2}{5} \right]$

$\qquad - 3(17 + 1)$

$= 14$

$H_{crit}(df = 2) = 5.99$, $\alpha = .05$. Because the value of $H_{calc}(14.00)$ is greater than the value of $H_{crit}(5.99)$, you can conclude that the treatment has produced differential effects.

16.16. $H = \dfrac{12}{12(12 + 1)} \left[\dfrac{(24)^2}{4} + \dfrac{(27)^2}{4} + \cdots + \dfrac{(27)^2}{4} \right]$

$\qquad - 3(12 + 1)$

$= 6.12$

$H_{crit}(df = 2) = 5.99$, $\alpha = .05$. Because the value of $H_{calc}(6.12)$ is greater than the value of $H_{crit}(5.99)$, you can conclude that the treatment has produced differential effects.

16.17. Wilcoxon signed-ranks T-test (shown below)

$T_{calc} = 9.5$ and $T_{crit} = 10$, $\alpha = .05$. $T_{calc}(9.5)$ is less than $T_{crit}(10)$, so you can conclude that the sums of the ranks are higher for the posttests scores.

16.18. A Friedman ANOVA will be used, because you are dealing with a Within-Groups design.

$FR = \dfrac{12}{4(3)(3 + 1)} \left[\dfrac{(24)^2}{4} + \dfrac{(27)^2}{4} + \cdots + \dfrac{(27)^2}{4} \right]$

$\qquad - 3(4)(3 + 1)$

$= 79.13$

$H_{crit}(df = 2) = 5.99$, $\alpha = .05$. Because the value of $H_{calc}(79.13)$ is greater than the value of $H_{crit}(5.99)$, you can conclude that the treatment has produced differential effects.

16.19. $r_S = 1 - \dfrac{6 \sum (R_Y - R_A)^2}{N(N^2 - 1)}$

$= 1 - \dfrac{6(-1^2 + 0^2 + -3^2 + 2^2 + 2^2]}{5(5^2 - 1)} = n = .1$

$r_{crit}(df = 3) = .878$, $\alpha = .05$. Because r_S is less than r_{crit}, there is insufficient evidence to conclude that a relationship exists between the student and teacher ratings.

Pilot	Pretest Score	Posttest Score	(Post-Pre) Negative	Difference (Negative)	(Post-Pre) Positive	Difference (Positive)
1	20	25			5	8
2	16	20			4	7
3	18	27			9	11
4	23	21	−2	4		
5	22	28			6	9
6	23	23				
7	20	19	−1	1.5		
8	25	23	−2	4		
9	19	22			3	6
10	21	23			2	4
11	22	23			1	1.5
12	19	27			8	10
			$\sum R = 9.5$		$\sum R = 56.5$	

Index

LICENSING AGREEMENT

You should carefully read the following terms and conditions before opening this disk package.
Opening this disk package indicates your acceptance of these terms and conditions.
If you do not agree with them, you should promptly return the package unopened.

Allyn and Bacon provides this Program and License its use. You assume responsibility for the selection of the Program to achieve your intended results, and for the installation, use, and results obtained from the Program. This License extends only to use of the Program in the United States or countries in which the Program is marketed by duly authorized distributors.

License Grant

You hereby accept a nonexclusive, nontransferable, permanent License to install and use the Program on a single computer at any given time. You may copy the Program solely for backup or archival purposes in support of your use of the Program on the single computer. You may **not** modify, translate, disassemble, decompile, or reverse engineer the Program, in whole or in part.

Term

This License is effective until terminated. Allyn and Bacon reserves the right to terminate this License automatically if any provision of the License is violated. You may terminate the License at any time. To terminate this License, you must return the Program, including documentation, along with a written warranty stating that all copies of the Program in your possession have been returned or destroyed.

Limited Warranty

The Program is provided "As Is" without warranty of any kind, either express or implied, including, but **not** limited to, the implied warranties or merchantability and fitness for a particular purpose. The entire risk as to the quality and performance of the Program is with you. Should the Program prove defective, you (and **not** Allyn and Bacon or any authorized distributor) assume the entire cost of all necessary servicing, repair, or correction. No oral or written information or advice given by Allyn and Bacon, its dealers, distributors, or agents shall create a warranty or increase the scope of its warranty.

Some states do **not** allow the exclusion of implied warranty, so the above exclusion may **not** apply to you. This warranty gives you specific legal rights and you may also have other rights that vary from state to state.

Allyn and Bacon does **not** warrant that the functions contained in the Program will meet your requirements or that the operation of the Program will be uninterrupted or error free.

However, Allyn and Bacon warrants the disk(s) on which the Program is furnished to be free from defects in material and workmanship under normal use for a period of ninety (90) days form the date of delivery to you as evidenced by a copy of your receipt.

The Program should **not** be relied on as the sole basis to solve a problem whose incorrect solution could result in injury to a person or property. If the Program is employed in such a manner, its is at the user's own risk and Allyn and Bacon explicitly disclaims all liability for such misuse.

Limitation of Remedies

Allyn and Bacon's entire liability and your exclusive remedy shall be:

1. The replacement of any disk **not** meeting Allyn and Bacon's "Limited Warranty" and that is returned to Allyn and Bacon or

2. If Allyn and Bacon is unable to deliver a replacement disk or cassette that is free of defects in materials or workmanship, you may terminate this Agreement by returning the Program.

In no event will Allyn and Bacon be liable to you for any damages, including any lost profits, lost savings, or other incidental or consequential damages arising out of the use or inability to use such Program even if Allyn and Bacon or an authorized distributor has been advised of the possibility of such damages of for any claim by any other party.

Some states do **not** allow the limitation or exclusion of liability for incidental or consequential damages, so the above limitation or exclusion may **not** apply to you.

General

You may **not** sublicense, assign, or transfer the License of the Program. Any attempt to sublicense, assign, or transfer any of the rights, duties, or obligations hereunder is void.

This Agreement will be governed by the laws of the State of Massachusetts.

Should you have any questions concerning this Agreement, or any questions concerning technical support, you may contact Allyn and Bacon by writing to:

Allyn and Bacon
A Pearson Education Company
160 Gould Street
Needham Heights, MA 02494

You acknowledge that you have read this Agreement, understand it, and agree to be bound by its terms and conditions. You further agree that it is the complete and exclusive statement of the Agreement between us that supersedes any proposal or prior Agreement, oral or written, and any other communications between us relating to the subject matter of this Agreement.

Notice To Government End Users

The Program is provided with restricted rights. Use, duplication, or disclosure by the Government is subject to restrictions set forth in subdivison (b)(3)(iii) of The Rights in Technical Data and Computer Software Clause 252.227-7013.